HISTORY OF THE GREAT WAR
SEABORNE TRADE
VOL. I

The Lords Commissioners of the Admiralty have given the Author access to official documents in the preparation of this work, but they are in no way responsible for his reading or presentation of the facts as stated.

HISTORY OF THE GREAT WAR

BASED ON OFFICIAL DOCUMENTS

BY DIRECTION OF THE HISTORICAL SECTION OF THE
COMMITTEE OF IMPERIAL DEFENCE

SEABORNE TRADE

Vol. I
THE CRUISER PERIOD

BY
C. ERNEST FAYLE

The Naval & Military Press Ltd

Published by

The Naval & Military Press Ltd
Unit 10 Ridgewood Industrial Park,
Uckfield, East Sussex,
TN22 5QE England

Tel: +44 (0) 1825 749494
Fax: +44 (0) 1825 765701

www.naval-military-press.com
www.military-genealogy.com

In reprinting in facsimile from the original, any imperfections are inevitably reproduced and the quality may fall short of modern type and cartographic standards.

PREFACE

THE object of this book is to show how seaborne trade was affected during the war by naval operations and conditions having their origin in the naval situation. In the history of past wars this effect has been very imperfectly traced. Although one of the most important functions of a navy in war is to deny passage to the enemy's seaborne trade and secure the free circulation of our own, the earlier naval historians were content to record the operations undertaken by the fleet to secure its ends, and little effort was made to describe the actual result of those operations, or to indicate their effects on the flow of trade. Vital as these matters are now seen to be, the old writers left too little material to enable the gap to be adequately filled by their successors.

It was essential that no such gap should be left in the history of a war in which the economic element attained unprecedented importance, and in order to avoid swelling the naval history to an unwieldy bulk, it was decided to supplement Sir Julian Corbett's *Naval Operations* by a separate work dealing with the effect of operations on seaborne trade. The Garton Foundation was already engaged in research on cognate questions for the Committee of Imperial Defence, and an arrangement was accordingly made with the Trustees—the Right Hon. A. J. Balfour, M.P., the Right Hon. Viscount Esher, G.C.B., and Sir Richard Garton, G.B.E.—that they should allow a member of their staff to undertake the work, in co-operation with the Historical Section. As a result of this arrangement the work was entrusted to the present writer, who was subsequently transferred to the regular staff of the Historical Section.

In the execution of this task it has been necessary to touch at some length on the effect of those financial and economic reactions of the war which powerfully affected seaborne trade, though they had no direct connection with naval operations. The treatment of these more general causes of economic disturbance has, however, been subordinated, so far as possible, to the development of the main theme—the effects, whether direct or indirect, of naval activity on the flow of trade, and the measures adopted to counteract them.

In order to avoid duplication, the description of naval dispositions, movements, and actions, even when arising directly from the attack or defence of commerce, has been restricted to such brief reference as was necessary to make clear their bearing on the interruption or maintenance of the flow of trade. In like manner, it has been left for Mr. Archibald Hurd in *The Merchant Navy* to deal with the effects of the war on the lives and fortunes of merchant seamen and to do justice to the heroism and resource which they displayed either as traders under war conditions or as members of the auxiliary services. It is not with the achievements of the Royal Navy and the Merchant Service but with the result of those achievements that this book is concerned.

Restriction of enemy trade was, in large measure, a matter of diplomatic arrangements with neutral countries, which lie outside the scope of this book. The full story of the blockade remains to be told, but an attempt will be made in this and subsequent volumes to give a general idea of the situation in which the Central Powers were placed by the severance of their maritime communications.

The period covered by the present volume embraces those early months of the war during which the German attack on commerce was carried on mainly by surface cruisers and armed liners. The force of this attack was broken at the Battle of the Falklands in December 1914; but the last of the original raiders was not accounted for till April 1915.

There are several reasons for devoting a volume to this

period. Before the war it was the initial economic crisis arising from a European conflict which caused the gravest apprehensions, and although the events of these early months have been overshadowed by the subsequent development of the submarine campaign, there is still much of special interest in the methods adopted to overcome the universal shock to credit and dislocation of trade which followed the outbreak of war, and the rapid readjustment of trade and shipping to the new demands and changed conditions so suddenly imposed. Moreover, the effect produced by the surface raiders was, in the main, local and temporary, and can only be made clear by detailed treatment, involving a separate study of each trade route affected. The effects of the submarine campaign, which struck at the very heart of our maritime communications, were far more serious; but for that very reason, individual losses lose their significance, and the development of the situation can be followed in broader outline. It is hoped, therefore, to complete the work in three volumes.

No attempt has been made to draw comparisons with the losses suffered in previous wars. Apart from the fact that the statistics of those wars are admittedly imperfect, both the character of naval warfare and the processes of trade have since undergone too radical a change to make any comparison of figures other than misleading.

The materials on which this volume is based have in large part been supplied by the Admiralty, the Board of Trade, the Ministry of Shipping, and other Government Departments. Such material, to which no specific reference can yet be made, includes not only official publications, but confidential reports received from naval officers, intelligence officers, and consular officials as to the movements of shipping and the effect of losses; depositions of masters and officers of vessels captured by the enemy; miscellaneous telegrams and correspondence; diaries and letters of captured German officers and sailors. For the use which the author has made of this material, he alone is responsible.

PREFACE

The non-confidential and unofficial material consulted has been voluminous and varied. Many references will be found in the notes, but special mention may be made of the valuable information contained in publications issued by Lloyd's, the Liverpool Steamship Owners' Association, the Chamber of Shipping, and the Liverpool and London War Risks Insurance Association; the files of *Lloyd's List*, the *Statist*, and *Economist*; and the economic material collected by the Garton Foundation. Among many who have assisted him with advice and information, the author is under very special obligations to Sir Julian Corbett, whose guidance has been invaluable throughout; to Sir Norman Hill, Bart., Admiral Sir Edmond J. W. Slade, and Mr. John Hilton, all of whom have read and criticised the volume in proof to its very great advantage; and to the staff of the Historical Section.

CONTENTS

CHAPTER I

INTRODUCTORY: THE MARITIME TRADE OF THE BELLIGERENTS

Dependence of Great Britain on seaborne trade—Importance of seaborne trade to other belligerents—Volume, character, and value of British trade and shipping—Importance of British shipping to the Allies—Trade and shipping of the Allies—Trade and shipping of Germany and Austria—Neutral shipping in its relation to the war—Effect of steam, cables, and wireless telegraphy on the attack and defence of commerce—Financial factors in modern commerce . . . . . . pp. 1-29

CHAPTER II

THE OUTBREAK OF WAR: DANGERS AND PRECAUTIONS

Effects of the political crisis on shipping and insurance—Financial crisis and panic on the insurance market—Threatened stoppage of trade and food shortage—Genesis of the State Insurance Scheme—Adoption of the scheme by the Government—Its provisions—Declaration of war—Opening of the State Insurance Office—Effects of the scheme in maintaining seaborne trade—Other measures taken for the protection and encouragement of commerce—Admiralty advice and instructions to shipping—Naval protection and the armed liner menace—Geographical features in the attack and defence of trade—The Grand Fleet as the shield of British commerce—The cruiser squadrons and the trade routes—Critical character of the first weeks of war . . . . pp. 30-53

CHAPTER III

THE FIRST CAPTURES: THE MEDITERRANEAN MENACE

Legal position of belligerent merchantmen in enemy ports—Seizure and detention of such vessels by Germany and by the Allies—Prompt protection given to British trade—Immediate paralysis of German shipping and capture of German merchantmen—Reduction in the volume of traffic under the British flag—Significance of British control of the Straits of Gibraltar—Anxiety with regard to the Mediterranean tracks—Failure of the GOEBEN and BRESLAU to interrupt Mediterranean traffic—Capture or immobilisation of enemy shipping in that sea—Declaration of war against Austria and watch on the Austrian Fleet—Navigation in the Adriatic restricted—The situation at the Dardanelles—Rush of shipping to clear from the Black Sea—The Mediterranean link secured pp. 54-68

CONTENTS

CHAPTER IV

THE CONTROL OF THE ATLANTIC TERMINALS

Heavy responsibilities laid on the cruiser squadrons—The Declaration of London and the question of contraband—Further captures of enemy merchantmen—The protection of trade in the terminal waters—Raid by the KAISER WILHELM DER GROSSE off the Canaries—British shipping diverted and the patrols reinforced—Destruction of the KAISER WILHELM DER GROSSE by the HIGHFLYER—Limited effect of her operations—Increased security afforded to trade in the terminal waters—Reviving flow of traffic under the British flag—All grain ships pass the Dardanelles—The situation in European waters and the approaches thereto at the middle of September . . . . pp. 69–86

CHAPTER V

MINES IN THE NORTH SEA

Inactivity of the German High Seas Fleet—The German minelayers and International Law—Counter-measures by the British Admiralty : Restriction of Navigation in the North Sea—Neutral losses—Sinking of the *Runo*—Effect of these disasters on trade—German shipping confined to port—Effect of German command of the entrance to the Baltic—Russian trade forced on to White Sea and transhipment routes: timber and dairy produce—Activity of neutral shipping in trade with Scandinavia ; heavy shipments of foodstuffs—Communication maintained with Holland and Belgium—The general situation in the North Sea at the middle of September . . . . pp. 87–99

CHAPTER VI

THE SAFETY OF THE NORTH ATLANTIC

Volume, character, and distribution of North Atlantic trade—Its protection and possible assailants—German liners in American ports—Vital importance of the route, especially to food supplies—First effects of the outbreak of war : financial crisis and suspension of sailings—Admiral Cradock's brush with the KARLSRUHE—The approaches to New York and the St. Lawrence secured—Rapid resumption of sailings from and to American ports—Search for enemy cruisers in the Caribbean—The watch on the German liners—Capture of German supply ships in the Caribbean—Heavy shipments from the United States and Canada—Contrast between immobilisation of German shipping and activity of British trade
pp. 100–114

CHAPTER VII

COVERING TRADE IN THE FAR EAST

Characteristics and trade of the Oriental Route—The forces protecting and threatening the route—Dislocation of trade by the outbreak of war—Immediate steps taken to secure the focal points—Detention and seizures of enemy merchantmen—German shipping everywhere flies to shelter—Capture of German liners at sea—The KÖNIGSBERG sinks the *City of Winchester*—Indian trade nevertheless revives—Admiral Jerram protects

CONTENTS

and encourages trade in the Far East : gradual recovery of confidence—Capture of German liners off Tsingtau—Security of Australian trade—Radical change in the situation due to declaration of war by Japan—Progress of trade recovery hampered by economic conditions—Obstacles to the recovery of Indian trade—Activity of Indian exporters checked by shortage of tonnage—Further steps taken to protect Eastern trade—Position and outlook in the second week in September . pp. 115–143

CHAPTER VIII

THE SITUATION IN THE PACIFIC

The German forces in the Pacific unlocated—Admiral von Spee at Ponape—The Pacific trade routes—Admiral von Spee concentrates his squadron—Restriction of his movements by British dispositions—He detaches the EMDEN to the Indian Ocean and goes East with his main force—Allied trade little disturbed by the war—Abortive cruise of the PRINZ EITEL FRIEDRICH and COMORAN against Australian trade—The NÜRNBERG cuts the Australia-Vancouver cable—Admiral von Spee's appearance at Apia—The *Southport* captured by the GEIER, but escapes—Reduction of German Colonies and security of trade in the Western Pacific—The threat to trade on the West Coast of South America pp. 144–153

CHAPTER IX

EARLY ATTACKS ON THE SOUTH AMERICAN ROUTE

Vulnerability of the route—Its characteristics and trade—Dislocation of trade on the North Pacific coast—The LEIPZIG off San Francisco—Effect of her operations : congestion at Puget Sound ports—Her departure and subsequent recovery of trade—Paralysis of German shipping on West Coast of South America : its significance—Economic reactions of the war in Chile and Peru—Chilean proposal to acquire the Kosmos Line—Steps taken to encourage shipping in the South Atlantic—Effect of the outbreak of war accentuated by economic conditions in Brazil and Argentina—The DRESDEN holds up and releases three steamers—Capture of the *Santa Catherina*—Continued paralysis of trade at the Plate : difficulty with regard to Brazilian coffee shipments—Sinking of the *Hyades* and *Holmwood* by the DRESDEN : acute anxiety of shipowners and traders—They are reassured by the Admiralty—Admiral Cradock ordered to cover trade in the South Atlantic—Capture of the *Bowes Castle* by the KARLSRUHE : trade unaffected—Argentine meat and maize begin to move—Commercial conditions in Brazil : coffee and rubber—Three-quarters of a million tons of enemy shipping idle—British trade moving freely in the Pacific—Dangers threatening the route at the beginning of September—The crisis nevertheless past . . . . pp. 154–180

CHAPTER X

THE BEGINNINGS OF TRADE RECOVERY

Anticipations as to initial losses not fulfilled—Extensions of the State Insurance Scheme and reduction of premiums : effect on war risks in the open market—Dislocation of trade by war conditions : financial chaos ; loss of markets and sources of supply ; restrictions on navigation ; prohibition of exports ; requisitioning of ships—Amazing power of recovery displayed—Coal export resumed—Serious situation in the cotton trade—Surcharges on liner rates—Improved position at end of August—Further reductions in State Insurance premiums and their effect—Glut of tramp tonnage and fall in freights—Shipping and trade figures for August—Situation at the beginning of September—Effects of the war on French, Russian, and Belgian commerce—Losses and immobilisation of German and Austrian shipping—German efforts to find new channels for trade—Effects of the war on economic position of Germany and Austria

pp. 181–202

CHAPTER XI

THE "EMDEN" AT WORK

The EMDEN appears in the Bay of Bengal—Shipping moving freely at the time of her arrival—Her first prizes—Shipping at Calcutta warned: the routes closed—Further captures in the Bay of Bengal—Measures taken to protect trade—Reappearance of the KÖNIGSBERG—Bombardment of Madras by the EMDEN—The Bay of Bengal tracks again closed—Serious effects of the suspension of sailings—Panic and financial dislocation in Southern India—Shipping West of Colombo permitted to sail—The EMDEN attacks shipping near Colombo: several prizes taken—The routes west of Colombo closed—Reopening of the routes—Effects of the EMDEN's operations on commerce—The Admiralty decide to keep routes open—General situation of trade in the Far East—Revival of Indian trade at the beginning of October . . . pp. 203–220

CHAPTER XII

COMMERCE AND COMMERCE DESTROYERS ON THE SOUTH AMERICAN ROUTE

The DRESDEN passes into the Pacific—The KARLSRUHE and armed liners in the South Atlantic—Abortive cruise of the CAP TRAFALGAR—Her destruction by the CARMANIA—Bombardment of Papieté by Admiral von Spee: its effects—Search for the DRESDEN: her chase of the *Ortega*—Increased volume of trade in the South Atlantic—News of the KARLSRUHE and KRONPRINZ WILHELM—The DRESDEN on the Chilean coast—The LEIPZIG moves south and captures the *Elsinore*—The NEWCASTLE searches the Californian coast—The LEIPZIG on the Peruvian coast: her capture of the *Bankfields*—The German Pacific squadron approaches South American waters—The Trans-Pacific services well maintained—News of the LEIPZIG's operations received in Peru—Sailings suspended at Peruvian ports: effects on trade—Admiral von Spee's intention to proceed to South America discovered—The GLASGOW and MONMOUTH at Valparaiso: paralysis of German trade—Sailings resumed from Peruvian ports—Precautions taken in the North Pacific—The Panama Canal and North Pacific trade—General situation on the route at end of October

pp. 221–237

CHAPTER XIII

TRADE PROTECTION IN THE SOUTH ATLANTIC

Necessity of additional protection for South Atlantic tracks—Increased shipments of meat and grain from the Plate and New Zealand—Evidences of hostile activity in the South Atlantic—Immunity of trade in the North

Atlantic and in terminal waters—Work of the patrols—West African trade and its protection—Big capture of German steamers at Duala—Admiral Stoddart goes to Pernambuco—Fourteen captures by the KARLSRUHE reported—The course of trade not interrupted . pp. 238-245

CHAPTER XIV

THE CAREER OF THE "KARLSRUHE"

Characteristics and early movements of the KARLSRUHE—Her capture of the *Bowes Castle*—Her supply ships and cruising ground—Her capture of the *Strathroy*—Captain Köhler's methods and good fortune—His capture of the *Maple Branch*—Movements of the KRONPRINZ WILHELM—Her capture of the *Indian Prince*—The KARLSRUHE takes the *Highland Hope* and turns westward in fear of interruption—Her capture of the *Indrani*, which is used as a tender—Further captures by the KARLSRUHE—The case of the *Maria*—The position in the South Atlantic at the beginning of October—The KARLSRUHE's eastward sweep: captures of grain ships—The KARLSRUHE goes west of the tracks: capture of the *Condor*—The *Crefeld* sent off to Tenerife with prisoners—Capture of *La Correntina* by the KRONPRINZ WILHELM—Capture of the *Glanton* and *Hurstdale* by the KARLSRUHE—Captain Köhler quits his cruising ground—Effects of the KARLSRUHE's depredations on trade—Small percentage of ships and cargoes captured—No suspension of sailings caused by KARLSRUHE's operations—Many vessels saved by deviation—The German cruisers handicapped by coaling difficulties and lack of bases—Position on the arrival of Admiral Stoddart . . . . . . pp. 246-267

CHAPTER XV

REAPPEARANCE OF THE "EMDEN"

The EMDEN goes to Diego Garcia and cruises fruitlessly for Australian meat ships—The search for the EMDEN—Capture of her colliers by the YARMOUTH—The EMDEN's second raid off Minikoi—Continued search for the EMDEN: little delay to shipping—Criticism of naval dispositions: Bengal Chamber of Commerce demands convoys—Admiralty Statement as to trade protection—Better observance of Admiralty instructions—Steady recovery of Indian trade—Commercial activity in the Far East and Australia—Increased shipments from the United Kingdom—The search for the KONIGSBERG: her inactivity—British control of the Western Pacific—The EMDEN raids Penang and sinks the *Zhemchug*—Trade little affected—The Oriental Route now well guarded—The KÖNIGSBERG located in the Rufiji River and blockaded . . . . . . pp. 268-279

CHAPTER XVI

TRADE ACTIVITY IN EUROPEAN WATERS

Immunity of British shipping on North American, Cape, and Mediterranean tracks, and in terminal waters—Mine losses in North Sea reduced during September—Further restrictions on navigation in North Sea—Further losses due to German mines—Maintenance of North Sea trade—German interference with wood cargoes from Baltic—Consequent irritation in Sweden threatens German iron supplies—Efforts to develop the trade of Archangel : Russian Insurance Scheme—Appearance of the submarine as a commerce destroyer : loss of the *Glitra*—New minefield off Irish Coast : loss of the *Manchester Commerce* : its restricted effects—The fight for the Channel Coast : Belgian steamship lines transferred to British ports—Congestion of French Atlantic ports hampers trade—Immunity of traffic with Spain and Portugal—Mines in the Adriatic—Mediterranean trade prosperous—Attempt to revive Black Sea chartering frustrated by closure of the Dardanelles—Turkish attack on Russian ports : War declared—Serious effects of suspension of Black Sea trade—Elasticity of British commerce—Neutral susceptibilities impede restriction of enemy supplies—Contraband reaching Germany through neutral countries—Further measures taken by British Government to restrict enemy trade

pp. 280–299

CHAPTER XVII

THE PROGRESS OF TRADE RECOVERY

Limited effect of the German attack on commerce—Steadily increasing volume of British trade, especially in imports of foodstuffs and raw materials—Comparison with August and September 1904—Continued fall in War Risk premiums: policy of State Office—Increased activity on the freight markets—Effects of requisitioning on supply of tonnage—Rise in freights—Slight recovery of French commerce—Economic condition of the Central Powers—General situation at the end of October . . pp. 300–312

CHAPTER XVIII

THE BATTLE OF CORONEL AND ITS EFFECT ON TRADE

Reviving trade of the South American Route threatened by Admiral von Spee—He proceeds to the Chilean coast—Search for the KARLSRUHE : her capture of the *Vandyck*—The German squadron off Valparaiso : Escape of the *Colusa*—Suspension of British sailings from Valparaiso—Battle of Coronel—British trade on the West Coast at a standstill—Effects of the battle and of the KARLSRUHE's captures on insurance markets and confidence—Argentine maize export undisturbed—Loss of the *Valentine* and *Helicon*—Measures taken to cover trade routes . . pp. 313–324

CHAPTER XIX

THE END OF THE "EMDEN" AND "KARLSRUHE"

Captain von Müller decides to raid Cocos I.—Precautions taken by Admiral Jerram—Destruction of the EMDEN by the SYDNEY—The KÖNIGSBERG also accounted for—Fall of Tsingtau and internment of the GEIER—Destruction of the KARLSRUHE—The careers of the EMDEN and KARLSRUHE compared—Percentage of losses due to the EMDEN's operations—Causes which limited her success—Serious indirect effects of her operations—Expansion of Indian trade follows her destruction—Fall in insurance rates—Anxiety as to possible Turkish attack on the Suez Canal—Protection of trade in the Persian Gulf—Complete control established over Oriental Route . . . . pp. 325–337

CONTENTS

CHAPTER XX

FROM CORONEL TO THE FALKLANDS

German cruisers unlocated in Pacific and South Atlantic—The KRONZ-PRINZ WILHELM captures the *Union*—Reasons for her comparative inactivity—Continued suspension of sailings on the West Coast—Loss of the *North Wales*—German liners meet Admiral von Spee with coal and provisions: annoyance of Chilean Government—Over 100,000 tons of British shipping held up—Paralysis of trade in Chile and Peru—Refusal of German liners to engage in trade—Chilean protection to shipping in territorial waters—North Pacific trade little disturbed—West Coast shipping begins to move at end of November—South Atlantic trade well maintained in spite of alarming rumours—British concentration in the South Atlantic—Admiral von Spee goes round the Horn—Loss of the *Drummuir*—Capture of the *Charcas* by the PRINZ EITEL FRIEDRICH—Destruction of the German Pacific Squadron—Its immediate results . . . . pp. 338–350

CHAPTER XXI

THE ADVENT OF THE SUBMARINE

Failure of the German cruiser campaign—Reduction of mine losses during November—Reappearance of the submarine as a commerce destroyer—Loss of the *Malachite* and *Primo*—Improved import figures for November—Reduction in State Insurance rates—General immunity of shipping—Admiral von Tirpitz foreshadows submarine campaign against commerce—Mine losses check Russo-Swedish traffic—German raid on East Coast followed by many losses due to mines—Effect on sailings and insurance rates—Minefield off Irish coast—Effect of restrictions on navigation in North Sea—Activity of North Sea trade—German attitude towards wood cargoes in neutral vessels—White Sea trade increases, but restricted by lack of equipment at Archangel and by ice—December trade figures reflect security of the trade routes—Shortage of tonnage and congestion of ports—Further reduction in State Insurance rates—News of the *Kronprinz Wilhelm*—Limited success of efforts to revive German trade—Continued expansion of British commerce—Opening of the submarine campaign . . . . pp. 351–368

CHAPTER XXII

THE END OF THE FIRST PHASE

Security and volume of South American trade after the Battle of the Falklands—The DRESDEN goes into hiding—The PRINZ EITEL FRIEDRICH captures the *Jean* and prepares to leave the Pacific—Further captures by the KRONPRINZ WILHELM; her narrow escapes—The PRINZ EITEL FRIEDRICH comes round the Horn and attacks the sailing trade—Operations of the three raiders subsequent to January 31st, 1915—Arrival and internment of the PRINZ EITEL FRIEDRICH at Newport News—Destruction of the DRESDEN—Final captures and internment of the KRONPRINZ WILHELM—Careers of the KRONPRINZ WILHELM and PRINZ EITEL FRIEDRICH—Limitations of the armed liner as a commerce destroyer . pp. 369–382

CHAPTER XXIII

COMPARISONS AND ACHIEVEMENTS

Activity of British trade contrasted with paralysis of German shipping—Comparison of tonnage losses suffered by belligerents—Effects of economic pressure on Central Powers—British losses insignificant when compared with volume and value of traffic—Economic factors limiting recovery in export trade—Volume of essential imports well maintained—Rise in the cost of living in the United Kingdom—Upward course of freights—Shortage of tonnage caused by redistribution of traffic and by requisitioning—Congestion of ports: its causes and effects—Economic factors a more potent cause of freight and price advances than naval operations—The campaign against British commerce hitherto frustrated at every point

pp. 383–410

APPENDIX . . . . pp. 411–419

INDEX . . . . pp. 421–442

LIST OF MAPS

IN SEPARATE VOLUME

1. THE WORLD ON MERCATOR'S PROJECTION, SHOWING PRINCIPAL TRADE ROUTES.

2. NORTH SEA AND BALTIC SEA, SHOWING EARLY MINEFIELDS IN NORTH SEA

3. NORTH ATLANTIC, SHOWING NORTH AMERICAN AND CARIBBEAN TRADE ROUTES.

4. ORIENTAL TRADE ROUTE.

5. SOUTH AMERICAN TRADE ROUTE, SHOWING POINTS OF ATTACK, AUGUST 1914—MARCH 1915.

6a. GULF OF ADEN, SHOWING CAPTURE OF *City of Winchester* BY "KÖNIGSBERG," AUGUST 6, 1914.

6b. VICINITY OF CANARIES, SHOWING CAPTURES BY "KAISER WILHELM DER GROSSE," AUGUST 15–16, 1914.

6c. PACIFIC COAST OF NORTH AMERICA, SHOWING CAPTURE OF *Elsinore* BY "LEIPZIG," SEPTEMBER 11, 1914.

6d. GULF OF GUAYAQUIL, SHOWING CAPTURE OF *Bankfields* BY "LEIPZIG," SEPTEMBER 25, 1914.

7. BAY OF BENGAL AND PART OF INDIAN OCEAN, SHOWING CAPTURES BY "EMDEN," SEPTEMBER 10—OCTOBER 30, 1914.

8. VICINITY OF CAPE SAN ROQUE, SHOWING CAPTURES BY "KARLSRUHE," "DRESDEN," AND "KRONPRINZ WILHELM," AUGUST 15 TO OCTOBER 27, 1914.

9. MID-ATLANTIC, SHOWING CAPTURES BY "KRONPRINZ WILHELM" AND "PRINZ EITEL FRIEDRICH," DECEMBER 4, 1914, TO MARCH 27, 1915.

Typographical Note.—Throughout the volume the names of warships and merchantmen commissioned as warships are printed in small capitals, thus—KÖNIGSBERG, KRONPRINZ WILHELM. The names of all other ships are printed in italics, thus—*Elsinore*.

SEABORNE TRADE

CHAPTER I

INTRODUCTORY: THE MARITIME TRADE OF THE BELLIGERENTS [1]

THE protection of seaborne trade has always ranked among the primary functions of the British Navy, but since the industrial revolution at the end of the eighteenth century its importance has immeasurably increased. Deprived of that trade Great Britain could neither maintain her industries, nor equip her armies, nor feed her people. The maintenance of maritime communications was, in August 1914, a consideration every whit as vital as the denial of passage to an invading force.

Indeed, the economic developments of the last hundred years had emphasised for every industrially developed State the danger of any interruption of its seaborne trade. Few such States were wholly self-sufficing as regards the production of foodstuffs, and practically all were dependent in some degree upon oversea supplies for the raw materials necessary, not only to the conduct of war, but also to the fulfilment of the minimum requirements of civil life. Nor could any of them find adequate markets for its surplus products if it were unable to avail itself of maritime transport. The conditions of modern warfare, involving the withdrawal of labour and transport on a gigantic scale from civil to military employment, intensified the dependence of belligerent Powers upon external sources of supply, and at the same time, the vast expenditure incurred emphasised the importance of maintaining the machinery of commerce and finance in working order.

In the great struggle which began in August 1914, all these considerations were strengthened by the wide spread of the conflict and the extent to which hostilities were prolonged. The insular position of Great Britain retained something at least of an exceptional character;

[1] See Map 1.

but all the continental belligerents were faced from the first with a restriction of their open land frontiers which rendered them increasingly dependent upon oversea traffic for important elements of their national strength. With every month that went by the greater became the effect, both military and economic, of commercial isolation. The steps by which British and Allied commerce was protected and encouraged, the measures adopted to check panic on the marine insurance market and avert the laying up of shipping, the sweeping of the enemy's merchant flag from the sea and the slow strangulation of his foreign trade, may lack, in general, the spectacular interest and vivid drama of actions such as those which took place off the Falklands or the coast of Jutland, but even their routine developments are equally significant in the history of the world war.

It is, indeed, by the effect of naval activity upon the economic situation that the success or failure of the operations undertaken by the naval forces of either belligerent group must to a great extent be tested; but in order to appreciate fully the relation between the events of the war at sea and the arrest or progress of commerce, it is necessary first of all to form some idea of the target presented to attack by the seaborne trade and mercantile fleets of the States participating in the conflict, and of their relative importance to the nations concerned. The extent and nature of their seaborne commerce, the degree in which it depended upon shipping flying the national flag, and the waters in which that shipping was mainly to be found, were all factors in the problem.

It was, of course, for Great Britain herself that both the monetary value of the interests exposed to attack and the relative importance of those interests to the national strength reached its maximum. During the three years (1911, 1912, 1913) which immediately preceded the war the average value of goods annually imported into the United Kingdom for home consumption was £623,000,000, of which £263,000,000 represented food, drink, and tobacco, and £205,000,000 raw materials for use in British factories. A considerable part of this total was received in payment of interest on British investments abroad, or in return for shipping, banking, and insurance services rendered to foreigners. To pay for the remainder, British produce and manufactures were exported to the extent of nearly

£489,000,000 annually. In addition, foreign and colonial produce to the value of £108,000,000 a year was consigned to this country and subsequently re-exported to other destinations.[1]

The most striking feature in these figures is the very large proportion which foodstuffs bore to the whole import trade. But a mere recital of import figures gives only a very imperfect picture of the extent to which this country was dependent on oversea supplies for the necessaries of life. Calculations made by a Committee of the Royal Society show that on an average of the five years 1909–1913, inclusive, nearly two-thirds, in nutriment values, of the annual consumption of foodstuffs in the United Kingdom came from abroad, and the proportion of imports was particularly high in the case of cereals—the most vital of all foods.[2]

With regard to the stocks at any time on hand, precise calculations are difficult to obtain, especially as the quan-

[1] The statistics in this chapter relating to British trade and to the net tonnage of vessels entered and cleared at British ports, are taken from the *Annual Statement of the Trade of the United Kingdom for* 1913 [Cd. 7585], and the *Annual Statement of the Navigation and Shipping of the United Kingdom for* 1913 [Cd. 7616]. Those relating to the trade of foreign countries are based mainly on the *Statistical Abstract for the Principal and Other Foreign Countries*, 1901–1912 [Cd. 7525]. Unless otherwise stated, all trade figures represent the average of the last three years for which statistics were available, or the mean percentages for such three years. The figures of the mercantile shipping owned in each country are from *Lloyd's Register*, 1914–15.

[2] *The Food Supply of the United Kingdom* [Cd. 8421], 1917. The figures given by the Committee in respect of some of the leading items show the following percentages:

	Imports.	Home Production.
Cereals	79	21
Meat (including bacon and hams)	40	60
Butter	64·5	35·5
Cheese	80	20
Eggs	50	50
Margarine	49·5	50·5
Vegetables (other than potatoes)	36	64
Fruit	73	27
Sugar, cocoa, and chocolate	100	*nil.*

Moreover, perhaps a quarter of the home supplies of meat and dairy produce depended upon the use of imported fodder, and the manufacturers of margarine drew almost the whole of their raw materials from foreign sources. This fact was not allowed for by the Committee, but taking it into account, it would appear that imports accounted for 55·2 per cent. of the protein (the chief body-building substance), 61·2 per cent. of the fats, and 69·5 per cent. of the carbo-hydrates contained in the food annually consumed by the population of the United Kingdom. Translating the whole into energy value, in terms of calories, the dependence upon seaborne trade amounted to 64 per cent.

tities showed a marked variation according to season. It appears, however, from the Report of the Royal Commission on the Supply of Food and Raw Material in Time of War that the stocks of the principal imported foodstuffs seldom exceeded four to eight weeks' supply. By rigid economy, the adoption of State rationing, the substitution of alternative foodstuffs for those in which stocks were low, and the forestalling of home supplies, these periods could be increased; but it was evident that in the event of any large proportion of imports ceasing to come forward, the limit of endurance must soon be reached.

Very much the same conditions were presented by the staple industries. Cotton, silk, petroleum, rubber, jute, hemp, and many minor but essential products were derived exclusively from foreign sources. Seventy-five per cent. of the annual wool consumption was imported. Of the iron ore employed in British foundries three-quarters was produced at home, but owing to the greater richness of Spanish ores, 40 to 50 per cent. of the total production of pig-iron was derived from imports, and the metallic manganese required by steel manufacturers was mainly of foreign origin. In the production of copper, tin, lead, and zinc, shipments from abroad accounted for a large, in some instances an overwhelming proportion of the ores smelted.[1] Some six or seven million tons of timber were brought into the United Kingdom every year, about a third of this figure representing pit-props required in the collieries. Indeed, it is not too much to say that almost all the staple British industries were dependent for their prosperity upon the uninterrupted flow of commodities from oversea. Stocks of several of the more important raw materials representing six months' consumption or over were normally available, but the assurance of adequate and regular supplies was an essential condition of continuous activity in factories and workshops.[2]

[1] See *Census of Production, Final Report* [Cd. 6320], 1912.
[2] *Report of the Royal Commission on Supply of Food and Raw Material in Time of War* [Cd. 2643], 1905. The average period in which stocks of certain important materials would be exhausted at the normal rate of consumption is given as follows:

Cotton . . about 7 months	Jute (Dundee only)	4–12 months
Wool, imported . 2–3 ,,	Silk, raw . .	a few months
,, home grown . 6 ,,	Other kinds .	a very short time
,, mohair, alpaca, etc. . . 6 ,,	Silk, Manufacturers' stocks . .	2–3 months
Flax (Dundee only) 4–9 ,,	Iron Ore, imported .	1–2 ,,

While the first essential in time of war was to secure the safe passage of food and raw materials, there were also certain manufactured articles of a specialised character, such as aniline dyes and optical instruments, for which Great Britain was almost wholly dependent on foreign countries. Moreover, the vast expansion called for in military equipment and the enormous accumulation of munitions and war material necessitated by the conditions of modern warfare, strained the manufacturing resources of the country to their utmost at an early stage of the conflict, and involved large purchases abroad. In order to avert a collapse of the national strength it was essential that each of the three great branches of the import trade should be maintained, and scarcely less important was the maintenance of the outward-bound traffic. For it was only by the uninterrupted flow of exports that imports could be paid for, and unemployment and distress amongst the industrial population avoided, without incurring crushing indebtedness to the producing countries.

The task imposed upon the Navy by the necessity of affording protection to this gigantic trade was a heavy one. The total weight of commodities imported during 1913 has been estimated at 55,000,000 tons, and that of exports and re-exports at 100,000,000, including 76,000,000 tons of coal. It can safely be assumed, therefore, that the trade of the United Kingdom involved annually the lifting of cargoes amounting to over 150,000,000 tons.[1]

In addition, the coasting traffic of the United Kingdom, which was carried on almost entirely under the British flag, involved the lifting of some 70,000,000 tons annually, and was a very important factor in the distribution of imports.

The carriage of these cargoes involved, as shown by the entrances and clearances in the foreign trade at ports in the United Kingdom, an average of 47,000 laden voyages inwards and 61,000 outwards each year, of which 26,000 and 31,000 respectively were made under the national flag. The proportion of the total trade carried by British ships

Timber—soft	1¾–8 months	Petroleum	. .	6 months
,, hard	unspecified	Rubber .	. .	4–8 weeks
Hides and leather	6–9 months			

The Royal Commission calculated the proportion of pig-iron produced from foreign ores at 41 per cent. In 1913 it was almost exactly 50 per cent.

[1] *Reports of the Departmental Committee on Shipping and Ship-building* [Cd. 9092], 1918, p. 75.

was, however, much higher, whether as regards volume or values, than these figures would suggest. Their average size was greater than that of their foreign competitors,[1] their average cargoes, especially in the import trade, were more than proportionately heavier, and they were responsible for the distribution of the greater part of the more valuable exports. Taking all these factors into account, their total share in maintaining the commerce of the United Kingdom may safely be put at 74 per cent.[2]

The carriage of cargoes from or to British home ports was, however, only a part of the work performed by the mercantile marine. The enterprise of many generations had rendered British shipowners and seamen pre-eminently the carriers of the world's commerce, and from 40 to 45 per cent. of the ocean-going tonnage was normally employed in trading between ports in the British Dominions oversea, or in foreign countries. It has, indeed, been estimated that British shipping carried no less than half the total volume of the world's seaborne trade, and if the value of the cargoes be taken as the criterion, the proportion rises to 52 per cent.[3] This general carrying trade had an important economic significance, for, as we have seen, no small portion of the goods annually imported into the United Kingdom represented payment for the services of the mercantile marine and for banking and insurance services closely connected with the carrying and *entrepôt* trade. Moreover, it was to a great extent the services of British ships, as carriers of cargoes between foreign countries, by which the resources of many of our principal markets and sources of supply had been built up. The protection of the routes between foreign ports was thus only second in importance to the safety of the tracks leading to the United Kingdom itself.

The mercantile fleet by which these functions were performed reached, on July 1st, 1914, a total of 8,587 steamers and 653 sailing vessels, with a tonnage of 19,250,000; and the total tonnage under the British flag, including ships owned in the Oversea Dominions, was 21,000,000, or about 43 per cent. of the world's shipping.[4] In the

[1] The proportion of British tonnage to the total tonnage entered and cleared was 68 and 62 per cent. respectively.
[2] Cd. 9092, p. 143. The percentage quoted refers to values.
[3] Cd. 9092, pp. 145–146.
[4] Statistics of shipping tonnage are variously given under three denominations, " Gross Tonnage," " Net Tonnage," and " Deadweight." *Gross*

LINERS AND TRAMPS 7

larger classes of ocean-going steamers, British predominance was still more pronounced, and in actual carrying power the tonnage under the British flag was at least equal to that of all other countries put together.

It was, however, on the steamers of 1,000 tons net (say 1,600 tons gross) and upwards, that the country relied for the maintenance of the ocean traffic—of all traffic, that is to say, with ports lying outside the Home Trade limits, stretching from Brest to the Elbe. The circumstances of the war, which cut off so large a proportion of the short distance trade, emphasised our dependence on this class of vessel, of which there were on the Register, on December 31st, 1913, 3,747.[1] Of these about one third, representing 42 per cent. of the tonnage, were liners running on fixed voyages and to a regular schedule of dates. A few of these vessels were constructed almost exclusively for the passenger traffic; but by far the greater number even of those holding a passenger certificate carried large cargoes in addition, and many liners were confined exclusively to the cargo trade. It was by the fixed services that British exports, other than coal, were mainly carried, and they brought in practically the whole foreign meat supply of the country, the greater part of the imported dairy produce, much of the grain, and a large proportion of the less bulky and more valuable imports of raw material and manufactured goods. The regularity of their sailings gave them a special importance in trades where a fixed date of arrival is a factor in the estimation of profits, and it had the additional advantage of avoiding the carry-

---

tonnage represents the total measurement capacity of a vessel, calculated at 100 cubic feet to the ton, and is the denomination most commonly employed. *Net tonnage* represents the measurement capacity after deducting space occupied by engine room and accommodation for the crew. It is commonly used in official statistics, and is always employed for figures of entrances and clearances. Roughly speaking, 8 tons gross may be taken as the equivalent of 5 tons net, though this gives no certain rule for calculating the tonnage of individual ships. *Deadweight*, seldom employed for statistics except in America, represents the weight of cargo and bunkers that the vessel can carry when fully loaded. When not otherwise specified, all tonnages given in this work represent the *gross* tonnage of steamers, and *net* tonnage of sailing vessels, except in figures of entrances and clearances and comparisons based thereon, when net tonnage only is employed. In computing the percentage of the world's shipping owned by different countries, American vessels confined to the navigation of the Great Lakes are, in every instance, excluded. All steamers under 100 tons gross and all sailing vessels under 100 tons net are excluded from the statistics given.

[1] Cd. 7616, p. xi.

ing of heavy stocks in this country, and thus reducing the cost of storage. The services of the great lines, such as the Cunard, the White Star, the P. & O., Union Castle, Orient, Blue Funnel, Shaw Saville and Albion Lines, the Pacific Steam Navigation Company, and the Royal Mail, connected the British Isles with almost every port throughout the habitable globe, and on their uninterrupted regularity depended not only a big percentage of the essential supplies, but the financial stability of the country, since it was mainly by them that the products of British factories were distributed in foreign markets.

On the other hand, it was mainly by the general traders or tramps that the bulkier commodities, which are usually shipped in whole cargoes, such as sugar, ore, timber, and to some extent grain, were brought to British ports. It was entirely by vessels of this class that the exports of coal were lifted, and in the general carrying trade their importance was very great. Running on no regular service, and ready to go wherever a charter could be obtained, and to take the goods to any port to which they might be ordered, these ships were an indispensable factor in the distribution of the world's commerce, while at the same time they constituted for Great Britain an all-important mobile reserve of surplus tonnage on which to draw in time of need. In times of peace they were to be found engaged in the trade of other countries to an even greater extent than in that of the United Kingdom, and while liners accounted for over 54 per cent. of the British tonnage employed in the carriage of our own imports and exports, 81 per cent. of the steamers and 75 per cent. of the tonnage trading between foreign ports consisted of general traders.[1] Whether privately owned or belonging to the fleets of big companies, this crowd of freighters was constantly on the move, presenting itself wherever trade happened to be brisk, in many cases only returning to British ports after an interval of many months, even of years, spent in going from port to port abroad, in response to the demand for tonnage.

While the ramifications of this world-wide trade defy

---

[1] These percentages are based on a table contained in a *Report presented to the Liverpool Steam Ship Owners' Association on the Shipping of the United Kingdom employed in Ocean Trade*, by Sir Norman Hill, Secretary to the Association, in October 1915.

detailed analysis, certain main Trade Routes are distinguishable, under which the greater part of ocean traffic may conveniently be grouped. These routes were common to the shipping of all nations, but the world-wide character of British commerce and the extent of British interests in the general carrying trade gave to this country a paramount interest in their security.

The North American Route ran from Canada and the United States to ports on the Northern and Western coasts of Europe, with a branch to the Mediterranean. In volume of annual trade and in the total tonnage engaged, it was the foremost of the ocean highways, and its preservation against attack was amongst the chief objects of British naval activity. Closely connected with it, but of lesser importance, was the *Caribbean Route* to the Gulf of Mexico, Central America, and the West Indies.

Of equal importance from the point of view of British trade was the *Oriental Route*, which had its home terminals in British and North Sea ports, and passed through the Straits of Gibraltar and the Mediterranean Sea, by way of the Suez Canal, to India, Australia, and the Far East. No other route played so large a part in the distribution of British manufactures, and in the early months of the war it derived a special interest from the fact that it became the scene of operations of the most daring and successful of the German raiders.

Third in importance was the *South American Route*, which was the object of sustained cruiser attack for a period of some months. The greatest volume of trade on this route was to be found on the track which stretches diagonally across the Atlantic, from the neighbourhood of Finisterre to Brazil and the River Plate; but the route was continued through the Straits of Magellan, or round Cape Horn, to the Pacific coast of America, and was joined off Cape Horn by the track of homeward-bound steamers from New Zealand.

The Cape, or South African Route, had lost much of its value as a result of the construction of the Suez Canal, but part of the outward-bound Australian trade still went by way of the Cape of Good Hope. Apart from this trade, the Cape Route derived its chief importance from the commerce of the South African Union; but it received substantial contributions from the branch lines which served the various ports created by the development of colonisation on both the West and East African coasts.

The West African trade, indeed, while its defence was bound up with that of the Cape Route, was commercially of sufficient importance to deserve separate reference.

The *North Pacific Route*, from the Far East to the West Coast of America, and the *Australian-American Route* across the Pacific were of somewhat minor significance so far as British shipping was concerned, and though the Panama Canal added greatly to their importance, this Canal was only opened after the commencement of hostilities and had little effect on shipping during the early months of the war.

In addition to these great trunk lines, there were innumerable cross tracks and branches which supplemented the main routes and assisted in the distribution of their trade. A great volume of commerce was also carried by vessels plying on the short sea passages to and from the North Sea and Baltic ports, the Mediterranean, or the Atlantic coast of Europe. With the exception of certain sections of the Pacific commerce and the coastal trade of foreign countries, there were few branches of ocean traffic in which British vessels were not extensively engaged at the outbreak of war.[1]

The field of operations thus presented to hostile attack was incomparably rich. The total value of the steam tonnage owned in the United Kingdom and engaged in the foreign trade was estimated in 1911 at £127,000,000, and at the outbreak of war it was probably in the neighbourhood of £150,000,000.[2] To this figure must be added, in estimating the extent of British interests afloat, the value of the cargoes, both British and foreign, carried by the ships; for even the foreign cargoes were mostly insured on the London market. It will be seen from the trade figures already given that the value of British cargoes afloat, whether in British or foreign bottoms, averaged £100,000,000 a month, and the total value of all cargoes carried by British ships during 1913 has been estimated at

[1] Sir Douglas Owen, *Ocean Trade and Shipping*, Cambridge, 1914, and B. Olney Hough, *Ocean Traffic and Trade*, London and Chicago, 1914, both rank the Cape Route before the South American. In assigning third place to the South American Route, special regard has been paid to the share of Argentina, Uruguay, and New Zealand in the food supplies of the United Kingdom, and to the fact that the homeward trade from Australia mostly comes through the Suez Canal. Sir Douglas Owen, writing from an exclusively British standpoint, places the Oriental Route first of all.

[2] In December 1914, 4,421 steamers entered in the various War Risks Associations were insured for £153,469,068. These included a number of coasting steamers, but on the other hand the insured values were often well below the actual value of the vessels.

£1,800,000,000.[1] On the other hand, the volume of the traffic rendered it difficult for an enemy to produce a material impression upon it by anything short of a commercial blockade of the British Isles. The number of ships engaged in British trade was so great that a score of captures, while it might bring serious loss to individual owners or underwriters, would represent only an insignificant percentage. So world-wide was our commerce, that even the temporary closing of a minor track could be looked upon with comparative indifference, so long as the safety of the main trade routes was not compromised.

To our Allies the free movement of British shipping was only less important than to ourselves, for while all were dependent, in varying degree, upon seaborne trade, no one of them possessed a mercantile marine of sufficient size to carry that trade without being supplemented by the services of vessels flying foreign flags, nor had they, like ourselves, a large reserve of surplus tonnage engaged in traffic between foreign ports, which could be drawn into their own trade should need arise. All were dependent, in greater or less degree, upon the ability of British shipowners to continue their activities in the general carrying trade.

Thus, in time of peace, between 60 and 70 per cent. of French imports and exports were seaborne; but only about 40 per cent. of the seaborne imports and less than 60 per cent. of the corresponding exports were carried in French bottoms.[2] The total value of the seaborne trade, including goods in transit, averaged some £435,000,000 a year, and though the home production of the principal foodstuffs was not far short of the amount consumed, French industries depended upon oversea supplies for a large proportion of their raw materials. It must be remembered, moreover, that the greater part of the trade across the land frontiers was brought to an end by the outbreak of war, while at the same time the vital necessity of importing materials, manufactured goods, and even foodstuffs, was emphasised by the insuperable difficulties in the way of maintaining home production at its normal level. The general mobilisation, the demands of the armies, and the German occupation, early in the war, of the richest metalliferous

[1] Cd. 9092, p. 74.
[2] The figures represent goods actually carried in French and foreign ships, not tonnage entered and cleared. French tonnage in the foreign trade was under 30 per cent. Cd. 7525 and *Report on Bounties and Subsidies in Foreign Countries* [Cd. 6899], 1913.

districts, all tended to increase the dependence of the country upon maritime trade.

Though inadequate to the demands of her commerce, the mercantile marine of France represented an important element of her national wealth, and exposed a considerable target to hostile attack. It amounted to very nearly 2,320,000 tons, including 1,025 steamers and 551 sailing vessels. The relative value of the sailing trade was greater to France than to most other maritime countries, and the two largest individual fleets of sailing vessels in the world were French.[1]

Five great steamship companies accounted between them for half the steam tonnage: the Compagnie Générale Transatlantique, whose chief services ran to North American and West Indian ports; the Messageries Maritimes, trading to the Levant and Black Sea, French Indo-China and the Far East, Australia, Madagascar, and Mauritius; the Chargeurs Réunis, with lines to the Far East, South America, and West Africa; the Compagnie de Navigation Sud-Atlantique, who owned the fastest liners under any flag on the South American Route; and the Société Générale de Transports Maritimes, whose vessels were mainly employed in the trade with Algeria and Tunis. There were few large fleets of tramp steamers, but the commerce between France and her African Colonies and Protectorates engaged the attention of numerous minor lines, and a great number of short sea traders ran from the northern ports to the United Kingdom. Havre and Bordeaux were the chief home terminals in the Atlantic trade, but neither of them approached the commercial importance of Marseilles, the centre of the Mediterranean traffic and the port of departure for East Africa and the Far East, which did something like twice the trade of any other French port.

In the case of Russia the disproportion between commerce and shipping was still more marked than in that of France. Although 45 per cent. of the imports and 72 per cent. of the exports were seaborne, only 21 per cent. of the tonnage entered with cargoes and 11 per cent. of the tonnage cleared flew the national flag. The total mercantile marine, exclusive of vessels on the Caspian Sea, amounted to about 1,000,000 tons, employed chiefly in the Baltic,

---

[1] Those of the Société Nouvelle d'Armament, Nantes, and A. D. Bordes et Fils, Dunkirk. The total French sailing fleet was 397,152 tons, more than half of which belonged to these two firms.

Black Sea, and Levant. The Russian Volunteer Fleet and the Northern Steamship Co. also maintained important services to the Far East, and there were a number of steamers engaged exclusively in the trade of the Siberian ports.

Unlike most of the other Great Powers, Russia was wholly self-supporting as regards foodstuffs, but the comparatively backward state of her industries involved a dependence upon foreign factories, which was emphasised by the demand for war material. On the other hand, the economic strength of the Empire rested to a very large extent upon the sale of its harvests in foreign markets. Both as a market and a source of supply, Germany took the foremost part in Russian trade, and the closing of the German and Austrian frontiers forced the Empire into almost complete reliance on the sea routes. At the same time, the capacity of Russia to use those routes was limited by the circumstances of her geographical position. With the Dardanelles in the hands of a hostile Power, the Black Sea ports, with nearly half the seagoing shipping of the Empire, became useless for the purposes of foreign trade. The outlet from the Baltic is a narrow bottle-neck easily closed by an active enemy, and at both the Baltic and White Sea ports navigation is impeded by ice throughout the winter months.

The foreign trade of Belgium, though large, was carried on almost entirely by foreign—mainly British and German —shipping. Japan, on the other hand, possessed a mercantile fleet with a steam tonnage of nearly 1,750,000 tons. But though the Nippon Yusen Kaisha, one of the leading shipowners of the world, maintained an important European service, Japanese shipping was mostly employed in the local trade of the Far East, or on the Pacific Routes.

Of far greater importance than the shipping owned by any Ally of Great Britain was the mercantile fleet of her principal adversary. The efforts of German shipowners and shipbuilders, backed by active support from the Government, had brought Germany into the second place on the world list. On July 1st, 1914, she owned 2,090 steamers and 298 sailing vessels, aggregating about 5,500,000 tons, or nearly 12 per cent. of the world's total tonnage.

Although the special export rates quoted by the German State Railways were not confined exclusively to goods shipped in German bottoms, it was by German shipping that a large proportion of the commerce of the Empire was handled. No less than 50 per cent. of the tonnage entered, and 60 per cent. of that which was cleared with cargoes at German ports flew the national flag; but like British shipping, that of Germany was to be found in every sea, carrying foreign as well as national goods, and several important services had been established by German companies between ports in distant seas.[1]

The German spirit, with its love of scientific organisation, tends rather to the creation of great lines and amalgamations than to the individualistic activities of the tramp steamer, and the support given by the State was confined mainly to the liner trade. Thus, the development of German shipping left British supremacy in the tramp trade unchallenged, but on every trade route the splendidly built and organised German liners competed for traffic.

The North Atlantic trade engaged the largest and fastest steamers of the Hamburg-Amerika Line and the Norddeutscher Lloyd; the commerce of South America was shared by the Hamburg-Amerika, Hamburg-Süd-Amerika, Kosmos, and Roland Lines; the whole coast-line of Africa was encircled by the numerous services of the Deutsche Ost-Afrika, Hamburg-Bremer Afrika, and Woermann companies. In the commerce of the Far East and Australia the Hamburg-Amerika and Norddeutscher Lloyd were again prominent; the Deutsch-Australische Line also provided frequent sailings to Australian ports, and the Hansa Company took a share of the Indian trade. Nearer home, the Deutsche Levante Line owned the largest fleet engaged in the traffic of the Mediterranean and the Black Sea, and a large number of companies found lucrative employment for their vessels in the commerce of the Baltic.

The connection between the majority of the larger shipping companies was very close, extending from working agreements and the running of joint services to the acquisition by the leading lines of large blocks of share capital in associated concerns. A single group of ten lines (including all those mentioned above with the exception of the Deutsche Levante Line) controlled practically the whole of the extra-European trade. The members of this "Rhederei-Vereinigung," or Shipping Association, owned

[1] Such were the Hansa service between New York and Calcutta and the Hamburg-Amerika service between New York and the West Indies.

between them over 3,000,000 gross tons of steam shipping, or 60 per cent. of the whole steam tonnage under the German flag, and they exercised a controlling influence over several companies which remained outside the group. In international competition the advantages derived from this compact and formidable organisation were strongly reinforced by the low through rates for rail and water transit, which amounted in effect to a handsome subsidy not only to the German exporter, but to the German shipowner at the expense of the State Railway revenue, and by the very close connection and co-operation which existed between the banks, the shipping companies, the merchants, and the manufacturers. Moreover, the strength of the great lines running the Atlantic services depended in no small measure upon the grip obtained on the continental emigrant traffic by a system of Control Stations, based on the denial by the Government of any right of passage through Germany to emigrants holding the tickets of non-German lines. On this well-organised and aggressive co-operation between the producing, transport, and financial interests, backed by the State, rested in large measure not only the expansion of German commerce, but the growth of German influence abroad. Yet in the very factors which formed the strength of German seaborne trade there was an element of weakness. It depended to a great extent on State support and on artificially created credit, and it was, for this reason, the less likely to recover rapidly from any prolonged interruption.[1]

During the three years immediately preceding the war, the value of German imports for home consumption averaged some £510,000,000, and of the domestic exports £445,000,000. No official figures are available showing the proportion of this trade crossing the land frontiers, but it is probable that nearly 70 per cent. in value of the imports and 60 per cent. of the exports were seaborne.[2] Moreover, the very considerable transit trade would mostly represent goods brought to Germany from oversea for distribution by the land routes. Of the imports for home consumption rather more than half consisted of raw materials for manufacture and about 30 per cent. represented live animals and foodstuffs. Cotton, wool, copper,

---

[1] For a detailed account of the organisation of German shipping, see Cd. 9092, pp. 5-18, 90-105.
[2] Cd. 9092, pp. 90-92 (paras. 210, 216, 217).

skins and hides, iron ore, nitrates, and rubber were the largest items among the raw materials, and these particular imports were mainly seaborne. In the matter of foodstuffs the Empire was to a considerable extent self-supporting; but one third of the wheat and flour annually consumed was imported, and 70 per cent. of the imports came from beyond the seas. Barley, to the extent of nearly half the annual consumption, was procured from Russia, and the loss of the Russian supplies could be made good, if at all, only from oversea sources. Maize and coffee were shipped in large quantities from South America, and the import of nitrates from Chile had an important bearing on German agriculture, as the comparatively poor soil of Germany could be made to yield heavy crops only by the free use of artificial fertilisers. The grazing and dairy interests, also, were to a great extent dependent upon imported fodder. Great as were Germany's internal resources, she could not face, without danger of severe suffering to her people and serious financial weakness, a prolonged interruption of her maritime communications.

As might be expected from the very restricted coast line of Austria-Hungary, the shipping of the Dual Monarchy was only of minor importance, amounting to about 1,000,000 tons. The Austrian Lloyd and other companies had services to North and South America and the Far East, and the Austrian flag was well represented in the trade of the Mediterranean, Levant, and Black Sea; but of the whole volume of foreign trade less than one-fifth was seaborne, and the security of the ocean routes was perhaps less important to Austria than to any other of the principal belligerents.

We have been dealing, hitherto, with the shipping of the belligerent countries only; but so long as either group could command the sea, they could of course employ neutral shipping as freely as their own for the carriage of their commerce. Should either group, however, fail to afford the necessary protection to their own ships, they must inevitably be forced into complete dependence upon neutral shipowners for the maintenance of their communications. In this case their prospects could hardly be considered encouraging. The right to capture enemy goods wherever found, which was claimed and exercised during the great naval wars of the eighteenth century, had been modified by the Declaration of Paris (1856), which forbade the capture of enemy goods, other than contraband, under a neutral flag; but the right of blockade remained unimpaired, and the definition of contraband was, in itself, shifting and uncertain. In warfare under modern conditions the whole resources of the State are organised and directed towards the attainment of victory, and every branch of trade by which those resources are maintained becomes, in greater or lesser degree, contributory to military strength. It was inevitable, in these circumstances, that the list of articles commonly classified as contraband should be extended, and that the belligerents should be brought by successive steps to aim at nothing less than the absolute interdiction of commerce with the enemy countries.

Apart from legal restrictions, there was the initial difficulty that few of the neutral Powers possessed mercantile fleets of a size which would enable them to take over any great part of the trade hitherto carried by belligerent ships. The United States was the largest neutral shipowner, having a mercantile fleet amounting (exclusive of vessels plying on the Great Lakes) to 8,000,000 tons; but the proportion of sailing tonnage was nearly one-third of the whole, and a large number of the steamers were employed exclusively in coasting traffic. The share of American shipping in the general carrying trade of the world was thus inconsiderable, and Norway, with 2,000,000 tons of steam shipping and 500,000 tons of sailing vessels, played a much more prominent part. In addition to regular lines connecting Norway with other European countries, North and South America, Africa, and the East, Norwegian shipowners controlled a large amount of tramp tonnage, which was managed with great enterprise and kept actively employed.

The other Scandinavian States, Sweden and Denmark, owned about 2,000,000 tons between them. Swedish and Danish, as well as Norwegian shipping, played an important part in the North Sea traffic, especially in the trade between the United Kingdom and Scandinavia. Though several Swedish lines connected the country with more distant ports, it was, in fact, in the numerous North Sea and Baltic services that Swedish shipping found its most profitable employment. The share of Denmark in the general carrying trade was larger, and out of £5,390,000 gross freight received by Danish shipowners in 1912, only £1,700,000 was earned on the routes between Denmark and foreign ports, all the rest representing Danish activity in the commerce of other lands.

Holland and Italy [1] each owned about 1,500,000 tons. Italian shipping was chiefly employed in the direct trade of Italy with Mediterranean countries, the United States, and South America; but Dutch shipowners had for some years shown increasing enterprise as general carriers. The regular lines were mainly engaged in the trade of Holland itself, especially with America, the United Kingdom, and the Dutch East Indies, but a fair amount of tramp tonnage was annually placed on the market for employment in the general carrying trade. Greek shipping was chiefly of the tramp class, and formed an important factor in the general traffic of the Mediterranean and Black Sea; but the fleets of the remaining minor shipowning Powers were mostly confined to the commerce of the several States themselves.

Seeing that the sea-going tonnage of all the neutral countries together was less than one-half of that possessed by the belligerent Powers, and that a considerable part even of this tonnage was tied to the service of neutral requirements, there was little prospect of either belligerent group obtaining cargo-space under a neutral flag for any large proportion of the goods usually carried by its own shipping.[2] The most that could be hoped was that the neutral tonnage available would suffice for the carriage of such imports as were essential to the feeding of the people or the manufacture of material employed directly or indirectly for war purposes. Yet to such cargoes a neutral flag could give no guarantee of protection.

[1] Italy is here counted as neutral, as she did not enter the war until May 1915.
[2] The States which became belligerent in 1914 owned between them 68 per cent. of the world's gross tonnage. In *net steam* tonnage the percentages were as follows:

	Thousand tons net.	Per cent.
United Kingdom	11,538·0	44·4
Dominions and Colonies	901·8	3·5
TOTAL BRITISH	12,439·8	47·9
France	1,098·0	4·2
Russia	498·5	1·9
Belgium	218·8	·8
Japan	1,048·0	4·0
TOTAL ALLIES	15,303·1	58·8

The position was not greatly affected by the possibility of rapid construction in neutral countries. Indeed, the shipbuilding figures for the three years previous to the war showed a disproportion between the capacities of belligerent and neutral yards still greater than that between the existing mercantile fleets. This disproportion was mainly due to the position of Great Britain as the only Power building ships for export on a large scale. In these years the average production of new tonnage, exclusive of American ships launched on the Great Lakes, was 2,962,000 gross tons, of which 1,825,000, or nearly 62 per cent., were launched in the United Kingdom. The German output was 365,000 tons, or 12·3 per cent.; and the French, 137,000. Of neutral Powers, only the United States, with 173,000 tons, and Holland, with 99,000, approached even the French figure.[1]

There was thus little hope of any rapid expansion of neutral shipping to a point at which it could replace the belligerent services; but it had sometimes been assumed that the outbreak of hostilities would be followed by extensive transference of belligerent shipping to neutral ownership. There were, however, obvious limitations to the relief which could be obtained in this way by a Power unable to protect its own merchantmen. In the first place, the transfer of flag would not enable a vessel to carry contraband or to enter blockaded ports. In the second place, the sudden

Footnote continued:

Germany	3,096·0	11·9	
Austria-Hungary	653·4	2·5	
Turkey	67·8	·3	
TOTAL ENEMY		3,817·2	14·7
United States	1,195·0	4·6	
Norway	1,153·4	4·4	
Sweden	578·5	2·3	
Denmark	453·0	1·7	
Holland	909·6	3·5	
Italy	871·4	3·4	
Greece	515·1	2·0	
Other Countries	1,193·6	4·6	
TOTAL NEUTRAL		6,869·6	26·5
WORLD TOTAL		25,989·9	100·0

Tonnage taken from *Lloyd's Register*. In this table all wood and composite steamers are excluded, as well as American vessels employed on the Great Lakes or in the Philippines.

[1] Figures based on annual returns published by "Lloyd's Register of Shipping," and *Shipping and Shipbuilding Record*.

acquisition of several hundred thousand tons of shipping by neutral owners would involve practical difficulties in respect of financing, manning, and handling the fleets acquired, which presented an almost insurmountable obstacle. Finally, the view of international law taken by the leading maritime Powers, and codified in the Declaration of London, 1909, authorised a belligerent to disregard the transfer of an enemy vessel in all cases where it could be proved that such transfer was effected to avoid the consequences to which a belligerent ship, as such, was exposed.[1]

It was clear, therefore, that whatever assistance might be obtained from neutral shipping, the ability of any belligerent to keep his seaborne trade on foot must depend mainly upon his power to afford adequate naval protection to his own merchantmen. This protection had to be given under conditions which were, in many respects, without precedent in the history of naval warfare. The campaigns which had taken place since the end of the eighteenth century threw only a very limited light upon the way in which the problems of trade defence had been modified by the advent of steam and electricity. The exploits of the ALABAMA and her consorts were performed by steamers attacking a sailing trade. The Franco-German war was fought while both the navy and the commerce of Germany were yet in their infancy. The Spanish-American and Russo-Japanese conflicts presented only a very imperfect analogy to the conditions of such a struggle as that which began in August 1914.

Perhaps the most obvious effect of the development of steam shipbuilding was the disparity in speed between the ships used in attacking commerce and those employed in trade.[2] The frigate or privateer of the sailing era had usually an advantage in speed over the majority of the vessels on which she preyed; but that advantage was very small compared with the discrepancy between the maximum speed of a modern cruiser and that of merchant shipping.

The maximum speed at sea of the German light cruisers

---

[1] The Declaration of London had not been ratified by Great Britain, but the Article (No. 56) dealing with the point in question, certainly expressed the views of British jurists.

[2] The new factors introduced by the use of submarines as commerce-destroyers may most fitly be set aside until it becomes necessary to deal with the opening of the submarine campaign.

on foreign stations at the beginning of the war varied from 20 to 25 knots. In actual practice, the fear of exhausting her coal supply would deter any cruiser from using habitually anything above a speed of 10 to 12 knots; but provided she had sufficient coal to keep up fires in her boilers, she could quickly work up to a speed sufficient to catch any merchantman near enough to be made out. Tramp steamers were usually content with a speed of 8 to 10 knots, and even in the case of the liners, other than those employed in the mail services, only a small proportion exceeded 12 knots at sea.[1] There was thus little chance of a merchantman escaping when chased by a hostile cruiser, and her prospects would be little better if she were sighted by a liner armed for the purpose of commerce destruction, for the vessels likely to be employed for this purpose were, generally speaking, several knots faster than the majority even of regular freighters, and in many seas a liner of 15 or 16 knots speed would find the greater part of the shipping on which she hoped to prey 25 or 30 per cent. slower than herself.

The visibility of smoke, enabling the presence of a steamer to be detected some time before any part of her hull could be made out, was another factor which favoured the attack. A raider cruising at low speed and burning the best Welsh coal would make little smoke, nor was it practicable for a merchantman in frequented waters to regard all smoke sighted as suspicious. Meanwhile the cruiser, so long as she possessed a reasonable reserve of coal, could chase every trail of smoke reported by her look-out, trusting to her own speed for escape if it should prove to proceed from an enemy warship.

On the other hand, the task of a commerce destroyer under steam was gravely complicated by the question of fuel. A warship of the sailing period could ship six months' stores and keep the sea, without putting into port, until they were on the point of exhaustion. The radius of action of a modern cruiser was limited by her bunker capacity. The limit of endurance might be increased by cruising at low speed and lying to at night; but every occasion on which it was necessary to raise speed for the purpose of over-hauling a prize or avoiding capture reduced the maximum

[1] Only one-sixth of the steamers under the British flag could maintain a speed of even 12 knots at sea (Cd. 9092, p. 140), and many of these were small, short distance, passenger vessels.

period. A considerable reserve must always be kept in hand for an emergency, such as a flight before superior force, and in practice, the German raiders seldom went without coaling for more than three weeks, and usually renewed their supplies every week or ten days.

When fuel ran low the cruiser must either go into port or replenish her bunkers from a collier. The only Power provided with a chain of accessible and defensible bases in almost every sea was Great Britain, and such coaling stations as an enemy possessed were certain to be reduced or blockaded early in the war unless the British main fleet should be defeated. The amount of coal which a belligerent warship could obtain in a neutral port was limited by international law to the amount necessary to enable her to reach the nearest port of her own country, and it was further provided that she might not obtain a second supply in the same neutral territory during a period of three months.[1] Moreover, for a raiding cruiser to go into port was to betray her whereabouts. The news would be instantly cabled to the hostile Admiralty, and communicated by cable or wireless to every ship engaged in searching for her.

Coaling from a supply ship avoided this disadvantage, but the process of coaling at sea was lengthy and difficult. It could be undertaken only in fine or moderate weather and in unfrequented waters where no hostile warship was likely to be encountered. To coal from a supply ship in territorial waters was forbidden, but it might be expected that a raider, unprovided with bases, would feel little scruple in filling her bunkers under the lee of a desolate island, or even in an unfrequented harbour. But this process, also, involved a departure of some days from the trade routes, with the probability of missing many valuable prizes. We shall see that the question of fuel was always an absorbing one for the German commerce destroyers. It is probably not too much to say that during the most active periods of their career, at least half the time was spent by them either actually in coaling, or in steaming to and from the rendezvous at which supply ships

---

[1] Hague Convention XIII of 1907 (Articles 19 and 20). It was provided, however, that a belligerent warship could fill her bunkers to their full normal capacity in the territory of neutral States which have adopted this rule regarding the supply of fuel. Great Britain protested against this extension, and made a reservation in respect of it. See A. Pearce Higgins, *The Hague Peace Conferences*, Cambridge, 1909, pp. 451, 475-8.

THE PROBLEM OF FUEL

were to be met or the transfer of fuel effected. It may be added that they were continually hampered by the difficulty of arranging for supplies and by the capture of vessels intended to provide them with fuel.[1]

Not only did the necessity of renewing their coal supply restrict the time during which the enemy cruisers could operate continuously on the trade routes, but the necessity of maintaining a reserve circumscribed their activities when actually so engaged. They dare not cruise in waters where British patrols were likely to be met, because every occasion on which they were compelled to use their full speed in order to escape would deplete their coal supply and lessen their endurance; they dare not devote much attention to the faster liners, because every hard chase would, in similar fashion, exhaust their powers of further activity.

Moreover, the space occupied on a modern warship by engines, machinery, and bunkers, had greatly reduced that available for *personnel* and provisions. A cruiser could not spare many men for prize crews. She must either take each batch of captures into port at once or sink her prizes. The circumstances under which a prize might be destroyed were rather vaguely defined by international law, but there was no doubt about the obligation to provide for the safety of the crew. The accommodation on board a cruiser was limited, and even if she were able to use a prize or tender as a " prison-ship," the difficulty of feeding a large number of prisoners would compel her to send them into port within, at most, a few weeks. But to send them into port was to furnish the enemy with news of her proceedings, and might involve the necessity of changing her cruising ground. A big liner, armed for the purpose of commerce-destruction, was rather better off in this respect, as she could herself accommodate some hundreds of prisoners and a large quantity of provisions.

While the attack was thus handicapped by considerations of coal endurance and supplies, the change from sail to steam had conferred upon merchantmen seeking to avoid capture an inestimable advantage in the power of dispersal and deviation. The sailing vessel was always at the mercy of winds and currents. The course to be followed by vessels wishing to take advantage of, for instance, the

[1] The process of oiling at sea is both easier and quicker than coaling, but the difficulty of arranging for supplies remains. Moreover, few cruisers available at the outset of the war were fitted for burning liquid fuel.

Trade Winds, could be foretold within tolerably certain limits. If attacked, the trader found twelve out of thirty-two points of the compass barred to her in her attempt to escape. A frigate hanging on to the skirts of a convoy could snap up straggler after straggler. A squadron strong enough to overpower the escort might hope to capture a large proportion of the convoy. The advent of steam rendered it far easier to keep a convoy together and avoid straggling, while even in the event of the escort being overpowered, the merchantmen could scatter to all points of the compass in the hope of minimising losses. It was not, however, anticipated before the war that the convoy system would be adopted at the outset, as mercantile opinion was apprehensive as to its effects on the flow of trade.[1] In the course of the submarine campaign the heavy losses incurred and the numerous delays due to fear of destruction led to the application of the system, which fitted in with the close regulation of trade then in force; but during the period of surface attack, convoy was confined almost entirely to vessels, such as transports, of special military importance. Against a surface raider, even the individual steamer was protected to a great extent by her own power of free movement, which was limited only by her coal capacity. Except when leaving or entering port, she could shape her course fifty, a hundred, two hundred miles on either side of the normal track. By altering course so as to leave any possible pursuer directly astern so soon as sighted, a merchant vessel could lengthen the chase to its utmost possible limit, in the hope of succour. If the fall of darkness or fog enabled her to escape observation, she could again alter her course at any angle, without the enemy being able to forecast her movements. Moreover, a steamer could choose her own time for traversing a dangerous area, such as narrow waters or the point of intersection between two trade routes, and could usually pass through it in a few hours. She could leave port at night, in any direction, and be well away from the coast before daybreak. She could arrange to enter port during the hours of darkness. She could frequently secure the protection of a neutral flag during part of her voyage, by keeping within the three-mile limit. She could follow

[1] Some doubts, which subsequently proved to be groundless, were also felt as to the ability of merchantmen to adapt themselves to the conditions of sailing in convoy

throughout her whole voyage a course assigned to her by the Admiralty or by her owners, instead of being dependent upon the action of external forces.

This power of deviation was intimately connected with the development of the means of communication. The network of submarine cables and telegraph systems laid during the last half-century had brought every considerable port into touch with all parts of the world. Within still more recent years the progress of wireless telegraphy had facilitated direct communication with ships at sea. In July 1914 all important warships and some 2,500 merchantmen of all nationalities were equipped with wireless apparatus;[1] The radius of ship installations was usually about 300 miles, with a minimum of 200, but might extend to 500. At night, especially in a north and south direction, the range was frequently doubled, and messages had been recorded up to a distance of over 2,000 miles.[2]

This development of the means of communication cut both ways. The linking up of ports by the submarine cable and the practice of publishing shipping movements to which it had given a great extension, were undoubtedly of advantage to the commerce destroyer, who was thus enabled to collect information as to merchant sailings. It is easy, however, to overrate the advantage thus obtained. Information that a certain ship had left port on a particular day was only of value if she could be intercepted near her port of departure or arrival. Her course between port and port might be widely varied by secret instructions, and though there were a number of focal areas through which nearly all vessels on a particular route passed in times of peace, it was only when these areas were determined by geographical conditions, that they must necessarily be traversed in war. In practice, deviation was always limited to some extent by the desire to economise coal and to arrive on time, and the successes of raiding cruisers were commonly achieved, not so much by chasing individual ships as by taking up a position on some great artery of commerce and keeping a good look out for smoke. But in this process it was the position itself, rather than any special information about particular vessels,

[1] See List in *Lloyd's Register* 1914-15.
[2] *Wireless Telegraphy in the Navy.* Commander C. F. Loring, R.N., *Naval Annual*, 1914.

which was the main factor of success. Like the ant-lion, the commerce destroyer set a trap across the path and waited almost passively for the prey to fall into it.

In maintaining such a position wireless telegraphy conferred indubitable benefits upon the attack. It enabled information as to the enemy's movements to be conveyed to a raider. It provided the captain of a commerce-destroyer with a ready means of calling up supply ships, and enabled him to command a wide stretch of sea by spreading his tenders as scouts. By listening for the enemy's call signs he could judge the distance of hostile vessels, and could form some approximate idea of their direction. And there was always the chance that he might intercept messages *en clair*, or in a known code, to enemy merchantmen, which would give him valuable information.

On the other hand, the submarine cable and wireless telegraphy enabled the operations of squadrons cruising in defence of trade to be co-ordinated to a degree hitherto unknown. Every scrap of information relating to the movements of an enemy cruiser could be disseminated in a few hours to all the ships engaged in searching for her, and the raider could only send out calls at the risk of their being taken in and interpreted by the patrols.

Even more important was the part played by cable and wireless in facilitating the control of merchant shipping. In the case of British ships, every foreign port at which there was a Consular Representative or a Lloyd's Agent, every bluff or headland on which there was a Lloyd's Signal Station, became a centre from which owner's instructions, Admiralty advice, or news of recent events could be distributed. Information as to special local dangers and instructions as to courses to be followed and precautions to be observed could be sent out by cable and wireless to all cruisers at sea and communicated by signal to every merchantman they met. The use of wireless by merchant ships themselves and by their owners or agents in direct communication with them involved the risk of the message being intercepted by a hostile raider, but the power to send out a call for assistance might prove invaluable in an emergency. The wireless system also frequently afforded the only means of recalling to port, or diverting, a vessel which had sailed in ignorance of danger, and at the beginning of the war it was extensively used to warn ships at sea of the outbreak of hostilities.

On a balance of advantages and disadvantages, the change from sail to steam and the development of communications had tended to favour the defence of commerce against the attack of raiding cruisers. Their effect on the ability of a superior naval Power to interrupt, by sustained pressure, commercial intercourse with an enemy country, remains to be considered.

In itself, steam had probably tended to increase the pressure thus exercised. It was no longer possible for a blockading force to be blown off by the same wind as enabled enemy ships to leave port. The necessity of coaling could be met by sending in two or three ships at a time, and the time lost by a ship going into port and returning was much less than that lost by a sailing man-of-war putting in to water or refit. But the whole question of blockade had been complicated by the introduction of entirely new factors in the torpedo, the mine, and latterly the submarine. The development of these new weapons rendered the close blockade of an enemy's coastline practically impossible, and threw back the blockading force upon the alternative of seizing and holding the approaches to his home waters. If those approaches consisted of comparatively narrow waters capable of being dominated by a cruiser cordon, the effect of a blockade could be obtained without the risk of actual coastal operations. The working of such a cordon was greatly facilitated by the certainty of communication conferred by wireless telegraphy, as were all cruiser operations having for their function the control of terminal waters or focal points. The power of co-ordination conferred on squadrons cruising in defence of commerce was equally advantageous to squadrons cruising for the interruption of commerce, as distinguished from isolated raiders acting only by evasion and surprise. Indeed, a squadron operating in terminal waters or in the neighbourhood of a focal point could discharge the functions both of attack and defence, for "since the lines of communication for both our enemy and ourselves are the same, it follows that the ships that we use to stop his trade will at the same time defend ours." [1]

[1] Vice-Admiral Sir Edmond Slade, K.C.I.E., K.C.V.O., in the *Naval Annual*, 1914, p. 93. See also Sir Julian Corbett, *The Principles of Maritime Strategy*, pp. 97, 98 and 264, 265. The continuation of the German lines beyond the British terminals was, of course, an important factor in the war.

So far, therefore, as the sea itself was concerned, the unification of control and rapid communication of intelligence due to modern conditions probably outweighed the disadvantages attendant upon the danger of too near an approach to the enemy's ports. But the great developments in land transport which had taken place since the introduction of steam had modified the situation in a manner unfavourable to the naval Powers. Every continental country was connected by a highly developed railway system with all contiguous countries. The greater cost of land transport, the capacities of neutral ports and of neutral shipping, all imposed limitations upon the extent to which the export and import trade of a belligerent could be diverted from the direct sea routes to transhipment channels, but a complete stoppage of his oversea trade could only be secured by exercising some form of control over shipping bound to every port with which he had rail, canal, or river communication.

It was not, however, the conditions of naval warfare alone which had undergone a revolutionary change since the last great world-conflict; the problem of maintaining seaborne trade in time of war was at least equally affected by the development of new processes in the course of that trade itself, and in particular, by the growth of international credit and the emergence of the financial interests as an independent and indispensible factor in the machinery of commerce. Owing to the colossal proportions to which the volume of trade had swelled during a century of unprecedented expansion, the capital of the merchants was now much smaller, relatively to the extent of their transactions, than it was at the beginning of the nineteenth century; yet the growers of the world's harvests still looked to be paid at the earliest possible date, while the consumers were ready to pay only when the goods were delivered. The gap was bridged by the Banks and Discount Houses, whose great resources enabled them to wait for their money, and who were willing, for a consideration, to finance the movement of goods in transit. By far the greater proportion of the cargoes at any time afloat belonged not to the producers, the merchants, or the consumers, but to those who had discounted the Bills of Exchange representing the purchase price of the goods, holding as their security the Bills of Lading and the policies of marine insurance. The bills by which the purchase price of any cargo was represented might be held in many countries, and might each have passed through many hands in the adjustment of international exchanges; but each financial interest concerned would look for the satisfaction of the bills which it had discounted or received for collection, to the realisation of the goods comprised in the Bills of Lading, or in the event of a loss at sea, to a claim under the marine insurance policy. Each would have as an additional security the names of all preceding financial interests as endorsers of the Bills of Exchange.

This complex web of international credit was exceedingly sensitive, and particularly responsive to the influence of war perils. Not only was the solvency of the great financial houses dependent upon the safe arrival of the cargoes which formed their primary security for the money advanced; but they were so closely inter-connected by the processes of international commerce and finance, that even the temporary collapse of any of the great credit markets of the world was bound inevitably to react on all the rest and throw out of gear, in a greater or less degree, the delicate machinery by which the commerce of the world was carried on. The vastly increased rapidity of communications which alone made the system possible was in this respect a source of weakness, since a report, or even a rumour of danger arising in any one financial centre, could in a few hours be flashed all over the globe and shake the fabric of credit in every commercial community.

In this way the problem of maintaining seaborne trade in time of war acquired a dual character; it was essential, in order to avert a collapse of credit, that the financial interests should be adequately protected against the risk of losing the goods which formed their security; it was essential to the continued free movement of cargoes that the fabric of credit should be maintained. For Great Britain, in particular, both phases of the problem were of vital importance; no other country was so dependent for the necessaries of life on the uninterrupted flow of seaborne traffic; no other country had so heavy a financial stake in the movement of the world's commerce. From the earliest moment of the war the preservation of credit against a collapse caused by panic or uncertainty became an object of wartime statesmanship as urgent as the protection of shipping against the attacks of hostile raiders.

CHAPTER II

THE OUTBREAK OF WAR: DANGERS AND PRECAUTIONS

FROM the moment when the Archduke Francis Ferdinand was murdered at Sarajevo on June 28th, 1914, the aspect of European politics became threatening; but it was not until July 26th, after the Austrian Minister had left Belgrade, that the menace became sufficiently acute to affect shipping interests in Great Britain to an appreciable extent. On that day the gravity of the situation was revealed by the publication of Admiralty orders to the effect that the First Fleet, which had just returned to Portland from manœuvres and was about to disperse for manœuvre leave, should be kept concentrated, and that the ships of the Second Fleet should remain at their home ports in proximity to their balance crews. The fact that the Admiralty considered such precautions to be necessary emphasised the danger which lay in the severance of relations between Austria and Serbia, and on the following day, Monday, July 27th, the tension was reflected in the marine insurance market, where premiums were paid in several instances to cover war risks on cargoes carried both by British and foreign owned vessels. As yet, however, the prospect of a general war was not sufficiently imminent to produce anything like a panic, and the rates paid did not exceed 5s. per cent.[2]

It was indeed a general dislocation of commercial activity rather than the prospect of an attack on British trade which, at this period, formed the chief ground of apprehension. So early as July 25th the effect of the political outlook abroad had begun to be felt in the Black Sea market, and the stagnation now became general, chartering for August loadings being almost entirely suspended. Meanwhile the anxiety with regard to goods at sea became more acute,

---

[1] See Maps 1 and 2.
[2] For insurance quotations the files of the *Times*, *Shipping World*, and *Economist* have been collated.

and on the 28th the war risk premiums on cargoes under a foreign flag rose to 7*s.* 6*d.* per cent., or 20*s.* on cargoes in Austrian vessels. There was as yet no serious expectation of Great Britain being involved in war, and the majority of cargoes in British bottoms could still be covered at 5*s.*; but the probability of Russia becoming a belligerent was considered sufficiently great to justify a charge of 10*s.* on cargoes from Baltic ports.

So far hostilities had nowhere actually broken out, but in the course of July 28th the Austrian declaration of war was delivered to Serbia, and in view of the obvious risk of the conflict extending to some at least of the Great Powers, the war risks market became very active on the 29th. Cargoes in Austrian and Russian bottoms were practically uninsurable, and rates for the Far Eastern voyage rose to 1 per cent. on cargoes in British, and 2 per cent. on those in foreign vessels. German underwriters displayed even greater apprehensions, and at Hamburg 5 per cent. was asked in respect of vessels bound for Petrograd and 4 per cent. in respect of the homewards voyage from Australia.

During the next two days, although efforts were still being made to localise the conflict, and Sir Edward Grey, in particular, was earnestly striving to preserve the peace of Europe, reports of mobilisation on a large scale were received from Austria, Germany, and Russia, and the hope of preventing the conflagration extending became almost hourly more remote. In these circumstances the rush of inquiries on the war risks market steadily increased, while the ordinary business of marine insurance was practically suspended. On July 30th the rate on goods carried by British steamers to Riga rose to 3 per cent., and premiums on cargoes under the French, German, Russian, and Italian flags varied between 1 and 4 per cent. On the 31st, premiums of 3 per cent. were paid on cargoes in British ships coming direct to ports in the United Kingdom, and 5 per cent. in the event of touching at continental ports. The owners of goods in French and Russian bottoms were obliged to pay 5 per cent. in order to obtain cover, and double that amount was demanded on the cargoes of German and Italian vessels.

Although chartering had been practically at a standstill since July 27th, there had hitherto been no actual interference with the course of shipping, except in the Adriatic, where the Austrian Lloyd services were suspended as early as the 29th; but on the 31st it was reported that Spanish shippers of iron ore at Vigo had received telegraphic instructions from Hamburg to discontinue loading cargoes for Germany until further notice. The gravity of the crisis was still more clearly indicated by the action of the leading German steamship companies. The Hamburg-Amerika liner *Imperator*, which was due to sail from Hamburg for New York on the morning of the 31st, was retained in port and no announcement was made with regard to her future movements. At the same time the sailings of the *Vaterland* and *Amerika*, from New York and Boston respectively, on August 1st, were cancelled by the New York office of the Company, and the *President Grant*, which had left New York, was recalled by wireless. The Norddeutscher Lloyd also cancelled their American sailings and recalled the *Friedrich der Grosse*, which had put out from Baltimore. It was evident that the German shipping companies regarded the danger of war as acute and imminent, for the *Imperator* and *Vaterland* were not only the largest steamers which flew the German flag, but ranked among the fastest liners in the world. The sailing of such ships would not be lightly cancelled, and a week's time would have seen them safe at their destination.[1]

The immediate danger was of war between the Central Powers and Russia, in which France would almost inevitably be involved by the terms of the Dual Alliance. The course to be followed by Great Britain was less definitely laid down, nor were British statesmen yet without hope that a general European conflict might, even at the last moment, be averted. Their hopes were shared by business interests and the public generally, and though heavy premiums were paid for policies against an outbreak of hostilities, no cancellation of sailings took place. It was reported, however, that a number of British, French, and Scandinavian vessels which had loaded barley at San Francisco were obliged to delay their departure owing to the difficulty of effecting insurance.[2]

[1] *Times*, 1 August, 1914. For *Friedrich der Grosse*, *Times*, 17 August, 1914.
[2] *Times*, 1 August, 1914.
On July 30th premiums of twenty to twenty-five per cent. were paid for insurance against Great Britain being involved in war with any Continental Power during the next three months, and premiums of forty to fifty per cent. against war between Germany and Russia only.

THE CRISIS BECOMES ACUTE

On the evening of Friday, July 31st, the markets closed for the August Bank Holiday week-end. By the time they reopened the whole situation had developed with startling rapidity. On August 1st war between Germany and Russia was imminent; France was mobilising; and the question of Belgian neutrality had become prominent. At the same time, the British Foreign Office was informed that the authorities at Hamburg were forcibly detaining British ships. Sir Edward Grey at once protested, pointing out that the detention of British shipping must have a deplorable effect upon public opinion in this country; and orders were accordingly given for the release of the vessels. The German Government, however, insisted on regarding the permission to sail as a special act of grace, stating that no other foreign vessels had been allowed to leave, owing to the precautions which it had been found necessary to take at the port.[1] During the night war was declared by Germany upon Russia, and early on the morning of the 2nd German troops penetrated into Luxemburg, and frontier incidents occurred between German and French detachments.

All hope of preserving peace between France and Germany had now almost vanished, and the chief element of uncertainty was the attitude of Great Britain. While the development of the Entente had been followed by a regrouping of the fleets, which left French shipping in the Atlantic exposed to serious danger in the event of British neutrality, no binding alliance existed between the two countries; but on the morning of August 2nd, Sir Edward Grey gave an assurance to the French Ambassador in London that, subject to the policy of the Government receiving the support of Parliament, the British Navy would give all the protection in its power in the event of the German fleet coming into the Channel, or through the North Sea, to take hostile action against French coasts or shipping.[2] The First Fleet had already left Portland on July 29th for a secret destination, and measures were adopted to make ready the ships of the Second and Third Fleets for any emergency which might arise; but the final step of calling up the Naval Reserves was not taken until 2.15 a.m. on August 2nd.

---

[1] *Correspondence respecting the European Crisis* [Cd. 7467], 1914, Nos. 130, 140, 145.
[2] *Ibid.*, No. 148.

THE OUTBREAK OF WAR

On that day the situation was still further strained by the receipt of information that sugar on board British vessels at Hamburg had been compulsorily unloaded and detained. A further energetic protest by the Foreign Secretary brought no reply from the German Government, and the tension between the two countries became acute.[1] The last hope of peace was practically destroyed by the presentation to the Belgian Government, on the evening of August 2nd, of a Note demanding right of passage for German troops through the territory of Belgium. The refusal of King Albert's Government to consent to this violation of their neutrality was followed, on August 3rd, by a formal declaration of war by Germany against France, and an intimation to Belgium that the German Government proposed to carry out the passage of their troops through Belgian territory by force of arms.

This was the situation—outlined in Sir Edward Grey's historic statement in the House of Commons on the night of August 3rd—by which shipowners and underwriters found themselves confronted when they reassembled on Tuesday, August 4th. It was reflected in the continued suspension of business at the banks, the closing of the Stock Exchange, the introduction of a partial moratorium, and the publication in the *London Gazette* of a long list of prohibited exports. In such circumstances, chartering naturally remained in abeyance, and war risk premiums rose to 10 and even 15 per cent.

For the nation as a whole the suspension of chartering and the violent fluctuations of the insurance market had a grave significance. What was threatened was not merely a rise in prices due to the high cost of insurance, but a disastrous diminution in the volume of imported foodstuffs and raw materials. From the moment when it became clear that Great Britain might not improbably become involved in the war, widespread apprehensions had arisen as to the possible interruption of our maritime communications. The prospect of war between Russia and the Central Empires had, in itself, been sufficient to send up the price of bread, in anticipation of the grain shipments from the Black Sea being blocked. As the likelihood of the conflict extending to this country increased, it became evident that there was real danger of a serious shortage in the food supplies. So early as July 30th

[1] Cd. 7467, Nos. 149, 150.

chartering had come to a stop at North American ports, and by the morning of August 3rd many vessels already laden with grain were held up, owing to the impossibility of effecting insurance at other than prohibitive rates. There was every indication that the interruption of imports, the rise of prices, and the hoarding of private stocks would, in a few days, cause terrible distress among the poorer classes of the population and seriously compromise the ability of the country to wage effective war. Opponents of intervention laid special emphasis on the possibilities of a collapse of credit and widespread starvation, and even the supporters of the Government plainly revealed their anxiety to know what steps were being taken to meet the menace.[1]

They had not long to wait. On August 3rd, as a preliminary measure, the Government agreed to guarantee war risks on wheat and flour shipped from American and Canadian ports on the Atlantic under existing contracts. This, however, was but a temporary and partial remedy, and in the course of the discussion which followed Sir Edward Grey's statement, Mr. Lloyd George, then Chancellor of the Exchequer, assured the House that the Government had taken the whole question of food supplies into consideration, and that he would be able on the morrow to declare their policy, not only with regard to that question, but with regard to the larger problem of the protection and encouragement of British shipping and seaborne trade in all eventualities.

In giving this assurance, the Chancellor was not speaking without justification. At the instance of Sir H. Llewellyn Smith, then Secretary to the Board of Trade, a strong Sub-Committee of the Committee of Imperial Defence had been appointed by the Prime Minister in May 1913, " to consider, without prejudice to the question of policy, whether an administratively practical scheme can be devised to secure that in time of war British steamships shall not be generally laid up, and that oversea commerce shall not be interrupted by reason of inability to cover the war risk of ships and cargoes by insurance, and which will also ensure that the insurance rates shall not be so high as to cause an excessive rise of price." The members of this Sub-Committee were all men of weight and eminence in shipping, insurance, or commercial circles.

[1] *Hansard*, 3 August, 1914.

They comprised: the Rt. Hon. Fredk. Huth Jackson (Director of the Bank of England), Chairman; Lord Inchcape (Chairman of the P. & O.); Sir A. Norman Hill (Secretary of the Liverpool Steamship Owners' Association and Manager of the Liverpool and London War Risks Insurance Association); Sir Raymond Beck (Deputy Chairman of Lloyd's); Mr. Arthur Lindley (a well-known Average Adjuster); Captain M. P. A. Hankey (Secretary of the Committee of Imperial Defence), Secretary. It would have been impossible to find a body entitled to speak with greater authority upon the question submitted to them, and by a happy coincidence, their Report, dated April 30th, 1914, was actually before the Government at the time when the European crisis arose.

The problem which Mr. Huth Jackson's Committee had to solve went to the very root of the maintenance of seaborne trade in time of war. Their task was on the one hand to provide the means of averting a collapse of credit which would dislocate the whole machinery by which the movement of cargoes was financed, and on the other hand to provide such reasonable security for the shipowners as would ensure their ability and readiness to carry the cargoes. It was, indeed, a general suspension of business on the part of underwriters and shipowners, rather than the actual losses that might be incurred, which competent judges dreaded as the result of an outbreak of hostilities. There were few who doubted the ability of the Navy to ensure, within a comparatively short period, a reasonable degree of safety on the main trade routes; but the Admiralty had never claimed, nor did the experience of previous wars suggest, that it would be possible, even with a working command of the sea, to guarantee immunity from danger. The chances of war had, it is true, been faced courageously and successfully in the past; but both the conditions of naval warfare and the processes of international commerce had changed so greatly since the Napoleonic struggle that it was now almost impossible to find any adequate measure of the risks. Yet it was vital that the measure of these risks should be ascertained. The business of the underwriter was based on the computation of averages. So long as he could assess the average loss he would cheerfully undertake big risks in return for a proportionate premium, but if the materials for assessing averages were not available, his business would become a pure gamble, and the leading underwriters would probably cease to operate. In that case the movement of the world's trade must come to a stop, for great as were the resources of the financial interests, they could not be expected to finance uninsured ventures. In like manner, the shipowner who was unable to cover himself by insurance, or to measure the war risks with sufficient accuracy to provide against them in fixing freights, could no longer expose the capital represented by his ships to the danger of total loss. Under such conditions it was almost certain that, should Great Britain become involved in conflict with a Naval Power, the movement of seaborne commerce would be practically suspended until the risk of capture could be estimated with some approach to accuracy.

It was indeed probable that the richer shipowners would run their own risks, and that as the extent of those risks was gradually ascertained, the underwriters would come slowly back into the market. As and when the facilities for insurance increased, shipping generally would resume its activities; but in the meantime the price of all imported commodities would be raised by the high freights charged by shipowners to cover their own estimate of the risks run, the freight and insurance markets would be subject to violent fluctuations as the risks varied, and no buyer or seller would be able to contract ahead. But far worse than any fluctuation of freights or prices would be the actual shortage of necessary commodities. For some weeks, perhaps for some months, the volume of imports would be reduced to very small proportions, and in view of the inadequacy of the stocks normally on hand to sustain the population for any considerable period, utter disaster might well be the result, even though few ships were captured by the enemy.

To meet this danger, it was proposed by Admiral Sir George Tryon and others, a quarter of a century before the outbreak of the great war, that the State itself should undertake the insurance of shipping against war risks, and this proposal was constantly urged upon successive Governments by the shipowners. Both national insurance and the alternative scheme of a complete indemnity against loss by capture were considered by the Royal Commission on the Supply of Food and Raw Material in Time of War; and in 1907 and 1908, a Treasury Committee, of which Mr. Austen Chamberlain was Chairman, sat to consider the question of a National Guarantee for the War Risks of Shipping. The report of this Committee was unfavourable to the proposal. They were unable to form any reliable estimate of the liabilities involved, which they expected to be very large, and they considered it impossible to devise any practicable machinery for the working of the scheme, or to provide adequate security against frauds being practised on the State. Moreover, some of the evidence given before the Committee suggested that the underwriters were, at that time, convinced of the capacity of the insurance market to undertake war risks, and were disposed to resent the prospect of State interference.

During the period which elapsed between the presentation of the Treasury Committee's Report and the appointment of Mr. Huth Jackson's Committee, the situation underwent a radical change. It became more and more clear that the underwriting market was in reality quite unprepared to deal with the risks of a war to which Great Britain was a party, and the uneasiness of shipowners on this point was reflected in the growth of the great War Risks Clubs. So early as 1899, the North of England Protecting and Indemnity Association had been formed for the purpose of insuring vessels against war risks on a mutual basis, and in 1913 this example was followed in the formation of the London Group of War Risks Associations and the Liverpool and London War Risks Insurance Association. At the date when Mr. Huth Jackson's Committee was appointed, over two-thirds of the British ships engaged in the foreign trade were entered in one or other of these associations, and it was mainly this fact which enabled the Committee to overcome difficulties which had previously appeared insuperable.

It is true that the existence of the Clubs did not, in itself, go far to ensure the maintenance of seaborne trade. The policies which they granted extended to all perils arising from wars in which Great Britain remained neutral, but in the case of this country itself being at war, the only risks covered were those of ships actually at sea or in an enemy port on the declaration of war, and even these ships were covered only until their arrival at a British port, or at the nearest neutral port in which it was safe to lie. Beyond this it was impossible for insurance on a mutual basis to go; but the obvious effect was to add greatly to the danger of a suspension of traffic, as no protection was given in respect of voyages undertaken after the outbreak of war, and the majority of ships at sea would be unable to complete their voyages without forfeiting their insurance.

If, however, the existence of the War Risks Associations did nothing to make State assistance less imperative, it did much to make it practicable, for they provided, for the first time, adequate machinery through which the business of hull insurance could be carried on with the same efficiency and despatch as ordinary commercial operations, and through which also the State could be secured against either fraud or negligence in the handling of the ships, and therefore of the cargoes insured. In a Memorandum presented to the Committee at the outset of their inquiry, Sir H. Llewellyn Smith suggested that the insurance of ships should be dealt with entirely through the Clubs, and the presence on the Committee of Sir Norman Hill, the Manager of the Liverpool and London Association, enabled them from the start to adapt their scheme to the rules of the Clubs in such a way that it could be brought into instant operation on the outbreak of war.

In the first place, Sir Norman Hill was able to lay before the Committee an estimate of the values actually on risk in ships and cargoes over a given period, and of the values actually on risk at any given time, and these figures being accepted by the Board of Trade, provided the necessary datum-line for the calculation of risks, which had hitherto been lacking. He was able, moreover, to indicate the practical possibilities of a partnership between the State and the Clubs in the business of hull insurance, and upon this basis the Committee worked out a detailed scheme for the insurance of war risks both on ships and cargoes. Throughout their proceedings they had the assistance of Sir H. Llewellyn Smith, as representing the Board of Trade, and the scheme was submitted in outline to Mr. J. Stanley Todd, Secretary of the North of England Protecting and Indemnity Association, Mr. H. R. Miller, Secretary of the London Group, and Mr. C. W. Gordon, President of the Chamber of Shipping. Evidence was also taken from representatives of the underwriters and cargo-owners, and in view of the composition of the Committee itself, there could be little doubt as to the practicability of the scheme.

Even so, the Government had hitherto hesitated to take action on the Report; but the imminence of the crisis and the signs of uneasiness which developed in the underwriting market during the last week of July brought home to them forcibly the peril in which the whole nation would be placed by the withdrawal of insurance facilities, and by August 3rd they had already decided to adopt the Committee's Scheme with some minor modifications. So early as July 31st the Report was issued confidentially to the three great associations. At midnight on Sunday, August 2nd, they were informed that the Government had decided to accept the scheme and to put it into immediate operation, and on the following day the Board of Trade initialled a slip covering the hulls of entered vessels. On the morning of August 4th, the Report was published in the press, and was well received by the shipping and commercial community.[1]

On the evening of the 4th the House met in a grave mood, and their anxiety to hear the promised statement with regard to trade and food supplies was intensified when the Prime Minister announced that His Majesty's Government had felt it necessary, in discharge of their treaty obligations, to despatch an ultimatum to Germany, requiring strict observance of Belgian neutrality. The time limit fixed by the ultimatum expired at 11 p.m. on the same date, and, as little hope of a satisfactory reply could be entertained, it was evident that the ability of the Government to deal with the menace to oversea supplies would soon be tested to the full.

Following on Mr. Asquith's statement, Mr. Lloyd George rose to explain the policy of the Government in this respect, and gave an outline of the scheme which had been based upon the Report of Mr. Huth Jackson's Committee. This scheme was, briefly, as follows:

(1) The Government would make an arrangement with the existing Shipowners' Clubs, or other approved associations, by which the Clubs would extend the existing standard forms of policy to cover war risks up to the arrival of the vessel at her final port of the voyage which she was making when war broke out, and for ten clear days after such arrival. Similar policies would be granted

[1] *Report of a Sub-Committee of the Committee of Imperial Defence on the Insurance of British Shipping in Time of War* [Cd. 7560].

THE STATE INSURANCE SCHEME

in respect of voyages undertaken after the outbreak of war.

(2) The Government would reinsure 80 per cent. of all war risks under policies issued by the approved associations.

(3) In respect of voyages current on the outbreak of war no premium would be charged; but in respect of voyages begun after the outbreak of war, premiums on a voyage basis would be fixed by the State from time to time, at a rate not exceeding 5 per cent. and not less than 1 per cent. The State would receive 80 per cent. of such premiums.

(4) The associations would run the remaining 20 per cent. of the risks and receive the remaining 20 per cent. of the premiums.

(5) The insurable value of any ship would be calculated on the basis of first cost, less 4 per cent. depreciation for each year from the date of completion.

(6) With regard to cargoes, a State Insurance Office would be set up, which would insure all cargoes carried in British ships on voyages commenced after the outbreak of war, provided that the ships themselves were insured under the State scheme.[1] Cargoes already afloat at the outbreak of war would not be covered by the State.

(7) The premium in respect of cargoes would be on a flat rate, irrespective of the character of the voyage and the nature of the cargo covered. The rate could be varied from time to time, with a maximum of 5, and a minimum of 1 per cent.

(8) Standard forms of policy were to be adopted, which would include a clause to the effect that ships insured under the scheme should obey all directions given by the Admiralty as to starting on a voyage, routes, ports of call, and stoppages.[2]

It will be seen that under this scheme the benefits of State Insurance were restricted to ships entered in the approved associations and to cargoes carried in such ships. With regard to the insurance of hulls, the entire

---

[1] In order to obtain cover for the cargo with the State Office, it was necessary that the ship should be insured under the State scheme up to 30 per cent. of her value.

[2] Specimen Agreements, Policies, etc., under the Scheme and its subsequent extensions will be found in the *Manual of Emergency Legislation*, *Supplement No. 3*, pp. 413–456, *Supplement No. 4*, pp. 272–295.

management of the business, as well as the communication of Admiralty instructions and the control of voyages, was left to the Committees of Management, to each of which a representative of the Admiralty and another of the Board of Trade were appointed. With regard to cargoes it was necessary to create a new organisation for the issue of policies and the adjustment of claims. Thanks to the ready co-operation of the underwriters, Mr. Lloyd George was able to announce that this office had already been established and provided with the trained staff and expert management necessary for its success, and that an Advisory Board of men well known in insurance and commercial circles was being formed to fix rates and supervise the working of the scheme.

The distinction which was thus drawn between the insurance of hulls and of cargoes, and the fact that different machinery was provided for dealing with the two classes of risk, must not be allowed to obscure the essential unity of the scheme. It was so framed as to give reasonable security against both the dangers which were apprehended as a result of the outbreak of war—the collapse of credit and the stoppage of supplies; but these dangers were themselves only two facets of a single problem—the maintenance of oversea trade; and the connection between the two parts of the scheme which dealt with them was close and vital. By guaranteeing adequate insurance of cargoes in transit, backed by the whole resources of the State, it enabled the Banks and Discount Houses to grant the credit required for financing the movement of commodities, and thus preserved the financial machinery of commerce from collapse; but this was of no avail unless ships were forthcoming to carry the cargoes, nor could the State reasonably undertake the liabilities involved, unless it received some measure of control over the movement of those ships. For while the primary value of the ships themselves lay in the cargoes which they carried, the movement of the cargoes could be controlled only by controlling the movement of the ships. Hence the immense value of the partnership which was established between the State and the War Risks Associations in the business of hull insurance. It was no negligible advantage that the insurance of the ships would be effected on the basis of values agreed by the Associations in their ordinary course of business, thus avoiding any risk of inflated claims;

but of still greater importance was the effect of this partnership on the course of trade. The fact that the Managing Committees of the Clubs were composed of shipowners, whose profits depended on the earning of freights, ensured that all reasonable risks should be run in the carrying of cargoes; the fact that the members of the Associations contributed the premium fund out of which losses were paid and remained liable to contribute to the settlement of any losses in excess of the premiums received, ensured that unreasonable risks should be avoided. The presence on the Committees of representatives of the Admiralty and the Board of Trade ensured close co-operation between the shipowners and the State. At the same time, the power vested in the Committees to refuse settlement of claims or otherwise to penalise the member concerned, in the event of their instructions being disregarded, enabled them to exercise an effective control over the movement of the ships, and therefore of the cargoes, which no State Department could otherwise have obtained.

It will be observed that the obligation of the shipowners to pay premiums and contribute towards excess losses was the pivot of the whole scheme. It had, indeed, been an instruction to Mr. Huth Jackson's Committee, in the Terms of Reference, that " any scheme prepared must be on the basis of reasonable contributions being paid by the owners of ships and cargoes towards the cost of insurance." The alternative of a free National Indemnity was thus excluded from their purview, probably because it was felt that, although the maintenance of the flow of traffic concerned the nation as a whole, such an indemnity would have the appearance of placing shipowners and cargo-owners in a preferential position as compared with other classes of the community, who were left to bear unaided all losses arising from the dislocation caused by war. But the strongest argument in favour of an insurance scheme, as opposed to an indemnity, was, in fact, that only under such a scheme was it possible to obtain that partnership between the State and the shipowners for the running of risks and the sharing of losses which was necessary to assure the State against fraud or negligence, to give control over the movement of shipping, and to ensure the development of the maximum effort in the carrying trade.

It was with this object of ensuring the maximum effort

that the scheme was extended to cover all cargoes, whether British or neutral-owned, carried in ships insured under the scheme, and all voyages made by such ships whether to British or neutral ports. Apart from the fact that the property in any cargo at a given moment might not be easy to ascertain, since many cargoes change hands many times in the course of a voyage, the cross voyages of British ships between foreign ports formed too important a factor in the development of British commerce and carrying power to be omitted from the scheme.[1]

Before the State Cargo Insurance Office had opened its doors, the contingency in view of which it had been created had actually arisen. The time limit contained in the ultimatum expired without any reply having been received, and from 11 p.m. on August 4th a state of war existed between Great Britain and Germany. Relations with Austria were not, as yet, formally broken off, as the ultimatum, being based upon the violation of Belgian neutrality by Germany, had been addressed only to that Power.

Rapidly as the situation had developed, the two or three days of preparation had been so well utilised that the State Insurance Office was able to open for business at 2 p.m. on the first day of the war. There had not been time to print the policies, but provisional cover slips were issued, and a certain amount of business was actually transacted that afternoon. For the most part, however, the officials and the fifty clerks with which the office was provisionally provided, were employed in answering a continual stream of inquiries by brokers and merchants anxious to understand fully the working of the scheme before placing risks. The general feeling was one of profound satisfaction at the step which the Government had taken, and confidence in the scheme was increased by the strength of the Advisory Board, the composition of which was now announced. The President of the Board was Mr. (now Sir) Douglas Owen, formerly Secretary of the Alliance Marine Assurance Co., Ltd., and an acknowledged authority on all matters relating to maritime insurance and seaborne trade. With him were associated representatives of Lloyd's and of the leading marine insurance companies; and it was widely recognised that the presence of these experts ensured the practical

---

[1] Cf. p. 6, *supra*.

and businesslike direction of the scheme.[1] The premium on cargoes had been fixed, for a start, at the maximum of 5 per cent.; but even this rate contrasted strongly with the rates of 15 and 20 per cent. which were now being quoted by underwriters for the more dangerous voyages. The premium on hulls was fixed at $1\frac{1}{4}$ per cent. for a single trip, or $2\frac{1}{2}$ per cent. for the round voyage, a quarter of the maximum rate contemplated in the original report of the Sub-Committee.

It would be difficult to exaggerate the debt owed not only by traders and shipowners, but by the nation as a whole, to those by whom the State Insurance Scheme was framed, and to the Government who had the wisdom and courage to adopt it at the very moment when hostilities were imminent. The economic strength of the nation was, indeed, to be severely tested by the loss of ships and cargoes; but when the Government decided to put into operation the scheme prepared by Mr. Huth Jackson's Committee, they averted once for all the danger of a general suspension of traffic more disastrous than a hundred casualties. To this one measure, above all else, was due the uninterrupted flow of seaborne trade through all the vicissitudes of the war.

Nor was this all. From the very first, its value as an instrument for the control of shipping movements was clearly apparent. Although the policy of the Admiralty was to interfere as little as possible with the normal course of commerce, it was, of course, necessary for them to keep closely in touch with the shipping which they were to protect. For this purpose, among others, a Trade Division of the Intelligence Department had existed from 1901 to 1909, and was replaced in 1913 by a Trade Section of the Operations Division. This Section quickly proved its utility, and on August 23rd, within three weeks of the outbreak of war, it was expanded into a separate Trade Division, with Captain Richard Webb, R.N., as Director. There was also in existence a Committee for the Diversion of Shipping, under Vice-Admiral Sir Edmond Slade, whose special function was the redistribution of trade normally handled

---

[1] In addition to the Chairman, the original members of the Board were: Sir Raymond Beck, Sir Edward Beauchamp, and Mr. Sydney Boulton, of Lloyd's; Mr. R. B. Lemon, of the Marine Insurance Company; Mr. H. T. Hines, of the Royal Exchange Assurance Company; Mr. R. A. Ogilvie, late of the Alliance Assurance Company; and Mr. W. E. Hargreaves, of C. T. Bowring & Co.

at ports which the exigencies of war might render useless for commercial purposes. It was no light task, however, to control the movements of some thousands of steamers engaged in a world-wide commerce, and would have been an impossible one, but for the high organisation of the shipping industry itself. The great Shipowners' Associations and the Corporation of Lloyd's, with its agencies at every considerable port at home or abroad, were allies of the utmost utility, and the State Insurance Scheme, with its provision for Admiralty and Board of Trade representation on the Management Committees of the War Risks Associations, provided an invaluable extension of the machinery of control.

Already, during the period of strained relations, the naval authorities, at home and abroad, had been busily engaged in communicating to the masters of British merchantmen instructions from their owners, which might otherwise have been held up by the general dislocation. When war became practically certain the exertions of the Admiralty were redoubled. All vessels bound for German or Austrian ports were recalled, and those about to enter the North Sea were diverted to Western ports. At the same time steps were taken to warn British shipping generally of the danger to which it was exposed and to furnish the masters of vessels at sea, or about to sail, with such instructions and advice as might contribute to the safety of their voyage.

The gist of the Admiralty advice was that all steamers should abandon the regular tracks, complete their voyages, so far as possible, without bunkering, and reduce the brilliance of the lights shown at night. It was strongly recommended that waters in which traffic is thickly concentrated should be traversed during the hours of darkness, and that as much use as possible should be made of territorial waters. Vessels homeward bound to the United Kingdom were further advised to call for orders as soon as possible after arriving in home waters.

These instructions were issued, in the first place, to naval officers, by whom they were passed on to every merchantman met at sea, or entering or leaving port. They were also sent to the Naval Intelligence Officers stationed at the chief British ports abroad. These officers had been appointed under a scheme first put into operation in 1911, for the purpose of providing means by which accurate intelligence might be collected and disseminated, and the movements of merchant shipping controlled in time of war. By the outbreak of war eleven such officers had been appointed, each having responsibility for a definite area, and it was part of their duty to collect, from the whole of the area entrusted to their charge, information as to the movements of enemy cruisers. This information enabled them to disseminate, through the medium of the consular offices, warning as to specific local dangers, as well as the general Admiralty advice.

In addition to these official channels of communication the instructions were handed to Lloyd's, by whom they were transmitted to their agencies and signal stations abroad. They were also given to the approved War Risks Clubs, for the information of their members, and it was here that the full value of the State Insurance Scheme became apparent. By offering strong inducements to shipowners to join the Approved Associations, it led to a great extension of their membership; and the Admiralty were thus provided with a ready and effective means of communicating confidentially with the majority of British shipowners. By making the cover conditional upon observance of Admiralty instructions, it furnished the strongest possible inducement to follow the advice received.

Meantime every possible preparation was made to secure for British commerce that adequate naval protection upon confidence in which the Insurance Scheme and the instructions to shipping were alike based. In considering the probable effects of a naval war on seaborne trade, it had always been assumed that the critical period would be the first few weeks after the outbreak of hostilities. The majority of German naval writers based their calculations upon the hope that the British navy would be taken more or less unawares, and even in this country it was frequently assumed that a certain period must elapse before adequate protection could be given to the trade routes. In naval circles little doubt was entertained of our ability to deal with the enemy's battle squadrons; and his cruisers in foreign waters were comparatively few in number. It was feared, however, that before our cruisers were on their stations or our defensive arrangements perfected, we might be confronted by the appearance on all the great ocean highways of large numbers of hostile liners, armed for the purpose of commerce destruction.[1] There were always to be found at sea and in foreign ports many German steamers of large size and good speed, which were believed to be so constructed as to permit of immediate conversion into auxiliary cruisers, and it was from these vessels that the gravest danger to British commerce was apprehended.

The Treaty of Washington, 1871, founded on the decision in the celebrated case of the *Alabama*, laid down as a rule of International Law that a neutral Government is bound to use due diligence to prevent the fitting out, arming, or equipping within its jurisdiction, of any vessel which it has reasonable grounds for believing to be intended to carry on war against a Power with which it is at peace, and to prevent the departure of such vessels from its jurisdiction. This rule was embodied in Article 8 of the Hague Convention, No. XIII, of 1907, but this Convention did not prohibit the conversion of merchantmen into warships on the high seas.[2] The British Government had earnestly pressed for such a rule, arguing that liberty to effect conversion in this manner was in fact an abrogation of the clause in the Declaration of Paris by which the right of privateering was abolished. Owing, however, to the inability of the Powers to come to an agreement, the point remained undecided, and it was believed that many of the German liners carried concealed armaments ready to be mounted on the outbreak of hostilities.[3]

For the purpose of affording protection against this menace, the Admiralty had decided, early in 1913, to arm a number of selected British liners with a pair of 4.7" guns, mounted at the stern, so as to preclude all possibility of offensive use, while providing means of defence against a lightly armed assailant. Of such defensively armed vessels there were, at the outbreak of war, 39, almost all of which were steamers engaged in the Australian and South American meat trade, and were thus easily provided with insulated magazines. No ammunition was carried by these vessels in times of peace, but it was stored ready for delivery on the outbreak of war, and trained gunners belonging to the Royal Naval Reserve were carried among the crews. No objection had been raised by foreign Powers

[1] See, especially, Mr. Winston Churchill's statement in the House of Commons, November 27th, 1914.
[2] A. Pearce Higgins, *The Hague Peace Conferences*, pp. 448, 464–466.
[3] *Ibid.*, pp. 316–321.

to the status of such ships, but there had not yet been time further to extend the system.[1]

The defensively armed ships were thus in a very small minority, even among liners, nor were they expected to stand up to anything more powerful than a converted merchantman, and in view of the expectation that the enemy would attempt to redress their numerical inferiority by a sudden blow before the British fleet was fully concentrated, and that this stroke would be accompanied by a surprise attack upon merchant shipping, it was of primary importance alike to the safety of trade and to the establishment of confidence among merchants and shipowners that the initial steps taken for the disposition of the naval forces of Great Britain should be prompt, vigorous, and effective. It may fairly be claimed that these conditions were, generally speaking, attained. In particular, the First Fleet, consisting of the most modern and powerful battle squadrons, with an attendant retinue of cruiser squadrons and flotillas, was already on its war station, under the command of Sir John Jellicoe, when hostilities broke out. At an early period of the war it became known as the Grand Fleet, and from the first it was the pivot upon which turned the defence of British trade throughout the world, as well as the free movement of our armies and the security of the British Isles from invasion.

It is a commonplace of naval strategy that both the attack and defence of trade rest ultimately upon the command of the sea, won by destroying or masking with superior force the enemy's battle squadrons; but in this case there were circumstances which rendered the Grand Fleet in a peculiar degree the direct safeguard of Allied commerce and enabled it to exert a paralysing influence upon the enemy's trade. These circumstances are to be found in the geographical situation of the principal belligerents.

Well placed, themselves, for receiving the commerce of every sea, the British Isles lie like a barrier between Germany and the ocean highways. With the exception of ships engaged in the coasting trade, or in short sea voyages such as those to the Scandinavian States,

---

[1] The details and working of this scheme for the defensive armament of merchantmen will be fully described by Mr. Archibald Hurd in *The Merchant Navy*.

every vessel approaching or leaving a German port must pass either through the English Channel or by the North-about Passage, the northern entrance to the North Sea. One or other of these courses must be followed, also, by every German cruiser or armed liner putting out from a German home port to prey on Allied shipping in the Atlantic or in more distant waters. The passage of the Channel by hostile cruisers or merchantmen was, from the first, practically impossible. The North-about Passage presents a wider doorway, more difficult to close, but the Orkneys and Shetlands extend the line of British bases almost half-way to the Norwegian coast. So long as the approaches to the North Sea were held by the British fleet in superior strength, the access and egress of enemy shipping were rendered at best extremely hazardous, and the way into the Atlantic could only be opened for German raiders by a force sufficiently powerful to offer battle. An isolated vessel, favoured by luck, might get through from time to time, but, in the main, the enemy were obliged to rely, for the attack on commerce, almost entirely on the ships already abroad.[1]

This combination of superior naval force with the advantages of geographical position accounts for much which at first sight appears incomprehensible in the effects of the war upon seaborne trade. All over the world German liners, laden with the copper, nitrates, cotton, and other commodities which Germany so sorely needed, were retained in harbour, even when no local danger prevented their free movement, because the British hold upon the approaches to home waters was too powerful to be disturbed. On the other hand, British trade in seas not immediately threatened by the presence of a German raider could move with perfect confidence, though the nearest friendly patrol might be a thousand miles away. Hidden away in the mists of the northern seas, deprived by the enemy's inactivity of any but the rarest opportunities of action, the battle squadrons, with the cruisers and flotillas which rested on their strength, formed the

---

[1] The successes obtained by the German submarines at a later period of the war were, of course, due simply to the fact that the submarine is a vessel possessing great possibilities of evasion, and has thus a very much greater chance of eluding the patrols than a surface ship. The superior success of the submarines was due, not only to the advantages conferred by their invisibility in the actual field of operations, but to their ability to reach it undetected.

dominant factor both in the attack and the defence of sea-borne trade.

Thus the early concentration and immediate readiness of the Grand Fleet for war went far to remove the menace to our maritime communications. It was necessary, however, to provide against the possibility of a stray raider slipping through the cordon, and to fetter the activities of the German warships in distant waters. The number of these was inconsiderable, but they included at least eight of the most modern and fastest cruisers flying the German flag, and it was possible that they might be largely reinforced by German liners at sea or in neutral ports, if these vessels should succeed in arming themselves for that purpose.

To deal with these actual or potential dangers, and to break up German trade between foreign ports, the British Admiralty could rely, in the first place, upon the ships serving permanently on foreign stations. The number of these had been diminished as a result of the policy of concentration in home waters forced upon the Admiralty by the rapid growth of the German navy; but political, no less than strategic reasons, still rendered it necessary to maintain squadrons in those waters where our chief interests lay. The Mediterranean Fleet, the strongest of our forces abroad, had been greatly reduced as a result of the agreement with France; but it was still a powerful and efficient force, comprising three battle cruisers, four armoured and four light cruisers, and a considerable torpedo flotilla. In more distant seas there were a battle cruiser, two battleships, six armoured cruisers, and seventeen light cruisers, with a proportion of torpedo craft, and a number of sloops and gunboats intended for the policing of coastal and inland waters. The distribution of these vessels comprised the Fourth Cruiser Squadron in North American and West Indian waters, the Cape, East Indies, and China Squadrons, the New Zealand Division, and the Australian Fleet, with two or three ships on the South American and Pacific coasts.

As soon as the danger of war became obvious, the officers commanding these squadrons were instructed to prepare for eventualities and to warn British shipping in their areas of the possible development of events. By August 4th their preparations were far advanced, and they had also entered into relations with the commanders of warships belonging to the prospective Allies of Great Britain. These ships were not numerous in the more distant seas. The main strength of the French Fleet was concentrated in the Mediterranean, and that of Russia was divided between the Baltic and the Black Sea. There were, however, some half-dozen French and Russian cruisers on foreign stations, and, in every case, these ships co-operated most cordially with the British forces in the task of commerce protection.

It remained to provide adequate cover for shipping traversing the waters in which the trade routes converge towards the home terminals, and to establish a watch on those enemy vessels by which the safety of such waters might be endangered. The Admiralty arrangements for this purpose contemplated the disposition of a series of intermediate squadrons to secure the focal points of trade which lay between the areas entrusted to the forces on foreign stations and those which were more immediately protected by the main fleets.

These squadrons were to be composed of ships on a Second and Third Fleet basis; that is to say, ships which were not permanently in commission, but were kept in an advanced stage of preparation for service, allowing of speedy mobilisation. In fact, as we have seen, the dispersal of Second Fleet ships and crews had been arrested on July 26th, and the calling out of the Naval Reserves on August 2nd enabled both the Second and Third Fleets to be placed on a war footing. During the days of supreme tension which preceded the delivery of the British ultimatum, the work of completing the ships for sea went rapidly forward, and when the ultimatum expired many of them were already on their war stations, while others were going out.

For the purpose of reinforcing the various squadrons, whether those permanently stationed abroad or those now specially mobilised for service in the Eastern Atlantic, a number of fast liners were requisitioned by the Admiralty for use as armed merchant cruisers, and many smaller vessels were taken up as boarding and examination steamers. These converted merchantmen could not, of course, be compared with the regular cruisers in fighting power, but they were admirably adapted for dealing with similar vessels commissioned by the enemy, or for exercising the control of shipping in protected areas.

THE REWARD OF READINESS

Thus, by the date on which hostilities broke out, the effective maintenance of British seaborne trade was already in large measure secured. The State Insurance Scheme ensured the maximum of effort to keep trade afoot on the part of shipowners, merchants, and the financial interests. The naval dispositions and the Admiralty instructions to shipping minimised the risk of loss.

The instant readiness for war which was thus displayed by those responsible for the direction of our naval forces and the encouragement of merchant shipping had results of primary importance. It is true that, although the danger of initial panic or of a surprise attack was thus averted, the German cruisers at sea were able, after some weeks of comparative inactivity, to strike heavy blows, by shifting their ground to the less defended waters. It is true also that the development of a hitherto untried weapon—the submarine—subsequently enabled the enemy to develop an attack of far greater intensity; but by the time this form of attack had been developed, the organisation of the nation for war had made such strides that it failed to produce the panic and dislocation which might have followed its appearance at an earlier date. In spite of all that happened during the prolonged struggle, the first few weeks of hostilities retain a very special interest. It was during that period, while trade and finance were still suffering from the shock and dislocation caused by the rapid development of the crisis, that a definite answer was given to the question whether British shipping would or would not prove able and willing to run the risks of maintaining the flow of trade. When once the machinery of trade had been re-established, and the confidence of shipowners and merchants confirmed, in their ability to carry on under the new and strange conditions, British finance and commerce were able to survive, albeit at heavy cost, blows which might have been disastrous if struck at the outset of the war.[1]

[1] For details of the defensive preparations see Sir Julian Corbett, *Naval Operations*. In addition to the scheme for State Insurance, the Committee of Imperial Defence had conducted enquiries into the diversion of shipping and control of railways, and had worked out the whole policy to be adopted with regard to enemy and neutral shipping, careful arrangements being concerted to give instant effect, in an emergency, to the decisions of the Government.

CHAPTER III

THE FIRST CAPTURES : THE MEDITERRANEAN MENACE [1]

So suddenly had the crisis developed that almost up to the last moment commercial intercourse between the States now involved in conflict had proceeded on the accustomed lines, and the declaration of war was immediately followed in all belligerent countries by the arrest of enemy merchantmen lying in their harbours. Thanks to the activity displayed by the Admiralty in warning British ships at sea, those which had been on their way to German ports during the period of tension had all been brought back or diverted to the United Kingdom, and many steamers which lay in German harbours at the end of July also succeeded in leaving before war broke out, though up to the last moment the German authorities continued to place obstacles in the way of their departure.[2] Their voyage home was one of some peril, for the mines which had been laid for defence of the German coast rendered navigation dangerous. Indeed, one ship was actually destroyed in this way prior to the declaration of war, though news of the disaster was not received until August 7th. This was the *San Wilfrido*, a tank steamer of 6,458 tons, owned by the Eagle Oil Transport Company, which put to sea from Hamburg on August 3rd, but struck one of the mines laid for the defence of the Elbe, and went to the bottom.

There remained in German ports, on August 5th, seventy-three British steamers and three sailing vessels of 100 tons and over, with a total tonnage of 170,000,[3] together with a few Allied ships, mostly Russians of small size. Of the British steamers twenty-three were ocean-going vessels of between 3,000 and 5,000 tons, the remainder being

[1] See Map 1.
[2] Cd. 7467, No. 156.
[3] Gross tonnage of steamers, net tonnage of sailing vessels. One small steamer was also detained by the German authorities in the Marshall Islands, but was subsequently released on the capture of those islands.

54

smaller ships, mostly engaged in direct trade between this country and Germany.

The position of a merchantman engaged in an ordinary commercial voyage and surprised in an enemy port by the outbreak of hostilities, had for a long time been recognised as one of peculiar hardship. During the second half of the nineteenth century a practice had arisen of allowing such vessels a reasonable period within which to withdraw before they could be seized. This practice had been recognised and regularised by Convention No. VI of the Hague Conference, 1907, which provided (Article 2) that merchant ships lying in an enemy port at the commencement of hostilities, or entering such port while still ignorant that hostilities had broken out, should not be liable to confiscation, but only to detention for the period of the war. They might, however, be requisitioned, on condition of compensation being subsequently paid. It was further stated by Article 1 of the Convention to be *desirable* that such vessels should be allowed to depart freely, either immediately, or after a reasonable number of days of grace, with a pass to their original port of destination, or such other port as might be indicated to them. Only vessels fitted by their build for conversion into warships were expressly excluded from the benefits of the Convention.[1]

It was provided that the Convention should only be binding in a war all parties to which were signatories of the Convention; and as the signatures of the Serbian and Montenegrin delegates had not yet been ratified, there was some legal doubt as to its applicability in the present case.[2] The articles in question had, however, been ratified by all the Great Powers, and on the first day of the war the British Government issued an Order in Council indicating their willingness to comply with the principle laid down by Article 1 as to "days of grace." They stipulated, however, that their action in this respect would depend on their being satisfied, not later than midnight of August 7th, that reciprocal treatment was being accorded to British ships and cargoes in enemy ports. In this event, German vessels would be allowed up to midnight on August 14th for loading or unloading, and

---

[1] Higgins, *The Hague Peace Conferences*, pp. 295–307.
[2] See Judgment of Sir Samuel Evans in the case of the schooner *Möwe*, in *Lloyd's Reports of Prize Cases*, vol. ii., London, 1917, pp. 85–6.

departure. Cable-ships, seagoing ships designed to carry oil fuel, and vessels whose tonnage exceeded 5,000 gross or whose speed was 14 knots or over, were excluded from this privilege, as well as vessels fitted for conversion into armed merchant cruisers, which, under the Convention, were liable not only to detention but to confiscation.[1]

The German Government, also, at first indicated its willingness to liberate merchant vessels in German harbours on receipt of a counter undertaking from the British Government.[2] The Foreign Office were, however, unable to obtain satisfactory information as to the treatment accorded in Germany to British ships and cargoes, and, in consequence, the Order in Council of August 5th never came into operation.[3] All German ships in British ports were accordingly seized, but in compliance with Article 2 of the Sixth Convention and in faith that it would be observed by the German Government, the Crown refrained from asking the Prize Courts for an Order of Confiscation in the case of vessels engaged in an ordinary commercial voyage, being content that they should be detained by the Admiralty Marshal until further orders.[4]

The total number of German vessels thus seized at ports in the United Kingdom was fifty-six, comprising thirty-four steamers and twenty-two sailing vessels, with a total tonnage of 81,000; and within a few days these were joined by three other steamers, arriving in ignorance of the outbreak of war.[5]

Among the ships seized the most important were the homeward bound Hamburg-Amerika liners *Kronprinzessin Cecilie*, *Prinz Adalbert*, and *Belgia*, all three of which had reached the entrance to the Channel when, on August 3rd, they learned that a state of war existed between Germany and France. Thereupon the *Kronprinzessin Cecilie* and *Prinz Adalbert* put into Falmouth, where they were still lying at the expiration of the British ultimatum; and as they had arrived in search of a port of refuge and not in the ordinary course of commerce, it was subsequently

---

[1] Published in *London Gazette*, 5 August, 1914. See *Manual of Emergency Legislation*, September 1914, p. 138.
[2] *Ibid.*, p. 141.
[3] *Ibid.*, pp. 141-2.
[4] The leading case is *The Ship " Chile," Lloyd's Reports of Prize Cases*, vol. i, London, 1915, p. 8.
[5] There were also four yachts, a steam trawler, and ten sailing vessels under 100 tons net.

SEIZURES AND DETENTIONS

held by the Prize Court that the Hague Convention did not apply. Both ships were accordingly condemned. The *Belgia* ran for safety to the Bristol Channel, and on August 4th arrived off Newport, where her appearance, in the existing state of tension, excited apprehensions of a German raid. She was therefore denied entrance to the port and ordered to an anchorage in the Channel, where she was taken possession of next day, after the declaration of war.

Still more important were the seizures at British ports abroad, where some fifty German steamers were detained, most of these being liners of fair size. At Antwerp, a port of call for several of the great German lines, over thirty steamers were detained, and though few enemy merchantmen were found in French harbours, a large number fell into the hands of the Russians. The total of German shipping detained in British or Allied ports on the outbreak of war, or subsequently seized on entering port, amounted to 223 steamers and thirty-five sailing vessels, with a tonnage of 650,000, or roughly 12 per cent. of the German mercantile marine. In addition, some fifty "interior vessels" and lighters, averaging 1,000 tons, were seized by the Belgians in canal ports.

The detention of German merchantmen in British harbours was speedily followed by the arrival of others brought in as prizes by our ships at sea. The restless activity of the Royal Dockyards during the days of suspense had borne good fruit, and almost before the ultimatum had expired, a chain of patrols, extending from the Shetlands to the Cape Verdes, had been flung out to cover shipping in the approaches to European waters. The Tenth Cruiser Squadron, under Rear-Admiral de Chair, in co-operation with the cruisers of the Grand Fleet, kept watch on the North-about Passage, with the double purpose of preventing German cruisers or armed liners from breaking out into the Atlantic, and of stopping homeward-bound merchantmen or cargoes of contraband in neutral bottoms from reaching German ports. The Eleventh Cruiser Squadron, commanded by Rear-Admiral R. S. Phipps Hornby, guarded the northern entrance to the Irish Sea and the area south-west of Ireland in which the North Atlantic Trade Routes approach the Irish Sea and English Channel. At the western entrance to the Channel itself was posted the Twelfth

Cruiser Squadron, under Rear-Admiral Wemyss, working in conjunction with a French force based on Brest. From the Channel to Finisterre, and from Finisterre to Madeira, British trade with French, Spanish, and Portuguese ports, together with the European ends of the Oriental, Cape, and South American Trade Routes, was under the charge of Rear-Admiral de Robeck, with the Ninth Cruiser Squadron. Finally, the extension of the South American and African Routes further south, to the Canaries and Cape Verdes, was protected by the Fifth Cruiser Squadron under Rear-Admiral Stoddart.

Even before the outbreak of hostilities the ships of the Ninth and Fifth Cruiser Squadrons were pushing out down the Trade Routes to Finisterre and the Canaries, warning all British merchantmen encountered of the imminence of war; and by August 5th, ships of all the various patrol squadrons were on or very near their war stations. On these stations they were equally well placed to protect British and to intercept German shipping, and within a few hours from the declaration of war a number of prizes fell into their hands. That these prizes were not more numerous was due to the passive policy enjoined on German shipping. We have seen that, as early as July 31st, when war with France and Russia only was in contemplation, the German transatlantic lines had cancelled their services and recalled steamers at sea. Had Great Britain remained neutral, an effort would, no doubt, have been made to cover the homeward passage of ships at sea and to re-establish the chief services; but in face of the British ultimatum no attempt to carry on trade seems to have been contemplated for a moment. To every port which could be reached by cable from Germany, and to every ship at sea which was within reach of a German wireless station, orders were flashed directing all steamers to suspend their voyage at the first port of call, or if it should appear dangerous to proceed even so far, to hurry into the nearest harbour where the shelter of a neutral flag could be obtained. Thus the seaborne trade of Germany, so far as it was carried on under the national flag, was completely wiped out by the mere existence of a state of war.

A few vessels engaged in the short sea trades were, however, still moving in the waters round the British Isles, and others, which were not equipped with wireless apparatus, were unsuspectingly completing their voyages from distant ports. The fate of these vessels illustrated convincingly the danger from which the bulk of German shipping was saved by its acceptance of an inactive rôle.

It had been contemplated by the Sixth Hague Convention of 1907 that merchant ships which had left their last port of departure before the outbreak of war, and were encountered on the high seas while still ignorant of the outbreak of hostilities, should receive the same treatment as those surprised in port, that is to say, they should not be confiscated, but merely be detained for the period of the war or requisitioned on payment of compensation. The German and Russian Governments, however, did not agree to the Article [1] which related to such ships, and made a reservation in respect of it. The provision, therefore, was inapplicable as regards German ships, and all those which were captured at sea became good prize, whether aware of the outbreak of hostilities or not.[2]

As the GRAFTON and GIBRALTAR passed up the Irish Sea, to join the Northern Patrol, they captured the *Marie Glasier*, returning from Barry in ballast to load at Archangel, and the *William Behrens* bringing timber from Archangel to Liverpool. Another vessel from the White Sea port, the *Ulla Boog*, bound for Barry with a cargo of pit-props, was taken by the CHALLENGER, keeping watch at the entrance to the Bristol Channel. In the English Channel, the *Franz Horn*, the *Perkeo*, a large sailing vessel, and the Austrian liner *Laconia* were brought in by destroyers of the Dover Patrol. The French were also on the alert, and two vessels, the *Porto* and the Austrian *Dinorah*, were captured by a destroyer of the Cherbourg Flotilla. As relations with Austria had not yet been definitely broken off, the *Laconia* was released and allowed to complete her voyage to Rotterdam. The *Dinorah* was subsequently requisitioned by the French Government.[3]

Further west, two small German sailing vessels were captured by the ISIS and DORIS of the Eleventh Cruiser Squadron, in the neighbourhood of the Scillies, and another by the DIANA of the Twelfth, and Admiral de

[1] No. 3 of the Sixth Convention.
[2] See *The Barque "Perkeo," Lloyd's Reports of Prize Cases*, vol. i, at p. 55.
[3] The aggregate gross tonnage of the five German steamers was 7,400 tons. The *Perkeo* was of 3,609 tons net.

Robeck, then one day out of port, sent the HIGHFLYER back to Plymouth with the Dutch liner *Tubantia*, which was carrying £100,000 in gold for the London branch of the Deutsche Bank, a number of German reservists, and 2,500 tons of grain.

On the morning of the 6th, the Norddeutscher-Lloyd liner *Schliesen* (5,586 tons) was captured by the VINDICTIVE, Admiral de Robeck's flagship, and sent into Plymouth with a prize crew on board. On the same day the VINDICTIVE stopped and boarded the Austrian steamers *Alfa* and *Polnay*. Both vessels were laden with grain, the *Alfa* from Taganrog for Bremen, and the *Polnay* from Braila for German consignees at Rotterdam. They were accordingly ordered to report at Falmouth, where their voyage was stopped. Another prize taken on August 6th was the *Syra* (2,017 tons), which was captured off Gibraltar by the CORNWALL on her way down to join Admiral Stoddart's flag.

Few of these early prizes were of much intrinsic value, but their capture gave welcome evidence of naval activity and afforded an effective contrast to the unimpeded arrivals and departures of British merchantmen. At first, indeed, the number of these was a long way below the normal, for the shutting down of trade with the Central Powers necessitated a redistribution of commerce which it took some time to effect, and the universal financial crisis produced by the outbreak of war opposed a serious obstacle to the flow of traffic to and from neutral ports. The requisitioning of several hundred ships as naval auxiliaries or transports was a further cause of disorganisation, and finally, although the State Insurance Scheme prevented any general laying up of shipping, a certain degree of caution was inevitable during the first days of the war, and homeward-bound vessels were in some cases temporarily held up at foreign ports to await owners' instructions or further light on the risks involved in continuing their voyage.

It was not long before the situation began to clear. Though the first shots of the war were fired in the North Sea in the early morning of August 5th, it soon became evident that unless some peculiarly tempting opportunity was offered, the High Seas Fleet had no immediate intention of offering or accepting battle, and in the meantime the cruiser patrols had secured the terminal waters, and in the Mediterranean, the only serious menace to British trade with Southern Europe and the Far East had been removed.

The opening day of the war had served to demonstrate the hold of Great Britain on the gateway of the Mediterranean as well as on the approaches to the North Sea. On August 5th the Gibraltar Flotilla brought in three German steamers, engaged respectively in the trade of the Mediterranean itself, of Africa and of the Far East. The *Adolf* was bound from Trangsund in the Baltic to Alicante. The *Emir* belonged to the Deutsche Ost-Afrika Company and was returning from Beira, in Portuguese East Africa, to Hamburg. The Hansa liner *Schneefels* was on her way from Calcutta to New York. It would be difficult to illustrate more effectively the world-wide influence of a naval force established on one of those focal points at which the tracks of vessels from many seas converge to a common centre.

Next day, another prize, the *Georg*,[1] was brought in to Gibraltar, but meanwhile a somewhat threatening situation had developed in the Mediterranean itself. The naval position within the Straits contained several elements of uncertainty. In the first place, it was obvious that relations of so equivocal a character as those existing between the Western Allies and Austria could not long be maintained, and that the Austrian fleet might at any moment be brought into play against their maritime communications. This was not, in itself, a very serious complication of the problem of trade defence, for the Austrian fleet was particularly deficient in fast light cruisers suitable for use as commerce destroyers, and was hampered by the position of its bases at the head of the Adriatic. Had the full strength of the Triple Alliance been brought into the field, the position, both with regard to comparative strength and the proximity of bases to steamer tracks, would have been much more threatening; but Italy had declared her neutrality on August 3rd, and with Italy neutral or friendly, the probable outbreak of hostilities with Austria could be faced with comparative equanimity.

There were, however, two units of the German fleet in the Mediterranean, the battle cruiser GOEBEN and the light cruiser BRESLAU. During the period of tension, Admiral Sir Berkeley Milne, who commanded the British

[1] Gross tonnage of the four prizes, 13,228.

forces in the Mediterranean, had received orders to shadow these ships, and to take such steps as might be necessary to prevent their passing through the Straits to attack trade on the Atlantic routes. He had not, however, succeeded in getting in touch with them, and after coaling at Brindisi on July 31st, they were not definitely located till August 4th, when, war having broken out between France and Germany, they appeared off the Algerian coast, where the GOEBEN bombarded Bona and the BRESLAU threw a few shells into Phillipeville. Some damage was done to the French steamer *St. Thomas* and the British steamer *Isle of Hastings*, but as the orders for embarking troops at these ports had already been countermanded, the effect of the bombardments was negligible. Still, unimportant as were their initial exploits, the hostile vessels constituted a serious danger to shipping, and an additional menace was the presence at Genoa of the liners *König Albert* and *Moltke*, both of which were suitable for conversion into armed merchant cruisers.[1]

In these circumstances it was considered advisable to instruct all east-bound steamers at Gibraltar to call for instructions at Valetta, where, however, the naval authorities sent them on, whenever owners were willing, with the minimum of delay. In the meantime the attention of the Italian Government was called to the possibility of an attempt being made to arm and equip the *Moltke* and *König Albert* within the limits of their jurisdiction. On the other hand, the GOEBEN and BRESLAU, after being sighted by the INDOMITABLE and other ships on the evening of the 4th, had again disappeared from sight. Admiral Milne's task was complicated by the necessity of lending support to the French fleet, which was engaged in covering the passage of the Algerian Army Corps to Marseilles, and although the enemy ships were located on the 5th at Messina, where they put in to coal, he did not succeed in bringing them to action. For some days, therefore, considerable anxiety was felt with regard to the safety of British shipping within the Straits, which amounted to some three-quarters of a million tons; but this anxiety was quickly relieved. The GOEBEN and BRESLAU had no intention either of escaping into the Atlantic or of attacking the Mediterranean trade. The

---

[1] *König Albert* : Norddeutscher-Lloyd ; 10,484 tons, 15 knots. *Moltke :* Hamburg-Amerika Line ; 12,335 tons, 16·5 knots.

German Government, who already contemplated bringing Turkey into the war, had ordered them to Constantinople, and after leaving Messina on the night of the 5th, they steamed eastward at high speed. Although the light cruiser GLOUCESTER at one time came near enough to exchange shots with the BRESLAU, the German ships ultimately succeeded in evading all attempts to bring them to action, and on August 10th they arrived at the Dardanelles, where they were at once permitted to enter. The first of their pursuers came up shortly after, but passage was denied to them. A close watch on the Straits was, however, established, and at the same time a squadron was left at the entrance to the Adriatic to observe the movements of the Austrian fleet.[1]

Regrettable as was the escape of the GOEBEN and BRESLAU, and serious as the consequences of their arrival at Constantinople were to prove, they had been run to earth, and for the flow of trade this meant a real gain. During the six days which had elapsed between the declaration of war and the arrival of the hostile warships at the Dardanelles, the anxiety of masters and shipowners had been reflected in constant and urgent inquiries as to the safety of the tracks. The Admiralty had given instructions that shipping should only be detained as an emergency measure, and there was little official interference with the flow of traffic, but many west-bound steamers were ordered into Valetta by their owners, and over eighty steamers, mostly of large size, were sheltering in Gibraltar harbour. There were, indeed, all the elements of a panic which might have paralysed for the time being, not only the trade of the Mediterranean itself, valued at over £125,000,000 a year, but also the still greater volume of traffic which passes through the Suez Canal. From this danger British commerce was now freed; the hostile cruisers, if not destroyed, were securely blocked, and the policy of the Admiralty in encouraging the movement of shipping was fully justified. Some alarm was excited during the second week of August by a rumour that German ships had laid mines near the entrance to the Suez Canal, but upon the channel seaward from Port Said being swept by the fleet, the report was ascertained to be without foundation. The German liners at Genoa were kept under strict surveil-

[1] For a full account of this episode, see *Naval Operations*, by Sir Julian S. Corbett.

lance by the Italian authorities, and British trade, both with the Mediterranean ports and with the East, was able to proceed without any appreciable risk of hostile interference.

On the other hand, here as elsewhere, the German flag had been absolutely driven from the sea. As early as August 1st, German steamers began to throw up their voyages and hurry into the shelter of neutral harbours. The *Czar Nicolai II*, an oil-tanker returning from Batoum, was caught by a French torpedo-boat off the African coast on August 4th; but by the expiration of the British ultimatum the majority of the enemy steamers were safe in port and few were left to fall into the hands of the British cruisers. The *Erymanthos*, of the Deutsche-Levante Line, was seized by destroyers off Valetta on August 5th, and the *Kawak* and *Kalymnos* of the same line were captured at sea during the next few days, but no further prizes were made. Half a dozen German steamers trading to the Mediterranean were, however, detained in Egyptian ports in which they had taken refuge.[1]

In the ports of Spain, Greece, and Italy, there lay also a number of Austrian steamers which feared to complete their voyages in the peculiar position of Austrian relations with the Western Powers. These relations, indeed, were fast coming to a crisis. On August 8th, an Austrian detachment bombarded the Montenegrin port of Antivari, and on the 10th a blockade of the Montenegrin coast was proclaimed, twenty-four hours being allowed for the departure of neutral and friendly ships. It was evident that so anomalous a position could not be continued, and on the same day it was terminated by a declaration of war by the French Government. Two days later a similar declaration by Great Britain was received in Vienna, and this was shortly followed by the beginning of offensive operations. On August 15th the British squadron which had been left in observation at the entrance to the Adriatic was joined by the main body of the French fleet, and next day the combined forces carried out a northward sweep which raised the blockade of Antivari and drove the Austrians back to their defended ports, with the loss of the light cruiser ZENTA.

On the declaration of war against Austria eleven

[1] The tonnage of these ships was 18,649; of the four prizes, 11,399.

Austrian steamers were detained in British ports, and five others were seized at Malta and Alexandria, or in the harbours of Algeria. The Austrian Government, however, came to an arrangement with the Allies for the mutual admission of days of grace, and five of the ships detained in the United Kingdom were released under this agreement.[1] The others, amounting to some 19,000 tons, were unable or unwilling to depart within the limited period, and remained in British hands, together with a steamer which was completing in a Tyne shipyard.[2] The five vessels seized in the Mediterranean all took advantage of the days of grace, and their arrival at Greek and Italian ports brought up the total number sheltering in neutral harbours in that sea to fifty-one German and twenty-three Austrian steamers, with an aggregate tonnage of a quarter of a million.

Thus, by August 16th, the Mediterranean had become practically an Allied lake, with the exception of the upper waters of the Adriatic. Since the end of July mines had been freely sown by the Austrians in these waters, with results disastrous to two or three of their own steamers and to several Italian fishing craft. In consequence of this danger, a dozen British steamers were detained at Venice by their owners' instructions, and even after the victorious sweep on August 16th, it was considered unsafe for merchantmen to move outside the limits of Italian territorial waters. In addition to the mine peril, it was impossible to guarantee absolute security against the activities of Austrian torpedo craft issuing from the fringe of islands on the Dalmatian coast, and it was decided by the Advisory Committee to exclude Adriatic voyages from the benefits of the State Insurance Scheme.

More serious than the stoppage of direct steamer communication with Venice was the threatened total extinction of Black Sea trade. Since the reorganisation of the Turkish army by German officers, German influence had been steadily gaining ground at Constantinople, and from the first day of the war the attitude of the Turkish Government had been equivocal. So early as August 4th, mines were laid in the Dardanelles, and, on the 5th, one of these exploded under the British steamer *Craigforth*, which had

---

[1] *Manual of Emergency Legislation*, September 1914, pp. 97-8, 142-3.
[2] These included the *Alfa* and *Polnay* (see p. 60, *supra*), whose cargoes had been pre-empted by the British Government.

to be run ashore to avoid sinking. Assurances were given that the explosion of the mine was purely accidental, and a score of steamers subsequently passed in safety during the same day, but the activity displayed in mining the channel was in itself suspicious. At Constantinople everything was in confusion. The financial chaos was complete and business came to a standstill. An embargo was laid on all grain ships and several cargoes were commandeered, with the ostensible object of securing the food supply of the city. Other vessels were prevented from leaving by the impossibility of completing their discharge, and the commercial and political outlook was exceedingly black.

The arrival of the GOEBEN and BRESLAU added to the difficulties of the situation, as their presence tended greatly to reinforce the influence of the pro-German section in the Government, which was strong and truculent. The German warships conducted themselves as if they were in one of their own ports, and the BRESLAU even boarded British steamers lying in the harbour without evoking any protest from the Turkish authorities. Under strong pressure from the British ambassador, due apologies for this and other outrages, together with promises of amendment, were obtained from the Grand Vizier, who was anxious to preserve a strict neutrality; but it became daily more doubtful how far he and his adherents would be able to control the actions of the military party.[1]

On August 12th the situation was complicated by the announcement that the GOEBEN and BRESLAU had been purchased from Germany for the Turkish navy. The transfer of belligerent warships which had put into port to avoid capture was not recognised by International Law, but the Turks had been greatly irritated by the preemption of two battleships building for them in England, and it was not considered desirable to contest the sale. No steps, however, were taken to hand over the ships or to replace the German officers and crews by Turks, and it soon became very doubtful whether the transaction was genuine. In these circumstances, it was necessary to contemplate the permanent closing of the Dardanelles to traffic, a prospect which could not be regarded without grave anxiety, as not only would the grain and oil of

[1] *Correspondence relating to the rupture of relations with Turkey* [Cd. 7628], 1914.

TURKEY AND THE DARDANELLES

Russia and Roumania cease to be available for the Western Allies, but Russia would be heavily hit financially by the stoppage of her principal export, and Roumanian products would be forced almost inevitably into the markets of the Central Powers.[1]

British trade with the Black Sea was carried on mainly under the national flag, and there was a considerable amount of British tonnage actually loading in Russian and Roumanian ports, in addition to that lying in the Bosporus and Dardanelles. It now appeared possible that the whole of these vessels might be cut off by the closing of the Straits, and great efforts were accordingly made to remove the ships while there was yet time. The financial crisis in Southern Russia greatly impeded the completion of cargoes, but as fast as ships could be cleared they stood over to Constantinople to await their turn for passing through the Narrows.

Even at Constantinople, however, the position of British merchantmen was precarious, and the danger to which they were exposed was emphasised by the preferential treatment accorded to German and Austrian shipping. All enemy steamers in Russian ports on the Black Sea had been detained on the outbreak of war,[2] but a considerable number which were already at sea had found their way to the Golden Horn, bringing up the total of German and Austrian ships in Turkish ports to nearly thirty, with a tonnage of about 100,000. These ships were allowed to use their wireless freely, a privilege which the Turkish Government denied to Allied merchantmen, nor was any attempt made to intern the Deutsche Ost-Afrika Liner *General*, which was known to have acted as a tender to the GOEBEN and BRESLAU.

So far as Black Sea trade was concerned, the situation was thus thoroughly unsatisfactory, but this was more than compensated by the position attained, as the result of the initial naval movements, in the Mediterranean itself. So long as the Allied fleets retained their hold upon the entrances to the Adriatic and the Dardanelles there was

[1] On an average of the four years 1910, 1911, 1912, and 1913, the percentage of Russian wheat to the total imports of the United Kingdom was 14·7. The years 1912 and 1913 saw a great diminution in the imports from Russia, but the first seven months of 1914 were marked by heavy shipments. France was also a large buyer, both from Russia and Roumania.

[2] They included 5 German steamers of 3,000 to 4,000 tons and a number of smaller vessels, with 10 Austrian steamers aggregating 37,000 tons.

no danger of hostile cruisers issuing to attack the Mediterranean trade. Best of all, the essential link in the great trunk route from India and the Far East had been definitely secured, and, meanwhile, the continuation of the voyage from the Straits of Gibraltar to the United Kingdom had been guaranteed by the cruiser squadrons entrusted with the safety of the Atlantic approaches.

CHAPTER IV

THE CONTROL OF THE ATLANTIC TERMINALS [1]

THE work of the patrols by which trade was covered in its approach to home waters proved, generally speaking, singularly devoid of incident. The expectation of a surprise attack upon commerce during the early weeks of the war remained almost entirely unrealised. The hold of the Grand Fleet on the entrance to the North Sea was too firm to be broken, and with one notable exception, no German cruiser or armed liner broke out into the Atlantic. The German cruisers on foreign stations confined their activities to distant seas, and made no attempt to come into the richer but more dangerous field presented by the terminal waters. Enemy merchantmen everywhere remained in port, and few prizes were to be made, simply because there was no trade under the German or Austrian flag to be attacked.

This absence of incident must not blind us, however, either to the value or to the difficulty of the work performed. It is true that, so long as the Grand Fleet remained undefeated, no enemy squadron could hope to operate undisturbed in the immediate vicinity of the British Isles, but even a flying raid on the North Atlantic terminals might well have inflicted a severe blow on the confidence of traders in naval protection, and to the South—where the Cape and South American routes converge, and their united traffic meets the trade of the Mediterranean and the Far East off the Iberian coast—there is a focal area second only in importance to the Channel mouth, and far more difficult to guard. So heavy was the strain on the resources of the Admiralty that the utmost difficulty was found in providing forces strong enough to cover the long stretch of the terminal waters from the Cape Verdes to the Scillies.

[1] See Maps 1 and 3.

For some time, indeed, the cruiser chain was dangerously weak. Yet, as we shall see, it proved sufficient. The one attempt made to disturb the security of the approaches was promptly parried and heavily punished. Nowhere was a more striking contrast presented between the paralysis of enemy shipping and the flow of British trade; but this result was not achieved without a great and incessant strain upon the officers and crews of the covering squadrons. The possibility that a solitary raider might elude the vigilance of the North Sea cordon, or that one or more of the German cruisers in the Western Atlantic might cross to the European or African coast, could never be ignored. In North American ports some of the fastest liners in the world were lying under the German flag and were believed to be awaiting their opportunity for a dash into the Atlantic as armed raiders. If the enemy merchantmen met at sea were few, there were a large number in Spanish and Portuguese ports, in the harbours of Madeira and the Azores, of the Canaries and Cape Verdes, all of which had to be kept under close and constant observation lest they should slip out either as commerce destroyers or as supply ships to German cruisers. All these anxieties were increased by the continual rumours as to the movement of enemy vessels which, even when not wholly probable in themselves, required to be sifted, checked, and reported to the Admiralty, in order that dispositions might be altered or initiated as occasion arose, and shipowners or masters informed of any impending danger. All the time, the flow of British and Allied shipping had to be shepherded and guided, warned of local dangers, directed as to the courses to be followed and advised in cases of difficulty. All the time, also, there was a continual stream of homeward bound neutrals to be visited and searched for contraband goods.

The provisions of International Law with regard to belligerent trade carried on by means of neutral shipping had been restated and codified by the Declaration of London in 1909. In one respect this Declaration constituted a triumph for British diplomacy, as it gave formal recognition to the doctrine of "continuous voyage," by which the ultimate destination of the goods, and not the port of discharge, was made the test of their character. The point was one of great importance, as the right of a belligerent to treat as contraband goods consigned to a

THE LAW OF CONTRABAND

neutral port for subsequent transport to an enemy country had not hitherto been admitted by continental jurists, but had become essential to the successful exercise of sea power, owing to the great development of land transport during the last hundred years. Some of the other provisions of the Declaration were, however, less satisfactory from the point of view of the naval Powers, and owing to the opposition aroused, the signatures of the British delegates had not been ratified by the Government. The Declaration was, therefore, without binding effect, though it remained in many respects an authoritative statement as to the accepted laws and practice of war at sea.

By the Declaration of London all goods destined for a belligerent State were divided into three classes—Absolute Contraband, Conditional Contraband, and Free.

Absolute Contraband was rigidly confined to war material and articles used exclusively for purposes of war. Such articles, if carried in neutral bottoms, were declared liable to capture if the ultimate destination of the cargo was in enemy territory or in territory occupied by the armed forces of the enemy, whether the carriage of the goods to the enemy destination was direct or entailed transhipment or transport by land.

Conditional Contraband included foodstuffs, fodder, fuel, bullion and specie, and a number of articles capable of employment either for warlike or peaceful purposes. It was stated that such goods would be liable to capture only if shown to be destined for the use of the enemy's armed forces or of a Government Department concerned with the carrying on of the war. In the case of Conditional Contraband the doctrine of " continuous voyage " was not applied, and its capture was made subject to the vessel herself being bound for territory belonging to or occupied by the enemy. Proof of ultimate enemy destination would, therefore, afford no grounds for the capture of goods to be discharged in a neutral port and forwarded by rail.

Free Goods, which might not be declared contraband, included textile materials, metallic ores, rubber, manures, agricultural, mining and textile machinery, and other industrial materials and manufactured articles.

It was further provided that in cases where contraband goods formed more than one-half of the cargo, either in quantity, value, or freight, the vessel herself should be subject to condemnation.[1]

The two most unsatisfactory points in these provisions, from the point of view of belligerent rights, were the wide extension given to the "free list" and the failure to apply the doctrine of continuous voyage to Conditional Contraband. It was obvious that such articles as metallic ores, cotton, and rubber would be extensively used for war purposes, and that manures and agricultural machinery would be employed to produce food for the enemy's fighting forces as well as for his civil population. Moreover, the placing of any article on the list of conditional contraband was stultified, under modern conditions, as long as it could be delivered at any port having railway communication with the enemy's territory.

Nevertheless there were considerable difficulties in throwing over the Declaration at the outset of the war. Measures having for their object the restriction of supplies reaching the enemy through neutral countries involved the restriction of imports by those countries themselves. To place on the list of contraband such articles as cotton and coffee might inflict on the chief producing countries —who were friendly neutrals—greater injury than that inflicted on the enemy. The refusal of the British Government to ratify the Declaration left it with its belligerent rights unimpaired; but it was necessary, in exercising those rights, to have regard to considerations of foreign policy as well as to the military situation.

Immediately on the declaration of war, a Proclamation was issued specifying articles which would be treated as Absolute and Conditional Contraband respectively.[2] These lists were practically identical with those contained in the Declaration of London, except that aircraft of all kinds and their accessories were transferred from the conditional to the absolute list. No further steps were taken at the moment to define the British position.

Even under the limitations imposed by tacit adoption of the Declaration of London, the regulation of neutral traffic formed a heavy addition to the work of the fleet. For the examination of ships passing north-about, the Admiralty relied mainly on the Tenth Cruiser Squadron,

[1] The Declaration of London is printed in Appendix H to the *Manual of Emergency Legislation*, pp. 447-463, and in Higgins, *Hague Peace Conferences*, pp. 540-566.
[2] *Manual of Emergency Legislation*, p. 108.

assisted by the cruiser squadrons of the Grand Fleet. The gate to be closed was a wide one, and though the Northern Patrol was reinforced by a number of Armed Merchant Cruisers, the task was, in the highest degree, arduous and exacting. Ships passing through the Channel could be more easily dealt with. The Twelfth Cruiser Squadron with its French consorts held the western entrance, and the Dover Patrol the eastern. By these forces vessels passing up Channel were intercepted and required to anchor in the Downs, where they were examined by the Downs Boarding Flotilla. Thus the dispositions in the Channel enabled the British Navy to exercise a high degree of control over the flow of trade. In conjunction with the Northern Patrol, they did much to relieve the outlying squadrons of the search for contraband; yet it was necessary for those squadrons to keep a watch on suspicious movements in their own area, especially those of possible colliers and supply ships to the German cruisers, and to report suspicious steamers passing through their area, for examination in home waters.

In the course of a few weeks it became evident that the right to capture conditional contraband on vessels bound for German ports was derisory, so long as supplies were permitted to flow into Germany, without interruption, through neutral countries. Accordingly, an Order in Council was issued on August 20th in which the position arrived at by consultation between the Allied Governments was defined. This position was, in effect, an acceptance of the provisions contained in the Declaration of London, with the very important modification that Conditional Contraband having an ultimate enemy destination would be liable to capture to whatever port the vessel was bound and at whatever port the cargo was to be discharged, whether in belligerent or neutral territory.[1]

This application of the principle of the "continuous voyage" to Conditional Contraband increased the need for activity and rigour in the work of examination. At the same time, every effort was made to cause as little delay as possible to neutral shipping; but the large cargoes carried by modern steamers, and their extensive subdivision, rendered it impossible to search them effectively at sea, and it was necessary to send into port, for more

[1] *Manual of Emergency Legislation*, p. 143.

thorough examination, those whose papers showed a *prima facie* case for suspicion.

With the prevention of contraband traffic added to the watch on German shipping and the protection and encouragement of British commerce, the task of the patrols was a heavy one, yet the difficulty of providing adequate forces to carry out that task grew greater every day. The transport of the Expeditionary Force to France and of the French troops brought home from Algeria and Morocco, imposed an immense strain upon the naval resources of the Allies. Escort for our own garrisons returning from South Africa and elsewhere, and for expeditions directed against the enemy's colonies, had to be provided to some extent by the patrols themselves. Whatever calls there might be for escort or for trade protection, the primary necessity of providing the Grand Fleet with its full complement of scouts could not be allowed to suffer for a day. Thus, in spite of the number of liners and yachts commissioned as auxiliary cruisers or examination vessels, the total forces available could be rendered adequate only by skilful dispositions, joined with sleepless vigilance and the utmost care to keep every ship in a state of continuous efficiency.

During August, the activities of the Northern Patrol and of the Eleventh and Twelfth Cruiser Squadrons at the western entrance to the Channel, were confined mainly to the stoppage of contraband. Admirals Hornby and Wemyss were, indeed, required to bear a part in protecting the passage of the Expeditionary Force from England and Ireland to France, but this operation was not disturbed by the enemy. British trade in home waters remained entirely unmolested, nor was any attempt made to cut the deep sea cables, or to destroy the cable landings at Valentia and St. Just, for the protection of which against possible attacks by disguised enemy trawlers, the Admiralty had detailed the fisheries protection gunboats SQUIRREL and THRUSH. On the other hand, the only enemy merchantmen met at sea after the two first days of war were the small German steamer *Nauta* (1,187 tons), three Austrian steamers,[1] and a few German sailing vessels returning from distant ports. None of these prizes were of great importance, but three sailing vessels captured by the Twelfth Cruiser Squadron on

---

[1] Aggregate tonnage, 9,592 gross.

September 10th were of some value, as they carried large cargoes of nitrate from Chile.

While the search for contraband, the protection of transports and of the deep sea cables, kept the patrols in home waters constantly on the alert, it was on the Ninth and Fifth Cruiser Squadrons to the south that the greatest strain was thrown. They had to cover between them the whole of the trade routes from Ushant to the Cape Verdes, a stretch of sea which is always crowded with British shipping, while it lies, in part at least, at a considerable distance from any British port. Under their care were the junction of the South American and African trade routes, between the Canaries and Madeira, and of both with the Oriental and Mediterranean trade. In addition to the communication of instructions and advice to British shipping and the examination of suspicious neutrals, they were called upon to keep watch on numerous German steamers in Iberian ports and those of the Atlantic islands, some of which were believed to be secretly arming for the purpose of attacking commerce. Among these were the Norddeutscher-Lloyd Liner *Goeben*, at Vigo, a steamer of 8,000 tons and 14·5 knots speed, and the Hamburg Süd-Amerika Liners *Belgrano* and *Cap Arcona*, at Coruña and Villagarcia respectively. Moreover, the cable-ship *Stephan*, at Vigo, was equipped with cable-cutting gear, and the Hamburg-Amerika Liner *Frankenwald*, at Bilbao, was also suspected of a design to cut the deep-sea cable. At Lisbon alone were over thirty German steamers, and many others were lying in the harbours of the Azores, Madeira, the Canaries, and the Cape Verdes. In view of the prevalent belief that several of these ships carried concealed guns and gun-mountings, and the proximity of the ports to the chief focal points of trade in the Eastern Atlantic, there was thus legitimate cause for anxiety, and the masters of homeward bound shipping were moving with extreme circumspection, passing through the danger points, so far as possible, under cover of darkness.

Admiral de Robeck, in the VINDICTIVE, arrived at Vigo on August 7th, and at once took steps to impress on the Spanish authorities the necessity for watchfulness. As the ships of the Ninth Cruiser Squadron came down the trade route to join his flag, they communicated with all British merchantmen met at sea, informing them that the route was clear and that trade for the Channel and Irish Sea could safely continue on its course. On their arrival, the cruisers were disposed in such a way as to constitute effective patrols in the neighbourhood of Finisterre and off the Portuguese coast from Oporto to St. Vincent. A close watch was kept off the mouth of the Tagus, and during the first fortnight of the war Vigo, Bilbao, Coruña, Lisbon, and Madeira were visited by members of the squadron. No German merchantmen were met at sea, but two Austrian steamers, the *Mediterraneo* and *Daksa*, laden with grain from the Black Sea for the Weser and Elbe respectively, were sent into British ports, where they were compelled to discharge their cargoes. At Lisbon and Madeira the Portuguese authorities, mindful of their country's long friendship and close association with Great Britain, were found to be keenly on the alert to prevent the equipment of German steamers as warships within territorial waters. Not only was the wireless apparatus of all German vessels at Lisbon disconnected, but an order was issued by the port authorities and strictly enforced by the Portuguese navy, forbidding any merchantmen to sail during the hours of darkness, a measure which went far to relieve the anxieties of the Tagus patrol. At the Spanish ports on the Atlantic and the Bay of Biscay, measures were also taken to protect the neutrality of the harbours. The wireless apparatus of the German steamers was dismantled, the *Frankenwald* was kept under surveillance, and the *Goeben* and *Stephan*, which were considered as naval auxiliaries, had essential parts of their machinery removed.

Meanwhile the LEVIATHAN, on special duty, had visited the Azores, where all was quiet, and the Fifth Cruiser Squadron was securing the point of junction between the South American and African trade routes. When Admiral Stoddart called at Gibraltar on August 3rd, he found that rumours were current to the effect that the German light cruiser BERLIN and the gunboat PANTHER had been seen in the neighbourhood of the Canaries; but a careful search of the Canaries and Cape Verdes revealed no trace of any suspicious vessels, and the only German ship encountered was the *Hochfeld*, homeward bound from Monte Video, which was captured on August 14th by the MONMOUTH, *en route* for South America. As it was important that the MONMOUTH should not be delayed, and the *Hochfeld* had only sufficient coal to take her to Madeira, the prize was released and made her way to Funchal, where she remained.

From this time onwards Admiral Stoddart's force was occupied in keeping watch on the Canaries and Cape Verdes and patrolling the trade route between them. The task was an onerous one and of great importance to the maintenance of British trade, for these islands were regarded as likely bases or rendezvous, not only for German, but for neutral vessels chartered to convey coal and supplies to enemy cruisers. The great number of British ships passing through the area, many of which call at the islands to coal, emphasised the necessity of adequate protection. His work was facilitated, however, by the establishment of Admiral de Robeck's patrols to the north, and by the British control of the Straits of Gibraltar. In the meantime, as we shall see, the safety of the North Atlantic tracks had been secured and a close watch established on the German liners in North American ports, while the enemy's main force in the North Sea had shown no desire to try conclusions with the Grand Fleet. The approaches to European waters from the west and south were thus rendered reasonably safe, and as the immunity of shipping at sea became manifest, the confidence of shipowners and merchants in the efficacy of naval protection steadily increased. There was as yet little chartering in British ports, for the effects of the financial disturbance and dislocation of trade caused by the war could not immediately be overcome, but homeward bound vessels were now moving with greater freedom, and a rapid fall in the rates quoted by underwriters for war risks on current voyages reflected the reviving confidence of trade, as well as the steadying effects of the State Insurance Scheme.

The first blow in the campaign against British commerce in the Eastern Atlantic was, however, about to fall.[1] Up to the third week of August all reports of German cruisers in the neighbourhood of the Canaries or off the African coast had proved to be baseless, but on August 16th, the Union Castle Liner *Galician* arrived at Tenerife with definite information as to the presence of a formidable raider on the trade routes.

Having left Cape Town on July 28th, the *Galician* had been advised by wireless of the outbreak of war and the

[1] See Map 6b.

suspected presence of German cruisers, and her master had accordingly shaped a course to carry his ship west of the Canaries. As, however, his coal was running short, he ventured, when nearing the islands, to inquire by wireless as to the safety of the track to Tenerife. To this inquiry he received a reassuring reply; but early on the afternoon of August 15th, when the *Galician* was still some sixty miles away from the ordinary track, a large four-funnelled steamer was seen approaching, and on coming nearer the stranger was seen to be the KAISER WILHELM DER GROSSE, a Norddeutscher Lloyd Liner of 13,952 tons and 22·5 knots.

Her presence was a complete surprise. She was, in fact, the one ship which had succeeded in running our northern blockade outwards. Leaving Hamburg on August 4th, under the command of Captain Rymann, she hugged the Norwegian coast as far as possible before turning westward, and was thus able to evade the Grand Fleet and pass round the north of Iceland, before the Northern Patrol was fully established. On August 7th she captured and sank the steam trawler *Tubal Cain*, fifty miles north-west of Staalbierg huk in Iceland, and, taking the crew of the prize on board, made boldly for the junction of the Cape and South American routes. Passing down outside the line of the patrols, she arrived at her field of operations without being sighted, and was fortunate enough to intercept the *Galician's* message to Tenerife. It was, in fact, from her that the reply to that message had been sent.[1]

On discovering the character of the approaching steamer the *Galician's* wireless operator sent out the S.O.S. call, but before he could complete the name of the ship a signal came from the German threatening to open fire if any further use was made of the wireless. At 2.45 p.m. the vessel was stopped and a boarding party came off from the cruiser. They found that in addition to a large general cargo, which included parcels of maize and ore for delivery at Antwerp, Hamburg, and Rotterdam, she carried nine first-class and thirty second-class passengers, among whom were women and children. Their presence on board was very embarrassing to the German captain, who appeared somewhat undecided as to what course he

---

[1] The principal German authority for the KAISER WILHELM DER GROSSE, is *Kreuzerjagd im Ozean*, by Kapitän-Leutnant Aye.

should follow. There was some talk of throwing the maize overboard, but nothing came of it, and finally, after the liner had been compelled to accompany her captor all night, she was released at 5 a.m. on August 16th. She had suffered no damage beyond the disablement of her wireless apparatus, and the only persons taken off were a military officer and a gunner, who were among the passengers. The intercourse between captors and captured had been throughout of the most friendly description, and the German captain's final decision was conveyed in a polite signal, " I will not destroy your ship on account of the women and children on board. You are dismissed. Good-bye."

On the 16th, the KAISER WILHELM was still more active. On that day she stopped three steamers, the *Kaipara* at about 6.30 a.m., the *Arlanza* at 1 p.m., and the *Nyanga* at 4.30 p.m. The *Arlanza*, like the *Galician*, had women and children among her passengers. She was a Royal Mail steamer of 15,044 tons, homeward bound from Buenos Ayres to Southampton, and having sailed before the outbreak of war, she was right on the regular track, across which the KAISER WILHELM was now working. In this case the Germans did not even send off a boarding party, being content to communicate with the master by signal. The ship was only detained for an hour or two, and after being compelled to throw overboard her wireless apparatus, was allowed to proceed on her way. The humanity of Captain Rymann saved the British mercantile marine from a serious loss, for the *Arlanza* was a fine new ship which had only been completed in 1912. His action both in this case and in that of the *Galician* forms a striking contrast to subsequent developments of the German war against commerce, and indeed, the whole record of the enemy cruisers during the earlier months of the war suggests that these developments must have been imposed upon the German navy by its Government, and were the result of a policy deliberately adopted.

The *Nyanga* and *Kaipara* were less fortunate. Neither of them carried passengers, and the people in both vessels, 101 in all, were transferred to the cruiser, after which the ships were sunk by the opening of their seacocks and the explosion of bombs, assisted, in the case of the *Kaipara*, by gunfire from the KAISER WILHELM. Of the two vessels thus lost, the *Nyanga* was an Elder Line steamer of 3,066 tons, homeward bound from the west coast of Africa with 2,400 tons of African produce originally consigned to Hamburg, though she had received instructions at Sierra Leone that, in view of the outbreak of war, she should go to a British port. The *Kaipara* was a more serious loss. She was a vessel of 7,392 tons, belonging to the New Zealand Shipping Company, and carried a general cargo of 4,000 tons, much of which was frozen meat. Like the *Galician* she attempted to send out a wireless call for assistance, but was compelled by the Germans to desist.

The wireless apparatus of the larger merchantmen was, in fact, already proving a double-edged weapon. Should a British cruiser be within a short distance of the spot where a steamer was stopped, the S.O.S. call might very well lead not only to the safety of the ship attacked, but to the destruction of the raider. On the other hand, the interception of messages passing between steamers at sea and the shore stations was a valuable aid to the enemy's cruisers in locating their quarry. In any event, it was essential to the assailant that the wireless of captured ships should be silenced at the earliest possible moment, and that of any vessels released thoroughly disabled. This, as we have seen, had all through been the KAISER WILHELM DER GROSSE's first care; but the Germans had been less successful than they supposed. Within six hours after her release the wireless operator of the *Arlanza* succeeded in rigging up a duplicate set of apparatus, and an emergency apparatus of moderate power was erected in the *Galician* with the aid of some spare parts obtained at Tenerife. With great prudence, the *Galician's* captain, while instructing the operator to listen carefully for wireless calls, forbade any messages to be despatched until the ship arrived in the Channel, and the captain of the *Arlanza* appears to have been equally discreet. No subsequent emergency arose to test the value of the skill and diligence displayed by the operators of both ships, but the rapidity with which they effected the refits illustrates in a striking way the difficulty of permanently silencing steamers equipped with wireless plant, and the consequent danger to a raider of releasing them after capture.

Apart from the possibility of wireless communication, the ships were released too near port for news of the raider's activity to be long delayed. The *Galician* arrived at Tenerife on August 16th, and the news she brought reached the Admiralty on the same day. On the morning of the 17th the *Arlanza* put into Las Palmas for the purpose of reporting her encounter with the KAISER WILHELM, and communicated by signal with the CORNWALL, then lying outside the port. The CORNWALL at once passed on the news by wireless to the CUMBERLAND and went off to look for the raider, while the British Consul reported to the Admiralty what had happened.[1] Startling as was the news, the situation was now too well in hand for it to cause any great alarm, and shipping was not detained; but the Admiralty issued instructions for all steamers to pass well to the westward of the Canaries. By this time Admiral Stoddart's squadron had been reinforced, and a number of cruisers and armed liners, on their way to other stations, were passing through the Canaries-Cape Verde area. By one of these, the KINFAUNS CASTLE, the German barque *Werner Vinnen*, of 2,962 tons net, was captured on her way from Cardiff to Antofogasta with a cargo of Welsh coal; and on August 23rd, the *Professor Woermann* was taken by the CARNARVON, then on her way to Sierra Leone to coal. This was an important prize, as the *Professor Woermann*, a liner of 6,061 tons, had been cruising off the African coast for some days, and was apparently intended to join the KAISER WILHELM DER GROSSE, or some other German warship.

Of the raider herself nothing was heard until the 24th, when it was ascertained that she had been seen on the 17th at Rio de Oro, a lonely anchorage on the African coast, in Spanish territory. Although a week old, the clue was too valuable to be neglected, and the HIGHFLYER (Capt. H. T. Buller), now under Admiral Stoddart's command, was sent to investigate it. On August 26th she arrived at Rio de Oro and found the quarry still at anchor. The KAISER WILHELM had, in fact, put over to this unfrequented roadstead immediately after sinking the *Nyanga*, and had remained there ever since. At the anchorage she found the German s.s. *Duala*, with whom she had been in communication on the 15th, and shortly after her arrival she was joined by the *Arucas*, which had succeeded in slipping out of Tenerife, and by the *Magdeburg* and *Bethania*, which had been at sea on the outbreak of war. From these ships she had obtained coal and provisions, but was not yet ready

[1] The fate of the *Kaipara* and *Nyanga* was unknown till August 26th, when it was announced by the German Consul at Tenerife.

for sea when the British cruiser arrived. She had committed a clear breach of neutrality by her prolonged stay, which the Spanish authorities on the spot were powerless to prevent; and as she refused to quit territorial waters, Captain Buller had no alternative but to attack her where she lay. The superior armament of the cruiser soon put the issue beyond dispute, and the action ended in the total destruction of the KAISER WILHELM. The *Magdeburg* and *Bethania* fled at the first shot, as did the *Arucas*, to whom Captain Rymann had humanely transferred his prisoners before the action commenced. The *Duala* had already left and had reached Las Palmas on the 22nd. The *Arucas* joined her there on the 28th, and was interned by the Spanish authorities on her arrival.

So ended the career of the first German raider to trouble British commerce in the Atlantic. She had been at sea twenty-one days since the declaration of war, and had sunk two merchant steamers and a trawler, amounting altogether to 10,685 tons. The value of vessels and cargoes was under £400,000—a poor return for the loss of so fine a ship—and the indirect effect of her operations was trifling. What it would have been but for the existence of the State Insurance scheme must remain a matter of conjecture, but there can be little doubt that the course of trade would have been seriously disturbed. As it was, the insurance and freight markets were scarcely at all affected and the only dislocation of shipping involved was the diversion of a few steamers to pass west of the Canaries. There seems little reason to criticise the manner in which she was handled, and the humanity displayed, as well as her resistance to a superior opponent, were honourable to the captain and crew; but little had been done to justify the expectations formed in Germany as to the effects of a surprise attack.

Yet no better area could have been chosen for the KAISER WILHELM'S first appearance. It represented the junction between two routes of the first importance, and was therefore a highly fertile point of concentration for British shipping. It had the disadvantage, however, that both the Canaries and the Cape Verde Islands lay within the chain of cruiser patrols by which British trade was covered. From the time her presence became known the raider's position was precarious, and it will be observed that her actual period of activity on the steamer tracks was confined to two days. From the diary of one of her officers which subsequently fell into British hands, it appears that Captain Rymann's intention was to cross the Atlantic into South American waters, and that her long stay at Rio de Oro was due to the difficulty of obtaining sufficient coal for this operation. Only 850 tons were obtained from the *Duala*, which was the first supply ship to join. The *Magdeburg*, with 1,400 tons, and the *Bethania*, with 6,000 tons, did not arrive till August 24th and 25th respectively. Hence she was still unready to put to sea when she was discovered by the HIGHFLYER, and not having steam up, was unable to make use of her superior speed.

The raid by the KAISER WILHELM DER GROSSE did not affect directly the work of Admiral de Robeck farther north. It emphasised, however, the necessity of watching the islands in the Atlantic which might be used as bases for German colliers, and at the end of August and the beginning of September, as ships became available for the work, the system of patrols carried on by the Ninth Cruiser Squadron was extended to Madeira and the Azores. Although nothing suspicious had been found when these islands were visited early in August, the Admiralty had now reason to believe that the Azores were being used as a base, both for enemy and neutral ships destined to supply the German cruisers in the Southern Atlantic. The whole neighbourhood was, in consequence, thoroughly searched; and on September 8th the VINDICTIVE, while so engaged, captured the German collier *Slawentzitz*, with 5,000 tons of coal on board, which was awaiting instructions at a rendezvous.

Admiral de Robeck was the more easily able to extend his patrols in this way, since he had been relieved of responsibility for the watch on enemy vessels in Galician ports. At the beginning of September a French cruiser squadron took over that part of the trade route which lies between Ushant and Finisterre, together with the Finisterre Patrol. The enemy ships in Ferrol and Vigo now included most of the Austrian steamers to which British passes had been given under the days of grace. The *Bathori* of the Austrian Lloyd Line, which had been released by the French with a pass for Rotterdam, also obtained permission to change her destination to Vigo, but through some misunderstanding was captured by the MINERVA before an intimation of the change had been received. As she had little coal on board and the MINERVA was unable to spare a prize crew, the *Bathori* was sunk; but in the circumstances, the British Government subsequently agreed to repatriate the crew and to consider the question of compensation after the war.

By this time the armed liner menace might be regarded as practically removed so far as the terminal waters were concerned. The career of the KAISER WILHELM DER GROSSE had been brought to an end so quickly that its effect was rather to inspire confidence than to deter merchant shipping from keeping the seas. No other hostile vessel had succeeded in passing from the North Sea into the Atlantic. In the ports of the Spanish Biscayan and Atlantic coasts, of Portugal, Madeira, the Azores, the Canaries, and the Cape Verdes, there lay over a hundred German and Austrian steamers, aggregating some 380,000 tons, but they were powerless alike to carry on trade or to put to sea for raiding purposes. Those which were regarded as capable of conversion into armed auxiliaries were closely watched by the Spanish and Portuguese authorities. Even if they should elude the vigilance of the port officials, they had little chance of slipping through the cordon of patrols maintained by the French in the Bay of Biscay and by the Ninth and Fifth Cruiser Squadrons farther south. Moreover it had become at least doubtful whether any of them had, in fact, guns on board, and there was no base available at which they could receive an armament. Finally, the home ends of the trade routes were now too strongly guarded to form a profitable field of operations. The German cruisers in the Western Atlantic were known to be at work on the South American coast, and any raider which succeeded in getting to sea, either from German or from neutral ports, was more likely to join them than to court destruction by an attempt to prey on commerce in the terminal waters.

In these circumstances, the British cruiser captains were able to assure all British and French merchantmen met at sea or found in port, that they could safely continue their voyages, and the number of steamers encountered afforded convincing evidence of the confidence felt by British traders. Under the shield of the patrols the trade with European Atlantic ports and the Mediterranean rapidly revived. French commerce had been heavily hit by the mobilisation, the enemy occupation of the north-eastern provinces, and the disorganisation caused by the German advance; but by August 20th the export of pit-props to the British coalfields was resumed from Bordeaux;[1] and when the retreat of the Allies in France rendered the northern ports unsafe, a constant stream of vessels, carrying supplies and material as well as troops, was poured into those on the Bay of Biscay.

The export of wine from Oporto to the United Kingdom suffered no interruption, as credit was maintained and shipowners displayed no anxiety with regard to the trade routes. Spanish shipments of iron and lead at first fell heavily, but this was due rather to financial conditions than to fear of capture, and by the beginning of September the steamers which carry coal to the Mediterranean and return with Spanish ore were running on more or less normal lines. Fruit and vegetables were also coming forward freely, and though some diminution was noticeable in the British tonnage employed in the Spanish trade, this was fully made good by the activities of Spanish shipping. The arrivals from Italy remained normal, and though August was marked by a very heavy drop in the clearances for Italian ports, due to restrictions imposed on the export of coal from the United Kingdom, the removal of these restrictions was followed by a prompt recovery.[2] The upper waters of the Adriatic were still closed, but on August 24th permission was given for vessels insured under the State Insurance Scheme to proceed as far north as Bari, and five days later this permission was extended to include Vieste. Brindisi was thus once more rendered available as a port of call, and British shipping was not otherwise greatly interested in the Adriatic.

The trade of the Black Sea alone remained at a standstill. Matters at Constantinople went from bad to worse. The pro-German party in the Turkish Government continually gained ground, and the original crews of the GOEBEN and BRESLAU were still on board. In these circumstances the sailings of British ships for Turkey and the Black Sea practically ceased, as it was impossible to say when the attitude of the Turks might become actively hostile. On the other hand, a large number of British ships from Russian and Roumanian ports were now on their way home.

[1] Consular Reports, Annual Series, 5525, Bordeaux.
[2] Consular Reports, Freight Market Reports, and Board of Trade Returns.

After much pressure on the part of the British Embassy, clearance of the homeward bound grain steamers at Constantinople was granted towards the end of August; on the 22nd the Straits were definitely reopened for traffic, and by the 24th all British vessels other than salvage ships had passed out of the Dardanelles. Great efforts were made to expedite the sailing of steamers left in the Black Sea, and by the middle of September most of them had passed through the Straits.

On the longer routes also shipping had begun to move more freely. The raid by the Kaiser Wilhelm der Grosse was so quickly brought to an end that it had little effect upon the South and West African trade, and though financial conditions retarded the recovery of South American commerce, we shall see that by the beginning of September this recovery had at least made some progress. On all hands the patrolling cruisers reported that British merchantmen were now sailing with perfect confidence, and that the majority of the ships met at sea flew the Red Ensign. It was a tribute to the work of the squadrons, which they accepted as full compensation for the monotony and anxiety of the patrols.

Whatever hopes the enemy may have entertained of interrupting British trade in European waters, or the approaches thereto, had thus been utterly dispelled by the end of the first five or six weeks of war, while their own shipping in these waters had come to a complete standstill. The Mediterranean was completely under Allied control from the Straits of Gibraltar to the Suez Canal, and from the Shetlands to the Cape Verdes a protected zone had been established, within which British merchantmen could move with hardly less security than in time of peace. The only attempt made to disturb the safety of this zone had resulted in the destruction of the raider before she had been able to inflict any serious damage. Even less success had attended a more insidious form of attack which had been employed in the North Sea.

CHAPTER V

MINES IN THE NORTH SEA[1]

THE predominance of British naval strength in the North Sea was such as to afford the enemy little hope of successful cruiser activity. The heavier ships of the German High Seas Fleet seldom moved far from their own bases, and though their light cruisers and destroyers made occasional dashes to sea, they were too intent on avoiding contact with superior force to attempt operations on the steamer tracks. It is true that the activities of their submarines were less restricted, but these craft were not used for the attack on commerce until a later period of the war, when the failure of the initial cruiser campaign had become manifest.

There remained the use of mines. Mine-laying as a method of interrupting enemy commerce is, indeed, objectionable, both from the point of view of humanity and of international comity. Electro-contact and observation mines, controlled by an observer on shore, can be employed only in the defence of harbours. The automatic contact type, which alone can be used on the high seas, is a blind and mechanical weapon, incapable of discrimination and as likely to prove destructive of neutral lives and property as of a belligerent's. For this reason its employment, outside territorial waters, had been held by British jurists to be inadmissible.

At the Hague Conference of 1907, the British delegates contended for the total prohibition of mine-laying, except for the defence of coasts and harbours or off the enemy's naval ports. The proposal was made on grounds of common humanity, and with special reference to the safety of neutral shipping. These arguments were urged by Sir Ernest Satow and Captain C. L. Ottley, R.N.,[2] with great force

[1] See Map 2.
[2] Now Rear-Admiral Sir Charles L. Ottley, G.C.M.G., C.B., M.V.O.

and cogency, and were strongly supported by the representative of China, who stated that five or six hundred Chinese lives had been lost as the result of vessels striking mines laid during the Russo-Japanese War, many of which had drifted on to the coast two years after the close of hostilities.

In opposition to the British proposal the German delegates contended strongly for the right of belligerents to lay mines on the high seas within the theatre of war, and throughout the discussions they consistently opposed all attempts to impose rigid restrictions on the use of mines, on the ground that such restrictions would bear hardly on the weaker naval Powers. It proved impossible to secure anything like unanimity upon the various points raised, and as a consequence of this divergence of policy, the Convention ultimately concluded took the form of a somewhat unsatisfactory compromise. So strongly were its defects felt by the British representatives that Sir Ernest Satow considered it necessary to make a formal statement of their objections. In this statement he laid special emphasis on the right of neutrals to security in navigating the high seas, and concluded by declaring that the British delegation could not accept the Convention as a complete exposition of international law on the subject, and that the fact of their having voted for it must not be taken as implying recognition of the legitimacy of acts which it did not specifically prohibit. In reply to Sir Ernest Satow, Baron Marschall von Bieberstein, of the German delegation, argued that the Conference should avoid the promulgation of rules " whose strict observance may be rendered impossible by the force of circumstances," and that ample security for the safety of innocent lives and neutral shipping would be found in the conscience and good sense of the belligerents, adding that the officers of the German navy would always " fulfil in the strictest manner the duties prescribed by the unwritten law of humanity and civilisation." With this exchange of views between the representatives of the two great naval Powers the discussion closed.[1]

The actual Convention (No. VIII of 1907) prohibited the laying of unanchored automatic mines not so constructed as to become harmless within one hour after those who

[1] Higgins, *The Hague Peace Conferences*, pp. 322–344; W. I. Hull, *The Two Hague Conventions*. Boston, U.S.A., 1908, pp. 93–100.

THE LAW AS TO MINES

laid them had lost control of them, and of moored mines which did not become harmless on breaking loose from their moorings. Powers which did not possess mines of the approved varieties undertook to convert those in their arsenals " as soon as possible," but no time limit was laid down, and in the meantime no restriction was placed upon the use of the older mines. The result of this proviso was, therefore, to stultify the whole effect of the prohibition.

In partial acknowledgment of the British contentions, it was further provided (by Article 2 of the Convention) that no mines should be laid off the coasts and ports of the enemy " with the sole object of intercepting commercial navigation." Here again the prohibition was practically worthless, as it was always open for a belligerent to contend that his mines were laid in the hope of catching a patrolling cruiser, or of denying to the enemy's warships access to their docks and harbours. Even such limited protection as might be given by the article was of no effect in the war, as both France and Germany were dissatisfied with its loose drafting, and made reservations with regard to it.

Finally, it was declared that so soon as was consistent with military exigencies, warning should be given, by a notice to mariners, communicated to all Governments through the usual diplomatic channels, of the areas in which mines had been laid. Strict adherence to this rule would modify the risk to peaceful shipping, but not the interruption to trade; while the danger of mines breaking away from their moorings and drifting with the current was in no way reduced. Obviously, the effect of the article depended entirely upon the interpretation given to military exigencies, and, generally speaking, the clauses of the Convention were so loosely worded and so full of loopholes, that the measure of restraint which they imposed would depend almost entirely upon the views entertained by the belligerent Governments.

The course followed by the two Powers on the outbreak of war was in strict conformity with the attitude taken up by their representatives at the Hague. The British Admiralty, at the outset, refrained altogether from mine-laying on the high seas; the Germans adopted it as an integral factor of their naval strategy. On the very first day of the war the AMPHION and the Third Destroyer Flotilla discovered the mine-layer KÖNIGIN LUISE off the coast of Suffolk, and sank her after an hour's chase. She had, however, already laid her mines, and to one of these the AMPHION herself fell a victim on the following day. The danger area, which became known as the Southwold Minefield, lay right in the fairway of shipping, well outside territorial waters, and while the Germans may conceivably have hoped that it would form an obstacle to the operations of any British naval units based on Harwich, it must have been obvious that it was at least equally likely to work havoc among peaceful merchantmen, whether British or neutral. In order to minimise the danger, the Admiralty not only set the mine-sweepers at work to clear a channel, but at once published particulars of the danger area so far as it could then be ascertained,[1] and drew the attention of neutrals to the risks run in traversing the North Sea. These risks were strikingly illustrated on the night of August 21st, when the Danish steamer *Maryland*, bound from Rosario to Copenhagen, struck a mine some thirty-five miles from land and sank. Fortunately all her people were saved, but the *Chr. Broberg*, another Danish steamer which had observed the casualty, failed to discover the *Maryland's* boats and anchored for the night in order to renew the search next morning. The result was that the *Chr. Broberg*, which was homeward bound to Copenhagen from Palermo, also struck a mine and foundered, her engineer being drowned.[2] It will be noted that neither vessel was taking any part whatever in the trade of the United Kingdom; they were following the ordinary track from one neutral port to another, and their destruction was due to the fact that the Germans had created a danger area right across this high road of peaceful commerce.

In consequence of these disasters the Admiralty issued, on August 23rd, a public statement drawing attention to the vital importance of all vessels, neutral as well as British, calling at British ports before entering the North Sea, in order to obtain the latest intelligence as to minefields and swept channels. At the same time they emphasised the fact that no mines had yet been laid by them, and that they were doing their utmost to keep the sea routes open for commerce.[3]

It was not long before further evidence of the activity

---

[1] *Lloyd's List*, 7 August, 1914.
[2] *Ibid.*, 24 and 25 August, 1914.
[3] *Times*, 24 August, 1914.

of the German mine-layers came to hand. On the night of August 26th a Danish trawler was blown up off the Tyne, and a British trawler, fishing off the Humber, fouled a mine in her nets and exploded it. At the time it was generally believed that these new minefields had been laid by disguised enemy fishing craft, but they were subsequently ascertained to be the work of a German force of light cruisers and destroyers, accompanied by a mine-layer, which came out on August 23rd. The cruisers themselves were equipped for mine-laying, and during the night of the 25th and the early morning of the 26th, two fields were laid, one about thirty miles east of Spurn Head, the other off the entrance to the Tyne. The next few days were marked by several casualties amongst British fishing craft and neutral steamers, and on September 5th, the Wilson Liner *Runo*, bound from Hull to Archangel, was blown up in the Tyne minefield, and went to the bottom with the loss of twenty-nine lives. A few days later the Admiralty issued a statement to the effect that her loss was due to departure from directions which would have assured her a safe voyage, and the urgency of their previous warnings was thus tragically emphasised.[1]

While the Tyne and the Humber might both be legitimately considered as British naval bases, they were primarily great centres of commercial traffic, and since the Germans, as in the case of the Southwold minefield, gave no notice whatever as to the position and extent of the danger area, it was due solely to the energy of the British fleet that the toll of non-combatant lives and neutral vessels was no larger. Immediately after the sinking of the KÖNIGIN LUISE the Admiral in charge of patrols was instructed to patrol the coast night and day to prevent mine-laying, and at the same time preparations were made to maintain a Swept Channel from the mouth of the Thames to the estuary of the Humber. This channel was marked by buoys, and as it was regularly and constantly patrolled, it afforded a safe passage for merchant shipping of all nations between the Channel and the northern area of the North Sea. The measures taken to secure this passage could not, of course, be made public, but through Lloyd's, the War Risks Associations, the Customs Officers at the

[1] *Times*, 10 September, 1914. As the result of a Board of Trade Inquiry, the master's certificate was suspended for six months. *Times*, 11 January, 1915.

ports, and the patrol flotillas, the Admiralty at all times furnished to the masters of British, Allied, and neutral merchantmen information as to the ascertained limits of the German minefields, and the courses which should be followed in order to secure a safe voyage. After the discovery of the Tyne and Humber minefields the work of the patrols and mine-sweepers was reorganised on a more elaborate basis, and the Swept Channel was extended to Flamborough Head, an inshore channel off the Tyne being also thoroughly cleared. In addition a branch track was swept through the northern portion of the Southwold danger area, to provide means of entrance and egress for vessels not desirous of touching at the more northerly ports.

Thanks to the existence of this Swept Channel the risks of navigation in the North Sea were far less than might reasonably have been anticipated. It was, of course, impossible to exclude altogether the risk of mines coming adrift from their moorings and floating far out of the known danger areas, or even into the Swept Channel itself. It was impossible also, in some cases, to induce masters to accept the necessity of deviating so widely from their normal track as was involved by following the inshore route; but the danger from floating mines was minimised by the activity of the patrols in exploding them, and experience soon showed the wisdom of adhering closely to the courses indicated. All through the war the regular procession of ships up and down the Swept Channel went on with a comparative freedom from interruption or accident which reflected the highest credit on the mine-sweeping service.

This service was, in large part, the creation of the war. The nucleus of a gunboat and trawler flotilla for mine-sweeping purposes was already in existence, but it soon proved necessary for this to be greatly extended in order to cope with the situation created by the activity of the enemy's mine-layers. Many scores of trawlers and drifters were taken up and converted into mine-sweepers, the skippers and crews being absorbed into the Trawler Section of the Royal Naval Reserve. By September 1st some 250 of these craft had already been taken up, either as mine-sweepers or as patrol vessels for watching the Swept Channel, and as the war went on this number continually expanded. Mine-sweeping flotillas were instituted at the principal ports all round the coast, but the heaviest work fell on those by whom the Swept Channel was maintained. At first under the Admiral of Patrols, and afterwards under a separate Admiral of the East Coast Mine-sweepers, they were continually engaged in sweeping for and exploding the enemy's mines, examining suspected vessels, and directing merchant steamers as to the courses to be followed. The gallantry, discipline, skill, and resource displayed in the execution of these arduous and dangerous tasks were beyond all praise, and no less credit was earned by the men of the Auxiliary Patrol, composed of armed yachts, trawlers, drifters, and motor-boats, with officers and crews drawn from the R.N.R. and R.N.V.R. These patrols took no part in the actual sweeping operations, but in addition to the detection and destruction of enemy submarines, they gradually took over from the destroyer flotillas a great part of the work of preventing mine-laying by the enemy and protecting the mine-sweepers at their work.

As a result of the prompt measures taken by the Admiralty the loss caused by mines in the North Sea during August and September was confined to two British and eight neutral steamers sunk, one British and one neutral damaged. Seven British fishing craft and a Danish trawler were also destroyed, but the total effect of the minefields in restricting navigation was comparatively small. The sinking of the *Runo* inflicted a temporary check on North Sea chartering, and several steamers from Holland and Scandinavia under orders for the Tyne were diverted to more northerly ports; but the success with which the Swept Channel was kept clear, enabled navigation to be carried on with a minimum of interruption, and the volume of trade at the East Coast ports was, as we shall see, maintained at a surprisingly high level.[1]

For the Grand Fleet and its attendant squadrons and flotillas, the early weeks of the war formed a period of incessant strain. The activity of the enemy's submarines, the possibility of a fleet action, and the necessity of covering the passage of the Expeditionary Force to France threw a heavy burden of anxiety and responsibility on to Admiral

[1] The British steamers sunk amounted to 3,816 tons, and the neutrals to 16,736. The total loss of life on board British steamers and fishing craft amounted to 59. The only victims of any size were the *Maryland* (5,136 tons) and the *Tysla* (4,676 tons), a Norwegian steamer which was blown up off Flushing on August 7th by a mine which appears to have drifted from the Dutch minefield in the Scheldt.

Jellicoe and his command; but so far as the effect on commerce was concerned, the mine peril at this time altogether overshadowed all other naval operations in the North Sea. Apart from the laying of minefields, the enemy made no attempt to disturb the security of the North Sea tracks, and the only British vessels captured were the little schooner *Frau Minna Petersen*, which was taken by a German torpedo boat on August 7th, and twenty-four fishing boats which were captured by enemy torpedo craft between August 22nd and 26th, mostly by the force which laid the Tyne and Humber minefields. On the other hand, the captures of German shipping were confined to half a dozen steam trawlers sunk by ships of the Grand Fleet,[1] and eight small sailing vessels which were brought in by the coast flotillas. These were the only enemy merchantmen met at sea. Not only were the entrances to the North Sea, by the North-about Passage and the English Channel, closed by the British fleet, but the daring and activity of its omnipresent light squadrons and flotillas prevented any commercial movements, even in the waters near the German coast. In Rotterdam and other Dutch ports, there lay sixty German and Austrian vessels, amounting to 160,000 tons, but the short passage which lay between their harbours of refuge and the Elbe or the Weser cut them off as effectually from home as if they had been on the other side of the Atlantic.

It was the same with the German steamers in Norwegian ports, of which there were thirty-two, with a total tonnage of 86,000, besides a large number of steam trawlers. Many of the steamers were already fully or partly loaded, but, in spite of the cover given by territorial waters for a great part of the homeward voyage, none of them attempted to leave, and several paid off their crews and laid up. The most important among them was the *Prinz Friedrich Wilhelm*, one of the largest steamers of the Norddeutscher-Lloyd, having a gross tonnage of 17,082 and a speed of 17·5 knots. She had taken refuge at Bergen at the beginning of the war, and as a possible armed auxiliary she became the object of watchful attention by British cruisers.

The action off Heligoland, on August 28th, emphasised the British command of the North Sea and the narrow limits within which it was safe for even the lighter

[1] These trawlers were sunk, after removal of their crews, because they carried pigeons and were presumably on some belligerent mission.

German warships to operate outside their defended waters. It was obvious that they could neither defend their own commerce nor venture, with any prospect of success, to attack that of the Allies in the open sea. Such restriction of British trade as took place was due almost entirely to the geographical features of the situation and, in particular, to the German command of the entrance to the Baltic.

From the beginning of the war the Baltic was a closed sea to commerce under the Allied flags. The Kaiser Wilhelm Canal enabled the Germans to maintain a preponderance of strength over the Russian Baltic Fleet without sacrificing their ability to concentrate their force in the North Sea whenever desired. On the other hand, it was impossible for Great Britain to introduce reinforcements, as the Sound and Great Belt had been mined by Denmark, and pilotage was refused to warships. Even if this had not been the case, the possession of interior lines by Germany would have rendered the operation extremely hazardous. There was, therefore, nothing to be done but to abandon the Baltic trade, except in so far as it could be kept on foot by neutral vessels, and all Baltic voyages were excluded from the benefits of the State Insurance Scheme. A number of British steamers which had been unable to clear before the outbreak of hostilities were locked up in Russian and Swedish ports, but their aggregate tonnage was comparatively small.[1]

Even for neutrals, the navigation of the Baltic was full of danger. No actions on a large scale between the opposing fleets took place, but there was constant desultory fighting, minefields were freely laid by both sides in defence of the coasts, and navigation lights were removed. Towards the end of August the Russian Admiralty found it necessary to close the Gulf of Finland altogether for outward navigation. The Germans, according to their usual practice, did not confine their mine-laying to belligerent waters, and during August two Dutch steamers were blown up off Dager Ort at the entrance to the Gulf.

In consequence of these obstacles, trade with the Baltic ports of Russia was brought to a complete standstill. The export of timber and pit-props from Finland ceased, and

[1] The total number locked up in the Baltic and Black Sea was 71. The majority of those in the Baltic were brought out at a later period of the war.

the interruption of this traffic threatened to affect British collieries to a very serious degree, as the supply from Southern France was also greatly diminished, owing to the congestion of the railways and the shortage of labour due to mobilisation. Equally serious to British food-supplies was the loss of Finnish dairy produce. While grain was mainly exported from the Black Sea, eggs to the rate of a hundred millions a month and butter were shipped to the United Kingdom from the ports of Northern Russia. These supplies were now threatened, but about the middle of August a determined attempt was made to revive the export trade by Swedish vessels between Raumo and Gefle, whence the cargoes were carried by rail to Bergen or Trondhjem for final shipment to the United Kingdom. The revival was at first only on a small scale, and was impeded not only by high freights across the Gulf of Bothnia, but by high insurance premiums for the North Sea passage. The latter, however, were reduced by competition, and in the course of a month or two the exports of Finnish dairy produce to the United Kingdom once more became considerable in volume.[1]

For the timber export and for imports of all kinds, except such as could be transhipped through Sweden, Russia was driven to depend on the White Sea ports, the closing of the Dardanelles, coupled with the dangers of the Baltic, having stopped all other avenues of trade. The White Sea outlet, however, was grievously insufficient, owing to the limited capacity of the port of Archangel and the railway system connected with it. Even in September the ships of all nationalities cleared from the United Kingdom for ports in Northern Russia amounted only to about 10 per cent. of the normal traffic, and the supply of the Russian armies was seriously impeded in consequence.

The traffic with Sweden also declined during August by over 50 per cent. each way; but here the recovery was quicker and more complete. By August 20th it was considered safe to send steamers to Gothenburg, as the entrance to the Kattegat could be navigated in territorial waters. The removal of the restrictions, however, made little difference to British shipping. The percentage of British tonnage engaged in the Swedish

[1] *Consular Reports*, A. S. 5546, *Finland*, and Board of Trade Returns.

trade is always small, and after the outbreak of war it became practically negligible. Swedish shipping, on the other hand, was greatly stimulated, towards the end of August, by the announcement of a State Insurance Scheme [1] and by the removal of the coal embargo in Great Britain. The export of coal from the United Kingdom to Sweden was carried on with such vigour that the August leeway was fully made up during the following month, and great quantities of wood-pulp, paper, and pig-iron were brought to this country in return. The Swedish exports of butter and timber also showed a measure of recovery.

Danish trade also fell completely into the hands of neutral shipowners. Copenhagen and Aarhuus were subject to the dangers of the Baltic; and Esbjerg, the only considerable port on the North Sea, was too near the German naval bases to be approached with safety by British vessels. But here again, less than 20 per cent. of the trade is normally carried in British bottoms, and Danish shipowners proved fully equal to maintaining the connection. By the end of the first week of war, the export of dairy produce to the United Kingdom was renewed with vigour, and very soon butter, eggs, and bacon were reaching this country in quantities which equalled or surpassed the figures of ordinary peace trade. The losses sustained through mines in the North Sea did not affect the volume of traffic, which was simply diverted to more northern ports, and Leith, in particular, became crowded with Danish shipping laden with food cargoes. As Denmark was the source of roughly one-half of our supplies of bacon, the enterprise displayed by Danish shipowners was of considerable importance to the feeding both of the troops and the civil population.

While British shipping disappeared almost entirely from the trade with Sweden and Denmark, it still persisted to some extent on the Norwegian tracks, though here, too, the majority of the ships employed, even in times of peace, were Scandinavian. The greater distance from the German bases and the open nature of the passage rendered the voyage to Norwegian ports comparatively safe, and it was not excluded from the State Insurance Scheme. Owners were advised to send a representative to the Admiralty to obtain instructions as to the route to be followed in order to avoid mine dangers, but

[1] *Times*, 22 August, 1914.

no other restriction was imposed. Nevertheless, there was a considerable reduction in the number of British vessels engaging in the traffic, though by the end of August the Wilson line had re-established regular sailings to Norwegian ports. The mercantile marine of Norway was, however, fully equal to the occasion, and the total tonnage arriving during August was little below the normal, while the clearances were actually above it. By September matters were still better. Wood-pulp was coming to the United Kingdom in very large quantities, and the timber trade showed a marked recovery. A considerable amount of fish was also received; but the interference with the fisheries caused by naval operations limited the supply. The export of British coal became brisk as soon as the restrictions were relaxed.

In addition to carrying the produce of their own country, Norwegian steamers played a considerable part in the revival of Danish and Swedish trade. That of the Netherlands was left almost entirely to Dutch and British shipping. In times of peace about half the tonnage plying between the United Kingdom and the Netherlands flies the British flag. It was now exposed not only to the risk of mines, but to possible interference by the German flotillas from Emden and Wilhelmshaven. The voyage to Dutch ports was therefore excluded from those covered by the State Insurance Scheme, though British vessels already in those ports were permitted to make the return voyage. On the outbreak of war all the British services to Rotterdam and Flushing were suspended, and though some of them were revived when the limits of German activity became clear, the resumption was only on a much reduced scale, employing about a quarter of the usual tonnage. Several of the services, notably those from Grimsby and the Forth to Rotterdam, were replaced by vessels under the Dutch flag, and the steamers of the Batavier and Zeeland lines continued to run with fair regularity. In fact the Batavier line's service of cargo boats to London was only suspended for a single day. Thanks to the activity of Dutch shipping the supplies of dairy produce and pork from the Netherlands were not only maintained but increased, though that of sugar was greatly reduced, owing to the necessity of providing for domestic consumption in view of the probability that Germany would cease to export.

With Belgium a certain amount of communication was kept up, both by British and Belgian steamers, but the German advance and the total absorption of the people's energies in their desperate resistance, left only a fraction of the normal trade on foot.

Thus the general situation in the North Sea at the middle of September was that the trade with Russian Baltic ports was completely at a standstill, but commerce with Scandinavia and Holland was proceeding briskly in neutral bottoms, and the dairy produce, which forms an important section of our food supplies, was freely coming forward. German shipping was at a standstill in the North Sea, and only a comparatively few small vessels were moving in the Baltic. Upon the whole, this situation was decidedly satisfactory. The percentage of British tonnage ordinarily engaged in North Sea and Baltic voyages is small, and could profitably be diverted to other seas. The important point was that our supplies of food and raw materials should not suffer, and that the coal and manufactured goods, by which we pay for these essential imports, should have free passage. In the main, these conditions had been secured. The effect of the German command of the Kattegat upon our supplies of timber was serious, and still graver were the consequences to Russia of the interference with Baltic traffic; but thanks to the daring and vigilance of the British Patrols and the magnificent devotion of the mine-sweeping service, the chief Dutch and Scandinavian tracks were immune from interference, and whatever hopes the enemy may have built upon their unscrupulous use of mines had been defeated. In the North Sea itself, as in the Mediterranean, and in the approaches to these seas from the Atlantic, the German navy had proved powerless to prevent the passage of British trade or to protect the movements of their own shipping. Meanwhile little greater success had attended the operations of their cruisers in distant waters.

CHAPTER VI

THE SAFETY OF THE NORTH ATLANTIC [1]

It was the safety of the North American Route which in the opening days of the war was the chief cause of anxiety. It has been estimated that the trade of this route employed one-sixth of the world's entire mercantile tonnage,[2] and the character of the trade gave it an importance even more than proportionate to its bulk. During the last two or three decades, the United States and Canada had become, to an ever increasing extent, the granaries of the world, and hardly less significant was their position as a storehouse of raw materials for the factories of Europe. Moreover, the character of the war itself, with its demands upon the Western Powers for an unprecedented expansion in the provision of military equipment and material, emphasised the importance of maintaining touch with the great manufacturing resources both of the States and the Dominion. Altogether, it is not too much to say that uninterrupted communication with North America was, for the Allies, an essential condition of success.

In the three years immediately preceding the war, the proportion of British imports of wheat and flour derived from this source averaged nearly 45 per cent., or about 36 per cent. of the whole annual consumption. About one-half the total imports of bacon and hams, nearly two-thirds of the cheese, and almost the whole of the lard brought from abroad came from Canada and the States. The annual value of these essential foodstuffs reached over £40,000,000, but even this figure gives a very imperfect indication of the importance of the traffic. This importance lay in the fact that, in the event of a prolonged stoppage, or even a serious diminution of the supplies, a large part of the population

---

[1] See Maps 3 and 5.
[2] Hough, *Ocean Traffic and Trade*, p. 72.

of the United Kingdom would be brought to the verge of famine.

Scarcely less vital than the question of food supplies, was the dependence of our greatest staple industry upon the cotton crop of the Southern States. The experience of the American Civil War, when the mills of Lancashire stood idle and thousands of British workers were reduced to misery by the blockade of the cotton ports, afforded a terrible illustration of the consequences of any interruption of the flow of trade along the North Atlantic tracks. Since that date, other sources of supply had been developed, but our purchases from the States, which averaged about £50,000,000, still amounted to 75 per cent. of the total import. Tobacco and leather from the United States and timber from Canada were other outstanding items of the import trade; but the importance of these was dwarfed, during the war, by the demands of the navy and the war industries for petroleum and copper. The total value of all imports amounted to some £161,000,000 a year, and British, foreign, and colonial products were shipped from the United Kingdom in return to the extent of £86,000,000.[1]

Of the shipping by which this vast trade was carried, by far the greater part was British owned. In the year 1913 alone, the carriage of cargoes from and to the United States, Canada, and Newfoundland involved over 4,000 steamer voyages, 87 per cent. of which were under the British flag, irrespective of the sailing traffic and of several hundred ballast voyages made by ships going out from Great Britain to load cargoes at American ports. But the interests of British shipping in the trade of North America were by no means confined to the direct traffic to and from the United Kingdom. The mercantile marine of the United States, in 1914, was wholly inadequate to its foreign commerce, nine-tenths of which was carried on under foreign flags. Among these flags the British predominated, and at least half the vessels which entered and cleared at ports on the Atlantic and Gulf coasts, with cargoes to or from every country in Europe and South America, were British owned.

[1] These figures are for the whole trade with the United States and Canada, on an average of the years 1911, 1912, and 1913; but the direct trade with ports on the Pacific Coast amounts only to a very small proportion of the whole.

In its normal character, the shipping of the North Atlantic route was mainly distinguished by the size, luxury, and speed of the liners employed in the mail and passenger traffic. The crack ships of the great British, German, French, and American lines represented the last word in marine architecture, whether as regards construction and engine power or the comfort and elegance of accommodation and fittings, and the loss sustained by the capture or destruction of a single liner would run into many hundreds of thousands of pounds, in some cases into over a million. The carrying capacity of the fastest ships was comparatively small, and their cargoes were restricted to goods having a very high value in proportion to bulk, such as bullion and specie; but these record-breaking vessels, though they attracted a large share of public attention, were very few in number, and the majority of the passenger liners carried big cargoes, ranging up to ten or fifteen thousand tons. There were also a great number of cargo liners pure and simple, of lower speed and carrying few or no passengers, but running to a schedule as regular as those of the mail services.

Inasmuch as North America provides its own coal, the export trade from the United Kingdom was almost entirely in the hands of the liner companies. The imports were more evenly divided. In the handling of the cotton crop, the leading part was played by regular lines running from the southern ports of the United States, with augmented services during the export season ; but even with augmented services, these lines were at times unable to cope with the demands of shippers, and at such periods there was heavy chartering at the cotton ports. Most of the grain imported by this country was also carried as liner parcels, but whole cargoes shipped "to order" were also numerous, and many tramps went out in ballast every year to load grain at North American ports, calling for instructions as to its delivery on their homeward voyage. Heavy and bulky goods of comparatively low value, such as timber, provided employment for a large amount of tramp tonnage, and there were always charters to be obtained at Norfolk and Newport News, where the product of the Virginian coal-fields was shipped to South America or Europe. A special feature of the route, also, was the large number of big " tank " steamers which distributed the petroleum of the American and Mexican oil-wells. Though mostly controlled by the great American combines, these vessels were generally run, prior to the war, under the British and German flags.

The whole of this great volume of traffic followed, generally speaking, very well-defined lines. The Great Circle Tracks from New York to the Fastnet, off the southwest coast of Ireland, represent the shortest route between the majority of North American ports and Europe; and not only steamers from Boston, New York, Philadelphia, and Baltimore, but those from the Carolina ports, and even from the Gulf, make for a focal point south-east of Cape Race, and from there set their course to run on the Great Circle to the Fastnet. They are joined by the bulk of the shipping from the St. Lawrence, coming through the Cabot Strait, or by steamers from Halifax, Nova Scotia, and St. John, New Brunswick, when the St. Lawrence is closed by ice.[1] Only during the summer months does a portion of the Canadian trade pass to the north of Newfoundland, through the Belle Isle Strait. Through, or very near, the same focal point passes the track from New York and Boston to the Mediterranean and the East. There is thus a concentration of shipping in the waters between Cape Race and New York which offers to a hostile raider a field of almost incomparable richness.[2]

To the trade coming from North Atlantic ports must be added a great part of that of the Caribbean Route, which serves the West Indies, ports on the Gulf of Mexico, and Central America. This route, indeed, is to a great extent merely a branch of the North American. Not only do steamers passing through the Florida Strait join the Great Circle Tracks, many of them first calling for bunkers at Newport News, but a considerable part of the trade is carried on by vessels running on a triangular service between Europe, New York, and the Caribbean. There are, however, direct routes of some importance which pass through the Windward Passage between Cuba and San Domingo, or

[1] During the winter months another portion of the Canadian trade comes through Portland, Maine, to which port the goods are carried by rail. This traffic, of course, also follows the Great Circle Tracks.

[2] There is another focal point half-way between Bermuda and Newport News, where the trade between New York and the Plate cuts the route of cotton steamers coming up to join the Great Circle Tracks. The main focal point for outward bound traffic from Europe to New York varies from 43 N. 50 W. to 40·30 N. 47 W., according to season, the southern limit of drift ice being the determining factor.

make for a focal point at St. Thomas or Barbadoes, and a network of minor tracks covers the whole Caribbean Sea with a series of branch or transhipment services. Apart from the commerce of the United States Gulf ports, which is included in the figures already given, British trade with the West Indies, Central America, and South American ports on the Caribbean, amounted before the war to some £14,500,000 a year of exports and re-exports, and £12,000,000 of imports, among which sugar, cocoa, coffee, and fruit were the most important items.

Taking the trade of the North Atlantic as a whole, it will be seen that its most vulnerable points in time of war are clearly and somewhat narrowly defined. They comprise, in the first place, the areas in which the various tracks converge to the English Channel and the Mediterranean; secondly, a belt of sea lying off the American coast from St. John's, Newfoundland, to the Chesapeake; thirdly, the entrance to the principal passages which pierce the Antilles. On the outbreak of war, the European ends of the tracks were almost immediately covered by the patrol squadrons whose work has already been described. The protection of shipping in North American and West Indian waters was entrusted to the permanent force on that station, the Fourth Cruiser Squadron under Rear-Admiral Sir Christopher Cradock. The CONDÉ and DESCARTES were placed at his disposal by the French Admiralty, and brought up his strength to five armoured and two light cruisers. In addition, the Canadian training cruiser NIOBE was completing for sea at Halifax; but she was not available at the outbreak of war.

On the other hand, the Germans had, at the end of July, two light cruisers, the KARLSRUHE and DRESDEN, in the West Indies; and a third, the STRASSBURG, at the Azores. The STRASSBURG had been seen returning up Channel by Admiral Stoddart on July 31st, and could therefore be left out of account in considering the problems of Atlantic trade; but the DRESDEN and KARLSRUHE remained, and were both modern ships of high speed. An even greater source of anxiety, however, was presented by the German liners in American waters.

We have seen that so early as July 29th the German steamship companies cancelled their sailings, and that those ships which had already sailed were recalled by wireless. On August 2nd the *Friedrich der Grosse* arrived at New

THE ARMED LINER MENACE

York, having crept back with darkened scuttles and every precaution that the fear of capture could suggest. On the same day the *Grosser Kurfürst* and *President Grant* also returned, and within forty-eight hours from the expiration of the British ultimatum, a quarter of a million tons of hostile shipping were lying in New York alone. Foremost among the vessels which crowded the harbour stood the huge Hamburg-Amerika liner *Vaterland*, of 54,282 tons and 24 knots. She was the latest addition to the company's fleet, and the largest merchantman afloat. Next in point of speed came two steamers of the Norddeutscher Lloyd, the *Kronprinzessin Cecilie* and *Kaiser Wilhelm II*, both of which were over 19,000 tons and could make 23·5 knots. A larger but slower vessel of the same line was the *George Washington* of 19 knots and 25,570 tons, and in addition there were seven other ships belonging to the same two companies, ranging from 10,000 to 18,000 tons, and with speeds of from 13·5 to 15·5 knots. At Boston lay the Hamburg-Amerika liner *Amerika*, of 17·5 knots; and somewhere at sea was the *Kronprinz Wilhelm* of the Norddeutscher Lloyd, of 14,908 tons and 23 knots, which had put out from New York on August 3rd and was believed to be armed.

The proximity of New York and Boston to the most vulnerable part of the North American Route gave to the presence of these vessels an aspect of the most serious menace. Even if they had not actually guns on board, it was believed that every effort would be made to get them out and to supply them with armament, either from the German cruisers or from ships sent out from Germany to run the gauntlet of the patrols and meet them at a sea rendezvous. Three at least possessed a capacity for sustained high speed greater than that of most cruisers, and even the slowest might work irreparable damage among the cargo liners and tramps which make up so large a proportion of the Atlantic trade. It was difficult to exaggerate the effect which such an attack upon the most vital artery of our commerce might have at the beginning of the war. The period of the year was that at which the American and Canadian grain shipments begin to come forward most freely, and it was essential that their movement should be unimpeded and secure.

The rapid development of the European crisis at the end of July, emphasised by the cancellation of sailings by the

German steamship companies, put a complete stop to chartering in American ports. The British liners, however, maintained their services according to schedule up to the outbreak of war. Among the arrivals was the crack Cunarder *Lusitania*, which reported having seen a cruiser, believed to be the DRESDEN, in the neighbourhood of New York on July 31st. On August 3rd two German cruisers were reported off Heart's Content, the Newfoundland landing of the British-American cables; and on the 4th, after the dispatch of the British ultimatum to Germany, shipping at New York was warned not to leave the port until sufficient force had been collected to secure the approaches. Nevertheless, the captain of the *Lusitania*, which was scheduled to commence her return voyage on August 5th, determined to put to sea, trusting to the speed of his ship (25 knots) to save her from any possible danger. The captain of *La Lorraine*, a 21-knot steamer of the Compagnie Générale Transatlantique was equally impatient of delay, and both vessels put to sea on the evening of the 5th. Those on board both the *Lusitania* and the French liner reported on their arrival that they had been chased by a German cruiser. We shall see when we come to consider the movements of the DRESDEN and KARLSRUHE, that the observers must have been mistaken; but this is easily accounted for by the tension of such a voyage, when every funnel or smoke patch seen on the horizon may be an enemy cruiser, and the air is full of wireless signals in unknown codes.

On the night of the *Lusitania's* departure it was reported from Long Island that firing had been heard at sea, and for some days rumours were rife as to attempts to intercept her by German cruisers. The anxiety of shipping circles was very great, as not only was the *Lusitania* herself at stake, but her sister ship, the *Mauretania*, was approaching the American coast, and the great White Star liner *Olympic* was due at New York on August 6th. In this strained atmosphere the most baseless reports found ready credence. They culminated in a circumstantial account of an action in which the DRESDEN, KARLSRUHE, and STRASSBURG, while in pursuit of the homeward bound Cunarder, were beaten off by the British cruisers SUFFOLK and ESSEX. The last named ship was in point of fact the only one of the five which was within a thousand miles of New York at the time of the *Lusitania's* sailing, and on August 6th

THE AMERICAN TRACKS SECURED

she appeared off New York to show the flag and restore confidence, having previously diverted the *Mauretania* by wireless to Halifax. On the same day the *Olympic* arrived safely, and on the 7th a message was received from Admiral Cradock that it was now safe for ships to leave.

In order to understand the change which had taken place in the situation to permit of this message, we must turn to the movements of the Admiral himself. On the outbreak of war he had been instructed to concentrate the bulk of his squadron in the northern part of his station, in order to protect the focal points of the North Atlantic trade, and he was moving north in the SUFFOLK, for this purpose, with the BRISTOL ahead of him in wireless touch, when on the morning of August 6th he sighted the KARLSRUHE, north-west of the Bahamas, apparently coaling from the *Kronprinz Wilhelm*. In point of fact, the German liner had just received from the cruiser the guns and men necessary to equip her as a raider, and on sighting the SUFFOLK she at once made off at full speed, while the attention of the two British cruisers was concentrated on an attempt to intercept the KARLSRUHE. Thanks to her superior speed the KARLSRUHE succeeded in making good her escape, under cover of darkness, but the fact that she had been located so far to the south went a considerable way towards assuring the immediate safety of the shipping on the northern tracks. Moreover, Admiral Cradock had by this time received information that reinforcements were coming out from Europe to join him, and as he had already ordered the ESSEX to New York and the LANCASTER to the Cabot Strait, he had little fear for the safety of trade.

After the chase of the KARLSRUHE, the Admiral sent the BRISTOL to co-operate with the BERWICK, CONDÉ, and DESCARTES in the West Indies, while he himself proceeded in the SUFFOLK towards New York. On August 8th he captured the big oil tanker *Leda* (6,766 tons), and took her into Bermuda. She was on her way from Rotterdam to Baton Rouge, and belonged to the Deutsch-Amerikanische Petroleum Co., a subsidiary of the Standard Oil Co. of New York. Though flying the German flag, the vessel was in effect American owned, and at a subsequent date the British Government, as an act of grace, released the prize after her condemnation by the Prize Court, and allowed her to be transferred to U.S. Registry.

On August 11th the SUFFOLK arrived at Sandy Hook. Here the Admiral found that, in spite of his authorisation for sailings to be resumed, British shipping was still mostly inactive, and even the sailings of American owned liners were suspended, presumably owing to the fear that grain consigned to British ports would be regarded as contraband. Fresh reports as to the presence of German cruisers off the port sprang up almost daily, and though these were entirely without foundation, they were not without effect on the confidence of traders and shipowners. A persistent rumour that the *Vaterland* and *Barbarossa* had taken on board abnormal supplies of coal and were preparing to break out of New York, added to the alarm. Nevertheless, the situation was rapidly changing for the better. With the arrival of the SUFFOLK, Admiral Cradock had sufficient force on the spot to keep a close watch on the approaches to New York and the Cabot Strait. A daily search of the Newfoundland bays was instituted, in order to prevent their being used as hiding places by enemy vessels. The ships which were coming out along the trade route to reinforce the North American Squadron had seen no signs of an enemy, and the outward bound liners from Great Britain were running with little delay and without interference. If, then, the United States Government was determined to prevent the escape of commerce raiders from American ports there was little to fear; and it soon became apparent that there was little prospect of any of these ships getting away. Moreover, the German cruisers had now been definitely located. The KARLSRUHE, after her escape from the SUFFOLK and BRISTOL, put into San Juan, Porto Rico, to coal, on August 9th, and was again reported on the 12th at Curaçao. On August 12th it became known that ships had been stopped by the DRESDEN on the 6th, off the mouth of the Amazon. It was clear, therefore, that danger was to be apprehended rather in the West Indies or off the South American coast than in the North Atlantic.

By this time, also, the squadrons under Admirals Hornby, Wemyss, de Robeck, and Stoddart had fully established the cruiser cordon covering the terminal waters and cutting off from the Atlantic the German ships in Spanish and Portuguese ports and in the island harbours. Most important of all, the control of the approaches to the North Sea by the Grand Fleet remained unchallenged.

In these circumstances the flow of trade, actively encouraged by Admiral Cradock, was quickly resumed. On August 18th it was announced at New York that the Western Atlantic was clear for shipping as far south as Trinidad, and by August 15th the whole of the British services to and from American ports were practically re-established, while the Canadian services were in a fair way to recovery. The Compagnie Général Transatlantique also made arrangements to resume their regular sailings.

The resumption of tramp traffic was a slower business. The financial dislocation and the practical elimination, for the time being, of the principal markets on the Continent of Europe had disorganised American commerce. Both in United States and Canadian ports many charters had been cancelled on the outbreak of war; and though the first panic soon died away, the stagnation of trade rendered it difficult to obtain cargoes. A number of vessels were fixed to take coal to the Mediterranean, owing to the restrictions placed on British exports, and towards the end of the month the situation was eased by heavy grain shipments, financed by the Allied Governments; but chartering for cotton and general cargoes was still practically at a standstill.[1]

This reduction of traffic had little or no relation to the fear of capture. It was an essential element of the State Insurance Scheme that risks should be run, and so far as the North Atlantic was concerned, these risks were now seen to be slight. Vessels which could arrange fixtures were sailing with as much confidence as in times of peace, and so early as August 14th the premium for insurance against war risks in the open market had sunk to 2 per cent., one half the flat rate then quoted by the State Office for all voyages.

The outward services had from the first been maintained with remarkable regularity by the leading British lines. Such dislocation as took place was due to the requisitioning of vessels by the Government and to the taking over of ports for military purposes. Thus, the Cunard S.S. Company had arranged thirteen sailings for American and Canadian ports from August 1st to September 5th inclusive. Almost immediately on the outbreak of war they found themselves under the necessity of recasting their programme, owing to the taking up of their

[1] Funch, Edye & Co.'s report in *Lloyd's List*, 15 September, 1914.

fastest vessels for use as armed merchant cruisers and the closing to commerce of Southampton, the starting point of their Canadian service.[1] Yet of the thirteen sailings only two were cancelled. In eight instances, the original or a substituted ship sailed on the scheduled date; in three there was a delay, varying from four to seven days, owing to the difficulty of rearranging the services. In none is there the slightest trace of delay due to fear of capture.

The situation in North American waters having been re-established, Admiral Cradock, on August 15th, transferred his flag to the GOOD HOPE, which had come out to join him, and went south to conduct operations against the KARLSRUHE and DRESDEN. A carefully planned sweep of the Caribbean and the north coast of Brazil brought no result, and by the end of August it was known that the DRESDEN had captured a steamer off the mouth of the Plate, five or six thousand miles to the south. In consequence of this new development, Admiral Cradock was ordered to take command of a squadron on the east coast of South America for the protection of the Plate and Brazilian trade. He was succeeded on the North American station by Admiral Hornby, who assumed direct control of the northern area, leaving Captain Clinton-Baker of the BERWICK as Senior Naval Officer in the West Indies.

Under Admiral Hornby's command a close watch continued to be kept on the approaches to New York, Boston, and the Chesapeake, and on the southern entrance to the St. Lawrence. On several occasions intelligence was received that the German liners in American ports, or some of them, were preparing to break out as raiders or supply ships; but in no case were the rumours followed by any definite attempt, nor did the searches made from time to time by the United States authorities reveal any preparations for arming the liners.

A few belated German steamers succeeded in slipping into American ports subsequent to the outbreak of war; and on September 8th the *Magdeburg*, which has been noted as one of the supply ships to the KAISER WILHELM DER GROSSE, arrived at New York, having successfully eluded the British patrols. Her consort, the *Bethania*, was less fortunate, as on September 7th she fell in with the ESSEX and was taken to Bermuda as a prize. In addition to

[1] Closed to commercial traffic, *sine die*, on August 26th.

6,000 tons of coal and 2,000 tons of general cargo, she carried 400 naval reservists, survivors of the ill-fated raider.

No attempt was made by any of the new arrivals to leave. The work of Admiral Hornby's squadron was conducted with all regard for American susceptibilities, and the cruisers were kept well outside the limits of territorial waters ; but the threat which they presented was sufficiently effective. Although no less than fifty-four German and Austrian steamers, aggregating half a million tons and including a large proportion of the most modern and fastest liners under the German flag, crowded the harbours of the Atlantic coast, the whole of this great fleet remained absolutely immobilised. So serious was the inconvenience to the United States arising from the suspension of the German services, that a project for the acquisition of the ships was warmly advocated, both in and out of Congress. If this scheme had been carried through the financial relief to the German shipowners would have been very great ; but in face of the opposition both of Great Britain and of interested parties in America, it was allowed to drop, and the vessels remained at anchor, with crews reduced in most cases to simple care and maintenance parties, involving serious expense to their owners for port dues and upkeep, and liable to constant deterioration in value through their enforced inactivity.

Meanwhile, Captain Clinton-Baker was mainly occupied in the task of circumscribing the activities of the KARLSRUHE, which had captured the *Bowes Castle* on August 18th, off the northern coast of Brazil, and was believed to be acting from a secret base in that neighbourhood. It was known that she had been joined by supply ships coming from St. Thomas and Curaçao respectively, and the former island called for special attention, as it was the local head-quarters of the Hamburg-Amerika Company, who had established there an important coal depôt. Apart from the presence of forty German and Austrian steamers in Caribbean ports, it was known that efforts were being made to charter neutral vessels in America for the purpose of conveying coal and supplies to the enemy cruisers. The majority of the steamers so chartered were Norwegian, but several of the masters refused to have anything to do with the contraband trade or to obey the instructions of the German supercargo. Instead of proceeding to the assigned rendezvous, they carried the ship into a neutral port, from which they could communicate with their owners and inform them of the use to which the charterers had attempted to put the vessel. Nevertheless, there was a strong suspicion that a number of neutral as well as German steamers had put to sea with contraband cargoes, and the Allied division in West Indian waters was fully occupied in preventing supplies from reaching the enemy, and in safeguarding British trade. A close watch was maintained on St. Thomas, suspected areas were searched, the main trade defiles patrolled, and a cruiser kept on guard at St. Lucia, the point where a large number of British ships engaged in the West Indian trade collected to await orders.

Early in September, Captain Clinton-Baker was successful in ascertaining some of the rendezvous appointed for German supply ships, and on September 9th and 10th, three of these vessels were captured by the BERWICK near Tobago. One of the prizes was the Hamburg-Amerika liner *Spreewald* (8,899 tons); the other two were neutral steamers, the *Thor* and *Lorenzo*, which had cleared from Newport News and New York respectively with papers made out for South American ports. All these vessels were laden with coal and provisions,[1] and clear proof was found that the cargoes of the neutral steamers as well as that of the *Spreewald* were intended for the use of German cruisers. Both vessels and cargoes were accordingly condemned by the Prize Court at Kingston.

On September 13th another Norwegian steamer, the *Heina*, was boarded by the CONDÉ at the entrance to the Mona Passage. On examination it was found that she was bound for St. Thomas, and that her cargo consisted of coal to the order of the Hamburg-Amerika Company. There could be no question that this cargo also was intended to assist the German raiders in keeping the sea, and the *Heina* was accordingly sent in and condemned.

A number of German reservists were taken off other neutral vessels, but no further captures of contraband were made at this period. As for the German liners in

[1] *Thor*, Wilhelmsens Dmpsk. Akties. Tonsberg, chartered by the Inter-American Steamship Co., 1,983 tons coal, 20 tons provisions; *Lorenzo*, New York and Porto Rico S.S. Co., chartered by the Hamburg-Amerika Co. 1,977 tons coal, 150 tons provisions. See Prize Court proceedings in *Lloyd's List*, 3 December, 1914.

THE ATLANTIC FOOD SUPPLIES

Gulf ports and in those of Central America and the West Indies, they gave little trouble. The control of the main channels by the Allied cruisers not only cut them off from the open sea, but made even an attempt to carry on local trade among the islands too hazardous to be risked. Two only succeeded in slipping out in the hope of carrying supplies to German cruisers in the South Atlantic—the *Macedonia* from New Orleans on August 30th, and the *Navarra* from Pensacola on September 3rd. The remainder were content to accept a passive rôle, and over a hundred and fifty thousand tons of enemy shipping lay idle in Gulf and Caribbean ports.

In striking contrast to the inactivity of German shipping, whether on the east coast of North America or in the Caribbean, was the volume of traffic under the British flag. The general dislocation of trade caused by the war had thrown a large quantity of tramp tonnage on to the market, much of which found its way to American ports, and though chartering was still somewhat restricted, owing to the inclination of owners to hold out for something better than the low freights obtainable, and of shippers to retain stocks in the expectation of rising prices, a fair number of vessels were fixed for the carriage of grain cargoes. The liner services were now running to schedule, and altogether, 580,000 net tons of shipping, of which about 540,000 were British, were cleared during August with cargoes for the United States, Canada, and the Caribbean. The arrivals of laden vessels, including, of course, some which had started before the outbreak of war, aggregated over 1,000,000 tons, 90 per cent. of which flew the Red Ensign.

The completeness of naval protection and the absence of attack were emphasised, in particular, by the imports of essential foodstuffs during the first two months of war. In spite of the interruption of sailings during the first ten days of hostilities, the total imports of wheat and wheat flour received from the United States and Canada during August and September, 1914, amounted to over 940,000 tons, an increase of nearly 70 per cent. on the figures for the same period in the preceding year. Oats, barley, bacon and hams, cheese, and lard, all came forward at about the normal rate; the supply of petroleum was also well maintained, and the only unsatisfactory feature of the position was the failure of the cotton crop to move, owing to the disorganisation of the trade by war conditions and the closing down of the Continental mills.

It is, indeed, in the absence of incident, rather than in the events to be recorded, that we must look for the real significance of the story of trade in the North Atlantic during the early months of the war. That the cream of the German mercantile marine should be content to remain shut up in neutral harbours was an illustration of their country's impotence at sea, which was bitterly felt in Germany and could not fail to impress neutrals. That a trade so vast as that of the North American Route, and so vital to the food supply, industries, and financial stability of Great Britain, should have been carried on for so long without even an attempt at interruption is without parallel in the history of naval warfare.

CHAPTER VII

COVERING TRADE IN THE FAR EAST [1]

THE Oriental Route presents, in its general characteristics, a striking contrast to the North American. Instead of a clear run of some 3,000 miles, which the faster liners can accomplish in less than a week, it involves voyages ranging from seven to twelve thousand miles, and occupying from a month to six weeks for the largest vessels engaged. For a great part of its length the trunk route passes through enclosed seas, and at half a dozen points the course of shipping is confined within narrow defiles. The more important of these defiles constitute focal points from which branch tracks radiate in all directions, many of them traversing an intricate maze of passages among archipelagoes which afford ample facilities for evasion and surprise to an enemy cruiser. Although the route is flanked by several British naval stations on which squadrons were based, the spheres of action of those squadrons were too distant to permit of speedy reinforcement from home ports. Such geographical conditions made it inevitable that trade should be far more deeply affected by the outbreak of war than was the case in the North Atlantic, and though it speedily recovered, its revival was accompanied by serious losses of ships and goods.

Since the Mediterranean trade is carried on, generally speaking, by vessels which do not pass through the Suez Canal, the Oriental Route proper may be considered as beginning at the southern outlet of the Red Sea, where the stream of outward bound shipping diverges to the eastern terminals. The volume and value of the trade which passes through the bottle-neck of the Straits of Bab-el-Mandeb renders the area immediately to the south one of the most important focal points of shipping

[1] See Map 4.

in the world; but its protection is facilitated by the fortified base and coaling station at Aden and by the ease with which the forces on the spot can be reinforced from the Mediterranean. It is not, therefore, until steamers have proceeded some way farther east that the real dangers of the route begin.

From Aden numerous tracks diverge, like the sticks of a fan, to all parts of the Indian Ocean. The two most northerly lead respectively to Karachi and Bombay. At Karachi the bulk of the Indian wheat export is shipped, and Bombay receives one-third of the total imports of India. As the principal base of the East Indies Squadron, it played an important part in the defence of the route.

Farther south, other tracks strike off from Aden to East African ports, to Mauritius, and to Australia, but the main trunk route proceeds almost due east for a distance of 2,100 miles to Colombo, the second point at which the trade of the Oriental Route is gathered up and distributed. Here the course of shipping is again confined within very narrow limits. The approaches to the port from the west are restricted by the fringe of islands and atolls forming the Laccadive and Maldive groups, which practically confine navigation to the Eight Degree and Nine Degree Channels, on either side of Minikoi. Moreover, since the passage between India and Ceylon is closed by Adam's Bridge, all vessels proceeding farther east than Colombo have to pass round the south of the island. Thus the whole traffic between Europe and ports on the Bay of Bengal, in the Malay Archipelago, and the Far East, together with a portion of the Australian shipping and of the Indian coasting trade, traverses the restricted area between Minikoi and Dondra Head, the southernmost point of Ceylon. Colombo itself is a defended port and affords a secure refuge, but the concentration of traffic offers a tempting field of operations to a raider, while the open waters to the south provide ample means of evasion, and numerous unfrequented anchorages for coaling can be found among the Maldives and the Chagos Archipelago to the south-west.

From Dondra Head a further portion of the Australian trade diverges from the trunk route, and a number of steamers make for ports in the Dutch East Indies by way of the Bali and Sunda Straits. From this point, too, three important

TRACKS AND FOCAL POINTS

tracks traverse the Bay of Bengal. The waters of this Bay form a rough triangle, at the apex of which stand Calcutta and Chittagong, the ports of shipment for the tea and jute of Bengal and Assam. At these ports a third of both the export and import trade of India is concentrated. Of the three tracks already mentioned, one proceeds for a little over 1,200 miles up the Indian coast to Calcutta, passing Madras and Negapatam. Another of about equal length strikes diagonally across the Bay to the great rice port of Rangoon, roughly bisecting the triangle. The third—the trunk route to the Far East—forms its base, proceeding straight across the entrance of the Bay to Penang (1,270 miles), at the entrance to the Malacca Strait, where it is joined by a subsidiary track from Calcutta and Rangoon.

Thus the Bay of Bengal, like the neighbourhood of Colombo, offers favourable opportunities for an attack on commerce. The entrance is too broad to be sealed with certainty except by a very large force, and once inside the Bay a hostile cruiser can seek its quarry on any of several clearly defined and well-frequented tracks, with a focal point at each angle of the triangle. On the other hand, Calcutta, Madras, and Rangoon are all defended ports, and a secure base for vessels guarding the Malacca Strait is found in Singapore, at its eastern exit.

Here again is one of the great trade defiles of the world, for not only is Singapore the chief port of shipment for the tin and rubber of the Straits Settlements and Federated Malay States, but, like Aden and Colombo, it is a centre from which tracks diverge to many markets and upon which they converge from many sources of supply. Of these tracks there are five of principal importance. The most northerly proceeds direct to Bangkok, the port of Siam. The second leads due east to Labuan and the oilfields of British North Borneo. The trunk route runs from Singapore to Hongkong (1,460 miles), at which point it splits up into a series of branch tracks leading to the principal Chinese and Japanese ports, while a few vessels, chiefly Russian, continue through the Korean Strait to Vladivostok and Nikolaevsk in Siberia. Another great track proceeds from Singapore direct to Yokohama (2,900 miles), throwing off a branch to Manila and other ports in the Philippines.

The waters traversed by all these routes are those of the China, Yellow, and Japan Seas, enclosed between the main land of Asia and the fringe of large islands, Borneo, the Philippines, and Japan, which follow its curve. At two points, the Formosa Strait between the island of that name and the Chinese coast, and the Korean Strait between the Korean peninsula and Japan, the traffic is confined within narrow limits and offers a tempting point of attack to any force capable of maintaining itself for a few days. A network of minor tracks connects the ports of China, Japan, Siberia, and the Philippines, and the coasting trade—especially that between Chinese ports—is of great importance.

The base of the British China Squadron was at Hongkong, in the very centre of the web. The French navy had a base at Saigon and the Russian at Vladivostok, while the strongly fortified port of Tsingtau on the Yellow Sea was the head-quarters of the German Pacific Squadron. The preponderant naval Power in the Far East, however, was Japan, and her geographical position gave the Japanese fleet virtual control over all the routes to the northward of Hongkong.

Fifth and last of the Singapore tracks is that which leads down the Karimata Strait to the sugar ports of Java and the other harbours of the Dutch East Indies. It is continued between the coasts of New Guinea and Australia to Brisbane; but it was only a small fraction of the Australian trade that passed this way in 1914.

The bulk of the mail and passenger traffic to Australia struck straight across the Indian Ocean from Aden or Colombo, and goods in respect of which a quick passage is an important consideration mostly followed the same course; but owing to the heavy dues imposed on vessels passing through the Suez Canal, some two-thirds of the outward bound shipping still followed the old route round the Cape of Good Hope, and this stream of shipping was further swelled by the outward bound New Zealand trade. On the return journey, the desire of Australian exporters to place their products on the London market by fixed dates led to a general preference being given to the Suez Route, which was adopted by some 60 per cent. of the homeward bound shipping, including practically the whole of the wool ships and about half of those laden with frozen meat.[1] Other meat laden steamers from Australia,

---

[1] The prevalence of westerly winds round the Cape of Good Hope is an additional reason for giving preference to the Suez Route on the homeward voyage.

together with most of those carrying New Zealand products, reached the United Kingdom by way of Cape Horn.

For the trade of so vast an area the services of a great body of shipping are required, and during the years preceding the war the outwards and homewards passages through the Suez Canal amounted to some 5,000 a year, of which 60 per cent. were under the British flag. In addition to these vessels, carrying on the direct trade with Europe, many hundreds of ships were engaged in the commerce between Asiatic ports, or on such cross-tracks as run from Bombay to Zanzibar, from various Indian ports to Mauritius, Durban, and Cape Town, and from Japan to Australia. The trunk route and its main branches are themselves fed by numerous minor tracks which distribute and collect the cargoes of the great liners. In the China and Japan Seas, especially, the coasting traffic reaches imposing proportions. Each Treaty Port gathers together the trade of a wide area, and several important services under European flags are concerned solely with the coasting and local traffic. At Chinese ports alone, British vessels were entered during 1913 on over 27,000 voyages in the coasting and transhipment trade.

In Eastern waters, therefore, the defence of trade was a matter of special difficulty, while the target offered to attack was very extensive. It was, moreover, one which offered special temptations to an assailant, owing to its nature and value.

The whole falls into three main categories. First comes the trade of the Middle East from Aden to Singapore, with its centre at Colombo. Secondly, the Far Eastern section comprises both the trunk and local traffic of the China and Japan Seas, the Philippines, and the Malay Archipelago, everything, in fact, which passes through or lies east of the Malacca Straits. Thirdly and lastly, there is the European-Australian trade, with its focal point at Fremantle.

From the Middle East, British imports amounted, in times of peace, to over £74,000,000 a year; of which wheat from India accounted for £9,000,000; jute and jute manufactures for £10,000,000; tea from India and Ceylon for over £11,000,000. The value of the imports from the Malay Peninsula, amounting to some £17,000,000 annually, was made up almost entirely of tin and rubber. The wheat crops of India provided, normally, between one-fifth and one-sixth of our foreign supplies; the plantations of Malaya and Ceylon about one-half of the total rubber import; and both these figures were capable of considerable expansion. Shipments from the Straits accounted for 86 per cent. of our imports of block tin, and about two-thirds in value of the total imports of this metal.[1] Barley, oil seeds, leather, and rice were other important items in the Indian export trade. On the other hand, the markets of the Middle East absorbed some £72,000,000 worth of British products, of which £62,000,000 were purchased by India alone, more than one-half of this amount representing cotton goods. The carriage of Government stores and treasure between India and Great Britain added some £46,000,000 to the annual value of the traffic.

These are large figures; but they are far from representing the whole extent of British interests in the Middle East. Of the foreign commerce of India, amounting, exclusive of stores and treasure, to £268,000,000 annually, over £150,000,000 was carried on with countries other than the United Kingdom. France, Germany, and the United States were all large buyers of Indian products, and about a fifth of the whole trade was done with other Asiatic countries. But though the ramifications of Indian commerce extended all over the world, 75 per cent. of the whole was carried on under the British flag, while the coasting trade, amounting to £70,000,000 a year, was practically confined to British and native vessels. Although the Hansa line employed many fine vessels in its Indian service, foreign shipping was, in fact, wholly overshadowed throughout the Middle East by the services of the great Ellerman Combination, the P. & O., Anchor, Bibby, Clan, and Henderson lines, the various branches of the British India Steam Navigation Company, and the tramp tonnage by which the wheat and jute of India and the Burmese rice crops were mainly lifted.

In the Far Eastern section of the route the distribution of the carrying trade was less unequal, for here the P. & O., Blue Funnel, Clan, Ben, and Glen services had to meet the competition of many foreign lines, including the Messageries Maritimes, the Hamburg-Amerika Company, the Norddeutscher Lloyd, the Nippon Yusen Kaisha, and

[1] A large proportion of the imports of block tin were re-exported to other countries.

the Russian Volunteer fleet; the trade of the Malay
Archipelago was largely in the hands of Dutch steamship
companies; and Japanese tonnage, both of the tramp
and liner class, was prominent in the local traffic of the
Eastern seas. We have already seen, however, that in
this traffic British shipping was well represented, and in
addition to the trade with the United Kingdom and India,
the British lines carried much of the general commerce
of the Far East. Silk, tea, straw plait, and copper from
China and Japan, hemp from the Philippines, and rubber
from the East Indies were prominent items in the homeward cargoes, and many tramp steamers were employed to
lift cargoes of sugar from Java and beans from Chinese
ports. The oil wells of Borneo required the services of
numerous tank steamers, and the total value of all commodities imported from countries east of the Malacca Straits
averaged about £17,500,000 a year. The chief commercial
importance of the Far East to this country was, however,
its position as a market for British products, which it
absorbed to an annual value of £38,500,000, mainly composed of textiles, iron and steel, and other manufactured
goods carried as parcels in liner cargoes.

In the Australian trade, which balanced at about
£37,000,000 each way, the outstanding items, so far as imports into the United Kingdom were concerned, were wool,
frozen meat, grain, and butter, which accounted between
them for over 70 per cent. of the homeward traffic. With
the exception of wheat these are all mainly liner trades,
and the Orient Line, the branches of the P. & O., Messageries Maritimes, and Norddeutscher Lloyd, which reached
Australian ports by way of the Suez Canal, were joined on
their homeward passage by the vessels of the Deutsch-
Australische line, as well as by those of several British
services which made the outward voyage round the Cape
of Good Hope. The exports from the United Kingdom
to New Zealand added another £11,000,000 a year to the
outward traffic round the Cape.

Such, in brief outline, was the commerce of the Oriental
Route, and it will be readily appreciated that the problem
of its defence was amongst the heaviest, as it was amongst
the most important tasks entrusted to the naval forces of
Great Britain. The volume and nature of the trade, the
length of the route and the number of focal points and
defiles, presented to a hostile cruiser peculiar opportuni-

ties both for the capture of ships and for the dislocation of traffic, and imposed upon the British squadrons by which trade in the Indian Ocean and Western Pacific was protected the necessity of unceasing vigilance.

Each of these squadrons had for its special function to cover one of the main divisions of the Eastern trade. The East Indies Squadron, under Rear-Admiral Sir R. H. Peirse, was in charge of the trunk route from Aden to Singapore, with all the branch tracks in the Arabian Sea and the Bay of Bengal. The peace strength of the squadron included the battleship SWIFTSURE, the light cruisers DARTMOUTH and FOX, and three sloops. Four vessels of the Indian Marine were also available for use as armed auxiliaries. The force was not a large one in proportion to the extent of the area to be covered and the value of the trade to be protected, but the bulk of the enemy's strength in Eastern waters lay in the Western Pacific, and was cut off from the Indian Ocean by the China Squadron and the Royal Australian navy.

These were both powerful forces. Vice-Admiral Sir T. H. M. Jerram, on the China Station, disposed of the battleship TRIUMPH, the armoured cruisers MINOTAUR and HAMPSHIRE, the light cruisers NEWCASTLE and YARMOUTH, eight destroyers, and a number of sloops and gunboats for coast and river work. His command extended over the whole of the narrow seas through which the trunk route passes east of Singapore, and in which so great a local and transhipment trade is carried on. It included also the northern waters of the Malay Archipelago. Within the area assigned to Admiral Jerram fell the base of the German Pacific Squadron at Tsingtau; but on the other hand, he could expect assistance from the French Pacific Division, the effective units of which were the cruisers MONTCALM and DUPLEIX, the torpedo vessel D'IBERVILLE, and three destroyers, and from the Russian cruisers ASKOLD and ZHEMCHUG at Vladivostok. In case of need, the fine "Empress" steamers of the Canadian Pacific Railway Company's Vancouver-Hong Kong service formed a valuable reserve.

To the south of the China Station, the protection of Australian trade and of traffic in the southern waters of the Malay Archipelago and Western Pacific was confided to the Australian Fleet under Vice-Admiral Sir George E. Patey. This force was of peculiar interest, inasmuch as it was a unit of the Royal Australian Navy, and was the first complete Dominion Naval Unit. With a correct appreciation of the strategical requirements, and in a fine spirit of loyalty and co-operation, the Commonwealth Government, immediately on the outbreak of war, placed the whole force unreservedly under the control of the Admiralty. It included two very fine light cruisers, the MELBOURNE and SYDNEY, two old light cruisers, the ENCOUNTER and PIONEER, and three destroyers; but its main strength lay in the flagship, the battle-cruiser AUSTRALIA. Three old light cruisers, PSYCHE, PYRAMUS, and PHILOMEL, forming the New Zealand Division under Captain H. J. T. Marshall, R.N., were also available in this area.

In close touch with these squadrons, by which the main Oriental Route was covered throughout its length, was the force under Rear-Admiral H. G. King-Hall on the Cape of Good Hope Station. His three light cruisers, HYACINTH, ASTRÆA, and PEGASUS, were primarily concerned with the defence of South African commerce; but in performing this function they covered the outward bound Australian trade at the only point at which it was vulnerable prior to its arrival in Australian waters. Moreover, since the limits of Admiral King-Hall's command extended up the East African coast to Zanzibar, his squadron covered the most important points on the cross-tracks between Africa and India, and was in a position to observe Dar-es-Salaam, the capital of German East Africa and the local head-quarters of the Deutsche Ost-Afrika Company, where there was a floating dock and an important coal depôt.

On this port, within a few days' steaming of the trunk route between Aden and Colombo, was based the German light cruiser KÖNIGSBERG. This ship had left Dar-es-Salaam fully coaled on July 31st, and was sighted by Admiral King-Hall on the evening of the same day; but he was unable to shadow her for long, owing to her superior speed, and her exact whereabouts on the outbreak of war were unknown. She presented, therefore, a serious threat to Allied commerce, either on the East African coast or the Oriental Route.

Still graver was the menace of the German "East Asiatic" or Pacific Squadron under the command of Vice-Admiral Graf von Spee. This force included two armoured cruisers of considerable fighting power, the flagship SCHARNHORST and her sister the GNEISENAU, neither of which could be accurately located during the period of tension. In addition there were three light cruisers, all of modern type. Of these, the EMDEN was at Tsingtau, the LEIPZIG was detached on the North American coast, and the NÜRNBERG, after being relieved by the LEIPZIG, had left Honolulu for an unknown destination on July 27th. The GEIER, an older and slower vessel, had sailed from Singapore on July 29th, and her movements had not since been reported. There were several gunboats at Tsingtau and in Chinese waters, and the Governments of the German Pacific Colonies possessed two or three lightly armed yachts and surveying vessels.

In addition to Tsingtau, Admiral von Spee possessed a subsidiary base at Rabaul in Neu Pommern,[1] and at two or three other points in the German Pacific Islands there were coal depôts and wireless stations. His force was thus both strong and well equipped, and the vast extent of trade open to his attack rendered it a very disturbing factor in the problem of trade defence. It was open to the German Admiral, after concentrating the scattered units of his command, to strike at the crowded shipping in the China Seas; to go south and attack the trade of Australia and New Zealand in its terminal waters; or to slip through the islands of the Malay Archipelago for the purpose of interrupting traffic on the great trunk route between Colombo and Singapore. Should he consider any of these courses as unlikely to give good results, it lay within his power to quit Asiatic waters altogether and transfer his field of operations to the Eastern Pacific, with the object of attacking shipping on the South American coast. Which, if any, of these courses he would adopt remained for the moment matter of pure conjecture.

With the KÖNIGSBERG in the Indian Ocean and Admiral von Spee's squadron in the Pacific, the Oriental Route was thus exposed to attack throughout its whole length, and an additional anxiety was the presence east of Suez of eight German liners, suitable for conversion into merchant cruisers. These were not, as in the North Atlantic, concentrated at one end of the route, but were widely scattered on the principal tracks: the *Tabora* at Dar-es-Salaam; the *Südmark* and *Zieten* somewhere between Colombo and Aden; the *Kleist* also at sea in the Indian Ocean; the *Yorck* and *Prinz Eitel Friedrich* at or

[1] Formerly New Britain.

near Tsingtau; the *Princess Alice* in the Philippines; and the *Seydlitz*, which had left Sydney hurriedly on August 3rd, in Australian waters. None of these had a speed exceeding 15·5 knots, but with the exception of a few mail steamers the shipping of the Oriental Route is not fast, and any one of the vessels named, might, if armed, have worked serious havoc on the crowded tracks.

In face of these dangers, and in view of the extent and complexity of the problem presented by the defence of commerce in the Eastern seas, it would not have been surprising if the outbreak of hostilities had produced a temporary paralysis of seaborne trade. For a week or two, indeed, it seemed as if this would be the case; chartering came to a standstill, and many of the regular lines cancelled their sailings, in whole or in part. Shipowners and shippers alike were apprehensive of immediate danger and unwilling to enter into engagements for the future, and the trade of the Far and Middle East was reduced to a small fraction of its normal proportions. It would be unjust, however, to attribute to the fear of capture the whole, or even the greater part of the diminution in traffic. Serious as were the perils to which shipping was exposed, and keenly as they were felt, they were covered by the State Insurance Scheme and would have produced no great reduction in the volume of trade but for the complications introduced by the universal financial dislocation and the necessity of suddenly readjusting the channels of commerce to new and strange conditions.

To Indian merchants the shock arising from the outbreak of war was very severe. The first six months of 1914 had been a period of flourishing trade, and the prospects for the latter half of the year were equally good, for the crops were above the average and importers anticipated a big demand for cotton goods as a result of their realisation. On the outbreak of war, however, the whole situation was immediately and disastrously changed. The banks and native moneylenders took fright, credit was restricted to the narrowest limits, and importers' stocks were left to accumulate on their hands. The financial stringency thus produced was accentuated by the loss of the German and Austrian markets, which had absorbed, during the last financial year, 14·2 per cent. of the total exports. With these elements of economic disturbance, added to the uncertainties of the naval situation, it is little wonder that the export trade of the Middle East dwindled, for the moment, almost to nothing.

In the Far East the immediate effects of the declaration of war were very similar. Here too the restriction of banking facilities rendered it difficult to finance shipments, and Chinese ports were blocked by the accumulation of stocks—tea for Russia, silks for Great Britain, France, and America. Japanese exporters of copper were severely hit by the closing of the London Metal Exchange, and the trade between Japan and India was almost completely interrupted by the disorganisation of the exchanges. As a result of these conditions, many shipowners and merchants cancelled their engagements for Europe, and business on the freight markets at Shanghai, Yokohama, and Manila came to a complete standstill.

Until the exchanges had settled down and traders were able to accommodate themselves to a state of war, it was impossible that traffic should be resumed to any but a limited extent; but there was no hesitation on the part of shipping to bring forward such cargoes as were available. Complaints were, indeed, received that the Indian Authorities were inclined to hold up ships on rumours of danger; but the Admiralty were confident that no unreasonable risk would be run by vessels putting to sea, so long as proper precautions were taken, and they so informed the local Intelligence Officers and the Commanders of the Eastern Squadrons. At the same time they took prompt steps to provide an adequate defence against hostile attack, and especially to cover the focal points at which such attack was most to be expected.

After sighting the KÖNIGSBERG on July 31st, Admiral King-Hall had returned in the HYACINTH to cover the South African and outward bound Australian shipping in the neighbourhood of Cape Town. The ASTRÆA and PEGASUS, however, were left on the East African coast to protect trade against the German cruiser, and farther north the SWIFTSURE and DARTMOUTH, of the East Indies Squadron, sailed almost immediately after the declaration of war to cut her off from the Gulf of Aden and to protect the great Aden-Colombo trade route.

Meanwhile the work of arming the Royal Indian Marine ships was put in hand at Bombay. The FOX and the sloop ESPIÈGLE were ordered to the neighourhood of Colombo, to prevent an attack by armed liners in the crowded area between Ceylon and Minikoi. The D'IBERVILLE and three French destroyers in the Malacca Strait performed a similar function with regard to the trade of Penang and Singapore.

In the Pacific, Admiral Jerram had used the period of suspense to concentrate the China Squadron at Hongkong, where he was joined by the DUPLEIX. On August 6th, he put to sea with his whole force to cover shipping in the China Seas against the German Pacific Squadron. Before leaving he had made arrangements for the Canadian Pacific Railway Company's " Empress " steamers to be requisitioned and armed as auxiliary cruisers on their arrival at Hongkong, and the big P. & O. liner *Himalaya* was also taken up for the same purpose.

To the south of Admiral Jerram's field of operations the Australian Fleet was concentrating for the purpose of barring a southward move by Admiral von Spee, or undertaking offensive operations against the German Colonies in the Pacific. Meanwhile, the PIONEER was detached to cruise off Fremantle, in anticipation of an attempt by armed German liners on the Aden and Colombo tracks at their point of convergence.

Thus, within a few days of the commencement of hostilities, the most vulnerable points had been covered on each section of the route. In the meantime, all German vessels in British and Allied harbours had been seized; and although many of those which were in port at the end of July had effected their departure during the period of tension, a considerable number fell into the Allies' hands. Among the ships thus detained at Aden and Indian ports, at Saigon, or in the harbours of Australia and Siberia, were no less than twenty-three liners, ranging from 4,000 to 7,000 tons, thirteen of which belonged to the Hansa Company. In the Suez Canal lay a dozen more steamers of the same type. These, of course, were immune from capture, but several of them, including the big Norddeutscher Lloyd liner *Derfflinger*, were detained by the Egyptian Government, on account of breaches of neutrality committed or reasonably apprehended within the neutral zone. The others were subsequently offered a free pass by the Egyptian Government, but refused to avail themselves of it, fearing capture in the Mediterranean if they put to sea.

A somewhat difficult situation was thus created, but it was never contemplated by the Conventions that the immunity conferred upon shipping while in the Canal should constitute it a permanent port of refuge, and eventually all German vessels in the Canal and Egyptian ports were forced to sea and captured, when outside the three-mile limit, by a British cruiser. On being brought before a Prize Court at Alexandria, those steamers which had originally put in for the purpose of avoiding capture were condemned as prizes, while others which had entered the Canal in ignorance of the outbreak of war were detained on the same terms as ships in British home ports.

During the first few days of the war, other German liners which had failed to receive news of the outbreak of hostilities continued to put into Allied ports on the route; and on the severance of relations with Austria, a number of Austrian steamers were added to the list. The total number of enemy ships seized or detained at ports east of Suez, in the Suez Canal zone, or at Cape Town on the outward voyage to Australia, was thus brought up to seventy steamers with an aggregate gross tonnage of over 300,000.[1]

[1] Particulars of enemy shipping detained or seized in port on the Oriental Route.

—	No. of vessels.	Tons Gross.	Nature.
In Suez Canal Zone .	15	79,018	3 Norddeutscher Lloyd, 3 Deutsch-Australische, 5 Hansa, 1 Rickmers, 3 Austrian.
At Aden and Indian Ports.	18	96,327	13 Hansa, 2 Hamburg-Amerika, 1 Deutsch-Australische, 2 Austrian.
At Singapore and Far Eastern Ports.	8	22,638	2 Hamburg-Amerika, 1 Hansa, 5 miscellaneous and local.
In Australian Ports .	26	110,740	8 Deutsch-Australische, 4 Norddeutscher Lloyd, 3 Hansa, 5 miscellaneous and local,* 5 sailing vessels, 1 Austrian.
At Cape Town .	3	15,176	2 Deutsch-Australische, 1 Hansa.
	70	323,899	

Of the above, seven steamers, aggregating 39,180 tons, were subsequently condemned by the Prize Court at Alexandria (3 Norddeutscher Lloyd, 3 Deutsch-Australische, one Austrian); one Hansa liner of 5,476 tons at Perim; another of 5,639 tons at Cape Town; one local steamer of 1,449 tons at Sydney; and two Hamburg-Amerika liners of 9,017 tons in Siberian ports.

In addition, one Austrian steamer of 2,650 tons was detained at Colombo, but released under the "days of grace."

* Under "miscellaneous and local" are included four small Norddeutscher Lloyd steamers exclusively engaged in local trade.

By those enemy merchantmen which had received notice of the outbreak of hostilities, no attempt was made to carry on trade, or even to complete their voyages. Under instructions issued to them as soon as war was seen to be imminent, those which were west of Colombo ran for Marmagao in Portuguese India or for the ports of Eritrea and Italian Somaliland. Those in the eastern area of the Indian Ocean sought shelter under the Dutch flag in Sumatra; while the harbours of Java, Borneo, and the Philippines were soon crowded with steamers engaged in the trade of Australia and the Far East. A smaller number took refuge in Bangkok or in Chinese ports, and three or four Australian liners made their way across unfrequented seas to Honolulu or American Samoa. In all, more than a hundred steamers, with a tonnage of well over 400,000, were thus laid up, and so prompt was the desertion of the trade routes by vessels flying the German flag, that few opportunities of making prizes were afforded to British cruisers.

There were, however, some German liners by which the warning was not received, or to whom it came too late. Several of these, as we have seen, put into Allied ports while still in ignorance that war had broken out, and were there detained; but others, still less fortunate, were picked up by the patrols engaged in securing the focal points of the route against German attacks. Thus, within the first week of the war, the FOX and ESPIÈGLE, operating off Colombo, made four valuable prizes. Two of these were Hansa liners, the *Moltkefels*, outward bound to Calcutta, and the *Rappenfels*, returning from Calcutta to Bremen. The other two were Deutsch-Australische steamers, the *Fürth* and *Australia*. Two or three days later, on the arrival of the GOEBEN and BRESLAU at the Dardanelles, the fast and powerful cruisers BLACK PRINCE and DUKE OF EDINBURGH were ordered from the Mediterranean to the Red Sea, to keep watch on any German liners in Massawa. On August 15th the BLACK PRINCE captured the *Südmark*[1] and *Istria* of the Hamburg-Amerika line, which were seeking to reach the shelter of the Canal; and two days later the DUKE OF EDINBURGH took the Argo Company's steamer *Altair*, whose master was still in ignorance of the outbreak of war. At the other end of the route, the PIONEER captured the Deutsch-

[1] See p. 124, *supra*.

Australische liner *Neumunster* on August 17th, and the *Thüringen*, of the Norddeutscher-Lloyd, on the 28th. On the Siberian coast the *Sabine Rickmers* was taken by the Russians at Castries Bay.[1]

While the patrols established at the focal points had thus proved their vigilance and the soundness of the dispositions adopted, they had not been successful in bringing the enemy's cruisers to action. The strength of the German Pacific Squadron had not been reduced and the KÖNIGSBERG remained unlocated in the Indian Ocean. The freedom of movement of the last named had, however, been circumscribed by the arrival of the two big Mediterranean cruisers at Aden and by the operations of the Cape Squadron.

The two ships left by Admiral King-Hall on the East African coast had lost no time in acting vigorously against the German bases. On August 8th the ASTRÆA bombarded Dar-es-Salaam, destroying the wireless station and causing so much alarm that the floating dock was sunk by the Germans themselves at the entrance to the harbour. The exit of the *Tabora* and two other large steamers of the Deutsche Ost-Afrika line was thus blocked, and the KÖNIGSBERG deprived alike of her principal fixed base and of the services of three possible tenders. Moreover, this blocking in of the *Tabora*, followed by the capture of the *Südmark*, went far to remove anxiety as to attacks by armed German liners in the western portion of the Indian Ocean, for the *Kleist* had put into Padang on August 7th, and only the *Zieten* remained at sea. On August 20th she too was located at Mozambique, but on the following day it became known that her arrival was not altogether a matter for congratulation, since she had on board prisoners taken by the KÖNIGSBERG from a British steamer.

The vessel whose loss was thus made public was the *City of Winchester*, a liner of 6,601 tons, belonging to the Hall Line, a branch of the Ellerman combine.[2] She left Colombo, homeward bound from Calcutta, on July 30th, and it was not until 6.30 p.m. on August 6th, when she was already within the entrance to the Gulf of Aden, that her master received news of the declaration of war. Two or three hours later she was stopped by the KÖNIGSBERG, which had come north from Dar-es-Salaam and was lying in

---

[1] The total tonnage of the above ten prizes was 49,395.
[2] See Map 6a.

"CITY OF WINCHESTER" SUNK

wait on the trade route near Socotra. The liner was compelled to follow her captor to Makalla on the Arabian coast, which was reached on the afternoon of the 7th. At this out-of-the-way anchorage they were joined by the *Zieten* and the Hamburg-Amerika liner *Ostmark,* and in the course of the evening the four vessels put to sea, but almost immediately parted company. The *Ostmark* arrived at Massawa on the 11th; the KÖNIGSBERG apparently went back to the trade route to look for further prizes or to communicate with German vessels; the *City of Winchester,* with a prize crew on board, accompanied the *Zieten* along the Arabian coast, getting farther and farther from the trade routes, until 4 p.m on August 9th, when they dropped anchor among the unfrequented Khorya Morya Islands. On the 10th, the prize was brought alongside the *Zieten* and about 300 tons of coal were transferred from her to the German steamer. The master, with most of the officers and the white members of the crew, were then put on board the *Zieten,* which was sent off with instructions to land them at a neutral port. Next day, the KÖNIGSBERG rejoined and took 250 tons of coal and some foodstuffs from the prize, the work continuing all night with carefully screened lights. Early in the morning of the 12th, the transfer of stores and coal having been completed, the remainder of the crew were taken on board the cruiser and the seacocks of the prize were opened. As the ship sank slowly, three shots were fired into her; but it was not until 3.30 on the 13th that she finally disappeared, having taken twenty-two hours to sink. In the meantime the Hansa liner *Goldenfels* had come up, and the remaining prisoners in the cruiser were transferred to her. The *Goldenfels* was homeward bound from Hankau and Colombo, but she now put back across the Indian Ocean for Sabang in Sumatra, evidently in order to keep back the news as long as possible.

The KÖNIGSBERG'S bold dash into the Gulf of Aden had thus been rewarded by the first prize which fell to any German cruiser. This was, however, the extent of her achievement. The Gulf is not a station on which a solitary raider could long maintain herself. Indeed, had the KÖNIGSBERG remained in the neighbourhood of Cape Gardafui, she must almost certainly have been caught by the combination of the BLACK PRINCE, DUKE OF EDINBURGH, and DARTMOUTH. Her captain appears to have been fully alive to the danger of his position. The time actually spent on the trade route was small, and after sinking his prize he steamed south into less frequented waters, where the risk of meeting a British cruiser was minimised, even if there were fewer opportunities for successful attacks on shipping.

Nevertheless the loss to British commerce was by no means negligible, for the *City of Winchester's* cargo, which included 30,000 chests of choice tea, was valued at no less than £250,000. There was, indeed, a temporary panic on the tea market, for the cargo loss was only very partially covered by insurance against war risks, and many merchants were hard hit in consequence. On the other hand, the effect on shipping was, fortunately, very small, for the news was a fortnight old at the time of its receipt, and several vessels had in the meantime passed safely through the danger area.

By this time, indeed, the evidences of British naval supremacy, both in Eastern and European waters, had produced a general revival of confidence, and as the first shock of the financial disturbance died away, trade began gradually to accommodate itself to the altered conditions. Although many of the usual markets for Indian produce were now cut off, new demands in several directions arose from the circumstances of the war itself. The export of Bengal coal, for instance, was quickly stimulated by a strong demand from Port Said, due to the increase of prices in Great Britain and the high freights payable on cargoes from the United Kingdom to the Mediterranean. Wheat chartering at Karachi recommenced at an early date, and the general outlook for Indian trade was distinctly more hopeful.

In the meantime a strong barrier had been erected against any attempt by the German forces in the Pacific to break through into the Indian Ocean. When Admiral Jerram put to sea from Hongkong on August 6th, his latest information indicated that the most powerful German ships were in the neighbourhood of the Caroline Islands, and it was probable enough that a rendezvous in the Southern Pacific would be chosen by Graf von Spee for his concentration. At the same time, the immediate interests entrusted to Admiral Jerram's care were too important for him to feel justified in uncovering the Chinese tracks for the purpose of seeking his enemy in the open waters to the east and south. Apart from the possibility of his opponent eluding him and coming down on the unprotected trade routes in his rear, there was a report that hostile merchant cruisers were fitting out at Tsingtau, and in the crowded waters of the China, Japan, and Yellow Seas, irreparable damage might be caused by even a single raider. Accordingly, he sent a strong division under Captain Fitzmaurice of the TRIUMPH to observe the German ships in Tsingtau, while with the rest of his squadron he endeavoured to cut off the EMDEN, which was reported to have left that base with four colliers on August 3rd for the purpose of joining Admiral von Spee.

This report was not wholly accurate. The EMDEN originally left Tsingtau on July 31st, and after receiving news by wireless of the declaration of war against Russia, shaped her course for the Korean Strait, where she would be in a position to cut off merchantmen bound for Vladivostok. On August 4th she captured the *Riasan*, a steamer of 3,522 tons, belonging to the Russian Volunteer fleet, and turned back towards Tsingtau with the prize. On the way she was informed of the outbreak of war with Great Britain; and when she arrived at Tsingtau on August 6th, she found preparations for the attack on commerce actively going forward. The *Prinz Eitel Friedrich*, a Norddeutscher Lloyd Liner of 8,897 tons and 15 knots speed, which had started on the homeward voyage, had been recalled and was in process of equipment as an armed merchant cruiser, her armament being supplied by the gunboats LUCHS and TIGER, which were themselves too small for operations on the trade routes. The *Yorck*, of the same line, had sailed on August 4th with supplies for Admiral von Spee, and the EMDEN herself now received orders to join the squadron.

After coaling at Tsingtau, the EMDEN again put to sea on the evening of August 6th, in company with the *Markomannia*, a Hamburg-Amerika liner of 4,505 tons and 14 knots, which had been allotted to her as a tender and was laden with 6,000 tons of coal. The *Riasan* being capable of 16 knots speed and suitable for employment as a commerce raider, was placed in the hands of the dockyard authorities for conversion, and armed with guns taken from the old gunboat CORMORAN, whose name she assumed. Meanwhile, a number of other German steamers in the port were filled up with coal and provisions in order that they might act as supply ships to the German cruisers.

On the evening of August 8th, as Captain Fitzmaurice steamed up the Chinese coast, reassuring shipping and keeping a sharp look out for hostile raiders, he was informed by wireless from Shanghai that the EMDEN had been sighted on the morning of the 7th, 120 miles south-east of Tsingtau. Had the German cruiser intended to attack trade in Chinese waters her career might very probably have been cut short at its commencement, either by Captain Fitzmaurice's division or by the ships retained by Admiral Jerram farther south. So far, however, from attempting operations in the China seas, she proceeded by an almost direct route to join Admiral von Spee's flag at Pagan Island in the Ladrones, which he had appointed as a rendezvous. Thus, although the EMDEN's wireless was heard in the TRIUMPH almost simultaneously with the receipt of the message from Shanghai, she was already out of chasing distance, and her subsequent course lay well outside the limits which Admiral Jerram's care for the China and Japan trade assigned to the operations of his squadron.

The Admiral's own cruise, however, was by no means fruitless, as on August 12th he destroyed the powerful wireless station at Yap, which was connected by cable with Shanghai and formed the chief link between the German forces in the Pacific and the mainland. The enemy's coal supply was also reduced by the capture of the German steamer *Elsbeth* of 1,651 tons, which had left Tsingtau for Yap on July 30th with 1,800 tons of Government fuel. As a prize crew could not be spared to take her into port, she was sunk by the HAMPSHIRE after removal of her crew.

Meanwhile, Captain Fitzmaurice had taken up a position at the entrance to the Yellow Sea, where he could keep watch on enemy vessels coming either from Tsingtau or Shanghai. The declaration of war with Austria on August 12th had added to his responsibilities, as the light cruiser KAISERIN ELIZABETH was at Tsingtau, and among the half-dozen German and Austrian steamers lying at Shanghai were the *China* and *Silesia*, of the Austrian Lloyd, which were suitable for conversion into armed cruisers, though they were not of high speed. On the other hand, a radical change in the whole position was foreshadowed on August 15th by the presentation to Germany of an ultimatum by the Japanese Government, demanding the retrocession of Kyau-Chau to China, and the withdrawal of all armed German vessels from Chinese and Japanese waters. This ultimatum was followed by preparations for immediate action in the event of an unfavourable reply, and a considerable number of steamers were taken up by the Government for use as transports and auxiliaries—a development which was not unwelcome to Japanese shipowners, as it tended to maintain freights at a normal level, despite the disorganisation of business.

It was thus evident that Japan was prepared, if necessary, to act with vigour, in which case the Allies would be placed in a position of overwhelming superiority throughout the Western Pacific; but there was still a week to elapse before the ultimatum expired, and in the meantime it was necessary to exercise the utmost vigilance in the defence of seaborne trade. This need was the greater because, now that the first shock of war had died away, shipping activity in Far Eastern waters was beginning to revive. Although business conditions in China were still bad, local merchants and financiers were making strenuous efforts to relieve the situation, and in the absence of any attack by the German squadron or its auxiliaries, shipowners were ready enough to allow their vessels to sail when cargoes were available. Admiral Jerram had, from the first, held that no unreasonable risk would be incurred by vessels obeying the general Admiralty advice, and all naval authorities were instructed that the free movement of merchantmen was to be encouraged. The only definite restriction imposed was the indication of a special course between Shanghai and Japan, which was designed to take the fullest possible advantage of territorial waters; and after the Yellow Sea Patrol had been established, even this restriction was removed, shipowners being advised that as from August 18th trade between China and Japan might be resumed without any limitation as to course.

Though the volume of traffic was still far below the normal, the number of ships which, encouraged by the attitude of the naval authorities, put to sea from Chinese and Japanese ports, was quite great enough to make the security of the tracks an object of grave consideration, and when Admiral Jerram returned to Hongkong on August 17th, from his eastward cruise, he immediately turned his attention to the protection of the routes. His force was depleted by the necessity of detaching the

NEWCASTLE to Esquimault, with the object of checking operations by the LEIPZIG on the Pacific coast of North America; but the armed merchant cruisers EMPRESS OF ASIA and EMPRESS OF JAPAN were now available, and the HIMALAYA was almost ready. With these ships added to those of his original squadron, the Admiral was able to organise an effective patrol from Singapore to Hongkong and from Hongkong to Shanghai and Japan, a particular ship or ships being allotted to each section of the route.

The division under Captain Fitzmaurice, as soon as the attitude of Japan was clearly defined, proceeded to close Tsingtau. It was too late to catch the PRINZ EITEL FRIEDRICH, which had completed her armament and sailed to join Admiral von Spee's flag on August 6th, with four supply ships in company. Four days later, the CORMORAN (ex-*Riasan*) also put to sea; but neither vessel made any attempt to attack trade in Chinese or Japanese waters, and the course which they followed took them clear of the British patrols.

There remained in Tsingtau the KAISERIN ELIZABETH and several German liners intended to act as supply ships. The Austrian cruiser was over twenty years old, and was considered unfit for the attack on commerce. She made no attempt to put to sea, and her guns were subsequently landed to assist in the defence of the port. On the other hand it was hoped that the supply ships might win clear before a close blockade was established, and every effort was made to hurry their departure; but it was already too late, and on August 21st and 22nd, three Hamburg-Amerika liners coming from Tsingtau were taken by the TRIUMPH and DUPLEIX. These were the *Senegambia*, *C. Ferd. Laeisz*, and *Frisia*, carrying coal, live cattle, and mails for the German cruisers. In addition, the *Paklat*, a Norddeutscher Lloyd steamer employed in the local trade, was captured by the destroyers attached to the division. She was carrying 250 refugees from Tsingtau to China ports, and her release was subsequently demanded by the German Government on this ground. It was considered by the Prize Court, however, that the sending away of the refugees was a war measure, and the *Paklat* was accordingly condemned.[1]

While the China Squadron was thus engaged in pro-

[1] The aggregate tonnage of these four German steamers was 15,365 tons.

tecting trade in Far Eastern waters, Admiral Patey was busied with preparations to cover the expeditions against the German Colonies in the Pacific which were preparing in Australia and New Zealand. The outbreak of war had been accompanied in Australia, as elsewhere, by a financial crisis which caused a temporary suspension of chartering, and there were grave fears that the wool export season, which was timed to begin on September 7th, might have to be postponed to the New Year. So long, however, as Admiral Patey's powerful force remained concentrated between the enemy and the trade routes, Australian shipping had little reason to fear attack in the terminal waters, and the revival of trade depended mainly on an improvement in business conditions.

It was not long before the risk of capture was practically eliminated in the Western Pacific. No reply having been received to the Japanese ultimatum, war was declared by the Mikado's Government on August 23rd, and the whole strength of the Island Empire was thrown into the conflict. Immediate preparations were commenced for the investment and attack of Tsingtau, both by land and sea; the protection of the trade routes north of Hongkong was undertaken by the Japanese fleet, and strong squadrons were fitted out to co-operate with the Western Allies against the German forces in the Pacific.

From this time onward Allied shipping in the China and Japan Seas was able to proceed without the slightest fear of interruption, and as business conditions gradually improved, with the recovery of the exchanges and consequent extension of credit, the volume of seaborne trade steadily increased. The chief obstacle to complete recovery was, in fact, the entire suspension of the German services. Heavy German purchases of cereals were thrown on to the hands of Chinese merchants, who were thereby deprived of the funds necessary to pay for imports, and the shippers of Congou tea for northern European ports were equally affected. Six and a half million pounds weight of tea shipped from Hankau and Fuchau was on board German liners sheltering in neutral ports, with little prospect of immediate delivery, and large stocks, which should have been carried by Norddeutscher Lloyd, Rickmers, or Hamburg-Amerika liners, were accumulating at Vladivostok, to await transport by the Siberian Railway.

[1] *Consular Reports*, A.S. 5480, *Shanghai.*

Several Chinese and Japanese ports also found themselves deprived of their principal means of communication; but both British and Japanese shipping in the local trade exerted itself vigorously to supply the place of the interned steamers. On the European run, the sailings of the chief British lines were, generally speaking, well maintained. The combined Glen and Shire service was suspended during the month of August, and the British India sailings to Shimonoseki were also temporarily cancelled; but the P. & O., Blue Funnel, Indra, and Indo-China lines continued to run with only minor irregularities, and to do good business. Indeed, the big Japanese lines were severely hit by the refusal of Eastern shippers to place goods in any but British bottoms—a striking testimony to the activity of the British navy and the effects of the State Insurance Scheme.

The results of the first three weeks of war in Eastern waters had thus been eminently favourable to the Allies. Despite the vast target offered to attack and the presence of formidable hostile forces within striking distance, only two Allied merchantmen had been lost, while a dozen enemy steamers captured at sea, a much larger number seized in port, and the immobilisation of those which remained, testified to the completeness of the control established over the main arteries of commerce. Best of all, the flow of trade had been resumed both from British and Eastern ports.

As was only natural, this resumption of trade was on a considerably reduced scale. The financial dislocation was too general and far reaching for its effects to pass away in a few weeks, and they were seen in decreased purchases of British goods as well as in diminished shipments of Eastern products. In no direction was the strain more severely felt than in the Manchester cotton trade, which found the demand from some of its principal markets reduced to an extent which threatened a crisis in the industry. Although the first shock of the war had passed away, Indian commerce was still suffering under a heavy handicap. In addition to the loss of the enemy markets it had become evident that neither from France nor Belgium were any considerable orders likely to be received for many months. Altogether some 25 per cent. of the export trade had thus to be written off, and the blow to certain special trades was even more severe than this figure would suggest. The principal markets for the oil seeds which form an important part of the exports of the East Coast were Hamburg and Marseilles, and Hamburg was also an *entrepôt* for West Coast products, such as copra, pepper, ginger, and fibres. Trade with Hamburg was now barred, and Marseilles was also practically closed owing to the financial conditions and the congestion of the port by military traffic. For all these products, therefore, new distributing centres had to be found, and in the meantime the trade in them was at a standstill. This diminution of Indian exports, with the accompanying restriction of credit, reacted on the volume of imports which could be absorbed. The buyers of cotton goods were unable to place new orders, and there was considerable difficulty in dealing with *ante-bellum* shipments on their arrival at Indian ports. Similar conditions obtained throughout the Far East, and the outlook for the mills of Lancashire was so black that many of them threatened to close down altogether.[1]

Nevertheless, the revival of trade in the United Kingdom and the gradual recovery of the exchanges had already produced a considerable effect, and the security of the route enabled shipping to take full advantage of the increasing demand for cargo space. By the beginning of September, all the lines engaged in the Indian trade had re-established their regular services, and chartering was in full swing on the Eastern markets. The increased cost of bunkering and the necessity of insuring vessels against war risks were reflected in rising freights and heavy surcharges on liner rates, but in spite of the extra cost of transport, the volume of traffic either way was steadily augmented.[2]

[1] The export of piece goods to India during August amounted only to 152,860,000 yards, valued at £1,745,000 ; as compared with 259,130,000 yards and £3,047,000 in August 1913.

[2] See, for example, the following figures of exports (in lakhs of rupees) from the chief Indian ports; taken from the monthly returns of Foreign Seaborne Trade issued by the Department of Statistics, Calcutta.

Week ending.	Calcutta and Chittagong.	Bombay.	Karachi.	Madras.	Rangoon.
Aug. 8	63	36	37	1	8
,, 15	29	12	9	1	22
,, 22	119	35	13	6	13
,, 29	163	21	2	1	8
Sept. 5	123	22	15	—	17
,, 12	159	11	28	—	12

By this time, indeed, the shortage of tonnage at Indian ports had become the chief obstacle to the flow of trade from the Middle East. The withdrawal of the German and Austrian services reduced the number of vessels calling at these ports by some thirty large vessels a month, and, in addition, the decrease in clearances from the United Kingdom during August was beginning to make itself felt.[1] An even more important factor was the decision to send Indian troops to replace the British garrison in Egypt, which subsequently developed into the despatch of a strong Expeditionary Force for service in Europe. For the carriage of this force a large number of steamers was required, and by the end of August a considerable proportion of those available in Indian ports had been withdrawn from commercial employment to be fitted up as transports. The result of this wholesale requisitioning, combined with the decrease in arrivals and the withdrawal of enemy shipping, was almost to paralyse some of the principal branches of Indian trade. At one time the export of Bengal coal was entirely stopped, owing to the fact that no ships to carry it could be procured at Calcutta; and although a certain amount of tonnage was secured during the first two weeks of September for this purpose and for tea shipments, shippers of jute were still unable to charter and importers of sugar were vainly clamouring for tonnage.

Nor was this the only effect which the preparation of the Indian Expeditionary Force had on the problem of maintaining the flow of trade. The naval dispositions by which the safety of the route was secured were also profoundly affected. From the time when the transports began to collect at Bombay, the whole strength of the East Indies Squadron was absorbed in providing the necessary escort. The task was complicated by the necessity of covering the minor expedition against German East Africa, and even the patrol at the great focal point off Colombo had to be abandoned. The result was to leave shipping in the greater part of the Indian Ocean altogether uncovered, but the paramount importance of the military considerations involved fully justified the risk to trade. Moreover, the risk itself was modified by the con-

[1] The steam tonnage entered with cargoes at Indian ports during September was only 278,000, as compared with 534,000 in 1913—a reduction of nearly one-half.

stant passage of British warships on convoy duty between Bombay or Karachi and Aden, which afforded a considerable measure of security against a dash by the KÖNIGSBERG into the Arabian Sea. Of the German cruiser herself very little had been heard since the *Zieten's* arrival at Mozambique. On August 30th she appeared off Majunga in Madagascar, but she effected nothing, and it seemed as if the destruction of her bases and the immobilisation of German shipping on the coast had reduced her to inactivity or impotence.

Indeed, the chief danger-point of the Oriental Route at the beginning of September was to be found farther east, in the neighbourhood of the Malacca Strait and the Malay Archipelago. Although Admiral von Spee's movements were circumscribed by the operations of the Australian Fleet and the entry of Japan into the war, his squadron was still unlocated, and there was always a possibility that he might endeavour to slip through the channels of the Archipelago and appear suddenly in the Indian Ocean. Both Admiral Jerram and Admiral Patey considered this course as among those likely to be adopted by their opponent, and their suspicions seemed to be confirmed by reports of activity on the part of German colliers in the Dutch East Indies, and by the evidence of charts found in one of the German ships captured off Tsingtau. It was of the first importance that if the German Admiral made any such attempt he should be met in force before he had time to scatter his cruisers on the crowded tracks, but the East Indies Squadron, as we have seen, was now wholly occupied in escort work, and Admiral Patey was detained in the eastern section of his station by the operations which were in progress against Samoa and Neu Pommern.

It remained for the China Squadron to fill the gap, and on August 25th Admiral Jerram sailed from Hongkong for Singapore with the MINOTAUR and HAMPSHIRE, leaving instructions for the bulk of his squadron to follow as soon as possible. The TRIUMPH and a destroyer were detached to co-operate in the reduction of Tsingtau, but in exchange, the Japanese Admiralty placed two of their cruisers under Admiral Jerram's orders, and the ASKOLD and ZHEMCHUG also received instructions to join up.

When he arrived at Singapore, on August 30th, the Admiral was informed that the *Goldenfels* had just put into Sabang, and that the KÖNIGSBERG was reported to have accompanied her almost into harbour. He accordingly sent the HAMPSHIRE to Acheh Head, the northern extremity of Sumatra, to protect the focal point at the entrance of the Malacca Strait; but investigation soon proved the rumour of the KÖNIGSBERG'S presence to be baseless, and he was able to exclude her movements from his survey of the situation.

That situation, as ascertained by Admiral Jerram during a careful search of the Karimata Strait and the Java Seas, was by no means unsatisfactory. During the early weeks of the war the call-signs of the GEIER were frequently heard among the islands, and it was strongly suspected that she was in touch with the larger enemy cruisers; but no British merchantmen had been stopped, and they were now moving freely, though vessels leaving Singapore for Java were advised to call at Batavia for instructions before proceeding to the more easterly ports, and the strictest precautions were urged in the neighbourhood of the Bali Strait. No sign of her presence or of a southward movement by the German Pacific squadron was now discovered, and the drastic measures taken by the Dutch authorities to protect the neutrality of their ports and territorial waters gave a satisfactory assurance that little support for the operations of any hostile cruiser could be expected from the German steamers in the Malay Archipelago.

In Philippine ports, where lay about a score of German merchantmen, the restrictions on coaling were less rigorous, but some check on the movement of these ships was provided by the armed merchant cruisers which, now reinforced by the EMPRESS OF RUSSIA, still sustained the Singapore-Hongkong patrol. As an additional precaution the sloops and destroyers were formed into a separate division, based on Sandakan in British North Borneo, where they served the double purpose of keeping a watch upon Manila and protecting the homeward bound tank steamers from Borneo, which had been directed to come round the north of that island. Meanwhile the DUPLEIX and the French torpedo craft maintained a guard upon the entrance to the Malacca Straits, and the remainder of Admiral Jerram's force was left disposable to meet any sudden emergency or reinforce a threatened point.

Thus, by the second week of September, the hold of

THE ONE WEAK LINK

the Allied fleets on the Oriental Route had been firmly established from Aden to Yokohama and Sydney. In the west, the KÖNIGSBERG appeared to have shot her bolt with the taking of a single prize, and her possibilities of mischief were restricted by the loss of her base and the collection of strong British forces in the Arabian Sea. In the east, a cordon which Admiral von Spee was unlikely to penetrate now stretched between his squadron and the trade of the China Seas and Australia, while Admiral Jerram's new dispositions cut him off from the channels leading through Melanesia into the Indian Ocean. All along the route the German liners which had escaped capture or seizure were blocked in the neutral ports where they had taken refuge, by patrols which rendered any attempt at evasion almost hopeless. The one weak link in the chain was the absence of any defence at the Colombo focal point, a defect which sprang inevitably from the numerical weakness of the British forces in the Middle East and the magnitude of the tasks imposed upon them, but which was yet to produce disastrous results. For the present, however, it seemed as if the close guard maintained on the eastern and western entrances of the Indian Ocean secured the central area from all danger of attack, and while the local protection was a sufficient safeguard against local dangers, the supremacy of the Allied fleets in the Mediterranean and the Atlantic gave a reasonable assurance of safety for the European end of the voyage. Hence, covered as they were against unforeseen contingencies by the cheap and adequate insurance provided by the State Scheme, shipowners and merchants alike responded readily to the reviving demand.

CHAPTER VIII

THE SITUATION IN THE PACIFIC [1]

ALTHOUGH by the beginning of September the Eastern trade routes were covered against the chances of an attack by Admiral von Spee, in such a way as to provide a reasonable degree of security, the possibilities of disturbance represented by his powerful squadron could not be ignored so long as it remained unlocated. The very fact that the wide, empty spaces of the Central Pacific, to which he was now confined, afforded no opportunities commensurate with the strength of his force, increased the probability that he would seek elsewhere a more fruitful field of operations, and every scrap of evidence which seemed to throw any light upon the whereabouts or intentions of the German Admiral was eagerly collected and carefully examined by the Allied commanders. For several weeks, however, his plans and position alike remained unascertained. It was known that at the end of July his two largest ships were somewhere among the islands of the Western Pacific, and it was tolerably clear that the EMDEN, when she finally sailed from Tsingtau, had proceeded to join his flag. Beyond this nothing was certain. From time to time reports were received which pointed to the presence of the squadron, or some of its units, in the channels of Micronesia or the Malay Archipelago, but these reports lacked definite confirmation, and the only ship whose presence could be traced with certainty was the slow and comparatively harmless GEIER. No attack was made on any of the French or British islands, nor was Allied shipping subjected to any interference. In these circumstances the German Pacific squadron remained a potential rather than an immediate menace; but the threat was no less disquieting on that account, as it was impossible to say when, or at what point, it might suddenly assume concrete form.

[1] See Maps 1 and 4.

THE PACIFIC TRACKS

In order to understand the reasons of this apparent inactivity on the part of the most powerful force by which the trade of the Allies was menaced at the outset of the war, it is necessary to go back to the outbreak of hostilities and to consider the situation as it presented itself to the German commander.

During the period of strained relations, Admiral von Spee was at Ponape, towards the eastern end of the Caroline Islands, with his two big cruisers, the SCHARNHORST and GNEISENAU. The position was a central one with regard to the German possessions in the Pacific, but it was a long way from Tsingtau and a thousand miles from his secondary base at Rabaul. Nor was it within striking distance of any frequented track of merchant shipping. The Oriental Route, as we have seen, goes up to Chinese and Japanese ports inside the Philippines; the most northerly route between Europe and Australia keeps south of Borneo and New Guinea; and in the Pacific itself, the trade routes of any importance are few and far apart. The chief of them is a Great Circle track which passes over 1,000 miles north of Hawaii and still farther from Ponape. It is used by nearly all steamers plying between ports on the east coast of Asia and those on the west coast of North and Central America, but a considerable number of them diverge from the main track to call at Honolulu, either for purposes of trade or for convenience of bunkering. Another route of some importance proceeds from Australia to Panama and North American ports by way of Samoa, Fiji or Tahiti, and Hawaii; and this is intersected, at the last named point, by the track of steamers bound from Yokohama to South America. Another route to South American ports runs from Sydney and Newcastle, N.S.W., and was followed in 1914 by considerable numbers of both steamers and sailing vessels laden with Australian coal, and by a smaller number of sailing vessels carrying wheat to Peru. From Sydney also, runs a track to Yokohama, followed by a branch of the Nippon Yusen Kaisha; and the trade of the Pacific Islands in fruit, sugar, copra, and phosphates employs many small vessels which sail mostly from Australian ports. Finally, far to the south of all other tracks, the homeward bound trade from New Zealand made direct for Cape Horn, to join the South American Route.

This being the course of trade, vulnerable focal points are few. Indeed, Honolulu is the only one of any consequence lying between the Asiatic and American coasts; and even Honolulu was, during the war, only of minor importance as regards British shipping. The extensive commerce of the United States with China and Japan was carried mainly in Japanese and American bottoms, and that between Hawaii and the States was restricted to the American flag. Indeed, British shipping in the Pacific was rarely exposed to serious risk of capture outside the terminal waters. The Canadian Pacific Railway Company's steamers followed the Great Circle track from Vancouver to Yokohama without divergence, and the big liners which carried the meat and dairy produce of New Zealand to the United Kingdom were strung out across one of the longest and most open ocean passages in the world.

It will be seen that none of the principal tracks pass within a thousand miles of Ponape, and so long as the German Admiral remained there, he could not hope to exercise any deterrent influence on British trade. On the other hand, the island was a favourable starting-point for a voyage of evasion, as it was far removed from the British bases, and the German squadron might cruise for many weeks in the waters of the Central Pacific without meeting any vessel by whom their presence was likely to be reported. For such a voyage, however, an adequate supply of coal and provisions was essential, and herein lay Admiral von Spee's greatest difficulty. In face of the superior strength opposed to him, he at once abandoned all idea of a return to Tsingtau; and the presence of the AUSTRALIA to the south was sufficient to keep him away from Rabaul. In these circumstances, his first care was to concentrate his scattered forces and to accumulate a sufficient stock of fuel and stores to give him freedom of movement. He therefore remained at Ponape until August 6th, in touch with the wireless station at Yap, from whence a cable ran to Shanghai and gave him communication with Tsingtau and the German ships in East Asiatic and Philippine ports, and then, having been joined by the NÜRNBERG from Honolulu, sailed for Pagan Island, in the Ladrones, his first war rendezvous.

There the three cruisers arrived on August 11th and remained until the 13th. Before they sailed again they were joined by the EMDEN and PRINZ EITEL FRIEDRICH, with a number of supply ships. From the new-comers Admiral von Spee learned that another auxiliary cruiser, the CORMORAN, was coming out to join him as soon as her equipment was completed. When she joined the concentration would be practically complete, for the GEIER, which was old, slow, and weakly armed, would have diminished rather than increased the effectiveness of the squadron, and was never called to the flag. Her movements at this time had little intrinsic importance, but, as we have seen, she contributed something to the mystery surrounding the squadron, as her wireless calls were frequently heard by the Australian stations, and gave rise to reports that the more powerful German vessels had ventured into the Malay Archipelago.

The move from Ponape to Pagan Island had not appreciably altered Admiral von Spee's position with regard to the trade routes. It was still open to him to strike at shipping in the China and Japan Seas, to go south into Australian waters or to slip through the channels of Melanesia into the Indian Ocean. Any one of these courses presented a tempting bait, but none of them was without its dangers. The idea of an attack upon Australian shipping was rejected by the Admiral from the first, as he dared not face the battle-cruiser, which was capable of destroying his whole force in detail. Similarly, an attack on British trade in the Far East must involve the risk of action with superior strength, and as he had reason to anticipate the entry of Japan into the war, any movement into the China Seas would court certain and irremediable disaster.

A brighter prospect was held out by the passage through the Malay Archipelago into the waters of the Middle East. If successfully accomplished, it would bring him on to one of the richest cruising grounds in the world, and afford him an opportunity of paralysing for a time the whole trade of the Allies with India, Australia, and the Far East. Here, too, were the German steamers in Philippine and Dutch East Indian ports, some at least of which might be expected to join the squadron with coal and provisions.

Nevertheless, this course also was rejected by the Admiral. He probably feared that the difficulties in the way of obtaining coal and supplies might prove insuperable, especially as the addition of a large fleet of supply ships would limit the emergency speed of his squadron. There was a possibility also that the movements of a considerable body of ships in the Java Seas might be reported to the British naval authorities, and lead to his being intercepted by the AUSTRALIA. The fear of this ship exercised a paralysing influence over all his actions, and it would seem that from a very early period he anticipated that the pressure of the AUSTRALIA to the south, and the Japanese menace to the north might render it necessary for him to quit his station altogether and cross the Pacific into South American waters. He accordingly contented himself with detaching his fastest cruiser, the EMDEN, with orders to make her way into the Indian Ocean, accompanied by the *Markomannia*, while he himself, with the rest of his squadron, went to the Marshall Islands, westward from Pagan Island, to await developments.

If Admiral von Spee had as yet accomplished little, he had at least avoided contact with the squadrons of Admiral Jerram and Admiral Patey, as his movements had kept him well outside the areas to which they were confined by the fulfilment of their immediate defensive tasks. His difficulties were, however, greatly increased by Admiral Jerram's destruction of the wireless station at Yap, on August 12th, as this event cut him off from all communication with the continent of Asia and rendered it impossible for him to locate the forces by which he was surrounded. In order to remedy, so far as possible, this weakness in his position, he detached the NÜRNBERG, on August 22nd, to Honolulu, for the purpose of obtaining information as to his enemy's movements and the progress of events.

During the three weeks which had elapsed since the declaration of war, no vessel flying the British flag had been interfered with by the squadron, and the deterrent effect of its presence on Pacific trade had been very slight. The Asiatic terminals of the Great Circle Route were, as we have seen, well guarded by Admiral Jerram, and subsequently by the Japanese. On the North American coast, British shipping was at first held up by the presence of the LEIPZIG, and for some days vessels in Chinese and Japanese ports bound for San Francisco were also delayed.[1] This menace, however, was soon removed by the departure of the LEIPZIG from Californian waters and the despatch of the NEWCASTLE from China to Esquimalt. The

[1] See Chapter IX, *infra*.

presence of the German squadron thousands of miles to the south had little effect on the situation, and Japanese cargoes for America were mostly forced on to the Pacific Route, not only because neutral tonnage was available, but because the freights and war risks on goods in British bottoms were considerably below those demanded on shipments to New York *via* Suez. Almost the only adverse factor affecting British trade was the requisitioning of the Canadian Pacific Railway Co.'s steamers, which put a stop to one of the two chief North Pacific services under the British flag.

At the beginning of the war, the Australian service of the Nippon Yusen Kaisha was temporarily discontinued, but an enterprising private owner chartered a large steamer for the route and had no difficulty in obtaining cargo. The trade carried on by Australian shipping among the Archipelagoes of the Western Pacific suffered some interruption, due to fear of capture either by Admiral von Spee's squadron or by the smaller German warships and armed vessels lurking among the islands; but the total volume of this traffic is inconsiderable. The main steamer tracks were effectively protected by Admiral Patey's force in the position from which it was covering the expeditions despatched or preparing for the reduction of the German colonies. In the early days of the war there was some nervousness in Australian shipping circles as to a possible southward movement by the German squadron, and the exports of coal from Newcastle, N.S.W., showed a diminution of 60,000 tons, or about 38 per cent., as compared with August 1913; but the absence of attack and the safe arrival of British vessels gradually restored confidence, and by the end of the month thirty-six vessels, with an estimated capacity of 160,000 tons, were loading, or about to load, in the port for foreign destinations.[1]

By this time the Allied forces were ready to take the offensive; and on August 30th the movements of the German squadron were circumscribed by the surrender of German Samoa, with the wireless station at Apia, to a New Zealand Expedition under the protection of a powerful escort, including the AUSTRALIA and MONTCALM. Preparations for the attack on Rabaul and German New Guinea were hastened; and with the Japanese squadrons

[1] *Lloyd's List*, 16 October and 5 November, 1914, giving reports from Newcastle dated August 10th and September 1st.

closing in from the north, the Commonwealth forces strengthening their hold upon the Southern Pacific, and Admiral Jerram cutting off the avenue of escape through the Malay Archipelago, it became more and more probable that the German Admiral would be forced out of the Western Pacific altogether and compelled to relinquish any idea of attacking either Far Eastern or Australian trade.

As a matter of fact, Admiral von Spee had already recognised the necessity of quitting his station. While at the Marshalls he was joined by the CORMORAN, with two supply ships which she had picked up at sea; but at about the same time he learned definitely that Japan had entered into the war. This information was decisive as to his future movements. It is probable, as has been said, that he had from the first considered the advisability of crossing the Pacific to the American coast, where he might draw to his flag the LEIPZIG and possibly one or more of the German cruisers in the South Atlantic. He had now practically no option. With the Japanese fleet opposed to him, it would be madness to turn back, and even to remain where he was would expose him to the risk of destruction by an overwhelming concentration of his enemies. Nor, indeed, was any adequate employment for his force to be found in that neighbourhood. In the absence of a landing force, he could do nothing of importance against the British and French possessions, while the widely scattered shipping of the Pacific trade routes afforded little opportunity for successful commerce raiding. The only course from which any considerable success, or even continued safety, could be expected, was to cross over to the American coast. Yet he was reluctant to quit the Western Pacific without striking a blow, and he hoped to obtain from the NÜRNBERG intelligence which would show him some opportunity for action.

In this hope the squadron quitted the Marshall Islands on August 29th, steering east towards Fanning and Christmas Islands, where a junction with the NÜRNBERG was to be effected. Such supply ships as had been emptied were sent back, to find their way into Philippine or Dutch East Indian ports. The PRINZ EITEL FRIEDRICH and CORMORAN were also detached to harry trade in the Southern Pacific and Australian waters. As no supply ship was sent with them, their prospects were not very brilliant, but the Admiral hoped that, in any case, their movements would serve to divert attention from the course which he himself proposed to follow.

With this object, and also in the hope of chance captures, the two armed auxiliaries proceeded in company towards the Australian coast; but their coal supply ran short, and, contrary to their expectations, they came across no vessels from whom they could replenish their bunkers. They also learned that the approaches to the trade routes were barred by British and Japanese squadrons which would render an attack too dangerous to be lightly risked. They accordingly decided to turn back to the German colonies and renew their supplies of fuel.

Meanwhile the main squadron had proceeded slowly on its way to Christmas Island. The NÜRNBERG arrived at Honolulu on September 1st, and left again on the evening of the same day, after taking on board some fresh provisions and as much coal as the authorities would permit. On September 6th she rejoined the squadron, bringing a piece of intelligence which seemed to offer that opportunity of striking an effective blow for which the Germans had been longing. This was the despatch of the expedition from New Zealand to Samoa, whither Admiral von Spee now went in the hope of catching any ships which might have been left on guard after the capture of the island.

First, however, the NÜRNBERG was detached to Fanning Island, to cut the Australia-Vancouver cable. This she successfully accomplished on September 7th, and, on the same day, rejoined the squadron at Christmas Island. On the 14th, the two big cruisers arrived off Apia, only to find that they were too late. The British flag was flying over the island and both the transports and their covering force had already left. The force left in occupation was already entrenched and was too strong for any landing party the ships could spare. There was nothing to be done, and the squadron again turned eastward.

Meanwhile the activities of Admiral Jerram and the Australian Fleet had rendered the Malay Archipelago too dangerous for the GEIER, and towards the end of August she shifted her ground to the islands of Micronesia. On September 4th she arrived at Kusaie, in the Carolines, in company with the supply ship *Tsintau*, which she had met at sea. At Kusaie she found the *Southport*, a tramp steamer of 8,588 tons under charter to the Pacific Phosphate Co., Ltd., which was waiting there for orders. The coal in the *Southport's* bunkers was transferred to the *Tsintau*, and the engines of the prize were disabled by the removal of the eccentrics and other essential parts. The GEIER and *Tsintau* then left the harbour on September 7th, informing the master (Captain Clopet) that they would return in about a fortnight, and that he would be responsible for the safe-keeping of the prize. Considering escape to be impossible they did not think it worth while to go through the formality of taking his parole.

The German captain had, however, underestimated the determination and resourcefulness of his prisoners. No sooner was the GEIER fairly out of sight than Captain Clopet consulted his chief engineer as to the possibility of repairing the engines. With great ingenuity a makeshift repair was effected, and on the afternoon of the 18th the *Southport* was warped out of the harbour. Skilfully as the work had been done, she was by no means fit to face the perils of navigation in the Coral Sea, and the stock of food was of the scantiest, but the daring of the master and crew were crowned with deserved good fortune, and after an adventurous voyage of eleven days the *Southport* limped into Brisbane, where she was enthusiastically received.

On September 11th, a week after the *Southport* was stopped, an Australian force occupied Herbertshöhe, and after some sharp fighting in the bush, the German Governor, on September 15th, signed a convention surrendering the whole territory of German New Guinea and the Bismarck Archipelago, including Neu Pommern. The local steamers *Sumatra* (584 tons) and *Madang* (194 tons) and the Government yacht NUSA (64 tons) were taken, during or immediately after the operations, by the covering force.

By this event the Germans were deprived of a coaling base and a wireless station, and the position of the GEIER, CORMORAN, and PRINZ EITEL FRIEDRICH became still more desperate. The capture of the *Elsbeth, Senegambia, C. Ferd. Laeisz,* and *Frisia* and the close watch kept upon the German steamers in the Philippines seriously reduced the stocks of coal available for the raiders. The gradual occupation of one after another of the German possessions in the Pacific threatened to leave them altogether without supplies or means of obtaining information. They were, in fact, reduced to the condition of helpless fugitives,

THE REAL MENACE

lurking in obscure harbours and unfrequented waters to escape capture, and powerless for mischief.

All fear of any serious attack on British trade in the Western Pacific was now practically at an end; but Admiral von Spee's squadron was still unaccounted for and continued to cause grave anxiety to the Admiralty. The fact that the EMDEN had been detached for service in the Indian Ocean remained unknown for some time after she quitted Pagan Island, but the possibility that Admiral von Spee might be forced over to the American coast by the pressure of the powerful forces behind him had become a contingency to be faced, at least as early as the entrance of Japan into the war. The contingency was the more serious because the elements of a powerful and persistent attack were already gathering on the South American coasts.

CHAPTER IX

EARLY ATTACKS ON THE SOUTH AMERICAN ROUTE [1]

THE trade of the South American Route was, on the whole, the most vulnerable branch of British commerce exposed to the German attack. Its chief importance lay in a stretch of 6,000 miles of open sea from the River Plate to the Scillies; but before the effect of the Panama Canal had made itself felt, there was a continuous track from Vancouver and San Francisco, through the Straits of Magellan, to the United Kingdom. Throughout this whole voyage of over 15,000 miles there was no port—with the exception of the ill-supplied Falkland Islands—on which a British squadron could be based, and no squadron, accordingly, was maintained on the route in time of peace. The Canadian light cruiser RAINBOW and a couple of sloops sufficed for the fishery patrols and general police work of the Northern Pacific, and the light cruiser GLASGOW served to represent British interests in South American waters. On the outbreak of war, the home end of the route, as far south as the Cape Verde Islands, came under the protection of the patrols established by the Fifth and Ninth Cruiser Squadrons; but it was not until after the lapse of some weeks that any considerable force could be collected on the South American coast.

Nevertheless, the desirability of reinforcing the Pacific and South American stations speedily became obvious. The LEIPZIG was already on the west coast of North America. The NÜRNBERG had last been heard of at Honolulu,[2] and it was uncertain whether she had gone west to join Admiral von Spee or returned to the Californian coast. Meanwhile Admiral Cradock's activity in the North Atlantic and the success with which the trade in this area was covered against attack tended to force the KARLSRUHE,

[1] See Maps 5 and 8. [2] See page 124, *supra*.

CHARACTER OF THE ROUTE

DRESDEN, and KRONPRINZ WILHELM southward on to the Plate and Brazilian tracks, and in the South American ports themselves were a large number of German steamers capable either of being armed as raiders or of acting as supply ships and tenders to the German cruisers.

The volume of trade thus threatened is considerably less than that which crosses the North Atlantic or passes through the Suez Canal; but it engages a large amount of tonnage and is of particular importance in relation to the food supply of the British Isles. In order to understand clearly the situation which arose during the first few weeks of the war it is necessary to give some consideration both to the nature of this trade and the characteristics of the route itself.

It has first to be observed that, although there was, at the outbreak of war, an unbroken track running from Vancouver to the Channel, the route is divided by the Straits of Magellan into two sections which differ greatly as regards local conditions and volume of trade. This division is accentuated by the barren and inhospitable nature of the territory forming the southern horn of the South American Continent. The most southerly port of any considerable size on the Pacific coast is Valdivia. The main body of the Atlantic trade comes no farther south than the River Plate and Bahia Blanca. In the Pacific there is a further subdivision, the commercial significance of the coast centring in the North American ports from Vancouver to San Francisco and in the ports of Peru and Chile from Callao to Valdivia. Thus the route presented to attack three distinct areas of commercial activity, separated by wide stretches of barren coast, and forming to some extent self-contained fields of operation for raiding cruisers.

The trade of the Northern Pacific now comes almost entirely through the Panama Canal; but in August 1914 the grain, lumber, and canned salmon of British Columbia and the Western States still followed the long route through the Straits. Even then, however, a considerable transhipment trade was carried on by the railway across the isthmus, and for this reason Panama was adopted as a terminal port by many of the chief steamship lines serving the west coast of South America. Compared with other sections of the South American Route, the direct trade of the Northern Pacific ports with the United Kingdom was of minor importance, but the need for adequate protection of shipping in these waters was emphasised by the position of Vancouver, the Puget Sound ports—especially Seattle and Tacoma—San Francisco, and Panama, as the eastern terminals of the Great Circle route from Asia and of the tracks between Australia and the Western States. Any danger which threatened the traffic of the South American Route in this area would necessarily menace, at the same time, British shipping on the principal trans-Pacific tracks.

Should a campaign in the North Pacific prove unremunerative, or the raider be driven from his station by superior force, it was open to him to pass, through a wide stretch of unfrequented waters, to the attack of commerce on the west coast of South America. In the trade of this coast one item is of supreme importance. The production of nitrate of soda is a Chilean monopoly, and many of the northern ports derive their sole importance from the nitrate export and the import of coal and petroleum for use in the nitrate industry. Prior to the war, a large proportion of the output, which averaged two and a half million tons a year, valued at over £20,000,000, found its way to Germany, where it was extensively used both for agricultural purposes and in the manufacture of explosives. British purchases averaged over £1,000,000—a figure greatly exceeded during the war—and, in addition, there was a large export to the United States which was mostly carried in British bottoms.

Wheat, barley, oats, and wool were shipped in considerable quantities from Valparaiso and the southern ports of Chile, and copper from Coquimbo. Of these the copper export was the most important, especially in time of war; but it was somewhat overshadowed by the more extensive production of the United States, and could not compare in importance with the Bolivian output of tin. Bolivian ore to the annual value of £1,500,000 was purchased by the United Kingdom alone, but as Bolivia has no coastline, the cargoes were shipped at Antofagasta in Chile and Mollendo in Peru. From Peru itself we derived raw cotton, sugar, alpaca, and rubber, but the rubber was all sent down the Amazon for shipment from Para in Brazil. In the imports from Ecuador, cocoa was the only important item.

It will be seen that the typical West Coast products were goods of high value in relation to bulk, and there was, therefore, little tramp chartering except at the nitrate ports, where a certain number of steamers were fixed for whole cargoes and large sailing vessels were also freely employed, most of these being under the French and German flags. The greater part, however, even of the nitrate export, was shipped in liner parcels, and a large proportion of the general traffic was handled by the ships of a few big companies. This tendency was accentuated by the nature of the coast, along which the ports are distributed at wide intervals, and often separated by tracts of desolate country with few longitudinal railways. Hence the regular lines, sailing to a fixed schedule, with frequent stoppages, provided an indispensable means of communication, and played an important part even in the internal trade.

These lines were mainly owned by British and German companies. The leading place was taken by the Pacific Steam Navigation Company, which provided frequent services to the principal centres of commerce on the West Coast, connecting with a coastal service which linked up all the Chilean and Peruvian ports, and continued to Guayaquil, in Ecuador, and Panama. Other British lines connected Chile and Peru, not only with the United Kingdom but with San Francisco and New York; and among the more important services may be mentioned those of the New York & Pacific Company, Ltd., (Messrs. Lamport & Holt) and the Gulf line, owned by the Nautilus Shipping Company, Ltd. At Callao, the chief centre of Peruvian trade, and at several of the larger Chilean ports, the average number of British steamers calling in the foreign trade was from two to four each week. At Valparaiso, the leading port in the import trade, the number rose to eleven or twelve every fortnight in the foreign services and three in the coasting trade. German shipping was represented by the joint services of the Kosmos and Hamburg-Amerika lines and by the Roland line, working in connection with the Norddeutscher Lloyd. The Kosmos line, with a fleet of over thirty steamers, played an important part in the coasting as well as the foreign trade, and its services extended not only to Panama, but as far north as San Francisco.

Thus the whole Pacific section, from Vancouver to the Straits, possessed a strongly marked character which had considerable effect on the course of trade during the war.

The concentration of ownership in the hands of a few large companies rendered it comparatively easy to control the movement of shipping, and the semi-coastal nature of the steamer tracks provides great facilities for seeking ports of refuge and for the use of territorial waters. On the other hand, a coastal trade is peculiarly liable to interruption by an attack at any one point; and the coast line of southern Chile offers a number of little used harbours, affording possible secret bases and hiding-places for a raider or his supply ships.

On the east coast of South America the ports of any considerable size are less numerous: the coasting trade is carried on exclusively under the national flags and the steamer tracks follow the coast line at a greater distance. The bulk of the West Coast traffic, after passing through the Straits, makes a clear run of some 1,800 miles to the River Plate, where many steamers put in to coal at Montevideo, before striking diagonally across the Atlantic, in company with the meat and grain ships from the Plate and Bahia Blanca. Other steamers continue up the coast to Rio de Janeiro, about a thousand miles from the Plate, before directing their course to Europe. From the great coffee port of Santos, from Bahia, and from Pernambuco, subsidiary tracks swell the volume of trade. But whether proceeding direct from the River Plate, or calling at Brazilian ports, the steamers engaged in the East Coast trade follow a well-defined track, parallel with the coast, as far as the neighbourhood of Cape San Roque. Here the stream diverges into two main currents. The greater number of vessels proceed to Europe, by way of the Cape Verde Islands and Madeira, while a smaller but substantial proportion branch off to United States Atlantic ports. Three great focal points are thus presented to attack—off the mouth of the Plate, where vessels coming through the Straits or round the Horn are joined by those from Buenos Aires, Monte Video, Rosario, and La Plata; near Cape San Roque, where the whole trade both with Europe and North America is gathered together; and in the neighbourhood of Madeira and the Canaries, where the European track merges with that from the African ports.

In the export trade of the Plate foodstuffs form by far the most important items. Under normal conditions the meat freezing and preserving establishments of the Argentine Republic and Uruguay shipped to the United Kingdom beef and mutton of an annual value of £16,000,000, and the British imports of maize, wheat, and oats from the same countries amounted to £18,000,000. Flax seeds and wool also figured prominently among the Argentine exports; but their importance as elements in the trade of the South Atlantic was altogether overshadowed by that of the food cargoes. It must be remembered that the meat exports of New Zealand, which come round the Horn and follow the same track as that of Plate shipping, have to be included in any estimate of the total volume of South Atlantic traffic, and in time of peace at least 84 per cent. of the beef and 67 per cent. of the mutton brought to this country from abroad came by the South American route. The proportion of Argentine maize to the total import was 78 per cent.; and shipments from the Plate and Bahia Blanca amounted to 13·6 per cent. of the total supplies of wheat and flour derived from abroad —too large a proportion to be easily replaceable.[1]

Brazilian commerce, though extensive, was built up almost entirely on two great staple exports. In the year 1913, out of shipments aggregating £65,000,000 in value, nearly £41,000,000 was represented by coffee and over £10,000,000 by rubber, and upon the demand for these two commodities depended the financial stability and purchasing power of the Republic. Of the production of rubber, 44 per cent. found its way to Great Britain, from whence a large proportion of the import was distributed to other countries through the London rubber market, but the chief market for coffee was the United States, which received nearly a third of the total exports of Brazil. Germany also was a good customer for coffee, and Hamburg was the distributing centre for the whole European continent. Indeed, German enterprise has taken a prominent part in the development of the trade, and most of the coffee shipping firms were, at the outbreak of the war, of German origin.

Both in volume and value the trade of the East Coast greatly exceeded that of the Pacific ports, and its character presented a marked difference, due chiefly to the nature of the Plate exports. The carriage of frozen meat is a liner trade, requiring large and costly vessels fitted with

[1] The maize figures have been calculated on an average of the two years 1912, 1913 only, as in 1911 the crop failed and the export was abnormally small. Other figures are on a three years' basis,

refrigerating machinery, and the Brazilian coffee export was also mainly in the hands of the liner companies; but it was by tramp shipping that the Argentine grain crops were lifted, and when the harvests were ready for shipment, chartering at the Plate ports was very heavy. On their outward voyage the tramps were chiefly employed in the carriage of coal, of which more than 7,000,000 tons were annually exported from Great Britain to South America. Of this total, about 800,000 tons went through the Straits, and the remainder was absorbed by the Brazilian, Argentine, and Uruguayan markets. In addition, many ships were drawn to the Plate ports in ballast by the demands of shippers.

Among the liner services, which it must be remembered handled nearly the whole of the British export trade other than coal, as well as the homeward cargoes of frozen meat, there were about a score of important British services. Those of the Royal Mail Steam Packet Company, of Messrs. Lamport & Holt, and of the Nelson, Houlder, Houston, and Donaldson lines, were prominent in the carriage of meat from the Plate; the New Zealand meat exports were handled by the steamers of the New Zealand Shipping Company and of the Shaw, Savill & Albion line, both of which called at Monte Video on the homeward run.[1] The Houlder and Houston lines, together with the Prince line and a Lamport & Holt service, were among those which connected the coast with New York as well as with the United Kingdom. Taking tramps and liners together, an average of twenty British steamers were entered at Plate ports every week, while at the leading ports on the east coast of Brazil, the numbers were—Rio Janeiro, seventeen; Santos, eight; Pernambuco and Bahia, four each. The trade of the northern Brazilian ports, from Ceara to Para, stands somewhat apart. The track from these ports proceeds straight across the Atlantic to Europe, well to the north and west of the main South American Route. Their importance is derived almost entirely from the export of Brazilian and Peruvian rubber, and the Booth line had something like a monopoly of the traffic both with the United Kingdom and the United States.

[1] The Royal Mail service was run in conjunction with that of the Pacific Steam Navigation Company; but only the steamers of the latter line proceeded to the West Coast.

In addition to the British lines there were French, Italian, American, Dutch, Spanish, and Scandinavian services; but all these were of minor importance in comparison with those of the Hamburg-Amerika and Hamburg-Süd-Amerika Companies, whose share—especially of the Brazilian trade—was second only to that of the leading British lines. German influence in South America was strong, thanks in large measure to the number of German settlers, and the trade of Germany with the Latin Republics amounted to some £50,000,000 a year of imports and £30,000,000 of exports. Even this figure, however, was exceeded by the extent of British commerce. The exports and re-exports from the United Kingdom to South America were valued at some £47,000,000 a year, and the imports derived thence at £60,000,000. Rather less than one-fifth in value of the exports and about one-sixth of the imports passed through the Straits. To these figures must be added, in order to arrive at the total volume of trade following the route, the imports from New Zealand, amounting to £19,000,000 a year, and the value of produce from the Pacific coast of North America.

The total British tonnage annually cleared from the United Kingdom with cargoes for South America amounted to nearly five and a half millions, and that entered to over three millions; but, as we have seen, British shipping was also actively engaged in the trade of South America with other foreign countries. The exports from the United States to Argentina and the imports into the States from Brazil employed a large amount of tonnage, and in the year 1912 no less than 170 British vessels from North America were entered at Buenos Aires, while from Rio Janeiro and Santos alone, 251 were cleared for the United States and 105 for the British West Indies.

Moreover, it must be remembered that British capital was very largely invested in South America. The banks, mines and railways of Bolivia were to a great extent British owned; our financial interests in Peru were large, and in Chile still larger, the nitrate industry having absorbed many millions of British capital. In Argentina and Brazil, railways, ports, lighting, drainage, and town planning schemes had been financed from London to the extent of several hundred million pounds. The foreign debts of all the South American Republics were held in great part by British investors. Inasmuch as these countries were financially and economically dependent upon seaborne trade, and the greater part of their exports were normally carried in British bottoms, any interference with the free movement of shipping on the South American Route must necessarily be felt indirectly through the diminution of receipts from investments, as well as directly through the loss of ships and cargoes.

Thus, the importance and the vulnerability of the route combined to render it a source of pressing anxiety at the outset of the war. The most serious danger lay in the possible interruption of the grain and meat traffic in the South Atlantic. It was, however, in the Northern Pacific that the menace first became definite and acute.

During the summer of 1914 the disturbances in Mexico had called the LEIPZIG to Mazatlan, where she was co-operating with the British sloop ALGERINE for the protection of Europeans and the preservation of order. On August 1st information was received that the European situation had become serious, and next day the LEIPZIG put to sea for Magdalena Bay, where she coaled on August 5th. Meanwhile the ALGERINE had steamed north to Esquimalt, and another British sloop, the SHEARWATER, had started from Ensenada. Though admirably adapted for the police work of peace, these old-fashioned ships were neither fast nor powerful enough to engage the LEIPZIG with any hope of success, and the task of covering the homeward bound grain ships from British Columbia fell to the RAINBOW, which was about to leave Esquimalt for the Behring Sea Fisheries patrol, and was now placed by the Dominion Government at the disposition of the Admiralty.

Up to the end of July 1914 the trade of British Columbia and the Western States was proceeding briskly, but this activity was rudely interrupted by the declaration of war. It was generally believed that the NÜRNBERG, as well as the LEIPZIG, was still on the coast, and in view of the frequent reports received as to the supposed movements of these ships, owners were generally unwilling to risk their vessels until the situation should be cleared up. Chartering was suspended at all ports on the coast, and most tramp steamers remained in port, while the liner services were curtailed and irregular. At the same time, the presence of the RAINBOW was even more effective in putting a stop to German trade. The few enemy steamers on the coast cut short their voyage at the nearest port, sending on their cargoes under the American flag, and numerous sailing vessels of large size were held up in Californian and Mexican harbours.

This widespread disturbance was caused by the mere proximity of belligerent warships and not by any active interference with the flow of trade, and so far as British shipping was concerned, it would probably have passed away within the first few days of the war if the danger had not, meanwhile, assumed a more definite form. On August 11th, however, while the RAINBOW was still engaged in covering the passage of the sloops to Esquimalt and searching the coast in the neighbourhood of Vancouver and Puget Sound, the LEIPZIG appeared off San Francisco. Cruising off the entrance to the harbour, just out of sight from the shore, she established a virtual blockade of the port, and her appearance at once put an end to any hope of an immediate improvement in the condition of North Pacific trade. It was currently, though erroneously, reported that she was accompanied by the NÜRNBERG, and that the two cruisers had actually effected captures off the Golden Gate. Against the LEIPZIG and NÜRNBERG combined, the RAINBOW would be able to do little, and the reports which spread all up and down the coast paralysed the movements of shipping from Vancouver to Panama.

At San Francisco itself no fewer than twenty-five British steamers were detained, and as some 60,000 tons of barley were awaiting shipment, the delay was serious; but it was at Seattle and the other ports on Puget Sound that the situation gave rise to the gravest concern. At these ports the export season was in full swing, and large stocks of salmon, grain, flour, and lumber were accumulating in the warehouses and on the quays. Many of the ships by which these should have been lifted were now detained in other ports, in some cases with their outwards cargoes still on board, and there was no immediate prospect of their coming forward. Further heavy consignments of salmon from Alaska were due to arrive for shipment during the next two months, and it was obvious that, if the paralysis of shipping should continue, a dangerous degree of congestion would soon be reached.[1]

So uncertain was the situation, and so gravely was

[1] *Lloyd's List*, 7 September, 1914 (Seattle Correspondent, August 17th).

confidence shaken by the rumours which multiplied every day, that even steamers on the trans-Pacific tracks were mostly held in port, though in their case there was little to fear when once an offing had been obtained. Sailings were suspended, not only on the American coast but at Yokohama and other Asiatic ports, and a good deal of trade was diverted to the two big Japanese lines, the Nippon Yusen Kaisha and Osaka Shosen Kaisha, whose services were maintained according to schedule.

The results of the LEIPZIG's appearance off San Francisco thus illustrated in the most striking manner the powers of dislocation possessed by even a single cruiser when able to maintain herself off a focal point of trade. She did not, however, hold her position for long. There had as yet been little time for her commander, Captain Hann, to make arrangements for the supply of fuel, and he had little reason to court an action with the RAINBOW, which, even if successful, might put a stop to his career by forcing him into a neutral port for repairs. Accordingly, after putting into San Francisco to coal on August 17th, he went to sea again the next day and quitted the neighbourhood of the port, thus escaping a meeting with the RAINBOW, which had come south to look for him.

In the meantime, the Admiralty had ordered Admiral Jerram to despatch one of his light cruisers from the China Station to Esquimalt, and the NEWCASTLE, a faster and more powerful ship than the LEIPZIG, actually sailed from Yokohama on the 18th. But before the arrival of the NEWCASTLE, and even before it was known on the coast that she was coming, British shipping had resumed its activities. By the date of the LEIPZIG's departure from San Francisco the first shock of the outbreak of hostilities had subsided; the rumours of the NÜRNBERG's presence had received no confirmation; and with the removal of the immediate local danger, the confidence of masters and owners rapidly revived. Within two or three days after the LEIPZIG put to sea, British steamers at San Francisco began to move, and as day after day went by without any further news of the raider, the trade of the North Pacific ports became active at all points. Sharp as the alarm had been while it lasted, its effects were hardly felt farther south than Panama. On the west coast of South America British shipping was subject to no hostile interference. There was no German cruiser on the coast, and though rumours as to the movements of the LEIPZIG and NÜRNBERG caused occasional delays, these interruptions were, in the aggregate, of little consequence. German shipping, on the contrary, was wholly inactive. Thirty-five steamers, mostly belonging to the Hamburg-Amerika and Kosmos Lines, were on the coast at the outbreak of war, or arrived at Chilean and Peruvian ports during the first month of hostilities; but with few exceptions they brought their voyages to an end at the first port of call, refusing even to proceed up the coast for the purpose of completing delivery of their cargoes. Nearly fifty sailing vessels were similarly immobilised.[1]

In view of the absence of any British force on this section of the route, the failure of the German liners to complete their outward voyages, or to take any part in the coasting trade, is certainly surprising; so far as the homeward run to Europe is concerned, their inactivity may be accounted for by the dangers of the South Atlantic voyage and the impossibility of penetrating the British cordon in the Channel and North Sea. The enormous importance of nitrates to Germany in the manufacture of fertilisers and explosives emphasises the significance of their refusal to face these risks, and the contrast between this refusal and the activity of British shipping affords a conspicuous example of the far reaching effects of a well-designed hold on focal points and terminal areas. While German shipping was paralysed by the presence of squadrons at a distance of ten thousand miles, British vessels were proceeding with the utmost confidence, although we had not a single cruiser nearer than the RAINBOW at Esquimault and the GLASGOW on the Brazilian coast.

Despite the immunity of British shipping from hostile attack, the commerce of Chile and Peru was seriously disorganised by the outbreak of war. The closing of the German market led to a crisis in the nitrate industry, and trade of all kinds was hampered by the collapse of the exchanges. While these conditions rendered it difficult to obtain cargoes at many points, a shortage of tonnage was produced at other ports by the scarcity of arrivals due to the world-wide cessation of chartering and by the withdrawal from traffic of the German liners. One result

[1] Gross tonnage of above steamers, 201,227. Net tonnage of sailing vessels, 104,186.

of this shortage was to dispose the Governments concerned to do everything in their power to facilitate the free movement of British shipping. For Chile, especially, the export of nitrate and the import of coal by the nitrate districts was a matter of vital necessity. If the German market was closed, the British and American remained open, and there could be little doubt that the British demand would increase as a result of the war. It was of primary importance to the economic stability of the country that tonnage should be available, both for the foreign and the coasting trade. Hence the Chilean Government, while they found it necessary to impose restrictions on the amount of coal to be taken by merchantmen, contrived, both in the framing and execution of the decree, to render it as little onerous as possible to British vessels. At the same time they kept a watchful eye on the German steamers lying in their ports, in order to guard against any breach of neutrality.

So serious were the consequences to Chile of the interruption of her maritime communications that the Chilean Government proposed to acquire all the Kosmos Liners then lying in their ports for the purpose of employing them in the foreign trade. For this, however, the consent of the Allied Governments was required, as the transfer of belligerent merchantmen to a neutral flag, in order to escape the consequences of belligerency, had always been regarded as inadmissible, and was definitely forbidden by Article 56 of the Declaration of London. In the special circumstances of the case, the Allied Governments were willing, as an act of goodwill, to recognise the transfer, but only on the understanding that the vessels should not be employed in trading, either directly or indirectly, with Germany or Austria-Hungary. Their insistence on this proviso and the emergence of other circumstances unfavourable to the transaction led to the abandonment of the project, and Chilean trade remained almost entirely dependent upon the British services, which were running with fair regularity, though generally some days behind their scheduled time.[1]

Thus, while the trade of Chile and Peru was seriously disturbed, the position as regards British shipping was not

---

[1] For the proposed acquisition of the Kosmos liners, see Alejandro Alvarez, *La Grande Guerre Européenne et la Neutralité du Chile*, Paris, 1915, pp. 261-265.

unsatisfactory, the only immediate danger being that the LEIPZIG might come south in order to find a safer and richer field of operations. On the opposite coast the situation presented very similar features, but the economic disturbance ashore affected British trade more seriously than in the Pacific, and the dangers to be apprehended were more menacing. At the outbreak of war there was, indeed, no German cruiser in the South Atlantic, but while lying in Rio Harbour during the period of tension, Captain Luce, of the GLASGOW, heard of the departure of the DRESDEN from St. Thomas, the KARLSRUHE from Havana, and the STRASSBURG from the Azores. There had also to be taken into consideration the possibility of cruisers breaking out from German home ports on to the European end of the trade route, and for a few days there seemed to be some danger of a panic which might seriously interfere with the arrival at British ports of food supplies from New Zealand and the Plate. The agents of the leading lines were instructed to retain their ships in port, and a general paralysis of British trade on the East Coast appeared to be within measurable distance. This danger, however, was happily and speedily averted by the effect of the State Insurance Scheme and by the local encouragement given to shipping by Captain Luce and by the British Ministers and Consular officers on the coast.

On receiving news of the declaration of war the GLASGOW left Rio, and Captain Luce proceeded to patrol the trade route, warning all British merchantmen of the outbreak of hostilities and communicating the Admiralty instructions as to the precautions to be adopted. To this he added the advice that masters of homeward bound vessels should call at Pernambuco in order to obtain the latest news as to the local situation before shaping their course across the North Atlantic. Meanwhile the sailings of German liners had been stopped all down the coast, and many of those which were at sea put at once into the nearest port, without attempting to complete their voyages. Among these were the Hamburg-Amerika liner *Blücher* of 12,350 tons and 16·5 knots, which put back to Pernambuco on August 4th, alleging engine troubles, and the Hamburg-Süd-Amerika liner *Cap Trafalgar* at Buenos Aires, an almost new ship of 18,710 tons, with a speed of 17·5 knots. Both these vessels were reported to be arming as commerce destroyers, and though careful investigation by the Brazilian and Argentine Governments failed to reveal any sign of warlike preparations, their presence added to the prevailing uneasiness. It was impossible, also, to ignore the possibility that the DRESDEN and KARLSRUHE might come south; and though Admiral Stoddart had been ordered to reinforce the GLASGOW, this was, of course, known only to the Admiralty.

There was thus ample cause for anxiety, but the confidence displayed by Captain Luce and the British diplomatic representatives went far to allay the alarm, and the chief impediment to an immediate resumption of activity was the existence of a financial and economic crisis ashore. At the time when war broke out, trade on the east coast of South America was in a far from flourishing condition. Brazilian exporters had suffered severely through the fall in the price of rubber in 1913 and the disorganised state of the coffee market. The prospects for the coffee crop of 1914–15 were poor, and with the two staple exports both adversely affected, the general commercial and financial situation was anything but satisfactory. In Argentina also the outlook was black. The prosperity of the country had reached high-water mark in 1910, and a burst of over-confidence, reflected in a fictitious boom in land values, was followed by a period of severe depression, which began in 1912 and had not yet spent its force.

In these circumstances, the financial reactions which everywhere followed the outbreak of war were felt here with exceptional severity. The position was serious in Brazil and critical in Argentina, where it was aggravated by the lateness of the principal crop. The greater part of the wheat surplus had already been shipped, but the export of maize, which the month of August should normally have seen in full swing, had been delayed by heavy rains, and shipments had barely begun when the crisis in Europe put a complete stop to all further movements. The freight on grain cargoes is paid in advance, and German financial houses were deeply interested in the business. These people were now wholly cut off from their resources, and financiers of other nationalities were almost equally affected by the collapse of the exchanges, the closing of the banks, and the proclamation of a moratorium. Thus, shippers were unable to obtain ⟨money for the payment of freight advances or the hire of labour;

chartering and loading were alike suspended at Plate ports, and the export of grain was at a standstill.

Both in Argentine and Brazilian ports difficulties with regard to coaling added to the perplexities of shipowners. The interruption of the fuel supply from Great Britain caused a shortage which, in Brazil particularly, assumed such proportions as to threaten the running of railways, coasting vessels, and factories, and abnormal prices had to be paid by masters desiring to fill their bunkers. The Governments of the two Republics were seriously alarmed by the restrictions placed on British exports, and decrees were issued limiting the amount which could be shipped by steamers to a quantity sufficient to take them to their first port of call. When, however, it was found that the British embargo extended only to coal required for Admiralty purposes and that colliers were able to come forward safely, confidence was quickly restored; and though the regulations were retained as a check upon infractions of neutrality, they were not enforced in such a manner as to cause any inconvenience to legitimate trade.

The obstacles placed in the way of renewed commercial activity by this combination of adverse conditions proved to be far more difficult to overcome than that presented by the fear of capture, the dislocation caused by which was very slight. For some time after the declaration of war there were constant inquiries at the Embassies and Consular Offices, but few vessels were held up for more than a few days, and the first actual news received of any hostile interference with South American trade was not of a nature to cause panic.

Immediately on the outbreak of war the DRESDEN quitted the Caribbean and turned south. On August 6th she was off the northern coast of Brazil, steaming down the track of vessels bound from South America to the West Indies. At about 1.30 p.m. she stopped and boarded the *Drumcliffe*, which in ignorance of the outbreak of hostilities was proceeding, in ballast, from Buenos Aires to New York. The DRESDEN'S commander, Captain Lüdecke, appears to have been somewhat at a loss as to what to do with his prize. He could not spare a prize crew, and had no desire to encumber himself with prisoners. Either from fear of the British cruisers in the Atlantic, or with a view to subsequent concerted operations in the Pacific, he had already decided to go round the Horn, and it was no part of his programme to delay his movements by immediate operations against commerce. Accordingly the *Drumcliffe* was permitted to pass on her way with no greater damage than the removal of her wireless apparatus. About an hour after her release, the Houlder liner *Lynton Grange* and the Houston liner *Hostilius* were stopped within a few miles of the same spot. Both vessels were from the Plate, the *Lynton Grange* bound for Newport News and the *Hostilius* for Cienfuegos in Cuba. Like the *Drumcliffe* they had left port in the last week of July, and were unaware that hostilities had broken out. The cargo of the *Hostilius* was neutral owned, and after some two hours' discussion among the German officers, both ships were finally released, the DRESDEN continuing on her voyage to the south.[1]

No news of this encounter was received until August 11th, when the *Hostilius* arrived at Barbados, and the effect was then rather to encourage than to deter shipping, as it suggested that the Germans were not prepared to go to the length of sinking prizes, in which case their lack of ports would confine their operations within very narrow limits.

A further encouragement to trade was the issue, on August 12th, of an Admiralty Statement as to the safety of the trade routes, which laid special emphasis on the security of the Atlantic tracks. Captain Luce also was doing his utmost to reassure shipping by cruising on the trade routes to show the flag and endeavouring to speak as many steamers as possible. While so engaged, on August 14th, he captured the Hamburg-Süd-Amerika liner *Santa Catherina*, of 4,247 tons, some 350 miles south of Bahia. This vessel had left New York for Santos on July 27th, and as she was not equipped with wireless, had received no news of the declaration of war. Unfortunately she was destroyed, by the accidental breaking out of fire in her bunkers, before she could be brought into a British port.

It was, of course, impossible for a single British cruiser to police effectively some two thousand miles of coast, and the German and Austrian steamers in Brazilian and Argentine ports were joined by several new arrivals, none of which, however, showed any signs of further commercial activity.

---

[1] A German account states that these three ships were released because they were in ignorance of the outbreak of war, but this is unlikely, in view of the German reservation with regard to Article 3 of the Sixth Hague Convention. The Register of the *Hostilius* was endorsed : " Let go because her destruction did not seem worth while."

On the other hand, the only regular British service suspended was that of the Royal Mail Steam Packet Company, which was temporarily held up owing to the closing of Southampton to commercial uses, and the requisitioning of a large proportion of the Company's fleet. Some difficulty, however, was found by the liners in obtaining cargoes for their refrigerated space, owing to speculative retention of meat stocks by holders in Uruguay and the Argentine, in hope of a rise in price. The cost of war risks insurance and a surcharge of 50 per cent. imposed by lines belonging to the Plate and Brazilian Conferences on both freight and passenger rates, proved an additional impediment to the revival of trade.

The majority of the Argentine banks reopened on August 12th, but it was some time before anything like normal business conditions were restored, and there was no immediate resumption of chartering on any considerable scale. On August 15th Congress prohibited the export of wheat and wheat flour, with a view to protecting domestic supplies, but as the greater part of the year's surplus had already been shipped, this was a matter of little consequence, and the chief obstacle to a revival of shipping at the Plate continued to be the financial difficulties which impeded the movement of the maize harvest. It was impossible to induce the banks to negotiate drafts drawn against bills of lading; and though vast quantities of maize were awaiting shipment, the owners of tramp tonnage were unable to secure charters, and over 400,000 tons of shipping suitable for the carriage of grain lay idle in River Plate harbours.[1]

Meanwhile the export trade of Brazil was seriously threatened by difficulties arising from the German nationality of the principal coffee shipping firms. Large consignments of this product were ready to be shipped to South Africa, the United States, and other British and neutral markets, but the shipping companies were honourably anxious to do nothing which might be of financial assistance to the enemy, and were doubtful as to the propriety of accepting the cargoes. In view, however, of the importance of retaining the carriage of Brazilian trade in British hands, it was eventually officially decided that there was no objection to the shipments being accepted, and the companies were advised to this effect.

[1] *Lloyd's List*, 8 and 19 September, and 1 October, 1914.

172   ATTACKS ON SOUTH AMERICAN ROUTE

It will be seen that there were still many causes of anxiety and perplexity to British shipowners and merchants quite apart from the menace presented by the enemy cruisers, but in the latter days of August this menace also assumed a more threatening aspect. After dismissing the *Hostilius* and *Lynton Grange* on August 6th, the DRESDEN coaled in secret off the northern coast of Brazil and then steered wide out into the South Atlantic, rounding Cape San Roque at a great distance. She was joined *en route* by two Hamburg-Amerika liners, the *Prussia*, which had sailed from Pernambuco on August 4th, before the declaration of war, and the *Baden*, which slipped out of the same port on August 11th.[1] The *Baden* brought a good supply of coal, but Captain Lüdecke made no attempt to attack trade in the focal area round Fernando Noronha. His whole care at this period was to avoid observation, and he kept steadily on his course till 10 a.m. on August 15th, when he encountered the Houston liner *Hyades*, about 180 miles east of Pernambuco. The *Hyades*, a steamer of 3,352 tons, had left Rosario, with 4,453 tons of maize, on July 31st and had been warned by Captain Luce of the outbreak of war. She accordingly put into Pernambuco for the purpose of obtaining instructions from the owners before proceeding farther on her voyage. Having been reassured by the release of the *Hostilius* and the arrival of two British steamers, neither of which had seen anything suspicious, she sailed again on the 14th; but in accordance with advice received from the Consul, her master shaped his course to pass 100 miles east of Fernando Noronha, thus keeping well away from the usual tracks. By a piece of singularly bad fortune this course, which would probably have carried him clear of danger if the DRESDEN had been actively engaged in commerce destruction, brought him right across the track which she was following for the purpose of concealment. Captain Lüdecke had now ample accommodation for prisoners, and although the cargo of the *Hyades* was consigned by a German firm at Rosario to another German firm at Rotterdam, for transhipment to Germany, he was persuaded that, if allowed to continue her voyage, she would be diverted to a British port. The crew of the *Hyades*

---

[1] *Prussia*, 3,557 tons, 12 knots; *Baden*, 7,676 tons, 12 knots. Both ships were equipped with wireless.

were accordingly taken off by the *Prussia*, after which the prize was sunk.¹

Next day, August 16th, the *Siamese Prince*, outward bound from London to the Plate, was stopped and boarded; but her cargo was neutral owned, and she was accordingly released after a parole had been taken from her people. At the same time, the *Prussia* was sent off with instructions to land the crew of the *Hyades* at the nearest Brazilian port.

Successful as the DRESDEN had been in avoiding observation, rumours of German activity on the coast sprang up, about this time, at several points. On August 16th, the BREMEN was reported off Bahia, and the sailings of several steamers from the Plate were delayed for fear of capture by the same ship. As a matter of fact, the BREMEN had been relieved by the DRESDEN in the early part of the year, and at no time during the war did she quit the Baltic and North Sea. The persistent rumours as to her presence in South American waters must, therefore, have arisen from some confusion between her and the DRESDEN, or have been spread by German agents for the purpose of creating alarm. On August 20th, however, the presence of the DRESDEN and the destruction of the *Hyades* became known through the arrival of the *Siamese Prince* and *Prussia* at Rio; and although the MONMOUTH, which had been despatched by Admiral Stoddart on the 18th, arrived at Pernambuco on the same day, and at once went south to join Captain Luce, the news brought by these vessels had a disconcerting effect. It was now evident that ships which fell into Captain Lüdecke's hands were liable to be sunk, and great anxiety was felt as to the safety of the *Hellenes*, another Houston liner, which was at sea with a cargo valued at £300,000, and of other steamers which had recently left port or were shortly due to arrive. As one after another of these ships reached her destination, or was reported at an intermediate port, the alarm gradually died down, but the general feeling of uneasiness was not entirely dissipated, and a wild rumour which arose shortly after the MONMOUTH sailed from Pernambuco, as to the presence of the GNEISENAU off the Brazilian coast, found sufficient credence to delay several steamers at that port. A more authentic cause of disturbance was the announcement of the sinking of the *Kaipara*, but this was followed so quickly by the news that

¹ See Map 8.

the KAISER WILHELM DER GROSSE had been destroyed, that its effect was negligible. On the other hand, the CAP TRAFALGAR slipped out of Monte Video on the 22nd, and as she was believed to be already armed, her escape caused considerable anxiety. The position, indeed, was not altogether satisfactory in view of the scanty force available for the defence of trade; and the Plate voyage was quoted in the open market at 70s., which compared unfavourably both with the State Flat Rate, then standing at 3 per cent., and with underwriters' quotations for the North Atlantic and the Far East.

On being joined by the MONMOUTH, Captain Luce proceeded to sweep the coast for the DRESDEN, but without success, as Captain Lüdecke kept well out in the Atlantic and made no attempt to approach the trade routes. After sinking the *Hyades*, he went, in company with the *Baden*, to Trinidada, an island lying some 500 miles from the Brazilian coast.[1] Here he found a German steamer from which he coaled on August 20th and 21st, after which he continued his voyage, gradually drawing nearer to the coast as he approached the South of Brazil, where the German element predominates. By August 26th the DRESDEN was cutting across the steamer tracks east of Rio Grande, where they begin to converge towards the Plate Estuary, and in doing so she ran across two British ships, the *Holmwood*, outward bound for Bahia Blanca, and the *Katherine Park*, on her way from Santa Fé and Buenos Aires to Rio de Janeiro and New York. The masters of both these vessels had departed from their usual track, but at this point in their voyage it was difficult to avoid frequented waters, otherwise than by hugging the coast within the three-mile limit, a course seldom followed except in cases of well ascertained local danger, on account of the prolongation of the voyage involved.

The *Holmwood*, which was boarded, after a short chase, at 8 a.m., was carrying about 6,000 tons of coal for the Buenos Aires and Pacific Railway Co. Her master protested strongly against his ship being sunk, on the ground that the consignees were neutrals, and that the coal had been bought before the declaration of war; but

[1] In most maps this island is spelt "Trinidad," but the use of the Portuguese form is a convenient means of distinguishing it from the large British island of Trinidad in the West Indies. For its importance in relation to the attack and defence of South American trade, see Chapter XII, *post*.

his protest was disregarded, and after the crew had been removed to the *Baden*, a bomb was placed in the hold of the prize. Meanwhile the *Katherine Park* had come up, and as her cargo of quebrecho wood was owned in the United States, the prisoners were transferred to her and she was dismissed at 2.20 p.m., on the usual parole being given by her master and crew. By this time the *Holmwood* had already disappeared.

The *Katherine Park* arrived at Rio on August 30th, and the news which she brought, coming so soon after the destruction of the *Hyades*, intensified the prevailing uneasiness. It was still believed locally that the BREMEN was also on the coast, and great anxiety was felt as to the fate of ships at sea. The departure of several steamers from Plate ports was delayed, and for a short time there seemed to be some risk of a general interruption of services. The Admiralty, however, intimated to shipowners and shippers, through the British Embassies and Consular Offices, that no undue risk would be run by vessels which left port at night, made a good offing, and avoided the regular tracks. At the same time they pointed out that the State Insurance Scheme was framed on the assumption of a certain percentage of losses, and that it was open to all British merchants and shipowners to insure themselves under the scheme. What was still more important, they were able to give an assurance that the British forces in the South Atlantic were being increased.

Already, on August 28th, the GLASGOW and MONMOUTH had been joined by the armed merchant cruiser, OTRANTO, but the reinforcements now sent were on a much larger scale. As we have seen, the safety of the North Atlantic had been completely secured before the end of August, and Admiral Cradock had turned his attention to the northern coast of Brazil, where he was searching for the DRESDEN and KARLSRUHE and their supply ships, when he received instruction from the Admiralty to take command on the South American coast. On September 3rd, when the Admiral received these orders, he was returning from the St. Paul Rocks, where he had hoped to find the CAP TRAFALGAR. Two days later he arrived at Pernambuco, and immediately proceeded to dispose the force assigned to him in such a way as to cover the trade routes and provide for an effective pursuit of the DRESDEN.

For this purpose he had, in the first place, the three ships already on the station, together with the GOOD HOPE and BRISTOL, which he brought with him from the West Indies; but this was not the limit of his resources. The destruction of the KAISER WILHELM DER GROSSE and the firm grip established by Admirals de Robeck and Stoddart on the European approaches permitted the outlying squadrons to be strengthened without exposing trade to undue risk in the terminal areas. The battleship CANOPUS, the cruiser CORNWALL, and the armed liners CARMANIA and MACEDONIA were accordingly placed under Admiral Cradock's orders, bringing up his total strength to nine ships, either in hand or on their way out.

On arriving at Pernambuco Admiral Cradock found that the German steamer *Stadt Schleswig* had arrived at Maranham on September 2nd, with the crew of the *Bowes Castle*, which had been sunk by the KARLSRUHE on August 18th, some 500 miles south-west of Barbados. This evidence of the KARLSRUHE's activity had little effect on shipping, as the *Bowes Castle* was many days overdue, and had already practically been given up for lost. It was, moreover, largely discounted by the increased naval protection given to the route.

Meanwhile Captain Luce had turned south on receiving news of the *Holmwood's* destruction by the DRESDEN, and on September 8th the GLASGOW and her consorts arrived at Monte Video. Their arrival went far to restore confidence in the Plate trade, especially as no further captures had been recorded, and by this time the economic conditions were also showing signs of improvement. The reduction of the State Flat Rate to 2 per cent. on September 1st was an encouragement to trade on this, as on all other routes, and this concession was accompanied by a reduction in hull premiums from $1\frac{1}{4}$ to 1 per cent.[1] Upon this the liner companies reduced the 50 per cent. surcharge on freight and passenger rates by one half, and were quickly rewarded by an increase of business. The demand for refrigerated space had already revived to some extent, owing to large contracts entered into by the War Office with the chief meat freezing establishments, but any tendency to a general revival had hitherto been checked by the rise in prices and the efforts of the American Meat Trust to corner the supplies. With a view to defeating these attempts and avert the

[1] See Chapter X, *post*.

danger of speculative retention of stocks, the Board of Trade now initiated a scheme for regular weekly purchases on a large scale, in order to assure a steady supply for the civil population of the United Kingdom. This arrangement removed one of the principal obstacles to recovery, as the liners no longer found difficulty in obtaining cargoes for the homeward voyage. The maize harvest had also at last begun to move. By September 7th, 107,000 tons of shipping had been fixed for the carriage of grain; and though 325,000 tons remained on the market, the financial position was so far ameliorated as to give good prospects of brisk chartering in the immediate future, provided confidence was maintained in the safety of the route.[1]

In Brazil, the recovery of trade was somewhat less marked than in the case of the Southern Republics, as the movement of the principal staple export was still severely handicapped. Although coffee could be shipped to Germany under neutral flags, little or no tonnage was available for the purpose, and shipments to Hamburg, whether for consumption within the Empire or for distribution to other European markets, had absolutely ceased. Buyers in the United States took advantage of this situation to reduce their offers, and the result was a heavy fall in the price of the product. In these circumstances importing firms in Brazil were unable to remit either to the United States or to Europe, as they were unable to furnish cover to the banks. The rate of exchange fell heavily, and both the export and import trade of the southern provinces were threatened with paralysis. The export of rubber, on the other hand, was well maintained, as Great Britain and the United States were by far the largest purchasers, so that the loss of the German market was not severely felt. The Booth line services, both to Europe and America, were running with comparatively little dislocation, and the outlook in the northern provinces was distinctly hopeful. The whole country, too, benefited to some extent from the general revival of confidence caused by Admiral Cradock's arrival, and a further improvement in the position was foreshadowed by the announcement that the Royal Mail Steam Packet Company had made arrangements to resume their regular sailings, using London and Liverpool as ports of departure. This was welcome news, for the immobility of the German liners

[1] *Lloyd's List*, 9 September, 1914.

which handled so large a part of the Brazilian trade left the supply of tonnage dangerously short. Even while the GLASGOW was the only British cruiser on the coast these vessels had made no effort to continue their voyages, though several of them had cargo on board for places farther down the coast than their port of refuge, and it was evident that they had not the slightest intention of running any risk of capture. Throughout the whole of August their number had steadily increased, as ship after ship put in for safety, and there were now well over thirty in Brazilian harbours, among the later comers being four Woermann liners and six or seven other steamers which the fear of capture had driven over from the African coast.

The German and Austrian steamers in Argentine ports and at Monte Video were equally inactive, as were those on the west coast. Altogether some three-quarters of a million tons of enemy shipping were lying idle at ports on the route,[1] and the only German vessel continuing to trade in South American waters was a small river steamer, plying between Monte Video and Asuncion.[2]

This immobility formed a striking contrast to the increasing activity of British shipping, which, now that the economic conditions had begun to improve and a reasonable measure of protection was provided, showed no reluctance to put to sea. It was indeed fortunate that the amelioration of the financial conditions which permitted the resumption of chartering at the Plate should have coincided with so great an increase in the available British force, but, as a matter of fact, the immediate danger had already disappeared. Even so important a focal point of

[1] The particulars of these, as on September 10th, 1914, were as follows:

—	German steamers.		Austrian steamers.		German sailing vessels.	
	No.	Tons gross.	No.	Tons gross.	No.	Tons net.
North American Pacific Ports	5	27,470			11	25,930
South American Pacific Ports	35	201,227			49	104,186
South American Atlantic Ports	60	326,549	10	43,205	2	2,206
Total	100	555,246	10	43,205	62	132,322

These figures are exclusive of about a dozen German steamers in South American waters which were at sea on September 10th, acting as supply ships to German cruisers.

[2] The *Dr. Kemmerich*, 526 tons.

commerce as the entrance to the Plate proved an insufficient bait to turn Captain Lüdecke from his purpose; and when the GLASGOW and her consorts arrived at Monte Video, the DRESDEN was already well to the south, heading for the comparatively empty waters of the Pacific.

In the Pacific also the situation had improved. Shipping in Chilean and Peruvian waters had as yet suffered no interruption, and the balance of naval strength in northern waters had now been turned in favour of the Allies.

The declaration of war by Japan added the cruiser IDZUMO to the Allied force on the west coast of North America, and on August 30th the NEWCASTLE arrived at Esquimalt. The appearance of the NÜRNBERG at Honolulu on September 1st finally disposed of the idea that she had returned to Californian waters, and on September 3rd, Captain Powlett of the NEWCASTLE, who had become Senior Naval Officer on the station, sailed from Esquimalt for the purpose of searching for the LEIPZIG, of whom nothing definite had been heard since she quitted San Francisco on August 18th. He left the RAINBOW to guard the northern trade routes against the possibility of a surprise, and the IDZUMO to keep watch off San Francisco.

Meanwhile shipping was moving freely both on the Pacific tracks and on the South American Route. The opening of the Panama Canal to commerce on August 15th acted as a stimulus, especially to the export of grain to Europe, and within two or three weeks from the LEIPZIG'S departure from San Francisco trade had become brisk all along the coast.

Thus, by the end of the first week in September, the general outlook on all sections of the South American Route showed a great improvement, both as regards the volume of trade moving and the protection provided. Nevertheless, the route was still threatened by serious dangers. While the KARLSRUHE was being searched for on the northern coast of Brazil she had in reality established herself in the focal area off Cape San Roque, where she had begun a brief but brilliant career as a commerce destroyer which will form the subject of a future chapter. Already she had captured two vessels on her new cruising ground, and favoured by rare luck, was preparing for further successes. The KRONPRINZ WILHELM, whose movements were wrapped in equal obscurity, had also found her way on to the trade routes, and on September 4th she captured the *Indian Prince* not far from the scene of the KARLSRUHE'S operations. Farther south, the CAP TRAFALGAR, having received an armament from the gunboat EBER, which had crept over from the African coast, was cruising, with a singular absence of success, on the look out for British merchantmen.[1]

The Plate trade was now, indeed, covered against the DRESDEN and that of the North Pacific against the LEIPZIG ; but the immunity hitherto enjoyed by shipping on the west coast of South America was threatened by the possibility that both these cruisers might be driven into Chilean or Peruvian waters by the pressure of the superior forces behind them. Moreover, the powerful squadron under the command of Admiral von Spee was still at large in the Pacific, and though his intentions were as yet uncertain, so strong a barrier had been erected against his return to Asiatic waters, that the probability of his making his way eastward to the South American coast was already fully recognised. The situation was thus full of menace, and in fact the period of maximum hostile activity on the South American Route was at its commencement. It is none the less true that, on this as on other routes, the initial crisis had been passed. The immediate effects of the dislocation produced by the war were rapidly passing away, and the flow of trade had recommenced. When once that flow had been resumed, no shock sustained from the activity of hostile raiders proved sufficient seriously to interrupt its progress.

[1] The EBER put into Bahia on September 5th, flying the merchant flag.

CHAPTER X

THE BEGINNINGS OF TRADE RECOVERY

BOTH in home and distant waters the course of the war, during the first five or six weeks of hostilities, had been in sharp contrast to the anticipations formed on either side of the North Sea. The readiness displayed by the Grand Fleet had put an end to any hope the enemy may have entertained of striking a surprise blow before the British forces were concentrated, and their inability or unwillingness to contest the command of Home Waters had been demonstrated in the most striking manner by their failure to interrupt the passage of the Expeditionary Force to France, the subsequent transfer of its base from the Channel ports to St. Nazaire, and the despatch of reinforcements and supplies. Such losses as merchant shipping had sustained had all been due to the German minefields, and their effect, as we have seen, had been insufficient to prevent the resumption of a brisk traffic on the North Sea tracks. In more distant seas the enemy had displayed a greater activity, but the fears which had been entertained as to the sudden appearance of a swarm of German cruisers and armed liners on the trade routes had not been realised. The covering squadrons had taken up their positions promptly and without interference, and the majority of the German steamers which had taken refuge in neutral harbours found themselves, almost from the first day of the war, closely and vigilantly watched by British patrols. Only one merchant cruiser had succeeded in running the gauntlet of the North-about Passage for the purpose of preying on Allied trade, and she had been brought to book at the very beginning of her active career.

By the middle of September the approaches to European waters, the Mediterranean Sea, and the North Atlantic were already fully controlled and could be traversed by Allied merchantmen without fear of attack. East of Suez, the KÖNIGSBERG was still unlocated on the East African coast, but after a single capture she had sunk into inactivity, and the focal point at Aden was strongly guarded against the possibility of a renewed attack. An almost impenetrable screen of Allied squadrons shut off Admiral von Spee from the Eastern trade routes, and his force had been driven into the comparatively barren waters of the Southern Pacific. The trade of South and West Africa had been immune from attack since the sinking of the *Nyanga*; and though the South American Route was menaced at more than one point, a strong covering squadron had been provided, and the losses were as yet comparatively insignificant.

The rapidity with which confidence in the safety of the trade routes revived may be clearly traced in the course of quotations on the war risks insurance market. The early and drastic reductions made in premiums charged under the State Scheme, and the more than corresponding fall in underwriters' quotations were at once a main factor in the recovery of seaborne trade and the most convincing testimony to the security of the ocean highways.

That the fear of a panic on the insurance market was not unwarranted had been shown during the week preceding the ultimatum, and the immediate result of the outbreak of hostilities was to send up the rates on cargoes in British bottoms, in some cases to as much as 20 per cent.[1] The contrast between these rates and the State Flat Rate of 5 per cent. was very marked, but the demand for cover under the Government scheme was at first affected by the exclusion from that scheme of cargoes afloat at the declaration of war. It was rather in respect of such cargoes than of new voyages that insurance was, at the moment, desired. Hulls, however, could be covered for current voyages, and there was an immediate rush of owners to join the three great Associations which had been " approved " for the purposes of the Scheme. By the night of August 4th, the value of tonnage entered in the Liverpool Club had risen from £30,000,000 to £50,000,000, and within forty-eight hours from the declaration of war all the principal liner companies and many owners of tramp steamers had become members of one or other of the Associations.

[1] For war risks quotations the *Times*, *Shipping World*, and *Economist* have been collated.

INSURANCE SCHEME EXTENDED

On August 6th it was decided that the benefits of the scheme should be extended to ships owned in the Oversea Dominions and Colonies, subject to their joining one of the approved Associations, and next day the first reduction was made in the cargo rate, which was now fixed at 4 per cent. At this rate a considerable amount of business was done, and at the same time the influence of the scheme began to be felt on the open market, where quotations during the next two or three days dropped rapidly to 10, 8, 7, and 6 per cent.

On August 10th the State Insurance Office announced its willingness to insure cargoes on current voyages as from the first port of call, and a further increase of business resulted. The scheme was, however, still insufficiently attractive to the owners of coasters and to short sea traders, to whom the cost of hull insurance on a voyage basis was much greater than to the owners of ocean-going vessels. A meeting of short sea traders was accordingly held on the 10th to discuss the project of forming a separate association for the protection of their interests, but on the 13th a concession was made under the State Scheme which avoided the necessity for their receiving separate treatment. This concession took the form of issuing time policies on hulls affording cover for three months (ninety-one days) at a premium of $2\frac{1}{2}$ per cent., the same rate as was charged for a single round voyage. It was further provided that should a ship so insured be at sea on the expiration of the policy, she should be held covered at a *pro rata* premium until her arrival at a safe port and for thirty days after arrival.

The owners of sailing vessels, which were excluded from the original scheme, were also pressing for consideration. Nearly all sailing vessels engaged in foreign trade were entered in War Risks Associations of their own, and on August 14th the Government agreed to cover 60 per cent. of the value of vessels so entered, for current voyages only. No arrangement was made in respect of cargoes.

Meanwhile quotations on the open market for the insurance of steamer cargoes were steadily falling. On August 11th, 4 per cent., the equivalent of the State Flat Rate, was quoted for goods in vessels which had passed Gibraltar homeward bound, but, not having called at that port, were excluded from the extension of the

Government Scheme. In the coasting and short sea trades cargoes were now being insured by underwriters more cheaply than by the State Office, and goods in coasters bound from London to Scotland, on which 5 per cent. had at first been demanded, could now be covered for 2 per cent. By August 14th, cargoes to the Far East could be insured on the open market at 3 per cent., and goods shipped from United States Atlantic ports to the west coast of England at 2 per cent. On the 17th a further fall took place in the North Atlantic rates. The big liners were now resuming their regular sailings, and goods carried in these fast vessels could be covered at a special premium of 30s.

The arrival of the GOEBEN and BRESLAU at Constantinople, the Allied command of the entrance to the Adriatic and the watch established on the German liners in neutral ports greatly decreased the risk of loss, and the first news received of German activity tended to strengthen confidence in the safety of the routes rather than to shake it. Whatever were the motives for the release of captured steamers by the DRESDEN and KAISER WILHELM DER GROSSE, the action taken by these ships suggested limitations to the effectiveness of the campaign against commerce. In these circumstances the Advisory Committee, who were working in close co-operation with the Board of Trade, deemed it desirable to reduce the Flat Rate on cargoes, which was now higher than the majority of quotations on the open market. The rate was accordingly reduced, on August 18th, to 3 per cent., and this step was immediately followed by a corresponding fall in the premiums required by underwriters. Cargoes for the Far East could now be covered at 50s.; on the North Atlantic passage at 30s. or 35s., according to the class of vessel; on the Plate voyage at 1 per cent.; and in coasters at rates varying from 10s. to 20s.

The result of these reductions was greatly to increase the amount of business done on the open market. From the first the State Office refused to accept insurances not effected before the commencement of the voyage in question, and this of itself threw a certain amount of business into the underwriters' hands; but the activity of the market was now redoubled, and while the State Office continued to receive a preference for the longer and more dangerous voyages, cover for the North Atlantic or the short sea passages was generally provided by the underwriters. The result was that the State Office took the worst and the underwriters the best of the risks; but inasmuch as practically all seagoing vessels were now entered in one or other of the Clubs, the amount of business done on the open market involved no loss of control over the movement of cargoes. In these circumstances the Advisory Committee were content to reduce premiums gradually, so as to steady rates, while building up a solid reserve of premium income against the contingency of losses not hitherto announced or a possible increase in the weight of the attack.

The main object of the Government in undertaking to accept liability for war risks on British ships and goods was to maintain as far as possible the oversea trade of the country, and the success achieved in this respect was beyond expectation. For about a week after the declaration of war the freight markets were, indeed, generally paralysed. It was inevitable that this should be the case. Apart from the natural desire of shipowners to obtain further light on the situation before committing their vessels, the universal financial dislocation caused by the war was an obstacle to trade which it needed time to remove. The conditions which we have traced in North and South America and in the Far East were felt everywhere in a greater or less degree. A moratorium had been proclaimed in twenty different countries, banks and exchanges were closed, money and credit were difficult to obtain and the impossibility of financing shipments was a bar to sailings even in cases where vessels were willing to leave port.

Moreover, the war had necessitated a readjustment both of the export and the import trade, which necessarily took time to effect. The whole trade of the United Kingdom with Germany and Austria, together with that carried on in British bottoms between the Central Powers and the British Dominions or other foreign countries, was suddenly wiped out, and it soon became clear that all traffic with Turkey also, must, for the time being, be written off. With the Allied countries, commerce could still be maintained, subject to the risk of capture, but the German command of the entrance to the Baltic, and the uncertainty of the situation with regard to the Dardanelles, blocked the two chief channels of Russian trade, and the German invasion paralysed the commercial activities of France and Belgium. The railways of these countries were choked by military traffic, their whole energies were absorbed by the task of resistance, and their richest provinces were already occupied or threatened. Whether as markets or as sources of supply they were, for the moment, practically eliminated.

The proportion of the whole volume of British commerce thus brought to a standstill was serious. In the year 1913 Germany, Austria, and Turkey accounted for 12 per cent. in values of the foreign trade of the United Kingdom, France, Russia, and Belgium for 14·6 per cent. Thus rather more than a quarter of our commerce was directly affected by the war, and of this a great part was, for the duration of the war, irretrievably lost, imports and exports being about equally affected.[1] But the dislocation did not end here, for apart from the general financial upheaval which acted as so serious an impediment to the resumption of trade, many neutral countries were gravely affected by the interruption of their communications with the Central Powers, to whom they were in the habit of shipping a large proportion of their exports, and from whom they dervied a large proportion of their supplies.

These conditions involved, of course, a serious diminution in the volume of trade; but still more important was the redistribution of traffic which they rendered necessary. It was impossible to write off so large a proportion of our commerce without an effort to replace it. If our ships were not to lie idle, if our merchants were not to break, if our people were not to starve, it was essential that other sources of supply, other markets, other employment for the tonnage concerned should forthwith be found, and the way in which this was done reflected unbounded credit, not only on the effectiveness of naval protection and the foresight which had framed the State Insurance Scheme, but on the courage, resource, and energy of shipowners and merchants. In spite of all difficulties, both of readjustment and of transport, the volume of trade was maintained at a surprisingly high level, but the wide range of the dislocation rendered it inevitable that the revival should be gradual.

From the difficulties caused by mobilisation Great Britain was as yet comparatively free, though recruiting

---

[1] Report of Joint Committee of the Chamber of Shipping and Liverpool Steamship Owners' Association, July 1917, vol. ii. p. 103.

for the New Armies was proceeding briskly; but the dislocation inseparable from a state of war had already begun to make itself felt at the ports. The Dover-Calais service was suspended from August 4th to August 26th in consequence of the despatch of the Expeditionary Force to the Continent, and the majority of the South Coast ports were similarly affected. Southampton, indeed, was practically closed to commercial traffic for the period of the war, and the lines using that busy centre were compelled to rearrange their services. The bases for cruiser squadrons and flotillas established at many ports, especially on the East Coast, restricted the dock and quay space available for commercial traffic, and at the same time a sudden strain was thrown on the resources of the harbours by the arrival of vessels diverted from their voyages to German, Baltic, or Scandinavian ports. Thanks to the knowledge possessed by its members as to the capacity of the various harbours, the Admiralty Committee on the Diversion of Shipping was able to carry out its work with a minimum of dislocation; but the demands made upon the available port facilities by naval and military requirements could not be other than a handicap to trade. All round the coasts, moreover, the requirements of port defence and of the Examination Service interfered to some extent with the loading and discharge of merchantmen; and although the Admiralty were careful to interfere as little as possible with lights and buoys, they were compelled to impose certain restrictions on the navigation of coastal waters.

A further interference with the course of the export trade was the issue by the British Government of a long list of prohibited exports, comprising not only warlike stores but a large number of articles to which the circumstances of the war gave a peculiar importance. Among the articles shipment of which was absolutely prohibited were foodstuffs and fodder, copper, lead, nickel, zinc, petroleum, cotton waste, saltpetre, and hempen cloth. It was also forbidden to export to any part of Europe except France, Russia (other than Baltic ports), Spain and Portugal, large steam coal, manufactured fuel, aluminium, manganese, tin, india-rubber, nitrates, carts, rope and harness, railway material, and other articles.[1]

[1] See lists of August 3rd, 5th, and 10th in *Manual of Emergency Legislation*, pp. 160, 162, 164, 165. The exception of Spain and Portugal was rendered possible by the fact that these countries had no communication with Germany or Austria otherwise than by sea.

In practice these restrictions did not, with one exception, hamper trade very seriously, since so long as sufficient stocks were available for home requirements, there was no difficulty in obtaining a licence for "prohibited" shipments, on affording satisfactory proof that they were intended for Allied or neutral consumers and that there was no danger of their reaching the enemy. In the case of large steam coal, however, licences were at first very sparingly granted, and even on shipments to the countries excluded from the general prohibition, shippers were required to give a bond in three times the value of the cargo, to be forfeited if the coal was not delivered at the port of destination named in the Bill of Lading. These restrictions, coupled with the difficulty of arranging payments and the general financial and commercial dislocation, reduced the coal export trade, for the time being, to a state of complete paralysis, and many thousand tons of tramp shipping were thrown out of employment.

In consequence of this multiplicity of adverse conditions the demand for cargo space, both in the commerce of the United Kingdom and in the general carrying trade of the world, dwindled to very small proportions during the first few weeks of the war. The majority of the fixed services were suspended or reduced, many existing charters were cancelled, and business on the freight markets was at a standstill. Indeed, the losses of shipowners, through the enforced idleness of their vessels, would have been very heavy but for the employment afforded by the war itself. A Royal Proclamation of August 3rd empowered the Government to requisition all ships required for naval or military purposes, and within a very short time several hundred thousand tons of shipping were taken up as transports, armed merchant cruisers, and colliers, or for other auxiliary services. Owing to the urgency of the need, there was no time to fix rates or sign charters, and the terms were left to be fixed by the Admiralty Transport Arbitration Board, on which shipping and trading interests were strongly represented.[1] The owners, as a class, were not only anxious from patriotic motives to comply with the requirements of the Admiralty, but glad to find any employment which would avert the necessity of laying up their ships. At the same time this wholesale requisitioning was not without its adverse effects upon commerce. The

[1] See *Manual of Emergency Legislation*, September 1914, pp. 386-95.

withdrawal of the largest and fastest liners put the shipping companies to considerable inconvenience through the necessity for continual rearrangement of their services, and the requisitioning of laden or partly laden freighters was a serious matter for the shippers of the goods on board. In many cases it was impossible to discharge these goods before the ship was put into her new employment, and in other cases great difficulty was found in keeping track of goods hastily transferred from requisitioned ships to substituted vessels.

Nevertheless, severely as trade was handicapped, it showed an amazing elasticity and power of recovery. The efforts of the Government to alleviate the financial situation and steady the money market met with early and striking success; the safe arrival of ships at sea and the evidence of naval activity given by the bringing in of German prizes restored confidence in the safety of the sea routes; and the effect of the State Insurance Scheme kept shipping on the move. The War Risks Associations themselves, fully realising the object with which the scheme had been adopted, issued an appeal to their members to do everything in their power to keep their ships running,[1] and as the exchanges began to settle down and the effects of the first shock died away, inquiries for tonnage became more numerous and the prospect of an early return to something approaching normal conditions more definite. The Admiralty Statement issued on August 12th marked the end of the period of acute paralysis. In that statement the Admiralty referred to the efforts which were being made to protect shipping and run down the few German cruisers known to be at sea. They continued:

" Although the principal difficulty was at the beginning, all British ships are arriving with the greatest regularity. With every day that passes the British Admiralty's control of the trade routes, including especially the Atlantic trade routes, becomes stronger. Traders with Great Britain of all nations should, therefore, continue confidently and boldly to send their ships and cargoes to sea in British or neutral ships, and British ships are themselves now plying on the Atlantic routes with almost the same certainty as in times of peace."[2]

[1] *Liverpool and London War Risks Insurance Association, Report for the year ending February* 19*th*, 1919, p. 7.
[2] *Times*, 13 August, 1914.

190 BEGINNINGS OF TRADE RECOVERY

This statement had a great effect in stimulating the demand for shipping. The Baltic became active, and fixtures were also recorded on the Liverpool, Cardiff, Newcastle, and Glasgow exchanges. North America and India were chartering for wheat and Java for sugar. The regular liners were gradually resuming their sailings, and though the demand for tramp tonnage was still very restricted, there were signs of an all-round revival.

This revival was greatly assisted by the reduction of the cargo rate to 3 per cent. on August 18th, and by the introduction of time policies on hulls. The latter concession was the more valuable to owners of tramp tonnage because it was shortly followed by a modification of the restrictions on the export of coal which enabled shipments to be made to Italy and Scandinavia. On August 20th the embargo was altogether removed,[1] and though a certain amount of supervision was still exercised by the Customs authorities over shipments of the better qualities of steam coal, the wider choice of markets now open and the lifting of the triple bond restored normal conditions sufficiently for business to be resumed at the coal ports. The Scandinavian States hastened to replenish their stocks, and the Italian Government placed very large orders for fuel for the State Railways, to lift which they took up a large number of British as well as neutral vessels.

From the tramp shipowner's point of view the resumption of coal shipments was all-important; but coal, although the bulkiest, was not the most valuable of our staple exports. In this respect it ranked well below the products of the Lancashire cotton mills, and here, unfortunately, the position was much less reassuring. The cotton trade had been heavily hit by the moratorium and the widespread financial crisis. The prohibition of code telegrams was also felt as a serious impediment to business, but the gravest feature of the situation was the fact that the stoppage of the Continental mills left the cotton industry of the world with an enormous surplus of raw cotton which necessitated artificial manipulations of price and produced a general feeling of uncertainty as to the future. Shippers of yarn were heavily hit by the loss of the German market, which normally accounted for a third of the total export. The chief markets for piece goods—India and China—

[1] *Manual of Emergency Legislation*, p. 168.

were in a state of grave financial disturbance, and unable to place orders.

Moreover, the export of cotton goods, which is a liner trade, was seriously interfered with by the interruption of the fixed services due to requisitioning and to the uncertainties of the first two or three weeks of war. When the regular sailings were resumed a new obstacle was found in the heavy surcharges announced by the principal liner companies on all routes. These surcharges, which were imposed both on freight and passenger rates, varied from 20 to 50 per cent. on the rates in force in July.[1] So great an increase in the cost of transport, added to the cost of insuring goods against war risks, naturally tended to hamper trade, and cotton exporters especially remonstrated strongly against the action taken by the companies. Shipowners, in reply, pointed out that their working expenses had greatly increased. Insurance against war risks on hulls, at $2\frac{1}{2}$ per cent. for the round voyage, might work out to anything up to £250 per 1,000 tons of cargo capacity. Ordinary marine insurance rates were higher than before the war; the cost of bunkering had greatly increased; receipts from passenger traffic had almost vanished; and the running of the lines was seriously interfered with by requisitioning and by delays in port, due to congestion arising from naval and military requirements.

Despite these heavy advances in liner rates, the trade position steadily improved during the latter part of August. The complete control established by the fleet in the North Atlantic, the revival of the coal export and of the imports of iron and fruit from Spain and the Mediterranean, the activity of mine-sweepers in clearing the North Sea passages, all contributed to restore the equilibrium. By the end of the month practically all the long distance liner services were running, with or without modifications due to altered circumstances and slackened demand. In many cases the ships were obliged to sail with part cargoes only,

[1] By August 15th the following surcharges had been announced by the leading lines and companies in the several trades:

India	. . . .	20 per cent on *ante-bellum* rates.
Australia	. . . .	25 ,, ,, ,, ,, ,,
South and East Africa	.	$33\frac{1}{3}$,, ,, ,, ,,
West Africa	. .	50 ,, ,, ,, ,,
Plate and Brazil	. .	50 ,, ,, ,, ,,
Pacific	. . .	$33\frac{1}{3}$–50 ,, ,, ,, ,,
Mediterranean	. .	50 ,, ,, ,, ,,

owing to the financial difficulties of shippers, and some of the services had to be run, temporarily, at a loss. Nevertheless the machinery of distribution was re-established, and there was no longer any doubt as to the ability and willingness of the mercantile marine to carry cargoes when the goods were available. On many of the short sea passages also renewed activity was visible, and the Continental trade generally, though still much restricted, showed signs of recovery. The coasting trade in the North Sea was hampered by the mine peril and by the restriction of port facilities due to naval requirements, but the West Coast and Irish services had suffered little or no interruption, and were now running on normal lines.

The loss of the *Hyades* and *City of Winchester* [1] had no appreciable effect upon the confidence of traders or shipowners. The contrast between the comparative immunity enjoyed by shipping and the heavy percentage of losses which had been anticipated was so marked that isolated captures could well be disregarded, especially in view of the assistance given by the State Insurance Scheme. The sinking of the *Nyanga* and *Kaipara*, at so important and vulnerable a focal point as the neighbourhood of the Canaries, might have had more serious consequences had not the announcement of the losses been preceded by news of the destruction of the KAISER WILHELM DER GROSSE.[2] As it was, these losses failed either to destroy the confidence of shipping or seriously to affect the insurance market. Although the rates on the open market showed some tendency to harden, underwriters' quotations for the longer voyages seldom exceeded the State Flat Rate of 8 per cent., and North Atlantic premiums varied from 45s. to 85s. Outward cargoes to the Mediterranean and certain ports in Northern Europe could be covered at 2 per cent., but 5 per cent. was asked on homeward cargoes from the White Sea.

On September 1st a considerable step forward was taken by the State Office. Nearly £600,000 had already been received in cargo premiums, and it was now clear that, thanks to the activity of the navy, the estimate of

---

[1] Published in late edition of the *Times*, August 23rd.

[2] The destruction of the raider was announced in the House of Commons on August 27th. The sinking of the two steamers was first reported by the German Consul at Tenerife on August 26th (see p. 81, *supra*) and was published, after investigation, on August 29th.

losses formed before the war was very unlikely to be approached. It was, of course, possible that ships might have been captured whose loss had not yet been reported,[1] and it was equally possible that one or more of the raiders known to be at sea might yet work serious mischief. On the other hand, there was considerable evidence that the rate of 3 per cent. was handicapping the recovery of trade. It was accordingly again reduced to 2 per cent. At the same time the premium on hulls was lowered from $1\frac{1}{4}$ to 1 per cent.; 2 per cent. for the round voyage or for a three months' time policy. A further concession was made by allowing a ballast voyage not exceeding 800 miles in length to count as part of the subsequent laden voyage. The effect of this was important. Hitherto the owners of a tramp steamer chartered to load cargo at any port other than that at which she was lying at the time, or her port of arrival, if she was at sea, were obliged to take out a time policy in order to cover the vessel while proceeding to the loading port. It was now possible for them, in most cases, to cover the whole risk by a single trip policy at 1 per cent.

The immediate result of the reduction in the cargo rate was that underwriters' quotations fell to 2 per cent. for the Plate and Eastern voyages. The North Atlantic rate dropped to 35s. and 30s., and then to 25s. Cargoes for Mediterranean and short sea voyages could be covered at 25s. and 30s., and coastwise traffic at 1 per cent. At the same time, important reductions in the liner surcharges followed on the reduction in hull premiums. The South and West African surcharges had already been lowered to 25 per cent. They were now further reduced to 20. The Plate and Brazilian lines and those engaged in the Mediterranean trade reduced their 50 per cent. surcharges by one half. The Australian and New Zealand lines met the situation by reducing their freights on fine goods by 2s. 6d., and on other classes by 1s. 3d. per ton.

These concessions were a distinct encouragement to shippers, and the export trade as a whole showed marked signs of recovery, with a corresponding improvement in the position of the liner companies, but the outlook for

---

[1] This was, in fact, the case. Such ships were the *Bowes Castle*, captured by the KARLSRUHE, August 18th; *Holmwood*, captured by the DRESDEN, August 26th; *Strathroy*, captured by the KARLSRUHE, August 31st.

owners of tramp shipping was still uncertain. Very heavy shipments of grain were now coming from North America, and the removal of the coal embargo had been followed, as we have seen, by a great expansion in exports ; but neither at the American nor the Welsh ports was the demand for shipping equal to the supply. At the beginning of the war a great number of vessels had crowded to these ports in the hope of finding the employment denied them elsewhere, and the cargo space available was far in excess of shippers' requirements. At North American ports an even larger proportion of the grain than usual was now being shipped on the liners, and anything like a full return to normal conditions in the coal trade was forbidden by the elimination of the German and Russian markets and the diminished purchasing power of many neutral countries.[1] The result was a glut of tonnage both on the Welsh and American freight markets, and at the same time the demand from other quarters was greatly restricted by the suspension of Baltic and Black Sea traffic and the delay in shipping the Argentine maize harvest. Not only were charters difficult to obtain, but freights fell to such an extent that many owners began to lay up their vessels on arrival as an alternative to running them at a loss.[2]

Owing to the large number of vessels following the longer routes which had begun their homeward passage prior to the outbreak of war, the tonnage of British ships entered with cargoes during August was only 13·3 per cent. less than in the same month of 1913, but foreign entrances were down by 44·6 per cent. in consequence of the withdrawal of the German liners and the all-round diminution in Continental traffic, and the clearances of all nationalities fell from 5,729,000 to 2,460,000 tons, a decrease of 57 per cent. These reductions were due in great part to the paralysis of the first few days of war; and the re-establishment of the fixed services, the resumption of chartering even on a limited scale, and the continued fall in insurance rates gave promise of better things in the immediate future. It was, at any rate,

---

[1] In August 1913, Germany took 798,000 tons and Russia 770,000, nearly 26 per cent. of the total export.

[2] For example, a steamer was chartered on August 28th to carry wheat from Galveston to the United Kingdom at 2s. 3d. per quarter, a drop of 1s. 3d., or nearly 36 per cent. on the rates prevailing in July (*Morning Post*, 29 August, 1914).

clear that the fear of capture was not an appreciable factor in the situation, and that when cargoes were more readily available there would be no difficulty in finding ships to lift them.

Meanwhile, if the protection provided by the navy and the encouragement to shipping given by the State Insurance Scheme had not sufficed to keep trade afoot on normal lines, in face of the obstacles presented by economic conditions, they had at least enabled the supply of food and essential raw materials to be well maintained. The total decrease in imports as compared with August 1913 was 29·7 per cent. in estimated weights and 24·3 per cent. in values. The essential food supplies, however, were coming forward freely enough. The imports of wheat and flour were actually larger, and those of meat little smaller than in the corresponding month of the previous year. In dairy produce there was a diminution, chiefly due to the loss of the Russian supplies. Fruit and vegetables also dropped, but the greatest decrease was naturally in sugar, which had now to be brought from countries at a much greater distance. Taking foodstuffs as a whole, the war had, as yet, showed no signs of producing any real shortage, and only in the case of shipments from the Baltic and Black Sea did naval conditions play any prominent part in the restriction of supplies.

In the class of raw materials, iron ore showed a decrease of nearly 27 per cent. on August 1913, but the trade was rapidly reviving. Copper and tin ores, coming chiefly by the longer routes, were as yet unaffected. Cotton, wool, and petroleum were up to the normal standard. By far the greatest decrease was in timber and pitprops, in respect of which the closing of the Baltic made itself severely felt.

Exports, on the other hand, were down in value by 45 and re-exports by 46 per cent. But in view of the many obstacles to the revival of the export trade, the fact that goods to the value of £28,600,000 were shipped from the United Kingdom during the first month of hostilities was in itself sufficient evidence of the capacity of the British merchant marine to maintain its activities, and of the elasticity with which finance and commerce were recovering from the shock of war. Including bullion and specie, the cargoes entered or cleared during the month amounted to over £88,000,000, a figure by the side of which the losses sustained shrink into insignificance.

The coasting trade, which had been invested with additional importance by the heavy demands made upon the railways for military transport, showed a much smaller shrinkage than ocean traffic. Its security had never been threatened, except to a limited extent by mines on the East Coast, and the total tonnage arrived and departed coastwise during August, including the intercourse between Great Britain and Ireland, was nearly five and a half millions, a decrease of only 9 per cent. as compared with August of the previous year.

No great change in the situation took place in the first few days of September. The loss of the *Holmwood* had only a very temporary and local effect, and the chief interference with trade arose from the rearrangement of North Sea services due to mine losses, which threatened to strain the resources of the Northern and West Coast ports. Chartering was still dull, and many tramps were laid up on arrival, but the prospects of reviving trade in South America, India, and the Far East held out hopes of recovery which were not seriously clouded by any threat presented by the German cruisers known to be at sea.

In the other Allied countries the position continued to be less satisfactory. Although a determined effort was being made, by the help of British and neutral shipping, to develop the trade of Archangel, the limited resources of the port were taxed to their utmost by military requirements, and even with the assistance of the transhipment route through Sweden, Russian commerce could only be carried on on a very limited scale. Belgium was already more than half overrun by the invaders, and though Antwerp and the coast still held out, the prostration of the country rendered commercial activity impossible. Communication with the United Kingdom was maintained by the Belgian packets as well as by British steamers, but the traffic was mostly confined to the carriage of refugees and the import of articles needed for military use. Of ordinary oversea trade there was little or none; and after the first week of the war the important service of the Red Star line ceased to run from Antwerp. By the beginning of September, however, arrangements were made to resume its sailings from English ports.

France was more favourably situated, inasmuch as she retained the free use of her ports and large tracts of her territory remained free from the invader. Yet she was terribly crippled. The German advance, which at one time threatened the Channel and even the Atlantic ports, was stopped at the Marne on September 6th, and by the 12th the tide of invasion had been rolled back to the line of the Aisne. But even so, the districts richest in coal and ores remained in the enemy's hands, and all commercial activities were suspended in the departments through which the storm had passed.

In normal years, Germany, Belgium, Russia, and Austria supplied about a quarter of the goods imported by France for home consumption, and took about 30 per cent. of the French products exported. All these countries were now, wholly or in great part, removed from the commercial arena, and the dislocation of trade must have been very great even if the frontiers had been held throughout. Moreover, while the strength of the French fleet in the Mediterranean and the security provided by the British squadrons in the Atlantic and distant seas enabled French vessels to sail in safety, the Northern ports, and subsequently St. Nazaire, were choked with the tonnage required for the landing of the British Expeditionary Force, its reinforcements and supplies, and Marseilles was seriously congested by the transport to France of the Algerian Army Corps and other troops from abroad. In these circumstances trade was necessarily restricted, but it was essential that the maritime communications should be maintained as far as possible, and on August 14th the French Government followed the lead of the British by agreeing to underwrite 80 per cent. of the war risks on French steamers. This step did much to encourage French shipping, which had hitherto been very nervous, and the Compagnie Générale Transatlantique at once set about reorganising its services to North, Central and South America, and the French Antilles. In view of the large proportion of French commerce carried in foreign bottoms, the encouragement of French shipping did not, however, fully meet the situation, and the benefits of the insurance scheme were, from the first, extended to cargoes carried under Allied or neutral flags.

Despite this encouragement the entrances of French ships during August decreased by 44 and the clearances by 60 per cent., and the arrivals and departures of foreign vessels showed a still larger falling off. Indeed, the French and foreign tonnage which cleared with cargoes for ports outside Europe (other than those in French Colonies) amounted to only 140,000 tons, as compared with 770,000 in August 1913. The imports decreased in value by 54 per cent. and the exports by 49 per cent. Nor did the early weeks of September show many signs of a revival.[1]

Nevertheless, the essential condition of recovery for French as for British commerce was already secured : the sea routes were open. The Central Powers, on the other hand, were faced by a complete severance of their maritime communications. By the middle of September the losses of German and Austrian shipping amounted to some 300 steamers and over 50 sailing vessels sunk, captured at sea, or seized or detained in Allied ports ; but the importance of these losses was completely overshadowed by the impossibility of making effective use of those which remained. Over 670 steamers, aggregating roughly 2,750,000 tons, and 72 sailing vessels were sheltering in neutral harbours, closely watched by Allied cruisers. Between thirty and forty steamers lay in German colonial ports, where their capture was not likely long to be delayed. Some thirty more were leading a precarious existence as supply ships to the German cruisers at sea, and about fifteen steamers and forty sailing vessels were still on their way to port, on uncompleted voyages. The remainder, with the exception of a few German steamers employed in the Baltic, lay as idle in their home ports as the ships which had taken refuge under neutral flags. Unless and until the German and Austrian fleets should prove themselves capable of contesting the command of the sea, there was no possibility either of the ships laid up abroad returning or of those in home ports putting to sea.[2]

To a limited extent it might be possible to replace the services of vessels under the national flags by the employment of neutral shipping, and at the end of August and the

[1] *Documents Statistiques sur le Commerce de la France*, Paris. These figures are, of course, exclusive of vessels employed in the transport of troops.
[2] A large number of the German ships laid up in neutral ports carried goods belonging to British consignees, and great difficulty was experienced in obtaining possession of the cargoes. Licence was given by the Board of Trade to pay freight and other charges in spite of the prohibition against trading with the enemy, but in most cases every obstacle was placed by the German companies in the way of obtaining delivery of the goods, and comparatively few of the ships had even begun to discharge their cargoes by the end of the year.

beginning of September determined efforts were made in Germany to find some means of carrying on the foreign trade. A "Sea Insurance Company," the capital of which was mainly provided by the State, was formed to insure against war risks cargoes carried either in German or in neutral vessels, and a special bank was created at Hamburg to support the export houses. Owing to the dangers of North Sea navigation and the high premiums demanded, great difficulty was experienced in attracting shipping to German ports, but as soon as the railways could be partially cleared of military traffic, the necessary steps were taken to resume both the import and export trade with Scandinavia, Holland, and Italy; and it was hoped that in addition to the special commerce with those countries, communications might be opened through their ports with oversea markets and sources of supply. Negotiations were entered into for services to be run from Gothenburg, Rotterdam, and Genoa for the carriage of German goods, and widespread efforts were made to enlist neutral merchants in the building up of a large transhipment traffic.

It was not, however, easy to improvise new channels of trade at a moment's notice. The export of foodstuffs and of many other commodities had been prohibited; and although the War Committee of Trade and Industry held out hopes that licences would be granted on an extensive scale, there was, in the disturbed condition of the Empire, little surplus production available for shipment. Moreover, the effects of the financial crisis caused by the war, and particularly the loss of the London money market, were severe and far reaching. Remittances from abroad ceased altogether, and few shippers could find the security demanded by the new export bank. Speaking in general terms, the shipment of German products to oversea markets at the middle of September was practically at a standstill, and with Russia, France, and Belgium enemies, this meant the stoppage of the greater part of the export trade.[1]

With regard to imports, the first fact which had to be faced was the loss of some 45 per cent. of the normal total

---

[1] Austria-Hungary and neutral countries having direct rail or river communication with Germany took, normally, about a third of the total exports. But even from this a certain proportion must be deducted for goods sent by sea.

which came from countries with which Germany was now at war. Of the remaining 55 per cent., such part as was drawn from oversea sources could be procured only by means of neutral shipping, and the employment of neutral vessels in the carriage of cargoes either direct to German ports or to neutral ports for subsequent transhipment to Germany was limited, so far as contraband goods were concerned, by the activities of the British patrols. Although foodstuffs and other commodities in the " Conditional " class could only be interfered with when there was reasonable presumption of enemy destination, many suspicious cargoes were brought in and were pre-empted by the British Government; and the Order in Council of August 20th, extending the doctrine of continuous voyage to conditional contraband, considerably extended the powers of the patrols in the restriction of illicit traffic.

Moreover, the merchants and shipowners of countries adjoining the German frontiers were not unanimously desirous of lending the shield of their neutrality to the restoration of German commerce. The high prices and freights to be obtained were, no doubt, a strong temptation. On the other hand, these countries were threatened by a failure in their own supplies, due to the withdrawal of the German services and the temporary dislocation of British shipping. Most of them were dependent upon the United Kingdom for the supply of coal and other essential commodities, and all had a strong interest in standing well with the Power which controlled the seas. On the outbreak of war both the Dutch and Danish Governments prohibited the export of grain from their territories, and during the first few weeks of war the list of exports prohibited from Holland was extended to include rice, cotton, liquid fuel, maize, hides, and several other articles. The transit of foodstuffs consigned " to order " or on through bills of lading, *via* the Rhine, was also materially checked by an arrangement made between the British and Dutch Governments, whereby cargoes to be discharged at Dutch ports were exempted from treatment as conditional contraband, on a specific declaration that they were intended for consumption in Holland itself.

Thus, though imports were still reaching Germany through Holland and Denmark (where German interests were strongly represented in shipping and commercial circles), this traffic was as yet on a very restricted scale

OBSTACLES TO TRANSIT TRADE

and was frowned upon rather than encouraged by the Governments concerned. Swedish shipments were confined to iron ore, and Norway had practically no trade whatever with the Central Powers. Indeed, Norwegian underwriters went so far as to refuse to insure shipments of herrings to Germany under existing contracts. In Italy and Switzerland German agents were busily endeavouring to arrange for the development of a transit trade, but no great progress in this direction had yet been made.

The effect of these conditions on German industries was very marked. Iron and steel manufacturers were heavily hit by the cutting off of ore supplies from France, Belgium, Spain, and Northern Africa, and the diminution of the import from Sweden, and by the stoppage of coal shipments from Great Britain. Many foundries and furnaces were temporarily shut down and a large number of workmen were thrown out of employment. The cessation of timber imports was a severe blow to the northern and eastern States, where no large local forests were available, and unemployment in the woodworkers' trades assumed alarming proportions. The jute mills estimated their stocks as only sufficient for two or, at the most, three months' consumption. The leather trade was seriously threatened by the loss of all foreign supplies of hides and skins. Petrol and benzol showed signs of running short, and the stocks of wool and cotton were rapidly diminishing, without any immediate prospect of replenishment.

As regards foodstuffs, the problem before the German Government was accentuated from the start by a panic rise in prices and by attempts to corner supplies. These influences were met by a complicated series of regulations and orders beginning so early as August 1st, the general effect of which was rather to increase than to alleviate the distress. So far as the loss of oversea supplies was concerned, there was no immediate fear of an actual food shortage, though the available supplies of wheat were seriously curtailed. On the other hand, there was reason to fear that maize, barley, and oil-cake for fodder purposes would shortly become almost unprocurable, owing either to the belligerency of the producing countries or to the severance of the maritime communications; and it was evident that any serious diminution in the supplies of these feeding stuffs must inevitably be reflected in a shortage of meat and dairy produce.

In Austria-Hungary also, food prices rose rapidly from the beginning of the war, but this was due rather to a bad harvest and other internal influences than to the stoppage of foreign trade, as the Dual Monarchy was practically self-sufficing as regards foodstuffs. Almost all industries, however, were heavily hit by the cessation of imports. In spite of the liberty enjoyed by neutral shipowners to carry cotton to the enemy countries, Austrian as well as German importers found so many difficulties in regard to freight, insurance, and finance, that little or no advantage of this liberty could, for the time being, be taken. Many other industries were similarly affected, and both the export and import trades, as in Germany, were reduced to a small fraction of the usual total.[1]

Compared with this paralysis the course of British trade might almost be termed normal, and no stronger contrast could be found than that between the enforced idleness of German and Austrian merchantmen and the immunity with which Allied shipping was plying in every sea. This immunity was, however, about to be disturbed in a manner which might have had serious consequences had it developed at an earlier period, before the confidence of shipowners and shippers in the safety of the trade routes had been restored and confirmed by experience of successful activity.

[1] The Austro-Hungarian imports and exports for August as compared with the same month in the previous year, were as follows:

	Imports Kr.		Exports Kr.
August 1914 .	. 94,700,000	August 1914 .	. 30,400,000
August 1913 .	. 268,600,000	August 1913 .	. 215,000,000

No statistics of foreign trade were published in Germany after the declaration of war.

CHAPTER XI

THE "EMDEN" AT WORK [1]

IT was in the Indian Ocean that the first heavy blow fell on British shipping. We have seen that, while Admiral von Spee considered a movement through the Malay Archipelago by his whole force to be unduly perilous, he had detached the EMDEN (Captain von Müller) for the purpose of attacking trade on the Oriental Route. Both the ship and her commander were well suited to the task. The EMDEN—completed in 1909—was a fine specimen of the modern light cruiser. She could make 22 knots at sea, and her bunkers carried sufficient coal for a cruise of 5,200 miles at 10 knots. Captain von Müller was in many respects an ideal cruiser commander, combining dash with prudence, fertile in resources, and eminently capable of playing a lone hand.

After leaving Pagan Island on August 13th, he made his way south through unfrequented waters, stopping to coal from his tender, the *Markomannia*, off Anguar, on August 19th. On August 22nd he entered the Molucca Pass and on the 25th he coaled again from the *Markomannia* off Timor. As he was anxious to reach his destination unreported, he made no attempt on the sugar ships from Surabaya, Samarang, and Batavia, but after traversing the Flores Sea, passed through the Bali Strait and followed the southern coast of Java and the south-western coast of Sumatra, well out from shore so as to avoid observation by coasting steamers.[2]

Captain von Müller was fortunate in the time of his arrival in Dutch East Indian waters. Had he been a few days later at the Bali Strait his career might have been terminated at its outset by one of Admiral Jerram's ships

---

[1] See Maps 4 and 7.
[2] The EMDEN appears to have met and communicated with the *Princess Alice* (see p. 125, *supra*) about August 20th and with the GEIER in the Flores Sea.

engaged in the search of the Java Seas.[1] Even as it was he had a very close call. On September 4th the EMDEN came inshore near Simalur Island, to coal, and in so doing she only escaped by some twenty-four hours an encounter with the HAMPSHIRE, which was then searching the coast and coming down in the opposite direction.

From Simalur the EMDEN steamed straight across the entrance to the Bay of Bengal, towards the Indian coast, with the *Markomannia* still in company. Neither vessel showed any flag, and all lights were extinguished at nightfall. By 10 a.m. on September 10th the cruiser and her tender had arrived on the Colombo-Calcutta track in about 11° N., where they met the Greek steamer *Pontoporos*, bound from Calcutta to Karachi with 6,000 tons of Bengal coal. As the cargo was regarded by the Germans as contraband, Captain von Müller considered the ship to be good prize, and she was accordingly commandeered as an additional collier and compelled to accompany her captor with a prize crew on board.[2]

The EMDEN was now on one of the richest cruising grounds in the world, and she was singularly favoured in the time of her arrival. It will be remembered that, towards the end of August, the urgent necessity for escorting the Indian Expeditionary Force had drawn the whole of Admiral Peirse's command into the Arabian Sea, while Admiral Jerram's sphere of activity did not yet extend west of Singapore. Thus the Bay of Bengal tracks and the great focal point of shipping at Colombo were uncovered at the very time when the trade of India was showing signs of renewed activity. On the other hand the inactivity of the KÖNIGSBERG and the rapidity with which the German liners in Eastern waters had been accounted for went far to remove the only sources of danger which had yet been ascertained. A spirit of somewhat exaggerated optimism had replaced the original uneasiness which had led to the holding up of shipping by the Indian authorities, and this optimism was so far shared by the masters of merchantmen that they were apt to regard the statement that a certain track was reasonably safe as overriding the general Admiralty instructions as to dispersal and reduction of lights.

As the EMDEN steamed up the track towards Calcutta she met two steamers, the *Indus* and *Lovat*, which had

[1] See p. 142, *supra*.
[2] She was subsequently condemned by the German Prize Court.

left the Sandheads on September 7th and 9th respectively, for Bombay, where they were to embark troops for Europe. The *Indus* was captured on the 10th, very soon after the *Pontoporos*, the *Lovat* at about 4 p.m. on the 11th. In each case the crew were transferred to the *Markomannia* and the prize sunk by gunfire within some three hours of the capture. Both vessels were steaming straight down the usual track, and in neither case had the master the slightest suspicion that the approaching cruiser was an enemy until the German flag was hoisted and he was signalled to stop. No attempt, therefore, was made by the *Indus* to use the wireless apparatus with which she was equipped, and the master of the *Lovat* actually took the EMDEN, *Markomannia*, and *Pontoporos* to be part of a British convoy which he was to join.

Having disposed of the *Lovat*, the EMDEN continued on her course for Calcutta, and about an hour before midnight on the 11th saw the lights of a steamer a little ahead. She promptly fired a gun across the bows of the stranger, which at once lay to and proved to be the *Kabinga*, of the Ellerman and Bucknall Line, which had left the Sandheads on the evening of the 11th for New York. Like the *Indus* she was equipped with wireless apparatus, but had no chance to use it. As the master had his wife and child on board, Captain von Müller consented to postpone the transfer of the crew till daylight, and as he ascertained next morning that the whole of the cargo was neutral owned, the *Kabinga* was not sunk, but was required to follow the movements of her captor.

The next day (September 13th) brought two more prizes. The lights of the *Killin* were seen between midnight and 1 a.m. and the *Diplomat* was captured a little after noon. Like the EMDEN's previous victims, both ships were entirely unsuspicious of danger. The *Killin*, two days out from the Sandheads, carried 5,000 tons of Bengal coal for Colombo. The *Diplomat*, which had left the Hoogly on the evening of the 12th, was a richer prize. She was a fine steamer of 7,615 tons, only two years old, and carried 7,000 tons of general cargo for London. The vessel herself was insured for £81,000, and the estimated value of the cargo, which included 30,000 chests of tea, was over a quarter of a million. By singular ill-fortune it was in this ship and the *City of Winchester* that the finest growths of the Indian tea-crop had been shipped, and the loss of these special cargoes was the more unfortunate as the general quality of the crop was moderate.

As Captain von Müller had already a large reserve of coal in the *Pontoporos*, in addition to the stock carried by the *Markomannia*, he did not consider it worth while to put a prize crew on board the *Killin*, especially as Bengal coal is not very suitable for cruiser work. Both the *Killin* and *Diplomat* were accordingly sunk, the crews being transferred to the *Kabinga*, which was retained as a prison ship.

At about 4.30 p.m., just before the *Diplomat* was sunk, a third steamer arrived on the scene. This proved to be an Italian vessel, the *Loredano*, bound to Calcutta from Trieste, and her master, Captain Giacopolo, was requested by Captain von Müller to take the crews of the captured steamers on board. This he declined to do, on the ground that he had not sufficient provisions for so many people, and the *Loredano* was accordingly allowed to go on her way. It would have been wiser from the German point of view if she had been detained. Captain Giacopolo's sympathies were, at least, not anti-British, and as a seaman his feelings were outraged by the destruction or threatened destruction of so many fine vessels. He accordingly made every effort to warn shipping of the EMDEN's presence, but as his steamer was not equipped with wireless, his powers in this respect were limited. Fortunately, on September 14th, when very near the mouth of the Hoogly, he met the outward bound Ellerman liner *City of Rangoon*, which carried a Marconi outfit. To this ship he conveyed the news by signal. She immediately turned back and sent a wireless message to Calcutta giving warning of the danger.

This warning, received at 2 p.m. on the 14th, came with the shock of complete surprise. No thought of danger was entertained at that port, and several vessels were about to sail. It was clear that prompt action was necessary in order to minimise the possible loss, and the Port Officer at once gave orders to stop all sailings. He also telegraphed the news to Chittagong and other ports in the district, and to the Intelligence Officer at Colombo. At the same time the pilot vessel was withdrawn from the mouth of the Hoogly and the navigation lights in the channels were ordered to be extinguished. At Colombo, the Intelligence Officer gave instructions for all vessels in the Bay of Bengal trade to be detained in port and for the

Colombo-Singapore Route to be closed. Thus the immediate effect of the EMDEN's appearance was to paralyse all shipping movements east of Colombo, in the northern portion of the Indian Ocean.

Mortifying and inconvenient as was this stoppage of trade, it had the effect of considerably diminishing the actual loss sustained, for the EMDEN was now very close to Calcutta, and but for the timely warning given by Captain Giacopolo, she would in all probability have captured several steamers which had just left or were about to leave the port, including the *City of Rangoon* herself, a fine new ship with a cargo valued at £600,000. Thanks to the prompt action taken all these vessels were saved, but at about 6 p.m. on the 14th the *Trabboch*, on her way from Negapatam to Calcutta in ballast, was captured thirty-three miles from False Point, for which headland the EMDEN was steering, in order to coal under its lee.

The weather was now very stormy, and it was not until 10.30 p.m. that the crew of the *Trabboch* had been transferred to the *Kabinga* and the prize sunk. By this time Captain von Müller had decided to shift his ground, for his wireless operators had taken in the instructions given by the Port Officer, and he was aware that his presence was known. He accordingly transferred all his prisoners to the *Kabinga*, and released her with a word of warning as to the removal of the lights in the Hoogly. The prisoners had been treated throughout with marked courtesy and consideration, and the parting was friendly on both sides.

Prompt as had been the action taken at Calcutta, it had been impossible to warn all vessels which had already left port, and about a quarter of an hour before midnight on the 14th, shortly after the *Kabinga* parted company, the EMDEN captured the *Clan Matheson*, on her way to Calcutta. Having been informed at Madras that the Bay of Bengal was absolutely safe, her master had not obscured his lights, and though she was equipped with wireless, she had no chance to use it, as her look-out did not see the EMDEN till the cruiser was alongside and had fired across her bows.[1]

After sinking the *Clan Matheson* the EMDEN remained for some twenty-four hours in the neighbourhood of

---

[1] The *Clan Matheson* had discharged a large part of her cargo at Colombo and Madras, but about 2,800 tons of general goods for Calcutta remained on board.

the Hoogly, but no further prizes were made, and on September 16th, after coaling from the *Pontoporos* near False Point, she ran across the Bay towards the Burmese coast. All sailings from Rangoon had been stopped on receipt of news of the EMDEN's presence in the Bay, and the only vessel met was the Norwegian steamer *Dovre*, which was boarded on the evening of the 18th, twenty-four miles south-east of the entrance to Rangoon River. By this steamer the crew of the *Clan Matheson* were brought into port on the morning of the 19th.

Meantime further details of the raid had reached Calcutta. The *City of Rangoon* arrived at the Sandheads at 4.45 p.m. on the 14th, and on the morning of the 15th wireless messages were received from the *Kabinga* to the effect that she was returning to Calcutta with the crews of five captured ships. The wireless apparatus of the *Kabinga* had been dismantled before her release, but the operator succeeded in restoring it by the aid of spare parts, which the Germans had failed to discover. Later in the day, the *Loredano* arrived at Calcutta, and on the 16th the *Kabinga* came into port and landed the crews of the *Indus, Lovat, Killin, Diplomat,* and *Trabboch,* as well as the chief engineer of the *Pontoporos,* who was British. Three days later came news from Rangoon of the capture of the *Clan Matheson,* bringing up the total loss of British ships to six steamers aggregating 29,477 tons.

The urgent necessity of re-establishing the maritime communications of India was evident; but the East Indies Squadron was wholly absorbed by escort duties in the Arabian Sea, and it became necessary to call upon the resources of the China Squadron. This could be done the more readily as the whereabouts of Admiral von Spee had been revealed on September 14th by his appearance off Apia, and Admiral Jerram accordingly detached from Singapore the HAMPSHIRE, YARMOUTH, and the Japanese light cruiser CHIKUMA, which had been placed at his disposal. With these ships Captain Henry W. Grant of the HAMPSHIRE was to undertake the immediate hunt for the raider, while the Admiral himself made arrangements for cutting her off if she should return to the Dutch East Indies to coal.

Captain Grant's task was a difficult one. The waters of the Bay of Bengal are broad, and by the time his ships were fairly in the Bay, the information brought by the *Kabinga* was two or three days old. That given by the people in the *Dovre* had not yet been received. He accordingly arranged to sweep for the EMDEN on what seemed to be the most promising lines, and also to search the Nicobar and Andaman Islands, to which she might possibly go for the purpose of coaling. On the 19th he heard that she had been seen off the entrance to Rangoon River on the previous evening, and altered his dispositions with the object of cutting her off, but the information had reached him too late for this move to be successful.

Meanwhile, the KÖNIGSBERG, also, had emerged from the obscurity in which her movements had been shrouded since the capture of the *City of Winchester*. On September 20th she suddenly appeared off Zanzibar, where the PEGASUS was lying at anchor to repair boilers. A short action resulted in the destruction of the PEGASUS, after which the KÖNIGSBERG again disappeared. An energetic hunt for her was at once organised by the Admiralty, but no further sign of activity followed her success, and trade remained practically unaffected.

The KÖNIGSBERG was probably hampered in her movements by the necessity of keeping in touch with German East Africa. The EMDEN was under no such restrictions, and during the next few weeks her incessant activity offered a marked contrast to the comparative sterility of the KÖNIGSBERG'S career. As nothing further had been heard of the raider since she stopped the *Dovre*, the Bay of Bengal trade routes were reopened as from 8 a.m. on September 22nd, but the respite was very brief. The Germans had intercepted wireless messages, from which Captain von Müller gathered that the entrance to the Bay was likely to be patrolled by British cruisers, and he resolved on a bold stroke to escape them. After coaling under way from the *Markomannia* in the Gulf of Martaban, he turned west on the morning of the 19th and steered right across the Bay to Madras, where he arrived at 9.20 p.m. on the 22nd. Approaching the shore closely under cover of darkness, he opened fire on the tanks of the Burmah Oil Company, standing near the harbour. The British India Steam Navigation Company's steamer *Chupra* was struck by a couple of shells while the EMDEN was getting the range, and slight damage was also caused in the town, but the principal result of the bombardment was the loss of some 425,000 gallons of oil in two of the tanks, which caught fire and burned furiously until consumed. Three other tanks were also struck, but one of them was empty, and the shell which struck another tank burst outside. The remaining tank contained liquid fuel, and, though a shell penetrated only two feet above the surface of the oil, no fire was caused by the explosion. Five people were killed and about a dozen wounded in the *Chupra* and ashore.

On the batteries opening fire in reply, the EMDEN made off in a southerly direction, and at 6 a.m. next morning she was sighted off Cuddalore. Eight hours later she was reported off Pondicheri, steering north-east; but this was a false course, adopted for purposes of deception. As soon as she was out of sight from land she again turned her head to the south and ran out of the Bay. With her usual good luck she steered clear of Captain Grant's cruisers, and her future movements remained quite uncertain.

As a result of this new evidence of the EMDEN's activity, the Bay of Bengal tracks were once more declared unsafe as from 2 a.m. on September 23rd. The prolonged interruption of trade was already producing serious consequences. The congestion at Calcutta had shown some signs of relief due to the release of vessels hitherto employed for transport purposes, but the cancellation of sailings and the cessation of arrivals from other ports aggravated the worst features of the situation. Enormous stocks of jute and tea were accumulating in the warehouses, with little prospect of early shipment, and these delays were the more unfortunate as tea retained for long periods in the moist climate of Calcutta is liable to deteriorate in value. The tanneries of Cawnpore and Agra had important contracts on hand for hides and leather needed for the manufacture of army boots and saddlery in the United Kingdom, and were being urged to expedite the shipments of these goods, but this too was now impossible. The thrice-weekly mail service between Calcutta and Rangoon was suspended, and Rangoon Harbour itself was full of shipping awaiting an opportunity to leave.

Still more serious, because more lasting, was the effect of the bombardment of Madras on the native population, by whom the limitations of the EMDEN's powers for mischief were very imperfectly understood. The alarm extended far beyond the port itself, and the majority of native moneylenders in East Coast towns packed up in wild panic and fled to the hills with all the money they could collect. As these men play an important part in the financing of commercial operations the effect of their withdrawal from business was to derange the whole course of trade, and the commerce of Southern India was plunged suddenly back into the chaos from which it had been gradually emerging.

Grave as was the situation at ports on the Bay of Bengal, it was little better at Colombo, where east-bound shipping was beginning to choke the berths. At the same time the closing of the Singapore-Colombo track stopped the export of tin from the Straits and threatened to hold up the supplies of sugar from Java, which were now being ordered in greatly increased quantities to take the place of continental beet.

Shipping in the Arabian Sea, on the other hand, was as yet permitted to proceed, subject only to instructions communicated to the masters at Aden, Colombo, or Indian ports. These instructions included confidential information as to the movements of warships on escort duty, which would allow the masters to avail themselves so far as possible of the protection thus provided. Nevertheless, the EMDEN's exploits had created uneasiness in the freight markets, and though there was still some demand for tonnage from Bombay and Karachi, little forward business was done. Outward sailings from Great Britain, however, remained unaffected. The State Flat Rate of 2 per cent. was now in force, and despite the news of the EMDEN's raid, cargoes for Indian ports could still be covered on the open market at the same rate. Thanks to the improvement in trade conditions at the beginning of September, the demand for cotton goods had revived, and the outward-bound liners had no difficulty in obtaining cargoes.[1]

The shock to trade had thus been almost entirely local, but locally it had been severe, and worse was to follow. The blow struck in the Bay of Bengal was quickly followed by another delivered in Cingalese waters. Captain von Müller had resolved to strike at the great focal point off Colombo, and after leaving the Bay of Bengal he shaped his course round the south of Ceylon on the usual steamer track. He had only the *Markomannia* with him, for the *Pontoporos*, from which little coal had yet been taken,

---

[1] The exports of piece-goods to India during September amounted to 266,024,000 yards, valued at £2,997,000, an improvement of 40 per cent. on the August figures, and almost exactly equal to the movement in September 1913.

had been sent away to a rendezvous off Sumatra, as she was too slow to make an ideal tender.

As the EMDEN came round Point de Galle on the 25th she met the *King Lud*, from Alexandria for Calcutta, which had not called at Colombo, and was following the usual steamer track in entire ignorance of her danger.[1] After sinking the prize, Captain von Müller took his ship up the western coast of Ceylon. Under cover of the sudden tropical nightfall he passed so close to Colombo that at 6 p.m. the watchers in the EMDEN saw a steamer coming out of the harbour stand out against the rays of the searchlight. The steamer was showing the ordinary navigation lights, and by means of these the cruiser— herself in complete darkness—followed her until 11.35 p.m., when both vessels were about fifty miles from Colombo. The EMDEN then signalled by Morse lamp code for the chase to stop, but the merchantman kept on her way until 11.50, when her pursuer was within a quarter of a mile. She was then stopped and boarded, and proved to be the *Tymeric*, homeward bound from Samarang to Falmouth.

By about 3 a.m. on the 26th the *Tymeric* was sunk, and at one in the afternoon another ship, the *Gryfevale*, was captured on her way from Bombay to Calcutta, and was retained as a prison ship. The EMDEN then turned westward towards Minikoi, working across the tracks which lead from the Eight Degree and Nine Degree Channels to Colombo and Point de Galle. At 1 a.m. on September 27th she saw the lights of a steamer which proved to be the collier *Buresk*, outward bound for Hongkong. Six hours later the *Ribera*, from Alexandria for Java, was captured on the direct track through the Nine Degree Channel, and at 7 p.m. the *Foyle*, bound from Venice to Rangoon, was stopped as she came out of the Eight Degree Channel. Both the *Foyle* and *Ribera* were sunk and their crews transferred to the *Gryfevale*, but the *Buresk* was retained as a tender to the cruiser.

During all this time the movements of the raider remained entirely unknown, and in fact the Colombo-Singapore Route was reopened on the 27th, the very day on which the EMDEN's record of captures reached its highest point. Captain von Müller did not, however, consider it safe to remain longer on the cruising ground he had worked so effectively. The *Gryfevale* was

[1] The *King Lud* passed Perim on September 14th.

accordingly released at 10 p.m. on the 27th, and at 8 o'clock on the morning of the 29th she arrived at Colombo, where she landed the crews of the sunken vessels and the *Buresk*. Meanwhile, the EMDEN made off to the south, where her captain proposed to coal and overhaul her in unfrequented waters.

The five steamers whose loss was thus announced had an aggregate tonnage of 18,948. The *King Lud*, *Ribera*, and *Foyle* were in ballast, and the loss in these cases was that of the hull only. The *Tymeric*, on the other hand, carried a cargo of 4,600 tons of sugar, worth about £80,000. The *Buresk*, from the captor's point of view, was a still more valuable prize. She was under charter to the Admiralty, and her cargo consisted of 6,000 tons of the best Welsh steam coal, a supply which was the more welcome as the stock on board the *Markomannia* was now running low.[1]

All the ships captured on this raid were taken on or very near the usual tracks. In the case of the *Gryfevale*, the position was practically unavoidable. She had been detained at Bombay until September 22nd, in consequence of the EMDEN's appearance in the Bay of Bengal, and when released had been directed to call at Colombo or Point de Galle for further instructions before proceeding on her voyage eastward. On her passage down the coast the master observed every possible precaution, but at the point where she was captured the convergence of the tracks renders wide deviation impossible. The *Tymeric* was also unfortunate, as she was sighted immediately on coming out of harbour, but like the *Buresk*, she facilitated the operations of the raider by showing lights. The *Buresk*, *King Lud*, *Ribera*, and *Foyle* had left Egyptian ports before the news of the EMDEN's arrival in Indian waters had been received, and their masters were apparently void of all suspicion as to any possible danger on the route.

The possibilities of deviation in the confined area between the Maldives and Ceylon, are, of course, somewhat restricted. A very wide departure from the normal track can only be effected by altering course to the south immediately after passing Minikoi, or leaving Colombo, and either such a sweep to the south, or the use of the alternative routes through the Khardiva channel or the passages of

[1] The master destroyed his sealed orders and instructions before the boarding party came on board.

the Laccadives, must prolong the voyage by many hours, and involve the burning of extra coal. Such a course, therefore, was not likely to be followed in the absence of special and definite instructions; but even without resorting to so extensive a deviation some departure from the direct track is possible, and had it not been for the complete confidence felt in the safety of the route, it is probable that several of the vessels captured might have got through. Coming straight down the route, or within a few miles of it, their loss was almost inevitable. The many rumours which credited Captain von Müller with special information obtained from secret wireless stations on shore appear to have had no foundation in fact. He may have gleaned something from intercepted messages and captured newspapers, but operating where he did, he had no need of such information to enable him to effect captures. The EMDEN had a crow's-nest which gave a range of vision extending in clear weather to some thirty miles. With a look out stationed in this point of vantage, she zig-zagged on either side of the track to an extent of thirty miles, chasing all smoke seen on the horizon, and the simplicity of the method employed was amply justified by its success.

To whatever cause it was due, the loss was serious, and the news brought by the *Gryfevale* excited widespread alarm. A few hours after her arrival the CHIKUMA put into Colombo, and on learning the news she sailed without delay for the neighbourhood of Cape Cormorin, in order to protect the focal point. At the same time the trade routes both east and west of Colombo were declared unsafe for shipping, and the greater part of the seaborne trade of India was thus brought to a standstill. Captain Grant was then patrolling the Colombo-Singapore route in the HAMPSHIRE, but on hearing by wireless of the EMDEN's new raid, he turned back to Colombo. In view of the protection afforded by his cruisers the Bay of Bengal routes were reopened on the morning of October 1st; but Captain Grant judged it safer to close that from Colombo to Singapore until he had received fuller information. The ships which had sailed from Colombo were accordingly recalled. On October 2nd, however, after he had received further particulars as to the position of the captures, all the Bay of Bengal routes were declared open, and ships held up at the various ports were instructed that they might leave. The track between Bombay and Karachi was also declared reasonably safe, and later in the day the routes westward of Colombo were reopened.

By this time the congestion had assumed still graver proportions. With the exception of a few hours on September 22nd–23rd and October 1st, the trade routes in the Bay of Bengal had been officially closed from September 14th to October 2nd. Some vessels had left Calcutta at their own risk and others had cleared during the short periods of reopening; but no fewer than forty-one steamers were still laid up in the port at the beginning of October. The exports of Calcutta and Chittagong had fallen from 159 lakhs in the week ending September 12th, to 35 in that ending September 19th. In the next two weeks they rose to 128 and 138 lakhs respectively, but even the last mentioned figure was much below the normal, and the accumulation of stocks was becoming increasingly serious.

An even greater inconvenience than the holding back of steamers already loaded was the delay to those which had been chartered at other ports, and were coming round into the Bay of Bengal to load. Heavy contracts had been entered into for the supply of gunny bags and cloth to Australia, for September shipment, but the steamers originally chartered for this purpose had been requisitioned for transport purposes, and the substitutes which had been obtained were prevented by the closing of the routes from arriving in time to fulfil the contracts by the specified date. The result was that the Australian importers threatened to cancel the contracts, and the shippers were thus placed in a situation of great difficulty. At the request of the Jute Fabrics Shippers' Association, the Indian Government took up the matter with the Commonwealth authorities, and it was eventually agreed that the contracts should stand for October shipment, but the delay in delivery was a source of no little trouble to the Australian farmers, who required the bags for putting up the harvest.

At Rangoon, the suspension of traffic due to the closing of the routes was acutely felt. The trade of the port had suffered severely from financial dislocation, and this check to its recovery was a heavy blow. There was, therefore, a rush of ships to clear as soon as the prohibition of sailings was withdrawn, and the week ending October 3rd showed a smart recovery in the export figures. At Madras no improvement in the situation was yet visible. The panic caused by the bombardment had thoroughly disorganised business throughout Southern India, and even the coasting movements were on a greatly reduced scale. In Ceylon also the nervousness of native merchants brought about a diminution in the local trade; but this was a small matter in comparison with the condition of the port of Colombo, which had now reached an acute stage of congestion owing to the cutting short of voyages at that point. The harbour was crowded with shipping, and fifteen steamers which had been unable to secure berths were lying outside the breakwater. Bombay and Karachi were naturally less affected, as there had been no appreciable suspension of traffic. The exports of wheat during September were, indeed, below the average, for the previous year's harvest had been poor, but trade was not much hampered by the fear of capture.[1]

Taking the trade of India as a whole, the decrease in the total value of goods exported, as compared with the previous year, was 61·2 per cent., as against 44·2 per cent. in the previous month; but in considering these figures it must be borne in mind that many other factors, besides the EMDEN's activity, still combined to depress trade. The elimination of the continental markets, the prohibition of various exports, and the shortage of tonnage involved an even greater dislocation of commerce than the captures in the Bay of Bengal or in the neighbourhood of Minikoi.

In these circumstances the primary concern of the Admiralty was to encourage the movement of shipping. The experience of the two raids had convinced them that little additional risk would be run by keeping the routes always open, except when the raider was known to be in the immediate vicinity of a port. There was, in truth, no logical middle course between allowing trade to move freely at all times and closing all the routes until the EMDEN should have been permanently disposed of, for it was evident that the crews of captured ships were never sent in until she was about to shift her ground. To close the routes indefinitely would be to present Captain von

[1] Exports figures in lakhs of rupees:

Week ending.	Calcutta and Chittagong.	Bombay.	Karachi.	Madras.	Rangoon.
September 19th	35	39	30	—	9
,, 26th	128	58	9	—	1
October 3rd	138	34	33	1	26

Müller with a success beyond his wildest hopes. To keep them open appeared to involve no excessive risk. During the six days on which the EMDEN was operating in the Bay of Bengal, with all the advantage of surprise, sixteen British steamers bound to or from Calcutta had escaped capture, against seven which were taken. During the three days of her activity in the confined area between Minikoi and Colombo, two homeward- and five outward-bound vessels got through between the port and the open sea. Moreover, several of the captured vessels owed their fate to a neglect of precautions which had some excuse in the attitude of the local authorities, but was not likely now to be repeated.

Instructions were accordingly given to the local authorities that shipping should be encouraged to move freely, and that vessels should not be detained upon mere rumours of hostile activity. At the same time, the urgent necessity of avoiding the normal tracks, obscuring lights, and refraining from sending unnecessary wireless messages was impressed upon the masters of all vessels bound to or from Indian ports. For some little time complaints continued to be received that the movement of trade was hampered by the refusal of port authorities to sanction sailings, except at ship's risk, but within the first few days of October the resumption of traffic had become general.

At its worst the loss of tonnage and dislocation of trade was a small matter in comparison with the great volume of British commerce, and apart from the failure to locate the EMDEN, the naval situation in the Indian Ocean and the Far East at the end of September was satisfactory. The KÖNIGSBERG had completely disappeared from view since her destruction of the PEGASUS, and it had become fairly certain that she was unlikely to operate far from the East African coast, where she was being hunted by the CHATHAM, DARTMOUTH, and WEYMOUTH, all faster and more powerful than herself. In the Pacific Admiral von Spee had been again located on September 22nd, when the SCHARNHORST and GNEISENAU bombarded Papieté, the reduction of the German possessions was going forward systematically, and no activity on the part of the enemy ships still in hiding was reported.

Meanwhile, the watch on German vessels in ports of the Philippines and Dutch East Indies was continued by the sloops, destroyers, and armed merchant cruisers of Admiral Jerram's command, with excellent results. The interception of a wireless message to the *Tannenfels*, a Hansa liner of 5,841 tons, which had left Manila on September 1st with 6,000 tons of coal for German warships, led to her capture by the destroyer CHELMER, in the Basilan Strait, on September 14th. Next day, the *Rio Passig*, an American steamer which had been chartered by the Germans, was taken by another of the flotilla, with 4,000 tons of coal on board.[1] Several German steamers which still lay at Manila had loaded large cargoes of fuel, but the watch was too close to allow them to get away, and the *Elmshorn*, which put to sea on the night of September 27th, was forced to return to port immediately by the approach of the HIMALAYA.

A further strain was placed on Admiral Jerram's resources by the necessity of providing escort for a number of minor convoys, British and French, from Hongkong and Saigon, and for the escort of the Expeditionary Force for Europe, which was collecting in Australian ports. Nevertheless he was able to send the EMPRESS OF ASIA to reinforce Captain Grant, who was continuing the search for the EMDEN and covering the focal points off the south of Ceylon and at the entrance to the Malacca Strait.

Under the protection of the China Squadron and of the Australian and Japanese forces operating in the Pacific, shipping east of Singapore proceeded without interruption and with abundant confidence. The capture of the *Tymeric* led, indeed, to some anxiety with regard to other sugar ships from Java, especially as a considerable number of Germans were employed by the sugar shipping firms, and it was feared that they might communicate to the raider information with regard to sailings. The masters of these vessels were therefore advised by the Consul at Batavia to proceed through the Malacca Strait, rather than by the west coast of Sumatra, and to call at Singapore for information and advice; but with this exception, shipping east of Acheh Head was free from all official restraint. The confidence of shippers had been greatly increased by the accession of local force due to the intervention of Japan, and both British and Japanese steamers found cargoes readily available.

[1] The cargo was released by settlement at Hongkong.

In Japan itself, though many merchants were hard hit by the capture of vessels engaged in the Far Eastern trade, the general feeling was optimistic. The obstacle to commerce presented by high rates for war risks had been overcome early in September by the adoption of a Government Insurance Scheme, and thus encouraged, Japanese shipping speedily became active. The effects of the early financial disturbance had not yet wholly passed away, and exports were still restricted by the lack of demand from Europe, but the Australian traffic was now brisk both ways, and Japanese tramp tonnage found plenty of employment in the local commerce of the China Seas and the carriage of rice from Saigon to France. With the German liners in Eastern waters laid up in port, and many French and British vessels withdrawn from commercial to naval or military use, there was every prospect that the supply of shipping would shortly become inadequate to the reviving demand, and Japanese shipowners could look forward with confidence to a rich harvest.

In the Middle East business conditions were still unsettled, but the worst of the financial crisis was now past, and the reopening of the trade routes was followed by a great expansion of the export trade. At Calcutta and Chittagong the totals for the weeks ending October 10th and 17th were in advance of anything yet attained since the outbreak of war. The improvement at Rangoon was well sustained, and even from Madras heavy shipments were recorded.[1] At the same time chartering for future cargoes went forward briskly. Business at Karachi was somewhat restricted by the high prices asked by Indian wheat shippers as compared with those ruling in the United States; but at Calcutta and other ports, available cargo space was eagerly sought for, and shippers were obliged to pay heavily in order to secure October loadings.

This expansion in the demand for tonnage brought into still clearer relief the shortage which had become manifest during the previous month. The tonnage cleared from

[1] Exports in lakhs of rupees:

Week ending.	Calcutta and Chittagong.	Bombay.	Karachi.	Madras.	Rangoon.
October 10th	190	35	37	18	12
,, 17th	156	81	12	26	44

the United Kingdom for India during September was nearly twice as great as in August, and though well below the figure for 1913, showed very little diminution as compared with 1912. Nevertheless the total for the two first months of the war showed a decrease of 72,000 tons on the previous year, and this decrease in outward sailings, combined with the laying up of the German and Austrian liners and the requisitioning of British ships for transport and naval purposes in the ports of India, Australia, and the Far East, reduced the supply of available shipping to a dangerous extent.

The shortage of tonnage, in its turn, emphasised the importance of preventing further depredations by the EMDEN. With so large a quantity of goods awaiting shipment, and only a limited amount of cargo space available, it was essential that ships should be turned round quickly in Indian ports, and that there should be no delays due to closure of routes or lack of confidence in their safety. For the moment there was no difficulty on this score. Captain Grant's cruisers were known to be actively engaged in searching for the raider; and though the fact that she had not yet been located was a natural cause of anxiety, it was not enough to keep British merchantmen in port. Yet the anxiety remained, and until Captain von Müller's career should be brought to a definite close, the situation in the Middle East could not be regarded as wholly satisfactory.

CHAPTER XII

COMMERCE AND COMMERCE DESTROYERS ON THE SOUTH
AMERICAN ROUTE [1]

WHILE the EMDEN was harrying commerce in the Bay of
Bengal and off Colombo, the great volume of British trade
throughout the world was proceeding without molestation
or alarm. Only on the South American Route did the
German cruisers occasionally make their presence felt.
It will be remembered that the beginning of September
was marked by a notable recovery in the volume of
traffic, especially at the Plate, and that at the same time
the British forces on the east coast of South America were
strengthened and placed under the orders of Admiral
Cradock. By September 17th the Admiral had concentrated the bulk of his force off Monte Video, and this
visible assurance of protection for the homeward-bound
grain and meat ships went far to revive the confidence
which had been so badly shaken by the DRESDEN'S
successive captures of the *Hyades* and *Holmwood*.

It was, naturally enough, upon the menace presented
by the DRESDEN that the attention both of the Admiralty
and of shipping circles was concentrated at the moment,
for her last capture had been made so near the Plate
estuary as to create legitimate anxiety for the safety of
this most important and vulnerable point; but we have
already seen that Captain Lüdecke's scheme of operations
excluded any idea of a sustained attack upon shipping
in the South Atlantic, and that after dismissing the
Katherine Park, he held his course southwards. Hitherto
he had, generally speaking, kept well outside the trade
routes, but from the Plate estuary to the Straits the main
steamer tracks lie at a considerable distance from the shore,
and so, as he was still bent upon concealing his movements,
he now hugged the coast, touching at Gill Bay, Argentina,
to coal, on August 30th. Even the concentration of

[1] See Maps 5 and 8.

British shipping by the narrow gut of the Straits of Magellan failed to tempt him into activity, and he preferred the less frequented route round the Horn to the passage of the Straits. On September 5th, when Admiral Cradock was off Pernambuco, the DRESDEN arrived at Orange Bay, a desolate inlet on the south-western coast of Tierra del Fuego, and here at last Captain Lüdecke considered himself safe from pursuit. He accordingly proceeded to overhaul his ship after her long voyage, and replenish her bunkers from the *Baden*, which was still in company.

Whatever were the motives of Captain Lüdecke's abandonment of the South Atlantic, he left behind him, unassailed, a volume of traffic far greater than he was likely to encounter in the Pacific. While Admiral Cradock's arrival would have rendered an attack on the Plate trade at or near the entrance to the estuary extremely risky, the prospects of seriously disturbing the flow of food ships from Argentine and Uruguayan ports and from New Zealand might well have tempted an enterprising officer. Whether through over-caution or through the nature of Captain Lüdecke's instructions, the chance was now lost; nevertheless the course of shipping from Plate and Brazilian ports was by no means immune from danger. The KARLSRUHE, as we have seen, was already at work in the neighbourhood of Cape San Roque, and both the KRONPRINZ WILHELM and CAP TRAFALGAR were at large in the South Atlantic.

Of none of these ships had any authentic intelligence been received by the middle of September. Of the KARLSRUHE it was known only that she had sunk the *Bowes Castle* off the northern coast of Brazil on August 18th, and the whereabouts of the KRONPRINZ WILHELM was equally uncertain. Indeed it was not yet known that she was in the South Atlantic. After her capture of the *Indian Prince* on September 4th, she took her prize away from the steamer tracks in order to transfer her coal and stores, and in the course of this process the ships worked gradually southward into unfrequented waters. By September 9th, when the *Indian Prince* was finally sunk, they were about 700 miles from the Brazilian coast and some 300 miles east of Trinidada.

It is possible that at this time the KRONPRINZ WILHELM intended to make for this island, which appears to have been regarded as a sort of head-quarters for German raiders

ANOTHER RAIDER DESTROYED

in the South Atlantic. Uninhabited and unproductive, it lies far from any steamer track, forming a convenient rendezvous for ships desiring to avoid observation. Under its lee the Germans had collected three colliers: the *Pontos*, a Hamburg-Amerika steamer which put out from Monte Video on August 7th; the *Eleonore Woermann*, which had crossed over from the African coast, and an American steamer, the *Berwind*, which had been chartered by the Hamburg-Amerika Company for the purpose of conveying coal and provisions to the German cruisers. It will be remembered that the DRESDEN had coaled here on her way down the coast, and had the KAISER WILHELM DER GROSSE succeeded in leaving Rio de Oro before the HIGHFLYER arrived, it is not unlikely that she would have come to Trinidada as her first rendezvous in South American waters, bringing with her the *Bethania* with her remaining coal supplies.[1]

Since the DRESDEN'S visit, the base had, in fact, been used only by the CAP TRAFALGAR. The big Hamburg-Süd-Amerika liner had been singularly unsuccessful in her operations as a commerce destroyer. Every time she approached the trade routes she was frightened away from them by hearing the wireless calls of British cruisers, and she had not a single prize to her credit. Her one achievement was to have remained entirely unlocated. Indeed, as we have seen, Admiral Cradock expected to meet her so far north as the St. Paul's Rocks. The British Admiral was not, however, blind to the advantages possessed by Trinidada as a possible base for the enemy's cruisers, and when he decided to move south in pursuit of the DRESDEN, he ordered the armed Cunarder CARMANIA (Captain Noel Grant, R.N.) to search the island on her way down.

On September 14th, the CARMANIA arrived at Trinidada and found the CAP TRAFALGAR and two other steamers lying off the island. The raider had, in fact, been at her base for about a week, either coaling or awaiting a consort. On the CARMANIA'S approach the German vessels made off in different directions, but after a short time the CAP TRAFALGAR turned and headed for her opponent. A smart action of some eighty minutes' duration ensued, which ended in the sinking of the German, whose surviving crew were picked up by the *Eleonore Woermann*,

[1] For her intention to cross over to South America, see p. 83, *supra*.

which then made off for Buenos Aires. The CARMANIA, pierced by seventy-nine shells and seriously afire, was in no condition to pursue.

Captain Grant's successful action not only freed British trade in the South Atlantic from a formidable menace, but broke up once for all the German base at Trinidada and forbade any idea of using it as a centre of concerted operations. The *Berwind* arrived at Rio de Janeiro on September 18th, and subsequently reverted to legitimate trade. The *Eleonore Woermann* landed the survivors of the CAP TRAFALGAR at Buenos Aires on September 24th, and remained at that port for many weeks. The *Pontos* put into Santa Catherina on October 9th. Neither the KRONPRINZ WILHELM nor any German supply ship subsequently ventured to make use of the island.

When Admiral Cradock received news (on September 20th) of the success which had attended his arrangements for a search of Trinidada, he was about to leave the Plate estuary. After taking in fresh water and provisions and coaling his ships outside territorial waters, he sailed from Monte Video on September 21st, with the GOOD HOPE, MONMOUTH, GLASGOW, and OTRANTO, intending to sweep for the DRESDEN as far as the Straits, and then send on the GLASGOW and MONMOUTH to the west coast, where German steamers were reported to be moving. The CANOPUS was ordered up to the Plate to act as guardship at the focal point, and the CORNWALL, BRISTOL, and MACEDONIA remained to patrol the trade routes off the Brazilian coast.

Meanwhile, the appearance of the SCHARNHORST and GNEISENAU at Apia [1] had emphasised the possibility that Admiral von Spee might cross over to the American coast, but almost immediately after Admiral Cradock's departure from the Plate intelligence was received which showed that the German squadron was still in the Western Pacific, and that, whatever might be their ultimate intentions, there was no immediate probability of their arrival in South American waters.

It will be remembered that following its fruitless visit to Apia, the German Pacific squadron had again turned eastward. After obtaining some fresh provisions at the Society Islands, they arrived, on September 22nd, off Tahiti. There they found, in Papieté harbour, the French

[1] See Map 1.

gunboat ZÉLÉE with a recently captured prize, the German steamship *Walküre*.[1] After a short bombardment in which both the ZÉLÉE and *Walküre* were sunk[2] and considerable damage was done in the town, the Germans steamed away in an easterly direction, and the squadron was once more lost to sight.

The positive results of this first achievement of Admiral von Spee's powerful force were small. The trade of the Society Islands, in which British shipping predominates, was temporarily disturbed, but this was a comparatively trifling matter. Nevertheless, the incident came as a welcome relief to the monotony of the cruise. It also contributed to increase the mystery of the German Admiral's destination, and excited a short-lived alarm lest he should turn back and repeat his performance at ports in Samoa, Fiji, or New Zealand.

On the other hand, the definite location of the German Pacific squadron at Papieté on September 22nd, enabled Admiral Cradock to turn his whole attention to the DRESDEN, and was sufficient guarantee of the safety, for the time being, of any ships detached to the West Coast. On September 25th, however, as he was making his way down from the Plate, he met the P.S.N. liner *Ortega*, and from her he obtained information which decided him to carry on and search the Straits with his whole force before sending on the GLASGOW and MONMOUTH into Chilean waters.

The DRESDEN had remained at Orange Bay until September 16th, when she quitted her anchorage and, still accompanied by the *Baden*, commenced her voyage up the Chilean coast. On the 18th, when rather to the north of the western entrance to the Straits, she fell in with the *Ortega*, and immediately gave chase, firing a round of blank as a warning to the liner to heave to. The *Ortega*, in addition to her valuable cargo, had taken 300 French reservists on board at Valparaiso, and her capture would have been a notable success for the German cruiser; but this disaster was happily averted by the courage and resource of her master, Captain Kinneir, who made for the narrow and uncharted channel known as the Nelson Strait, through which the Germans declined to follow him.

[1] 3,836 tons. Oceana Rhederei A. G. Captured at Makatea, outward bound from Wellington.
[2] The *Walküre* was subsequently raised.

With Captain Kinneir's report to encourage him, Admiral Cradock arrived at Punta Arenas on September 28th. Here he was informed by the British Consul that the Germans were believed to be using Orange Bay as a base, and on the 30th his ships closed in on the bay, where he hoped to surprise, not only the DRESDEN but the LEIPZIG and NÜRNBERG, of whom nothing had been heard for some weeks.[1] To the bitter disappointment of the whole force, however, the bay was empty, and later in the day the wireless operators picked up a message from the Peruvian to the Chilean authorities, stating that two German cruisers had been seen off the southern coast of Peru on the 29th. Admiral Cradock accordingly sent on the GLASGOW, MONMOUTH, and OTRANTO to the West Coast, while he himself in the GOOD HOPE, after a second search of Orange Bay, went back to the Falklands to coal.

Disappointing as was the result of the search, it proved, at least, that the DRESDEN was no longer to be feared by shipping on the East Coast. This fact and the destruction of the CAP TRAFALGAR were the more important, inasmuch as the recovery of trade at Plate ports, which set in at the beginning of September, was now fully developed. Heavy purchases of meat by the Allied Governments ensured satisfactory cargoes to the liners, and now that the financial conditions had improved and confidence in the safety of the routes was re-established, there was no longer any impediment to the movement of the maize harvest. By the end of the month the greater part of the available tonnage had been fixed, and there was even some fear that the glut might be changed into a shortage, owing to the decreased arrivals from Great Britain and the departure in ballast from the Plate of a number of steamers attracted by the high freights offered on other routes, especially in the Far East. In consequence of these conditions the competition for the remaining tonnage was brisk, and shipowners had no difficulty in securing remunerative charters.[2]

This renewed activity in the movement of the staple exports reacted favourably on the import trade of Argentina and Uruguay, and led to a notable increase in the number of ships cleared from British ports with cargoes

---

[1] The NÜRNBERG was not in company with the big cruisers at Papieté, having been left behind to guard the supply ships.

[2] *Lloyd's List*, 31 October and 2 November, 1914 (Buenos Aires Reports, September 16th and 25th, 1914).

for those countries; but Brazilian commerce was still hampered by the slow movement of the coffee crop owing to the closing of the German market and the withdrawal of German shipping. The Royal Mail service was now, however, running, and as the Booth line's sailings from northern ports had never been interfered with by any of the hostile cruisers in the Atlantic, the rubber export continued on approximately normal lines.

Taking the three East Coast countries, Brazil, Argentina, and Uruguay together, the clearances from the United Kingdom during September showed an increase of nearly 70 per cent. on the August figures. The volume of homeward-bound shipping is more difficult to estimate, owing to the varying length of passages represented by the tonnage entered during any particular month; but taking as a rough basis for comparison the tonnage entered in September and October respectively, the increase during the latter month works out at 54 per cent. for all vessels, or 64 per cent. for British ships.[1]

With the DRESDEN driven into the Pacific and the KAISER WILHELM DER GROSSE and CAP TRAFALGAR disposed of, the only enemies which remained to threaten this reviving trade were the KARLSRUHE and KRONPRINZ WILHELM. Of both these ships definite news was received during the last days of September. On the 24th, the Hamburg-Amerika liner *Prussia*, which had sailed from Rio on the 5th, put into Santos, and there landed half the crew of the *Indian Prince*. Next day the *Ebernburg*, of the Hansa line, which had accompanied the *Prussia* from Rio, returned to that port with the remainder of

[1] Net tonnage of vessels entered and cleared with cargoes at ports in the United Kingdom from and to Brazil, Uruguay and Argentina:

	British.		Total.	
	Net tons.	Increase or decrease on previous month.	Net tons.	Increase or decrease on previous month.
Entered :				
August	197,467	—	217,519	—
September	103,793	− 47·4	124,802	− 42·6
October	170,231	+ 64·0	192,718	+ 54·4
Cleared :				
July	317,247	—	399,470	—
August	127,252	− 59·9	147,468	− 63·3
September	213,822	+ 68·0	250,353	+ 69·8

the crew. From the report made by the master of the *Indian Prince* it transpired that between September 4th, when his ship was captured, and September 17th, when the prisoners were transferred from the KRONPRINZ WILHELM to the supply ships, no other vessel had fallen a victim to the raider. In these circumstances the news had little effect on shipping, nor was the course of trade disturbed when the Italian steamer *Ascaro* arrived at St. Vincent, Cape Verde, on September 28th, and reported that she had been boarded by the KARLSRUHE on the 22nd between the St. Paul Rocks and Fernando Noronha. Two or three steamers bound for South American ports were already some days overdue, and it was evident that their non-arrival might be connected with the operations of the German cruisers, but in the absence of more definite proofs of hostile activity shipping was not to be restrained now that the demand for tonnage had revived.

It was, in fact, rather to the Pacific than to the Atlantic that attention was directed at the end of September and the beginning of October. The report that two German cruisers had been sighted off the Peruvian coast on September 29th was incorrect, but it was not without foundation. The NÜRNBERG, as we have seen, was with Admiral von Spee's flag, but the LEIPZIG and DRESDEN, though they were not together, were both in South American Pacific waters.

After the unsuccessful chase of the *Ortega*, the DRESDEN pursued her course up the Chilean coast, keeping well inshore until she arrived at the latitude of Valdivia. On her way she coaled from the *Baden* at St. Quentin Bay in the Gulf of Peñas, an unfrequented harbour on the desolate coast of Southern Chile. She subsequently cruised for some days in the neighbourhood of Coronel and Valdivia, but without meeting any British ships. By this time her presence had become known, and a number of ships were held up in consequence; but sailings were quickly resumed at the desire of the Admiralty, who considered that if ships obeyed the advice given them, the risk of capture was small, except when a hostile cruiser was in the immediate neighbourhood of the port.

Whatever risk there may have been was speedily removed, for on September 80th, while Admiral Cradock was searching Orange Bay, the DRESDEN suddenly turned her head to the north-west and struck out towards Mas-a-fuera. Thus she never approached the Peruvian coast, and the intercepted message of September 30th was, in reality, founded solely on the movements of the LEIPZIG, which had once more come into sight after a long period of obscurity.

After sailing from San Francisco on August 18th, the LEIPZIG went to the Gulf of California, where she remained in hiding for the next few weeks, engaged in the organisation of supplies and making no further attempt to interfere with British shipping. On September 8th she coaled at Guaymas from the German steamer *Marie* and from the trucks of the Sonora Railway Company, and on the following day proceeded south, accompanied by the *Marie*.

In the small hours of September 11th the cruiser was steaming down the track between San Francisco and Panama, when she encountered the *Elsinore*, a new tank steamer of 6,542 tons, owned by the Bear Creek Oil & Shipping Company, Ltd., Liverpool, and insured for £75,000. The *Elsinore* was bound from Corinto to San Luis Obispo, California, in ballast. Her master had received the Admiralty directions in August from the Consul at San Francisco, and he was accordingly proceeding with reduced lights, but he had little apprehension of immediate danger and had struck straight across the entrance to the Gulf of California, instead of keeping to territorial waters as far as Cape Corrientes on the Mexican coast. Even so he might have escaped unobserved had the look-out been able to distinguish the LEIPZIG in time for the course to be altered, but blinding rain squalls rendered it impossible to make out objects at a short distance from the ship, and at 2.30 a.m., when the *Elsinore* was seventy-three miles south-west of Cape Corrientes, she came suddenly under the glare of the cruiser's searchlight. At such close quarters any attempt to escape was hopeless, and as soon as the *Marie* came up the crew of the tanker were transferred to her, and the prize herself sunk by gunfire.[1]

As the *Elsinore* had still the greater part of her voyage to perform when she was captured, some little time elapsed before her loss could be suspected; but in the meantime valuable information as to the LEIPZIG's movements had been received.

It will be remembered that Captain Powlett sailed from Esquimalt in the NEWCASTLE on September 3rd. On

[1] See Map 6c.

September 17th he arrived at Santa Rosalia, at the entrance to the Gulf, after carrying out a very thorough search of the Californian coast and the waters of the Gulf itself. He had received information of the LEIPZIG's coaling at Guaymas and had satisfied himself that the German cruiser, after spending a considerable time in and about the Gulf, had probably quitted his station altogether. He inclined to the belief that she had gone south to the Galapagos Islands or Callao, with a view to joining the NÜRNBERG, of whom nothing had been heard since she left Honolulu on September 2nd, in an attack on the unprotected shipping from Chilean and Peruvian ports. In this case, however, she would have too long a start to justify him in quitting his station in pursuit, particularly as there was always a possibility that the NÜRNBERG might appear on the northern trade routes. He accordingly turned back for Esquimalt, to cover the North Pacific terminals, searching the coast again on his way. During his southward cruise he had established a look-out and intelligence system, by which he was assured of early information if the LEIPZIG should return to her old cruising ground.

Captain Powlett's forecast of the LEIPZIG's immediate movements was remarkably correct. After sinking the *Elsinore*, the raider continued to steam south, with the *Marie* in company. At this period, Captain Hann appears to have been more anxious to conceal his movements than to effect captures, and the course followed lay well outside the ordinary track of steamers plying between Panama and South American ports. The *Marie* had taken out papers for Callao, and the master of the *Elsinore* was told that he and his crew would be landed at that port; but on September 17th the cruiser and her attendant arrived at the Galapagos Islands, a desolate group some 600 miles from the coast of Ecuador, and here the prisoners were put ashore on the 21st, after the LEIPZIG had coaled from the *Marie*. Captain Hann had made up his mind to attempt a surprise attack on British shipping off the Ecuadorian and Peruvian coasts, and was therefore anxious to interpose the longest possible delay before news of his movements could be received. This remote group of islands, far removed from the track of shipping, presented itself as an ideal place of detention for his purpose, and leaving an officer in charge of the prisoners he stood over to the coast, with the *Marie* in company. By the morning of the 25th he had arrived at the entrance to the Gulf of Guayaquil.

In spite of the secrecy in which the movements of the LEIPZIG had been shrouded, her arrival was not altogether unexpected, owing to the appreciation of the position received from Captain Powlett, and instructions to detain British shipping until the situation should be cleared up were sent to all consular officers in Peru on the evening of September 22nd, through the Vice-Consul at Callao. There was then lying at Eten the British s.s. *Bankfields*, of 3,763 tons, owned by the Bank Shipping Company, Liverpool. She had just loaded a cargo consisting of 5,950 tons of sugar and 9 tons of copper ore, valued at £120,000. The shippers of a large part of the cargo were a German firm, and as the LEIPZIG was undoubtedly in communication with German agents ashore about this time, it is perhaps not astonishing that the telegram to the Vice-Consul at Eten, instructing him to detain shipping, was delayed in delivery. In fact, it did not reach him until 2 p.m. on the 24th, ten hours after the *Bankfields* had put to sea for Holyhead *via* Panama. It was, however, just in time to save the *Guatemala* of the Pacific Steam Navigation Company's coastal service, which arrived shortly after receipt of the telegram.

The master of the *Bankfields*, being in ignorance of any immediate danger, steered straight out across the Gulf of Guayaquil to join the Panama track, and at 8 a.m. on September 25th, when about thirteen miles from the track, he sighted the LEIPZIG, by whom he was stopped. At 8.55 a boarding party came off from the cruiser and the *Bankfields* was then compelled to follow the LEIPZIG until 3.20 p.m., when, the crew having been previously transferred to the *Marie*, the sea-connections of the prize were opened and five shots were fired at her, of which four hit.[1]

After sinking the *Bankfields*, the LEIPZIG and *Marie* proceeded to the Lobos de Afuera Islands, some sixty miles west of Eten, where, on September 28th, they met the Kosmos liner *Amasis*. This ship had been at Callao in the early days of the war and sailed on September 4th with a clearance for Punta Arenas. She had since been reported off the Ecuadorian coast, and now attached

[1] See Map 6*d*.

herself to the LEIPZIG, which only remained at Lobos de Afuera long enough to coal from her new tender. The British s.s. *Tamar* was loading guano at the islands, but as she lay within territorial waters the cruiser could not touch her, and steamed south on the evening of the 28th, with both the *Marie* and *Amasis* in company. On the night of the 30th, when very close to Callao, the *Marie* was sent off to that port.

It was on the 30th, as will be remembered, that the DRESDEN quitted the Chilean coast and set her course for Mas-a-fuera. There can be little doubt that the two German cruisers were now in communication, either directly by wireless or through German agents ashore. The LEIPZIG, indeed, was also about to turn westward, but it was first necessary for her to pick up her supply ships, three of which had put out on October 1st or 2nd, in obedience to Captain Hann's instructions. They comprised the *Anubis* from Pisagua, the *Karnak* from Iquiqui, and the *Abessinia* from Mollendo. All three, like the *Amasis*, were Kosmos liners, and all three were heavily laden with coal and provisions. On the following day (October 3rd) Captain Hann came into direct communication with his Admiral.

After bombarding Papieté, the German Pacific squadron went to the Marquesas Islands, where they arrived on September 25th. Here nothing was done beyond the seizure of some French Government funds and the procuring of a welcome supply of fresh provisions, and on October 1st the whole force bore away for Easter Island, which belongs to Chile and lies about 1,500 miles from the Chilean coast.

Up to this date the record of the squadron was singularly barren of achievement. In its slow and anxious passage across the Pacific it had seldom approached frequented waters, and the visit of the NÜRNBERG to Honolulu, the appearance of the SCHARNHORST and GNEISENAU at Apia, and the bombardment of Papieté had failed to disturb the main Pacific trade routes. The Canadian Pacific Railway Company's service was wholly discontinued, owing to the requisitioning of their steamers as armed merchant cruisers or transports, but a partial substitute was found in chartering steamers of the Russian Volunteer fleet for occasional voyages between Canada and Japan. The Blue Funnel Line continued to run with fair regularity between Asiatic ports and Vancouver and Puget Sound, and the Japanese services to North and South America were absolutely undisturbed. To some extent Admiral von Spee's movements undoubtedly contributed to the EMDEN's success, by compelling the Allied Admiralties to retain in the Pacific forces which might otherwise have been released for service in the Indian Ocean; but the direct effect of his operations on trade was, as yet, negligible.

The German Admiral was now, however, entering upon a new and more promising stage of his career. On October 3rd, two days after leaving the Marquesas Group, his wireless operators brought him into touch with the LEIPZIG on the Peruvian coast and with the DRESDEN at Mas-a-fuera. Both these cruisers were summoned by the Admiral to join his flag, and he was thus able to reckon on beginning his campaign on the South American coast with a considerable accession of force.

Almost simultaneously with the receipt of Admiral von Spee's summons, the LEIPZIG met the three supply ships which had sailed on October 2nd. She coaled from the *Abessinia*, near Mollendo, on the 3rd and 4th, and sent her in to Callao, after which she turned westward to meet the Admiral, taking the *Amasis*, *Anubis*, and *Karnak* with her. Meanwhile the *Marie* had put the crew of the *Bankfields* ashore at Callao on October 1st, and on the same day the master of the *Elsinore*, with part of his crew, also came to land, having left the Galapagos Islands in a small sailing vessel on September 24th. The German officer left in charge of the prisoners made an attempt to prevent any of them from sailing, but the Governor, very properly, refused to admit German jurisdiction over them in Ecuadorian territory.

British shipping in Peruvian ports had already been detained for more than a week, and the suspension of sailings was causing grave anxiety to the Government of the Republic. With the German liners withdrawn from trade, the country was more than ever dependent upon British tonnage, and in order to reassure masters and owners as much as possible, they ordered a cruiser to patrol the coast with the object of preventing any attack upon merchantmen in territorial waters. This step, however, was almost immediately followed by the arrival of the *Marie*, and the belief that a serious attack on West Coast trade was in contemplation was supported by the sudden departure of the three Kosmos liners and the subsequent return of the *Abessinia* to Callao, on the 6th, with her holds empty. The movements of the supply ships were naturally connected with those of the LEIPZIG and DRESDEN, and, in fact, gave rise to exaggerated reports as to the number of German cruisers on the coast. All British vessels in Peruvian and Ecuadorian ports continued to be detained, the sailings of vessels bound southward from Panama were also suspended, and the entire seaborne trade of the Republics was paralysed.

Although the trade of the United Kingdom with Peru was, comparatively speaking, small, this continued suspension of traffic had its serious side for British commerce as well as for that of the Republic. The *Bankfields'* cargo represented roughly the average monthly export to Great Britain of the Peruvian sugar industry; but this formed so small a proportion of the total supply, that the loss was not seriously felt. Of graver consequence was the check inflicted on the recovery of the alpaca export, which had already been heavily hit by the economic disturbance of August and September; and still more serious was the interruption of the shipment of Bolivian tin from Mollendo. Nevertheless the importance of the LEIPZIG'S operations was outweighed, in the eyes of the Admiralty, by a new development which threatened British trade in South American waters with a far more dangerous menace than it had yet had to face. In the evening of October 4th (local time), the wireless station at Suva, in the Fiji Islands, intercepted a message from the SCHARNHORST to the DRESDEN stating that the flagship was on her way from the Marquesas to Easter Island, and all doubt as to Admiral von Spee's ultimate intentions was thus set at rest. The all-important news was at once sent out by the Admiralty to the commanders of the forces concerned, and Admiral Cradock was instructed to concentrate the bulk of his squadron on the West Coast with a view to meeting this new and powerful opponent.

When the Admiral received this message, on October 7th, he was on his way to the Falklands, after his second unsuccessful search of Orange Bay, and the GLASGOW, MONMOUTH, and OTRANTO were already steaming up the West Coast. He accordingly took steps to inform Captain Luce of the change in the situation, and called up the CANOPUS from the Plate to complete the concentration of his squadron.

The GLASGOW and MONMOUTH arrived at Valparaiso on the 15th. Captain Luce's original instructions indicated the breaking up of German trade as one of the main objects of his mission, for the movements of the LEIPZIG's supply ships and of one or two other vessels, which may have been connected with the DRESDEN, had given rise to a report that the Germans were resuming commercial operations on the coast. He found, however, that the harbour of Valparaiso was crowded with German ships laid up for fear of capture, and that enemy trade was at an absolute standstill. The only vessels which had moved since the beginning of the war were those which had sailed to coal or provision German cruisers, and the Chilean Government was taking steps to prevent those ships from again putting to sea. Captain Luce accordingly turned back to join Admiral Cradock.

As yet, the probability of Admiral von Spee's approach was not realised in shipping circles, and British trade with Chile was proceeding normally. The suspension of sailings from Peruvian and Ecuadorian ports also came to an end shortly after Captain Luce's visit to Valparaiso. As day after day went by without further news of the LEIPZIG, masters and owners became anxious for their ships to leave. By October 17th shipping had begun to move, and within another couple of days every ship had been released and trade was again in full swing.

The intercepted message from the SCHARNHORST to the DRESDEN indicated as Admiral von Spee's most probable course of action an attack on shipping in Peruvian and Chilean waters or an attempt to pass into the South Atlantic, through the Magellan Straits or round the Horn. Nevertheless our interests in the Northern Pacific were too valuable to be neglected, and while Admiral Cradock was concentrating in the south, arrangements were made to collect an Anglo-Japanese squadron off the Californian coast to bar the Germans from access to the Panama Canal or the terminal waters of the northern trade routes.

So early as the end of September, when Captain Powlett returned to Esquimalt, he was preoccupied by the possibility that the German Pacific squadron might be driven over to the North American coast by the pressure of the forces behind him. He was apprehensive that, in that case, they might not only break up British trade, but venture an attack upon the shipping and coalfields at

Vancouver. He accordingly gave considerable attention to suggesting improvements in the shore defences, and made preparations for mining the channel. In these precautions the Admiralty fully acquiesced, but in pursuance of their usual policy of interfering with trade as little as possible, they gave instructions that, except in emergency, no mines should be actually laid which would interfere with the free movement of shipping.

Shortly after his return, Captain Powlett was informed that wireless messages had been passing between German steamers and cruisers off the Peruvian coast, and that three ships at Seattle were loading with coal and stores for the enemy. As these signs of activity might portend either further operations by the LEIPZIG or preparations for the arrival of the Pacific squadron, he decided on a second search of the coast with the NEWCASTLE, leaving the IDZUMO and RAINBOW to protect the North Pacific trade routes. With this object he sailed from Esquimalt on September 30th, and spent the next fortnight or three weeks in a very thorough examination of the coastal waters and the Gulf of California. In the course of this search he captured the German barque *Harvesthude* with coke from Hamburg, but consented to release her on the earnest representations of the Franco-Belgian mining company at Santa Rosalia to whom the cargo was consigned. He also diverted to Esquimalt two steamers bringing coal to Guaymas for the Sonora Railway Company, which was under suspicion of acting as an agent for the German cruisers; but he was unsuccessful in an attempt to cut off the *Sacramento* (*ex-Alexandria*), a German steamer which had left San Francisco with a cargo of coal and provisions, after a bogus transfer to American owners. No other sign of German activity was, however, discovered, and Captain Powlett accordingly returned to Esquimalt to await reinforcements.

The chief importance of this concentration in the Northern Pacific lay in the quantity of foodstuffs which were now passing through the Panama Canal. The shipment of grain, flour, and salmon from Puget Sound and Vancouver had recommenced as soon as the LEIPZIG'S departure from San Francisco became certain, and her suspected presence in and about the Gulf of California did little to retard the recovery. The news that the *Elsinore* had been sunk off the Mexican coast caused a temporary detention of vessels bound northward from Panama, but the interruption of sailings was very short and had no appreciable effect on trade. During the first two months in which the Canal was open for traffic (August 15th to October 15th, 1914) ten steamers, carrying between them 71,500 tons of grain, passed through to Europe, and nine others passed into the Pacific to receive grain cargoes. The number of British ships using the Canal steadily increased, and the general trade conditions presented a marked contrast to the semi-paralysis of the first half of August. The lumber industry, indeed, had not yet recovered from its depression, and the exports of tinned salmon from Puget Sound during August, September, and October showed a drop of 25 per cent. as compared with the preceding year; but the grain exports increased by some 50 per cent.[1]

Thus, the middle of October was marked by something of a pause in the operations on the west coast of America. The LEIPZIG and DRESDEN had disappeared from the coast and British shipping was moving with perfect freedom from Vancouver to the Straits. Admiral Cradock's squadron in the south and the Anglo-Japanese force in the north were concentrating for the defence of the trade routes against the threatened attack. Of Admiral von Spee no reliable news had been received since the Suva report. In point of fact his main force arrived at Easter Island on October 12th, and during the next two days he was joined there by the DRESDEN and LEIPZIG with their supply ships. But he was not immediately ready to move, and before anything further was heard of him the attention of the Admiralty and of traders had again been called to the South Atlantic.

[1] *Lloyd's List*, 9 December, 1914.

CHAPTER XIII

TRADE PROTECTION IN THE SOUTH ATLANTIC [1]

WHEN Admiral Cradock received orders, early in October, to concentrate his force in the Pacific, it became necessary, at the same time, to provide for the safety of shipping on his old station. The CARMANIA had been obliged to go to Gibraltar to refit after her action with the CAP TRAFALGAR, and the only ships which he could spare for the protection of the East Coast trade were the CORNWALL, BRISTOL, and MACEDONIA. However vigilant they might be, it was impossible for these three ships to guard effectually the whole stretch of the trade routes from the mouth of the Amazon to the estuary of the Plate, and the Admiral accordingly suggested that a second squadron should be formed in the South Atlantic for the purpose of dealing with the KARLSRUHE and providing against the contingency of Admiral von Spee eluding his search and coming round the Horn to appear suddenly on the Plate tracks.

The importance of providing for the security of trade in the South Atlantic was emphasised by the continued improvement of economic conditions in Argentina. Although the export of wheat was still restricted by the Government and was practically negligible, the maize harvest was now coming forward at the rate of 250,000 tons a month, and shipments of beef and mutton were not far from the normal figures.[2] In wool, hides and skins, and oil seeds the recovery was also very marked.

Whereas the chief difficulty of shipping during the earlier weeks of the war was to obtain cargoes, the active resump-

[1] See Map 5.
[2] Imports from Argentina and Uruguay into the United Kingdom.

	Nov. 1914. cwts.	Nov. 1913. cwts.	Dec. 1914. cwts.	Dec. 1913. cwts.
Maize	5,001,355	3,331,759	5,072,684	2,345,144
Beef and mutton	592,324	584,944	493,960	747,621

The meat figures for 1914 are exclusive of cargoes sent to France for the supply of the armies.

tion of trade, coupled with the reduction of available tonnage, had now brought about a situation in which the supply could no longer keep pace with the demand. Shippers were obliged to pay high freights to ensure October loadings, and good rates were quoted for November and December shipments. Although neutral steamers enjoyed a preference for voyages to Dutch and Scandinavian ports and were also in demand for the Mediterranean, the bulk of the tonnage employed was British, and the volume of traffic under the Red Ensign was now very great.[1]

Not only was the Plate trade itself expanding vigorously, but an increased tonnage was coming round the Horn from New Zealand, bringing beef, mutton, and dairy produce to the United Kingdom. The position of the New Zealand meat trade was, in fact, very satisfactory. It was preserved from any rise in freights by the existence of long-term contracts, and despite the requisitioning of eleven vessels usually engaged in the carriage of meat and dairy produce for transport purposes, sufficient refrigerated space was available to meet all probable demands up to the end of the year.[2] Shippers were thus able to respond freely to the demands of the Mother Country and the meat exports rose to abnormal figures.[3]

The only disturbing factor in the situation was the fact that the KARLSRUHE and KRONPRINZ WILHELM remained at large. Up to the middle of October nothing further was heard of either of these ships, but disquieting evidence of their activity was afforded by the non-arrival of several vessels bound from or to Argentine or Brazilian ports, which were already greatly overdue. Thanks, however, to the financial security enjoyed by shipowners and traders the unlocated presence of the two raiders in the South Atlantic did not deter steamers from putting to sea.

The peculiar importance of the Plate and New Zealand trade to the food supply of the United Kingdom rendered

[1] *Lloyd's List*, 23 and 26 November, 1914 (Buenos Aires Reports, October 16th and 23rd).
[2] Report of Shipping Freights and Charges Committee presented to the New Zealand House of Representatives.
[3] Imports of meat from New Zealand into the United Kingdom.

	Nov. 1914. cwts.	Nov. 1913. cwts.	Dec. 1914. cwts.	Dec 1913. cwts.
Beef	35,092	10,734	54,791	801
Mutton	145,262	70,884	93,820	6,571

it specially desirable that this expansion in its volume should not be checked by the infliction of such losses as might shake the confidence of shipping, and the Admiralty, who were fully alive to the requirements of the situation, readily concurred in Admiral Cradock's suggestion. They were the more easily able to do so as there was now less difficulty in finding ships available for the purpose.

Outside the Indian Ocean and South American waters the course of the war at sea since the beginning of September had been singularly uneventful, and the strain placed upon the naval resources of the Allies during the first few weeks of hostilities had sensibly diminished, both in the main theatres of war and on the trade routes. No attempt was made by the German and Austrian fleets to contest the command of the North Sea or the Mediterranean, and the immunity of the North Atlantic from attack was demonstrated, not only by the activity of merchant shipping, but by the undisturbed passage of the First Canadian Convoy in the early part of October. The arrangements for protecting this convoy did, indeed, draw off Admiral Wemyss' force from the entrance to the Channel about the middle of September, but its place was taken by the Seventh Battle Squadron under Vice-Admiral Bethell, and during the last few days of the month another haul of homeward-bound German sailing vessels was made by this squadron.[1]

The capture of sailing vessels was, however, a very minor incident in the war, and the chief duty of the cruiser squadrons in Home Waters continued to be the restriction of contraband traffic. By the end of the second week in October some fifty neutral vessels with suspicious cargoes had been sent into port or detained on calling at the British Isles, while the number of steamers boarded and examined at sea ran into many hundreds. In addition, enemy cargo had been seized in over 200 British and Allied vessels which had sailed before the declaration of war or had unwittingly accepted cargoes intended by neutral importers for transhipment to the Central Powers. But while many traces of illicit trade were discovered by the British cruisers or by the boarding and examination steamers at the ports, no German steamer was to be met

---

[1] From September 20th to 27th inclusive five such vessels, with a net tonnage of 6,682, were captured by Admiral Bethell or by the French. Two were laden with nitrate and one with grain.

SAFETY OF TERMINAL WATERS 241

with at sea, nor was any attack made in Home Waters on British trade.

This tranquility extended also to the eastern portion of the South Atlantic. Since the destruction of the KAISER WILHELM DER GROSSE, the area in which the South American and South African Routes converge had not been troubled by a hostile raider. The squadrons under Admirals de Robeck and Stoddart had been employed in watching the German vessels in Portuguese and island ports, and covering the passage of convoys, without any noteworthy incident occurring to break the monotony of the patrols. On September 28th Admiral de Robeck in his flagship, the ARGONAUT, visited Lisbon, where he was received with an enthusiasm which testified to the strong sense entertained by the Portuguese people of the traditional friendship between the two nations. There was at this period a rumour that Portugal was about to enter the war, and it was anticipated that this might lead to an attempt to escape by the German steamers in the Tagus; but if any such design was in contemplation, it was completely defeated by the vigilance of the Ninth Cruiser Squadron and the strict enforcement of neutrality by the authorities at Lisbon.

In addition to his close watch on the Portuguese coast, Admiral de Robeck was able to carry out a further search of the Azores, in the course of which, on October 10th, the ARGONAUT boarded a steamer flying Norwegian colours and calling herself the *Björgvin* of Bergen. On examination, this vessel proved to be the Hamburg-Amerika liner *Graecia*, of 2,799 tons, which had left New York on August 29th, and had been hovering for some time in the neighbourhood of the Azores, waiting for a chance to transfer her cargo of coal and stores to a German cruiser.[1]

The work of the Fifth Cruiser Squadron during September and October was even more uneventful; but to the CUMBERLAND, detached from Admiral Stoddart's command for service on the west coast of Africa, there fell the richest haul of prizes obtained by any single British cruiser.

At an early stage of the war arrangements were made for joint expeditions by French and British naval and military forces against the German Colonies of Togoland and

---

[1] There was actually a Norwegian ship *Björgvin*, registered at Bergen, of similar size, age, and build to the *Graecia*, so the disguise was well chosen.

the Cameroons. Apart from political motives, the reduction of these territories was desirable as a measure of trade protection, since the long range wireless station at Kamina in Togoland formed an important link in the intelligence system of the German naval forces abroad, and there were two or three ports which might be used as bases by German cruisers. The direct route to South Africa crosses the entrance to the Gulf of Guinea at a distance of some hundreds of miles from the shore, and the defended seaport of Sierra Leone, at the angle of the coast, was one of the bases of Admiral Stoddart's squadron. The South African trade was also, to some extent, secured by the constant passing and repassing of cruisers escorting the homeward-bound transports from the Cape. On the other hand, the trade of our West African Colonies, amounting to some £15,000,000 a year each way, was exposed to the attack of any German ships based on Togoland and the Cameroons, and it was the more important to protect it as the outbreak of war coincided with the flood season, during which the commerce of Nigeria is at its height.

With the exception of some river gunboats on the Niger, the only British man-of-war on the coast at the beginning of August was the gunboat DWARF; but the Admiralty having issued strict instructions that trade was not to be held up, the confidence of traders and shipowners in the control of the routes was exhibited in a striking manner, and commerce and navigation proceeded from the first on normal lines. German trade, on the other hand, came to a complete and immediate standstill. A large number of steamers belonging to the Woermann and Hamburg-Bremer Afrika lines were on the coast or coming out, but by none of them was any attempt made to continue trading. One small steamer was detained in a Nigerian port; three or four vessels sought shelter under a neutral flag at Loanda or Fernando Po; several fled across the Atlantic to Brazil; and about a dozen took refuge in the harbours of Madeira, the Canaries, and the Cape Verdes. The *Professor Woermann*, as we have seen, was converted into a supply ship, and captured by the CARNARVON on August 23rd, just before the destruction of the KAISER WILHELM DER GROSSE, whom she may have been intended to meet. The remainder were collected at Duala, up the Cameroon River, where they were under the protection of the German military forces and might hope for an additional measure of security from the difficulties presented by navigation to heavy ships. Among these was the Woermann liner *Max Brock*, which was reported to be arming. This ship, however, never put to sea, and the only German vessels which gave any signs of activity were two or three small local steamers which received a light armament on the outbreak of war. Even these confined their activities to unimportant attacks on British trading stations and French Customs Houses, and made no attempt against shipping.

The loss of a valuable cargo of West African produce in the *Nyanga* was too quickly followed by the destruction of the KAISER WILHELM DER GROSSE to have much effect on trade; but it was clearly desirable that the possibilities of mischief represented by the German Colonial forces should be removed as early as possible. Togoland was occupied during August by forces from the adjacent British and French Colonies, and early in September the naval force provided to cover the joint expedition to the Cameroons arrived on the coast. Two small armed steamers were sunk by the French gunboat SURPRISE in Corisco Bay; but the main operations were those conducted against Duala by a squadron under Captain Fuller of the CUMBERLAND, and a military force under General Dobell. The clearing of the narrow and tortuous channels, which had been carefully obstructed by the enemy, proved to be no light task, and had to be accomplished in the face of considerable opposition, but a gap having been blown in the principal barrier, the CHALLENGER was at length able to get within range, and on September 27th the town surrendered.

The operations ashore continued for some months, but the capture of Duala put an end to any menace from German shipping on the coast. Besides the Hamburg-Amerika liner *Kamerun*, of 5,861 tons, which had been acting as a look-out ship and wireless station, and was run ashore on the approach of the squadron, Captain Fuller obtained the surrender of nine vessels of the Woermann and Hamburg-Bremer Afrika lines, ranging from 2,229 to 5,528 tons, and several local steamers. In addition, two steamers of over 2,000 tons and seven smaller vessels had been sunk by the Germans in an attempt to block the fairway. Altogether, the capture of Duala cost the enemy over 45,000 tons of merchant shipping, together with a floating dock and numerous motor boats, dredgers, and other small craft.[1]

With all danger from West Africa at an end, Admiral Stoddart's position was considerably simplified. The German steamers in island ports gave no sign of activity, the North Atlantic had been brought completely under control, and no raider had escaped from German home ports on to the high seas since the departure of the KAISER WILHELM DER GROSSE. He therefore suggested to the Admiralty on October 12th, that he should go down the trade route to Pernambuco with the object of searching the focal area off Cape San Roque. This suggestion chimed in with that made by Admiral Cradock for the creation of a new squadron on the East Coast, and on October 14th, the Admiralty telegraphed to Admiral Stoddart to turn over the Canaries—Cape Verde patrol to Captain Buller of the HIGHFLYER, and proceed in the CARNARVON to Pernambuco. In addition to the CORNWALL, BRISTOL, and MACEDONIA, the armed merchant cruisers EDINBURGH CASTLE and ORAMA were placed under his orders, and the powerful armoured cruiser DEFENCE was also sent out from Gibraltar to join him.

The CARNARVON arrived at Pernambuco on October 21st, on which date Admiral Cradock finally quitted the Falklands for the West Coast. Nothing definite was yet known as to the movements of the German Pacific squadron, but on the 23rd, intelligence was received by the Admiralty which amply justified their decision to strengthen the forces protecting the Plate and Brazilian tracks. On this date a telegram was received from the Consul at Tenerife announcing that the Norddeutscher Lloyd Liner *Crefeld* had arrived the previous day (October 22nd) with the crews of no less than fourteen steamers (thirteen British and one neutral) captured by the KARLSRUHE in the Fernando Noronha area between August 31st and October 11th, inclusive. Of the KRONPRINZ WILHELM nothing was known, but that either she or the KARLSRUHE was still at work might be inferred from the non-arrival of vessels not included in the list reported by the *Crefeld*.

The news of these captures naturally produced some effect in shipping and insurance circles, but the extent of the disturbance was extraordinarily small. Heavy as

[1] The vessels which had been sunk in the fairway were subsequently raised by the British.

A SATISFACTORY POSITION

was the loss, it represented only a very small percentage of the traffic which had passed safely along the South Atlantic tracks. Thanks to the State Insurance Scheme, ships and cargoes could be insured at rates which, even at their highest, were far below what had been contemplated as a result of war conditions. With so strong a demand existing for South American products and such heavy stocks to go forward, shipping was not to be deterred by the comparatively small risk disclosed, and Admiral Stoddart's arrival at Pernambuco gave promise of increased protection for future movements.

CHAPTER XIV

THE CAREER OF THE "KARLSRUHE"[1]

THE thirteen captures announced by the *Crefeld* on her arrival at Tenerife were the fruits of a remarkable career which illustrated to the full both the possibilities and limitations of commerce destruction, under modern conditions, by an isolated raider. The KARLSRUHE, Captain Erich Köhler, was the fastest and most modern of the German cruisers on foreign stations.[2] She was ably handled, well supplied, and had at least her fair share of luck. Operating at a focal point of trade, she achieved a greater measure of success than any other of the original raiders, with the exception of the EMDEN. Yet, as has already been shown, she failed to disturb to any appreciable degree the current of South American trade.

Her escape from the SUFFOLK and BRISTOL and her subsequent movements up to the middle of August have already been mentioned.[3] After taking 1,100 tons of coal at Curaçao on August 12th, she proceeded along the northern coast of Brazil towards Cape San Roque, keeping some way out from the shore. Captain Köhler's war orders gave him wide discretionary powers to attack British trade in the Atlantic, and he had resolved to make for the great focal point at which the shipping of the South American Route is most thickly concentrated.

When he called at San Juan, Porto Rico, on August 9th,

---

[1] See Maps 5 and 8. The story of the KARLSRUHE has been told by two of her officers : by Kapitän-Leutnant Aust in *Die Kriegsfahrt S.M.S. "Karlsruhe,"* Karlsruhe, 1916, and by Korvetten-Kapitän Studt in *S.M.S. "Karlsruhe," Eines deutscher Kreuzers Gluck und Ende*, Leipzig, 1916. These narratives have been checked and supplemented for the purposes of this chapter by the depositions made by masters of captured vessels and diaries kept by prisoners.
[2] Completed 1913. Sea speed, 24·8 knots. Coal endurance, 6,600 miles at 10 knots. Also carried oil fuel.
[3] Pages 107–8, *supra*.

Captain Köhler made arrangements with the master of the Hamburg-Amerika liner *Patagonia*[1] to go to St. Thomas and fill up with coal with a view to meeting the cruiser at sea. At Curaçao he found another German steamer, the *Stadt Schleswig*,[2] whose master he instructed to proceed to a rendezvous off the Brazilian coast with a further supply of fuel. The cruiser herself, after leaving Curaçao, steamed east, along the coast of Venezuela, but without sighting any British ships until August 18th. During the night of the 17th she came into wireless touch with the *Patagonia* and turned somewhat to the north to meet her. Shortly after daybreak the tender was sighted and the two ships then steamed south in company. They had arrived at a point about 180 miles east of Barbados and sixty or seventy miles north of the usual track of shipping, when, at 4.45 p.m. on the 18th, Captain Köhler made his first prize. This was the *Bowes Castle*, whose capture has already been referred to.[3]

She was on her way from Antofagasta to New York with a cargo consisting of 5,980 tons nitrate, 692 tons silver ore, and 232 tons copper ore. Her master had received instructions from Captain Luce of the GLASGOW on August 17th, and had accordingly deviated widely from his normal course. Had the KARLSRUHE been actually at work on the trade route, he would almost certainly have escaped, and it was sheer bad luck which at this moment threw him across her path.

Despite the neutral ownership of the cargo, Captain Köhler decided to sink the ship, though he admitted to the master that this would involve liability to compensate the cargo owners. The crew of the prize were accordingly transferred to the *Patagonia* with such effects as they could hastily collect, and at 6.15 p.m. the seacocks of the prize were opened and several charges were exploded in her hold. She was a fine new ship, and the captors themselves could not repress a feeling of regret for her destruction.

The KARLSRUHE now went inshore to meet the *Stadt Schleswig*. On August 21st she coaled from the *Patagonia* near the mouth of the Amazon, and on the 25th, she found

[1] 3,016 tons, 11·5 knots.
[2] 1,103 tons, 9·5 knots; owner, H. C. Horn.
[3] Pages 111, 176, and 193n, *supra*. See Map 5.

the *Stadt Schleswig* at São João Island, about 120 miles north-west of Maranham. Having transferred, either to his own bunkers or to the *Patagonia*, her 800 tons of coal, Captain Köhler had the prisoners removed from the *Patagonia* to the *Stadt Schleswig*, which then parted company and took them into Maranham.[1]

Meanwhile the KARLSRUHE and *Patagonia* continued their voyage along the Brazilian coast. On August 30th the cruiser coaled again in a secluded inlet, and next day she picked up by wireless three additional tenders, the Hamburg-Süd-Amerika liners *Asuncion*[2] and *Rio Negro*[3] and the *Crefeld*[4] of the Norddeutscher Lloyd. At 5.30 p.m. on the 31st she was in company with the *Patagonia*, about fifty miles north-west of Rocas Reef, to which the *Asuncion, Crefeld*, and *Rio Negro* had been ordered. Here she was in the angle made by the tracks diverging from Cape San Roque to New York and Europe respectively, an ideal position for a commerce raider, so long as she could maintain her position.

Captain Köhler's choice of a cruising ground was speedily justified. His first blow fell on the trade between Brazil and North America. The *Strathroy*, a tramp of 4,486 tons under charter to the Lloyd Braziliero, left Norfolk, Virginia, for Rio on August 15th with 5,600 tons of coal for the Brazilian Government. Her master kept some eighty-five miles north of the usual track, but in the afternoon of the 31st, as she was passing through the focal area between Rocas and Fernando Noronha, she was sighted by the KARLSRUHE, which at once gave chase. The *Strathroy* made off at full speed, but was quickly overhauled and compelled to follow her captor to Rocas Reef, where she was boarded at 8 a.m. the next day.[5]

The swell at Rocas Reef was too heavy to allow of coaling, but the boats of the little squadron were busy during September 1st. A prize crew from the cruiser was put on board the *Strathroy*, provisions went off from the *Asuncion* to the KARLSRUHE, the commanders of all the ships were assembled for a conference, mails were collected and taken to the *Patagonia*, and the European prisoners,

[1] See page 176, *supra*.
[2] 4,663 tons, 10·5 knots. Sailed from Santos, August 17th.
[3] 4,556 tons, 12 knots. Sailed from Para, August 8th.
[4] 3,829 tons, 12 knots. Sailed from Santos, August 12th.
[5] See Map 8.

CRUISING GROUND AND METHODS 249

with two coloured men, were transferred to the *Asuncion*. The Chinese, who formed the majority of the steamer's crew, were retained to assist in working out the coal, and in the evening the *Strathroy* was sent off, in charge of the *Patagonia*, to a sheltered harbour on the Brazilian coast, which Captain Köhler had selected for a secret base. It was true that the use of this base would involve three or four days' absence from the trade routes every time the cruiser went in to coal, but even this interruption was preferable to the risks of coaling at sea.[1]

Having disposed of the *Strathroy* the KARLSRUHE turned north-east and cruised up the trade route from Pernambuco towards St. Vincent. Captain Köhler was fortunate in the time of his arrival. The capture of the *Hyades* and *Holmwood*, reported in quick succession,[2] had drawn the bulk of the British force on the East Coast southward in pursuit of the DRESDEN. Indeed, the GLASGOW, MONMOUTH, and OTRANTO began their sweep of the Brazilian coast at Rocas Reef on August 28th, just three days before the KARLSRUHE arrived there. Admiral Stoddart's squadron was fully occupied in watching the Canaries and Cape Verdes, assisting to secure the safety of homeward-bound transports from South Africa, and acting as a covering force to the Cameroons Expedition. He was therefore unable to make any detachment towards Pernambuco; and though British warships on their way to South America, or patrolling the Brazilian tracks, frequently passed through the focal area, no cruiser was permanently stationed off Cape San Roque.

The scheme of operations adopted by Captain Köhler was very similar to that employed by Captain von Müller in the Indian Ocean, but the KARLSRUHE had one advantage over the EMDEN, in the number of her tenders. The *Patagonia*, after taking the *Strathroy* in to the secret base, arrived at Pernambuco to deliver her mails on September 6th, and never rejoined the cruiser. The *Asuncion*, *Crefeld*, and *Rio Negro*, however, still remained, and all were equipped with wireless apparatus. During the day the KARLSRUHE steamed or drifted on the trade routes, with her attendants spread out as scouts on either side. The range of vision for smoke was thus extended to some

[1] The exact position of the KARLSRUHE'S secret base has not as yet been definitely ascertained.
[2] See pages 172–176, *supra*.

hundred miles of sea.[1] At nightfall the scouts usually closed in on the cruiser and all the ships lay to till morning.

In addition to their utility as scouts, the tenders served a useful purpose as prison-ships for captured crews. By distributing coal and stores amongst the several units of the squadron, it was possible to reserve accommodation of a sort for several hundred prisoners. Captain Köhler was thus able to avoid the necessity of sending ships into port at frequent intervals, with the result, as we have seen, that for a period of seven weeks [2] no definite intelligence of his operations was obtained by the Allies.

He had a further advantage over Captain von Müller in being able to coal at a secure anchorage. At an early period of the war the British Admiralty became suspicious that the Germans possessed a base of this kind somewhere on the northern coast of Brazil, and more than one careful search for it was undertaken. Indeed, the BRISTOL was actively engaged in this work during a great part of the KARLSRUHE's career. The coast to be searched extends, however, for over a thousand miles. The ports are few, the land sparsely inhabited, and communications restricted. The number of unfrequented harbours is large, and neither the British Admiralty nor the Brazilian Government succeeded in identifying the inlet to which the *Strathroy* was taken, and to which, from time to time, the KARLSRUHE and her tenders came in to replenish their bunkers.

It is possible that on some of these occasions the Germans were able to enter into communication with residents of their own nationality, but there is no evidence that Captain Köhler's operations were appreciably assisted by information thus obtained. On several occasions the cruiser's officers told the masters of captured vessels that they were informed by wireless or otherwise of sailings from Brazil and the United States, but in most cases, if not in all, these statements were admittedly false. Indeed it is not necessary to credit Captain Köhler with the possession of special intelligence as to steamers' movements in order to account for the success of his operations in an

---

[1] It has been variously estimated at from 50 to 200 miles. As it appears that the wing ships were frequently on the extreme horizon, or even out of sight from the cruiser, 100 miles is probably by no means an excessive estimate. The addition of other scouts (see *infra*) may have raised it at times to 150 miles or more.

[2] From the *Stadt Schleswig's* arrival at Maranham, September 2nd, to the *Crefeld's* arrival at Tenerife, October 22nd.

A WELCOME PRIZE

area through which, in normal times, an average of sixteen British steamers pass every day. His own use of wireless was limited to occasional short distance communications with the scouts, who usually received their orders by semaphore.

The KARLSRUHE's first victim in September was the *Maple Branch*, of 4,838 tons, which had left Liverpool on August 20th with 2,000 tons of general cargo for West Coast ports. Her master had heard a rumour that the Germans were aware of the advice given to merchantmen, and he accordingly decided to close the Brazilian coast as quickly as possible and run down within territorial waters. At 6 a.m. on September 3rd he was about twenty miles west of the trade route from St. Vincent, making for Fernando Noronha. At this point he was stopped and boarded. Among the cargo were some prize cattle, sheep, pigs, and poultry, on their way to an exhibition in South America. They formed a very welcome addition to the cruiser's stock of provisions, and after they had been slaughtered the meat was taken off to the KARLSRUHE and *Crefeld*. Some useful stores, such as tools and spun-yarn for making fenders to use while coaling, were also found on board, and the greater part of the day was spent in ransacking the prize. Her people were taken on board the *Crefeld*, and after she had been stripped of everything useful the connections were opened and a bomb exploded in the shaft tunnel.

On this day the *Asuncion* was not with the cruiser. She had fallen in with the KRONPRINZ WILHELM some distance to the south and remained with her all day, transferring a quantity of provisions. This was the first time that the KARLSRUHE and the KRONPRINZ WILHELM had been in proximity since August 6th. In the meantime the career of the KRONPRINZ WILHELM had been comparatively uneventful. After escaping from the SUFFOLK she crossed over to the neighbourhood of the Azores, where she coaled from the German steamer *Walhalla*,[1] and then turned south-west towards the trade routes. On August 27th she stopped the Russian barque *Pittan* in mid-Atlantic, but allowed her to proceed.[2] The *Pittan* was too small for her destruction to be worth the inconveni-

---
[1] Left Las Palmas with excess coal and provisions, August 2nd. Returned August 26th.
[2] 273 tons net. She had sailed before the outbreak of war. See Map 8.

ence of taking off her crew and feeding them for an indefinite period, and as she was not a steamer, she was unlikely to give information in time to be of any use to the Allies. The barque did not, in fact, arrive at Liverpool until September 26th, but on her passage she spoke the steamer *Manx Isles*, which reported at the Azores on September 11th. Even so, the intelligence was a fortnight old, and the locality of the incident was too remote from any important trade route to throw much light on the raider's intentions.

By September 3rd the KRONPRINZ WILHELM had arrived in the neighbourhood of the trade routes some 200 miles east of Cape San Roque. Here she met the *Asuncion*, and next day, after the *Asuncion* had gone off to join the KARLSRUHE, she made her first prize.[1] This was the liner *Indian Prince*, of 2,846 tons, which had left Bahia for New York on the previous day, with a valuable cargo of coffee, cocoa, salted hides, skins, rosewood, and rubber. In accordance with instructions received from the Consul at Rio, the master had carefully shaped his course to avoid the focal point off Cape San Roque, and he would undoubtedly have cleared the KARLSRUHE; but the KRONPRINZ WILHELM, though approaching the trade routes, was not yet actually on them, and at about nine o'clock in the evening of the 4th the *Indian Prince* was captured, after a short chase, 125 miles east of the usual steamer tracks.

During the 4th, the wireless calls of the KRONPRINZ WILHELM were heard by the KARLSRUHE, but Captain Köhler did not consider it prudent to reply, as he could also hear the calls of British cruisers in the neighbourhood. His prudence was justified, for Admiral Cradock in the GOOD HOPE was then on his way to Pernambuco to take up his new command, and other ships were also within touch. The result, however, was that the two raiders never came into direct communication, and thenceforth their courses lay far apart. Captain Thierfelder of the KRONPRINZ WILHELM took his prize over 500 miles away from the trade route before he considered it safe to stop and ransack her. On September 8th the liner's stores and coal were removed and her people taken off, and next morning the *Indian Prince* was sunk. A few days later (September 12th and 13th) the *Prussia* and *Ebernburg* arrived, and on the 17th they took off the prisoners, whom

[1] See Map 8.

they subsequently landed at Rio and Santos, as already narrated.[1]

Meanwhile the KARLSRUHE had been rejoined by the *Asuncion* on September 5th, and on the same day Captain Köhler intercepted wireless messages to the effect that the EBER had come into Bahia and that the CAP TRAFALGAR had been equipped as a raider. For the moment it looked as if British trade in the South Atlantic was about to be made the object of a concerted attack by the KARLSRUHE off Fernando Noronha and by the two big armed liners off the Plate, with Trinidada as their base.[2] This prospect was destroyed, as we have seen, by the CARMANIA's successful action with the CAP TRAFALGAR on September 14th, but whatever the plans of the armed liners may have been, they did not affect the movements of Captain Köhler, who had no intention of leaving the focal point. On September 6th the crew of the *Strathroy* were transferred from the *Asuncion* to the *Crefeld*, and the KARLSRUHE went off with the *Asuncion* to the spot where the captured collier was lying, narrowly escaping a meeting with both the GOOD HOPE and the CORNWALL. Here the cruiser coaled from the prize, and by the 9th she was back on the trade routes with the *Crefeld* and *Rio Negro* in company. From the 10th to the 13th the three ships drifted on the tracks in extended formation without meeting with any success, but at about 2 a.m. on the 14th they caught sight of a vessel steaming without lights, which was accordingly followed until daybreak, when she was seen to be British. As a blank shot fired to stop her was disregarded by the chase, a shell was sent over the steamer's bridge and she was brought to and boarded about six o'clock. She proved to be the Nelson liner *Highland Hope* (5,150 tons), which had left Liverpool on August 31st, in ballast, to load a meat cargo at Buenos Aires. While the crew of the prize were being transferred to the *Crefeld* and her wireless apparatus and stores removed, the Spanish steamer *Reina Victoria Elene* passed the group of ships and showed some curiosity with regard to them. Captain Köhler persuaded her that they were a British convoy, but shortly afterwards wireless messages were heard passing between the Spaniard and a British warship, and after opening the sea connections of

---

[1] See pages 227–8, *supra*.
[2] There is, however, no certain evidence that the KRONPRINZ WILHELM intended to go to Trinidada. See pages 222–4, *supra*.

the prize, the KARLSRUHE and *Rio Negro* turned westward away from the tracks, leaving the *Crefeld* to watch the sinking of the prize. When last seen by her crew, as the *Crefeld* bore away, about 9 p.m., the *Highland Hope* was settling down, with her decks already awash.

The ship met by the *Reina Victoria Elene* was the CANOPUS, on her way down to join Admiral Cradock. The story told by the Spaniards aroused the suspicions of the British captain, but by the time he came up the KARLSRUHE was already well to the westward. Captain Köhler had decided, in view of this disturbing incident, to leave the focal area for a time and try his fortune on the North American— Brazilian trade route at a point well removed from his ordinary cruising ground. By 2.80 p.m. on the 17th the KARLSRUHE was about 250 miles west of the European tracks and fifty miles north of that running from Cape San Roque to North American ports. Here she captured the collier *Indrani*, bound from Norfolk, Virginia, to Rio with 7,000 tons of Pocahontas coal. She was a comparatively new ship of 5,706 tons and was equipped with Marconi apparatus which, like the *Highland Hope*, she did not use, presumably because the hostile character of the cruiser was not discovered until too late. She had a speed of 12 knots, and in view of her character and equipment Captain Köhler decided to add her to his squadron as a collier and scout. Her officers and Europeans were transferred to the *Crefeld*, but her forty-eight Chinese sailors and firemen were kept on board to assist the prize crew. She was then left with the *Crefeld* and *Rio Negro* while the cruiser went off, with the *Asuncion*, which had now rejoined, to coal from the *Strathroy*. After spending September 18th and 19th in replenishing his bunkers, Captain Köhler considered it safe to return to the neighbourhood of Fernando Noronha, and on the 20th he was met there by the *Rio Negro, Crefeld,* and *Indrani*.

There were now nearly 120 prisoners in the *Crefeld*, and within the next two days another fifty persons had been added to the number, while the *Rio Negro* had also received a complement of captives. During these two days five steamers were stopped, two on the 21st and three on the 22nd. Of the latter two were neutrals and were allowed to proceed on their way, the Italian steamer *Ascaro* to St. Vincent and the Swedish *Prinsessan Ingeborg* to Buenos Aires. It will be remembered that the *Ascaro's* report of this incident, when she arrived at St. Vincent on the 28th, was the first definite news of the KARLSRUHE received since the arrival of the *Stadt Schleswig* at Maranham.[1]

Of the three prizes, the *Maria*, captured at about 1 p.m. on the 21st, was also a neutral. She was a steamer of 2,863 tons, belonging to the Holland Gulf Stoomvaart Maatschappij, and was bound from Portland, Oregon, to Dublin and Belfast with a cargo of wheat. While her crew were being transferred to the *Crefeld* the smoke of another steamer was seen on the horizon, and the KARLSRUHE and *Rio Negro* went off in pursuit. The newcomer, which was captured about twenty miles west of the track from St. Vincent to Brazilian ports, proved to be the *Cornish City*, a collier of 3,816 tons, which had left Barry Dock on the 3rd with 5,500 tons of Welsh coal consigned to the Brazilian Coaling Company, a British firm established at Rio Janeiro.

Unlike the *Indrani*, the *Cornish City* was some years old and a slow steamer. Moreover the coal she carried was of a soft variety, giving thick black smoke, and as Captain Köhler was now in no want of fuel he was unwilling to spare another prize crew. He was content to take off the stores, and after the prisoners had been removed to the *Rio Negro*, the prize was sunk about 7 p.m. The *Crefeld*, which had in the meantime scuttled the *Maria*, came up in time to witness the sinking.

During the night the KARLSRUHE heard the wireless call of the Royal Mail liner *Amazon* and chased in the most probable direction, but found at daybreak that she had been pursuing the *Ascaro*. An hour or two later Captain Köhler was consoled for this disappointment by meeting the *Rio Iguassu*, of 3,817 tons, outward bound from the Tyne with 4,800 tons of coal for the Tramway, Light and Power Company, Rio. The master had kept well to the eastward of the usual track until nearing the Equator, when he altered course to make the Brazilian coast as quickly as possible, in order to go down within territorial waters. Unfortunately for him, the point at which his course cut the St. Vincent—Pernambuco track was that at which the KARLSRUHE was then lying. An attempt was made by the cruiser to coal from the prize, but the sea was too rough, and as her coal was not of high quality, Captain Köhler did not consider it worth while to keep her.

[1] See page 176, *supra*.

Accordingly, at 6 p.m., after her crew had been removed to the *Crefeld*, the *Rio Iguassu* was sunk by explosives.

It will be observed that both the colliers were bound for a neutral country, but in each case the consignees of the coal were British and no great exception could be taken to the treatment of the vessels. The sinking of the *Maria* was a more questionable step. Her cargo of wheat was, undoubtedly, conditional contraband, and the test to be applied was, therefore, its destination. When the case came before the Prize Court at Hamburg it was contended on behalf of the captors that Belfast served " as a base of operations and supplies for the British forces," and that although a part of the cargo was to be discharged at Dublin, Belfast, which was the first discharging port, must be taken as the destination of the entire cargo. The owners appealed, but the Imperial Supreme Prize Court at Berlin considered themselves bound by a retrospective statement which had, in the meantime, been issued by the Chief of the German Admiralty Staff, declaring that Dublin also had served as a base for the British forces since the beginning of the war. The Bills of Lading were made out " to order," and though it was proved that they had been sold before war broke out to a British importer who required the wheat for the supply of his regular customers, the Court refused to accept this as conclusive evidence as to the destination of the cargo. They maintained that as the purchaser of the Bills of Lading was not the actual consumer and was unable to prove definite allocation of the cargo to existing contracts, it would have been possible for the British Government to acquire the wheat, and that in any case it was not, ultimately, a question of where the corn would be ground, but for what purpose the flour to be produced from it was intended. They therefore confirmed the condemnation of ship and cargo. The point was a fine one, and some of the arguments employed by the Court appear to go a long way towards annulling the distinction between " Absolute " and " Conditional " Contraband ; but in cases of cargoes consigned " to order," very clear evidence of innocent destination was insisted on by both sides throughout the war.[1]

[1] Judgment of Imperial Supreme Prize Court, Berlin, October 5th, 1915, citing judgment of Hamburg Prize Court, April 1915. The Supreme Court distinguished this case from that of the *Alfred Hage* (See Chapter XXI, *infra*) on the ground that in the last named case the cargo of pit-props was " regularly sold on the spot where they were and would be used." In the

After the capture of the *Rio Iguassu*, the KARLSRUHE steamed away from the tracks to the westward in order to overhaul her engines, and on September 28th she turned towards her coaling place. On her way she met the *Asuncion*, which had finally gutted the *Strathroy* and taken her out to sea, where she was sunk. The *Asuncion* had on board two or three of the *Strathroy's* officers, who were now transferred to the *Crefeld*. Next day the cruiser went off to coal in company with the *Asuncion* and *Indrani*, the *Crefeld* and the *Rio Negro* being left to await them. Shortly afterwards a steamer was sighted from the *Crefeld* going south, and a wireless message was sent to inform Captain Köhler, but nothing came of it. On October 1st the *Asuncion* rejoined, but the KARLSRUHE did not arrive till next day and one or two steamers which were sighted by the scouts had to be allowed to pass, as there was no one to chase them.

The KARLSRUHE had spent September 29th and 30th in coaling, and when she rejoined, in company with the *Indrani*, she was deeply laden with fuel, even the upper deck and quarter-deck being piled a yard deep with coal and only the space round the guns kept clear. By this time the captured collier had been disguised with black paint and was ready to play her part as a tender to the cruiser, under the new name of *Hoffnung*. Captain Köhler had now four steamers in attendance, all equipped with wireless, and on October 2nd he returned to the trade route, the *Asuncion* and *Hoffnung* steaming off on either side of the cruiser until they were only just visible on the horizon, while the *Rio Negro* and *Crefeld* remained in closer touch with the KARLSRUHE.

While coaling, the Germans heard of the EMDEN's brilliant success in the Bay of Bengal, but on the 2nd information was received by the *Asuncion* which bore more

case of the *Maria* there was only a statement of the buyer that it was his *intention* to sell to millers. The case of the *Modig*, a Norwegian steamer carrying small coal from Hartlepool to Raumo for the Helsingfors Gasworks, and captured in the Baltic during October 1914, was similarly distinguished on the ground that "the private person who receives the goods is at the same time the consumer, so that the goods fulfil the object for which they exist while in his hands." In this case the Court refused to consider the supposition that the cargo might have been commandeered by the Russian Government, on the ground that to act on such an assumption would altogether exclude importation for private purposes. (The judgment in the case of the *Modig* was delivered on the same date as that in the *Maria*.)

closely on their own activities. This was to the effect that the CAP TRAFALGAR had been sunk, but that the GOOD HOPE, MONMOUTH, and GLASGOW had gone south, and that Admiral von Spee was crossing to South American waters.

On the whole this was good news. The sinking of the CAP TRAFALGAR was discounted by the knowledge that the bulk of Admiral Cradock's force was removed, for the time being, from the KARLSRUHE's sphere of operations, and the prospect of an eventual junction with the German Pacific squadron opened out wide possibilities. With the news of the EMDEN's exploits to excite their emulation and a tolerably clear field before them, the Germans were in high spirits, while the prisoners, on the other hand, were becoming increasingly depressed. Their personal treatment was good, but the people in the *Crefeld* were suffering much inconvenience from overcrowding, and food was also running short.

On October 3rd the *Asuncion* and *Hoffnung* parted company, and during this day and the 4th no British ships were seen; but about 4.30 p.m. on the 5th, the *Crefeld*, which had been scouting to the east, reported a chase in sight. The KARLSRUHE promptly went off in pursuit, and at 6 p.m. the new-comer was stopped by a shot being fired across her bows. Again the prize was a collier, the *Farn*, of 4,393 tons. She was bound from Barry to Monte Video with 5,800 tons of the best Welsh coal and coke. The master had come down west of Madeira and subsequently steered some forty miles east of his ordinary course, but unfortunately came between the tracks from Pernambuco to Tenerife and Las Palmas respectively, with the result that he was sighted by the scout.

The *Farn's* cargo was too valuable to be willingly sunk by the Germans, and fortunately for Captain Köhler the prize crew and Chinese of the *Strathroy* were now available for another ship. Accordingly, the *Farn* was sent off to meet the *Asuncion* and take off the Chinese, after which both ships were to await the cruiser's return.

After the *Farn* had parted company, the KARLSRUHE, with the *Crefeld* and *Rio Negro* in company, steered still farther east. The wireless of a British cruiser had once more been heard in strength which showed her to be dangerously close, and Captain Köhler considered it desirable to leave the tracks for a time. His movement was a fortunate one, for it brought him into the area through which homeward-bound steamers were then passing in considerable numbers. On the afternoon of the 6th the *Rio Negro* reported a ship which proved to be the *Niceto de Larrinaga*, homeward bound from Buenos Aires to London, and having found his detour remunerative, Captain Köhler decided to remain for a few days in his new position. The *Lynrowan* from Buenos Aires for Liverpool was captured on the 7th, and the *Cervantes*, also homeward bound to Liverpool, on the 8th. At 11 p.m. on the same day the lights of another steamer were seen and shortly after midnight she was stopped and boarded, when she proved to be the *Pruth*, from Chile and Monte Video to St. Vincent " for orders."

All these ships were captured between forty and fifty miles to the east of the most easterly tracks between Brazil and the Canaries and all carried valuable cargoes consisting in great part of foodstuffs. In the *Niceto de Larrinaga* were some 8,000 tons of oats and maize. The *Lynrowan* had shipped at Rosario and Buenos Aires 5,500 tons of grain, sugar, and tallow. She also carried a number of motor cars ordered in Belgium. The *Cervantes* was bringing 4,500 tons of general cargo from West Coast ports, including cattle fodder, sugar, hides, and wool. Finally, the *Pruth* was laden with 2,300 tons of barley and 3,800 tons of nitrate.

It was sheer bad luck which led to the capture of these vessels. The masters were faithfully carrying out the Admiralty instructions for dispersal, and but for Captain Köhler's eastward movement, undertaken for his own safety, they would have escaped his clutches. They were all dealt with in the same way. The crews were removed to the *Crefeld*, the stores were taken off and the vessels themselves sunk by explosives. They represented an aggregate loss to British shipping of 17,445 tons.[1] The grain laden vessels took, in some cases, a long while to sink, and the *Niceto de Larrinaga*, which began to

---

[1] *Niceto de Larrinaga*, 5,018 tons. Miguel de Larrinaga S.S. Co. Ltd., Liverpool. Sailed from Buenos Aires, September 24th.
 Lynrowan, 3,384 tons. Liver Shipping Co. Ltd., Liverpool. Sailed from Buenos Aires, September 24th.
 Cervantes, 4,635 tons. Liverpool, Brazil and River Plate Steam Navigation Co. (Messrs. Lamport & Holt). Sailed from Rio de Janiero, October 1st.
 Pruth, 4,408 tons. Mercantile S.S. Co., London. Left Monte Video, September 23rd.
 The *Niceto de Larrinaga* was equipped with wireless.

go down at about 7 p.m. on the 6th, did not finally disappear till 2 a.m. on the 7th.

While the *Niceto de Larrinaga* was alongside the KARLSRUHE for the purpose of transferring her stores, another outward-bound vessel was sighted a few miles away, but she was out of sight before the cruiser could get clear. On the afternoon of the 9th yet another vessel was chased, but on being boarded she proved to be a Spaniard, the *Cadiz*. She was accordingly released and arrived at Tenerife on October 4th, the day after Admiral Stoddart left the Canaries for Pernambuco.

By this time there were over 350 prisoners on board the *Crefeld*, and they were very closely packed. The food was rather better, thanks to the stores found in the latest batch of prizes; but it could not be expected to last for long, and even before the capture of the *Pruth*, Captain Köhler had decided to send off the prison-ship to Tenerife. As a preliminary step the crew of the *Cornish City* were transferred to her from the *Rio Negro*. The only ship sighted on the 10th was a Norwegian, and on the evening of that day the KARLSRUHE and her consorts again turned westward in order to meet the *Farn* and *Asuncion*. Their eastward sweep had given excellent results, as five steamers had been captured in as many days, but it was now necessary for them to get in touch once more with their coal supplies. By the afternoon of the 11th they were well over 100 miles west of the track to St. Vincent, and approaching the rendezvous with the *Asuncion* and *Farn*. At 3 p.m. the *Asuncion* was sighted. She at once made off, taking the KARLSRUHE for a British cruiser, but on being recalled, reported that a British steamer was close at hand and was being detained by the *Farn*.

A very pretty little comedy was, in fact, in progress. The *Condor*, of 3,053 tons, belonging to the New York and Pacific S.S. Co., had sailed from Fernandina, Florida, on September 25th with 4,000 tons of general cargo shipped at New York and Philadelphia for various ports on the east and west coast of South America. The master had steered a careful course well away from all tracks, but at 3.15 p.m. on the 11th he met a steamer flying the red ensign whom he signalled to know if she had seen any British cruisers. The stranger replied that she could not see the signal clearly and asked the *Condor* to come closer. When the ships were about a mile apart, the master of the

Condor was amazed to see his new acquaintance suddenly replace the red ensign by the German flag. All this time, a second steamer, showing no colours, had been lying about six miles away, and shortly after a cruiser was seen, about ten miles away and coming up fast. By 3.45 she was alongside and sent off a boarding party. The master then learned that he had been in communication with the *Farn*, and that the other unknown steamer was the *Asuncion*, by whom the KARLSRUHE had been called up.

The *Condor* turned out to be a very welcome prize, as amongst her cargo were large quantities of stores, including 2,000 cases of condensed milk and 800 barrels of oil. The next two days were spent in transferring stores and oil from the prize, her crew being put on board the *Crefeld*. The release of the prison-ship was delayed by the necessity of using her boats in the transfer of the oil, but at 4.30 p.m. on the 13th she was sent off to Tenerife. Her master was instructed not to arrive before the 22nd, as Captain Köhler was anxious to delay the news of his operations as long as possible.

The passage to Tenerife was one of great discomfort for the prisoners, as the crew of the *Condor* brought up the numbers on board to 419, and food was very short. On approaching the Canaries, the *Crefeld* was obliged to exercise the utmost caution, in order to avoid the British cruisers who were on the watch. Indeed, she narrowly escaped capture at the hands of the armed merchant cruiser VICTORIAN. She succeeded, however, in slipping in to Santa Cruz on the appointed date, and next morning the prisoners were landed. They had not been searched and were able to retain diaries and memoranda relating to the KARLSRUHE's operations during the whole period of their captivity; but they were, of course, unable to give any reliable indication of Captain Köhler's future movements, beyond the fact that he still had four tenders, the *Asuncion*, *Rio Negro*, *Farn*, and *Hoffnung*, at his disposal, and was well supplied with fuel.[1]

So far as the movements of the KARLSRUHE were con-

---

[1] Some complaints as to the treatment received by the prisoners were made on their arrival at Tenerife, but they are not borne out by the master's statements or by the diaries kept on board the *Crefeld* and *Rio Negro*, all of which give Captain Köhler a good character for humanity. The inevitable overcrowding and the scarcity of supplies were serious sources of discomfort, but it is generally admitted that the Germans did as well as was possible in the circumstances.

cerned, the news brought by the prisoners in the *Crefeld* was the first which had come to hand since the *Ascaro* reported at St. Vincent on September 28th. But the *Ascaro's* intelligence was confined to the fact of her having been boarded by the German cruiser, and no particulars of captures in the South Atlantic had been received since the *Prussia* and *Ebernburg* landed the crew of the *Indian Prince* on September 24th and 25th. The story of the KARLSRUHE'S depredations was now brought up to October 18th, but the full extent to which shipping had suffered from the activity of German raiders was not known for some time after the *Crefeld's* arrival. Since September 3rd the KARLSRUHE had not been in communication with the KRONPRINZ WILHELM, and the people in the *Crefeld* could say nothing as to the movements of the armed liner, but that ship had already to her credit a prize more valuable than any the KARLSRUHE had yet made.

Captain Thierfelder had been informed by wireless of the destruction of the CAP TRAFALGAR, but he had also learned from South American papers brought off by one of the colliers that large contracts for meat for the United Kingdom had been concluded in Argentina,[1] and about the beginning of October he made his way towards the Plate with the object of intercepting the homeward-bound meat ships. On October 7th he was lying on the track between Fernando Noronha and Punta Arenas, some 270 miles from the entrance to the Plate Estuary, where he captured the Houlder liner *La Correntina*, of 8,529 tons, two days out from Buenos Aires.[2]

If the KRONPRINZ WILHELM had been somewhat slow in getting to work, the prize was one that might well console her people for their previous inactivity. *La Correntina* had a larger insulated cargo space than any other steamer in the world, and was now carrying about 8,500 tons of frozen meat, shipped under a War Office contract and valued at £210,000. The ship herself was insured against war risks for £148,600. She was defensively armed with two 4·7-inch guns, but owing to the disorganisation of the meat trade, the vessel which should have brought out her ammunition did not do so, and she left port without a round on board. It was afterwards rumoured that intelligence of this fact was conveyed by Germans on shore

---

[1] Journal of Paymaster A. Mahlstedt, in *Kieler Zeitung*, 25 September, 1915.   [2] See Map 5.

to the KRONPRINZ WILHELM, and some colour is given to
the statement by the fact that no other defensively
armed merchantman was held up during this period of
the war; but this fact cannot be considered as conclusive,
in view of the small number of defensively armed
ships, and the small percentage of all ships on the route
stopped by the enemy. Her master had deviated from
the ordinary track on leaving port, but when he altered
course to the north-east on the morning of October 7th he
blundered on to the track between Fernando Noronha and
Punta Arenas and was steaming up this track when captured. Although the KRONPRINZ WILHELM was first
sighted at a distance of ten or twelve miles, he does not
seem to have suspected her character till she was alongside, and in consequence he failed either to use effectively
or to disable his wireless apparatus, or even to throw overboard the breech blocks of the guns. A bag containing
dispatches from the British Legation was, however, sunk.[1]

As in the case of the *Indian Prince*, the next few days
were spent by the KRONPRINZ WILHELM in ransacking her
prize far from the track of shipping. By October 14th the
steamer's stores, 60 tons of frozen meat, and about 800
tons of bunker coal had been transferred, and the prize
was then sunk. At midnight on the 16th the KRONPRINZ
WILHELM was back on the trade routes, off Cape Frio, a
little north of Rio de Janiero. On the same date the
Hamburg-Süd-Amerika liner, *Sierra Cordoba*, put out from
Buenos Aires, ostensibly for Bremen, but really to join
the raider. The two ships met on October 20th, and on
the 22nd and the two following days the *Sierra Cordoba*
took off the prisoners and transferred coal and stores to
the cruiser. On the 24th she parted company, leaving
the KRONPRINZ WILHELM to continue her cruise.

Meanwhile the KARLSRUHE had again got to work. When
Captain Köhler dismissed the *Crefeld* he was, of course,
aware that the information given by the crews of the
sunken ships would render it dangerous for him to remain
in the neighbourhood of Rocas Reef and Fernando Noronha;
but as she had orders not to arrive until October 22nd,
he had a week or so of comparative safety in prospect
before he need shift his ground.[2]

[1] When the capture became known accusations of collusion were brought
against the master, but he was exonerated by a Naval Inquiry.
[2] See Map 8,

The removal of stores from the *Condor* was completed on the night of the 13th. As she carried a large consignment of dynamite, it was not considered safe to blow her up, but her sea-cocks were opened and the *Rio Negro* stood by to see her sink while the cruiser went off to coal. The 15th and 16th were spent in coaling, and by the 18th the Karlsruhe was back off Fernando Noronha, with the *Rio Negro* and *Asuncion* in company. With the *Farn* and *Hoffnung* to draw upon, the raider was now very well provided with coal. Indeed, she had been so successful in the capture of colliers that her original stock, obtained at Curaçao, remained almost untouched. Moreover, an experiment had been made with the oil obtained from the *Condor*, and it was found to give excellent results as liquid fuel. Curiously enough, the first prize made after the departure of the *Crefeld* was another collier, the *Glanton*, of 3,021 tons, from Barry Dock to Monte Video with 3,800 tons of coal and marine stores. Rather than spare another prize crew, Captain Köhler sank the *Glanton* after taking off her provisions and a quantity of oil and rope. Her people were put on board the *Rio Negro*.

Two other steamers sighted on the same day proved to be neutrals, and no further prize was made until the 23rd, when the *Hurstdale*, of 2,752 tons, was captured between twenty and thirty miles west of the track from Monte Video to the United Kingdom. She was on her way from Rosario to Bristol with 4,644 tons of maize, and was treated in the same way as the *Glanton*. While she was sinking, the Swedish steamer *Annie Johnson*, outward bound to Pernambuco, was stopped and released.

By this time Captain Köhler knew that the *Crefeld* should have arrived at Tenerife and it was high time for him to seek another cruising ground. Even apart from this consideration, he had come to the conclusion that a change was desirable, as the experience of the last few weeks showed, both by the actual captures made and the blank days spent in drifting on the trade routes, that British steamers were now deviating widely from the normal tracks. He would thus be obliged to rely mainly on chance encounters, and this was too uncertain a method to give good prospects. On the other hand, with the revival of South American trade, many more neutral ships were using the route, and the risk of being constantly sighted and reported was greatly increased. The alternative he had in mind was a raid on the West Indies, and on October 25th he finally turned westwards, after calling together the officers in charge of the *Rio Negro, Farn, Asuncion,* and *Hoffnung* to receive instructions.

Up to this date the KARLSRUHE had captured fifteen British steamers and one neutral, of which four were engaged in the trade between the United States and South America and the remainder were bound to or from the United Kingdom. No such record stood to the credit of any other German raider except the EMDEN, but in comparison with the total volume of trade on the route, the effect of her depredations was small. Of the outward bound prizes, four, with a net tonnage of 9,549 tons, had sailed from British ports during September. But during that month 233,483 net tons of British shipping were cleared for South America, so that the percentage of loss was under 5 per cent. Again, the four outward-bound colliers [1] carried between them about 20,000 tons of coal, all shipped during September, as against a total export to South America of 289,450 tons.[2]

In the homeward-bound trade the percentage was only a little higher. Including the *Pruth,* bound to St. Vincent " for orders," five British vessels were captured, with a total net tonnage of 12,826. If to these is added *La Correntina,* captured by the KRONPRINZ WILHELM, the total net tonnage is raised to 18,009, all of which had left East Coast ports on or before October 7th. The cargoes of the KARLSRUHE's five prizes amounted to 28,000 tons, of which 3,800 tons were nitrate and the remainder consisted mainly of maize, oats, and barley, with a certain amount of sugar, wool, hides, and tallow. *La Correntina,* as we have seen, carried 3,500 tons of meat. With these figures we may compare the ships entered with cargoes from South America and the imports from South American countries during the month of October. The net tonnage entered was 201,701. The imports included 149,000 tons of maize, 27,700 tons of meat, and 20,000 tons of nitrate, besides several thousand tons of other products. In November the maize import rose to 250,000 tons. Of the rubber and

[1] *Cornish City, Rio Iguassu, Farn,* and *Glanton.* The *Strathroy* and *Indrani* came from North America.
[2] Board of Trade Returns for Brazil, Uruguay, Argentina, Chile, and Peru. Clearances for Colombia are not included, as these belong rather to the Caribbean Route, and the vessels would not come within the KARLSRUHE's sphere of operations.

coffee from Brazil and the mutton from New Zealand which comes round the Horn, not a ton fell into the hands of the raiders.

The indirect effect of the captures, as we have seen, was slight.[1] In fact, the news brought by the *Crefeld* on October 22nd disturbed trade less than the sinking of two steamers by the DRESDEN at an earlier period of the war. The demand for tonnage caused by the recovery of South American trade was too strong an incentive for either the uncertain fate of overdue vessels or the actual announcement of losses to deter steamers from putting to sea. In this respect the career of the KARLSRUHE presents a striking contrast to that of the EMDEN; but Captain von Müller was operating in comparatively confined waters and in close proximity to great ports. The scene of Captain Köhler's operations was the open sea, and with so many British cruisers on the coast, he found it undesirable to approach Rio de Janeiro or the Plate. Thus, while her prizes were comparatively numerous, the KARLSRUHE caused no such stoppage of trade as did even the LEIPZIG by her quasi-blockade of San Francisco or her attack on the semi-coastal trade route on the Peruvian coast. Indeed, the chief point of interest in the KARLSRUHE's career is the light which it throws upon the limitations of sporadic raiding. From the first, as we have seen, she was excellently handled and exceptionally favoured by fortune; yet the effect of her operations was hardly appreciable even on the trade of the route which she attacked: in comparison with the world-wide volume of British commerce it was almost negligible.

There can be no doubt that observance of the Admiralty instructions to deviate from the usual tracks was a prominent factor in restricting the number of losses on the South American route. It is true that several ships which had departed widely from their normal course were captured; but during the days on which the KARLSRUHE was waiting fruitlessly on the trade routes many steamers must have passed her on either side, while her successful detour to the east of the tracks opened a safe passage to all those steering to the west of them. Many others, no doubt, passed the focal point in safety during the hours of darkness, for the instructions to obscure lights appear in general to have been carefully observed.

[1] See pages 177, 228, 239, 244–5, *supra*.

THE FUEL HANDICAP

A further limitation of Captain Köhler's success arose from the necessity under which he lay of leaving the trade routes from time to time to coal at his secret base. From August 30th, when he made his first prize in the focal area, to October 25th, when he finally quitted his station, is fifty-seven days, and at least a third of this time was spent away from the tracks, coaling, overhauling the engines, or steaming to and from the base. His changes of position when the wireless calls of British cruisers indicated danger consumed further time, and yet more was taken up in removing the crews and stores from the prizes. Many of these were sunk within a few hours of their capture, but two days were spent in removing the oil from the *Condor*, the ransacking of the *Maple Branch* occupied the greater part of a day, and a considerable time was wasted in attempting to coal from the *Rio Iguassu*. The *Lynrowan*, *Glanton*, and others which carried stores useful to the Germans also took some time to dispose of. Captain Thierfelder was still more severely handicapped, as he had no fixed base, and the KRONPRINZ WILHELM was accompanied by no regular tender. He was obliged to rely mainly on his prizes, both for coal and provisions, and to perform all his coaling at sea. Hence the capture of the *Indian Prince* and *La Correntina* was followed in each case by a long period of inactivity.

Captain Köhler's decision to abandon the South American Route was unknown and the KRONPRINZ WILHELM was still unlocated when Admiral Stoddart arrived at Pernambuco on October 21st. On her way down the CARNARVON had passed through the area in which the KARLSRUHE was then still operating, but without sighting her. A few days after his arrival the Admiral received a message informing him of the news brought by the *Crefeld*, and he proceeded to dispose his available force in such a manner as to afford the best protection to the trade routes. Under cover of his squadron the products of the East Coast continued to come forward in increasing volume, and shipping was also moving freely in Peruvian and Chilean waters, where Admiral Cradock was preparing to meet the German Pacific Squadron on its expected arrival. In the meantime the attention both of the Admiralty and of commercial circles was again directed to the progress of events in the East.

CHAPTER XV

REAPPEARANCE OF THE "EMDEN"[1]

WHILE the KARLSRUHE was taking toll of shipping in the South Atlantic and Admiral von Spee was making his way across the Pacific, the EMDEN was again busy in the Indian Ocean. The immunity enjoyed by traffic on the Oriental Route during the early part of October was only a lull. Although prudence had dictated the temporary retirement of the raider from the neighbourhood of Colombo, he had not yet done with that great nerve centre of the Eastern trade.

After dismissing the *Gryfevale* on September 27th, Captain von Müller went to the Maldive Islands, where he coaled from the *Markomannia*. As the fuel in this ship was now almost exhausted, she was sent off, on September 30th, to refill from the *Pontoporos*. The EMDEN, with the *Buresk* in company, steamed south, and on October 4th arrived in the neighbourhood of the Chagos Archipelago. Diego Garcia, in this group, had at one time been a coaling station for the vessels of the Orient Line,[2] and Captain von Müller appears to have anticipated falling in with some of the homeward-bound meat ships from Australia. Their track, however, now passed some distance to the north, and after four or five days' fruitless cruising, October 9th and 10th were devoted to heeling the cruiser and cleaning her bottom, preparatory to a return to the Minikoi area. She also coaled from the *Buresk*, and a welcome supply of fresh provisions was obtained from the islands, where the people were still in ignorance that war had broken out.

On his passage north the German captain experienced his usual good fortune, for after looking for him near Minikoi, Captain Grant had decided on a search of the southern archipelagos, and as the EMDEN was steaming

[1] See Map 7.
[2] *Islands in the Southern Indian Ocean Westward of Longitude 80° East*, 2nd ed., p. 352.

up the western side of the Maldives her pursuers were coming down on the eastern side. When, on October 4th, Captain von Müller passed through the Khardiva Channel to place himself between Minikoi and Colombo, they were already a considerable distance to the south.

At Diego Garcia Captain Grant learned that he had missed his quarry, and he accordingly turned back for Colombo. Some solace for his disappointment was provided by news of a success achieved by another of the ships under his command. He had been informed by Admiral Jerram, on October 9th, that a steamer flying the Greek flag had been sighted off Pulo Tapak, in Sumatra, four days previously, and had ordered the YARMOUTH from Acheh Head to investigate. She arrived at Pulo Tapak on the 12th, and found there not only the *Pontoporos* but the *Markomannia*. As both ships were caught outside territorial waters no question of neutrality arose. The *Markomannia*, which had now 1,300 tons of coal on board, was sunk, and the *Pontoporos*, with some 5,000 tons remaining, was taken into Singapore.[1]

Captain von Müller was, of course, ignorant of the fate which had overtaken his detached colliers. He coaled from the *Buresk* on October 15th, and by midnight on that date had arrived within a few miles of Minikoi. During the next four days seven British vessels were captured. At 12.50 a.m. on the 16th the EMDEN's look-out saw the lights of a steamer which proved, when stopped twenty minutes later, to be the liner *Clan Grant*, with 4,000 tons of general cargo for Calcutta. Before the prize had been disposed of smoke was seen on the horizon, and a short chase resulted in the capture of the *Ponrabbel*, a newly built steam dredger on her way out to Launceston, Tasmania. She was a low-powered vessel, and had not sufficient coal supply to allow of deviation. Like the *Clan Grant*, therefore, she was on the direct track to Colombo.

The crews of the *Clan Grant* and *Ponrabbel* having been transferred to the *Buresk* and the prizes sunk by about 2.30 p.m., the EMDEN stood across the Nine Degree Channel till she was sixty or seventy miles north-west of Minikoi. At 8 p.m. the lights of another steamer were seen, and shortly afterwards the new-comer was stopped and

---

[1] She was subsequently restored to the original owners and the coal was sold at Singapore for the benefit of the cargo owners.

boarded. Again the prize was an outward-bound liner, the *Benmohr*, with 6,000 tons of general cargo for Yokohama. Her master had received instructions at Port Saïd or Perim and was making a course well to the north of the ordinary track through the Nine Degree Channel. It was unfortunate that he had not been equally careful to obscure his lights. These were now extinguished by the boarding party, who proceeded to ransack the ship with the aid of electric torches and remove the crew. By an hour after midnight this operation was completed and the *Benmohr* was sunk.

Captain von Müller now turned east, and on October 18th he captured two more steamers between Minikoi and Ceylon, the *Troilus* at 2 p.m. and the *St. Egbert* at 9.30. The *Troilus* was a Blue Funnel liner homeward bound from Yokohama and was only twenty-five hours out from Colombo. The *St. Egbert* had also left Colombo on the 17th and was bound for New York. The masters of both ships had received instructions as to their course at Colombo and were doing their best to comply with them, though the master of the *St. Egbert* had neglected to obscure his lights. Unfortunately for them, both were captured before they had time and sea room to depart very far from the normal route.

Neither the *Troilus* nor the *St. Egbert* was immediately sunk, and on the 19th two other vessels were added to the little fleet of prizes. On this day Captain von Müller made a sweep somewhat to the north of the direct track through the Nine Degree Channel, with the result that he captured the collier *Exford*, on her way to Hongkong, and the British India Steam Navigation Company's *Chilkana*, outward bound for Calcutta, with a general cargo amounting to nearly 6,800 tons. The *Exford* had reached a point at which wide deviation becomes very difficult; nevertheless, her master had departed from his course as widely as was possible without getting on to another of the converging tracks. The *Chilkana* was forty miles north of the trade route.

With this success Captain von Müller was, for the moment, satisfied. His prisoners were mounting up, he would shortly require to coal the cruiser, his outward-bound prizes would soon be posted as overdue, and he did not consider it safe to remain any longer so near Colombo. The captured vessels were accordingly rounded up and the crews of the *Troilus, Exford,* and *Chilkana,* together with the prisoners in the *Buresk,* were transferred to the *St. Egbert,* the only prize carrying neutral cargo. At 5 p.m. on the 19th the *St. Egbert* was released, with instructions to land the crews at any port between Cape Comorin and Calicut, but not to go to Bombay, Colombo, or Calcutta, under pain of being sunk if discovered. The *Troilus* and *Chilkana* were sunk as soon as the crews had been removed, but the *Exford* was retained as a tender to the cruiser, which then ran to the south.

The German captain's decision to shift his ground before any rumour of his presence could reach the British naval authorities was fully justified. The HAMPSHIRE and EMPRESS OF ASIA returned from the Chagos Islands to Colombo on October 18th, and as no further news of the raider had been received Captain Grant left, after coaling, to patrol off Dondra Head, where he would be within touch with Colombo and at the same time could cover the junction of the Calcutta, Rangoon, and Singapore tracks. The ZHEMCHUG was searching the Nicobar and Andaman Islands for German coaling bases and the CHIKUMA was also in the Bay of Bengal. Finally, the YARMOUTH was approaching Colombo in charge of a convoy, and was very near that port when, on October 20th, the *St. Egbert* arrived at Cochin on the Malabar coast.

The information brought by the captured crews reached Captain Grant on the same day, and he immediately ordered the YARMOUTH to quit her convoy and proceed at high speed for the purpose of covering trade between Minikoi and Colombo. He considered it probable, however, that the EMDEN would have left the tracks in order to coal after her raid, and he accordingly proceeded with the HAMPSHIRE and EMPRESS OF ASIA to search the Upper Maldives, each ship examining one side of the group.

The search of the Maldives proved unsuccessful, but Captain Grant's dispositions provided so effective a cover for the trade routes that it was unnecessary to delay shipping for more than a few hours. On the first receipt of the *St. Egbert's* news homeward-bound steamers at Colombo and Bombay were officially detained; but those passing Aden and Perim outward bound were allowed to proceed, as it was unlikely that the EMDEN could maintain herself off Colombo until their arrival. At 9 p.m.

on the 21st shipping at Bombay was released, and twenty-four hours later the Colombo route was also reopened. The total interference with trade was thus very slight.

Nevertheless, the blow struck by Captain von Müller was again severe. Six steamers, aggregating 26,477 tons, had been lost and the four liners all carried valuable cargoes. The *Troilus* was the heaviest loss as yet sustained in the capture of any single ship. She was a fine new vessel of 7,562 tons, insured for £130,000, and the value of her cargo was at least £700,000. It is probable, however, that the prize most valued by the Germans was the *Exford*, in which they found 6,000 tons of Admiralty coal to replenish their fast dwindling supplies.

The apparent failure of the navy to check the activities of the EMDEN gave rise at this time to much criticism in Indian shipping and commercial circles. The Bengal Chamber of Commerce, in particular, reflected bitterly upon the presumed inadequacy of the naval dispositions, and urged the establishment of a system of commercial convoys with a view to avoiding further losses.

To this appeal the Admiralty considered it unnecessary to respond. They had little force to spare for such a purpose, nor was the situation, in their opinion, such as to render the adoption of this course imperative. The success obtained by the EMDEN was due, in part at least, to neglect of precautions, proceeding from over-confidence, and there was good reason to hope that with more careful attention to instructions the percentage of captures would diminish. It had never been anticipated that, even with the utmost skill and vigilance on the part of the defence, immunity from occasional losses could be guaranteed. This, indeed, seems to have been overlooked by the critics. The success of the navy in keeping the sea routes clear from the very outbreak of the war had given rise to an exaggerated optimism, in which the earlier apprehensions of heavy initial losses were forgotten, and there was a tendency to ignore the fact that the State guarantee of insurance was based upon the running of risks, and to expect from the British command of the sea not merely the limitation, but the total elimination of danger to merchant shipping. Nor was it fully recognised how greatly the task of the Admiralty had been complicated by the progress of military events in Europe, which rendered it necessary to employ a large proportion of our cruisers on foreign stations in covering the passage of essential reinforcements. The good fortune which had more than once narrowly saved the EMDEN from destruction was also, of course, unknown.

These factors in the situation were reviewed in a statement published by the Admiralty on October 24th, with a view to calming such apprehensions as might have been excited by the continuance of the EMDEN's activity and the news brought by the *Crefeld* as to the KARLSRUHE's depredations. They explained the difficulty of hunting down isolated raiders on the high seas and the great strain thrown upon the navy by the necessity for military convoys, but emphasised the fact that large numbers of fast cruisers were already employed in the hunt for the hostile commerce destroyers and that others were about to be released by the diminution of transport requirements. On the other hand, they pointed out that the total number of losses recorded was only thirty-nine, or less than 1 per cent of some 4,000 British ships engaged in foreign trade, and that out of eight or nine thousand voyages made to or from the United Kingdom since the outbreak of war, less than five per thousand had been interfered with by the enemy. In these circumstances they considered it undesirable to impose on trade the delays and restrictions inseparable from a system of mercantile convoys, and they reiterated that British trade could safely continue to rely upon the adequacy of naval protection so long as the instructions given to merchantmen were faithfully observed.[1]

How negligible were the depredations of the hostile cruisers in comparison with the total volume of British trade may be seen in the fact that during the months of September and October, when both the EMDEN and the KARLSRUHE were at the height of their activity, the cargoes lost represented less than 1·3 per cent. in value of those afloat in British bottoms.[2] It is true that the risks were unevenly distributed, and were at their highest in the case of ships bound to India or the Far East, but the

---

[1] The thirty-nine ships referred to in the statement may be accounted for as follows: Captured by EMDEN, 17; by KARLSRUHE, 13; by KAISER WILHELM DER GROSSE, 2; by LEIPZIG, 2; by DRESDEN, 2; by KÖNIGSBERG, 1; by KRONPRINZ WILHELM, 1; by submarine (*vide infra*), 1. The loss of the *Glanton, Hurstdale,* and *La Correntina* had not yet been reported.

[2] Estimate prepared for the Liverpool and London War Risks Insurance Association.

experience of the second Minikoi raid was not, itself, without its consolatory side. During the four days of the EMDEN's operations in the confined area between Minikoi and Colombo, no less than nineteen steamers, fourteen outward and five homeward bound, passed through in safety, as against seven which were captured. It was evident that the Admiralty instructions were now being more carefully observed, and though the difficulty of effecting a wide dispersal of shipping in confined waters was strikingly illustrated, the results went far to prove that deviation could at least be relied upon to reduce the risk of capture to a minimum.

In these circumstances, the dislocation of trade arising from the EMDEN's second raid in Cingalese waters was kept within very moderate bounds. Forward chartering continued to be hampered by the prevailing uncertainty and the withdrawal of native bankers and money-lenders from business, but the sailings of the liners and of tramps already fixed were little, if at all, disturbed. It is true that underwriters' quotations for war risks on cargoes to India and the East rose from 2 to 3 per cent., but this was of little consequence, since the State Flat Rate remained at the lower level, and the total number of steamers clearing with cargoes from Indian ports during October was only 10 per cent. less than in the same month of 1913, a decrease barely equivalent to the withdrawal of the German and Austrian services. How little the news brought by the *St. Egbert* affected the flow of trade could be seen especially in the figures of exports from Calcutta and Chittagong during the last fortnight of October, which surpassed even the record of the two preceding weeks. The returns from Rangoon were equally satisfactory, and both at Bombay and Karachi the shipments were heavy. Indeed, the only branch of Indian commerce in which exports were seriously restricted by the fear of capture was jute, large stocks of which were held back by the producers owing to nervousness as to the safety of the routes. Tea, both from India and Ceylon, wheat, cotton, hides, and oil-seeds from India, and rubber from the Cingalese plantations, were all going forward to the United Kingdom at or above the normal rate of shipment, and the gravest feature in the situation was the loss of the Continental markets, for which, especially in the case of oil-seeds, the British demand supplied inadequate compensation. The British market could, indeed, readily have absorbed the total ouput of oil derived from these seeds, but the crushing machinery was lacking, as this country had hitherto taken only a restricted part in the industry.[1]

From the Malay Peninsula, also, British imports were well maintained. Nearly a thousand tons of tin from the Straits had gone down in the *Troilus*, but thanks to the policy of the Admiralty in keeping the Colombo—Singapore track open, the supply was steady and sufficient for all requirements. Shipments of rubber rose far above the normal level. The export of this commodity to foreign countries had been prohibited early in the war, and the result of this prohibition was a fall in price which attracted to the Malay plantations a portion of the orders usually placed by British importers in Brazil. These orders were the more welcome as the impossibility of shipping rubber to Germany had already caused financial difficulties among the local merchants both in the Malay Peninsula and in Burma, which prevented them from buying British goods to the extent of their usual requirements.

A similar revival of prosperity was visible in the trade of the Far East. Here the local seas were completely immune from attack, and the possibility of interference by the EMDEN in Cingalese waters was too remote to exercise much influence. The financial difficulties of the early weeks of the war had been in great part overcome, and silk from Japan, silk and tea from China, came forward in large quantities to make up the leeway of the previous months. At the Javanese ports a continual stream of tramp tonnage arrived to load sugar cargoes, and during November and December some 250,000 tons of sugar reached the United Kingdom from this source. In Australia the export trade was still hampered by shortage of tonnage, but the reservation of refrigerated space on steamers requisitioned as transports went some way towards satisfying the requirements of shippers.

Meanwhile the outwards traffic, whether to the Far or Middle East, continued to be practically unaffected by

[1] Exports in lakhs of rupees:

Week ended	Calcutta and Chittagong	Bombay	Karachi	Madras	Rangoon
October 24th	191	76	62	7	15
October 31st	205	60	33	4	39

the EMDEN's operations. The export of British goods was restricted both by war conditions at home and by the disturbed state of the Eastern markets, and shipments to China and Japan were a long way below the normal; but the recovery of trade in India led to a revival of demand, and the quantity of piece-goods consigned to Indian merchants was only about 15 per cent. less than in October 1913. British purchases of sugar also stimulated the demand from the Dutch East Indies. Altogether, the tonnage of all nationalities cleared with cargoes during the month amounted to 130,000 tons for India and 120,000 for other Eastern ports, as compared with 165,000 and 135,000 tons respectively in the previous year. The export trade to Australia, whether by way of the Canal or the Cape, was well up to the normal level.

By the end of October all danger to trade on the route, other than that presented by the EMDEN herself, had practically passed away. The KÖNIGSBERG had remained inactive since her destruction of the PEGASUS, and the search for her was too vigorous to leave much fear of her attacking either the transports in the Arabian Sea or merchant shipping. On October 10th, the DARTMOUTH captured, near Mozambique, the tug *Adjutant*, which was suspected of having been in communication with the German cruiser. On the 19th, an indisputable tender to the KÖNIGSBERG was discovered by the CHATHAM in the Lindi River. This was the *Präsident*, a steamer of 1,849 tons, normally employed in the Deustche Ost-Afrika Line's service between Bombay and East African ports. Papers found in the prize proved conclusively that she had supplied coal to the KÖNIGSBERG during September in a branch of the Rufiji River, and the swampy delta of the Rufiji was thus indicated as a probable hiding-place of the raider. A close watch on the entrances was at once instituted, and there was every reason to hope that she would soon be finally brought to book. Her presence had ceased to have any appreciable effect on trade, and on October 27th the Union Castle Line reduced the East African surcharge from 25 to 20 per cent.

Meanwhile the SCHARNHORST's intercepted message of October 4th [1] had relieved the Admiralty of all fear that Admiral von Spee might turn back towards the Far Eastern routes; and though their possession of this know-

---

[1] See page 234, *supra*.

ledge was of too great strategic importance to be made public, the successive appearances of the German squadron at Samoa and Papieté gave sufficient indication of his movements for shipping on the Oriental Route to disregard them as a factor in the immediate situation. Tsingtau was closely invested by land and sea; the German steamers in Philippine and Dutch East Indian ports gave no sign of movement; and the enemy's possessions in the Pacific were almost all effectively occupied. Nauru, the last of the German wireless stations, fell on September 22nd, and a little later the Japanese occupied the Marshall Islands, where they released the *Induna*, a small British steamer which had been detained there on the outbreak of war.

With the reduction of the German Colonies, the small vessels, armed or armable, whose existence had troubled the communications, were gradually rooted out, while the GEIER and the two auxiliary cruisers left behind by Admiral von Spee were reduced to impotence by lack of coal and provisions and fear of capture by the overwhelming forces of the Allies. The PRINZ EITEL FRIEDRICH, after obtaining 2,000 tons of coal at Malakal before its reduction, set out across the Pacific to follow her Admiral. The GEIER achieved no further success after the escape of the *Southport*, and finally put over to Honolulu. Here she arrived, in need of extensive repairs on October 17th, and was promptly blockaded by Japanese warships lying off the port. The CORMORAN, after narrowly escaping capture by the SATSUMA at Yap, found her way to the Western Carolines, where she remained in hiding.

Thus the EMDEN was now the only real menace to trade remaining either in the Indian Ocean or the Western Pacific; but three successive raids had shown that even by herself she was capable of working serious mischief, and until she should be accounted for, there was little hope of conditions becoming normal, greatly as they had improved since the passing of the crisis produced by her first appearance. For a week after the arrival of the *St. Egbert* at Cochin, nothing was heard of her movements, but experience suggested that she might reappear at any moment and at any point. On the other hand, the focal area off Colombo and the Bay of Bengal were now both well guarded, and there was good reason to hope that a repetition of her previous easy successes would prove impossible.

When the next blow was actually struck, it lacked nothing in surprise and dramatic effect. Having decided that it was unsafe for him to remain longer in Cingalese waters, Captain von Müller resolved upon an exploit even more daring than those which had preceded it. He had become convinced that the trade routes were now too well guarded for a further attack upon them to be profitable, and he accordingly determined to make his appearance at a point as far removed as possible from the scene of his recent activities and to act directly against the forces by which Allied shipping in the Middle East was protected. For this purpose he disguised his ship with a dummy funnel, which gave her an appearance resembling that of the British YARMOUTH class, and after coaling from the *Buresk* sent her to a rendezvous off the coast of Sumatra, and the *Exford* to another near the Cocos Islands, farther south. He then ran across the entrance of the Bay of Bengal, carefully avoiding the track of shipping, and in the early morning of October 28th entered the harbour of Penang. Sweeping in out of the morning mist he sank the ZHEMCHUG, which had recently returned from her search of the Andamans and Nicobars, and then turned and made off before the D'IBERVILLE and two French destroyers, lying farther up the harbour, could cast loose from their moorings to attack him.

As she came out of the entrance the EMDEN met the liner *Glenturret* coming in. She was flying the " explosives " flag, and the Germans at once hailed to know the reason. They were answered that she had paraffin on board, for the master was unwilling to acknowledge that his ship carried a quantity of ammunition and explosives, which would have rendered her a valuable prize. A short respite was thus gained, but the EMDEN was about to send off a boat when the French destroyer MOUSQUET, returning from a patrol, appeared on the scene. Despite a gallant resistance, the MOUSQUET was speedily sunk, but in the meantime the *Glenturret* had entered the harbour, and Captain von Müller, who was unwilling to engage the remaining torpedo craft in narrow waters, made off, after picking up the survivors of the destroyer's crew, without attempting to follow up the liner.

This exploit was a remarkable illustration of the German captain's daring and activity, and coming so soon after the news of the second Minikoi raid, it assisted to

THE PENANG RAID

retard the recovery of chartering, but its effect on the immediate movements of shipping was surprisingly small. Some alarm indeed was excited at Calcutta, where an unfounded rumour that the Japanese steamer, *Kamasaka Maru*, had been captured, obtained wide credence; but though the port was closed for a few hours and several steamers which had just put to sea returned to the Hoogly, the interruption of trade was too short to be appreciable. There was, in fact, no cause for panic, for the naval protection given to trade in the Middle East became more complete with every week that passed. Captain Grant's division was concentrated in the neighbourhood of Colombo and Minikoi, and the ASKOLD was also near Colombo. The CHIKUMA was still in the Bay of Bengal, and besides the D'IBERVILLE and destroyers at Penang, the passage of the Malacca Strait was protected by the presence of the Japanese light cruiser YAHAGI at Singapore. The destroyer division at Sandakan was also under orders for the Straits, as the watch on German steamers in Manila had become a less urgent task. Finally, a new Japanese squadron, under Vice-Admiral Tochinai, was being formed to operate in the neighbourhood of Rangoon, Acheh Head, and the Sunda Strait, absorbing the CHIKUMA and YAHAGI.

There was thus ample force at hand to give protection to shipping between Singapore and Colombo, and on October 30th the situation was still further improved by the CHATHAM's discovery of the KÖNIGSBERG up a branch of the Rufiji River. She had been considerably lightened and was too far up for the CHATHAM to get at her effectively, but prompt measures were taken to block her exit, and the fast cruisers which had been searching for her were thus rendered available for operations against the one unlocated raider.

CHAPTER XVI

TRADE ACTIVITY IN EUROPEAN WATERS [1]

WHILE the EMDEN was holding up the trade of the Middle East, and shipping on the South American Route was exposed to the depredations of the KARLSRUHE and threatened by the approach of the German Pacific squadron, the general course of British commerce was but little impeded by hostile activity. The all-important North Atlantic tracks were immune, as we have seen, from interference, or even from alarm. All fear of attack on shipping from South African or West African ports disappeared with the capture of Duala, and no enemy troubled the great terminal area which stretches from the Straits of Gibraltar to the entrance to the Channel. Practically the only waters in which serious risk was still to be apprehended were those of the North Sea, where the danger arising from the German mine-fields called for unceasing vigilance on the part of the British flotillas, and the strictest supervision over the course of shipping.

From the beginning of the war a strict examination service had been imposed at all East Coast ports, and as time went by the restrictions on navigation in estuaries and coastal waters continually increased. At an early period, Harwich and Immingham were partially closed by their use as naval bases, and with the immense increase in the number of mine-sweepers and Auxiliary Patrol vessels employed, it became necessary to set aside more and more of the harbour accommodation on the coast for naval and military use. Partly for the purposes of port defence, and partly in order to ensure closer supervision over both British and neutral shipping, vessels were prohibited from leaving port at night, and stricter regulations were issued as to compulsory pilotage and the use of particular entrances and exits. The closing of certain of the channels in the estuary of the Thames on September 14th was only

[1] See Maps 1 and 2.

one of a long series of such measures announced by Notices to Mariners which appeared almost weekly in the shipping papers. From October 1st, the use of East Coast ports was prohibited to foreign trawlers, in order to guard against the supposed misuse of neutral flags by German mine-layers, and at the beginning of October the increasing activity of the enemy's submarines obliged the Admiralty to depart from the policy hitherto adopted, and to lay a British mine-field in the southern part of the North Sea.

In strict accordance with the Hague Conventions, the limits of this mine-field were publicly announced, and orders were issued to our patrols to warn all east-bound shipping of the danger. The mined area lay between latitude 51° 15′ N. and 51° 40′ N., and longitude 1° 35′ E. and 3° E. That is to say, its southern boundary ran from the Goodwins to Ostend, and the northern from the mouth of the Thames towards the north of Walcheren. The eastern boundary ran directly north from Ostend, leaving the approaches to Antwerp and the Scheldt free; while on the west a clear channel was left extending some miles from the Kentish coast. The southern limit of the ascertained German mine-field was 52° N., and a passage twenty miles broad was thus left between it and the new danger area for the use of shipping; but owing to the danger of mines—whether German or British—coming adrift in heavy weather, no part of the southern waters of the North Sea could be considered altogether safe for navigation.[1]

Although neutrals were inclined to grumble at these further restrictions, they could hardly protest against measures which fell so far short of those taken by the enemy, and thanks to the clear notice given, no neutral vessel fell a victim to the new mine-field. On the other hand, the Tyne, Humber, and Southwold fields each claimed a neutral victim during October, and another was blown up off the German coast. One British steamer, the *Cormorant*, was also lost in the Southwold area, and two others, the *Dawdon* and *Ardmount*, were destroyed off the Belgian coast, having blundered into the British field.[2]

---

[1] Admiralty Statement published October 3rd, 1914. See Map 2.
[2] The total tonnage lost through mines in the North Sea during October was: British, 6,425; Neutral, 3,273. Two British fishing craft were also blown up. In all, 15 British lives were lost.

Thanks to the existence of the Swept Channel along our Eastern Coast and to the precise and accurate information given by the Admiralty to both British and neutral shipping, the trade of the North Sea was less impeded than might have been expected by the mine-peril. The losses, after all, were small compared with the body of shipping employed; they were easily covered by insurance either on the London market or with the war risks offices which were set up in the neutral States concerned; and the demand for tonnage was too strong for the Dutch and Scandinavian shipowners to forgo their opportunity. Several services, both under the British and neutral flags, were transferred from East Coast ports to Tilbury or the West Coast, either on account of the mine danger or through the closing of ports to commercial use;[1] but these services were only diverted, not suspended, while at London and at the northern ports on the East Coast, from Grimsby to Leith, the dairy produce of Holland and Denmark continued to arrive in large quantities. The bulk of the tonnage employed was still neutral, though British shipping began to be a little more active in the Dutch and Norwegian trade; but the point of chief importance was that, under whatever flag, the flow of traffic should be maintained. This the German mine-layers wholly failed to prevent. The imports of butter and eggs from Scandinavia and the Netherlands, of Dutch cheese, and of bacon from Denmark, rose in October to well above the normal figures, and even the consignments received from Russia showed a very marked recovery, due to the development of the transhipment route through Sweden.

There was, however, one branch of Scandinavian trade which was directly threatened by the German command of the entrance to the Baltic. The arrivals of vessels laden with wood cargoes from Sweden were very numerous during October, and to some extent compensated for the diminution of supplies from Russia, but about the middle of the month this recovery was suddenly and roughly checked. At an early period of the war the German Government had notified the Governments of Sweden and Norway that unworked or roughly worked timber,

---

[1] Thus, the Wilson Line passenger service to Christiania, transferred from Hull to Liverpool; the Great Eastern Railway's Antwerp service, transferred from Harwich to Tilbury; the United Steamship Company of Copenhagen, whose food ships now ran direct to Manchester.

including pit-props, would be considered as fuel, which was classed by Article 24 of the Declaration of London as Conditional Contraband. For rather over two months from the outbreak of war no particular attempt was made to enforce this contention, but between October 10th and 16th, inclusive, about a score of Scandinavian vessels laden with wood cargoes for the United Kingdom were stopped by German cruisers or torpedo-boats in the Baltic and taken to Swinemunde. In the course of a few days the majority were released by order of the Imperial Prize Commissioner, on the ground that their cargoes had been decided by experts to be building timber, which could not be used for fuel without incurring a prohibitive commercial loss. On the other hand, five steamers which were carrying pit-props or similar timber were only allowed to depart on giving a bond for the value of ship and cargo, in order that the legality of the captures might be tested before a Prize Court.

These seizures caused great excitement in Sweden, as timber was the most valuable of the Swedish exports and was shipped almost exclusively from Baltic ports. It was now evident that cargoes of pit-props from these ports were liable to capture by the Germans, and that even sawn and planed wood was by no means immune from interference, as the ultimate decision as to its character would rest with the German Prize Courts, and the commanders of German warships were not likely to err on the side of leniency in deciding whether there was a *prima facie* case for suspicion. Most of the British ports to which such cargoes were usually shipped were regarded, or likely to be regarded, by the Germans as " fortified " or as bases of supply, and there was no guarantee that any wood cargo would not be taken in by the Kattegat patrols. To divert the traffic to Gothenburg or to Norwegian ports was almost impossible, owing to the limited capacity of the harbours and the difficulties of rail transport. The future prospects of the trade were thus precarious, and the anxiety of Swedish shippers was extreme. For the time being, however, the matter went no farther; no more steamers were taken in by the German cruisers, and wood cargoes from Sweden, other than pit-props, continued to come forward freely.

At the same time, the prevailing uncertainty as to the German attitude with regard to various categories of timber and lumber gave rise to an amount of irritation which was very prejudicial to German interests. Thanks to the German command of the Baltic a considerable traffic had by this time been built up between Lübeck, Stettin and Danzig, and Swedish ports. Iron ore, of which Germany was sorely in need, was shipped from Lulea in large quantities, and the Sassnitz—Trelleborg ferries were busily employed in the carriage of foodstuffs, either produced in Sweden or imported for the purposes of transhipment. So valuable was this trade to the Swedes that strong resentment was excited by a Proclamation issued by the British Government on September 21st, adding hæmatite and magnetic iron ore, together with unwrought copper, lead, glycerine, rubbers, hides and skins, and ferrochrome, to the list of Conditional Contraband.[1] This resentment was now diverted to Germany, and for a time there seemed to be a prospect of Germany losing, to some extent, the benefit of the Swedish supplies.

With this exception, very little of interest took place in the Baltic during this period. The only event which directly affected seaborne trade was that, on October 16th, the Russian Government announced that the activity of German submarines and mine-layers had compelled them to mine the entrances to the Gulfs of Finland and Riga and the coastal waters of the Aaland Isles, and to close both the Gulfs altogether to merchant shipping. This step, however, did not affect the route between Raumo and Gefle,[2] and as the trade of Riga and Petrograd was already practically extinct, the situation was not appreciably changed. The greater portion of Russian trade was still confined to the White Sea tracks, and great efforts were being made to develop the capacities of Archangel. Icebreakers were procured from the Canadian Government, with a view to keeping the port open as long as possible during the winter months, and though the usual date of closing was about October 20th, the end of the month saw British, Russian, and neutral steamers arriving and departing in considerable numbers, and chartering still in progress. Further, to encourage this trade and that of the Raumo-Gefle route, the Russian Government undertook, towards the end of October, to bear 75 per cent. of

---

[1] *Manual of Emergency Legislation*, p. 111. As a result of the Swedish protests the inclusion of iron ore was, for a time, withdrawn.

[2] See p. 96, *supra*.

the war risks on Russian, Allied, or neutral vessels engaged either in foreign commerce or in the coasting traffic; but the imperfect development of the northern railways continued to impede the revival of commerce.

The activity of German submarines in the Baltic, mentioned by the Russian Government, had its parallel in some daring work by either side in the North Sea. The activity of the submarines rendered the work of the cruiser patrols engaged in examining neutral shipping very dangerous; but during the first ten weeks of the war the enemy made no attempt to employ these craft for attacking merchant shipping. On October 20th, however, an incident took place which was to acquire a formidable significance from later developments. On that day the British steamer *Glitra*, of 866 tons, bound from Grangemouth to Stavanger with a cargo of coal, coke, iron plates, and oil, amounting to 1,050 tons, was stopped by U 17, fourteen miles from Skudesnaes. Although there would probably have been little difficulty in navigating the prize to a German port, the submarine could not spare a prize crew. The *Glitra's* people were given ten minutes to take to their boats and the ship was then sunk. The boats were subsequently picked up and towed in by a Norwegian torpedo craft.

The use as commerce destroyers of vessels which could not take their prizes into port, nor make proper provision for the safety of the crew, raised grave questions of international law, but for the time no further attempt of this kind was made against British merchantmen. On October 26th, however, the French steamer *Amiral Ganteaume*, of 4,590 tons, belonging to the Chargeurs Réunis and engaged in carrying 2,000 refugees from the Pas de Calais to Havre, was seriously damaged by an explosion which was at first thought to have been caused by a mine, but was subsequently proved to have been the effect of a torpedo fired by a submarine without warning. Between thirty and forty people were killed and many others injured by this outrage.

This was the last submarine attack on Allied merchantmen for some weeks, but on the same day, October 26th, a new extension of the mine menace both to Allied and neutral shipping was revealed by the sinking of the *Manchester Commerce*, twenty miles from Tory Island, off the coast of Donegal.[1] The sunken ship was a steamer of

[1] The AUDACIOUS fell a victim to the same mine-field on the following day.

5,363 tons belonging to Manchester Liners, Ltd., and was outward bound for Montreal. Unfortunately her loss was accompanied by that of fourteen lives, including the master. No notice of any kind had been given by the Germans, either to the Allied or to neutral Governments, of this new mine-field laid on the main trade route from America to Liverpool round the north of Ireland, crowded as it was with shipping of all nations, but thanks to the activity of the British mine-sweeping service and patrols in warning merchantmen and sweeping the infested waters, no further merchant losses were recorded for the time being. The rates charged by underwriters for war risks on cargoes to and from North American ports, which had fallen as low as 10*s.* or, in the case of fast liners, 7*s.* 6*d.*, rose, however, to almost double those figures.

Meanwhile the security of British shipping in the Channel was seriously menaced by the progress of events on land. While the fighting on the Aisne had settled down into the beginnings of trench warfare, the German invasion had now overflowed practically the whole of Belgium. Antwerp fell on October 9th, and the occupation of Ghent, Bruges, and Ostend followed during the next few days. During the latter part of October the Allied armies, supported by a British coastal squadron, were struggling desperately against the German attempt to push on to Dunkirk and Calais and thus gain a footing on the Channel coast. At great cost the line of the Yser was successfully held, but the possession of Zeebrugge gave the Germans a base for submarines and mine-layers dangerously near the mouth of the Thames. No British vessels fell into the enemy's hands in the captured ports, but the invaders recovered possession of the German and Austrian steamers which had been detained at the outbreak of war. Most of these, however, were sunk or disabled by the Belgians before the fall of Antwerp, and the exit of the remainder was blocked by the refusal of the Netherlands Government to allow them to pass through the Dutch territorial waters at the mouth of the Scheldt. Belgian commerce itself was, of course, brought to an absolute standstill, but many of the Belgian shipping companies followed the example of the Red Star Line, by establishing fresh services from British ports, and by arrangement between the British and Belgian Governments, these ships were brought within the scope of the State Insurance Scheme.

A further effect of the German advance was to increase the congestion at French Atlantic ports. The diversion of shipping from the Channel, and the crowd of steamers arriving with troops and supplies from Great Britain choked the harbours and brought about a state of disorganisation which gravely impeded the progress of trade. At Bordeaux, for example, twenty-two British steamers, over and above the regular traders to the port, were lying in the outer harbour and at the river anchorages on October 28th, most of them laden with coal or foodstuffs to Government orders. The knowledge that a delay of three weeks or more might be expected before steamers could begin to discharge was a serious obstacle to chartering, and though the tonnage cleared from the United Kingdom for France rose from 285,000 tons in August and 388,000 in September, to 639,000 in October, it was clear that the situation would not become really satisfactory until the congestion was relieved.[1]

While the benefits of the naval protection given to French trade were thus, to some extent, discounted by other less favourable factors, the commerce of the United Kingdom with Spain and Portugal went on, under the protection of Admiral de Robeck's force and the French squadron in the Bay of Biscay, as smoothly as in times of peace. Iron ore from Santander, iron ore and copper pyrites from Huelva, wine from Oporto and the south of Spain came forward in quantities little if at all below the normal, and in the Mediterranean, the main tracks of shipping were as free from attack as in the North Atlantic.

The position within the Straits was, indeed, very similar to that in the North Sea, except that the mine danger was much less serious and that a larger proportion of the mercantile tonnage employed was British. As in the chief theatre of war, the enemy's main forces were still intact, but were preserved from destruction only by their own inactivity, and exercised no direct influence upon the course of trade. The superior strength of the Allied forces in the Mediterranean kept the Austrian fleet sealed in its home ports, and the GOEBEN and BRESLAU, though secure from attack under the Turkish flag, could not

[1] Consular Reports, A.S. 5,525; *Times*, 29 October, 1914; *Morning Post*, 20 October, 1914.

venture to issue from the Dardanelles. The only waters in which navigation was unsafe were those of the Upper Adriatic, where the Austrian mines had been laid with no regard for the restrictions imposed by the Hague Conventions. Towards the end of September a Roumanian brigantine and two or three Italian fishing craft were blown up, and the sailings of Italian steamers from Brindisi to Dalmatia, Montenegro, Albania, and Greece, as well as the service between Venice and Trieste, were all suspended for fear of further disasters. The French Admiralty, upon whom the conduct of operations in the Adriatic mainly devolved, felt themselves obliged to adopt retaliatory measures, and during the first week of October they gave notice that they had mined the enemy's territorial waters and the channels between the Dalmatian Islands. So far as Austrian commerce was concerned, the mine danger was not a factor of importance, as the activity of Austrian shipping was confined to the despatch of an occasional steamer from Trieste to Venice or the Dalmatian coast, and all efforts to build up either the export or the import trade by means of neutral tonnage had been defeated by the difficulty of arranging payments. To Italy, on the other hand, the suspension of the Adriatic services was a serious matter, and urgent representations were made to Austria as to the reckless manner in which peaceful commerce was endangered by her policy. So strong was the pressure brought to bear by the Italian Government that the Austrians finally gave way and agreed to refrain from laying unanchored mines, to strengthen the moorings of those which were fixed, and to replace old mines which were furnished with defective mechanism. By October 22nd it was considered that the danger to navigation had been effectively removed and all the Italian services resumed their sailings.[1] The British State Insurance Office still refused to insure the cargoes of vessels bound farther north than Vieste, but this restriction affected British shipping to no very serious extent.

The conditions in the Mediterranean were thus favourable to commerce. Since the removal of the restrictions on the export of coal, the shipments to Italy had been heavy and gave employment to a large number of British,

[1] *Lloyd's List*, 2, 8, 23 October, 1914.

Greek, and Italian steamers. Lead from the Spanish Mediterranean ports and currants from Greece were imported freely, and in October the imports of fresh fruit rose to a considerably higher figure than in previous months of the war.

On the other hand, just as the British command of the North Sea was powerless to protect Allied shipping in the Baltic, so the Allied control of the Mediterranean stopped short at the Dardanelles. For some weeks after the reopening of the Straits on August 22nd, no attempt was made to prevent British vessels from leaving the Black Sea, and by the end of September nearly all the steamers which were loading at the outbreak of war had passed through the Narrows, bringing large quantities of barley from Russia and maize from Roumania to the United Kingdom, with a smaller amount of wheat and oats. The attitude of the Turkish Government was, however, altogether unsatisfactory, and German influence, greatly assisted by the presence of the GOEBEN and BRESLAU, still dominated the situation. Towards the end of September an attempt was made to revive Black Sea chartering; but on the 27th of that month an incident took place which put an end to all prospect of such revival. On that day a Turkish destroyer, issuing from the Dardanelles, was turned back by the British squadron, which had orders not to allow any Turkish warship to come into the Mediterranean so long as there was reason to suspect the presence of Germans on board. The Turkish authorities thereupon closed the Straits to traffic, and three or four British and neutral steamers which had arrived at Constantinople put back to Black Sea ports in order to avoid the danger of their cargoes being requisitioned. The British Government protested strongly, but they were unable to obtain a reversal of the decision, and all hope of lifting the remainder of the Russian and Roumanian harvests had to be indefinitely postponed.[1]

Although outward-bound British steamers had ceased to arrive at Constantinople practically from the beginning of the war, the Messageries Maritimes, the Italian lines and the Khedivial Mail steamers had continued to call; but with the closing of the Straits the whole of this traffic

[1] Cd. 7628.

was brought to a standstill. The chief mail and passenger liners under the French and Italian flags transferred their calls to Dedeagatch, in Bulgaria, the Khedivial Mail suspended its service altogether, and the Roumanian packets from Kustendji also cancelled their sailings. In fact, the only foreign service which still ran to Constantinople was that of the Russian Steam Navigation Company from Black Sea ports.[1]

Relations between Turkey and the Allied Powers were now severely strained, and during October the attitude of the Turks became so threatening that it was necessary to take into serious consideration the protection of the Suez Canal. On October 12th the Turkish fleet entered the Black Sea, and when they returned on the 14th, the BRESLAU was seen to be escorting two German steamers, the *Zeros* and *Eresos*, which had been lying at Sulina since the outbreak of war. As if to emphasise the identity of Turkish and German interests, both vessels flew the Turkish flag until they reached the entrance to the Bosporus. Worse, however, was to come, for on October 27th the Turko-German squadron again entered the Black Sea, and on the 29th they appeared suddenly off the Russian coasts, where they proceeded to attack ports and shipping. Odessa, Sevastopol, Theodosia, and Novorossisk were bombarded, and damage, more or less serious, was inflicted on the Messageries Maritimes liner *Portugal* and the British steamer *Frederike*, as well as several Russian vessels. The oil tanks at Novorossisk were also destroyed. In addition, the Russian steamers *Shura* and *Grand Duke Alexander* were captured and sunk at sea on the 29th and 30th respectively, and two more, the *Kazbeck* and *Yalta*, were destroyed on the 29th by mines laid at the entrance to the Kertch Straits.

These acts of unprovoked and treacherous aggression removed the last hope of peace, and on October 30th the British, French, and Russian Ambassadors at Constantinople demanded their passports. No time was lost in commencing hostilities. Admiral Carden bombarded the outer forts of the Dardanelles on November 3rd, and immediate steps were taken for the protection of the Suez Canal and Red Sea. On the 5th war was formally declared

---

[1] *Lloyd's List*, 27 October, 1914 (Braila Report, October 5th, Constantinople Report, October 15th); 30 October, 1914 (Constantinople Report, October 1st).

by Great Britain against Turkey. A British protectorate was proclaimed over Egypt, Cyprus was annexed, and some fifty small Turkish sailing vessels were seized in Egyptian and Cypriote harbours. At Bombay the Indian authorities detained the *Kara Deniz* of 5,012 tons, one of the few large steamships flying the Turkish flag, and three or four smaller vessels were seized in British home ports.

Except for the fact that the safety of the Suez Canal and Red Sea now became a more definite object of anxiety, the outbreak of war with Turkey affected British commerce only in so far as it rendered permanent adverse conditions which already existed, for the British ships seized in Turkish ports were few and unimportant,[1] Nevertheless, the open breach of relations was a bitter disappointment to traders, who had been hoping against hope for an opportunity of resuming the Black Sea traffic. It was a serious matter for the Western Powers that so many thousand tons of grain as were lying in the warehouses of Odessa, Novorossisk, and Braila should be withheld from the world's markets, and exceedingly discouraging reports which were received as to the prospects of the Australian harvest accentuated the misfortune of losing the Russian supplies. To the economic strength of Russia herself, inability to realise on the crops was a heavy blow. The whole situation, in fact, was most unfortunate for the Allies, and it afforded a striking illustration of the effects of geographical conditions on war-time trade. Even after Turkey acquired the GOEBEN and BRESLAU, the Russian fleet in the Black Sea was stronger than the Turkish. The security of the Mediterranean tracks was absolute. But the short passage between the two seas presented an insurmountable barrier.[2]

[1] The ships seized amounted to seven steamers of 11,872 tons, including the *Craigforth* (see p. 65, *supra*) which had not completed her repairs in time to leave before the final closure of the Straits. Three Allied steamers —one French, one Russian, and one Belgian—aggregating 9,666 tons, also fell into the hands of the Turks, together with about a dozen salvage steamers and tugs, British and French, at Constantinople or in the Dardanelles.

[2] It will be seen from the following figures of grain imported into the United Kingdom from Russia and Roumania, how vigorously Black Sea trade was proceeding up to the time when the Straits were first closed, and how serious were the effects of the closure. During the first eight months of 1914 the imports were well ahead of the two previous years, but the arrivals during the last four months (mostly representing August

It was not, however, by the loss of a single source of supply that a Power possessing the command of the sea could be reduced to starvation or distress. While it was possible for an inland sea, the entrance to which lay through a narrow and strongly fortified strait, to be closed even against the strength of Great Britain, the enemy was impotent to disturb the use by British commerce of the great ocean routes, and the result of the loss of the Black Sea trade was to throw an even greater proportion of British shipping than usual upon the North Atlantic tracks. This diversion of the course of trade and shipping did indeed have the effect of forcing up both the price of North American wheat and the freights payable for the Atlantic passage, but at the same time it afforded a striking illustration of the elasticity which British com-

shipments) show how sudden and severe was the blow to trade. The figures represent thousands of cwts.

	WHEAT.			BARLEY.		
	1912.	1913.	1914.	1912.	1913.	1914.
January to August	4,624·6	2,330·5	7,216·3	741·6	1,038·2	3,531·0
September to December	5,077·4	2,719·2	362·0	4,515·2	6,455·6	2,777·7
Total for year	9,702·0	5,049·7	7,578·3	5,256·8	7,493·8	6,308·7

	OATS.			MAIZE.		
	1912.	1913.	1914.	1912.	1913.	1914.
January to August	2,139·9	1,252·7	1,425·9	6,415·8	1,589·6	6,706·6
September to December	1,183·4	2,141·6	16·2	436·1	1,096·8	1,116·0
Total for Year	3,323·3	3,394·3	1,442·1	6,851·9	2,686·4	7,822·6

	TOTAL OF GRAIN.		
	1912.	1913.	1914.
January to August	13,921·9	6,211·0	18,879·8
September to December	11,212·1	12,413·2	4,271·9
Total for Year	25,134·0	18,624·2	23,151·7

merce derived from the protection provided by the fleet
and the ease with which the channels of trade could be
readjusted so long as the high seas remained clear for
shipping. Meanwhile the oversea traffic of the Central
Powers was still confined almost entirely to the transit
trade through neutral countries, and with the exception
of a few steamers in the Baltic, the shipping which remained under the enemy flags in home or neutral ports,
was as useless for the purpose of supplying their needs as
if it had actually fallen into the hands of the Allies.[1]

Such part of the enemy's ocean trade as could be kept
afoot was carried on wholly by means of neutral shipping,
and the chief difficulty in the way of restricting contraband supplies lay in the necessity of showing consideration
for the susceptibilities of neutral countries. At the beginning of October, for instance, some little friction with
the United States was threatened by the interference of
British cruisers with American shipments of copper to
Rotterdam; but in this case it was proved beyond question that the consignments were destined for Krupps, and
the American Government accordingly withdrew its protest and issued a warning to shippers against engaging in
the contraband trade. Another source of irritation was
the action of the North American Squadron in stopping
vessels, as was alleged, too near to United States territorial waters; but again the matter passed off without
incident, owing in this case to the forbearance of the
British Government, which instructed the patrols to keep
at a greater distance from the coast.

About the middle of the month a new question was
raised by the seizure of three steamers, the *John D.
Rockefeller*, *Brindilla*, and *Platuria*, belonging to the Standard Oil Company. The *John D. Rockefeller* was carrying
petroleum " to orders," and was consequently taken into
Kirkwall for examination on October 17th. It was
proved, however, that her cargo was destined for the
Danish Petroleum Company, and as the Danish Government had prohibited the export of petroleum, the vessel
was released, to the great satisfaction of the American
public. The cases of the *Brindilla* and *Platuria* raised a

[1] The only German merchantmen encountered at sea during October
were two belated sailing vessels—the *Ulrich* of 2,201 tons net, captured on
the 20th, with a cargo of nitrate from Antofogasta, and the *Carl* (1,085
tons) taken on the 28th, laden with guano for British consignees at London,
to whom the cargo was released.

wider issue. The *Brindilla*, taken into Halifax as a prize, was formerly the *Washington*, of the Deutsche Amerikanische Petroleum Gesellschaft, Hamburg. The *Platuria* was the *Diamant*, lately belonging to the same owners, and was seized at Stornoway on October 19th. Both ships had been lying at New York at the outbreak of war and had since been transferred to the American Register. The importance of the seizures lay in the fact that twenty-four other tankers belonging to this Company were lying in American ports, all of which had been or were about to be transferred to the United States' flag. In all, 180,000 tons of shipping were involved. The case of these ships was differentiated from that of an ordinary attempted transfer from a belligerent to a neutral flag by the fact that the German company was only a subsidiary of the Standard Oil Co. It could, therefore, be contended that their being placed on the American Register was only the formal recognition of previously existing American ownership. In these circumstances, the British Government decided to recognise the transfer, and the *Brindilla* and *Platuria* were accordingly released without being brought before a Prize Court.

The release of these ships did a good deal to calm the angry feeling which had been aroused in the United States, and still greater satisfaction was given by two notes presented by the British Ambassador at Washington towards the end of October. In these notes the British Government pointed out that so far from having abused their rights as belligerents, they had in all cases purchased and paid for the cargoes of ships diverted from German or neutral ports, even in the case of undoubted contraband, such as copper for Krupps, which might legally have been condemned without compensation. At the same time, they gave certain assurances with regard to the future treatment of American exports. In the case of oil cargoes, they stated that all ships would be allowed to proceed if their papers showed clearly that the oil was destined for neutral consignees, and that only shipments " to order " would be brought in for further examination. With regard to cotton, an absolute assurance was given that it was not in contemplation to place this product on the list of contraband and that shipments for Germany would be exempt from molestation. This was a very important concession, for the enormous surplus thrown back upon the producers' hands through the diminution of demand in Great Britain and on the Continent had already brought about a serious crisis in the Southern States.

Notwithstanding these concessions, the sensitiveness of the American people to any interference with commerce under their flag continued to place obstacles in the way of an effective control of contraband traffic, and on October 29th orders were issued to the United States port authorities, forbidding them to make public particulars as to the character and destination of outward cargoes until thirty days after the clearance of the vessels concerned. The result of these instructions was to increase the necessity for a rigorous examination of all east-bound shipping on the Atlantic tracks.

All through the month, very heavy shipments of grain to Scandinavian countries, and especially to Sweden, were recorded both in the United States and at South American ports. In many cases the freights paid were so high as to afford a reasonable presumption that the prices to be obtained were also abnormal, and there was a strong suspicion that a large part of these imports found their way ultimately to Germany. The same suspicions were aroused with regard to oil and coal, but on October 29th a statement was issued by the Swedish Chamber of Commerce in London, pointing out that the crops in Sweden had been bad, that the supply of mineral oil from Russia had ceased, and that all imports had fallen into arrears during the first few weeks of the war. The Chamber declared that the export prohibitions were rigidly enforced, and went so far as to affirm that " not a ton of coal, not a bushel of corn, not a gallon of petrol, not a bale of cotton had left Sweden for any belligerent country since the outbreak of hostilities." [1] Similar explanations were given on the part of Denmark and Norway. In Denmark special stress was laid on the shortage of cattle fodder caused by the loss of the Russian, German, and Roumanian supplies and the pre-emption by the British Government of maize cargoes diverted at the beginning of the war. Attention was also called to the shortage of mineral oils, due to the fact that the Danish Government had requisitioned all stocks of petroleum, benzine, and naphtha, and to the diminished import facilities arising from the laying up of the large German tank steamers. Both in Denmark and

[1] *Times*, 29 October, 1914.

Norway the high freights secured by Scandinavian shipowners were attributed mainly to the general withdrawal of British shipping from the Scandinavian trade.[1]

So far as coal was concerned, the explanations given were satisfactory. The total shipments from the United Kingdom to the three Scandinavian countries and to Holland during the nine months ending September 30th, 1914, were actually less than in the corresponding period of the previous year, in spite of the fact that the German supplies—normally of equal magnitude—were now cut off. Nor was there much cause for suspicion with regard to the import trade of Norway as a whole. The Norwegian Government had given an undertaking on September 16th that foreign goods consigned to Norway should not be re-exported without special permission, and though there might be some leakage through re-exports to other Scandinavian countries having different regulations, the total amount of contraband goods reaching Germany in this way was certainly small. On the other hand, there was good reason to believe that the Swedish export prohibitions were continually evaded and that a considerable transhipment trade with Germany was carried on either from Swedish ports direct or through Denmark. Danish imports themselves gave equal or greater cause for anxiety. Lard, which in ordinary times Denmark usually exports, was imported in October 1914 to the amount of 1,005,000 lbs. Rubber was shipped from Copenhagen to Lübeck in answer to the inquiries of a " small unknown German firm "; and though no copper was sent to Germany direct, it was freely exported to Malmo, in Sweden, with every prospect of its ultimately reaching the enemy. There was, in fact, little doubt that Copenhagen was becoming an *entrepôt* on a large scale for German trade.

With regard to Holland the position was much more satisfactory. The increased services of the Holland-Amerika Line gave rise to a certain amount of criticism in the British press, but this criticism was vitiated by forgetfulness of the degree to which legitimate neutral traffic was affected by the withdrawal of the German steamship companies from business, and the closing of the port of

---

[1] *Times*, 20 October, 1914. Interview with Mr. Karl Knudsen, President of the Norwegian Chamber of Commerce in London, in the *Times*, 17 October, 1914, and interview with Mr. Pedersen, Chairman of the Norwegian Food Commission, in *Lloyd's List*, 24 October, 1914.

Antwerp. To a great extent Rotterdam had now replaced Antwerp as a distributing centre, and Dutch shipowners were quick to profit by the opportunities presented to them; but successive prohibitions of export had reduced to a minimum the passage of supplies to Germany, and the Holland-Amerika Line itself refused to accept any cargo from the United States unless consigned to the Netherlands Government, who exercised a rigorous control over its ultimate destination.

It was evident, however, that through Swedish, Danish, and Italian ports a large amount of contraband still found its way to the Central Powers, and under the existing regulations the restriction of this traffic presented great difficulties. It must be remembered that foodstuffs and other articles in the " Conditional " category could only be interfered with if destined for the use of the enemy's armed forces, and even where a moral certainty existed as to the enemy destination of contraband cargoes, definite legal proof was exceedingly difficult to obtain.

It was clear that the regulations with regard to contraband needed drastic revision if their purpose was not to be defeated, and on October 29th two Proclamations [1] were issued by the British Government which went far to free their hands as regards the restriction of enemy supplies. The first of these Proclamations transferred to the list of Absolute Contraband a number of articles, including hæmatite iron ore and hæmatite pig-iron, iron pyrites, nickel ore and nickel, ferrochrome and chrome ore, copper, lead, aluminium, motor vehicles of all kinds, rubber, and mineral oils other than lubricants. The second related chiefly to the treatment of Conditional Contraband, and modified Articles 33, 35, and 38 of the Declaration of London in the following respects:

(a) A neutral vessel cleared for a neutral port, but proceeding to an enemy port, would be liable to capture and condemnation if encountered before the end of her next voyage.

(b) Enemy destination would be presumed in the case of goods consigned to or destined for an agent of an enemy State.

(c) Conditional contraband in a ship bound for a

[1] *Manual of Emergency Legislation, Supplement No. 2*, pp. 52-54, 78-80.

neutral port, would be liable to capture if the goods were consigned " to order," or if the consignee of the goods was not clearly shown on the ship's papers, or if the consignee was located in enemy territory. In all such cases it would lie upon the owners of the goods to prove that their destination was innocent.

The effect of these Proclamations was to bring the provisions of the Prize Law into much closer accordance with the conditions of modern war and modern commerce, and greatly to reduce the advantages derived by Germany from rail communication with neutral ports. A few days later another step was taken which, while its primary purpose was to enable more effective action to be taken against enemy mine-layers and submarines, had the incidental effect of facilitating in no small measure the regulation of neutral traffic. This was the declaration by the British Government that the whole of the North Sea would henceforth be treated as a Military Area, within which no vessels of any kind or nationality could navigate in safety except in accordance with Admiralty directions. The Admiralty Statement in which this decision was announced was dated November 2nd, a week after the sinking of the *Manchester Commerce*, and began by recapitulating the evidence as to indiscriminate mine-laying by the Germans on the high seas, without respect to the safety of non-combatant lives or neutral shipping. In these circumstances the Admiralty declared that, having regard to the security of neutral trade no less than to British interests, they felt it necessary to adopt exceptional measures to restrict the enemy's unlawful activities either in the North Sea itself or on the Atlantic Routes. They therefore warned all merchant shipping and fishing craft moving to the east of a line drawn from the northern point of the Hebrides through the Faroe Islands to Iceland, that they would be exposed to the gravest dangers from mines and from warships searching for suspicious craft. Neutral vessels trading to and from Scandinavia and Holland were advised to pass through the English Channel and the Straits of Dover, where inward-bound vessels would obtain directions that would pass them safely up the East Coast to Farn Island. At this point a safe route would be indicated as far as Lindesnaes, whence they could turn north or south, according to their destination, keeping as near the coast as possible. Similar instructions would also be given to outward-bound vessels.[1]

Although it was, of course, impossible to compel neutral vessels to follow the course indicated by the Admiralty, the advantages of doing so were obvious, and the consequent concentration of trade within narrow waters was of considerable assistance to the patrols. It was, in particular, a great advantage that as large a proportion of neutral traffic as possible should be induced to adopt the Channel Route, for on this route they had little chance of escaping the vigilance of the Dover Patrol, by whom they were diverted to the Downs, for examination by the Downs Boarding Flotilla. Even in the case of lines which persisted in the use of the North-about Passage it was usually possible to obtain some measure of assurance against their engaging in enemy trade, in return for immunity from detention and assistance in escaping the dangers of the North Sea.

Thus, while the enemy's inability seriously to interrupt the flow of traffic to and from the United Kingdom became every week more evident, the conclusion of the first three months of war witnessed a marked tightening-up of the British grip on the maritime communications of the Central Powers. Bearing in mind how formidable were the dangers to which British commerce was exposed, how heavy were the losses and how widespread the dislocation originally anticipated, and on the other hand, how numerous were the obstacles interposed by commercial developments and by considerations of foreign policy to the exercise of economic pressure by the Allied fleets, the situation at the end of October afforded many grounds for legitimate satisfaction.

[1] Admiralty Statement, published November 3rd, 1914.

CHAPTER XVII

THE PROGRESS OF TRADE RECOVERY

IN surveying the position of British trade at the end of the first few critical weeks of war, we saw that it had shown an elasticity and power of recovery which gave good hopes for the future. As soon as the initial financial crisis had died away and the transaction of business became possible on something approaching normal lines, there was a general resumption of activity both in the import and export trades, and shipping, encouraged by the security given by the State Insurance Scheme, responded with very little hesitation to the demands of traders. Since the middle of September, however, the fortitude of merchants and shipowners had been tested by heavy blows struck simultaneously in the Indian Ocean and the South Atlantic, and even on the Pacific Coast of America evidence had been given of a new activity on the part of the German cruisers at sea. Although two raiders had already met their doom, others whose commanders had given signs of abundant ability and enterprise were yet at large, as was the formidable force which Admiral von Spee had collected in the Pacific.

The immediate and local effect of these losses and perils on the trade of India and the Far East, of South America and the North Sea, had indeed been insufficient to arrest permanently or generally the revival of trade at the ports mainly concerned; but under modern conditions, the repercussion of such blows as were struck by the EMDEN in the Bay of Bengal and off Colombo, upon the sensitive and complex web of British commerce, was not necessarily limited to the particular route or section of a route attacked, and it becomes necessary to inquire in

SMALL EFFECT OF LOSSES

what manner the new developments of hostile activity had affected the general progress of trade recovery.

It may be said at once that the dislocation caused by the operations of hostile commerce destroyers was limited almost exclusively to the actual loss sustained in ships and cargoes captured, and to the suspension of sailings from ports directly and immediately threatened by the presence of a raider. In preserving trade from a collapse of credit, and from the doubts and hesitations caused by an unknown and immeasurable risk, the State Insurance Scheme had deprived the operations of hostile cruisers of the greater part of that widespread indirect influence which they might otherwise have exerted, and the apprehension of positive and immediate danger on the majority of the ocean tracks was so reduced by the naval protection afforded as to have little deterrent effect. We have already seen how small was the effect of the losses sustained in distant seas upon outward sailings from the United Kingdom, or upon homeward sailings from ports not immediately threatened. Still less did the potential menace of the cruisers in German home ports, or of a possible change of cruising ground on the part of those at sea, deter shipping from putting out on the routes as yet unassailed. The course of trade was, indeed, shackled in many directions by circumstances arising out of the financial and economic reactions of the European conflict, but the fear of molestation had practically no place among the obstacles to recovery.

As was only natural, the elasticity of British trade was most strikingly manifested in the North Atlantic traffic, which had never been attacked, and which was of peculiar importance to the safety and welfare of the United Kingdom under war conditions. The demand for North American wheat, which had been so greatly stimulated by the outbreak of war, was still further increased by the closing of the Dardanelles and the unfavourable reports received as to the Australian harvest. The volume of grain crossing the North Atlantic during September and October was, indeed, phenomenal. The oil tankers—stimulated by the demands of the Admiralty for liquid fuel—were exceptionally busy, and the import of other items of smaller bulk but of great importance to the conduct of the war industries, such as copper, bore equal witness to the security of the Atlantic tracks.[1] The only staple import which still showed a heavy decrease was that of raw cotton, for which, in the disorganised state of the industry, there were few purchasers.[2]

On other routes, where trade was stimulated by no such special demands and where the financial stability of producing centres and markets had been more severely shaken, the recovery was less rapid and complete; but we have seen that by the beginning of October the commerce of the Far and Middle East had revived at all points, and that the improvement in economic conditions in Argentina was reflected in an increase both of the inwards and outwards traffic. The disturbed conditions at the Cape arising from De Wet's rebellion prevented full advantage being taken of the security established on the South African Route, but West African trade was flourishing, and nearer home there was a steady flow of traffic to and from the Mediterranean ports, and no diminution in the arrivals of foodstuffs or the shipments of coal at North Sea ports.

In spite of these encouraging signs of renewed activity, the tonnage entered at British home ports during September was nearly half a million tons less than in August, for the effects of the initial dislocation on the arrivals from the more distant countries had now begun to tell. As compared with September 1913, the British entrances were down by nearly 40, and those of all ships by nearly 41 per cent. On the other hand, the corresponding reduction in weight of imports received was only 25 per cent., as against 29·7 per cent. in the preceding month. This discrepancy was due almost entirely to the fact that British ships were now bringing, on the average, larger cargoes to this country than before the war. The influence of war conditions led to an increased proportion of deadweight cargoes such as grain or ore, and a decreased proportion of measurement cargoes such as cotton or

[1] Imports from United States and Canada:

	September 1913	September 1914	October 1914
Wheat, in 1,000 cwts.	4,198	10,476	7,599
Wheatmeal and flour, do.	1,058	604	829
Barley, do.	354	253	1,111
Oats, do.	245	733	305
Copper, unwrought and partly wrought — tons	4,981	13,682	13,837
Petroleum (from all sources) in 1,000 galls.	47,899	52,109	62,379

[2] The import of American cotton during October was less than half a million centals, as against two millions in 1913, and nearly two and a half millions in 1912.

manufactured goods like typewriters and pianos, thus increasing the carrying power of the ships. Moreover, many liners which formerly discharged part cargoes only in British ports, going on to a continental port such as Antwerp or Rotterdam to complete their discharge, now delivered the entire contents of their holds in this country, and in the North Atlantic trade especially, a good deal of space formerly allotted on the liners to passengers and stores was now occupied by foodstuffs and other essential commodities. The result was that the average weight of imports carried per 100 net tons of shipping entered, rose from 115 tons in August to 145 tons in September. This increase in the carrying power of the ships employed in the import trade proved to be a permanent feature of war conditions, and in October, with an increase over the previous month of over 400,000 tons in the total tonnage entered, the estimated weight of all commodities received from overseas was only 16·3 per cent. below the figures for 1913. The decrease in *values* was greater, amounting to 28·1 per cent., but this was due mainly to the continued disorganisation of the cotton industry and to reduced purchases of manufactured articles.

As regards the export trade, the two dominant factors, when once the regular sailings of the liners had been re-established, were in the first place the loss of enemy, and restricted purchasing power of neutral markets; in the second place, the redirection of national effort in the United Kingdom. There was no lack of cargo space on the outward voyages, for the tonnage cleared at British ports was greater by 1,200,000 tons in September than in August, and a further rise of 200,000 tons was recorded in October, but the demand abroad was too greatly reduced, and the manufacturing and labour resources of the United Kingdom too extensively directed to war industries, for the normal volume of trade to be approached. Nevertheless the total value of exports and re-exports was greater by £3,300,000 in September than in August, and in October there was a further increase of nearly £4,000,000, bringing the total up to £35,780,000.

The increase on the August figures shown both by imports and exports is the more remarkable inasmuch as the records for any month include goods landed or shipped during the last few days of the previous month, so that the August returns reflected in some degree the conditions of *ante-bellum* trade. Moreover, the import figures for August were swollen to some extent by the inclusion of cargoes diverted from German ports on or immediately before the outbreak of war. The progress made during September and October was thus greater than is indicated by the statistics.

Some qualification is also necessary in comparing the 1914 figures with those for the preceding year. In taking the imports and exports of 1913 as a basis of comparison, it must be remembered that 1913 was the culminating year of a trade boom, and even if war had not broken out, it is doubtful whether traffic on so vast a scale could have been maintained without a lapse. If the figures for the two opening months of the war are compared with those for August and September 1904, itself a record year, it will be found that in spite of all the obstacles thrown in the way of commerce by financial dislocation and the perils arising from a state of war, the imports were rather greater in value and the exports only slightly less than under peace conditions. It is true that prices had been rising continually during the intervening decade and that this increase in values accounts to some extent for the apparent volume of war traffic; but on the other hand, a great quantity of stores and supplies shipped to France for the use of the Army is excluded from the 1914 figures.

If, therefore, the war had brought about a large reduction in the total volume of traffic, it was at least evident that unless the British control of the trade routes should be far more effectively challenged than had hitherto been the case, nothing approaching paralysis was to be feared, and in particular, all danger of any serious interruption in the supply of foodstuffs and essential raw materials had become exceedingly remote. In fact, the actual diminution in the volume of trade was due almost entirely to the disturbance of economic conditions by the war, rather than to the operations of the German cruisers.

The evidence thus afforded as to the comparative security of the ocean routes was clearly reflected in the course of quotations on the war risks insurance market. Throughout September and October the State flat rate remained unchanged, at 1 per cent. on hulls and 2 per cent. on cargoes, but in respect of cargoes it was usually possible to obtain a cheaper cover on the open market. In fact, it was considered in some quarters that the State cargo rate, low as it was when compared with the rates universally anticipated as the result of a state of war, imposed an unnecessary burden on commerce. This opinion was very prevalent in Lancashire, where the difficulties from which the cotton trade was suffering rendered shippers particularly anxious for the removal of every obstacle to increased exports, and strong pressure was brought to bear upon the Government, with a view to securing a substantial reduction.

It must be remembered that the extent of the dangers to which trade was exposed did not immediately appear. Up to the middle of September, only seven British ships were definitely known to have been lost by enemy action,[1] but during the latter part of the month there arrived in rapid succession the news of the EMDEN's early captures in the Bay of Bengal, of her subsequent sinking of the *Clan Matheson* and of the destruction of the *Indian Prince* by the KRONPRINZ WILHELM. In the face of these losses, however, the Manchester Shipowners' Association passed a resolution on September 25th, urging a reduction in cargo premiums, and suggesting that, after the war, the State Office should return to the contributors all excess of premiums received over claims paid.[2] On the very day after this resolution was passed, the *Gryfevale* put into Colombo with the crews of five more ships captured by the EMDEN off Minikoi, and within the next few days came news of the sinking by the LEIPZIG of the *Elsinore* and *Bankfields*. Yet notwithstanding this fresh evidence of the increasing activity of the German cruisers, business men in Lancashire continued to regard the cargo rate as excessive and to urge its reduction at least to 1 per cent.[3]

Since the sole object of the Insurance Scheme was to encourage the free movement of ships and cargoes, it was undoubtedly desirable that the premiums charged should be the very lowest compatible with the solvency of the scheme, but so long as the German raiders remained at large and capable of further mischief the Advisory Board felt themselves unable to recommend any further concessions. The premium on hulls already stood at the minimum contemplated by the report of the Committee

[1] *City of Winchester, Kaipara, Nyanga, Hyades, Holmwood, Bowes Castle*, and *Runo*.
[2] *Lloyd's List*, 29 September, 1914.
[3] See for instance the *Manchester Guardian*, 8 October, 1914.

responsible for the scheme, and although the cargo rate was undoubtedly more than sufficient to cover losses on the scale hitherto experienced, there could be no guarantee that much heavier blows might not yet be struck by the enemy warships already operating, or by others which might succeed in putting to sea.

The Flat Rate remained, therefore, at 2 per cent., but it must be remembered that this represented a maximum. On the Oriental and South American Routes, where German raiders were known to be at work, underwriters' quotations ruled about level with the State rate, and on those routes the cargoes were mostly covered with the State Office; but in respect of voyages on which there was no immediate visible danger, the greater part of the business was done on the open market at lower rates. Even in the North Sea, where the German mine-fields presented so serious a menace, the premiums seldom exceeded 1 per cent., and the North Atlantic rates sank from 25s. and 20s. at the end of September to 10s. and 7s. 6d. during the following month.[1]

Thus, although the month of October closed with the announcement of heavy losses, there was little reason to fear that the effect of those losses, or of any which there was immediate reason to apprehend, would be sufficient to check the course of that steady progress towards recovery which had been exhibited by British commerce during the first three months of war. The outlook for both shipowners and traders was hopeful, and to shipowners especially the month of October brought a radical improvement in the position. Nearly all the regular lines had now resumed their services, and although several of them were suffering severely from the paucity of outward cargoes due to diminished exports, and from the requisitioning of their largest and fastest vessels, they continued to maintain their sailings with regularity. Most of the fixed services to the Continent, other than those to German, Baltic, and Black Sea ports, were also running, and the coasting trade was kept fully employed owing to the demands of military traffic on the railways and the redistribution of the foreign trade between the various ports. Best of all, the demand for tramp tonnage

---

[1] It will be remembered, however, that North Atlantic rates rose somewhat at the end of October, as a result of the sinking of the *Manchester Commerce*.

had revived, and chartering was again brisk both at British and foreign ports.

In this resumption of tramp chartering the removal of the restrictions on the export of coal and the heavy shipments of grain from North America to Europe played a prominent part. By the end of September the glut on the North American and Welsh markets had to a great extent disappeared, and throughout October the demand for tonnage at New York steadily increased. Another factor of importance was the activity of the Royal Commission on Sugar Supplies in purchasing from the cane-producing centres stocks wherewith to make good the loss of the beet sugar normally derived from the Continent. Even in September large shipments of cane sugar were received from Cuba and the British West Indies, and in October these were supplemented by the arrival of numerous cargoes from Java and Mauritius. Still heavier shipments were on their way, and chartering for the Java ports was brisk and steady. At the Plate, too, the stagnation of the early weeks of the war had wholly passed away, and so far from tonnage lying idle, every available ship was now speedily snapped up.

The effect of this growth in the demand for tonnage was the more pronounced inasmuch as the available shipping had been greatly reduced by the cessation of German and Austrian sailings and by the requisitioning of British and Allied vessels. We have already seen how seriously the combination of these factors impeded commerce in the East, and as soon as the freight markets became really active they were felt also in the general trade of the world. The demands of the navy for merchant cruisers, boarding and examination steamers, colliers, oilers, mine-sweepers, and other auxiliaries grew with every month. The reinforcement and supply of the Expeditionary Force; the transport to Europe of the Indian Army Corps, the Canadian Expedition, and the Australian and New Zealand forces; the South African Expedition against German South-West Africa; the numerous minor operations against German colonies in Africa and the Pacific, the return of French and British garrisons from foreign stations—all these absorbed some hundreds of thousands of tons of shipping, and there was every probability that the requisitioned tonnage would increase rather than diminish in the near future.

As yet there was no general shortage of a serious character, nor had the competition of shippers forced up freights to a level imposing any appreciable burden upon trade; but the turn of the tide was strongly marked, and ship-owners were already able to obtain better rates than those ruling in 1913, though the general level was still below that of 1912. As was natural, it was at Plate ports that the most notable advance was recorded, and by the end of October 25s. or 26s. per ton could be obtained for a steamer ready to load at once, as against 13s. or 14s. in September.

The effect of this all-round rise in freights was on the whole beneficial to commerce, as it tended to draw into active employment every available freighter, and the demands of reviving trade in the United Kingdom attracted a large proportion of the world's unfixed tonnage to British ports. While the tonnage of British ships entered during October showed a decrease of 30·8 per cent. as compared with 1913—due mainly to the requisitioning of British shipping and the greater average length of voyages under the new conditions of trade—the corresponding decrease in foreign tonnage was only 26·3 per cent. A great part of this decrease was accounted for by the withdrawal of enemy shipping; and though the arrivals of Scandinavian vessels were still somewhat below the normal, owing to the cessation of the Baltic traffic in which they were usually active, tonnage under the Dutch, Spanish, Greek, and Italian flags showed an actual increase on the preceding year.

So far as British trade was concerned, the position was thus more satisfactory than could have been anticipated at so early a period of the war. Confidence had been restored; supplies had been maintained; there was little lack either of cargoes for the shipping available or of shipping to carry the cargoes on offer. If the state of French commerce presented a decided contrast, it was not through lack of the naval protection which Allied shipping shared with that of Great Britain, but through the effects of the German invasion on the whole social fabric of the country. And even in France, the end of October brought at least some prospect of improvement. Both in imports and exports, in tonnage entered and in tonnage cleared, the September figures were below those for August, though a slight improvement was recorded in the tonnage of vessels under the national flag, owing to the resumption of sailings by the big liners. By October, however, the turn of the tide at the Marne had had some effect, and though imports dropped still further, exports rose to a figure half way between those for August and September. The movements of shipping showed signs of greater activity on the part of both French and foreign vessels, but the congested state of the ports operated as an obstacle to further recovery.

Far more serious was the situation produced in the enemy countries by the continued severance of their maritime communications. Although the efforts made at the beginning of September to revive the foreign trade of Germany began, to some extent, to bear fruit during the succeeding month, the progress made was inconsiderable in comparison with the needs of the Empire. Apart from the activity of the British patrols in the interception of contraband, the difficulty of procuring tonnage and arranging payments opposed serious obstacles to the resumption of trade. The restricted and diminishing stocks of raw materials were mostly required for the execution of Government orders in connection with the war, and the claims of the army and of the war industries had absorbed a very large proportion of the available labour. Both these factors restricted the manufacture of surplus commodities for export, and the only German product of which large stocks were available was beet sugar, the export of which had been prohibited. Towards the end of October it was announced that services had been arranged from Genoa for the carriage of German goods to Spain, the Levant and Black Sea, America, and the East, and very moderate insurance premiums were quoted for these voyages.[1] In practice, however, the shipments that could be made were too meagre to pay even for the restricted supplies which Germany was now obtaining, and by October 31st, the German exchange on New York had fallen to six or seven points below par and was still going down. It was necessary, if possible, to do something to redress this inequality, and on October 31st a special law was passed permitting the export of beet sugar up to a total of 1,100,000 tons.

In passing this law there may have been some hope on the part of the German Government that they would be able to improve the financial situation of the country at

[1] *Lloyd's List*, 26 October, 1914, quoting *Börsen Halle*,

the expense of the enemy, through the re-export to the United Kingdom of sugar exported to neutral countries. Some such project was, in fact, anticipated by the British Government, who were watching the progress of events in Germany with close attention. All immediate danger of a sugar shortage in Great Britain had now passed, as the Sugar Commission had already in hand stocks sufficient for several months' consumption, and on October 26th, a week before the passing of the German export law, they prohibited for the time being all further imports.[1]

This paralysis of the German export trade was in itself an obstacle sufficient to prevent the resumption of the import traffic on anything approaching the normal scale. Even when the British Government had given a definite assurance that cotton for Germany would not be treated as contraband, the difficulty of arranging payments, the shortage of available tonnage, the dangers of navigation, and the delay in cable communications impeded business to an extent which went far to render the concession nugatory, and the supplies received by Germany through neutral countries were mainly confined to foodstuffs and a few materials, such as copper, essential to the war industries. Even the import of these commodities was subject to great difficulties, in addition to those arising from the omnipresence of the British cruisers, and this in spite of the restrictions under which those cruisers lay in respect of the treatment of food cargoes. A very large proportion of the tonnage engaged in the carriage of grain to neutral countries was British owned, and when a great increase in the shipments to Genoa, coupled with a corresponding increase in the railway traffic between Italy and Switzerland, and the Central Powers, indicated that this port had become an *entrepôt* for German trade, many British shipowners absolutely refused to accept cargoes for any Italian port or to insert a Mediterranean option in their charters.[2] The tonnage available for the transit trade was thus reduced to that supplied by neutral countries, and this was further restricted by the extensive employment of neutral shipping in British commerce and by the influence exercised by London as the chief marine insurance market of the world. On Octo-

---

[1] *Supplement No. 2 to Manual of Emergency Legislation*, December 1914, p. 185.
[2] *Times*, 23 October, 1914.

ber 19th a formal warning was issued by the Board of Trade against the granting to neutral ships of policies which included the risks of capture or detention, but even before the issue of this order, the London Institute of Underwriters had itself taken action in the matter, and the impossibility of covering ships and goods against the risk of seizure by British or Allied cruisers led to the cancellation of many suspicious contracts.[1]

Thus, many causes combined to restrict the supplies which Germany could draw from abroad even by means of the transhipment trade, and the greater rigour introduced into the British examination service by the Proclamation of October 29th and the declaration of a Military Area in the North Sea threatened a further reduction in the German imports of copper, nickel, lead, aluminium, and petroleum, which were already running short. Nor was the situation much better with regard to textiles and other materials. The stocks of cotton, wool, jute, flax, and leather were already much diminished, and the scanty supplies obtained by indirect means barely sufficed for the fulfilment of Government requirements. There was as yet no absolute shortage of foodstuffs, but the situation with regard to fodder was becoming serious, and agriculture was threatened by the cessation of nitrate imports, especially as the stocks in hand were all required for the manufacture of explosives. The fixing of maximum retail prices had led to great difficulties in respect of the distribution of supplies to consumers, and on October 28th the first order regulating wholesale prices was issued by the Federal Council.

Thanks to the stocks in hand before the outbreak of war, the great internal resources of the Empire and the development, even on a restricted scale, of the transhipment trade, the state of Germany was far from desperate; and now that the initial dislocation caused by mobilisation had passed away, hopes of its improvement were entertained; but it was already obvious that unless imports could be greatly increased, the strain of a prolonged conflict would be severe and would constitute a serious drain upon the national strength. In Austria-Hungary the conditions were very similar, and speaking generally, the economic pressure on the Central Powers at the end of October, while it held out to the Allies little

[1] *Times*, 19, 20 October, 1914.

hope of shortening the war, was sufficient to cause grave anxiety to the enemy Governments, the more so as no radical change in the situation could be expected unless the German and Austrian fleets should prove capable of contesting the command of the sea.

Of any such development there was at this period no sign. The enemy's submarines were, indeed, active in the North Sea, and their persistent attacks were not only harassing to the battle-fleet, but had achieved some measure of success against the cruiser squadrons. Their light cruisers and destroyers were also frequently at sea, though they accomplished little or nothing; but no operation of importance was attempted by their heavier ships until November 3rd, when the gunboat *Halcyon* and two destroyers had a narrow escape off Gorleston from a German squadron which included battle cruisers. A few shells, possibly ricochets, fell on the beach at Yarmouth, but no damage was done, and before the British forces which were instantly set in motion could come up with them, the Germans had disappeared. During their retreat, they laid a line of mines in the exit from the Swept Channel, and it is at least possible that this was the primary object of the expedition. If so, its success was very limited, for apart from a British submarine blown up during the pursuit, the only victims of the new mine-field were a couple of neutral steamers and some half-dozen fishing craft. The rapidity with which a passage was cleared was, indeed, a remarkable testimony to the efficiency of the mine-sweeping service.

Whatever may have been its object, the course of the Gorleston raid displayed no eagerness on the enemy's part to accept action, and confidence in the ability of the British fleet to retain its hold remained unshaken. Two days later, however, attention was again directed to the trade routes, where, it will be remembered, the EMDEN, the KARLSRUHE, the KRONPRINZ WILHELM, and the German Pacific squadron were still at large and unlocated. The approach of Admiral von Spee to South American waters had for some weeks been the most threatening factor in the naval situation, and on November 5th the Admiralty announced that reports had reached them from German sources of an action off the Chilean coast between his squadron and that of Admiral Cradock, in which the Germans claimed the victory.

CHAPTER XVIII

THE BATTLE OF CORONEL AND ITS EFFECT ON TRADE [1]

THE action referred to in the Admiralty statement of November 5th was the most considerable which had yet arisen directly from the attack and defence of commerce. Not only did it threaten to inflict a serious set-back on the revival of trade at South American ports, but its effects were felt far and wide as a disturbing influence in the problem of trade protection.

It will be remembered that the concentration of the German Pacific squadron was completed, on October 14th, by the arrival of the LEIPZIG at Easter Island, and that on the same date Admiral Stoddart received instructions to proceed to the east coast of South America and there take charge of a squadron intended to cover Plate and Brazilian shipping against attack, in the event of the enemy eluding Admiral Cradock and coming into the South Atlantic. At this time, Captain Köhler, having sent off his prisoners to Tenerife, was about to coal the KARLSRUHE, preparatory to a final raid in the Fernando Noronha area, before the arrival of the *Crefeld* should furnish the British Admiralty with intelligence as to his operations. The KRONPRINZ WILHELM, which had been occupied for a week in transferring coal and stores from *La Correntina*, was also about to return to the trade routes.

On both sides of the South American continent British trade was active. In the Atlantic, the volume of traffic was already very large and was steadily increasing. On the West Coast, the sailings from Peruvian ports had been interrupted for some three weeks by the appearance of the LEIPZIG, but were now about to be resumed. In Chilean waters British steamers were moving freely, and the visit of the GLASGOW and MONMOUTH to Valparaiso, on Octo-

[1] See Maps 1 and 5.

ber 15th, added to the general feeling of confidence in the safety of the tracks.

There was thus a great body of shipping exposed to attack, and the force by which South American trade was now menaced was the strongest which had yet been collected by the enemy at any point on the ocean trade routes. By his junction with the LEIPZIG and DRESDEN the strength of Admiral von Spee's command was brought up to two armoured cruisers and three light cruisers, all modern and all at least moderately fast. The PRINZ EITEL FRIEDRICH was following him across the Pacific; and if he should make his way into the Atlantic, the KARLSRUHE and KRONPRINZ WILHELM might also become available for concerted operations.

Of the supply ships which had accompanied the squadron across the Pacific only three—the *Yorck*, *Göttingen*, and *Titania*—remained in company, and by this time even they were almost empty. With the DRESDEN, however, had arrived the *Baden*, which had still some coal on board, and the LEIPZIG brought with her the *Amasis*, *Anubis*, and *Karnak*. Moreover, both on the West Coast and in Argentine and Brazilian ports, there were many German liners, some at least of which might be counted on for the renewal of supplies.

From Captains Lüdecke and Hann the Admiral learned that the GOOD HOPE, MONMOUTH, and GLASGOW had arrived at the Straits at the end of September, and that the IDZUMO and one or two British light cruisers were in the Northern Pacific. He learned also that British shipping was moving freely on the South American coast. For the first time since the outbreak of war, he found himself within striking distance of an important trade route which was not covered by a force presenting an absolute bar to attack. He had no reason to believe that his approach was expected by his enemies, and it only remained for him to choose the point at which he would strike. The most obvious course was to go direct to Valparaiso and hold up British trade in Chilean waters, but this by no means exhausted the possibilities of the situation.

It will be remembered that Captain Powlett was apprehensive of a raid on the shipping and coalfields at Vancouver, and a still more attractive bait was offered by the growing traffic of the Panama Canal. On the other hand, a northward move would take the German Admiral away from the ports in which lay the steamers on which he must mainly depend for his future supplies of coal. The passage of the Canal would bring him into a very rich field of operations and one in which it might be possible to arrange for the service, as supply ships, of some of the German liners laid up in American and West Indian ports. This course, however, was open to the objection that his squadron would be definitely located by its arrival at Panama, giving merchant steamers in the Atlantic and Caribbean warning of their danger and enabling the Allies to concentrate their forces for the purpose of opposing him.

Far more promising would be a move southward, round the Horn. If he could elude Admiral Cradock and appear unexpectedly in the South Atlantic, he would be in a position to strike a really serious blow at British trade. The grain and meat ships homeward bound from the Plate, the liners laden with New Zealand beef and mutton, the shipments of nitrate and barley from the West Coast, would all be open to his attack. While the NÜRNBERG, LEIPZIG, and DRESDEN were scattered on the trade routes, he could keep his two big cruisers together, and so compel the British to concentrate their forces. The effects of such an attack, combined with the operations of the KARLSRUHE and KRONPRINZ WILHELM, must have been serious in the extreme, especially in their relation to the food supplies of the United Kingdom. At the same time, alarm would have been excited for the safety of the North Atlantic tracks, for Cape and West African shipping, and for the outward-bound Australian trade. While a movement into Chilean waters was undoubtedly the easiest and most direct means of striking at British commerce, and shipping on the West Coast is peculiarly liable to complete interruption, no blow which could be struck in the Pacific would have a tithe of the economic importance of any considerable interference with the South Atlantic trade.

It may be questioned, however, whether Admiral von Spee fully appreciated the commercial factors of the situation. Both the Admiral himself and his crews were weary of their long inactivity and eager for an opportunity of accomplishing something worthy of the fighting strength of the squadron. In this mood, the prospect of finding a British squadron on the Chilean coast was an attraction rather than a deterrent. It is possible, also, that the Admiral was doubtful as to his ability to secure adequate coal supplies in the Atlantic. From the very first the lack of bases and the difficulty of procuring fuel had hampered his operations, and the supplies brought by the *Amasis, Anubis,* and *Karnak* would not last for very long. Should it prove impossible to arrange for an adequate service of supply ships, a dash into the Atlantic could only lead to the speedy internment, if not the destruction of his squadron.

Whatever his reason, Admiral von Spee decided to go at once into Chilean waters. In the event of his finding himself unmolested or of his defeating whatever British force might be on the coast, he would be able to put a stop for a time to all sailings from Chilean and Peruvian ports, and would have an opportunity of making arrangements with the Germans on shore or in the liners laid up in Chilean ports, for his future supplies of fuel. Nevertheless, this course involved the relinquishment of any attempt at a surprise attack on the Plate trade—a heavy price to pay for the advantages to be gained.

Several days were spent in coaling at Easter Island, and it was not till October 18th that the squadron was ready to leave. By this time the *Anubis* and *Karnak* had been cleared, and they were accordingly sent off to port, together with the *Yorck* and *Göttingen.* The *Titania, Baden,* and *Amasis* remained with the squadron, which arrived at Mas-a-fuera on the 26th. There the cruisers again coaled, and on October 27th they were joined by the PRINZ EITEL FRIEDRICH, which had hitherto pursued her lonely way across the Pacific without incident and without achievement. The abortive Australian cruise still rankled in the minds of her crew, and all on board were depressed, as " much coal had been burnt without any tangible result." [1] On the same day the whole squadron left for Valparaiso, and by the 29th they were in the neighbourhood of the port. They did not enter, however, as the Admiral wished to obtain further information as to the movements of the British cruisers before revealing his presence. He accordingly remained out of sight from the land, in wireless communication with Germans ashore. Among other news received was that of the raid on Penang, which gave

[1] *Weser Zeitung,* 14 April, 1915. Interviews with Captain and First Officer of PRINZ EITEL FRIEDRICH.

LOSS OF THE "VANDYCK"

special satisfaction to the Germans, inasmuch as the EMDEN had originally been a member of the Pacific squadron.

While the German squadron was making its way eastward, Admiral Cradock was concentrating his force in the south and the attention of Admiral Stoddart was directed mainly to the protection of trade against Captain Köhler's depredations. His more powerful cruisers were so disposed as to admit of rapid concentration in the event of Admiral von Spee coming into the Atlantic, but the BRISTOL, MACEDONIA, and EDINBURGH CASTLE were busily hunting for the KARLSRUHE in the focal area where she had made so many prizes.

As we have seen, however, Captain Köhler had already finally quitted his cruising ground and was on his way to the West Indies, where he hoped to effect a surprise attack. As he passed up the Brazilian coast he approached the trade route leading to Trinidad, and on the morning of October 26th he made the most valuable prize which had yet fallen to him. This was the Lamport & Holt liner *Vandyck*, of 10,328 tons, which had left Bahia on the 23rd, *en route* from Buenos Aires to New York.[1]

The haul was indeed a rich one. The *Vandyck* was a splendid ship, only three years old and valued at £200,000, while her cargo included 1,000 tons of frozen meat. Moreover, she carried some 200 passengers, and in consequence her store-rooms were filled with large quantities of provisions of all kinds which formed a welcome addition to the KARLSRUHE'S restricted supplies. Such a ship was not to be disposed of hastily, and Captain Köhler announced to the passengers that, in order to give them time to pack, the sinking of the vessel would be deferred to the next day.

In the meantime the KARLSRUHE, with the prize and the *Farn*, which was in attendance, steamed north, away from the tracks, and the *Asuncion*, *Rio Negro*, and *Hoffnung* were called up by wireless. Early on the morning of the 27th the transfer of the passengers and crew to the *Asuncion* began, and continued until evening. As soon as it was completed the *Asuncion* was sent off to Para, with instructions not to arrive before November 1st, as Captain Köhler wished to keep back the news of the capture as long as possible. Longer it could not be delayed, as the *Asuncion* was an old ship with poor accom-

[1] See Map 8.

modation for the prisoners, some fifty of whom were women and children. For these the Germans did the best they could, the officers of the *Asuncion* giving up their own cabins for the purpose; but even at the best the conditions in the crowded ship, under a tropical sun, were such as to forbid further prolongation of the voyage.

Having dismissed the *Asuncion*, the Germans turned their attention to removing the stores from the *Vandyck*, and this work went on far into the night. A little before midnight the *Royal Sceptre*, bound from Santos to New York, arrived upon the scene and was stopped and boarded. She carried coffee valued at £230,000, a large part of which was for delivery in Toronto *via* New York, but by the ingenuity of her master this rich cargo was saved from loss. Concealing his Bills of Lading, he produced the Manifest made out for the Customs at New York, and succeeded in persuading the boarding officer that the entire cargo was neutral owned. The *Royal Sceptre* was accordingly released, and the ransacking of the *Vandyck* continued without further incident. At 6.30 a.m. on the 28th she was sunk, and the KARLSRUHE, with the *Farn, Hoffnung*, and *Rio Negro* in attendance, proceeded on her way to the West Indies.[1]

Meanwhile, British steamers in steadily increasing numbers were passing safely through the area which the KARLSRUHE had just quitted and which Admiral Stoddart's dispositions had secured. In the Pacific also, shipping was proceeding with perfect confidence. The German squadron off Valparaiso lay too far out from the coast to interfere with the liners engaged in the West Coast trade, and the only steamers which they sighted were neutrals. The *Karnak* arrived at Antofagasta on October 28th and the *Anubis* at Callao on the 29th, but their arrival was not, at the time, connected with the movements of Admiral von Spee; nor was that of the *Yorck*, which put into Valparaiso on the 28th, left the port during the night and returned next morning. During the last four days of October, five British steamers entered or left Valparaiso, including the P.S.N. liner *Orita*, of 9,290 tons,

---

[1] As the *Asuncion* parted company before the *Vandyck* was sunk, there was, for some time, a doubt as to her ultimate fate. The Germans told the prisoners that they intended to arm her as an auxiliary cruiser, and in February, 1915, there was a rumour that she had reached Wilhelmshaven.

and the *Colusa*, of 5,732 tons, belonging to Messrs. Lamport & Holt. Had the Germans arrived a day or two earlier and been less anxious to conceal their movements, they might have made some valuable prizes.[1] As it was, the only one of these ships to see anything of an enemy was the *Colusa*, which narrowly escaped capture by the PRINZ EITEL FRIEDRICH.

The PRINZ EITEL had been ordered into Valparaiso to make further arrangements for the coal supply of the squadron. On the morning of the 31st, when very near the port, she sighted the *Colusa* and at once gave chase. In her eagerness to obtain a first success, she even continued the pursuit after the *Colusa* was within territorial waters, but at this point a Chilean gunboat intervened to prevent any further breach of neutrality, and the Germans were compelled to forgo their prize.

By this time Admiral Cradock was on his way up the Chilean coast, and on October 31st, the GLASGOW, which was cruising off Coronel, on the look out for an enemy sailing vessel whose presence had been reported, heard the call signs of the LEIPZIG. During the evening she put into Coronel to despatch and collect telegrams, and her arrival was reported by wireless to Admiral von Spee, who at once moved south with his whole force, in the hope of cutting her off. On the same day the Hamburg-Süd-Amerika liner *Santa Isabel*, which had sailed from Valparaiso, ostensibly for Hamburg, joined the German squadron. At 8 o'clock next morning the PRINZ EITEL FRIEDRICH entered the harbour, and later in the day the *Göttingen* arrived. The PRINZ EITEL made only a short stay, leaving at 1 p.m. with the object of intercepting British steamers moving on the coast, but her presence was sufficient to cause the suspension of all sailings from Valparaiso.

Meanwhile the GLASGOW had rejoined Admiral Cradock, and the two squadrons were steadily converging. While both commanders were aware that a meeting might at any time become imminent, neither anticipated it at the moment. Admiral von Spee expected only to encounter the GLASGOW, and Admiral Cradock hoped to surprise the LEIPZIG. His available force consisted only of the GOOD

[1] The *Orita* and *Quillota* sailed on the 28th for Coquimbo and Coronel respectively. On the 29th, the *Earl of Elgin* arrived from Punta Arenas, and on the 31st the *Inca* came in from the same port, in addition to the *Colusa*. The *Inca* and *Quillota* belonged to the Pacific Steam Navigation Co., the *Quillota* being one of the steamers in their coastal service.

HOPE, MONMOUTH, GLASGOW, and OTRANTO, as the CANOPUS, which he considered too slow to work effectively with his cruisers, had been left to escort the colliers, and was over 250 miles to the southward. He appears to have had no immediate expectation of encountering the main force of the enemy, and it was not until 4.40 on the afternoon of November 1st that he was finally undeceived by a message from the GLASGOW that she had sighted the SCHARNHORST, GNEISENAU, and one of the enemy's light cruisers.

The rival forces were now fairly in contact. Admiral Cradock found himself in face of greatly superior strength, but he was not the man to count the odds; nor indeed would it have been easy for him to evade an action.

After some manœuvring, the first shot was fired by the SCHARNHORST at about 7 p.m., just after the sun went down. The odds were all on the side of the Germans. More modern and better armed, they had also an advantage in speed which enabled them to choose their range and to gain and keep the advantage of the light. They were thus able to take full advantage of their superiority in gun power, a handicap against which the gallantry and devotion of the British Admiral and his crews strove in vain. Within an hour and a half the GOOD HOPE and MONMOUTH had gone to the bottom with their flags still flying, the GLASGOW and OTRANTO were driven to seek safety in flight, and the command of the sea in Chilean waters had passed temporarily into German hands.

To Admiral von Spee and the German Pacific squadron it had fallen to deal the heaviest blow which had been struck at the British fleet for well over a century; but the effect on the balance of naval power was not appreciable. Whether the victory was to yield tangible results or remain a barren exploit depended upon the subsequent action of the victors. The light in which Admiral von Spee himself viewed his success remains doubtful. In a letter dated November 2nd, he says, " We have at least contributed something to the glory of our arms, although it may not mean much on the whole and in view of the enormous number of British ships." There is here no mention of the trade routes uncovered by the defeat of Admiral Cradock's squadron; and whatever may have been the ultimate intentions of the German commander he made no immediate attempt to follow up his success by an attack on shipping.

His first move was to go to Valparaiso with the SCHARN-HORST, GNEISENAU, and NÜRNBERG. His principal object was to obtain definite news of the GOOD HOPE, whose fate had been hidden from him by the darkness, and to persuade the authorities to intern and disarm her, if she had escaped to a Chilean port. The LEIPZIG and DRESDEN were detached to Mas-a-fuera. The LEIPZIG went direct to the island, but the DRESDEN made a wide cast to the north, in order to pick up the *Sacramento*, with her valuable cargo of coal and provisions.[1]

The main division arrived at Valparaiso on November 3rd. They found British trade on the coast at an absolute standstill. We have seen that all sailings from Valparaiso had been suspended on November 1st, in consequence of the chase of the *Colusa* by the PRINZ EITEL FRIEDRICH. On the 2nd there arrived a Chilean steamer which had been stopped by the NÜRNBERG, on the previous day, sixty-two miles north of Talcahuano, and had seen two other German cruisers not far off. Other reports soon followed, and it became apparent that the whole German Pacific squadron was on the coast.

The PRINZ EITEL FRIEDRICH had been only thirty miles from the scene of the action on November 1st, and after the battle she turned back to rejoin the Admiral. Her bad luck still clung to her, and once more she narrowly missed a valuable prize. This was the *Oronsa*, a P.S.N. liner of over 8,000 tons. The *Oronsa* was at Calbuco, south of Valdivia, on the 2nd, and as she was bearing the body of the late Argentine Minister to Bolivia, the British Minister at Santiago persuaded the Chilean Government to send a destroyer to escort her into Valparaiso. Being thus secured against attack while in territorial waters, she reached port safely on the night of the 3rd. The PRINZ EITEL herself came into the harbour on the 4th.

Although the defeat of Admiral Cradock had not been followed by the loss of merchantmen, it was a severe blow to British trade on the West Coast. In the face of so formidable a hostile force and in the temporary absence of naval protection, it was impossible for steamers to put to sea, and all ships remained in port from Panama to Punta Arenas. The facility with which trade on this coast can be controlled had already been illustrated when the LEIPZIG was operating in Peruvian waters, and the

[1] See p. 236, *supra*.

measures now taken were successful in stopping all steamers before they could run into danger, but at the cost of a grievous delay to commerce.

Nothing having been heard of the GOOD HOPE, the SCHARNHORST, GNEISENAU, and NÜRNBERG left Valparaiso for Mas-a-fuera on November 4th, but the PRINZ EITEL FRIEDRICH remained behind, taking in coal from German steamers in the Bay. After taking 1,000 tons, she sailed on the 6th, being presumably afraid of internment if she outstayed her time. The departure of the German cruisers led to some inquiries as to whether it was now safe for ships to leave, but with Admiral von Spee's squadron still at large, it was not considered prudent to permit a resumption of the services. The whole shipping of the coast thus remained paralysed, whether engaged in the foreign or the coastal trade.

The first reports of the battle of Coronel received in London were based on statements made by the Germans at Valparaiso and were looked upon with some suspicion, but information was soon received from Captain Luce which put the fate of the GOOD HOPE and MONMOUTH beyond reasonable doubt, and on November 6th the Admiralty issued a further statement, confirming the loss of the two big cruisers.[1] The news caused a profound sensation, particularly in shipping circles. Steamers about to sail for the West Coast were delayed; and even on shipments from New York for Chile and Peru, insurance premiums on the open market rose to 6 per cent.[2]

Serious as was the suspension of the West Coast services, especially in its effect upon the supply of nitrate, it was not in itself a vital matter; but the possibility that the Germans might follow up their victory by coming round into the Atlantic could not be ignored, and the anxiety felt with regard to East Coast trade was increased by the fact that the *Asuncion* had arrived at Para on November 2nd with the crews of the *Glanton, Hurstdale*, and *Vandyck*. *La Correntina*, also, was now seriously overdue, and the alarm felt at Buenos Aires was such that there was some talk among ship-masters of petitioning the Admiralty to provide convoys twice a month for British vessels entering and leaving the River Plate.[3] Never-

---

[1] *Times*, 7 November, 1914.
[2] *Shipping World*, 11 November, 1914.
[3] Buenos Aires *Standard*, 3 November, 1914.

theless, there was no diminution in the volume of traffic. In accordance with instructions received from the Admiralty, Admiral Stoddart proceeded to concentrate the bulk of his force off the Plate estuary, and under his protection the export of the maize harvest went forward as actively as if there were no fear of hostile cruisers arriving on the route. As day after day went by without any sign of their arrival, the feeling of confidence increased and the danger of any serious interruption of the food supplies from New Zealand and the Plate sensibly diminished.

Admiral von Spee arrived at Mas-a-fuera on November 6th. He found the LEIPZIG awaiting him there with a prize in company. This was the *Valentine*, a big four-masted barque, belonging to Messrs. A. D. Bordes et Fils, of Dunkirk, which she had captured on November 2nd.[1] A marked feature in the trade of the Pacific Coast was the number of large sailing vessels which cleared every year from British ports with coal for Chile, returning to Europe with nitrate cargoes.[2] A large proportion of these were under the French flag, and although the outbreak of war brought about a great diminution in this traffic, many such ships were already on their way out, and among these was the *Valentine*, bound from Port Talbot to Valparaiso with a cargo amounting to over 3,500 tons. To a force so situated as was the German squadron she was a more valuable prize than the majority of steamers, and next day, November 7th, brought a further slice of luck in the arrival of the *Baden*, towing the Norwegian three-master *Helicon*, which had been captured by the *Titania*. She too was a collier, bound from Port Talbot to Caleta Caloso, and her seizure was subsequently justified by the German Prize Court on the ground that the 2,634 tons of coal which she carried might have been used for the supply of British warships; but the decision was reversed on appeal, and the German Government agreed to pay compensation. Meanwhile her cargo formed a valuable addition to the German Admiral's stock of fuel, and during the next two or three days this stock was further increased by the arrival of the DRESDEN with the *Sacramento* in company. The PRINZ EITEL FRIEDRICH also joined, with the coal which she had obtained at Valparaiso.

[1] See Map 5.
[2] In 1913 the number of French sailing vessels cleared from U.K. ports for Chile was seventy, and the tonnage 152,495.

Meanwhile the British Admiralty was taking every possible step to deal with the dangerous situation which had arisen. The GLASGOW, CANOPUS, and OTRANTO were instructed to concentrate on Admiral Stoddart and the KENT was sent out from Sierra Leone to join his flag. The AUSTRALIA, which had been working eastward across the Pacific, was ordered to join the Anglo-Japanese Squadron assembled for the defence of the northern trade routes, and the possibility of the Germans eluding this force and passing through the Panama Canal to attack trade in the Caribbean, was provided against by the presence of the battle cruiser PRINCESS ROYAL in the West Indies. This ship had already been ordered out to American waters for the purpose of protecting the North Atlantic Trade Routes against German cruisers breaking out from the North Sea, and her departure was now hastened. A powerful Japanese squadron was moved to Suva to cut off Admiral von Spee if he should attempt to return on his tracks towards the Western Pacific, and a covering force was provided for General Botha's base at Luderitzbucht and the South African trade. Most important of all, Vice-Admiral Sir F. Doveton Sturdee, K.C.B., was ordered to go out from home with the battle cruisers INVINCIBLE and INFLEXIBLE, take Admiral Stoddart's force under his command, and follow the German squadron wherever it might go.

These arrangements, especially the despatch of the battle cruisers, were veiled in profound secrecy, nor was anything definite heard for some time of Admiral von Spee, the KARLSRUHE, or the KRONPRINZ WILHELM. Shipping in the South Atlantic continued to display an admirable confidence and enterprise, but the sailing of all ships on the West Coast remained suspended. Shipowners, merchants, and the public generally awaited with anxiety but without panic the progress of events, and their confidence in the ability of the navy to deal promptly and adequately with the situation was strengthened on November 11th by the announcement of good news from the East.

CHAPTER XIX

THE END OF THE "EMDEN" AND "KARLSRUHE"[1]

By the end of October, as we have seen, the intelligence received as to the movements of Admiral von Spee and the discovery of the KÖNIGSBERG in the Rufiji River permitted an increase of the forces operating against the EMDEN. While the net woven around the German cruiser was thus drawn tighter, the capture of her two supply ships by the YARMOUTH threatened to restrict her freedom of movement, and had it not been for the capture of the *Exford*, she would have been placed in a position of some peril. Captain von Müller had ascertained from the survivors of the MOUSQUET that the *Pontoporos* had been captured, but the *Buresk* was awaiting him at Simalur with between four and five thousand tons still on board, and the *Exford*, whose cargo of 5,500 tons had not yet been touched, was at the southern rendezvous, off Cocos Island. In these circumstances the loss of the inferior fuel in the Greek collier was of less importance, and, after quitting Penang, he proceeded down the south-east coast of Sumatra to pick up his tenders and prepare for fresh operations.

At half-past four on the afternoon of October 30th the EMDEN cut the direct track between Colombo and Sabang, about 140 miles from the coast of Sumatra. Here she stopped the s.s. *Newburn* from the Tyne, with a neutral cargo for the Far East, and sent her into Sabang with the survivors of the MOUSQUET. An hour or so later she met the *Buresk*, with whom she kept on as far as the Sunda Strait, which was reached by November 5th. On the way, on November 2nd, another 500 tons of coal were taken from the prize.

These movements were quite unknown to the British authorities, for the report made by the *Newburn* at Sabang on October 31st, though it established the position of the

[1] See Map 7.

EMDEN on the previous day, gave no clue to Captain von Müller's intentions for the future. From Singapore to the Arabian Sea the atmosphere was one of strained expectancy, as it was impossible to tell in what direction the next blow might fall. Indeed, the Bombay—Colombo route was closed for a few hours on November 6th–7th, pending investigation into the identity of a cruiser sighted off the Travancore coast, as it was thought that the EMDEN might have returned to the scene of her previous exploits.

At this point, however, the good fortune which had hitherto attended Captain von Müller finally deserted him. From the Sunda Strait he had turned back to the rendezvous off Cocos Island, where he joined the *Exford* on the morning of November 8th. After obtaining some stores from the tender he sent her off to another rendezvous on the afternoon of that day, and, with the *Buresk* in company, held on for Cocos Island, where he proposed to cut the cables and destroy the wireless station.

It was this movement which sealed his doom. Though Admiral Jerram had been unable to spare a cruiser to be permanently stationed off Cocos Island, he had not been unmindful of the possibility of an attack on this important link in his communications, and he had given the officials of the Eastern Extension Telegraph Company full instructions as to the procedure to be adopted in the event of a surprise. For this purpose he furnished them with a list of the secret call signs of all British and Allied cruisers in that part of the Indian Ocean, so that they might communicate by wireless with the commanders of ships at sea, as well as by cable with himself at Singapore. The Admiral also communicated his apprehensions to Captain Kiddle of the MINOTAUR, who commanded the escort of the Australian convoy which sailed from St. George's Sound on November 1st.

The route of the convoy passed very near to the Cocos Group, and on the morning of November 8th, when the EMDEN met the *Exford* at the rendezvous 40 miles north of the islands, the convoy was about 230 miles to the south-east of them. At this point Captain Kiddle received orders to proceed to South Africa in the MINOTAUR, in order to join the covering force provided for the protection of the Union Expedition against Admiral von Spee. He accordingly turned over his command to Captain Silver of the MELBOURNE, at the same time repeating

THE TRAP FOR THE "EMDEN"

to him Admiral Jerram's warning with regard to Cocos Island. Besides the MELBOURNE, the escort still included her sister ship the SYDNEY and the big Japanese cruiser IBUKI.

In complete ignorance of the powerful force which was approaching, Captain von Müller arrived off Cocos Keeling Island at daybreak on November 9th. Resistance was impossible, but on the first sight of the EMDEN the telegraph operators sent off a cable to Admiral Jerram at Singapore. In spite of persistent jamming by the EMDEN they also contrived to get through a wireless message to the MINOTAUR, which was still in touch both with the islands and with the convoy.

They could do no more before a German landing party disembarked, but what they had done was enough. They had set in motion the whole elaborate machinery which had been prepared for dealing with the raider. On receipt of the cable from Cocos, Admiral Jerram instructed Captain Grant to proceed from Colombo to meet the convoy with the HAMPSHIRE, EMPRESS OF ASIA, and EMPRESS OF RUSSIA. He had already arranged with Admiral Tochinai to establish a patrol of the Sunda Strait, and on the evening of the 9th, the YAKUMO, with three British destroyers, left Singapore for that purpose. They were to be met at the Strait by the PHILOMEL and PYRAMUS of the New Zealand Division, which were on their way to Singapore. The Japanese Admiral himself arranged to leave Singapore in the TOKIWA next day for Acheh Head. The NISSHIN also would shortly be available. In the Bay of Bengal, or near Colombo, were the CHIKUMA, YAHAGI, and ASKOLD, ready to meet the EMDEN if she should double back for another raid on Indian commerce. The GLOUCESTER was coming out from the Mediterranean; and though the DARTMOUTH had been ordered to South Africa after the battle of Coronel, the WEYMOUTH was now ready to join the hunt. Thus practically every avenue of escape was blocked and, whatever happened at Cocos Island, the termination of the EMDEN's career in the Indian Ocean was now only a matter of time.

The efficacy of these arrangements was not, however, destined to be tested, for the wireless message to the MINOTAUR had brought about a swifter catastrophe. This message was passed on by Captain Kiddle to Captain Silver, who had arrived with the convoy at a point fifty-five miles north of Cocos Island. Its receipt placed him in a position calling for prompt and sound judgment. His first duty was to the convoy, which covered a wide area of sea and to guard which he had only three ships. He decided, however, that the most effective method of protecting it would be to get into immediate touch with the enemy, and for this purpose he detached the SYDNEY, Captain John C. T. Glossop, which went off to Cocos Island at a speed of 20 knots.

At 9.15 a.m. the SYDNEY came in sight of the German cruiser. Captain von Müller made no attempt to escape. His long cruise had, no doubt, reduced the speed of his ship and he must have felt that in any case he was coming to the end of his tether. He accordingly stood out to fight, and within twenty-five minutes from the time the EMDEN was first sighted from the SYDNEY, the two cruisers were hotly engaged. It was the first serious engagement of the Australian Navy, and the opportunity was brilliantly turned to account. The EMDEN'S resistance was worthy of her previous career, but the SYDNEY was so handled by Captain Glossop as to take the utmost advantage of her heavier armament, and her 6-inch guns, excellently served, soon began to tell. At 11.20, one hour and forty minutes after the first shot was fired, the EMDEN ran ashore on North Keeling Island, heavily punished, and with two-thirds of her crew dead or wounded. The SYDNEY then went in pursuit of the *Buresk*, which was captured after an hour's chase. The German prize crew, however, had opened the Kingston valves and damaged them beyond the possibility of repair. The *Buresk* was accordingly left to sink and the SYDNEY returned to receive the surrender of the EMDEN. In the meantime the German landing party had made their escape in the little schooner *Ayesha*, which they found at the island and armed with a couple of maxims. Their mission had not been wholly successful, as though they had destroyed the wireless installation and telegraph instruments, only one cable—that to Perth—had been actually cut before they were disturbed.[1]

[1] They were subsequently picked up by the German steamer *Choising*, which came out from Padang to meet them. Having sunk the *Ayesha*, they proceeded in the *Choising* to the Arabian coast, and continued their journey overland. The *Choising* put in for safety to Massawa.

THE INDIAN OCEAN CLEAR

The tide of events in the East had now turned strongly against the Germans. On the same day that the EMDEN met her fate a small Indian force, covered by the DUKE OF EDINBURGH, destroyed the Turkish fort at Sheikh Syed, opposite to Perim, and thus removed a possible menace to navigation in the Red Sea. On the following day the KÖNIGSBERG was at last definitely accounted for. All attempts to get at her had failed, owing to the difficulties of navigation and the impossibility of accurate spotting in the densely wooded delta of the Rufigi; but on November 10th, the collier *Newbridge* was sunk in the only navigable channel, which was completely blocked, and the escape of the German cruiser was thus rendered impossible.[1] Indeed, the first few days of November witnessed practically a clean sweep of the German ships whose existence had troubled British trade in the Indian Ocean and Western Pacific. Tsingtau surrendered on the 7th, and all the vessels in the harbour fell into the hands of the blockading squadron, including the KAISERIN ELIZABETH, five German gunboats, and three merchant steamers, whose aggregate tonnage was 9,482.[2] On the night of the 8th the GEIER was interned at Honolulu, and the only German warship remaining at large east of Suez was the CORMORAN, which was still in hiding in the Carolines.

Thus, so far as seaborne trade was concerned, no small off-set to Admiral von Spee's victory on the Chilean coast was provided by the removal of all serious danger threatening the Oriental Route. Moreover, though it did not become known till some weeks later, the destruction of the EMDEN was actually preceded by that of her most successful rival in the South Atlantic.

It will be remembered that the last intelligence received of the KARLSRUHE was that provided by the *Asuncion's* arrival at Para on November 2nd, with the prisoners from the *Glanton, Hurstdale,* and *Vandyck*. The capture of the *Vandyck* pointed to an intention on Captain Köhler's part to abandon the track between South America and Europe for that which ran between Plate and Brazilian ports and

---

[1] The *Somali* (2,550 tons) of the Deutsche Ost-Afrika Line, which had been acting as a supply ship to the KÖNIGSBERG, and was with her in the Rufigi, was set on fire and destroyed on November 7th, in the course of these operations.

[2] All these vessels were sunk by the Germans before the surrender, but the merchant steamers were subsequently raised and put into service by the Japanese.

the United States; but we have seen that his real design was one of a more daring nature. He had, in fact, made up his mind to attempt a surprise attack on Barbados, with the object of destroying the shipping in the harbour and interrupting British commercial communications in the West Indies.

What success would have attended this daring project, in face of the Allied Squadron in the Carribean, must always remain a matter of conjecture, for on November 4th, as the officers of the KARLSRUHE were sitting at supper and the crew were listening to the band on the forecastle, a violent explosion occurred on board from some unknown cause, breaking the ship absolutely in two. The fore part sank almost immediately, with the greater part of the crew. The after part remained afloat for some twenty minutes, enabling the survivors to be picked up by the *Rio Negro* and *Hoffnung*, which were in company. To their infinite regret, Captain Köhler was amongst those who were lost.

So complete was the destruction of the cruiser that little or no wreckage remained to mark the spot where she had sunk. In order to conceal her loss as long as possible, the survivors decided to sink the *Hoffnung* (ex *Indrani*) and attempt to reach Germany in the *Rio Negro*. The *Farn* was detached at the time of the explosion and had to be left to herself. After an anxious and trying voyage the *Rio Negro* reached Aalesund in Norway on November 29th, and a few days later arrived at Kiel, but the secret was well kept and it was many weeks before British cruisers ceased their search for the vanished raider. Of the *Farn* nothing was heard until 1915.[1]

The careers of the two German cruisers whose activities were thus brought to an end at the beginning of November present several interesting points of similarity and contrast. They were by far the most successful of the German commerce destroyers at sea on the outbreak of war. They were both well adapted for their purpose and commanded by men of enterprise and ability. Both attacked British trade on one of the great highways of ocean traffic, where shipping is thickly concentrated and follows well-defined routes. Both were deserted by fortune when engaged in changing the sphere of their operations, after

[1] She arrived at San Juan, Porto Rico, on January 12th, 1915, and was there interned.

having made their chosen cruising ground too hot to hold them; but the EMDEN fell a victim to the foresight of her opponents, at a moment when she was hemmed in by a well-designed combination which she could not hope long to have escaped; the KARLSRUHE was sunk by accident at a time when her whereabouts was unknown to her enemies. The active careers of the two ships extended over practically the same period, and both inflicted considerable damage on British trade; but the mischief done by the KARLSRUHE was confined to the destruction of ships; the EMDEN's success extended to the interruption of traffic.

By the capture of the *Vandyck*, the total of British steamers taken by Captain Köhler was brought up to sixteen, with a tonnage of 72,805. In addition he had captured and sunk one neutral of 3,804 tons with a British cargo, and had stopped and released the *Royal Sceptre*. The value of the ships and cargoes lost has been estimated at well over £1,000,000.[1]

The EMDEN captured, in all, twenty-four steamers, with a total gross tonnage of 105,413. Twenty-two of these were British, one Russian, and one neutral; but the neutral had already been retaken, four of the British steamers were released for the purpose of taking prisoners into port, one escaped before a prize crew could be put on board, and one was recaptured at a later date.[2] Thus, the actual loss to the British mercantile marine was reduced to sixteen steamers of 70,360 tons, which, with their cargoes, represented an estimated loss of £2,200,000.[1] In addition, considerable damage was done to the oil tanks at Madras and to the cable and wireless station at Cocos Island, and the raid on Penang involved the destruction of a Russian light cruiser and a French destroyer.

In the actual tonnage captured (exclusive of vessels released) the records of the two cruisers show little difference, but the monetary loss inflicted by the EMDEN was much greater, chiefly owing to the valuable cargo carried in the *Troilus*. On the other hand, she sank no cargoes of essential foodstuffs, with the exception of the *Tymeric's* 4,500 tons of sugar, while the KARLSRUHE, as we have seen, sent several thousand tons of wheat, maize, oats, and barley to the bottom. While the field of

[1] Estimates prepared for Liverpool and London War Risks Insurance Association.
[2] The *Exford* was recaptured by the HIMALAYA in December.

operations chosen by Captain von Müller enabled him to work havoc on the trade of the Bay of Bengal and the Far East, it precluded any attack on the grain ships from Karachi, and indeed, the presence in the Arabian Sea of so many cruisers engaged in escort duties would have rendered such an attack extremely hazardous. Nor did he succeed in capturing a single homeward-bound meat ship from Australia. Excluding vessels in ballast, his chief success was obtained against outward-bound steamers. The net tonnage of British ships cleared from ports in the United Kingdom, during August and September, with cargoes for India and the Far East, was 316,596.[1] Of such ships six were taken by the EMDEN,[2] with a net tonnage of 17,485, or 5·5 per cent. of the whole. If two vessels which escaped or were released [3] are included in the captures, the percentage rises to 7·2. On the other hand, while 412,650 net tons of shipping from India or the East were entered with cargoes at British home ports during October and November, only three laden homeward-bound vessels were captured.[4] The aggregate net tonnage of these ships was 11,856, and if this be added to the tonnage entered, the percentage works out at the low figure of 2·8.

Even if Indian trade alone is taken into consideration, the percentage of loss is surprisingly low. During the months of September and October, 300 British steamers were cleared with cargoes at Indian ports, and 262 entered.[5] Adding three vessels which were captured before they arrived in port, we get a total of 565 voyages, of which only six were interfered with by the raider.[6] Nor was the loss of cargoes much heavier, in proportion to the volume of trade. The total of Indian imports, exports, and re-exports for the two months, exclusive of treasure and Government stores, amounted to £25,384,000.[7] The cargoes of laden prizes bound to or from Indian ports have been estimated at £750,000, or under 2·5 per cent. of the trade afloat.

It must be remembered, of course, that a large number

[1] Monthly Board of Trade returns of steamers entered from and cleared to British India, Mauritius, Ceylon, Straits Settlements and Hongkong, China, Japan, and Java.
[2] *Clan Matheson, Buresk, Clan Grant, Benmohr, Exford, Chilkana.*
[3] *Glenturret, Newburn.* [4] *Diplomat, Tymeric, Troilus.*
[5] *Foreign Seaborne Trade* (monthly) Calcutta.
[6] *Killin, Diplomat, Clan Matheson, Clan Grant,* and *Chilkana* sunk, *Kabinga* released.
[7] *Accounts Relating to the Trade and Navigation of British India,* 1914.

A RAIDER'S DIFFICULTIES

of vessels sailed or arrived during the first ten days of September, before the EMDEN arrived on the tracks, and that a considerably higher percentage would be shown if West Coast shipping was excluded and only vessels bound to or from Bay of Bengal ports and the Far East taken into consideration. But in any case the proportion of prizes was low in comparison with the volume of trade attacked. The explanation is to be found in the very small part of the raider's career which could be devoted to actual operations against commerce. From August 6th, when she left Tsingtau for the second time, to November 9th, when she was destroyed, is ninety-five days. Of this period thirty-five days were occupied in effecting a junction with Admiral von Spee and in the subsequent passage through unfrequented waters to Captain von Müller's chosen sphere of operations. During the five days from September 10th to September 14th inclusive, eight steamers were captured; after which ten days were spent in coaling, cruising in the Bay of Bengal, bombarding Madras, and steaming into Cingalese waters. During these ten days no prizes were made, owing to the detention of shipping at Indian ports. Having arrived on her new cruising ground the EMDEN made six prizes in three days, but this burst of activity was succeeded by a blank period of eighteen days, during which she was in hiding or cruising fruitlessly for the Australian meat ships near Diego Garcia. On her return to the Minikoi area, four days of activity gave seven captures; but during the remaining twenty-one days of her career she never approached the trade routes except at the actual moment of her attack on Penang, on October 30th, when she cut the track between Colombo and Sabang, and on November 5th, when she looked into the Sunda Strait. Her periods of successful activity were more remunerative than those of the KARLSRUHE, which only on one occasion captured more than a single prize in a day, but Captain von Müller's lack of accommodation for prisoners prevented his activities from being sustained for more than three or four days at a time, since the dismissal of a prize with the crews and passengers of sunken ships was necessarily followed by an immediate shifting of his ground.

On the other hand, the arrival of these released prizes contributed materially to the alarm which was excited and the dislocation of trade caused by the EMDEN's operations.

The indirect effects of her activities were far greater than those which can be traced to her rival in the South Atlantic. It is one of the most remarkable facts in the early history of the war that the KARLSRUHE's numerous captures of British ships left the volume of trade on the Argentine and Brazilian tracks practically unaffected. It was generally a long time before they were known, and the suspicion, or even the certainty, that a hostile cruiser was at work somewhere on the route did not prevent merchantmen from leaving Rio de Janeiro or the Plate. There was always the possibility that she would have been driven from her station before they arrived on it; and even if she was still at work, the wide dispersion of shipping which was possible in the South Atlantic held out to any individual ship good chances of escape. It was quite another thing when the *Kabinga* came into Calcutta, the *Gryfevale* into Colombo, or the *St. Egbert* into Cochin, and reported that the EMDEN had been holding up shipping within fifty to two hundred miles of a great port, in waters where geographical conditions and the convergence of numerous tracks render dispersion difficult. Important as were her captures, their effect on trade was perhaps less serious than the delays and uncertainties arising from the holding up of shipping, whether due to the official closure of the routes or to the anxiety of shipowners and masters.

Still more serious was the effect of the captures and of the bombardment of Madras in shaking the confidence of Indian, especially of native, shippers and financiers. The flight of the moneylenders to the hills crippled the commerce of Southern India, and the holding back of stocks by producers was to a great extent responsible for the heavy decreases in the export of tea and jute goods. The position with regard to jute and jute manufactures was, in fact, fast becoming serious when the destruction of the EMDEN finally relieved the situation. The fears of Australian farmers had been relieved by large shipments of gunny bags during the latter part of October, but in all other directions the export of jute manufactures was in arrear, and the Dundee mills were threatened with an acute shortage by the delay in shipping the raw material. Up to November 13th only nine cargoes had arrived, as against twenty-one in the previous year, and the stocks in hand were running dangerously low.[1]

[1] *Lloyd's List*, 30 November, 1914, Leith Correspondent.

INDIAN TRADE EXPANDS

When once the menace to the route was removed and confidence re-established, a remarkable expansion took place in all branches of the Indian export trade which had been most affected by the EMDEN's activities. Heavy shipments of tea during November fully made up the leeway of previous months, and the figures for gunny bags and gunny cloth rose to considerably above the normal level. Those for raw jute still showed a large decrease on the previous year, due in part to the cutting off of the German market, but nearly twice as much was shipped to the United Kingdom as in the previous month. The total exports of Indian products rose from £6,656,000 in October to £10,532,000 in November, and, indeed, the November total was only 17 per cent. less than in 1913, despite the loss of enemy markets and the restriction of the continental demand.[1]

[1] Export trade of the principal ports in lakhs of rupees :

Week ending.	Calcutta and Chittagong.	Bombay.	Karachi.	Madras.	Rangoon.
November 7th	165	46	15	—	17
,, 14th	157	70	33	2	19
,, 21st	148	38	21	40	18
,, 28th	291	51	18	1	24
December 5th	125	55	40	23	19

In comparing these figures with those for the previous month (p. 216 n, 219 n, 275 n, *supra*), it must be remembered that the October figures are swollen by cargoes held back during the closing of the routes in September. It is noteworthy that the total exports from the Bay of Bengal ports (Calcutta, Chittagong, Madras, and Rangoon) for the two weeks ending November 14th were only 360 lakhs, but that in the two succeeding weeks they rose to 522 lakhs.

The following figures indicate the effect of the menace presented by the EMDEN, and its removal, on the shipments of tea and jute :

—		September.	October.	November.
Tea to United Kingdom	1000 lbs.	30,847	22,830	61,369
Raw jute to United Kingdom	tons	20	23	41
Gunny bags to United Kingdom	no.	2,906	1,117	8,237
,, ,, ,, Australia	,,	221	16,179	9,080
,, ,, ,, United States	,,	1,242	1,741	4,306
Gunny cloth ,, United Kingdom	yds.	2,720	1,587	10,223
,, ,, ,, Australia	,,	37	3,354	3,501
,, ,, ,, United States	,,	58,027	39,613	81,120
,, ,, ,, Argentina	,,	22,733	—	25,113
Total Exports of Tea	lbs.	33,679	27,368	69,773
,, ,, ,, Raw jute	tons	24	41	75
,, ,, ,, Gunny bags	no.	22,474	29,657	50,001
,, ,, ,, Gunny cloth	yds.	89,236	47,466	126,457

Hitherto the insurance of cargoes for the Eastern markets had been left mainly to the State Office, but the destruction of the EMDEN was followed by an immediate fall in underwriters' quotations for war risks from 60s. to 40s., and they would have gone still lower had not the outbreak of war with Turkey led to some anxiety concerning the safety of the Suez Canal.[1] By the latter part of the month, when it became clear that the situation in Eygpt was well in hand, the premiums dropped to 35s. and 30s., bringing them below the State Flat Rate, and they soon fell to a still lower level.

Anxiety as to the safety of the Canal also led, during November, to some temporary restriction in chartering, as owners were inclined to hold out for higher freights than shippers were willing to pay,[2] but the figures of Indian trade show how small was the effect of this disturbance, and the only branch of the Oriental Route which seemed likely to be seriously affected by the war with Turkey was the minor track which ran up the Persian Gulf to Muhammerah and the Euphrates. So long as Turkey remained neutral, the small force of light vessels maintained in the Gulf for police purposes had been considered sufficient to protect British interests in the grain and date harvests of Mesopotamia and more particularly in the valuable oil fields of Persia. Under cover of this force trade went forward normally, except for irregularities caused by shortage of tonnage; but during October, when the situation became more threatening, arrangements were made to provide military co-operation with further naval support, at the shortest possible notice. So complete were the preparations that the advanced guard of the expedition crossed the outer bar of the Shatt-el-Arab[3] on November 5th, the very day on which war was declared, and by the 11th the position had been rendered comparatively secure, and the oil tankers from and to Muhammerah were arriving and departing freely. On the 21st Basra was occupied, and thenceforward the Mesopotamian campaign affected commerce only in so far as the requirements of transport added to the shortage of tonnage both in India and on the Euphrates.

[1] *Times*, 12 November, 1914; *Shipping World*, 18 November, 1914.
[2] *Lloyd's List*, 6 November, 1914: London Freight Market Report.
[3] The German steamer *Ekbatana* of 4,753 tons was found sunk in the channel.

Thus the month of November witnessed the establishment of complete Allied control over the Oriental Route—over its minor branches as well as over the great trunk highway. With the EMDEN sunk, the KÖNIGSBERG blockaded and the GEIER interned, with Tsingtau, the Shatt-el-Arab, and the German Pacific Colonies in the hands of the Allies, the fear of any further attack on trade east of Suez was reduced to vanishing point. The stimulus of the successes achieved extended beyond the limits of the Eastern trade and gave a welcome fillip to public confidence in naval protection, which had been somewhat shaken by the battle of Coronel. All eyes were turned to the Southern Pacific, in expectation of a similar stroke to that which had freed British commerce from the most active and successful of the German raiders.

CHAPTER XX

FROM CORONEL TO THE FALKLANDS [1]

FOR some time after the battle of Coronel, little or no news was received from which any deduction could be drawn as to the subsequent intentions of the German Admiral. Although units of his force were constantly reported all up and down the Pacific coast, the majority of these rumours were entirely without foundation, and it was not, in fact, until November 13th that enemy cruisers were again seen in a Chilean harbour. On that day the DRESDEN and LEIPZIG put into Valparaiso; but after taking in a quantity of stores and provisions, they sailed on the 14th, and the veil was once more drawn over the movements of the squadron.

The same ignorance prevailed with regard to the German raiders in the South Atlantic. The destruction of the KARLSRUHE remained for some weeks unknown either to the public or the Admiralty, and the movements of the KRONPRINZ WILHELM were equally mysterious. Nothing definite had been heard of her since September 24th, and the only indication of her activity was given by the fact that *La Correntina* was missing and was not among the ships known to have been captured by the KARLSRUHE. In view of the large number of steamers at this time leaving and arriving at Plate ports the comparative inactivity of the KRONPRINZ is, at first sight, a little surprising, but the explanation is to be found in her lack of any such organisation of tenders and supply ships as contributed to the success of the KARLSRUHE'S operations, or of a base to which captured colliers could be sent.

After parting from the *Sierra Cordoba* on October 24th, Captain Thierfelder went back to the trade routes, and on the 28th he captured the four-masted iron barque *Union*, belonging to the great sailing fleet of Messrs. A. D. Bordes et Fils, off the mouth of the Plate Estuary. The German

[1] See Map 5.

captain now found himself faced with an awkward dilemma. He was right on the track of Plate steamers, and if he could maintain his position, he might hope to work havoc among the homeward-bound grain and meat ships from Buenos Aires and Monte Video. On the other hand, his prize was laden with Welsh coal, from Port Talbot to Valparaiso. He had nowhere to send her and no tender who could take her in charge. The daily coal consumption of a 15,000-ton liner is necessarily large, and it was long since he had received any substantial supplies. The imperative necessity of replenishing his bunkers carried the day, and he accordingly took the *Union* in tow and went off to join the *Sierra Cordoba*, leaving the main current of South American trade unmolested. On November 1st he rejoined the *Sierra Cordoba*, and during the following week some further stores were taken from this vessel. Two attempts were also made to coal from the *Union*, but the high seas which were running rendered this operation impossible, and the barque was accordingly kept in tow to await calmer weather.

On November 9th the *Sierra Cordoba* was sent off to look for the *Navarra*,[1] which had put into Pernambuco on September 24th and sailed again about the beginning of October. She was laden with stores and munitions, and appears to have been intended at one time to meet the German Pacific Squadron; but after rounding the Horn, she put back, presumably for fear of capture by Admiral Cradock's cruisers, and on November 11th, two days after the *Sierra Cordoba* had gone off to meet her, she arrived off the entrance to the Plate. Here she was sighted and chased by the armed merchant cruiser ORAMA. The ORAMA gained fast, and seeing that the prospects of escape were hopeless, the crew of the *Navarra* took to their boats and blew up the ship. The *Sierra Cordoba*, being unable to find her, went back to rejoin the KRONPRINZ WILHELM.

The operations of Captain Thierfelder were, however, only a minor factor in the situation. The question of real importance to the safety of British trade with South America was what use the victorious German Admiral in the Pacific would make of his opportunity. Already the great combination designed to restrict his further activities and protect the trade routes had been put in motion.

[1] See page 113, *supra*.

Admiral Stoddart's concentration off the Plate was completed by November 10th, and he then went a little north to await Admiral Sturdee. The GLASGOW joined his flag on the 11th and was sent in to refit at Rio de Janeiro, where she received a most friendly and gratifying welcome. The CANOPUS, which had developed engine-room defects, remained at the Falklands as guardship, but the KENT was already well on her way out, and on the 11th Admiral Sturdee left Devonport with the two battle cruisers, whose departure was kept a profound secret.

For the time being, however, there was no British squadron in a position to cover the Pacific tracks, and with Admiral von Spee's cruisers still unlocated, it was necessary to impose severe restrictions on the movements of shipping. At Valparaiso and the Southern ports as far as Punta Arenas all vessels were detained. At Antofagasta, farther to the north, the Consul permitted steamers to leave, provided they sailed before daylight, kept within territorial waters, and made a port each night, but the departure of sailing vessels was prohibited. No vessels were officially detained in Peruvian and Ecuadorian ports, where the immediate risk was smaller, but both at Callao and Guayaquil, P.S.N. liners were held up by instructions of the Company's West Coast manager.

In the meantime the German squadron was engaged in coaling at Mas-a-fuera, in preparation for a renewal of activity. The DRESDEN and LEIPZIG, having filled their bunkers, were sent off on the 11th to Valparaiso, but the main division did not leave until the 15th. By that time the *Valentine*, *Helicon*, and *Sacramento* had all been cleared, such part of the 13,000 tons of coal which they carried as could not be taken into the cruisers' bunkers being transferred to the *Baden* and *Amasis*. The *Helicon* was then released, but the *Valentine* was towed outside territorial waters and sunk, her crew being sent off in the *Sacramento*. The *Titania*, which was now empty, was also sunk.

On November 17th, two days after leaving the island, the main division was joined by the DRESDEN and LEIPZIG, in company with whom was the Kosmos liner *Rhakotis*, which had left Valparaiso on the 12th, cleared for Panama, with marine and engine-room stores for the squadron. She had now on board the master and crew of the *North Wales*, a prize captured by the DRESDEN on the 16th. This ship was a collier under charter to the British Admiralty, and had been ordered from Juan Fernandez to the base at the Falkland Islands. Recognising that the voyage was a perilous one, her master kept well clear of all the ordinary steamer tracks, and on the morning of the 16th he was 200 miles west of the track from Valparaiso to the Straits and over forty miles east of the direct route from Panama; but when roughly abreast of Concepcion he sighted two cruisers of unknown nationality, and at once made off at full speed, altering course to the north-east. One of the cruisers was soon seen to be moving in pursuit, and after an hour's chase the collier was overhauled by the DRESDEN and compelled to strike her flag. As she had only about 700 tons of coal on board, she was sunk without any further loss of time than was necessary to take off her crew and stores. The master was, of course, interrogated as to his destination, but fortunately he had had time to destroy his secret orders, and in order to avoid betrayal of the Admiralty's plans, he informed his captors that he was bound for Monte Video. Next day, just before the LEIPZIG and DRESDEN met the main division, the *Rhakotis* joined company and the prisoners were transferred to her.

After effecting the junction, the whole squadron proceeded towards Captain Lüdecke's old hiding-place in St. Quentin Bay, where further supplies of coal and provisions were expected. From the people in the *Rhakotis* they learned of the destruction of the EMDEN, the bottling up of the KÖNIGSBERG and the fall of Tsingtau, disquieting evidence of the control which was being established by the British and Allied navies even in the most distant seas. They heard nothing, however, to indicate that any British concentration was taking place in South American waters, and their chief preoccupation at the moment was the question of coal supply. This was, to some extent, solved when they arrived at St. Quentin Bay on November 21st, as they found awaiting them the Norddeutscher Lloyd liner *Seydlitz*,[1] which had sailed from Valparaiso on October 20th with 6,000 tons of coal, and the Kosmos liner *Memphis*, which had slipped out of Punta Arenas, without clearance, on the night of November 19th, with 2,400 tons. During the next two or three days they were joined by two more Kosmos liners. One of these, the *Ramses*, had sailed from Valparaiso on

[1] See p. 125, *supra*. She arrived at Valparaiso during October.

the 12th. The other, the *Luxor*, had been lying at Coronel. As she was loading large quantities of coal, the Chilean Government, suspecting her intentions, sent orders that no more was to be supplied. With 3,600 tons which she had already on board, she ran out of port, without clearance, on the night of the 18th, and joined the squadron in St. Quentin Bay on the 23rd.

The action of the German liners in leaving without clearance or on false declarations gave great offence to the Chilean Government, who had every reason to resent the use of their ports as bases for the attack on British trade. The continued suspension of commercial sailings was becoming a serious matter for the West Coast Republics. Hardly any ships had arrived or sailed since October 31st; the foreign trade of Chile and Peru was practically in abeyance, and even the coastal traffic was hampered by the stoppage of the Pacific Steam Navigation Company's service. Seven P.S.N. liners, with a tonnage of 49,572 gross, and five of their coastal steamers were laid up in Pacific ports, and in addition, the *Ortega*, which arrived at Monte Video, outward bound, on November 23rd, suspended her voyage at that port. In all, over 100,000 tons of British shipping were affected.

The result of this long continued suspension of British sailings was to put almost an entire stop to the exports of copper, copper ore, and tin ore to the United Kingdom, and the shipments of alpaca from Peru, though they had somewhat recovered from the paralysis caused by the LEIPZIG's earlier operations, were still very far below the normal. It is true that steamers from the Northern Peruvian ports could still reach the United Kingdom by the Panama Route without incurring unreasonable risk, but so long as the German squadron was actually on the coast, the Canal tracks, as well as that through the Straits, were closed to Chilean trade. With very few neutral vessels available, it was impossible to send nitrate in any large quantities either to the United Kingdom or to the United States, and the condition of the chief Chilean industry was deplorable. It had already been severely crippled by the loss of the German market and the collapse of the exchanges, and now that it was impossible to procure tonnage for shipments to those markets which were still open, the outlook was black. Out of 134 *officinas* which were working in July, only about forty-three were now open, and the drift of

PARALYSIS OF WEST COAST TRADE

labour away from the coast threatened serious difficulties in re-opening those which had closed, even when the situation improved. At the same time, the diminished purchasing power of the country, the stoppage of German traffic, and the danger to British shipping, restricted the import trade; few vessels were cleared for the West Coast from the United Kingdom, and there was a grave prospect both of deficiency in the supplies of coal and of an increased shortage of tonnage at the opening of the New Year.

The loss to Chilean trade and the annòyance of the Chilean Government were increased by the refusal of the German liners to take any part in relieving the situation. Although their activity as supply ships showed clearly that, for the time being, there was nothing to prevent their moving freely on the coast, they would neither accept cargoes nor even complete the voyages which had been cut short by the outbreak of war. The Kosmos Line gave particular offence by refusing to deliver goods to merchants at the Chilean ports in which they were lying, and by denying the competence of the Chilean Courts to decide actions brought by the consignees.[1]

If the coast had been everywhere under effective control, it would have been possible for British steamers to complete their voyages between port and port within territorial waters; but the great length of the coast-line and its desolate character rendered the position of the Chilean authorities very difficult. Although nothing was definitely known of the use made by the Germans of Mas-a-fuera and St. Quentin Bay, shipowners were justly apprehensive that the enemy would not be too scrupulous in his observance of the laws of neutrality. A suggestion was therefore put forward by the British Foreign Office that the Chilean Government should send a cruiser to patrol the coast, but the Chileans, though most anxious to get trade on foot, felt some difficulty in acceding to this proposal in view of the expense involved. They did, however, give such notice of the movements of their warships as would allow merchantmen of all nationalities, engaged in legitimate traffic, to take advantage of their protection while within the three-mile limit.[2]

Although the interference with trade arising from the disastrous situation created by the battle of Coronel was

[1] Alvarez, *op. cit.*, pp. 215, 216; *Lloyd's List*, 24 December, 1914,
[2] *Ibid.*, pp. 163, 164,

naturally felt most acutely in the commerce of Chile and Peru, it was not confined to the Southern Pacific. Among the many rumours circulated as to movements of German cruisers were some which related to their supposed presence farther north, and these culminated in a circumstantial report of a desperate action fought by the RAINBOW and MONTCALM against the LEIPZIG and NÜRNBERG, off the Oregon coast. In consequence of these rumours a number of steamers were detained at North Pacific ports, but the dislocation of trade in these waters was short-lived and not very extensive. The falsity of the reports was soon exposed and, on the whole, shipping north of Panama showed no reluctance to put to sea.

Towards the end of November the situation on the South American coast also began to improve. The loss of the *North Wales* was unknown, and as week after week went by without any further signs of hostile activity, shipowners became anxious for a resumption of traffic. This desire was shared by the Admiralty, but in view of the uncertainty which existed as to the whereabouts of the German cruisers they were unwilling to take the decision, in any particular case, out of the hands of the local authorities. They accordingly gave instructions that the question of permitting sailings should be left to the discretion of the Consular officials at the various ports, on the general understanding that trade should be held up as little as possible. In accordance with these instructions, the Consul-General at Valparaiso informed the steamers there that they might proceed as from November 26th, and shipping was also released at Antofagasta, Coquimbo, Iquique, and Talcahuano. The masters were instructed to keep their hour of sailing secret and to make full use of territorial waters as far south as Punta Arenas, so as to secure the utmost protection from the movements of Chilean warships. The first steamer left Valparaiso on the 26th, and sailings from Callao recommenced at about the same time, the Peruvian Government having despatched a cruiser to patrol the coast. It was not, however, until the beginning of December that shipping began to move with any approach to normal freedom.

Meanwhile the trade of the East Coast was proceeding in a wholly satisfactory manner, and had been subjected to no interference by the KRONPRINZ WILHELM. That ship had begun coaling from the *Union* on or about

November 12th, and the process continued until the 20th, by which time 2,000 tons had been transferred. On the 13th the *Sierra Cordoba* returned from her unsuccessful search for the *Navarra*, and on the 14th she was sent off to port with the crews of the *Union* and *La Correntina*. On the 20th, after the last of the coal had been taken, the *Union* was sunk, having been in tow for twenty-three days. Next day the *Anne de Bretagne*, another big French barque, was captured about 600 miles from the steamer tracks to Rio and the Plate. She was on her way from Frederikstad in Denmark to Melbourne, with a cargo of timber valued at about £15,000, and was scuttled by her captors on the 23rd.

The *Sierra Cordoba* arrived at Monte Video on November 22nd. Her report of the sinking of *La Correntina* had no great effect on trade, as the loss of the liner had already been taken for granted. Towards the end of the month a rumour sprang up that Admiral von Spee had come round into the Atlantic, that two German battle cruisers had broken out of the North Sea to join him, and that a battle was imminent off the River Plate. The insurance market was slightly disturbed in consequence, and the Royal Mail liner *Alcantara* was detained for a day or two at Santos, but the course of trade was not appreciably affected. In fact, the volume of traffic both ways was practically as great during November as it was in October, before Admiral Cradock's defeat.[1]

This confidence and enterprise on the part of merchants and shipowners was the more remarkable and the more admirable, inasmuch as it rested solely on the support given to credit by the State Insurance Scheme, and not on any specific knowledge as to the nature of the measures which were being taken to protect trade. It was not long, however, before their faith was openly justified. When Admiral von Spee put into St. Quentin Bay on November 21st, the period of most acute anxiety was, in fact, already almost past. Five days later (on Novem-

[1] *Shipping World*, 25 November, 1914.

	Net tonnage of vessels with cargoes from Brazil, Argentina, and Uruguay entered at United Kingdom ports.			Net tonnage of vessels cleared with cargoes from United Kingdom ports for Brazil, Argentina, and Uruguay.	
	British.	Total.		British.	Total.
November	216,677	244,865	October	182,681	238,597
December	221,484	235,505	November	182,909	225,504

ber 26th), Admiral Sturdee met Admiral Stoddart off the Brazilian coast and took over the command of the combined squadrons. From this time all danger of the British forces being attacked and defeated in detail was at an end; and even if the Germans came round into the South Atlantic, they would find a squadron of greatly superior strength between them and the Plate tracks. On his way down Admiral Sturdee had picked up the BRISTOL and MACEDONIA. The DEFENCE had been sent over to South-west Africa, but the KENT had arrived and the GLASGOW had rejoined, so that the force under Admiral Sturdee's command provided amply for all contingencies.

Very little information was available with regard to the movements of the enemy's ships. An intercepted telegram of November 28rd pointed to the German Pacific squadron being at St. Quentin Bay on or about that date, but even this was uncertain and their subsequent movements were altogether unknown. There was, therefore, nothing for Admiral Sturdee to do but to carry on and search for them in the neighbourhood of the Magellan Straits. He had, however, before him the report brought by the crew of *La Correntina*, from which it appeared that the *Sierra Cordoba* had parted company with the KRONPRINZ WILHELM at a point between three and four hundred miles east of Santos, and on this information he proceeded to sweep for the KRONPRINZ WILHELM on his way down the coast. This operation proved fruitless, as Captain Thierfelder, after sinking the *Anne de Bretagne*, had moved up into the area between Fernando Noronha and the St. Paul Rocks, in which the KARLSRUHE had formerly operated and from which the BRISTOL and MACEDONIA had just been withdrawn. Admiral Sturdee could not afford to spend further time in looking for her, and after the failure of his sweep kept steadily on his way to the south.

Meanwhile the rumours of Admiral von Spee's presence in the South Atlantic had again become strong, and in the first days of December they were accompanied by a report that the battle cruiser VON DER TANN had broken out from the North Sea to join him. Unconfirmed as these rumours were, some colour was given to them by a sudden outburst of activity among the German liners on the East Coast. Three of these ships sailed from Monte Video or Buenos Aires on December 2nd and 3rd with cargoes of coal and provisions, and two others endeavoured to escape from Pernambuco, but were detained by the captain of the port. One of these, however, the Hamburg-Amerika liner *Otavi*, succeeded in getting to sea on the 4th, the German Consul certifying that her destination was Fernando Po. It subsequently transpired that she had gone to join the KRONPRINZ WILHELM.[1]

The arrival of the battle cruisers was still unknown outside official circles, and the effect of this suspicious activity, coupled with the rumours as to German movements, was that several British ships hurried into a port of refuge and the sailing of others was postponed. The dislocation of trade was hardly appreciable, but it gives a hint of what might have happened had Admiral von Spee come round the Horn immediately after the battle of Coronel, or, still more, had he been able to make a surprise incursion into the Atlantic without showing himself on the Chilean coast.

Events were now once more hurrying to a crisis. Admiral Sturdee paid no attention to the rumours of German activity in the Atlantic, and shaped his course for the Falklands with his whole force, except the ORAMA, which was left to show the flag off Monte Video. Unknown to him, and in ignorance of his movements, his opponent was coming round to meet him.

On November 26th, the day of the junction between the two British Admirals, the German squadron left St. Quentin Bay. They were accompanied by the *Baden*, *Seydlitz*, and *Santa Isabel*. The other supply ships, having been cleared of their cargoes, were sent off to various Chilean and Peruvian ports, where they were mostly interned on their arrival. The PRINZ EITEL FRIEDRICH

[1] *Otavi* 5,173 tons, 10·5 knots.
Patagonia, arrived at Monte Video from Bahia Blanca, November 22nd, sailed December 3rd, nominally for Callao, with provisions and 1,400 tons coal. This was the KARLSRUHE's old tender, which had come down from Pernambuco to Bahia Blanca during September.
Mera, Kosmos liner, 4,798 tons, 9 knots, sailed from Monte Video on the night of December 3rd, declaring her intention of running the gauntlet to Germany. Cargo: livestock, provisions and 1,200 tons coal in addition to her bunkers.
Eleonore Woermann, formerly tender to CAP TRAFALGAR, cleared from Buenos Aires, December 2nd, for German South-west Africa, with coal, provisions and stores.
Gudrun, Hamburg-Bremer Afrika liner, 4,772 tons, 12 knots. Detained at Pernambuco when endeavouring to leave the inner harbour.
The Hamburg-Süd-Amerika liner *Bahia Blanca*, 9,349 tons, 13 knots, was also reported to be preparing to sail from Port Madryn.

was also detached. She was not a fighting ship, and Admiral von Spee never seems to have considered her a regular member of his squadron.

In all, a further eleven or twelve thousand tons of coal had been obtained at St. Quentin Bay, and on December 2nd, just after rounding the Horn, the supply was increased by 2,800 tons through the capture of the sailing vessel *Drummuir*, outward bound for San Francisco. She was stopped by the LEIPZIG about thirty miles from Staten Island and was towed to the east side of Picton Island, where three days were spent in transferring her cargo to the *Baden* and *Santa Isabel*. On December 6th she was towed outside territorial waters and sunk.

On the day after the *Drummuir* was captured the reviving confidence of trade in the Pacific received a set-back through the appearance of the PRINZ EITEL FRIEDRICH off Valparaiso. The West Coast manager of the Pacific Steam Navigation Company at once telegraphed to stop the company's south-bound steamers at Antofagasta and those bound north at Talcahuano. There was, however, no official prohibition of sailings, and at 8 p.m. the s.s. *Charcas*, belonging to the New York and Pacific Steam Navigation Co. (Messrs. Lamport & Holt), left Corral for New York *via* Panama. She was a steamer of 5,067 tons, but fortunately she had only 220 tons of nitrate on board. In accordance with the Admiralty instructions, her master endeavoured to keep within territorial waters, but the prevalence of thick fog rendered it dangerous to hug the coast and obliged him to go outside the three-mile limit. He was, however, only nine miles out and some forty or fifty miles inside the ordinary track of steamers between Valparaiso and the Straits when, at 9 a.m. on the 5th, he encountered the PRINZ EITEL FRIEDRICH, some fifty miles south of Valparaiso. In spite of the proximity of territorial waters, escape was impossible, as the German cruiser was not seen until the *Charcas* was fairly under her guns. The liner was boarded and sunk without waste of time, her crew being taken on board her captor, by whom they were landed at Papudo on December 6th. The PRINZ EITEL FRIEDRICH had thus scored her first success after 120 days of cruising. It was nearly three months before she was again definitely located.

This fresh loss at the moment when sailings were being generally resumed, was decidedly unfortunate, but its effects

DESTRUCTION OF VON SPEE

were immediately discounted, for two days after the crew of the *Charcas* were landed the situation in South American waters underwent a revolution as dramatic as that of November 1st, and more decisive. After sinking the *Drummuir*, the German Pacific squadron sailed from Picton Island on the evening of December 6th and proceeded towards the Falklands. Admiral von Spee himself appears to have desired to steam straight into the Atlantic for the purpose of destroying the weak British squadron which he expected to find there, and subsequently scattering his cruisers upon the trade routes; but he was persuaded by his staff to attempt first an attack upon the British base at Port Stanley. It was an unfortunate resolve. The German Admiral's leisurely movements since the battle of Coronel and the successive delays at Mas-a-fuera, St. Quentin Bay, and Picton Island, whether or no they were rendered inevitable by his position with regard to coal supplies, had given time for an overwhelming force to be assembled at the very point which he now proposed to attack. Admiral Sturdee's squadron arrived at Port Stanley on the morning of December 7th and at once commenced coaling in order to resume the search for the enemy next day. When Admiral von Spee approached the Falklands on the morning of the 8th he was, in fact, playing straight into his opponent's hands.

The leading German ships were sighted from the shore at 8 a.m., and at 9.20 the CANOPUS opened fire with her 12-inch guns at the GNEISENAU and NÜRNBERG. The enemy then turned away, and shortly afterwards they seem to have observed the tripod masts of the battle cruisers, with the result that the whole squadron made off at full speed. As the British ships came out of the harbour the Admiral flew the signal for a general chase, and by 12.55 p.m. the INFLEXIBLE was near enough to the enemy to open fire. The German Admiral's chances were no less hopeless than those of Admiral Cradock at Coronel. By 6 p.m. the SCHARNHORST and GNEISENAU, despite a spirited and vigorous resistance, had both been sunk by the fire of the battle cruisers and the CARNARVON. The light cruisers continued their attempt to escape for some time longer, but in the case of the LEIPZIG and NÜRNBERG the end was only deferred. The LEIPZIG was sunk by the CORNWALL and GLASGOW. The KENT, although nominally a slower ship than the NÜRNBERG, succeeded in overtaking her owing to the splendid work of the engine-room department, and the NÜRNBERG also went to the bottom. The DRESDEN alone succeeded in escaping. Of the colliers the *Baden* and *Santa Isabel* were sunk; the *Seydlitz* got away. Owing to the refusal of the Germans to strike their colours it proved impossible to save more than a comparatively small number of lives, and to the general regret of the victors, Admiral von Spee himself went down with his ship.

With the battle of the Falklands all danger of an organised attack on the South American Trade Route came to an end, and the British cruisers were now free to scatter for its defence against the few isolated raiders that were still at large. The effects of the long interruption of communications continued to be felt in Chile for many months, in financial stringency, dislocation of labour, and shortage of tonnage; but the regular services, both foreign and coastal, were soon running, and supplies of nitrate, tin, copper, alpaca, and sugar came forward freely to the United Kingdom. But the resumption of West Coast trade was the least of the results of Admiral Sturdee's victory. Of far greater importance was the freedom of shipping on the Plate tracks from any fear of an organised attack, and the security afforded to British commerce throughout the world by the destruction of the only powerful squadron which the enemy had been able to throw upon the trade routes.

CHAPTER XXI

THE ADVENT OF THE SUBMARINE [1]

THE battle of the Falklands practically marked the end of the first period of war at sea, in which the enemy endeavoured to destroy or hold up British commerce by means of cruisers and armed liners operating on the trade routes. Of fourteen such ships which were at sea on the outbreak of war, or left port during the first few days of hostilities, ten had been definitely accounted for. The SCHARNHORST, GNEISENAU, LEIPZIG, NÜRNBERG, EMDEN, CAP TRAFALGAR, and KAISER WILHELM DER GROSSE, had been sunk in action and the KARLSRUHE destroyed by an accidental explosion; the KÖNIGSBERG was blockaded beyond the possibility of escape and the GEIER was interned.[2] Within a week after the battle the CORMORAN shared the fate of the GEIER. On December 12th, want of provisions compelled her to weigh anchor and quit her hiding-place in the Carolines; on the 14th she arrived at Guam, and on the following day she accepted internment by the United States authorities. Thus the DRESDEN, KRONPRINZ WILHELM, and PRINZ EITEL FRIEDRICH were now the only survivors of the original raiders, not merely on the South American Route, but in any sea.

So close was the watch on the German fleet and on German shipping that these original raiders had never been reinforced. Since the CORMORAN left Tsingtau on August 10th, no cruiser had put to sea from a German port at home or abroad for the purpose of preying on commerce; nor, with the exception of the KRONPRINZ WILHELM and CAP TRAFALGAR, had any of the German liners

---

[1] See Map 2.
[2] Although a rumour as to the destruction of the KARLSRUHE sprang up towards the end of November, the truth as to her fate was not finally ascertained until March 1915; but by the middle of December it was apparent that she was no longer operating on her old cruising ground, and by the beginning of January the presumption of her loss was very strong.

lying in neutral harbours succeeded in obtaining the armament necessary for their equipment as cruisers. One big merchantman, indeed, had left the Weser, with guns mounted, at the end of September, although nothing was known of her movements till a later date. This was the BERLIN, a Norddeutscher Lloyd liner of 17,342 tons and 18 knots speed, which might have proved herself a formidable rival to the KRONPRINZ WILHELM, had such been her instructions. The BERLIN, however, had been specially equipped as a mine-layer, and after laying the Tory Island mine-field, by which the *Manchester Commerce* was destroyed, she endeavoured to make her way back to Germany. On November 16th she put into Trondhjem, with only two days' coal in her bunkers, and asked permission to make good engine room defects; but the result was her immediate internment by the Norwegian authorities and her disappearance from the dwindling list of fast German liners suitable for employment as commerce destroyers.

It was still, of course, possible that the gauntlet might be run by isolated ships; but the grip of the Grand Fleet on the North Sea exits, and the strength of the British squadrons abroad, rendered it highly improbable that the cruiser attack would ever again reach its original intensity. It was, indeed, doubtful whether the enemy could readily spare ships to make the attempt, as they had already lost heavily in cruisers,[1] while out of fourteen completed liners with a speed of 17 knots and upwards, only four now remained in German ports.[2]

The cruiser and armed liner menace was thus reduced almost to vanishing point, and the mine peril in the North

---

[1] In addition to those lost in the attack on the trade routes the German cruisers sunk in the North Sea and Baltic up to the end of November included the KÖLN, MAINZ, ARIADNE, MAGDEBURG, YORCK, and UNDINE. To these the FRIEDRICH KARL and BREMEN were added on December 12th and 17th respectively. The BRESLAU also was no longer available outside the Black Sea.

[2] Sunk . . 2 KAISER WILHELM DER GROSSE ($22\frac{1}{2}$); CAP TRAFALGAR ($17\frac{1}{2}$).
Interned . 1 BERLIN (18).
At Sea . 1 KRONPRINZ WILHELM (23).
In Neutral   *Vaterland* (24); *Kaiser Wilhelm II* ($23\frac{1}{2}$); *Kron-*
  Ports . 6   *prinzessin Cecilie* ($23\frac{1}{2}$); *George Washington* (19); *Amerika* ($17\frac{1}{2}$); all in the United States: *Prinz Friedrich Wilhelm* ($17\frac{1}{2}$) in Norway.
In German   *Imperator* ($23\frac{1}{2}$); *Cap Polonia* (18); *Kaiserin Auguste*
  Ports . 4   *Victoria* (18); *Victoria Luise* (18).
              ──
              14

Sea was also held well in check, thanks to the ceaseless activity of the mine-sweeping service and the Auxiliary Patrol. Six British fishing craft were blown up during November, with a loss of forty-two lives; but the only merchant steamer sunk was the *Khartoum*, of 3,020 tons, bound from the Tyne to Oran with coal, which struck a mine twenty miles from Spurn Head on November 27th. Four Scandinavian steamers were also sunk, but the largest of these was only of 1,500 tons and the percentage of loss was negligible.

A more serious development was the reappearance of the submarine as a commerce destroyer. On November 23rd, rather more than a month after the sinking of the *Glitra* by U 17, the *Malachite* was stopped in the Channel by U 21. She was on her way from Liverpool to Havre and had arrived within a few miles of her destination when she was captured. As in the case of the *Glitra*, the crew were compelled to take to their boats and the prize was then sunk. Three days later, the *Primo*, with coal from the Tyne for Rouen, encountered U 21 about ten miles from the French coast, and was treated in the same way.

Although the vessels thus lost were small steamers of no great value,[1] the indication given that the Germans were experimenting with the submarine as a weapon to be used against seaborne trade was disquieting. At the same time, there was, as yet, no apparent probability of the U boat taking the place of the cruiser as an instrument of organised interference with commerce, and the loss of the *Malachite* and *Primo* did little to shake confidence in the safety of the trade routes. Nor did the effect of Admiral von Spee's victory at Coronel extend beyond the waters immediately open to his attack. Both in the tonnage of British and foreign shipping entered at British ports and in the weight of imports received, the November trade figures compared more favourably with 1913 than those for the two preceding months. Exports, on the other hand, showed something of a set-back, but very little of this can be attributed to hostile interference with trade. It was due rather to the heavy shipments effected in October for the purpose of making up the August leeway and to the fluctuations of demand abroad.

With the expansion of foreign trade, the demand for

[1] *Malachite*, 718 tons; *Primo*, 1,366 tons.

a reduction in the State Insurance rates increased in urgency, but so long as Admiral von Spee's powerful squadron was still at large, the Advisory Board considered themselves unable to respond to this appeal. Admiral Sturdee's victory, however, completely changed the situation, and on December 11th, only three days after the battle, they reduced the cargo premium to 1½ guineas. On the 17th the rate on hulls was reduced to ¾ per cent., or 1½ per cent. for a round voyage or a three months' policy. Even these concessions, however, did not allow the State Office to compete very successfully for cargo business, except in respect of the South Atlantic passage and some of the longest voyages, such as that to Australia or the Far East. On all other routes the bulk of the business was done on the open market, where cargo for India or the Cape could be covered at 1 per cent. and for North America at 7s. 6d.[1]

Towards the end of December, the fact that one or two steamers in the South American trade were long overdue created a strong suspicion that the KRONPRINZ WILHELM was still at work; but in the other theatres of war at sea there was little to cause alarm to merchants or shipowners. Throughout November and December there was desultory fighting between the Russian and Turko-German squadrons in the Black Sea, but Black Sea trade had been at a standstill since the closing of the Dardanelles, and the subsequent operations had no commercial significance beyond the interruption of local traffic.[2]

The possibility of an attack on the Suez Canal was a much more serious matter, and for this contingency every possible preparation was made. The defences were strengthened, a flotilla of armed launches was organised for Canal patrols, and plans were worked out for the control of shipping in the event of attack. Meanwhile the Allied

---

[1] The rise in North Atlantic rates which followed the sinking of the *Manchester Commerce* was followed by a fall as soon as it became clear that the danger on the Irish coast had been removed.

[2] The following enemy merchantmen were sunk in the Black Sea during November and December:

Derindje (German), 3,373 tons, sunk near Kerasund, December 14th.

Nilufer (Turkish), 1,088 tons, blown up by mine near the entrance to the Bosporus, previous to November 25th.

Georgios (Turkish), 795 tons, a Greek steamer seized by the Turks. Sunk outside Sinope on December 17th, while on a voyage from Sulina to Constantinople.

Newa (Turkish), 549 tons, a British steamer seized by the Turks at Constantinople. Sunk previous to December 31st.

cruisers kept a careful watch on the Syrian and Anatolian coasts, in the course of which the ASKOLD captured the German steamer *Haiffa* (1,790 tons) on December 15th.

In Home Waters there was greater cause for apprehension. For some weeks after the sinking of the *Primo*, no further submarine activity against merchant shipping was recorded with the exception of an unsuccessful attack on the Great Eastern Railway Co.'s packet-boat *Colchester*, on December 11th. On December 22nd, however, an interview with Grand Admiral von Tirpitz appeared in the *New York Sun*, in which the German Minister of Marine foreshadowed a much more extensive use of the submarine against merchant shipping, and hinted that Great Britain could be starved into submission by the torpedoing of every ship which approached a British home port under an Allied flag. This suggestion was readily caught up by the German press, and Rear-Admiral von Schlieper contributed an article to the *Berliner Lokalanzeiger*, explaining that the German had always been hampered in his contest with the Briton by "a certain sentimental feeling of justice and delicacy which is especially peculiar to him," and that the time had now come to put this feeling aside and wage a "systematic and reckless war of retaliation against British commerce," by means of the new weapon which Germany had perfected and with which she could neutralise the "alleged supremacy" of Great Britain on the seas.[1]

It remained doubtful for some time whether the German Admiralty would really adopt a course involving a gross violation of International Law and the certainty of serious friction with neutral States. For not only was the submarine incapable of providing for the safety of crews and passengers on board sunken vessels, particularly if the torpedo was employed, but any such wholesale destruction as was threatened must necessarily result in sending to the bottom vast quantities of neutral, and especially of American goods. For these reasons, as well as through scepticism as to the practicability of the programme, the general inclination, both in Great Britain and in America, was to disregard the threat. On the other hand, it was obvious that the destruction of the German cruiser squadron, the frustration of the push for the Channel coast and the economic pressure exercised by the Allies through their command of the sea, might

[1] Quoted in *Lloyd's List*, 29 December, 1914.

force the Germans into the adoption of reckless measures in the attempt to injure the only enemy whom they were as yet unable to strike direct.

Whatever the actual intentions of the German Government might be, no immediate attempt was made to translate Admiral von Tirpitz' threats into action; but the losses from mines during December were heavier than they had been since the beginning of the war, and bore continued witness to the indifference with which the enemy regarded the destruction of non-combatant lives and of neutral property. The first of these disasters occurred in the Baltic, where three Swedish steamers were blown up on December 6th, with the result of inflicting a severe check on the increasing traffic between Sweden and Finland. In the North Sea, no vessels were lost during the earlier part of the month, but the closing weeks of 1914 were marked by a series of catastrophes which were preceded by one of the rare sorties of the heavier German ships. Since the Gorleston raid at the beginning of November, the High Seas Fleet had given little sign of activity, but on December 16th the German battle cruiser squadron appeared off Scarborough, Whitby, and Hartlepool and threw a number of shells into these towns, with the result of sinking or damaging half a dozen steam trawlers and other fishing craft, and inflicting some injury on two British steamers at Hartlepool, besides causing numerous casualties on shore. The raid was very brief and was followed by a hurried retreat to German waters, and the actual damage done was small; but the rates for insurance of property on the East Coast against damage by bombardment rose from a few shillings a year to 2 per cent. for six months. Underwriters also increased their quotations for war risks on the North Sea Passage, in the anticipation that fresh mine-fields would have been laid by the Germans under cover of the raid. For the same reason, the Hull—Copenhagen service and the coasting trade between the Tyne and the Humber were temporarily suspended.

These apprehensions proved to be well founded. During the bombardment of Scarborough the Germans laid a new mine-field very close in to the shore, by which four British and five neutral steamers were destroyed from December 16th to 31st inclusive, and a fifth British steamer was damaged. At one time there were very nearly fifty steamers held up in the Humber awaiting permission to leave; but no time was lost in sweeping the infested area, and within a week navigation had been rendered tolerably safe. By January 5, 1915, the Swept Channel had been buoyed as far north as Hartlepool, and now extended unbroken from the Thames to the Tees. The effect of the raid on commerce was thus comparatively small, but the insurance premiums on cargoes in neutral bottoms went up from 5s. to 10s. per cent., and on some ships much higher rates were paid.[1]

Meanwhile, only three days after the Scarborough raid, alarming evidence was afforded that the Tory Island minefield was still a menace to navigation. The area in which mines had been scattered by the BERLIN was large, and the stormy weather which is usual off the North Coast of Ireland not only hampered the mine-sweepers in their work, but added to the risk of mines breaking loose from their moorings and drifting into waters previously swept. Nevertheless, no merchant casualty subsequent to the loss of the *Manchester Commerce* was reported until December 9th, when the outward-bound Donaldson liner *Tritonia*, of 4,272 tons, was blown up in very nearly the same position. Within the next few days a dozen mines were swept up and exploded by a group of mine-sweeping trawlers at work in this area.[2]

The increase of hostile activity in Home Waters rendered it necessary, during November and December, to impose still further restrictions on navigation. Thus, owing to the frequent changes in the position of lights and buoys made with a view to baffling the enemy's submarines, pilotage became compulsory in all East Coast estuaries and firths as from November 27th; the waters of the

[1] The British ships sunk were as follows:
Elterwater, 1,228 tons, sunk December 16th, 3 miles E. of Scarborough (6 lives lost).
Princess Olga, 998 tons, sunk December 16th, 5 miles E.N.E. of Scarborough.
Gem, 464 tons, sunk December 25th, 3½ miles S.E. by E. of Scarborough (10 lives lost).
Linaria, 3,081 tons, sunk December 26th, 2½ miles N.N.E. of Filey.
The *Gallier*, of 4,592 tons, struck a mine near Scarborough on December 25th, but succeeded in reaching port.
In addition to the above, the steam trawler *Ocana* was sunk on December 23rd, with the loss of 8 lives, and another trawler, the *Manx Queen*, was captured and sunk by a German torpedo boat on December 16th.

[2] Total mine losses during December, exclusive of fishing craft:
British . . . . . 5 s.s. 10,043 tons
Neutral . . . . . 5 ,, 10,373 ,,

Firth of Forth, above the bridge, were closed to commercial navigation at the beginning of December; and a few days later the whole area of the Firth was prohibited to fishermen. Moreover, the regulation of shipping by the Admiralty was so extensive and precise as to amount practically to direct control of all commerce in the North Sea. Whatever inconvenience was thus inflicted, either on British or neutral vessels, was, however, more than compensated by the resulting freedom from serious risk. The volume of trade maintained within the "Military Area" bore witness to the judicious supervision of sailings and courses by the Naval authorities, as much as to the energy of the mine-sweeping flotillas in keeping the free channels safe for navigation.

Perhaps the most onerous of the restrictions was the closing of the inner waters of the Firth of Forth, as the result of this measure was that Bo'ness and Grangemouth practically ceased to be commercial ports. The collieries of Lanarkshire and Stirlingshire were thus deprived of their chief port for the landing of pit-wood and their principal place of shipment. Arrangements were made, however, for some part at least of the trade of the closed ports to be carried on from Leith, Granton, Methil, and the Clyde, and generally speaking, the volume of traffic in the North Sea was not much affected, either by the dangers arising from the German mine-fields, or by the restrictive measures taken to counteract them or to facilitate the work of the British fleet.

In spite of all obstacles the export of coal to the Scandinavian countries and Holland was well maintained, although the heavy shipments made during September and October led for a time to some reduction in the demand. Foodstuffs from these countries continued to arrive in large quantities, and in November the arrivals of wood pulp and timber from Sweden were also very large. Since the release of the vessels taken into Swinemunde at the middle of October, there had been no further interference with the Scandinavian timber exports, and it was only in the case of pit-props that the fear of capture seriously impeded business. On November 17th, however, a Proclamation was issued by the German Government, stating that all woods and lumber would be considered as fuel, and therefore as Conditional Contraband, with the exception of " certain very hard foreign woods" and "woods which have become considerably advanced in value in consequence of working by hand or machine, so that their use as fuel would be out of all proportion to their increased commercial value on account of such treatment."[1] Six days later they added to the list of contraband comprised in the German Prize Regulations, "woods of all kinds, rough or treated (particularly hewn, sawn, planed, grooved)."[2]

It was subsequently held by the Prize Court at Kiel that the cargoes of the vessels released in October came within the definition of Conditional Contraband laid down in the Proclamation of November 17th, and the claim for compensation brought by the owners was accordingly dismissed; but on appeal, this decision was reversed and compensation paid.[3] In the case of the five vessels released on bond, the cargoes of pit-props and the ships themselves were condemned by the Prize Courts. This decision also was reversed on appeal, as it was proved before the Supreme Court that the cargoes in question were intended for the fulfilment of ordinary commercial contracts; but inasmuch as the cargoes were found to be Conditional Contraband and the ports of destination were regarded by the German Admiralty as fortified places or bases, it was held that there was sufficient *prima facie* evidence to justify the captures, and compensation was refused.[4]

In the meantime this renewed threat to the timber export caused widespread consternation in Sweden. The Swedish State Insurance Office refused to insure wood cargoes, many charters were cancelled, and the railways to Trondhjem and Gothenburg were choked with cargoes diverted from the Baltic ports. In ordinary years the shipments made during the winter season are somewhat restricted owing to the presence of ice in the Baltic, but the decrease in shipments at the end of 1914 was very

---

[1] Proclamation of November 17th, 1914, amending Article 23, No. 9, of Prize Ordinance of September 30th, 1909.

[2] Supplement of November 23rd, 1914, to Prize Ordinance of September 30th, 1909.

[3] Judgment of the Imperial Supreme Prize Court, Berlin, in the case of the Norwegian s.s. *Belle Ille* and other ships. Judgment delivered July 6th, 1915.

[4] Judgment of the Imperial Supreme Prize Court, Berlin, in the case of the Danish s.s. *Alfred Hage*. Judgment delivered June 18th, 1915.

marked in comparison with the previous winter, as well as in comparison with the activity of the previous months.[1]

While British imports of wood from Sweden were thus restricted by the action of the German Government, those from Russia were menaced by the approach of winter. Thanks to the energetic work of the Canadian ice-breakers in the White Sea, the arrivals of timber-laden vessels at British ports during November were numerous, but towards the end of December ice began to impede navigation and the shipments fell away. The accumulation of ice was, indeed, a serious threat to the general trade of Russia, for which the White Sea now provided the only direct outlet. But even while a navigable channel could be kept open, the congestion of the port of Archangel formed a serious obstacle to trade. The shipping entered and cleared during two months of war was equal to the whole annual traffic of other times, and the resources for dealing with this increased trade were still gravely insufficient. There were neither quay space, nor cranes, nor railway accommodation to handle goods expeditiously. Such facilities as existed were practically monopolised by the Government for the import of munitions and military stores and the export of hemp and flax for the use of the British navy, and private commerce was only carried on with the greatest difficulty.

Mainly in consequence of the decrease in wood shipments from Sweden and Russia, the estimated weight of British imports in December compared rather unfavourably with the previous month, but the values rose by £11,500,000 and approached very closely to the figures for December 1913. This rise in value was due in part to the upward tendency of prices, but it was also due to the fact that while the import of the bulkiest raw material had diminished, other more costly products were coming forward with greater freedom. The crisis in the cotton trade was now passing away, and the imports for December once more reached a respectable figure. Imports of

[1] Imports of timber (other than pit-props) from Sweden, in loads.

	1913.	1914.
September	174,000	100,000
October	188,000	279,000
November	120,500	286,000
December	105,000	55,500
	1914.	1915.
January	73,000	37,500

wool were above the average, thanks to large shipments from Australia, New Zealand, and the Argentine. The arrivals of Eastern products, such as silk, jute, and tea, reflected the effect of the destruction of the EMDEN on the trade of the Oriental Route, and a great increase in the shipments of rubber from Ceylon and the Straits raised the total import of this material to above the normal level. In foodstuffs as a class the increases were very pronounced. Although the Australian wheat crop had failed, large purchases from India and Canada nearly made up for the loss from this source, and thanks to the comparative security established in the South Atlantic, maize from the Plate came forward in unprecedented quantities. Heavy shipments of Java sugar also arrived, and the total estimated weight of food imports was 10·8 per cent. greater than in December 1913.

While the volume of trade was thus increasing, the supply of tonnage was fast becoming unequal to the demand. To the withdrawal of German and Austrian shipping and the wholesale requisitioning of British steamers, there was now added the effects of serious congestion at British as well as French ports. Caused partly by lack of labour and partly by dislocation due to the diversion of trade from its accustomed channels, this congestion led to great delays in the discharge and loading of steamers, and consequently to a decrease in the carrying power of the tonnage available. The growing disproportion between demand and supply was accompanied by a rise in freights which was already serious and showed no signs of approaching finality. At the same time, prices, especially those of foodstuffs, rose in still greater measure, and the public, ignoring the financial factors of price inflation, were inclined to lay the whole blame for the dearness of food upon shipowners' profits.

In these circumstances it was very desirable to relieve trade as far as possible of the burden of war risks insurance, and on the last day of 1914, the State cargo rate was further reduced to 1 per cent., which was at that time about the market rate for the longer voyages, such as those to Australia, the Far East, and South Africa, while it was slightly under that then charged for the West Coast of South America or for the North Sea Passage to Holland and Norway. As was always the case, the reduction in the State rate was immediately followed by a fall in underwriters' quotations, and by the middle of January cargo for India and the Far East could be covered for 10s. and 12s. 6d. respectively, for South Africa at 15s. or 17s. 6d., and for the North Sea Passage at 15s. or 20s. Only quotations for voyages to the Plate, the West Coast of America *via* the Horn, and, in some cases, Australia, remained level with the State rate.

Any further reduction in the premium for the Plate voyage was forbidden by the continued activity of the KRONPRINZ WILHELM. On January 3rd the German s.s. *Otavi* arrived at Las Palmas with the crews of two steamers, one British and one French, which had been sunk by the raider during December. No great sensation was caused by the news, as both ships had already practically been given up and no others were seriously overdue; but it was evident that until the KRONPRINZ WILHELM should be finally accounted for, occasional losses might still be expected. On the other hand, the British forces in the South Atlantic were now too strong for any serious attack on the trade routes to be probable, and although the PRINZ EITEL FRIEDRICH and DRESDEN were also unlocated, the risk of capture was too small to affect appreciably the flow of trade.

The movements of British shipping outside the North Sea, Baltic, and Black Sea, were now, indeed, wholly uninfluenced by considerations arising from fear of hostile action, save in so far as obedience to Admiralty instructions required deviation from the usual tracks, and this security was reflected in the increased arrivals at British Home Ports. The withdrawal from commercial use of ships requisitioned for naval and military purposes had been in part made good by the employment in the trade of the United Kingdom of vessels normally engaged in the traffic between foreign ports, and the entrances of British tonnage during December 1914 and January 1915 showed a decrease of less than 25 per cent. on the previous year. On the other hand, those of foreign vessels employed in British trade diminished by no less than 41 per cent., so that the total tonnage entered compared unfavourably with the figures for October and November.

This decrease in foreign shipping entered was due, in part at least, to its increased employment in the trade of the countries by which it was owned, and there was reason to believe that a considerable proportion was used for the carriage of goods to Scandinavia, Holland, and Italy which were destined to be reshipped or forwarded by rail to the enemy countries. The abnormal exports of copper from the United States to Sweden and Italy particularly attracted the attention of the British Government, and it became necessary, so early as November 8th, to stop at Gibraltar all shipments of this metal which were not guaranteed by the Italian Government. The increased rigour of search and the number of ships brought in for examination naturally caused considerable inconvenience to neutral traders, and with a view at once to the avoidance of friction and to the restriction of enemy supplies, agreements were made during November and January with several of the Governments concerned, by which contraband cargoes consigned to named firms were exempted from examination if they were guaranteed by the neutral Governments, or if the goods in question were among those whose export from the receiving country was prohibited. In Holland a body called the Netherlands Oversea Trust Company was formed for the regulation of the import trade, and the leading shipping lines associated themselves with its work. The conclusion of these agreements rendered it possible to minimise interference with legitimate neutral traffic; but the loopholes for evasion of the regulations were numerous, and it was impossible to doubt that a large amount of contraband was now reaching Germany through neutral countries.

In these circumstances, the patrols were still required to exercise the utmost vigilance, and their activity led to the presentation, on December 28th, of a Note by the American Government protesting against the detention of Absolute Contraband consigned to neutrals on the ground of non-prohibition of export, and of Conditional Contraband consigned " to order," on mere suspicion of enemy destination. The ground taken by the United States was that there must be clear, positive evidence of the enemy destination of each cargo detained; but the Foreign Office were able to show, in their reply, that the presumptions based upon a comparison of the trade figures with those of normal times were so strong, that they had no alternative but to consider the bulk of the increase as due to the growth of Germany's transhipment trade. They were unable therefore to modify their attitude.

Although the Central Powers had in this way achieved

a measure of success in their effort to procure foodstuffs, copper, and other commodities from abroad, the attempted revival of their export trade was still hampered by the lack of tonnage and by financial and insurance difficulties. The same factors hampered their import of American cotton, and with a view to overcoming the tonnage difficulty, the project of American acquisition of the German steamers laid up in United States ports was revived. One ship, the Hamburg-Amerika liner *Dacia*, was actually purchased by Mr. Breitung, an American citizen of German extraction, and transferred to the United States registry. After loading a cargo of cotton at Galveston, she sailed for Norfolk on January 31st, to bunker in preparation for a voyage to Rotterdam; but the British Government refused to recognise the transfer, and gave notice that if the ship should be encountered by a British cruiser, she would be seized, and the validity of the transaction tested before a Prize Court. In these circumstances the American State Insurance Department refused to accept risks on the voyage, and pending the decision of a test case, no further transfers were attempted. The Central Powers were thus left to depend almost entirely upon the tranship-ment trade for such supplies as they could procure.

Meanwhile the expansion of British commerce was limited only by economic conditions and by the effects of shortage of tonnage and congestion of ports, which were felt with increasing severity every month. Notwithstanding these obstacles, the imports for the first month of the New Year were practically the same in value as in January 1914, and the decrease in estimated weights was only 10 per cent., the diminution in tonnage entered being compensated by a great increase in the proportion of cargo carried per ton of shipping. Exports also were greater than during any previous month of the war.

In the January trade figures the immunity of shipping on the Oriental Route was again reflected, and increased imports of South American products bore witness to the good work accomplished by Admiral Sturdee in the destruction of the German Pacific squadron. On the other hand, trade with Russia was fast dying away to nothing. Ice was steadily accumulating in the White Sea, and an accident to the ice-breaker *Canada* left little hope of keeping the passage open at all after the first few days of February. The projected railway to the ice-free ports of

Kola and Alexandrovsk was still non-existent, and practically the whole foreign trade of Russia was forced on to the transhipment route through Sweden, by way of Gefle and Raumo or by rail and road through Haparanda and Tornea. Even the transhipment route, however, was uncertain, for the traffic between Gefle and Raumo was again interrupted for several days, during the earlier part of the month, owing to the destruction of another Swedish steamer by a mine.

Of direct hostile interference with British trade there was very little until the last two days of the month. On the first day of 1915, the *Westergate*, of 1,742 tons, struck a mine in the Downs, but was brought safely into port; and on January 7th, the *Elfrida* (2,624 tons), bound for London from the Tyne, was blown up two miles from Scarborough. A couple of British trawlers and four or five small neutral steamers were also lost, but the risk to vessels following the Admiralty advice as to courses, continued to prove very small.

Towards the end of the month the German battle cruiser squadron again issued from port, but on January 24th it was met and defeated by Admiral Beatty before it had done any damage, and the only result of its cruise was to emphasise the British control of the North Sea. This control, in fact, had never been seriously challenged except by the enemy's mine-layers, and while the action off the Dogger Bank was satisfactory as a check to the new German policy of coastal raids, it had little effect on the situation from the point of view of seaborne trade. Far more significance attached to an incident, in itself of small importance, which occurred on the same day, and which, though its bearing on the defence of commerce could hardly be realised at the moment, marked the definite entry of the war into a new stage, in which the cruiser and the armed liner were relegated to an altogether subordinate position as factors in the attack on merchant shipping. This was the sinking of the *Durward*, a small steamer, bound from Leith to Rotterdam, which was captured by U 19, twenty-two miles from the Maas light-vessel. It is true that three ships had already been sunk by enemy submarines without any appreciable effect on the confidence of British shipowners and merchants; but the new departure in German policy foreshadowed by Admiral von Tirpitz gave to the sinking of the *Durward* an aspect more disturbing than that of the previous isolated attacks, and from January 21st we may date the appearance of the U boat as the chief weapon used in the attack on commerce.

For rather more than a week, however, the general uncertainty as to the real intentions of the German Government continued; but though no official endorsement of the Tirpitz interview had as yet appeared, the German submarines had already received orders to begin the attack, and on January 30th the new phase of the campaign was opened both in the Irish Sea and the English Channel, and the loss of half a dozen British steamers gave warning that a serious attempt might be expected to carry the threatened programme into practice.

In the Irish Sea, the *Ben Cruachan*, of 3,092 tons, bound from Cardiff to Liverpool, was stopped by U 21 at 10.15 a.m., fifteen miles from the N.W. light-ship, off the entrance to the Mersey. Ten minutes were allowed for the crew to collect their personal belongings and take to their boats, and the prize was then sunk by bombs placed on board. The crew, after drifting for five hours, were picked up by a smack and landed at Fleetwood.

Shortly after the *Ben Cruachan* was sunk, U 21 came to the surface some eighteen miles from the Liverpool Bar light-vessel and stopped the small steamer *Linda Blanche* (580 tons), bound from Manchester to Belfast, which was treated in the same way. Early in the afternoon the *Kilcoan* of 456 tons, from Garston for Belfast with coal, was stopped in almost the same position as the *Linda Blanche*. Before she could be disposed of, another small collier, the *Gladys*, appeared on the scene and was compelled to take the *Kilcoan's* boats in tow. The *Kilcoan* was then sunk, but she did not disappear until 3.40 p.m., and was seen, with the submarine still beside her, by the s.s. *Graphic* of the Belfast Steamship Company, which was approaching Liverpool at that time. The U 21 then went in chase of the new-comer, but the *Graphic*, unlike the colliers, was a fast steamer (18 knots), and succeeded in shaking off her pursuer.

These captures in the Irish Sea, like the previous exploits of U 21, presented some degree at least of regularity, in that the ships were stopped, their papers examined and the crews allowed time to take to their boats before the destruction of the prizes. A striking contrast was presented by the operations of U 20 in the Channel. Here also three ships were sunk, but the manner of their destruction was widely different from that employed by the commander of U 21. There was no examination of the ship's papers, no time given to the crew to leave the ship, and in fact no capture. In each case the first intimation given by the submarine of its presence was a torpedo fired without warning at the unsuspecting and defenceless merchantman.

All three vessels were attacked in the neighbourhood of Havre, and the fear of destruction by the French coastal flotillas, or by British destroyers, may explain, though it cannot excuse, the manner of the attack. The largest of the three was the *Tokomaru*, a Shaw, Savill & Albion liner of 6,084 tons, homeward bound from New Zealand. At about 9 a.m., when seven miles from Havre light-ship, she sighted a periscope on the port side of the ship, and simultaneously she was struck by a torpedo which exploded with great violence. The ship at once took a heavy list to port and filled so rapidly that the master was unable to fetch his papers from his cabin. There was time, however, to get the crew into the boats, and they were almost immediately picked up by a French mine-sweeper, in which they stood by until the *Tokomaru* finally disappeared at 10.30 a.m.

Half an hour after noon the *Ikaria* (4,335 tons), belonging to the Leyland Shipping Co., arrived off Havre. She was homeward bound from Santos and other Brazilian ports, with a cargo of coffee, sugar, and hides, part of which was to be discharged at Havre. She had stopped her engines about twenty-five miles from the port, for the purpose of obtaining a pilot, when the master observed the wake of a torpedo coming towards the ship at a distance of about 30 feet. A few seconds later it exploded, and the steamer immediately began to sink by the head. The master thereupon ordered the crew to take to the boats, and went on board a tug which had come out from Havre; but about an hour later, as the vessel was still afloat, he went on board again with some of the crew and passed a rope to the tugboat. As the ship would not steer, a second tug was called in to assist, and at 9.30 p.m. she reached port. It was, however, too late to save the ship, which sank in the outer harbour and became a total wreck; but a large part of the valuable cargo proved to be undamaged and was discharged into lighters.

Thanks to the promptness of the masters and the discipline of the crews, the torpedoing of the *Tokomaru* and *Ikaria* was unattended by loss of life, but the third disaster in the Channel was, unhappily, more destructive. In this case the victim was the General Steam Navigation Company's *Oriole*, of 1,489 tons. She left London for Havre on January 29th, but nothing more was ever seen of her, or of her crew of twenty-one all told, with the exception of two lifebuoys picked up near Rye on February 6th, and there was little reason to doubt that she had fallen a victim to the lawless operations of U 20.[1]

Although received with rapturous applause in Germany, as heralding the total interruption of British commerce and the starvation of the United Kingdom, these first exploits in the new phase of the attack on commerce failed to produce any marked effect on British trade and shipping. Several of the fixed services in the Irish Sea were temporarily suspended, but within a few days all had been resumed and coasters and colliers were again busy. The State Insurance rates remained unchanged, and though underwriters raised their quotations, there was no sign of panic. The freight markets were undisturbed, and the general attitude of shipping and commercial circles was one of full confidence in the ability of the navy to deal with the new menace as it had done with the cruisers in distant seas.

[1] A bottle subsequently came to hand containing a written message, "*Oriole* torpedoed, sinking." See judgment of Bailhache, J., in *General Steam Navigation Company* v. *Commercial Union Assurance Company*, *Times*, 30 July, 1915.

CHAPTER XXII

THE END OF THE FIRST PHASE [1]

IT will be remembered that when Admiral Sturdee met the German Pacific squadron on December 8th, 1914, the DRESDEN was the only German cruiser present which escaped destruction at his hands. The PRINZ EITEL FRIEDRICH, which had been detached by Admiral von Spee before the battle, was on the Chilean coast, where she had just captured the *Charcas*. In the South Atlantic, the KRONPRINZ WILHELM had abandoned her desultory attacks on trade off the entrance to the River Plate and had gone northwards into the area between Cape San Roque and the St. Paul Rocks. So long as these ships retained freedom of movement, they represented considerable possibilities of mischief; but the necessity for concentration of the British forces had passed away with the destruction of Admiral von Spee's big cruisers, and they were now dispersed in a series of detachments which were constantly engaged in searching the coasts, sweeping suspected areas, and patrolling the trade routes; so that while the extensive possibilities of evasion open to the surviving raiders might prolong their careers, there was little chance of their being able to maintain themselves near a focal point, or to effect other than isolated captures. We shall see that such captures were indeed effected by them from time to time, but the days of organised attack on South American trade were over, and the flow of traffic was never appreciably disturbed by these occasional losses. The opening months of 1915 saw meat, maize, wheat, oats, wool, and oil seeds from the Argentine Republic, meat and dairy produce from New Zealand, coffee from Brazil, nitrate and tin from the West Coast, arriving in very large, in some cases in unprecedented quantities, and the exports to those countries also exhibited a marked recovery. It would be too much to attribute the whole of this expansion

[1] See Maps 5 and 9.

to Admiral Sturdee's victory, for we have seen how great a part economic conditions played in the restriction of trade during the earlier months of the war, and how little its recovery was retarded by the depredations of the KARLSRUHE or the approach of Admiral von Spee. But remembering how formidable was the menace presented by the German squadron, it is difficult to over-estimate the importance of the success which freed this great volume of commerce from any further interference than spasmodic attacks by isolated and hunted raiders.[1]

Of the three surviving raiders, the DRESDEN gave the least trouble. Although a vigorous search was made for her after the battle of the Falklands, she succeeded in eluding it, and on December 11th she arrived at Punta Arenas, where she obtained 800 tons of coal from the Roland liner *Turpin*. On the 13th she again put to sea, fourteen hours before the arrival of the BRISTOL, which was looking for her, and for the next two months she remained in hiding among the uncharted passages to the south of the Magellan Straits. At one of her hiding-places she was joined by the *Sierra Cordoba*, which, in spite of having acted as a supply ship to the KRONPRINZ WILHELM, was allowed to leave Monte Video on December 18th, with a clearance for Callao. From her the DRESDEN obtained a further supply of coal, but no thought of active operations against commerce appears to have entered Captain Lüdecke's mind. The hunt for his ship by British cruisers was close and constant, her boilers were in bad condition, and he judged it imprudent to leave the unfrequented anchorages among which he had taken refuge.

Captain Thierichsens of the PRINZ EITEL FRIEDRICH adopted a bolder course. After landing the crew of the

[1] Principal imports following South American Route during the first three months of 1915.

—			1915.	1914.	1913.
Wheat from Argentina	1,000 cwts.		1,416	1,406	4,316
Oats from Argentina	,,	,,	2,386	2,103	1,951
Maize from Argentina	,,	,,	13,038	3,819	6,171
Meat from Argentina and Uruguay	,,	,,	1,202	2,320	2,345
Meat from New Zealand	,,	,,	511	442	442
Wool from Argentina	,,	lbs.	42,982	18,449	34,010
Nitrate	,,	tons	36	23	28
Tin ore	,,	tons	10	6	5

Charcas at Papudo on December 6th, he continued to cruise off the Chilean coast, compelling British shipping to move with some circumspection and to take advantage as much as possible of the protection afforded by the movement of Chilean warships in territorial waters. On the 10th, he intercepted wireless messages from which he gathered that Admiral von Spee's squadron had been destroyed, and he accordingly turned away from the coast in order to escape the search which was certain to follow the British victory. Next day (December 11th), he captured the French sailing vessel *Jean*, bound for Antofagasta and carrying 3,500 tons of Welsh coal.[1] Overjoyed at this lucky windfall, which secured his freedom of movement for a considerable period, he decided to tow his prize to Easter Island, where he might hope to transfer the cargo without fear of interruption. Next day he captured the British barque *Kildalton*, outward bound from Liverpool for Callao, but in this case the cargo was of no value to the captors, and after the crew had been taken off the prize was sunk and the PRINZ EITEL FRIEDRICH proceeded on her way to Easter Island with the *Jean* in tow.[2]

The PRINZ EITEL arrived at Easter Island on December 23rd, and the next fortnight was employed in removing the *Jean's* cargo of coal and obtaining a supply of fresh mutton from the island. Captain Thierichsens had no intention of remaining in hiding longer than was necessary for this purpose. It was obvious that he could do nothing further on the Pacific Coast, where both the British cruisers and merchant shipping would be on the alert; but he had now coal and provisions sufficient for a long voyage, and as soon as his preparations were completed he intended to slip round into the Atlantic and endeavour to reach a German port.

Meanwhile the KRONPRINZ WILHELM, of whom nothing had been heard since the arrival of the *Sierra Cordoba* at Monte Video on November 22nd, had got to work in the area recently vacated by the KARLSRUHE, and from which the BRISTOL and MACEDONIA had been withdrawn to join Admiral Sturdee's concentration. Captain Thierfelder's first success in these waters was obtained on December 4th,

---

[1] See Map 5.
[2] Many details as to the proceedings of the PRINZ EITEL FRIEDRICH subsequent to the battle of the Falklands are given in interviews with her Captain and First Officer in the *Weser Zeitung*, 14 April, 1915.

when he captured the collier *Bellevue* of 3,814 tons, and the French liner *Mont Agel* of 4,803 tons, about 150 miles to the east of the track between the St. Paul Rocks and Fernando Noronha.[1] Both ships had deviated widely from their ordinary course, and the *Mont Agel*, which was equipped with wireless, endeavoured to send out a call for help; but all her messages were jammed by the raider, and, indeed, there was no British cruiser near at hand to receive them.

The *Mont Agel* was bound from Marseilles to Santos, in ballast, and was sunk without loss of time; but the *Bellevue* had a coal and general cargo of 5,400 tons for Monte Video and Buenos Aires, and was thus too valuable to be summarily disposed of. The KRONPRINZ WILHELM and her prize accordingly steamed north-west, away from the trade routes, until December 8th, when Captain Thierfelder considered himself safe from interruption. The next twelve days were occupied in removing the *Bellevue's* stores and cargo to the raider, both vessels drifting with the current during this operation. On the 12th they were joined by the *Otavi* [2] with further supplies of coal, water, and provisions, and to this ship the prisoners were transferred, including the crew of the *Anne de Bretagne*, who were still on board the KRONPRINZ WILHELM. By December 20th the whole of the *Bellevue's* cargo had been taken off and the collier was accordingly sunk. Next day (December 21st) the *Otavi* was dismissed, with instructions to land the prisoners at Las Palmas, and Captain Thierfelder proceeded to steer back to the trade routes.

At a point about 300 miles south of the St. Paul Rocks and 170 miles east of the most easterly tracks, the *Hemisphere* was captured on December 28th. Captain Thierfelder's good fortune in the matter of captured cargoes still held good, for the new prize was a collier of 3,486 tons, with a cargo of 4,145 tons for Buenos Aires. Again the prize was taken well away from the trade routes in order to transfer the fuel, and it was not until January 7th that the *Hemisphere* was cast off and scuttled. On the previous day the KRONPRINZ WILHELM was joined by another supply ship. This was the *Holger*, a Roland liner of 5,555 tons, which put out from Pernambuco, without clearance, on the first day of the New Year.[3]

[1] See Map 9. [2] See page 347, *supra*.
[3] Strong action was taken by the Brazilian Government in consequence of this breach of neutrality, and the Roland line were penalised therefor.

She received the prisoners from the cruiser on January 8th, and next day the KRONPRINZ WILHELM steamed back once more toward the trade routes, leaving her tender to await her at a rendezvous.

Both the raider herself and the *Holger* had a narrow escape from capture or destruction at this time, as a telegram, giving the original rendezvous for the meeting of the two ships, was intercepted by the Admiralty, and led to a search of the suspected area by the HIGHFLYER, MARMORA, and EMPRESS OF BRITAIN from the Cape Verde Station. Indeed, during the latter part of her career, the KRONPRINZ WILHELM was continually favoured by fortune in escaping encounters with British cruisers patrolling between Fernando Noronha and St. Vincent. Even if Captain Thierfelder's necessities had not compelled him to depart from the steamer tracks every time he captured a prize with coal or stores on board, he would still have been unable, with any regard to the safety of his ship, to remain on the trade route for more than two or three days at a time.

On resuming his operations Captain Thierfelder struck the route at a point much farther north than the scene of his previous captures. Information as to these had, of course, been given by the prisoners landed from the *Otavi*, which arrived at Las Palmas on January 3rd, narrowly escaping the ARGONAUT and VICTORIAN, and he may have considered it desirable for this reason to change his cruising ground for a time. It was some 400 miles north-east of the St. Paul Rocks that, on January 10th, he captured the *Potaro*, of 4,419 tons. She was a Royal Mail steamer and had left Liverpool for Buenos Aires, in ballast, on December 25th. Her master had kept a very careful course, steaming without lights, and he now made a determined effort to escape and to summon assistance by wireless; but all his calls were jammed, and as the KRONPRINZ WILHELM had approached very close, under cover of haze, the chase was not a long one.

For Captain Thierfelder to go any farther north would have been to risk an encounter with the British cruisers on the Cape Verde patrol, and having sent off the *Potaro*, with a prize crew, to join the *Holger*, he turned and swept down the route. The positions in which the *Bellevue* and *Hemisphere* had been captured seemed to indicate that British steamers were now deviating widely from their ordinary course, and the *Potaro* herself was seventy miles off the track. He accordingly kept well to the east of the direct route between Fernando Noronha and St. Vincent, and on January 14th his tactics were rewarded by the capture of the *Highland Brae*, about 230 miles north-east of the St. Paul Rocks. The small wooden three-masted schooner *Wilfred M.* was taken on the same day.

The *Wilfred M.* was bound from St. John's, Nova Scotia, to Bahia, with a cargo of dried fish, which the Germans did not think it worth while to remove; and after her crew had been taken off, she was rammed and left derelict. The *Highland Brae* was a Nelson liner of 7,634 tons, outward bound from Gravesend to Buenos Aires, with 1,000 tons of general cargo. She had a large amount of coal in her bunkers and a quantity of desirable stores. In her case, therefore, the usual programme was repeated, and until January 30th, the KRONPRINZ WILHELM lay well off the trade routes, taking in fuel and provisions from the prize. During this period the *Holger* and *Potaro* rejoined. On the 30th the work was completed and the *Highland Brae* was sunk.

Meanwhile the PRINZ EITEL FRIEDRICH had come round into the Atlantic. By January 6th, or thereabouts, the whole of the *Jean's* cargo had been taken on board at Easter Island and she was accordingly towed off shore and sunk. Her crew and that of the *Kildalton* were landed on the island, on which the Germans had maintained an armed look out during the period of their stay. The whole proceedings of the PRINZ EITEL FRIEDRICH at Easter Island constituted a gross violation of international law and were subsequently made the subject of a strong protest by the Chilean Government;[1] but Captain Thierichsens was more concerned with the replenishment of his bunkers and stores, and the fact that his long detour had thrown his enemies off the scent. He was determined, however, to run no risks, and shaped his course to round the Horn in 61° S. By coming so low he encountered very bitter weather and much ice, but he escaped the British cruisers engaged in searching for the DRESDEN, and succeeded in making his way into the Atlantic without any suspicion of his movements being aroused.

The situation of the PRINZ EITEL FRIEDRICH was now

[1] See Alvarez, *op. cit.*, pp. 231, 243, where, however, there is some confusion of dates.

one of complete isolation. The squadron to which she was attached had been destroyed; she was in communication with neither the DRESDEN nor the KRONPRINZ WILHELM; and no supply ship bore her company. In view of the naval position in South American waters, Captain Thierichsens dared not approach the coast with a view to communicating with the German ships in Chilean or Argentine harbours, nor had he been able to do so would there have been much prospect of any of them putting out to join him. The British cruisers which were hunting for the DRESDEN had been joined by the Anglo-Japanese Squadron from the North Pacific, and in addition to the protection which they provided for Allied trade, the Chilean and Peruvian authorities were taking steps to prevent any repetition of the breaches of neutrality which had marked Admiral von Spee's stay on the coast. Of the steamers which had accompanied the German Pacific squadron the *Seydlitz* alone remained unaccounted for.[1] The *Amasis* had arrived at Punta Arenas on December 19th and was there interned. The *Memphis, Karnak, Ramses*, and *Sacramento* were also interned at Chilean ports, and the *Luxor* at Callao. The remaining German steamers on the coast, especially those of the Kosmos line, were under strict supervision; both in Chilean and Peruvian waters cruisers were on the move; and the coaling regulations were rigidly enforced.[2] A very similar state of things existed on the East Coast. The *Patagonia* had been arrested by an Argentine cruiser and brought into Bahia Blanca on December 21st. The *Mera* returned to Monte Video on December 22nd. The *Eleonore Woermann*, after a month of dodging and hiding from British cruisers on the Argentine coast, was captured and sunk by the AUSTRALIA, on January 6th, in the neighbourhood of the Falklands. On the same day the *Josephina*, a Dutch steamer which had been chartered by the Germans and laden with coal, was captured by the CARNARVON. She was taken into the Falklands on January 9th. Here too, especially in Brazil, the local authorities were now on the alert, and it was a difficult matter for a German ship to put to sea.

[1] She arrived at Port San Antonio Oeste, with the crew of the *Drummuir*, on December 20th, but subsequently put to sea, and finally arrived, on February 1st, 1915, at Bahia Blanca, where she was interned.

[2] Alvarez, *op. cit.*, pp. 209–219. In addition to the ships mentioned, several others were temporarily interned.

THE END OF THE FIRST PHASE

Entirely dependent as he was upon his own resources, and incapable of raising a speed within 5 knots of any British cruiser that he might encounter, Captain Thierichsens not only refrained from approaching an Argentine port, but made no attempt to assail the stream of richly laden merchantmen issuing from the Plate. Keeping well away from the steamer tracks, he followed the sailing route, some 800 miles from the coast, and was rewarded, during the last few days of January, by a little group of prizes. These were the Russian barque *Isabel Browne*, captured on the 26th; the four-masted American ship *William P. Frye* and the French barque *Pierre Loti*, taken on the 27th; and the *Jacobsen*, another French barque, on the 28th. The French and Russian vessels were sunk at once; but the case of the *William P. Frye* presented greater difficulties. She was bound from Seattle for Queenstown with a cargo of wheat valued at about £60,000, and Captain Thierichsens' first idea was to jettison the cargo and allow her to proceed.[1] This process, however, proved so lengthy that he became impatient, and on the morning of the 28th he took the extreme step of sinking the vessel, an action which subsequently gave rise to a warm controversy between the German and American Governments.

Thus, on January 31st, 1915, the situation on the South American Route was as follows. The DRESDEN was still in hiding to the south of the Magellan Straits, undiscovered but inactive. The KRONPRINZ WILHELM was about to return to the trade routes, after sinking the *Highland Brae*. The PRINZ EITEL FRIEDRICH was working up the sailing track in mid-ocean, where she might possibly add to her sailing victims, but could in no way affect the main current of South American trade. Within the next few weeks the development of the submarine campaign in the waters round the British Isles overshadowed altogether the further operations of these survivors of the original German raiders on the high seas, and the whole character and impact of the attack on commerce was completely changed. For that very reason, however, it will be convenient, at this point, to continue the story of the three raiders to the end of their careers, rather than to leave them as an isolated episode in the history of the new phase.

Captain Thierfelder's return to the steamer tracks at

[1] Interview with Master in *Times*, 12 March, 1915.

the beginning of February was not very productive, the only prize made being the Norwegian barque *Semantha*, captured on the 3rd, in about the same position as the *Highland Brae*. She was carrying 3,161 tons of wheat from Astoria to the Channel, and as in the cases of the *Maria* and the *William P. Frye*, the Germans decided to sink the ship rather than allow the cargo to reach a British port. The next week was spent by the KRONPRINZ WILHELM in ransacking and sinking the *Potaro*, and transferring the prisoners, now over two hundred in number, to the *Holger*. On February 12th the *Holger* was sent off to Buenos Aires, but whether owing to the frequency with which the call signs of British cruisers were heard, or through the wide dispersal of shipping now insisted on by the Admiralty, no further capture was made for another ten days.

Meanwhile the PRINZ EITEL FRIEDRICH was coming into the same area. On February 12th she captured and sank another sailing vessel, the British barque *Invercoe*, bound from Portland, O., for the Channel with 2,336 tons of wheat, but it had now become apparent to Captain Thierichsens that his stock of coal would be insufficient to enable him to reach Germany, and he accordingly decided to make for an American port, doing as much damage as possible on the way. By February 18th the PRINZ EITEL was within 250 miles of the Cape Verde—Pernambuco track, and on that and the two following days she captured three steamers which were following the route at a great distance.

The first of these was the *Mary Ada Short*, homeward bound from the Plate, with 5,000 tons of maize. Next day the *Floride*, of the Compagnie Générale Transatlantique, was taken; and on the 20th the *Willerby*, outward bound from Marseilles to the Plate, fell into Captain Thierichsens' hands. All three ships were sunk and the PRINZ EITEL proceeded to cut across the track between Fernando Noronha and the St. Paul Rocks.

Since his capture of the *Jean* on November 11th, Captain Thierichsens had not had the luck to encounter a coal-laden vessel. His more fortunate colleague, who had again returned to his old cruising ground, south-east of Fernando Noronha, was happy enough to meet yet another collier on February 22nd, when he captured the *Chasehill* with 2,860 tons of coal for the Plate, as well as the *Guadeloupe*, another liner belonging to the fleet of the Compagnie Générale Transatlantique, homeward bound.[1]

It will be observed that the KRONPRINZ WILHELM had thus actually crossed the track of the PRINZ EITEL FRIEDRICH, and had the two captains possessed attendant squadrons of scouts and supply ships such as accompanied the KARLSRUHE, they might have come into touch and framed a plan of concerted operations; but there is no evidence that either of them knew of the other's presence, and as both were in desperate straits for coal, they did not remain long in proximity. On board the PRINZ EITEL FRIEDRICH, the supply was running very low, and the engines and boilers had also begun to develop defects. She was in no state for further cruising, and Captain Thierichsens' one desire was to reach a safe port. The KRONPRINZ WILHELM was a little better off, as the cargo of the *Chasehill*, supplemented by the coal in her bunkers, would give her a few weeks' further lease of life. In the *Guadeloupe* also had been found a quantity of uniform cloth, shoes, and leather, intended for the French army, which were very welcome to the ill-supplied Germans. After these had been removed, together with the crew and 148 passengers, the French liner was sunk, and the KRONPRINZ WILHELM went off with the *Chasehill* to remove her coal and stores.

The arrival of the *Holger* at Buenos Aires on February 17th brought the Admiralty's information with regard to the KRONPRINZ WILHELM further up to date, but though many cruisers were patrolling the Atlantic tracks, her spells of activity were so short and so infrequent that they failed to get in touch with her. Of the PRINZ EITEL FRIEDRICH and DRESDEN nothing certain was known. On February 26th a British steamer which put into Coronel reported the presence of the prisoners on Easter Island, and thus made clear the fate of the *Jean* and *Kildalton*, but beyond this all was silence. In fact, the first intimation of Captain Thierichsens' depredations in the Atlantic was afforded by the arrival of the PRINZ EITEL FRIEDRICH herself at Newport News on March 11th. Here she landed the 800 odd prisoners with which she was encumbered and proceeded to effect the necessary repairs. For some time the German captain continued to declare his intention of putting to sea again as soon as his ship was ready,

[1] These ships were 270 miles from the ordinary tracks when captured.

but he was closely watched by British cruisers, and on April 8th, being informed that he could no longer stay in the port, he decided to accept internment.

On the day after the PRINZ EITEL FRIEDRICH arrived at Newport News, the *Chasehill* put into Pernambuco. Her holds, bunkers, and store-rooms having been completely gutted, she had been released on March 9th, the crew and passengers of the *Guadeloupe* being put on board. So greatly had the ship been damaged by rubbing alongside the KRONPRINZ WILHELM that the underwriters decided to acknowledge a constructive total loss.

The news brought by the *Chasehill* as to the continued activity of the KRONPRINZ WILHELM was somewhat disquieting, but it was counterbalanced two days later by the destruction of the last remaining unit of the German Pacific squadron. The DRESDEN had quitted Tierra del Fuegan waters on February 14th, with the *Sierra Cordoba* in company; but Captain Lüdecke's object was to avoid observation rather than to effect captures, and she kept well away from the steamer tracks. On the 25th, she dismissed her tender, and on the 27th she captured and sank the British barque *Conway Castle*, with 2,401 tons of barley from Valparaiso.[1] For the next ten days she remained stationary at or near a rendezvous where she expected to meet a supply ship, but on March 8th she was chased off by the KENT, who only lost her at nightfall. Her end, however, was not long delayed, as on the 14th she was surprised at anchor in Cumberland Bay, Juan Fernandez, by the KENT, GLASGOW, and ORAMA. In view of her repeated infractions of Chilean neutrality and the absence of any force to compel her internment, the British cruisers opened fire, and after her flag had been hauled down, she was blown up by her own officers.[2]

The first phase of the war on the South American Route was now fast drawing to a close. The KRONPRINZ WILHELM, indeed, made two further prizes, but Captain Thierfelder's extraordinary run of good fortune had come to an end, and neither of them was a collier. The *Tamar*, captured on March 24th, was a Royal Mail liner of 3,207 tons, which had sailed from Santos on the 15th with be-

---

[1] See Map 5.
[2] A formal apology was made to Chile by the British Government for this technical violation of territorial waters.

tween three and four thousand tons of coffee for Havre.¹ The *Coleby*, whose navigation lights betrayed her to the raider on the night of the 27th, was homeward bound from Rosario with 5,500 tons of wheat. From neither of these ships could the Germans replenish their almost empty bunkers, and since the departure of the *Holger*, no supply ship had joined them with coal or stores. The *Odenwald*, which attempted to leave San Juan, Porto Rico, on the night of March 20–21st, was stopped by the United States authorities, and the *Macedonia*, which broke from internment at Las Palmas, was captured by the GLOUCESTER on the 28th. Thus, left to himself, Captain Thierfelder was compelled to recognise that the game was up. His fuel was almost exhausted, some sixty of the crew and prisoners were down with beri-beri owing to the lack of proper provisions, and the KRONPRINZ WILHELM herself was in a very bad condition, having been badly damaged by vessels bumping alongside during coaling.² He therefore decided to make for a neutral port, and his fortune still held good so far as to enable him to arrive safely at Newport News on April 11th; but his ship was in no state to put to sea for another cruise, and by the end of the month he submitted to be interned.

With the internment of the KRONPRINZ WILHELM the first period of German cruiser activity came to an end. Its success had been very small in comparison either with the expectations formed prior to the war or with the size of the target offered to attack. Such as it was, the KRONPRINZ WILHELM herself might claim a fair share of the achievement, having captured nine British steamers aggregating 42,300 tons, and two French with a tonnage of 11,400, besides four sailing vessels, of which one was British, two French, and the other a neutral.³ The PRINZ EITEL FRIEDRICH also had moderately good results to show—at least for the last period of her activities—but of her eleven prizes, only four were steamers, so that her depredations had little effect on the shipping resources of the Allies.

The career of these vessels is particularly interesting, because they represented the type of armed German

¹ See Map 9.
² Interviews with her officers, *Times*, 13 April, 1915; *Weser Zeitung*, 8 May, 1915.
³ All sunk except the *Chasehill*, which was released, severely damaged. See p. 379, *supra*.

liner from whom so much was feared at the beginning of the war. They were, indeed, the only ships of this class which met with any appreciable success during the first stage of the struggle. So far as concerned the PRINZ EITEL FRIEDRICH this success was limited, first by her long period of unproductive cruising in the Pacific, and afterwards by the lack of speed which forbade her to approach the steamer tracks. It was her fate to operate for the greater part of her career in waters where prizes were few, and to be cut off by strong Allied forces from the focal points of trade. At no time, except during her brief association with the German Pacific squadron, had she any supply ships in attendance, and the necessity of husbanding carefully the precious supply so fortunately obtained from the *Jean* was an additional impediment to her later activities. While Captain Thierichsens' movements subsequent to the battle of Coronel exhibited both enterprise and judgment, the majority of his captures were obtained by a temporary reversion to older conditions, the attack of a steamer on sailing vessels, and they left the great volume of Allied trade in the South Atlantic unaffected.

The KRONPRINZ WILHELM was a better example of the type. Her armament was very light, and a defensively armed merchant vessel would probably have given a good account of her; but, whether by accident or design, the only ship of this class encountered was *La Correntina*, which had no ammunition on board. On the other hand, her speed was high—23 knots—and though her large coal consumption rendered it impossible for her to employ anything like full power for long together, the possibility of working up to a high speed in an emergency justified the taking of greater risks than were possible to the PRINZ EITEL FRIEDRICH. Captain Thierfelder was thus able to attack the steamer routes at or near the focal points, and the chief factor which militated against his achieving still further success was the difficulty of coal supply. Unlike the KARLSRUHE and EMDEN he had neither bases at which he could coal in safety, nor an adequate system of supply ships. The CARMANIA's victory broke up the German base at Trinidada before he could use it, and when he returned to the north the conditions had so far changed that he dared not make use of anchorages on the Brazilian coast, even if the great size of his ship had permitted him to do so. Neither the *Sierra Cordoba*, *Otavi*, nor *Holger* brought any large amount of fuel, and Captain Thierfelder was thus obliged to rely mainly upon replenishing his bunkers from prizes. In this respect he was fortunate, obtaining some 15,000 tons from the *Union*, *Bellevue*, *Hemisphere*, and *Chasehill*; but coaling at sea in the heavy South Atlantic swell entailed a certain amount of structural damage to the ship and long periods of absence from the trade routes. Every few days of activity were followed by two or three weeks spent in hiding, and while these detours may have assisted to preserve the KRONPRINZ WILHELM from the British cruisers who were searching for her, they greatly restricted her opportunities of making prizes. These opportunities were still further restricted by the wide dispersion practised by British shipping, which obliged Captain Thierfelder to rely on steaming parallel with the tracks at a considerable distance from them and taking advantage of chance encounters. Hence, in a career extending to eight months at sea, he accomplished considerably less than was achieved by Captains Köhler and von Müller in less than half that period. On the other hand, his record as a commerce destroyer compares very favourably with that of Captain Lüdecke. The DRESDEN's career also extended to some eight months, during which she steamed over 20,000 miles and took in 10,000 tons of coal; but the damage which she inflicted was small, and the tonnage sunk was actually little more than half of that captured and released during her hurried flight into the Pacific.

CHAPTER XXIII

COMPARISONS AND ACHIEVEMENTS

For some weeks before the destruction of the DRESDEN and the internment of the PRINZ EITEL FRIEDRICH and KRONPRINZ WILHELM, attention had been diverted from the operations of these three survivors of the original raiders by the new menace which had developed in Home Waters; but before dealing further with the effects of the submarine campaign, it is desirable to take stock of the situation in which the contending Powers found themselves at the moment of transition from the first to the second phase of the war at sea.

It is a striking contrast which is presented. On the one hand, the Central Empires were reduced to reliance upon an inadequate supply of neutral shipping for the export of their own products or the fulfilment of their requirements from abroad. In the case of contraband goods, they were still further restricted to the receipt of such cargoes as, with the connivance of neutral merchants, could evade the Allied examination service and the regulations imposed by neutral Governments. On the other hand, every sea route in the world, with the exception of those from Black Sea and Baltic ports was open for the distribution of British products or the supply of British needs. Goods of whatever category could be carried to or from the United Kingdom with a very slight degree of risk, whether in British or in neutral bottoms, and the benefits of this freedom extended also to the Allies of Great Britain. Russia, it is true, was less happily situated, inasmuch as the two chief channels of her trade were wholly interrupted, and France was prevented by the dislocation consequent on the German invasion from profiting to the full by the security of the seas. But so long as the White Sea and Swedish tracks were open, Russia could at least depend upon the fulfilment of her primary requirements for war material; and severely as French commerce was suffering, the activity of British shipping assured to France the uninterrupted arrival of additional foodstuffs for her armies, and the iron and coal wherewith to replace the loss of those rich metalliferous districts which were now occupied by the enemy.[1] By the end of 1914, both the movement of shipping at French ports and the figures of the import and export trade showed a distinct improvement, and although the volume of traffic was even now considerably less than half of that carried on in times of peace, the stream of shipping from British ports was well up to the normal level, and all anxiety with regard to essential imports was at an end. On the economic and commercial side Great Britain was the soul of the Alliance, and the essential condition of success in a prolonged conflict was the maintenance of her import and export trade in such measure as would enable her to place her financial and industrial resources freely at the disposal of her Allies.

Compared with this broad distinction between the situation of the two belligerent groups, the details of losses suffered by either side sink into insignificance; yet the figures of these losses are not without interest as showing how promptly and how thoroughly the control of the trade routes was established by the British fleet. So precipitate was the withdrawal of the German and Austrian merchantmen from traffic, and so large was the target exposed by shipping under the British flag, that it would not have been surprising if, as in the Napoleonic wars, the prizes taken by enemy cruisers had been far more numerous than those brought into British ports. Yet in point of fact the exact contrary was the case, and the losses sustained by the mercantile fleets of the Central Powers were not only comparatively but actually greater than those of British shipowners.

The total loss which the German cruisers, mine-layers, and submarines had inflicted on British shipping down to January 31, 1915, amounted to seventy merchant steamers,

---

[1] "In November 1914, when the Germans were in occupation of the basin of Briey and the industrial regions of the North and East, we in France were deprived of more than three-quarters of our blast-furnaces, and consequently of our usual production of steel and iron. If Great Britain had not been able to assure to us the freedom of the seas, we could not have continued the struggle; we must have capitulated through sheer lack of armaments" (M. André Lebon, in *Quarterly Review*, July 1917).

a steam dredger, and thirty-six steam trawlers, with a total tonnage of 282,000 gross. Considerable in itself, this figure represents no more than 1·37 per cent. of the steam tonnage flying the British flag at the beginning of the war, and if the vessels detained in German and Turkish ports be included, the ratio of loss is still under 2·3 per cent.[1] Nor had the losses fallen appreciably more heavily on the larger ships by which the ocean trades were mainly carried on ; for of some 3,750 steamers of 1,000 tons net or over on the Register of the United Kingdom, only ninety-seven, or less than 2·6 per cent. were sunk, captured, or detained.

There had also to be deducted a number of vessels which, as a consequence of the war, had been transferred to a foreign flag. These were mostly ships registered in the United Kingdom, but owned in the United States. Thus, some thirty steamers hitherto run by subsidiary companies under the control of the United Fruit Company of America and the United States Steel Corporation were now transferred to American Registry. But all deductions, whether due to hostile operations, to ordinary marine casualties, or to transfer of flag, were more than made good by the output of the British shipyards, and by the acquisition of foreign ships by capture or purchase. During the first five months of the war, 450,000 tons of steam shipping built in the United Kingdom were added to the Register, and after allowing for all additions and deductions, the gross steam tonnage on the Register on December 31st, 1914, was greater by 462,000 tons than on January 1st.[2]

The actual situation was not quite so satisfactory as these figures would suggest, for the effects of recruiting in the shipbuilding and allied industries, coupled with the greatly increased demands of the Royal Navy, had already begun to affect the time required for the completion of mercantile orders, and the monthly average of 90,000 tons added to the Register in August—December, represented a decrease of 33,000 tons on the average for January—July. Nevertheless, the fact remains that during six months of war, the enemy had proved powerless, not merely to

[1] For details see Appendix, Table I.
[2] Returns supplied to *Lloyd's Register* by the Registrar of Shipping. The figures include steamers under 100 tons gross, but the aggregate tonnage of such vessels is too small to affect the comparison. Ships detained for the period of the war were not removed from nor added to the Register.

diminish the British mercantile fleet, but to prevent its expansion.[1]

Light as were the British losses, those of the other Allies were still lighter, owing to the fact that their vessels were less exposed to attack. Those of France and Russia amounted together only to 30,000 tons of steam shipping sunk, captured, or detained,[1] and not a single Japanese ship had been molested. In the case of Belgium, the leading lines had simply transferred their offices and operations from Antwerp or Ostend to British ports, so that, although practically the whole of Belgium was now occupied by the German armies, the Belgian mercantile marine had been preserved from falling into the enemy's hands.

On the other hand, no less than 182 German and Austrian steamers had been sunk, captured, or condemned as prizes subsequent to their seizure in Allied ports, and 188 more were detained for the period of the war. Thus the total number which had fallen into the hands of the Allies was 320, representing 915,000 tons gross, or very nearly 15 per cent. of the steam tonnage owned by the Central Powers.[2]

Compared with the losses of steam tonnage, those of sailing vessels had no great significance, but here too the comparison was overwhelmingly against Germany. While the Allied losses amounted only to thirty-two vessels, mostly Russians of very small size, the Germans had lost sixty-four, with a total net tonnage of 71,000, many of those captured being big vessels employed in the grain or nitrate trades.

These were heavy losses, but they were a small matter compared with the blow inflicted on enemy shipowners by the suspension of traffic. While the entire British mercantile marine, with the unimportant exception of the ships locked up in the Baltic and Black Sea, was busily employed either in Government service or in trade, the fleets of the German and Austrian steamship companies had ceased altogether to earn money for their owners, save for a few naval auxiliaries and some small vessels employed

[1] See Appendix, Tables II. and III.
[2] For details see Appendix, Tables IV., V., and VI.
The above figures include four steamers in German Colonial ports captured and disabled but not yet removed by the British. They do not include the KAISER WILHELM DER GROSSE, CAP TRAFALGAR, and KÖNIGIN LUISE, sunk while acting as warships.

on the coasting and Swedish tracks. Over 700 steamers and 100 sailing-vessels, representing some 3,000,000 tons, or roughly half the remaining tonnage, were blockaded in Belgian and Turkish ports, or sheltering in neutral harbours whence they dared not move, and where they daily deteriorated in value. The remainder lay equally idle in their home ports. With heavy charges for upkeep and depreciation and little or no revenue coming in, most of the companies were obliged to pass their dividends for 1914, or to pay them on a reduced scale by drawing on the reserves built up in more prosperous years.

Yet for the Central Powers, as for Great Britain, it was not the carrying trade itself but the volume of imports and exports, by whomsoever carried, which was the vital matter, and as we have seen, the traffic which still reached them was sufficient to ensure the essential minimum supply of commodities required under war conditions. Moreover, now that the railways had been cleared, in some degree, of military traffic, and that German industries and finance had recovered from the first shock of the war, it had been found possible to resume the export of goods, not only to the neutral countries immediately across the frontiers, but also to oversea markets. The available cargo space, however, was small, the surplus production of the German factories limited, and the obstacles to commercial intercourse numerous and formidable. Hence the resumption of trade was confined mainly to shipments to the United States, and these shipments were on a much reduced scale. On all the foreign exchanges the balance was still heavily against Germany, and the shrinkage in the value of the mark was a matter of grave concern to German financiers.

With regard to foodstuffs the position in Germany was still one of inconvenience rather than of danger. The margin of supplies which had been cut off was insufficient to reduce any part of the population to want, but it was enough to disturb the equilibrium of distribution and consumption. Local shortages and shortages of particular commodities were productive of considerable irritation, and this irritation was increased by the failure of the measures taken by the Government to remedy the deficiency. The emergency legislation relating to food was already bulky and complex, and the constant revision of the regulations showed no signs of approaching finality; but nothing of importance had been done to increase production or to diminish consumption, and little success had been achieved in eliminating inequalities of distribution. A fruitful source of popular discontent and of friction between competing interests was thus created, and the outlook for the current year was overshadowed by the prospect of more serious dangers. While the deficiency in wheat and barley could be made good, to a great extent, by more extensive use of other cereals and the restriction of brewing and distilling, the situation with regard to fodder was not so easily to be remedied, and threatened an appreciable shortage in meat and dairy produce if the war should be prolonged. It remained to be seen, moreover, what effect the shortage of fertilisers and of labour would have on the coming harvest.

Thus, while the situation presented no immediate occasion for alarm, it afforded ample grounds for anxiety, and the possibility of a still greater restriction of oversea supplies, as the result of the adoption of more stringent measures by the Allies, had always to be faced. Meanwhile the economic strength of the Allies themselves, so far from having been seriously impaired, was increasing with every month, as the elasticity of British commerce found opportunity to display itself under cover of the naval protection so amply provided.

How complete that naval protection had been has already been seen in the small percentage of mercantile tonnage sunk or captured, but in order to appreciate fully the narrowness of the limits within which the success of the hostile raiders was confined, it is necessary to compare the losses incurred not only with the tonnage owned but with the volume of shipping exposed to attack. The total net tonnage of British ships entered and cleared with cargoes in the foreign trade of the United Kingdom during the first six months of the war was over 23,000,000, and of vessels of all nationalities 37,000,000. Of the foreign ships the great majority were neutrals, and were therefore exempt from capture unless they carried contraband, but all those coming to London or East Coast ports were exposed to the danger of the German mine-fields. Yet the total number of vessels sunk or captured by the enemy while carrying cargoes to or from the British Isles, was only forty-three British, with a net tonnage of 110,000, and twenty foreign, with a tonnage of 20,000. The proportion of loss to the tonnage entered and cleared works out at approximately one-half per cent. in the case of British and a little more than one-third in the case of all ships.[1]

Thus, compared with the volume of traffic the losses due to hostile activity were negligible, and we have already seen that they were very small in relation to the total tonnage on the Register; nor is the result less satisfactory if the basis of comparison be shifted from tonnage to values. Among ships entered in the War Risks Associations, comprising practically all foreign-going steamers and a considerable number of coasters, the losses represented no more than 1·78 per cent. on the entered values, and on the cargoes it was smaller still. With regard to cargoes indeed, it must be remembered that about a quarter of the imports and exports of the United Kingdom were carried on foreign ships, most of which were neutrals, and of such cargoes very few were lost. On the other hand, the cargoes carried by British ships between foreign ports were, to a great extent, financed and insured in this country, and the safest basis of comparison is that afforded by taking into account *all* cargoes carried in British ships during the six months. The estimated value of these cargoes was £651,000,000, of which those carried in ships captured or destroyed amounted to £4,283,000 or two-thirds of 1 per cent.[2]

Not only had the enemy's cruisers and mine-layers failed to inflict any appreciable percentage of loss, but they had failed to force up the rate for insurance against war risks to a level which would impose a serious obstacle to trade. Up to December 15th, 1914, the premium for insurance of hulls under the State Scheme to cover a single voyage was 1 per cent.; for a round voyage or a three months' time policy, 2 per cent. Since that date the premium had been reduced to ¾ and 1½ per cent. respectively. Allowing for time in port, and for a certain amount of insurance effected with underwriters at lower rates, the total cost of insurance on an average merchant steamer for the six months was probably little, if at all, over 3 per cent. representing about ·75 per cent. for each voyage actually

---

[1] Ships captured or sunk which sailed before August 1st, 1914, or would not have arrived until after January 31st, 1915, were, of course, excluded from this calculation.

[2] See Appendix, Table IX.

made.¹ In some of the most important branches of British commerce, cargoes, as we have already seen, could be covered on the open market, during the latter portion of the period under review, at 10s. or 7s. 6d., and the average cost of cargo insurance for a single voyage may be taken as about 1½ per cent.

So far, therefore, as the direct effects of hostile activity were concerned, the position was exceedingly satisfactory, but the dislocation of British commerce by the war was not confined to the capture of ships and cargoes or the temporary interruption of particular tracks by hostile cruisers. The export trade in particular was too severely handicapped in other ways to take full advantage of the freedom of movement accorded to merchant shipping. Apart from the elimination of the enemy markets and the direct effects of the war on Allied and neutral trade, the export of British capital had been to a great extent suspended since the outbreak of war. During the first seven months of 1914, £152,000,000 of British capital was invested in the Overseas Dominions or in foreign countries, an excess of £11,000,000 over the figure for the corresponding period in the previous year. It was owing to the effect of these investments that the export trade during the first seven months of the year suffered comparatively little from the general commercial depression; but with the outbreak of war the flow of British capital abroad automatically ceased. Although investments continued to be made on a reduced scale, they were neutralised by the calling in of floating capital, and, on balance, little or no British capital was exported during the war months. The result was a corresponding diminution in the effective demand for British products, which was of itself almost sufficient to account for the decrease in the export figures.²

At the same time, the obstacles to the revival of the export trade were not confined to the conditions abroad. The diversion of capital and labour in Great Britain from civil to military purposes was a still more important factor. By January 1915, the formation of the new armies was in full swing, well over a million men had been withdrawn from trade and industry, and the work of feeding, clothing, and arming the fighting forces absorbed

¹ Taking the average length of each voyage, including time occupied in loading and discharging, at forty-five days.
² *Statist*, 9 January, 1915.

a great part of the labour which remained. At first, indeed, the demands of the war industries and the depletion of the labour market by recruiting were, generally speaking, beneficial in their effects. It was thanks to these demands that the economic crisis produced no serious results in the way of unemployment; indeed, the percentage of unemployed fell steadily from August onward.[1] As commerce revived, however, the injurious results of this diversion of effort began to be apparent. The demands of the armies interfered seriously with the execution of commercial orders, and while the great volume of goods sent overseas for the use of the troops provided employment, it did not affect the balance of exchange between the United Kingdom and foreign countries.

In these circumstances, a diminution of 40 per cent. in values in the export trade was not surprising, and it might well be considered as satisfactory that, under so heavy a handicap, no less than £194,000,000 worth of goods had been exported or re-exported during the six months. It is noteworthy that September and October, when the cruiser attack was at its height, were actually the months in which the percentage of decrease was lowest, and ample evidence of the protection afforded to shipping was given by the fact that, seriously as the coal trade had been hit by the loss of the German and Russian markets and by the restrictions on export, over 22,500,000 tons had been sent out of the country, with only a negligible percentage of loss.

It is, nevertheless, by the import figures that the value of naval protection is mainly to be judged. We have already seen that the import values show a steady increase throughout the six months, from £42,000,000 in August to £67,000,000 in December, and the same in January. This increase, however, is partly accounted for by rising prices, and partly by the fact that imports are always particularly heavy during the last quarter of the year. A truer criterion is provided by the figures of percentage decrease in estimated weights, as compared with six months of peace, August 1913 to January 1914. Yet even when tried by this standard the diminution is surprisingly small, and the progress during half a year of war surprisingly great. For the months of August, September, and October, when commerce was still suffering from the effects of the financial crisis produced by a sudden change to war conditions, the

[1] *Board of Trade Labour Gazette, passim.*

decrease averaged 23·6 per cent. For November, December, and January, it averaged only 12 per cent., and it was actually lowest in November, the month which was ushered in by the disastrous action off Coronel.[1]

When we turn to details, the results are even more striking. All through, the decrease was heaviest in the class of manufactured goods. Here, the decisive factor was the cessation of trade with Germany and Belgium, from whence we were accustomed to draw 40 per cent. of our imports in this class. The stoppage of the German and Belgian trade accounted almost entirely for a diminution of over half a million tons in the import of steel blooms, billets, and slabs, steel girders, and wrought iron bars, and it was equally felt in the shortage of other articles of smaller bulk but greater proportionate value, notably chemicals and dyestuffs. A further 15 per cent. of our manufactured imports came from France, and here, too, although the communications were secure, the condition of the country forbade manufacture and export on an extensive scale.

Whatever security was afforded to shipping, it was impossible that fresh sources of supply should suddenly be found for goods formerly procured from these sources, and in many cases the result was to stimulate home production; but it was still imperative that the supply of foodstuffs and raw materials should be maintained, and the figures in these classes bear eloquent testimony to the completeness of naval control, the preservation of credit by the State Insurance Scheme and the enterprise of shipowners and merchants.

The fear of starvation had, indeed, passed away during the first few weeks, or even days of hostilities, for that fear was based mainly upon the anticipation of a financial panic, and so soon as it was seen that the support afforded to credit was strong enough to keep trade afoot, a bare sufficiency at least of actual necessaries might be regarded as secured. In fact, far more had been achieved; it proved possible to provide on a liberal scale and with ample reserves for the feeding of the armies in the field, without infringing upon the accustomed standard of life for the civil population. In spite of the activity of the German cruisers, in spite of the closing of the Dardanelles and the partial suspension of the Baltic trade, the imports of food-

[1] See Appendix, Table XII.

stuffs during the first six months of war actually exceeded in quantity those brought in during the corresponding months of 1913–14.

In some directions, it is true, the obstacles interposed by the war to the maintenance of supplies at their normal level, proved too great to be overcome. The loss of the Russian and Roumanian barley was only partially made good by increased imports from the United States, and it was not only the Black Sea supplies of oats which were cut off, but those (normally one-fifth of the whole) obtained from Germany itself. But with an increase of 250,000 tons in the imports of wheat, and of 130,000 tons in the imports of maize, the position as regards cereals, whether for human consumption or for fodder, was eminently satisfactory.

As regards foodstuffs other than cereals, the most important decreases were recorded in meat, fish, and eggs. The shortage in eggs is accounted for by the diminution in supplies from Russia; and restrictions on fishing in the North Sea, coupled with the requisitioning of so many trawlers and drifters, played havoc with the fisheries; but the drop of 20 per cent. in the imports of meat must be traced mainly to financial difficulties in Argentina at the beginning of the war, to the requisitioning of ships with insulated space at British and Australian ports, and to the sudden springing up of a demand from France.[1] In no case is there the slightest evidence of any diminution in the supply of foodstuffs due to active operations by the enemy at sea, as apart from the local effects of their command of the Baltic and Black Sea entrances.

An examination of the figures for raw materials gives very similar results. In this class there was a decrease ranging from 33 per cent. in August to 11·8 per cent. in November, and amounting to 26 per cent. for the six months. But this decrease is to a great extent accounted for by a single bulky article—timber—which fell off by about 1,500,000 loads, owing to the difficulties of Baltic navigation. Next in importance, so far as bulk is concerned, was a diminution of 800,000 tons in the imports of iron ore; but this must be traced, not to any threat of

---

[1] In normal times the French imports of refrigerated meat were negligible, but large purchases were now made, through the British Government, for the feeding of the French armies, and the emergence of this new demand naturally diminished the supplies available for the United Kingdom.

hostile interference—for the security of our communications with Spain was never in doubt—but to the slackening of demand, due to the restriction of markets for iron and steel manufactures abroad. Similarly, the drop of 5,200,000 centals in imports of raw cotton is entirely accounted for by the world-wide dislocation of the cotton trade, to which reference has already been made.

Of the other textiles, silk showed a large increase, in spite of the EMDEN's activity on the Oriental Route, and the supply of wool was fairly maintained, except as regards alpaca and mohair, which suffered respectively from the interruption of shipping on the west coast of America by the German cruisers, and from the entry of Turkey into the war. The supply of mohair from South Africa was, however, adequate to the demand, as the loss of the continental markets set free a large proportion of the spinners for the manufacture of khaki worsteds. The jute trade suffered both from the limitation of supplies in India and from the operations of the EMDEN; but here again, although the delay in shipments threatened at one time to be a serious inconvenience, the curtailment of exports prevented any real shortage from being felt. Hemp came forward in good quantities, but the imports of flax diminished by one-half, owing to the German occupation of Belgium and the difficulty of effecting shipments from Russia.

The direct effect of the LEIPZIG's operations and those of Admiral von Spee could be seen in a great reduction in arrivals of tin and copper ore from South America; but any fear of a copper shortage was averted by heavy shipments of unwrought or partly wrought metal from the United States. On the other hand, the EMDEN's activity did not greatly interfere with the supply of block tin from the Straits Settlements.

Among miscellaneous products, the supply of rubber was well maintained, mainly, despite the EMDEN, from the Malay Peninsula and Ceylon. Thanks in part to the arrival of captured cargoes, but still more to the rapidity with which Admiral von Spee was brought to book, the imports of nitrate rose by nearly 50,000 tons; but the most remarkable increase was in petroleum, the imports of which advanced by 56,000,000 gallons, or 20 per cent., owing to the Admiralty demand for liquid fuel.

So far, therefore, there was little evidence of any shortage caused by the war, either in the supply of food or of those raw materials which were necessary to the conduct of the war or the maintenance of British industries. Where a considerable diminution of imports was recorded, the cause was more frequently to be found in financial and economic conditions than in the activities of the German cruisers. The enemy had, in fact, proved powerless to obstruct the passage of commodities. It remains to be seen what effect his operations had had upon their price.

Although the apprehensions of famine prices due to the laying up of shipping and consequent shortage of supplies had been completely falsified, and the institution of the State Insurance Scheme had at once checked the tendency to inflated war risks, the first six months of war were marked by a very considerable rise both in the cost of transport of seaborne goods and in the price charged to the consumer. The rise in the price of foodstuffs was already serious, and by January 31st, the cost of living in Great Britain had risen by 23 per cent. in the large towns, and 20 per cent. in small towns and villages.[1] This rise in prices was generally connected in the public mind with the rise in freights which began in October 1914, but an examination of the phenomena renders it very doubtful whether the increased freight rates played a leading part in producing the rise in prices, and still more doubtful whether the advance in freights was due, in any appreciable degree, to hostile activity.

We have seen that at the beginning of the war the liner companies imposed surcharges, amounting in some cases to 50 per cent., on both freight and passenger rates, but that, on the other hand, tramp tonnage was in so little demand as to be almost unable to secure remunerative charters. As the preliminary dislocation died away and trade begun to accommodate itself to the new conditions, the position was gradually reversed; the liner surcharges were considerably reduced, but tramp shipping became in greater and greater demand, and freights rose in many cases to an altogether abnormal level. In October 1914, the average grain freights from North America, India and the Plate were rather higher than in the same month of 1913, but were well below the level of 1912. By November they were higher than in either 1913 or 1912 in

[1] *Board of Trade Labour Gazette.* Weighted percentage increase for twenty-three principal articles.

the case of North America and the Plate, lower than 1912 for shipments from Karachi; but by the end of the six months, they had reached, in each case, an unprecedented level.[1]

It would, however, be altogether erroneous to attribute this rise in freights simply to the influence of naval operations. In the first place, the freight on grain from North America rose greatly, although the North Atlantic Route was at no time subject to attack. Secondly, the advance in freights was altogether disproportionate to the cost of insurance against war risks, and increased as that cost diminished. Thirdly, the greatest advance in freights occurred during the months of December and January, after the destruction of the EMDEN and KARLSRUHE and of Admiral von Spee's squadron. It is evident, therefore, that the explanation must be sought elsewhere than in the fear of capture or the cost of insurance against it.

One cause of the increased freights was, no doubt, an increase in working expenses, due to the rise in the price of coal—especially at foreign ports—the prolongation of voyages by deviation, and the greater cost of loading and discharging cargoes at the ports. Another cause was the shrinkage in British exports and the general redistribution of the foreign trade, owing to the necessity for finding new sources of supply. Many of the liner companies were so hard hit by the reduction in the amount of outward cargo available and the partial disappearance of the passenger traffic, that even when full homeward cargoes could be procured at advanced rates, they had some difficulty in maintaining their services. At the same time, the necessity of drawing supplies from new sources obliged tramp steamers, in cases where an outward cargo for the substituted port was not immediately available, to make long voyages in ballast, the cost of which had to be considered in fixing the homeward freights.

The actual increase in working expenses per ton carried was estimated at the beginning of January at an average of 3s. 9d., or 6s. for the Plate voyage, and does not, therefore, go very far to account for the rise. The increase due to the necessity of covering the cost of outward voyages in ballast or partly laden cannot be exactly

[1] See Appendix, Table XIII.

estimated, but ballast voyages are a common incident of the tramp trade, and the direct effect on freights of a certain increase in their number was probably less than the indirect influence exercised on the course of the freight markets by the redistribution of commerce, through the reduction in the carrying power of the available tonnage. Indeed the growing disproportion between the demand for cargo space and the supply was by far the most potent factor in the production of freight advances. Reference to this shortage has already frequently been made, but it is necessary to examine it somewhat more closely in its general bearings, for it was the most important complication as yet introduced by the war into the problem of maintaining British trade.

Taking the world as a whole, it is probable that the tonnage available for commerce was not, in itself, inadequate to the work to be performed. The figures of British exports and imports show a diminution of about 30 per cent., and it is safe to assume that the total seaborne trade of the world had diminished in about the same proportion. That of Germany, Austria, and Belgium, which accounted between them for about 22 per cent. of the world's commerce, had practically ceased to exist, and that of France, Russia, and many neutral countries was greatly reduced in volume. On the other hand, the mercantile fleets of the Central Powers, amounting to 14 per cent. of the world's steam shipping, had been withdrawn from traffic, and although the losses of the Allies in ships captured or detained had been comparatively small, there were other circumstances which imposed serious limitations on the employment of their remaining tonnage for the purpose of commerce. Of the British steamers employed in ocean voyages, some 20 per cent. were now withdrawn from trade for use as transports or naval auxiliaries; the demands upon French shipping for similar purposes were considerable; and many Japanese steamers were taken up in connection with the expedition against Tsingtau. A certain amount of tonnage, Russian, British, and French, was also locked up in the Baltic and Black Sea, though these vessels, as well as those detained in enemy ports, included many small steamers unsuitable for employment on the ocean routes.

Allowance must also be made on the one hand for losses due to ordinary marine risks, and on the other for new construction in belligerent and neutral yards, and for the increased cargoes carried by British ships in the import trade, which showed a margin over the previous year of 17 per cent. for the whole six months, and of 28 per cent. for January 1915. When all these factors are taken into consideration it appears that the reduction in the available shipping was very fairly balanced by the diminution in the volume of goods to be carried; notwithstanding which there was evident, in the general carrying trade of the world, a shortage of tonnage which threatened gravely to impede the course of commerce.

The main cause of this shortage, as has been suggested, must be sought in the redistribution of traffic. It must be remembered that the carrying power of any ship over a given period varies with the conditions of her employment. The reduction which had taken place in British trade affected mainly the traffic with Continental ports, to or from which many cargoes could be carried by a single steamer in the course of a year. Essential imports hitherto derived from the Continent had now to be drawn from countries at a much greater distance, necessitating the employment of a larger number of vessels, because fewer voyages could be performed by each ship. At the same time the average length of all voyages was increased by the withdrawal of the fastest steamers and the best firemen for use in the navy or the transport service. While the volume of goods which could be carried during a given period by laden vessels was thus reduced, the long ballast voyages required by the development of new channels of trade and the waste of cargo space involved in the clearance of liners from British ports with part cargoes only on board, had the result of causing a still graver disproportion between the tonnage afloat and its capacity to carry on the trade of the world.

These factors were general to the whole carrying trade, but the demands of requisitioning upon the world-pool of shipping operated by no means evenly as between route and route, and this inequality in their incidence added to the difficulties of the freight markets. It will be remembered that the ships required for naval and military purposes were not all taken up in home ports. Many large steamers were requisitioned in British ports abroad, especially in those of India and Australia, and as we have seen, the withdrawal of these ships from trade, coupled with the cessation of the German services and the decrease in arrivals from Great Britain, created a local shortage which could only be made good by sending out vessels from home or redirecting them from distant seas. Some relief was found in the use of prize vessels and of German and Austrian steamers detained for the period of the war, but several of the prizes were required for naval or military use; and owing to the heavy work thrust on the Prize Courts, especially in dealing with the cargoes of the detained vessels, there was a considerable delay before the remainder became available for commercial use. Thus, it was not until the middle of December, 1914, that the whole of the ships interned at Sydney had been put into commission. Even then the relief afforded was only very partial, and meantime the competition of shippers in the markets affected had not only forced up freights, but had led to the departure of vessels in ballast from congested ports, such as the Plate, to those where cargo was more readily obtainable, with the result of producing a subsequent shortage on the routes from which they were withdrawn.

Every such local shortage thus assisted to disturb still further the general equilibrium between demand and supply, and the effect of the dislocation was increased by circumstances unconnected with the war, such as the failure of the Australian harvest, which powerfully reinforced the demand for tonnage on the North Atlantic tracks. Throughout the whole world shipping was kept continually on the move in response to the fluctuating requirements of charterers, and always the tendency was towards increased length of voyages and narrower concentration of demand.

Associated partly as cause and partly as effect with this world-wide redirection of trade and shortage of tonnage was the port congestion which we have already noticed, and which by the opening of 1915 had assumed formidable proportions. Even during the first three months of the war we have seen that the French Atlantic harbours were choked with shipping diverted from the northern ports owing to the German advance. When that advance was checked, the northern ports again came into use, but both at those on the Channel and those on the Atlantic coast, the depleted labour staffs and disorganised railway system proved quite unable to cope with the rush of vessels which poured in to make up the leeway of the previous months, and of transports and store-ships supplying the British Expeditionary Force. The equipment of the ports was, in several cases, altogether insufficient to deal with the volume of trade which had to be handled, and its dual control—by the Government and the local authorities—created additional difficulties.[1] In many cases the delays in unloading amounted to three or four weeks, or even longer, above the usual time of discharge, and the carrying power of the tonnage employed was correspondingly reduced. At Genoa, the situation was much the same. The course of Italian commerce had been seriously affected by the partial closure of the Adriatic and the development of a large transit trade with the Central Powers, and towards the end of January 1915 there were no less than seventy-five steamers awaiting their turn at the berths.[2]

Unfortunately, it was not only at foreign ports that the problem of congestion had assumed serious proportions. Although the trade of the United Kingdom had been diminished by the war, the handling of even that reduced trade at British ports presented grave difficulties.

In the first place, the replacement of imports normally derived from the Continent by supplies brought from more distant sources led to an unusually large proportion of the import trade being carried by big, ocean-going ships. The effect of this was to diminish the utility of the smaller ports, and to concentrate the trade at the comparatively few large ports where alone such vessels could be received. This tendency to concentration was reinforced by the exclusive allocation of certain harbours, and of quay and water space at other harbours, to naval and military use, which had the result, in the aggregate, of putting a very considerable strain upon the resources of the substituted ports. Moreover, the German mine-fields in the North Sea, while they failed to interrupt traffic with Holland and Scandinavia, did appreciably affect the dis-

[1] A deputation from the Special Advisory Committee of the Newcastle Chamber of Commerce visited Havre and Rouen and arranged for additional moorings to be laid down in the river for vessels whose cargoes were to be transhipped into lighters—thus releasing quay space—and for additional equipment and labour to be procured, with assistance from England.

[2] *Lloyd's List*, 20 January, 1915. Report of Annual Meeting of Glasgow Chamber of Commerce.

tribution of the trade. We have seen that from the beginning of the war there was a tendency for the East Coast services to be shifted, first from the more southerly to the more northerly ports, and afterwards from the East Coast as a whole to West Coast harbours. As the dangers of the North Sea increased and it became necessary to subject navigation to greater and still greater restrictions, the concentration of trade at particular harbours, and in some cases at altogether new centres, increased in like proportion, and long lines of food-laden steamers were often to be seen awaiting their turn at the berths.

The strain placed upon the ports generally by these alterations in services was further increased by the accumulation in the docks and sheds of military stores, prize cargoes, and the heavy purchases made by the Sugar Commission, all of which tended to be very slowly cleared off, and thus to occupy valuable space for a long period. In Liverpool alone, at the middle of January, there were over 100,000 tons of sugar on Government account, and six sugar-laden vessels were awaiting discharge. The occupation of quay space by prize cargoes was not yet the nuisance which it afterwards became, but the cargo of the *Alfred Nobel*, which was discharged at Liverpool at the beginning of December, was still on the quays at the end of January, and at Leith considerable inconvenience was caused by vessels brought in for examination.

The capacities of the leading ports would thus have been severely taxed, even if their ability to deal with cargoes had remained unimpaired; but the facilities for loading and discharge were in most cases seriously diminished. Tugs, motors, horses, carts, and barges had been requisitioned in large numbers for military and naval use, and the demands of military traffic upon the railways constituted a still greater impediment to trade. Engines, trucks, and siding accommodation were withdrawn from commercial use to an extent which gravely hampered the distribution of goods, and the shortage of trucks, in particular, was already acute. The difficulty was increased by the lack of any arrangement for pooling the trucks which remained available. In default of an agreement between the various owners, it was impossible to use a surplus in one direction to make good a deficiency in another, and sidings were choked with "empties" while cargo was accumulating on the quays. The delay in removing cargoes from the docks led to an extensive use of transit sheds as warehouses, with the result of still further impeding the flow of traffic, and the deficiency of these sheds at some of the older and smaller ports proved a serious obstacle to their development.

An additional source of pressure on the railways was the decrease in coasting traffic. The cost of insurance against war risks bore more heavily on the owners of coasters than on any other branch of the shipping industry. Even a cargo rate of 1 per cent. and a premium on hulls of 1½ per cent. for three months, rendered it difficult for them to compete successfully with railway transport, and their activities were further impeded by requisitioning, and by the congestion of the large ports whose imports they were accustomed to distribute. In spite of these disadvantages the West Coast services continued to run with fair regularity, but those on the East Coast were severely handicapped by the mine-fields and navigational restrictions in the North Sea, and the carriage of coal from the Tyne to London was affected by the general shortage of tramp tonnage. Altogether the arrivals and departures of coasting tonnage decreased by 14 per cent. during the months of November, December, and January, and if the intercourse between Great Britain and Ireland be excluded, the decrease shown is still greater.

This decrease in coasting traffic was a serious obstacle to the distribution of cargoes landed at the larger ports and limited the amount of relief which could be given by the smaller harbours. Moreover, the diversion of the coal supply of London to the railways added to the congestion of the railways themselves and led to a very considerable advance in the price of coal. In the hope of relieving the strain, over thirty interned German and Austrian steamers were placed in the hands of Messrs. Everett & Newbiggin, of Newcastle, to be managed for Government account in the coasting trade, especially in the carriage of coal to London, and the first four of these were ready to commence running by the middle of January. The others were not expected to be ready for some weeks, as all required docking before use could be made of them.

CAUSES OF PORT CONGESTION

The greatest difficulty at the ports, however, was the supply of labour. Large numbers of dockers had enlisted —5,000 to 7,000 at Liverpool, 1,000 at Manchester, 1,000 to 1,200 at Glasgow—and these were, in most cases, the pick of the men employed. At most ports there was an actual shortage of dock labour, and at many the labour available was of an unsatisfactory character. Even where the men were willing and time-keeping regular, the withdrawal of the strongest and most skilful workers reduced the average of efficiency, and in some ports the position was complicated by the existence of an unsatisfactory spirit among the men employed. Dock labour is mostly of a casual character, and in many cases men who now found themselves able to earn in three or four days sufficient for their requirements failed to put in a full week's work in spite of the efforts of the Trade Union leaders.

While the attitude of the men may fairly be traced, in large measure, to the unsatisfactory conditions of their normal employment, the effect of this attitude upon the loading and discharge of ships at Liverpool, London and the Clyde, was very bad. At the same time, it must be recognised that even where labour was contented and willing, as at Dundee and the Tyne, very serious delays occurred, due to sheer insufficiency of numbers to perform the work required.

This shortage of labour, which extended beyond the actual dockers to carters and others engaged in the work of distribution, presented a problem by no means easy to solve, for while the demand for labour, as between port and port, varied from time to time in accordance with the redirection of traffic, there were many difficulties in the way of transferring large bodies of workers from one port to another in order to meet the fluctuations of demand. It was not until a later period of the war that any effectual remedy was found, and in January 1915 the situation was growing steadily worse and worse.

The conditions were, naturally, most unsatisfactory at London and the West Coast ports. London was specially affected by the diversion of traffic from East Coast and South Coast ports and from the Continent, by the requisitioning of sheds and warehouses, and by the necessity of finding berths for transports. Early in January no less than forty-three ships were waiting at Gravesend for dock accommodation to become vacant; and though this number had been reduced to eleven at the end of the month, as the result of strenuous efforts by the Port Authority, the port was still greatly congested. Of the four great ports on the West Coast capable of dealing with general trade, Manchester alone was just able to cope with immediate requirements, though it possessed no margin for expansion. Liverpool was short of space, trucks, and labour, and on one day forty-five vessels were awaiting berths. The transit sheds were in use as warehouses, the quays were encumbered with tobacco, owing to the importers' decision to hold a two years' supply, and delays of three weeks in the discharge of cargoes were common. Bristol was seriously hampered by shortage of labour and by military demands upon the accommodation at Avonmouth, and was unable to cope satisfactorily either with the import or export trade. Glasgow was short of tugs, lighters, and cartage, and was peculiarly affected by labour troubles. The South Wales coal ports, Swansea, Cardiff, Newport, and Barry, were just holding their own, but had only limited facilities for dealing with general trade. Most of the smaller West Coast ports were incapable of affording any great relief, owing to their limited equipment and inability to receive large vessels. On the East Coast conditions were naturally better, as the reduction in the Continental trade and in the export of coal had diminished the demands on their resources. It was doubtful, however, whether they would be able to cope satisfactorily with any increase of traffic.

Taking the United Kingdom, France, and Italy together, it was estimated by a leading shipowner that at the end of January not less than 1,500,000 tons of shipping were held up by the congestion of the ports.[1] There can be no question that this delay in discharge and loading, which reduced the yearly carrying power of the ships concerned by perhaps 20 per cent., was one of the main factors, perhaps the chief factor, in producing shortage of tonnage and forcing up freights. It was, moreover, one which tended continually to increase in importance, and towards the end of January a strong deputation of shipowners who waited on the President of the Board of Trade at his request,

---

[1] Mr Philip Runciman, in *Morning Post*, 30 January, 1915.

made urgent representations as to the necessity of taking steps to ameliorate the position.[1]

We have seen, therefore, that the increase in freights was due to the operation of a large number of causes, only a very few of which—and those not the most important—were connected with hostile operations against seaborne trade. The Navy could, and did, keep the sea routes clear for shipping, but it could not secure the course of trade against the operation of industrial, commercial, and financial reactions of the great upheaval. It enabled the necessities of life and the raw materials of industry to be introduced in scarcely diminished volume, but the cost of transport was ruled, as always, by the law of supply and demand and by working conditions.

The cost of transport, however, was only one factor, and by no means the most important, in producing the increased cost of commodities. As a general rule, the price of imported goods is regulated mainly by the ratio of supply to demand, and is but little affected by fluctuations in freight rates, except when those rates become so high as to discourage importation and thus restrict the supply.[2] During the six months which succeeded the outbreak of war, the course of trade, as we have seen, was violently disturbed. Primary sources of supply for many products were closed, supplies were restricted, and prices rose to an abnormal level at a time when the freight markets were still easy. The demand for other products slackened, owing to the falling off of the export trade, with the result of a slump in prices which persisted even after the great advance in freights. There was yet a third class, in respect of which imports into the United Kingdom were maintained at, or very near, the level of 1913, but prices nevertheless showed a marked advance due, in the first place, to a shortage in the total world supply, and in the second place, to the elimination of competition by a narrowing of the range from which supplies were drawn.

Of this third class, the most notable example was wheat.

---

[1] *Times*, 28 January, 1915. The remedies proposed by the shipowners will be discussed in Vol. II, in connection with the steps actually taken at a later date.

[2] Thus, in the twelve months ended July 31st, 1914, the average rates of freight on wheat fell 1*s*. 4*d*. per quarter as compared with the year 1912–13, but the price fell only 6*d*. per quarter.

The imports of wheat and flour during the first six months of the war actually exceeded those for the corresponding period 1913–14, and the home crop was well above the average, yet the *Gazette* average price of British wheat at the end of January, 1915, was 51*s*. 6*d*. per quarter as compared with 34*s*. 2*d*. on August 1st, or 30*s*. 11*d*. at the end of January 1913, and the price of foreign wheat showed a still greater advance.[1]

It is to be noted, however, that the tendency to price inflation was strongly marked before the rise in freights became serious, and that the advance in freights was, by itself, quite insufficient to account for the increase in price. Something must be allowed for the cost of war risks insurance and the collapse of the exchanges, but it is evident that the full explanation of the advance cannot be given without entering into the question of supply and demand.

When the war broke out, Australia and Argentina had already shipped the greater portion of their surplus, and owing to the comparative failure of the last Indian crop, it was not anticipated that large supplies would be forthcoming from Karachi until the new harvest. The Russian crop was, however, about to be reaped, and prospects in North America were fairly good. The total requirements of importing countries for the season 1914-15 were estimated on August 15th at 81,500,000 quarters, and the available surpluses at 82,000,000, showing a narrow margin of 500,000 quarters of supply over demand.[2] But in this estimate, Russia, Roumania, and Australia accounted between them for 25,500,000 quarters, and it soon became clear that very little of this would be forthcoming. The closing of the Dardanelles blocked the Russian and Roumanian exports, and the Australian crop failed so completely that all idea of export had finally to be abandoned. Meanwhile the Argentine Government prohibited further exports of the 1913–14 crop, and Indian shipments for the six months August–January showed a decrease of some 20 per cent. Although the American and Canadian harvest exceeded expectations, and Canada was able to liberate considerable stocks of the old crop, there was a real and serious shortage in available supplies, particularly in those available for immediate shipment. More-

[1] See Appendix, Table XIV.
[2] *Statist*, 1 August, 1914,

over, these supplies had to be sought almost entirely in a single direction.[1]

It must be remembered that France, Italy, and Greece, who were large buyers from Russia and Roumania, were now also compelled to turn almost exclusively to North America for their supplies, and the French requirements were greatly increased owing to the havoc wrought by the German invasion. Bad harvests in the Scandinavian countries added to the keenness of competition, and the ample supplies secured for Great Britain were only obtained at a heavy cost.

While allowing full weight to the influence exerted by increased freights, it is clear that the predominant factor in the advance in wheat prices was the keenness of competition for the restricted supplies available, and this was true also of other cereals. The price of oats was forced up from 19s. 10d. in July to 27s. 6d. in January, owing to the restriction of supplies, but barley, owing to the greater relative importance of the home production, rose only from 24s. 2d. to 30s. 5d. The position with regard to maize was peculiar. When once the Argentine harvest began to move freely, it was, by itself, almost capable of supplying British requirements; but neutral competition was keen, owing to the locking up of some ten million quarters in the Black Sea; and meanwhile, freights from the Plate rose to an unprecedented extent. For the months of November, December, and January they averaged 27s. 11d., 38s., and 61s. 4d. respectively, as compared with 9s. 10d., 10s. 10d., and 10s. 1d. in the same months of 1913–14. It was during these three months that the heaviest shipments were made, yet the increase in the c.i.f. import values (cost, insurance, and freight) for

[1]

	Imports of Wheat into the United Kingdom (in millions of cwts.). Six months ended January.		
	1912–13	1913–14	1914–15
U.S. and Canada	24·8	30·6	44·6
Black Sea and Germany	5·8	4·4	·5
India	16·0	9·1	7·7
Argentina, Australia and Chile	12·1	5·4	2·0
Other countries	·3	·4	·1
Total	59·0	49·9	54·9

the six months, was only 16 per cent. The explanation is that maize is not an essential food, but a substitute feeding-stuff subject to the competition of the barley, oats and pulse of the temperate zone, and is thus unable to bear an unlimited advance in price without restricting the demand.

With regard to other imported foodstuffs, the chief increases were in the price of sugar, meat, and eggs. Sugar, it is true, had now to be brought from much greater distances, and the cost of transport was thus increased, but the dominant factor was the shutting out of Continental beet and the very heavy purchases made by the Sugar Commission in cane-producing countries during the early months of the war, with the object of creating reserve stocks. The rise in meat freights amounted, at the most, to $\frac{1}{2}d.$ a pound, and both the New Zealand lines and one, at least, of the chief Plate services, were bound by existing long-term contracts which forbade any advance on the rates ruling before the war. On the other hand, the supply, as we have seen, was restricted by various causes, and abnormal consumption on the part of the troops further diminished the quantity available for domestic purposes in Great Britain. The consequence was a considerable increase in both the wholesale and retail price of imported meat, though this was not as yet reflected by any great advance in the price of home-grown beef and mutton. The advance in eggs was, of course, mainly due to the shutting off of the Russian supplies. On the other hand, bacon, butter, margarine, and cheese showed little more than the usual seasonal increase until quite the end of the six months, thanks to the ample supplies brought by Dutch and Scandinavian vessels, and milk was, as yet, hardly affected by the increased cost of imported feeding stuffs.

In the case of raw materials and partially manufactured articles, the increases were generally much smaller, owing to the slackening of demand by reason of reduced production and the withdrawal of Continental competition. In many cases an actual decrease in price was recorded, notably in that of cotton, the price of which, even in January, stood far below that for January 1914, though the freight was nearly double. Copper also, in spite of the military demand, sank in price, as the cessation of direct trade between America and Germany threw large quantities on to the market. Tin, rubber, jute, and silk were all cheaper on January 30th than on the corresponding date in the two previous years, and the price of wool varied from a little below to a little above the normal level, according to the suitability of the various descriptions for Army purposes.

It is apparent, therefore, that the rise in freights, while it undoubtedly aggravated the tendency to price inflation, was by no means the most important factor, even in the case of import values, and retail prices were affected by still further complications introduced by war conditions and war finance, which it is not necessary to discuss here. But the rise in freights itself has been shown to have arisen mainly from other causes than the operations of the enemy commerce destroyers, and broadly speaking, the vicissitudes of the war at sea may be set aside as having no appreciable influence on the cost of living.

Thus, up to this point, the German campaign against seaborne trade had been everywhere frustrated. It had neither prevented the arrival of ample supplies of all essential commodities; nor shaken the fabric of British credit; nor forced up prices to a level involving any real hardship. One solid success had been achieved in the arrival of the GOEBEN at Constantinople, which assisted to force Turkey into the war and thus to cut off the grain shipments from Black Sea ports. Apart from this, the successes achieved by the German cruisers were at most of a local and temporary character, and were negligible in comparison with the volume of British trade. As a tactical achievement Coronel might well be balanced against the Falklands and the escape of the GOEBEN against the action off Heligoland; but it is not by the computation of losses or the issue of minor actions that the success or failure of naval warfare can be measured. By confining the German fleet to its own home waters and forcing the enemy back upon the weak alternative of sporadic raiding, the British Navy had achieved a silent victory whose fruits were to be seen in the steady stream of shipping, laden with munitions, food, and raw materials, which poured into British ports.

For the cruiser warfare which had proved so limited in its achievements, there was now about to be substituted a new and more deadly form of attack, directed not against the minor arteries of British commerce, but against its very heart, in the waters immediately surrounding the British Isles themselves. Henceforth it will not be necessary to study in detail the local effects of individual captures on particular routes; the course of the submarine campaign is more broadly marked by the steady diminution of the tonnage available for any voyage.

There were, indeed, losses to be suffered, both in ships and cargoes, compared with which those inflicted by the original raiders were trifling; yet now that the initial dislocation had been overcome and trade had settled down into its new channels, even these losses proved insufficient to stay its course. It was this which was the great achievement of the first phase of the war. The prompt and well-designed dispositions made by the Admiralty secured seaborne trade from the outset against the more drastic forms of surface attack, such as blockade or the concerted operations of powerful raiding squadrons. The instant adoption of the State Insurance Scheme preserved it from the effects of a collapse of credit. Thus relieved of their gravest apprehensions, British merchants, financiers, and shipowners adapted themselves readily to the exigencies of a state of war, and re-established with a minimum of delay the machinery of a wide-world commerce. Still greater exertions, a sterner fortitude, and a vast development of naval and economic organisation were to be called for during the course of the long struggle, but though much remained to be done, it was, in no small measure, the success with which British trade was brought through the first few months of war which enabled it at a later period to surmount a still more dangerous crisis.

APPENDIX

TABLE I. LOSSES OF BRITISH SHIPPING TO 31 JANUARY, 1915.
,, II. LOSSES OF FRENCH SHIPPING TO 31 JANUARY, 1915.
,, III. LOSSES OF RUSSIAN SHIPPING TO 31 JANUARY, 1915.
,, IV. LOSSES OF GERMAN SHIPPING TO 31 JANUARY, 1915.
,, V. LOSSES OF AUSTRIAN SHIPPING TO 31 JANUARY, 1915.
,, VI. TOTAL LOSSES OF GERMAN AND AUSTRIAN SHIPPING TO 31 JANUARY, 1915.
,, VII. GERMAN AND AUSTRIAN SHIPPING BLOCKADED OR HELD UP ABROAD.
,, VIII. NEUTRAL SHIPPING SUNK BY MINES TO 31 JANUARY, 1915.
,, IX. BRITISH LOSSES IN SHIPS AND CARGOES, SHOWN AS PERCENTAGE OF VALUES.
,, X. ENTRANCES AND CLEARANCES WITH CARGOES OF SHIPS IN FOREIGN TRADE AT PORTS OF THE UNITED KINGDOM.
,, XI. BRITISH IMPORTS AND EXPORTS-VALUES.
,, XII. PERCENTAGE INCREASE OR DECREASE IN ESTIMATED WEIGHT OF IMPORTS.
,, XIII. AVERAGE GRAIN FREIGHTS PER TON.
,, XIV. WHEAT PRICES, MONTHLY AVERAGE IN UNITED KINGDOM.
,, XV. WHEAT PRICES, MONTHLY AVERAGE IN EXPORTING COUNTRIES.
,, XVI. WEIGHTS AND AVERAGE IMPORT VALUES OF TYPICAL IMPORTS.

Note on Tables I.—VIII.—The figures in these tables are based on a collation of statistics prepared by Lloyd's with Admiralty Records. Steamers under 100 tons gross and Sailing Vessels under 100 tons net are excluded. Tonnages checked with *Lloyd's Register.*

Note on Tables X.—XVI.—A full statistical record of the effects of the war on Seaborne Trade would necessarily be very lengthy and has not been attempted here, especially as the figures are already available in the Board of Trade Returns and elsewhere. The tables here given have been constructed solely for the purpose of illustrating points specifically raised in the text, especially in the final chapter.

TABLE I

Losses of British Shipping to 31 January, 1915 [1]

(a) *Steamers*

Sunk or captured by:	s.s.	tons gross.	s.s.	tons gross.
KARLSRUHE	16	72,805		
EMDEN	16	70,360 [2]		
KRONPRINZ WILHELM	6	30,728		
DRESDEN	3	11,266		
KAISER WILHELM DER GROSSE	2	10,458		
LEIPZIG	2	10,305		
KÖNIGSBERG	1	6,601		
PRINZ EITEL FRIEDRICH	1	5,067		
			47	217,590
Sunk by Submarines			10	20,237
Sunk by Mines			14	37,739
			71	275,566
Steam trawlers Sunk or Captured by torpedo boats, etc.	26	4,578 [3]		
Sunk by Mines	10	1,958		
			36	6,536
Total Sunk or Captured.			107	282,102
Detained:				
In German ports	73	169,839		
In Turkish ports	9	12,496		
			82	182,335
Total, Sunk, Captured, or Detained			189	464,437

In addition 3 steamers were damaged by mines, 5 steamers and 3 steam trawlers damaged by bombardment.

(b) *Sailing Vessels*

	s.v.	tons net.	s.v.	tons net.
Sunk or Captured by Cruisers	3	3,587		
Captured by torpedo-boat	1	142		
Total Sunk or Captured			4	3,729
Detained in German ports			3	1,710
Total Sunk, Captured, or Detained			7	5,439

[1] Exclusive of vessels released, recaptured, or escaped.
[2] Includes dredger *Ponrabbel*.
[3] Includes 1 sunk by KAISER WILHELM DER GROSSE.

APPENDIX

TABLE II
LOSSES OF FRENCH SHIPPING TO 31 JANUARY, 1915

	s.s.	tons gross.	s.v.	tons net.
Sunk or Captured by Cruisers	1	4,803	6	12,170
Detained in German and Turkish ports	11	5,285		
	12	10,088	6	12,170

TABLE III
LOSSES OF RUSSIAN SHIPPING TO 31 JANUARY, 1915

	s.s.	tons gross.	s.v.	tons net.
Sunk or Captured by Cruisers on Trade Routes	1	3,522	1	1,231
Sunk or Captured in North Sea and Baltic	3	2,580	5	2,271
Sunk or Captured in Black Sea	3	4,673		
Sunk by Mines in Black Sea	3	2,981		
Detained in German or Turkish ports	3	6,720	13	3,309
	13	20,476	19	6,811

TABLE IV
LOSSES OF GERMAN SHIPPING TO 31 JANUARY, 1915

(a) *Steamers*

	s.s.	tons gross.	s.s.	tons gross.
Sunk or Captured by British at Sea or in German Colonial Ports	76	246,358[1]		
Sunk or Captured by Allies	17	39,863		
Seized in British or Allied ports and condemned	21	103,577[2]		
Steam trawlers Sunk or Captured	6	883		
Total Sunk or Captured			120	390,681
Detained in British or Allied Ports			167	404,684[3]
Total Sunk, Captured, or Detained			287	795,365

(b) *Sailing Vessels*

	s.v.	tons net.	s.v.	tons net.
Captured by British	27	37,292		
Captured by Allies	4	4,220		
Total Captured			31	41,512
Detained in British or Allied ports			33	29,656
Total Sunk, Captured, or Detained			64	71,168

[1] Includes 4 disabled but not yet removed.
[2] Includes 12 forced out of Egyptian ports.
[3] Includes 3 steam trawlers.

TABLE V

LOSSES OF AUSTRIAN SHIPPING TO 31 JANUARY, 1915

	s.s.	tons gross.	s.s.	tons gross.
Sunk or Captured by British	3	9,002		
Sunk or Captured by Allies	3	9,829		
Seized in Egyptian ports and condemned	2	6,189		
Sunk by Mines	3	3,468		
Total Sunk or Captured			11	28,488
Detained in British or Allied ports			21	83,131
Total Sunk, Captured, or Detained			32	111,619

TABLE VI

TOTAL LOSSES OF GERMAN AND AUSTRIAN SHIPPING TO 31 JANUARY, 1915

	s.s.	tons gross.	s.s.	tons gross.
German Steamers Sunk or Captured	120	390,681		
Austrian Steamers Sunk or Captured	11	28,488		
			131	419,169
German Steamers Detained	167	404,684		
Austrian Steamers Detained	21	83,131		
			188	487,815
Total Enemy Steamers Sunk, Captured, or Detained			319	906,984
German Sailing Vessels Sunk, Captured, or Detained (tons net)			64	71,168
Total Enemy Losses			383	978,152

TABLE VII

GERMAN AND AUSTRIAN SHIPPING BLOCKADED OR HELD UP ABROAD

	s.s.	tons gross.	s.v.	tons net.
German Shipping blockaded in Belgian ports	33	102,923	2	1,982
Austrian Shipping blockaded in Belgian ports	2	5,873		
German Shipping blockaded in Turkish ports	18	69,723		
Austrian Shipping blockaded in Turkish ports	10	36,982		
German Shipping sheltering in Neutral ports [1]	572	2,307,492	98	196,648
Austrian Shipping sheltering in Neutral ports	89	355,540		
	724	2,878,533	100	198,630

[1] Exclusive of ships transferred to Neutral Flags.

APPENDIX

TABLE VIII
NEUTRAL SHIPPING SUNK BY MINES TO 31 JANUARY, 1915

	s.s.	tons gross.
Norwegian	10	13,751
Swedish	10	12,900
Danish	7	11,909
Dutch	4	7,770
Italian	1	1,703
Persian	1	758
Total	33	48,791

One Danish and one Roumanian sailing vessel were also sunk, in addition to a few fishing craft.

TABLE IX
BRITISH LOSSES IN SHIPS AND CARGOES SHOWN AS PERCENTAGES

(a) *Ships*

Number of Ships entered in War Risk Associations . . 4421
Values entered £153,469,068

Month.	Lost.		Percentage on Total.	
	Number.	Value.	Numbers entered.	Values entered.
		£		
August, 1914	8	426,771	·18	·28
September	23	857,595	·52	·56
October	18	956,806	·40	·62
November	6	85,263	·14	·06
December	7	137,797	·16	·09
January, 1915	8	268,328	·18	·17
Total—Six months	70	2,732,560	1·58	1·78
Average per month	11·7	455,426	·26	·30

(b) *Cargoes*

Month.	Estimated value of Cargoes carried in British ships.	Estimated value of Cargoes lost in British Ships.	Percentage of loss on Values carried.
	£	£	
August, 1914	88,000,000	1,015,100	1·15
September	95,000,000	903,535	·95
October	108,000,000	1,768,220	1·64
November	108,000,000	83,550	·08
December	124,000,000	53,190	·04
January, 1915	128,000,000	459,664	·36
Total—Six months	651,000,000	4,283,259	·66
Average per month	108,500,000	713,876	·96

This table is taken from an estimate prepared by the Liverpool and London War Risks Insurance Association. It excludes two or three small vessels not entered in the Associations, but includes two steamers seized by the Turks and one damaged by bombardment in the Black Sea.

TABLE X

ENTRANCES AND CLEARANCES WITH CARGOES OF SHIPS IN FOREIGN TRADE AT PORTS OF THE UNITED KINGDOM

(a) *Entrances*

	British. 1,000 tons net.	Foreign. 1,000 tons net.	Total. 1,000 tons net.	Percentage decrease as compared with same month of the previous year.		
				British.	Foreign.	Total.
August, 1914	2,429	800	3,229	13·3	44·6	23·9
September	1,828	905	2,733	39·6	43·2	40·8
October	2,046	1,126	3,172	30·8	26·3	29·3
November	2,002	1,007	3,009	22·6	24·9	23·6
December	2,156	832	2,988	23·1	41·2	29·1
January, 1915	1,828	737	2,565	24·3	41·4	30·2
Total	12,289	5,407	17,696	25·9	37·0	29·7

(b) *Tons of Imports Carried per 100 tons net of Shipping*

	Tons.	Increase or Decrease as compared with same month of the previous year.
August, 1914	115	− 9
September	145	+ 31
October	152	+ 23
November	140	+ 22
December	129	+ 20
January, 1915	145	+ 32

(c) *Clearances*

	British. 1,000 tons net.	Foreign. 1,000 tons net.	Total. 1,000 tons net.	Percentage of decrease as compared with same month of the previous year.		
				British.	Foreign.	Total.
August, 1914	1,424	1,041	2,465	58·9	54·5	56·9
September	1,917	1,717	3,634	45·6	24·4	37·3
October	2,121	1,707	3,828	43·3	31·6	38·6
November	1,658	1,459	3,117	49·9	36·6	44·5
December	1,842	1,600	3,442	43·9	30·6	38·4
January, 1915	1,848	1,571	3,419	44·2	29·5	38·3
Total	10,810	9,095	19,905	47·5	34·5	42·3

APPENDIX

TABLE XI
IMPORTS AND EXPORTS FROM THE UNITED KINGDOM DURING THE SIX MONTHS ENDING 31 JANUARY, 1915, SHOWING PERCENTAGE OF DECREASE IN VALUES AS COMPARED WITH THE SAME MONTHS OF THE PREVIOUS YEAR.

—	Imports.	Percentage Decrease.	Exports including Re-Exports.	Percentage Decrease.
	£1,000		£1,000	
August, 1914	42,343	24·4	28,631	45·2
September	45,007	26·6	31,948	35·2
October	51,379	28·4	35,782	36·3
November	55,518	18·9	30,245	42·7
December	67,317	5·3	32,149	39·4
January, 1915	67,246	1·1	35,143	38·8
Total	328,810	17·1	193,898	39·6

TABLE XII
PERCENTAGE INCREASE OR DECREASE IN ESTIMATED WEIGHT OF IMPORTS IN EACH MONTH FROM AUGUST 1914 TO JULY 1915 INCLUSIVE, AS COMPARED WITH SAME MONTH IN THE PREVIOUS YEAR

—	Food, Drink, and Tobacco.	Raw Materials and Articles mainly unmanufactured.	Articles wholly or mainly manufactured and miscellaneous.	Total Imports.
August	− 9·7	− 33·0	− 61·4	− 29·7
September	− 10·0	− 28·5	− 51·4	− 25·0
October	+ 13·8	− 27·3	− 52·9	− 16·3
November	+ 6·7	− 11·8	− 46·2	− 9·4
December	+ 10·8	− 26·7	− 47·2	− 16·5
January	+ 17·8	− 21·6	− 38·1	− 10·3

TABLE XIII
AVERAGE GRAIN FREIGHTS PER TON FROM NORTH AMERICA, INDIA, AND ARGENTINA

—	United States and Canada.			India.			Argentina.		
To Liverpool from	New York.			Karachi.			River Plate Down River.		
	1912	1913	1914	1912	1913	1914	1912	1913	1914
	s. d.	s. d.	s. d.	s. d.	s. d.	s. d.	s. d.	s. d.	s. d.
August	9 8	7 11	—	20 9	18 7	—	20 8	17 4	—
September	15 0	7 7	10 1	22 0	18 2	17 4	27 5	14 3	12 0
October	16 2	8 8	12 8	23 4	16 1	17 3	26 9	11 0	16 10
November	16 9	8 0	18 2	21 6	—	16 7	23 1	9 10	27 11
December	14 8	6 11	24 8	18 5	14 8	—	19 4	10 10	38 0
January	14 10	7 2	29 10	18 9	13 9	35 0	22 5	10 1	61 4

TABLE XIV

WHEAT PRICES—MONTHLY AVERAGE IN THE UNITED KINGDOM

	(1) British Gazette. Averages (last Saturday in month). Per qr. 480 lbs.		(2) No. 2 North Manitoba Mid-monthly prices at Liverpool. Per qr. 480 lbs.		(3) North Atlantic. Grain Freights. First Saturday in month. Per qr. 480 lbs.		(4) North Atlantic. Grain Freights. Monthly Average. Per ton.	
	1913-14	1914-15	1913-14	1914-15	1913-14	1914-15	1913-14	1914-15
	s. d.	s. d.	s. d.	s. d.	s. d.	s. d.	s. d.	s. d.
July	33 6	34 1	36 8	35 1	2 7½	2 1½	7 3	8 2
August	33 7	38 9	36 1	44 5	2 9	2 6	7 11	no quotation after first week
September	31 7	38 3	36 6	47 5	3 0	1 9	7 7	10 1
October	30 7	37 2	35 3	43 1	2 6	2 3	8 8	12 8
November	30 4	41 0	33 6	47 5	2 0	4 6	8 0	18 2
December	31 2	42 7	34 3	50 3	1 10½	5 0	6 11	24 8
January	30 11	51 6	34 10	55 7	1 9	7 6	7 2	29 10

(1) From *Statist*.
(2) From *Statistical Tables Relating to Wheat*, Department of Statistics, Calcutta.
(3) Messrs. Farrar, Groves & Co.'s quotations, from *Statist*.
(4) Liverpool Shipowners' Report, extracted from *Corn Trade News*.

TABLE XV

WHEAT PRICES—MONTHLY AVERAGE IN EXPORTING COUNTRIES

	United States.				Canada.		India.	
	New York. Red. Per bushel 60 lbs.		Chicago. No. 2 Hard Winter. Per qr. 480 lbs.		Winnipeg. No. 2 Northern. Per qr. 480 lbs.		Karachi. White. Per qr. 492 lbs.	
	1913-14	1914-15	1913-14	1914-15	1913-14	1914-15	1913-14	1914-15
	cents.	cents.	s. d.	s. d.	s. d.	s. d.	s. d.	s. d.
July	95¾	95¼	29 1	26 11	30 10	34 2	30 3	30 0
August	95¼	98⅛	29 1	—	30 11	35 6	28 11	31 6
September	98	123	29 3	36 10	28 9	36 10	29 0	36 3
October	96¼	119¼	27 3	36 10	25 5	35 3	29 0	35 6
November	98	124¼	28 11	37 10	26 8	37 8	30 0	41 0
December	101	nom.	29 7	40 2	27 4	38 6	30 0	41 0
January	102	153	29 11	47 8	28 0	45 2	30 3	42 6

N.B.—First column from *Statist*; other three columns from *Statistical Tables Relating to Wheat*.

TABLE XVI

WEIGHTS AND AVERAGE IMPORT VALUES OF TYPICAL IMPORTS

Articles.	Unit.	Weight of Imports.		Average Import Values.			
		6 months ending 31 Jan. 1914.	6 months ending 31 Jan. 1915.	6 months ending 31 Jan. 1914.		6 months ending 31 Jan. 1915.	
		000	000	*s.*	*d.*	*s.*	*d.*
Wheat	cwt.	49,915	54,887	8	0	9	7
Wheatmeal and Flour	,,	6,567	5,459	10	8	12	6
Barley	,,	14,230	9,762	6	10	7	6
Oats	,,	7,282	4,702	6	0	8	7
Maize	,,	26,860	29,548	5	7	6	6
Beef, Chilled	,,	2,812	1,283	38	1	54	0
,, Frozen	,,	1,733	2,247	33	3	51	10
Mutton, Frozen	,,	2,202	1,773	39	3	48	7
Bacon	,,	2,482	2,553	72	3	75	7
Butter	,,	1,994	1,727	118	10	131	10
Cheese	,,	1,248	1,323	62	6	69	2
Eggs, estimated	,,	1,126	691	96	6	119	10
Fish, Fresh	,,	580	410	16	6	17	6
Lard	,,	1,000	869	55	10	54	11
Margarine	,,	784	796	51	10	53	4
Sugar, Refined and Candy	,,	9,797	8,057	13	2	24	7
Sugar, Unrefined	,,	9,514	13,110	10	0	20	4
Tea	,,	2,233	2,352	86	4	87	0
Iron Ore	ton	3,254	2,454	18	10	18	1
Copper Ore	,,	43	26	224	5	250	1
Tin Ore	,,	17	13	1,910	9	1,725	11
Timber, Hewn	load	449	286	90	4	101	0
,, Sawn, etc.	,,	3,771	2,390	63	1	68	5
Cotton	cental	13,850	8,655	66	4	45	10
Wool	lb.	296,040	269,904	0	10	0	11
Alpaca	,,	2,705	1,805	0	11	1	1
Flax	ton	31	18	923	8	1,368	10
Hemp	,,	70	54	567	10	598	1
Silk	lb.	573	730	12	10	12	5
Tallow	cwt.	907	699	33	8	31	10
Rubber	cental	782	782	183	2	209	3
Wood Pulp, Chemical Dry	ton	228	252	164	6	175	8
Wood Pulp, Mechanical Wet	,,	294	276	44	10	48	2
Steel Blooms, etc.	ton	493	60	97	4	113	9
Copper	,,	75	101	1,253	0	1,066	5
Lead	,,	100	115	382	11	377	7
Tin	,,	23	18	3,636	4	2,873	9

ND# INDEX I

SHIPS AND SQUADRONS

Abbreviations: A.M.C., Armed Merchant Cruiser; B., Battleship; B.Cr., Battle Cruiser; Cr., Cruiser; Gbt., Gunboat; L.Cr., Light Cruiser; Sl., Sloop; S/m., Submarine; Sq., Squadron; S.V., Sailing Vessel; T.-b.-d., Destroyer; Austr.Fl., Australian Fleet; E.I.Sq., East Indies Squadron; N.Z.Div., New Zealand Division.

A., Austrian; Br., British; D., Dutch; Dan., Danish; Fr., French; Ger., German; Gr., Greek; It., Italian; Nor., Norwegian; Sp., Spanish; Sw., Swedish; T., Turkish; U.S., American.

Merchant ships marked with an asterisk (*) acted or were intended to act as tenders or supply ships to German cruisers. Enemy merchantmen marked with a dagger (†) were suspected of being armed or fitted to receive armament.

Where Admirals' or Captains' names are given, they will be found in Index II.

Australian Fleet (Ad. Patey), 51, 122-3, 127, 151, 218
Cape Sq. (Ad. King-Hall), 51, 123
China Sq. (Ad. Jerram), 51, 122, 127, 141, 208, 218
Dover Patrol, 59, 73, 299
Downs Boarding Flotilla, 73, 299
East Indies Sq. (Ad. Peirse), 51, 122; absorbed by escort duty, 140, 204
Gibraltar Flotilla, 61.
Grand Fleet (Ad. Jellicoe), the pivot of trade defence, 49; 51, 69, 73, 77, 108, 181
High Seas Fleet, German, inactivity of, 60, 87, 356
Mediterranean Fleet (Ad. Milne), 51, 61-3
New Zealand Division (Capt. Marshall), 51, 123
Pacific Squadron, German, menace of, 123-4, 127, 132-3, 141, 143, 144; concentration of, 146-7, 150, 233, 237, 313; movements of, 148, 150-1, 224-5, 237; bombards Papieté, 224-5; located, 208, 217, 225, 234, 276; preparations to meet, 234, 238, 317; on Chilian coast, 316, 318-23, 338, 340-2, 347-50; combination against, 324; destruction of, 349-50; tenders and coal supply of, 133, 136, 146-7, 314-6, 319, 323, 340-2, 347-8; effect of its operations on trade, 148-9, 225, 232-3, 321-3, 339-40, 342-7, 350, 354, 394; mentioned, 180, 182, 267, 300, 312, 370, 396
7th Battle Sq. (Ad. Bethell), 240
4th Cr.Sq. (Ad. Cradock), 51, 104
5th Cr.Sq. (Ad. Stoddart), 58, 75-7, 81, 84, 108, 154, 176, 241
9th Cr.Sq. (Ad. de Robeck), 58, 75, 83-4, 108, 154, 176, 241
10th Cr.Sq. (Ad. de Chair), 57, 72-3
11th Cr.Sq. (Ad. Hornby), 57, 74, 108
12th Cr.Sq. (Ad. Weymss), 57-8, 73, 74 108, 240

Abessinia, Ger., 232-4
Adjutant, Ger., captured, 276
Adolf, Ger., captured, 61
Alcantara, Br., 345
Alexandria, Ger., See "*Sacramento*"
Alfa, A., 60, 65 n
Alfred Hage, Dan., 256 n, 359 n 4
Alfred Nobel, Nor., 401
ALGERINE, Br.Sl., 162
Altair, Ger., captured, 129

Amasis, Ger., 231–3, 314, 316, 340, 375
Amazon, Br., 255
†*Amerika*, Ger., 32, 105, 352 n 2
Amiral Ganteaume, Fr., torpedoed, 285
AMPHION, Br.L.Cr., sunk, 89–90
Anne de Bretagne, Fr.S.V., sunk, 345, 372
Annie Johnson, Sw., 264
*Anubis, Ger., 232–3, 314, 316, 318
Ardmount, Br., mined, 281
ARGONAUT, Br.Cr. (9th Cr.Sq.), 241, 373
ARIADNE, Ger.L.Cr., 352 n 1
Arlanza, Br., captured and released, 79–81
*Arucas, Ger., 81–2
Ascaro, It., 228, 254–5, 262
ASKOLD, Russ.Cr., 122, 141, 279, 327, 355
ASTRÆA, Br.L.Cr. (Cape.Sq.), 123, 126, 130
*Asuncion, Ger., 248–9, 252–4, 257–8, 260–1, 264–5, 317–8, 322, 329
AUDACIOUS, Br.B., 285 n
AUSTRALIA, Br.B.Cr. (Austr.Fl.), 123, 146–8, 149, 324, 375
Australia, Ger., captured, 129
Ayesha, Br.S.V., sunk, 328, 328 n

*Baden, Ger., 172, 174, 222, 225, 228, 314, 316, 323, 340, 347–8; sunk, 350
*Bahia Blanca, Ger., 347 n
Bankfields, Br., sunk, 231, 233–4, 305
†*Barbarossa*, Ger., 108
Bathori, A., sunk, 83–4
Belgia, Ger., seized, 56–7
Belgrano, Ger., 75
Belle Ille, Nor., 359 n 3
Bellevue, Br., sunk, 372–3, 382
Ben Cruachan, Br., sunk, 366
Benmohr, Br., sunk, 270
BERLIN, Ger.L.Cr., 76
BERLIN, Ger.A.M.C., lays Tory I. minefield, 352
BERWICK, Br.Cr. (Capt. Clinton-Baker), in 4th Cr.Sq., 107, 110, 112
*Berwind, U.S., 223–4
*Bethania, Ger., 81–83, 223; captured, 110–1
Björgvin, Nor., 241 n
BLACK PRINCE, Br.Cr., 129, 131
†*Blücher*, Ger., 167
Bowes Castle, Br., sunk, 247; 111, 176, 222

BREMEN, Ger.L.Cr., false reports of, 173, 175; 352 n 1
Brindilla, U.S. (ex-*Washington*, Ger.), 293–4
BRESLAU, Ger.L.Cr., in Mediterranean, 61–3; under Turkish flag, 66, 85, 287, 289–91, 352 n 1; mentioned, 67, 129, 184
BRISTOL, Br.L.Cr., in West Indies, 107–8; on S. American coast, 176, 224, 238, 244, 246, 250, 317, 346, 370, 371
Buresk, Br., captured, 212–3; tender to EMDEN, 212, 268, 278, 325–6; sunk, 328

Cadiz, Sp. 260
Canada, Br. ice-breaker, 364
CANOPUS, Br.B., 176, 224, 234, 254, 320, 324, 340, 349
Cap Arcona, Ger., 75
†*Cap Polonia*, Ger., 352 n 2
CAP TRAFALGAR, Ger.A.M.C., at Buenos Aires, 167; cruise of, 174, 180, 223; sunk, 222–4; coal supply of, 223; mentioned, 175, 227, 253, 258, 262, 347 n, 351, 352 n 2
CARMANIA, Br. A.M.C. (Capt Noel Grant), on S. American coast, 176; sinks CAP TRAFALGAR, 223–4, 238, 253
CARNARVON, Br.Cr., in 5th Cr.Sq., 81, 242; on S. American Coast, 244, 267, 349, 375
Cervantes, Br., sunk, 259
*C. Ferd. Laeisz, Ger., captured, 136, 152
CHALLENGER, Br.L.Cr., 59, 243
Charcas, Br., sunk, 348
Chasehill, Br., captured 377–8; released, 379; 382
CHATHAM, Br. L.Cr., in search for KÖNIGSBERG, 217, 276, 279
CHELMER, Br.T.-b.-d., 218
CHIKUMA, Jap.L.Cr., 208, 214, 271, 279, 327
Chile, Ger.S.V., detained, 56 n 4
Chilkana, Br., sunk, 270–1
†*China*, A., 134
Choising, Ger., 328 n
Chr. Broberg, Dan., mined, 90
Chupra, Br., damaged, 209–10
City of Rangoon, Br., 206–8
City of Winchester, Br., sunk, 130–2; 192, 205
Clan Grant, Br., sunk, 269
Clan Matheson, Br., sunk, 207–8, 305
Colchester, Br., attacked by s/m, 355
Coleby, Br., sunk, 380

INDEX I

Colusa, Br., chased, 319, 321
CONDE, Fr.Cr., 104, 107, 112
Condor, Br., captured, 260-1; sunk, 264; 267
Conway Castle, Br.S.V., sunk, 379
CORMORAN, Ger.Gbt., 133
CORMORAN, Ger.A.M.C. (ex-*Riasan*, Russ.), armed, 133; joins Ad. von Spee, 136, 147, 150; detached in Pacific, 150-1, 277, 329; interned, 351; coal supply of, 150-1, 152-3, 277
Cormorant, Br., mined, 281
Cornish City, Br., sunk, 255
CORNWALL, Br.Cr., in 5th Cr.Sq., 60, 81,; on S. American coast, 176, 224, 238, 244, 253, 349
Craigforth, Br., mined, 65; seized by Turks, 291 n
*Crefeld, Ger., 244, 248-9, 250 n, 251, 253-264, 267, 273
CUMBERLAND, Br.Cr. (Capt. Fuller), in 5th Cr.Sq., 81; at Duala, 241-3
Czar Nicolai II, Ger., captured, 64

Dacia, Ger., transferred to U.S., 364
Daksa, A., captured, 76
DARTMOUTH, Br.L.Cr., in E.I.Sq., 122, 126, 131; in search for KONIGSBERG, 217, 276; 327
Dawdon, Br., mined, 281
DEFENCE, Br.Cr., 244, 346
†*Derfflinger*, Ger., 127
Derindje, Ger., sunk, 354 n 2
DESCARTES, Fr.L.Cr., 104, 107
Diamant, Ger. See "*Platuria*"
DIANA, Br.L.Cr. (12th Cr.Sq.), 59
D'IBERVILLE, Fr.Gbt., 122, 127, 278-9
Dinorah, A., captured, 59
Diplomat, Br., sunk, 205-6, 208
Dr. Kemmerich, Ger., 178 n 2
DORIS, Br.L.Cr. (11th Cr.Sq.), 59
Dovre, Nor., 208-9
DRESDEN, Ger.L.Cr. (Capt. Lüdecke), in W. Indies, 104; early movements and reports of, 106, 108, 110, 155, 167-8; captures and releases *Drumcliffe*, *Hostilius*, and *Lynton Grange*, 169-70; sinks *Hyades* and *Holmwood*, releases *Siamese Prince* and *Katherine Park*, 172-5; moves into Pacific, 179, 221-2; chases *Ortega*, 225; search for, 226; on Chilian coast, 228-9; joins Ad. von Spee, 232-5, 237; with Ad. von Spee, 314-5, 321, 338; sinks *North Wales*, 340-1; at Falklands, 350;

in hiding, 370; sinks *Conway Castle*, 379; sunk, 379; her tenders and coal supply, 172, 174, 223, 370, 379, 382; news of her captures received, 170, 173, 175; effect of her operations on trade, 170, 173, 175, 184, 192, 228, 382, 412; mentioned, 176, 180, 227, 351, 362, 369, 375, 378
Drumcliffe, Br., captured and released, 169-70
Drummuir, Br.S.V., sunk, 348, 375 n 1
*Duala, Ger., 81-3
DUKE OF EDINBURGH, Br.Cr., 129, 131, 329
DUPLEIX, Fr.Cr., 122, 127, 136, 142,
Durward, Br., sunk, 365-6
DWARF, Br.Gbt., 242

Earl of Elgin, Br., 319 n
EBER, Ger.Gbt., 180, 180 n
*Ebernburg, Ger., 227, 252, 262
EDINBURGH CASTLE, Br.A.M.C., on S. American coast, 244, 317
Ekbatana, Ger., 336 n 3
*Eleanore Woermann, Ger., 223-4, 347 n; sunk, 375
Elfrida, Br., mined, 365
*Elmshorn, Ger., 218
*Elsbeth, Ger., sunk, 134, 152
Elsinore, Br., sunk, 229-30, 233, 236, 305
Elterwater, Br., mined, 357 n 1
EMDEN, Ger.L.Cr. (Capt. von Müller), at Tsingtau, 124; captures *Riasan*, 133; joins Ad. von Spee, 133-4, 144, 147; detached, 148, 153, 204; raid in Bay of Bengal, captures *Pontoporos*, *Indus*, *Lovat*, *Diplomat*, *Trabboch*, *Clan Matheson*, releases *Kabinga*, 204-8; bombards Madras, 209-10; first raid off Colombo, captures *King Lud*, *Tymeric*, *Buresk*, *Ribera*, *Foyle*, releases *Gryfevale*, 211-4; second raid off Colombo, captures *Clan Grant*, *Ponrabbel*, *Benmohr*, *Troilus*, *Exford*, *Chilkana*, releases *St. Egbert*, 268-72; raids Penang, stops *Glenturret*, 278-9; stops *Newburn*, 325; raids Cocos Is., captures *Ayesha*, 326-8; sunk, 328; search for, 208-9, 214, 268-9, 271, 326-7; her tenders and coal supply, 133, 148, 204, 206, 211-2, 213, 269, 270, 325; news of her captures received, 206, 208, 213, 271, 305; effect of her operations on trade,

INDEX I

206–7, 210–11, 214–20, 271–6, 279, 330–6, 361, 394, 412; mentioned, 233, 246, 349, 257–8, 265, 266, 312, 341, 351, 396
Emir, Ger., captured, 61
EMPRESS OF ASIA, Br.A.M.C. (China Sq.), 136; in search for EMDEN, 218, 271, 327
EMPRESS OF BRITAIN, Br.A.M.C., 373
EMPRESS OF JAPAN, Br.A.M.C. (China Sq.), 136
EMPRESS OF RUSSIA, Br.A.M.C. China Sq.), 142; in search for EMDEN, 327
ENCOUNTER, Br.L.Cr. (Austr.Fl.), 123
Eresos, Ger., 290
Erymanthos, Ger., captured, 64
ESPIÈGLE, Br.Sl. (E.I.Sq.), 126, 129
ESSEX, Br.Cr. (4th Cr.Sq.), 106–7, 110
Exford, Br., captured, 270–2; tender to EMDEN, 271, 278, 325–6; recaptured, 331 n

Farn, Br., captured, 258; tender to KARLSRUHE, 258, 260–1, 264–5, 317–8, 330; interned, 330 n
Floride, Fr., sunk, 377
FOX, Br.L.Cr. (E.I.Sq.), 122, 126, 129
Foyle, Br., sunk, 212–3
Frankenwald, Ger., 75–6
Franz Horn, Ger., captured, 59
Frau Minna Petersen, Br.S.V., captured, 94
Frederike, Br., damaged, 290
†*Friedrich der Grosse*, Ger., 32, 104–5
FRIEDRICH KARL, Ger.Cr., 352 n 1
*Frisia, Ger., captured, 136, 152
Fürth, Ger., captured, 129

Galician, Br., captured and released, 77–80
Gallier, Br., mined, 357 n 1
GEIER, Ger.Gbt., in Western Pacific, 124, 142, 144, 147; captures *Southport*, 151–2; at Honolulu, 277; interned, 329; her tenders and coal supply, 151–3, 277; effect of her operations on trade, 142; mentioned, 203 n 2, 337, 351
Gem, Br., sunk, 357 n 1
*General, Ger., 67
Georg, Ger., captured, 61
†*George Washington*, Ger., 105, 352 n 2

Georgios, Gr., seized by Turks and sunk by Russians, 354 n 2
GIBRALTAR, Br.Cr. (10th Cr.Sq.), 59
Gladys, Br., 366
Glanton, Br., sunk, 264, 267, 322, 329
GLASGOW, Br.L.Cr. (Capt. Luce), on S. American coast, 154, 165, 167, 175–6, 179, 224, 226, 234–5, 249, 258, 313–14, 319–20, 324, 340, 346, 349, 379
Glenturret, Br., escapes EMDEN, 278
Glitra, Br., sunk, 285
GLOUCESTER, Br.L.Cr., in Mediterranean, 62; in search for EMDEN, 327; in mid-Atlantic, 380
GNEISENAU, Ger.Cr., with Ad. von Spee, 123, 145, 217, 224, 232, 320–2; sunk, 349–50; rumour concerning, 173; mentioned, 351
GOEBEN, Ger.B.Cr., in Mediterranean, 61–3; under Turkish flag, 66, 85, 287, 289–91; effect of her operations on trade, 62–3, 66, 409; mentioned, 67, 129, 184
†*Goeben*, Ger., 75–6
Goldenfels, Ger., 131, 141
GOOD HOPE, Br.Cr., flagship of Ad. Cradock, in Caribbean, 110; on S. American coast, 176, 224, 226, 252–3, 258, 314; sunk, 319–20
*Göttingen, Ger., 314, 316, 319
*Græcia, Ger., captured, 241
GRAFTON, Br.Cr. (10th Cr.Sq.), 59
Grand Duke Alexander, Russ., sunk, 290
Graphic, Br., attacked, 366
†*Grosser Kurfürst*, Ger., 105
Gryfevale, Br., captured and released, 212–4, 305
Guadeloupe, Fr., sunk, 378
Guatemala, Br., 231
*Gudrun, Ger., 347 n

Haiffa, Ger., captured, 355
HALCYON, Br.Gbt., 312
HAMPSHIRE, Br.Cr. (Capt. H. W. Grant), in China Sq., 122, 134, 141–2, 204; in search for EMDEN, 208, 214, 271, 327
Harvesthude, Ger.S.V., captured and released, 236
*Heina, Nor., captured, 112
Helicon, Nor.S.V., captured 323; released, 340
Hellenes, Br., 173
Hemisphere, Br., sunk, 372; 382

INDEX I

HIGHFLYER, Br.L.Cr. (Capt. Buller), 60; sinks KAISER WILHELM, 81-3; in mid-Atlantic, 244, 373
Highland Brae, Br., sunk, 374
Highland Hope, Br., sunk, 253-4
HIMALAYA, Br.A.M.C. (China Sq.), 127, 136, 218, 331 n
Hochfeld, Ger., captured and released, 76-7
Hoffnung, Ger. (ex-*Indrani*, Br.), tender to KARLSRUHE, 257-8, 261, 264-5, 317-8; sunk, 330
*Holger, Ger., 372-4, 377-8, 381
Holmwood, Br., sunk, 174-5, 176, 196, 221, 249
Hostilius, Br., captured and released, 170, 172
Hurstdale, Br., sunk, 264, 322, 329
HYACINTH, Br.L.Cr. (Cape Sq.), 123, 126
Hyades, Br., sunk, 172-3, 192, 221, 249

IBUKI, Jap.Cr., 327
IDZUMO, Jap.Cr., 179, 236, 314
Ikaria, Br., torpedoed, 367-8
†*Imperator*, Ger., 32, 352 n 2
Inca, Br., 319 n
Indian Prince, Br., sunk, 252; 180, 222, 228, 267, 305
INDOMITABLE, Br.L.Cr. (in Mediterranean), 62
Indrani, Br., captured, 254. See also "*Hoffnung*"
Induna, Br., 277
Indus, Br., sunk, 204-5, 208
INFLEXIBLE, Br.B.Cr., 324, 349
Invercoe, Br.S.V., sunk, 377
INVINCIBLE, Br.B.Cr., 324, 349
ISIS, Br.L.Cr. (11th Cr.Sq.), 59
Isle of Hastings, Br., damaged, 62
Isobel Browne, Russ.S.V., sunk, 376
Istria, Ger., captured, 129

Jacobsen, Fr.S.V., sunk, 376
Jean, Fr.S.V., captured, 371; sunk, 374, 378
John D. Rockefeller, U.S., 293
*Josephina, D., captured, 375

Kabinga, Br., captured, 205-6; released, 207-8
Kaipara, Br., sunk, 79-80, 173, 192
KAISER WILHELM DER GROSSE, Ger.A.M.C. (Capt. Rymann), sinks *Tubal Cain*, 78; sinks *Nyanga* and *Kaipara*, releases *Galician* and *Arlanza*, 78-80; destroyed, 82; her tenders and coal supply, 81-3, 223; news of her captures received, 78, 80-1, 81 n, 192 n 2; effect of her operations on trade, 81-2, 86, 173-4, 184, 192, 243, 412; mentioned, 176, 227, 241, 242, 244, 351, 352 n 2
†*Kaiser Wilhelm II*, Ger., 105, 352 n 2
†*Kaiserin Auguste Victoria*, Ger., 352 n 2
KAISERIN ELIZABETH, A.L.Cr., at Tsingtau, 134, 136, 329
Kalymnos, Ger., captured, 64
Kamasaku Maru, Jap., 279
Kamerun, Ger., captured, 243
Kara Deniz, T., seized, 291
KARLSRUHE, Ger.L.Cr. (Capt. Köhler), in W. Indies, 104, 106-8, 110-11; reports and conjectures as to, 167, 227-8, 239; early movements of, 246-7; captures *Bowes Castle* and *Strathroy*, 247-8; captures *Maple Branch*, 251; captures *Highland Hope* and escapes CANOPUS, 253-4; captures *Indrani*, *Maria*, *Cornish City*, *Rio Iguassu*, *Farn*, *Niceto de Larrinaga*, *Lynrowan*, *Cervantes*, *Pruth*, and *Condor*, 254-61; captures *Glanton* and *Hurstdale*, 264; escapes CARNARVON, 267; captures *Vandyck*, releases *Royal Sceptre*, 317-18; blown up, 329-30; her tenders and coal supply, 108, 111, 246-50, 254, 255, 257, 258, 261, 264; her secret base, 249-50, 249 n, 267; news of her captures received, 176, 244, 261-2, 322; effect of her operations on trade, 176, 228, 239, 264-7, 273, 322, 331, 334, 412; mentioned, 175, 179, 222, 238, 312, 313-5, 324, 338, 346, 347 n, 351, 370, 371, 396
*Karnak, Ger., 232-3, 314, 316, 318, 375
Katherine Park, Br., captured and released, 174-5
Kawak, Ger., captured, 64
Kazbek, Russ., mined, 290
KENT, Br.Cr., on S. American coast, 324, 340, 346, 349, 379
Khartoum, Br., mined, 353
Kilcoan, Br., sunk, 366
Kildalton, Br.S.V., sunk, 371, 374, 378
Killin, Br., sunk, 205-6, 208
KINFAUNS CASTLE, Br.A.M.C., 81
King Lud, Br., sunk, 212-3
†*Kleist*, Ger., 124, 130
KOLN, Ger.L.Cr., 352 n 1
†*König Albert*, Ger., 62

KÖNIGIN LUISE, Mine-Layer, 89–90
KÖNIGSBERG, Ger.L.Cr., on E. African coast, 123–4, 126; loses her base, 130; sinks CITY OF WINCHESTER, 130–2; inactive, 141, 143, 204; destroys PEGASUS, 209; search for, 142, 209, 217, 276; blocked in Rufiji R., 279, 325, 329; her tenders and coal supply, 131, 276; news of her capture received, 130; effect of her operations on trade, 132, 192, 209, 276, 412; mentioned, 182, 337, 351
Kronprinzessin Cecilie (Hamburg-Amerika), Ger., seized, 56–7
†*Kronprinzessin Cecilie* (N.D.L.), Ger., 105, 352 n 2
KRONPRINZ WILHELM, Ger.A.M.C. (Capt. Thierfelder), at sea, 105; armed from KARLSRUHE, 107; captures and releases *Pittan*, 251–2; captures *Indian Prince*, 179–80, 222, 252; captures *La Correntina*, 262–3; captures *Union*, 338–9; captures *Anne de Bretagne*, 344–6; captures *Belle-vue*, *Mont Agel*, *Hemisphere*, *Potaro*, *Wilfred M.*, and *Highland Brae*, 371–4; narrow escapes of, 373; captures *Semantha*, *Chase-hill*, *Guadeloupe*, *Tamar*, and *Coleby*, 376–80; interned, 380; her tenders and coal supply, 222–4, 251, 252, 263, 338–9, 347, 372–3, 374, 378, 380, 381–2; news of her captures received, 228, 345, 362, 373, 378, 379; effect of her operations on trade, 227–8, 239, 345, 362, 380–2, 412; mentioned, 155, 244, 267, 305, 312, 313–5, 324, 351, 352 n 2, 354, 369, 370, 375

Laconia, A., captured and released, 59
La Correntina, Br., sunk, 262–3, 265, 267, 322, 338, 345, 381
La Lorraine, Fr., 106
LANCASTER, Br.Cr. (4th Cr.Sq.), 107
Leda, Ger., captured and released to U.S., 107
LEIPZIG, Ger.L.Cr., in N. Pacific, 124, 154, 162; off San Francisco, 163–4; goes south, captures *Elsi-nore* and *Bankfields*, 229–32; joins Ad. von Spee with supply ships, 232–4, 237; with Ad. von Spee, 313–5, 319, 321, 323, 338, 340–1, 348–9; captures *Valentine*, 323; captures *Drummuir*, 348; sunk, 349; her tenders and coal supply, 164, 229, 232–3; news of her captures received, 233; effect of her operations on trade, 148, 163–5, 231, 233–5, 236–7, 266, 394, 412; mentioned, 136, 150, 226, 228, 305, 344, 351
LEVIATHAN, Br.Cr., 76
Linaria, Br., mined, 357 n 1
Linda Blanche, Br., sunk, 366
Loredano, It. (Capt. Giacopolo), 206, 208
Lorenzo, U.S., captured, 112
Lovat, Br., sunk, 204–5, 208
LUCHS, Ger.Gbt., 133
Lusitania, Br., 106
Luxor, Ger., 342, 375
Lynrowan, Br., sunk, 259, 267
Lynton Grange, Br., captured and released, 170

MACEDONIA, Br.A.M.C., on S. American coast, 176, 224, 238, 244, 317, 346, 371
Macedonia, Ger., 113; captured, 380
Madang, Ger., captured, 152
MAGDEBURG, Ger.L.Cr., 352 n 1
Magdeburg, 81–83, 110
MAINZ, Ger.L.Cr., 352 n 1
Malachite, Br., sunk, 353
Manchester Commerce, Br., mined, 285–6, 298, 306 n, 352, 354 n 1
Manx Isles, Br., 252
Manx Queen, Br. trawler, mined, 357 n 1
Maple Branch, Br., sunk, 251, 267
Maria, D., sunk, 255–6, 256 n
Marie, Ger., 229–33
Marie Glasier, Ger., captured, 59
Markomannia, Ger., 133, 148, 203–6, 209, 211, 213, 268; sunk, 269
MARMORA, Br.A.M.C., 373
Mary Ada Short, Br., sunk, 377
Maryland, Dan., mined, 90, 93 n
Mauretania, Br., 106–7
†*Max Brock*, Ger., 243
Mediterraneo, A., 76
MELBOURNE, Br.L.Cr. (Capt. Silver) in Austr.Fl., 123; with Australian Convoy, 326–7
Memphis, Ger., 341, 375
Mera, Ger., 347 n, 375
MINERVA, Br.L.Cr. (9th Cr.Sq.), 83
MINOTAUR, Br.Cr. (Capt Kiddle), in China Sq., 122, 141; with Australian convoy, 326–7
Modig, Nor., 256 n
†*Molike*, Ger., 62

Molikefels, Ger., captured, 129
MONMOUTH, Br.Cr., on S. American coast, 76,' 173–5, 224, 226, 234–5, 249, 258, 313–4; sunk, 320
Mont Agel, Fr., sunk, 372
MONTCALM, Fr.Cr., 122, 149, 344
MOUSQUET, Fr. T.-b.-d., 278, 325

Nauta, Ger., captured, 74
Navarra, Ger., 113; destroyed, 339
Neumunster, Ger., captured, 130
Newa, Br., seized by Turks and sunk by Russians, 354 n 2
Newbridge, Br., sunk to block Rufiji, 329
Newburn, Br., captured and released, 325
NEWCASTLE, Br.L.Cr. (Capt. Powlett), in China Sq., 122, 136; on N. Pacific station, 148, 164, 179, 229, 236
Niceto de Larrinaga, Br., sunk, 259–60
Nilufer, T., captured, 354 n 2
NIOBE, Br.Cr., 104
NISSHIN, Jap.Cr., 327
North Wales, Br., sunk, 340–1
NÜRNBERG, Ger.L.Cr., in Pacific, 124; joins Ad. von Spee, 146; with Ad. von Spee, 148, 150–1, 315, 321–2; cuts cable at Fanning Id., 151; sunk, 349–50; rumours and conjectures relating to, 154, 162–5, 226, 230, 344; mentioned, 179, 228, 232, 351
NUSA, Ger.Govt.Yacht, captured, 152
Nyanga, Br., sunk, 79–80, 182, 192, 243

Ocana, Br. trawler, mined, 357 n 1
Odenwald, Ger., 380
Olympic, Br., 106–7
ORAMA, Br.A.M.C., on S. American coast, 244, 339, 347, 379
Oriole, Br., torpedoed, 368
Orita, Br., 318, 319 n
Oronsa, Br., 321
Ortega, Br. (Capt. Kinneir), escapes DRESDEN, 225; 342
Ostmark, Ger., 131
Otavi, Ger., 347, 362, 372–3, 381
OTRANTO, Br.A.M.C., in S. American coast, 175, 224, 226, 234, 249, 320, 324

Paklat, Ger., captured, 136
PANTHER, Ger.Gbt., 76

*Patagonia,' Ger., 247–9, 347 n, 375
PEGASUS, Br.L.Cr. (Cape Sq.), 123, 126; sunk, 209
Perkio, Ger.S.V., captured, 59, 59 n 3
PHILOMEL, Br.L.Cr. (N.Z.Div.), 123, 327
Pierre Loti, Fr.S.V., sunk, 376
PIONEER, Br.L.Cr. (Astr.Fl.), 123, 127, 129–30
Pittan, Russ.S.V., captured and released, 251–2
Platuria, U.S. (ex-*Diamant*, Ger.), 293–4
Polnay, A., 60, 65 n
Ponrabbel, Br.dredger, sunk, 269
Pontoporos, Gr., captured, 204; tender to EMDEN, 204–6, 208, 211, 268; recaptured, 269, 325
*Pontos, Ger., 223–4
Porto, Ger., captured, 59
Portugal, Fr., damaged, 290
Potaro, Br., captured, 373–4; sunk, 377
*Präsident, Ger., captured, 276
†*President Grant*, Ger., 32, 105
Primo, Br., sunk, 353
†*Princess Alice*, Ger., 125, 203 n 2
Princess Olga, Br., mined, 357 n 1
PRINCESS ROYAL, Br.B.Cr., 324
Prinsessan Ingeborg, Sw., 254
†*Prinz Adalbert*, Ger., seized, 56–7
PRINZ EITEL FRIEDRICH, Ger.A.M.C. (Capt. Thierichsens), at Tsingtau, 124; armed, 133; joins Ad. von Spee, 136, 147; detached in Pacific, 150–1; rejoins Ad. von Spee, 277, 314, 316; chases *Colusa*, 319; on Chilian coast, 321–3; captures *Charcas*, 348; captures *Jean* and *Kildalton*, 370–1; at Easter I., 371, 374; rounds Horn, 374–5; sinks *Isobel Browne, William P. Frye, Pierre Loti*, and *Jacobsen*, 376; sinks *Invercoe, Mary Ada Short, Floride*, and *Willerby*, 377; interned, 378–9; coal supply of, 150–1, 152–3. 277, 319, 371, 375, 377–8, 381; news of her captures received, 348, 378; effect of her operations on trade, 319, 348, 380–1, 412; mentioned, 351, 362, 369
†*Prinz Friedrich Wilhelm*, Ger., 94, 352 n 2
*Professor Woermann, Ger., captured, 81, 242
*Prussia, Ger., 172–3, 227, 252, 262
Pruth, Br., sunk, 259

428 INDEX I

PSYCHE, Br.L.Cr. (N.Z.Div.), 123
PYRAMUS, Br.L.Cr. (N.Z.Div.), 123, 327

Quillota, Br., 319 n

RAINBOW, Br.L.Cr., in N. Pacific, 154, 162–5, 179, 236, 344
*Ramses, Ger., 341, 375
Rappenfels, Ger., captured, 129
Reina Victoria Elene, Sp., 253–4
*Rhakotis, Ger., 340–1
Riasan, Russ., captured, 133. See also "CORMORAN"
Ribera, Br., sunk, 212–3
Rio Iguassu, Br., sunk, 255–6; 267
*Rio Negro, Ger., 248–9, 253–5, 257–61, 264–5, 317–8, 330
*Rio Passig, U.S., captured, 218
Royal Sceptre, Br., captured and released, 318
Runo, Br., mined, 91, 93

Sabine Rickmers, Ger., captured, 130
*Sacramento (ex-Alexandria) Ger., 236, 231, 233, 340, 375
St. Egbert, Br., captured and released, 270–1
St. Thomas, Fr., damaged, 62
San Wilfrido, Br., mined, 54
Santa Catherina, Ger., captured, 170
*Santa Isabel, Ger., 319, 347–8; sunk, 350
SATSUMA, Jap.B., 277
SCHARNHORST, Ger.Cr., flagship of Ad. von Spee, 123, 145, 217, 224, 232, 234, 320–2; sunk, 349–50; mentioned, 235, 276, 351
Schliesen, Ger., captured, 60
Schneefels, Ger., captured, 61
Semantha, Nor.S.V., sunk, 377
*Senegambia, Ger., captured, 136, 152
*Seydlitz, Ger., 125, 341, 347, 350, 375, 375 n
SHEARWATER, Br.Sl., in N. Pacific, 162
Shura, Russ., sunk, 290
Siamese Prince, Br., captured and released, 173
*Sierra Cordoba, Ger., 263, 338–9, 345–6, 370, 379, 381
†Silesia, A., 134
*Slawentzitz, Ger., captured, 83
Somali, Ger., destroyed, 329 n
Southport, Br. (Capt. Clopet), captured and escapes, 151–2
†*Spreewald, Ger., captured, 112
SQUIRREL, Br.Gbt., 74

*Stadt Schleswig, Ger., 176, 247–8, 250 n, 255
Stephan, Ger. cable ship, 75–6
STRASSBURG, Ger.L.Cr., 104, 106, 167
Strathroy, Br., captured, 248–50, 253–4; sunk, 257
†Südmark, Ger., 124; captured, 129–30
SUFFOLK, Br.Cr.(4th Cr.Sq.), 106–8, 246
Sumatra, Ger., captured, 152
SURPRISE, Fr.Gbt., 243
SWIFTSURE, Br.B. (E.I.Sq.), 122, 126
SYDNEY, Br.L.Cr. (Capt. Glossop), in Austr.Fl., 123 ; sinks EMDEN, 327–8
Syra, Ger., captured, 60

†Tabora, Ger., 124, 130
Tamar, Br., 232; sunk, 379–80
*Tannenfels, Ger., captured, 218
*Thor, Nor., captured, 112
THRUSH, Br.Gbt., 74
Thüringen, Ger., captured, 130
TIGER, Ger.Gbt., 123
*Titania, Ger., 314, 316, 323, 340
TOKIWA, Jap.Cr., in search for EMDEN, 327
Tokomaru, Br., torpedoed, 367–8
Trabboch, Br., sunk, 207–8
Tritonia, Br., mined, 357
TRIUMPH, Br.B. (Capt. Fitzmaurice), in China Sq., 122, 133–4, 136, 141
Troilus, Br., sunk, 270–1, 272, 275, 331
*Tsintau, Ger., 151–2
Tubal Cain, Br. trawler, sunk, 78
Tubantia, D., 60
*Turpin, Ger., 370
Tymeric, Br., sunk, 212–3, 218, 331
Tysla, Nor., mined, 93 n

Ulla Boog, Ger., captured, 59
UNDINE, Ger.L.Cr., 352 n 1
Union, Fr.S.V., captured, 338–9; sunk, 345 ; 382
U. 17, Ger. S/m, sinks Glitra, 285
U 19, Ger. S/m, sinks Durward, 365–6
U 20, Ger. S/m, torpedoes Ikaria, Tokomaru, and Oriole, 367–8
U 21, Ger. S/m, sinks Ben Cruachan, Linda Blanche, and Kilcoan, 366

Valentine, Fr.S.V., captured, 323 ; sunk, 340

INDEX I

Vandyck, Br., sunk, 317-8, 318 n; 329, 322
Vaterland, Ger., 32, 105, 108, 352 n 2
†*Victoria Louise*, Ger., 352 n 2
VICTORIAN, Br.A.M.C., in mid-Atlantic, 261, 373
VINDICTIVE, Br.L.Cr. (9th Cr.Sq.), 60, 75, 83
VON DER TANN, Ger.B.Cr., 346

*Walhalla, Ger., 251
Walküre, Ger., captured, 225
Washington, Ger. See " *Brindilla* "
Werner Vinnen, Ger.S.V., captured, 81
Westergate, Br., mined, 365
WEYMOUTH, Br.L.Cr., in search for KÖNIGSBERG, 217; in search for EMDEN, 327
Wilfrid M., Br.S.V., sunk, 374

Wilhelm Behrens, Ger., captured, 59
Willerby, Br., sunk, 377
William P. Frye, U.S.S.V., sunk, 376

YAHAGI, Jap.L.Cr., 279, 327
YAKUMO, Jap.Cr., 327
Yalta, Russ., mined, 290
YARMOUTH, Br.L.Cr., in China Sq., 122; in search for EMDEN, 208, 269, 271
YORCK, Ger.Cr., 352 n 1
*†*Yorck*, Ger., 124, 133, 314, 316, 318

ZELÉE, Fr.Gbt., sunk, 225
ZENTA, A.L.Cr., sunk, 64
Zeros, Ger., 290
ZHEMCHUG, Russ.L.Cr., 122, 141, 271; sunk, 278
*†*Zieten*, Ger., 124, 130-1, 141

INDEX II

GENERAL

Acheh Head, patrol off, 142, 269, 279, 327

Actions, Naval, their effect on trade, HIGHFLYER and KAISER WILHELM DER GROSSE, 82, 84, 86, 192, 243; off Heligoland, 94–5; CARMANIA and CAP TRAFALGAR, 223–4, 226, 253; off Coronel, 320–3, 340, 342–4; SYDNEY and EMDEN, 328, 335–6; off Falklands, 349–50, 351, 354, 369–70; off Dogger Bank, 365

Aden, focal point at, 116; KÖNIGSBERG'S raid near, 130–2; instructions to shipping at, 211

Admiralty, British, and State Insurance Scheme, 42–3, 46–7; advice and instructions to shipping, 45–6, 62–3, 81, 91–2, 97, 175, 217, 266, 282, 298–9, 344, 358, 365, 377; policy as regards trade, 63, 126, 187, 216–7, 228, 236, 344; statements and warnings by, 90, 91, 170, 189–90, 273, 281, 298–9, 312; criticised in India, 272–3; mentioned, 30, 234, 244, 323, 324

—, Trade Division of, 45

Adriatic, trade in, 31–2, 64–5, 85, 288; watch on, 63, 184, 287

Alexandrovsk, ice-free port, 365

Alpaca, stocks and imports of, 4 n 2, 156; effect of war on supply of, 234, 342, 350, 394, 419; price of, 419

Alvarez, Señor Alejandro, cited, 166 n, 343 n, 374 n, 375 n 2

Andaman Is., search of, 209, 217, 278

Antofagasta, trade of, 156; shipping held up at, 340, 344, 348

Antwerp, fall of, 286

Apia, occupied, 149; Ad. von Spee at, 151, 208, 224

Arabian Sea, protection of trade in, 122, 126, 140–1, 211, 276, 332; trade routes closed in, 214, 271–2

Archangel, trade of, 96, 196, 284, 360

Argentina, trade and communications of, 158–62; economic crisis in, 168–9, 171; trade with, 176–7, 226–7, 238–9, 238 n 2, 322–3, 345 n 2, 369–70, 370 n

Armed Merchant Cruisers, speed of, 21; accommodation in, 23; law as to conversion, 48

—, British, ships requisitioned as, 52, 122, 127

—, Enemy, dangers apprehended from, 47–8, 57, 351–2, 352 n; in Mediterranean, 62, 63–4; in North Atlantic, 70, 75–6, 84, 105, 108, 110; in North Sea, 94; on Oriental Route, 124–5, 127, 130, 133; in South Atlantic, 167–8, 242–3. *See also* Index I

Asquith, Rt. Hon. H. H., Prime Minister, 35, 40

Aust, Kapitän-Leutnant, cited, 246 n 1

Australia, Commonwealth of, communications and trade of, 116, 118–9, 121, 145–6; naval cooperation by, 122–3; effect of war on trade of, 137, 149, 215, 275, 276; failure of harvest in, 291, 361, 406

Austria-Hungary, trade and shipping of, 16, 18 n 2; Allied relations with, 61, 64; economic position in, 202, 311–2, 386–7

Austrian Lloyd, service suspended, 32

Auxiliary Patrol, formation and services of, 92–3, 353

Avonmouth, congested, 404

Aye, Kapitän-Leutnant, cited, 78 n

Azores, enemy ships at, 70, 75, 84, 104, 167, 251; search of, 76, 83, 241

Bacon, imports and consumption of, 3 n 2, 97, 100; effect of war on supply of, 97, 113, 282, 419; price of, 419, 408

INDEX II

Bali Strait, 116, 203; warning as to, 142
Baltic Sea, German command of, 13, 95, 185, 393; trade in, 95–9, 194, 195, 282–4, 308, 358–60
Barbados, projected raid on, 330
Barley, effect of war on supply of, 32, 113, 120, 156, 163, 291 n 2, 302 n 1, 393, 419; price of, 407, 419
Barry, congested, 404
Batavia, instructions to shipping at, 142, 218
Batavier Line, service maintained, 98
Beck, Sir Raymond, member Insurance Committee, 36
Belgium, dependent on foreign shipping, 13; effects of war on, 99, 186, 196, 286
Bengal, Bay of, trade routes in, 116–7; protection of, 122, 204, 271, 277, 279, 327; EMDEN in, 204–10; trade routes closed in, 206–7, 209–12, 214–15
Bethell, V.-Ad. Sir Alexander E., commands 7th B.Sq., 240
Bieberstein, Baron Marschall von, 88
Bilbao, watch on, 75–6
Biscay, Bay of, patrols in, 76, 83–4, 287
Black Sea, trade of, 30, 65–7, 85–6, 194–5, 289–92, 291 n 2, 393, 407, 409; operations in, 290, 354
Blockade, under modern conditions, 27–8
Blue Funnel Line, services maintained, 138, 232
Board of Trade, and State Insurance Scheme, 35, 39, 40, 42–3, 46, 184; meat purchases by, 176–7; and cargoes in enemy ships, 198 n 2; and port congestion, 404
Bolivia, trade and communications of, 156, 161; tin exports held up, 234
Bombay, British Base, 116, 126, 140; trade of, 116, 139 n, 211, 216, 216 n, 219, 219 n, 274, 275 n, 335 n; ships held up at, 213–5, 271–2, 326
Bo'ness, closed, 358
Booth Line, immunity from attack, 177, 227
Bordeaux, trade of, 12, 85; congested, 287
Borneo, oil-fields of, 117, 121, 142
Boston, U.S.A., German liners at and watch on, 105, 110
Brazil, trade and communications of, 158–62; economic crisis in, 168–9, 171, 177–8; trade with, 227, 345 n, 369; neutrality of, enforced, 167–8, 169, 347, 372 n 3; KARLSRUHE's base in, 249–50, 249 n
Bristol, congested, 404
British Columbia, trade and communications of, 155–6; effect of war on trade of, 162–4, 232–3, 236–7
British India Steam Navigation Co., branch service suspended, 138
Buenos Aires. *See* Plate, River
Buller, Captain Henry T. (HIGHFLYER), destroys KAISER WILHELM DER GROSSE, 81–2; S.N.O. in mid-Atlantic, 244
Butter, imports and consumption of, 3 n 2, 121; effect of war on supply of, 96–7, 282, 419; price of, 408, 419

Cables, Deep-sea, influence of, on attack and defence of trade, 25–8; protection of, 74, 75–6; cut, 151, 328
Cabot Strait, protection of, 107–8
Calcutta, trade of, 117, 139 n, 215, 216 n, 219, 219 n, 274, 275 n, 335 n; shortage of tonnage at, 140; shipping held up at, 206–10, 215, 279
California, Gulf of, LEIPZIG in, 229; search of, 230, 236
Callao, commercial importance of, 157; shipping held up at, 231, 233, 340, 344
Cameroons, occupation of, 241–3
Canada, trade and communications of, 100–4, 145–6; trade with, 106–10, 113–4, 301–2, 302 n 1
Canadian Pacific Railway Co., A.M.C.'s requisitioned from, 127, 149, 232
Canary Is., focal point at, and its protection, 58, 70, 75–7, 84, 158, 244, 249; KAISER WILHELM DER GROSSE's raid off, 77–82. *See* also "Las Palmas," "Tenerife"
Cape Verde Is., focal point at, and its protection, 58, 70, 75–7, 84, 154, 158, 244, 249, 373; *See* also "St. Vincent"
Carden, R.-Ad. Sackville, H., at Dardanelles, 290
Cardiff, congested, 404
Cargoes, of ships sunk or captured by enemy, percentage values, 389, 415, Table IX; barley, 259, 379; coal, 174, 204, 205, 213, 248, 254, 255, 258, 272, 285, 323,

339, 340–1, 348, 353, 366, 371, 372, 377; coffee, 252, 367, 379–80; copper ore, 247; fish, 374; maize, 172, 259, 377; meat, 80, 262, 317; nitrate, 247, 259, 348; oats, 259; silver ore, 247; sugar, 213, 231, 259, 367; tea, 132, 205–6; timber, 345; tin, 275; wheat, 255, 376, 377, 380; general, 78, 207 n, 251, 252, 259, 260, 269, 270, 285, 367, 374, 378

Caroline Is., 132, 151, 329, 351. *See also* "Ponape"

Cereals, imports and consumption of, 3 n 2. *See* also under "Wheat," etc.

Ceylon. *See* "India, British"

Chamberlain, Rt. Hon. Austen, Chairman, Committee on National Guarantee of War Risks, 38

Channel, English, defence and attack of trade in, 50, 57–9, 73–4, 94, 240, 240 n; services suspended in, 187; threat to, 286; submarines in, 285, 353, 367–8

Cheese, imports and consumption of, 3 n 2, 100; effect of war on supply of, 113, 282, 419; price of, 408, 419

Chemicals, effect of war on supply of, 392

Chesapeake, watch on, 110

Chile, trade and communications of, 156–7; effect of war on trade of, 165–6, 235, 342–4, 350; proposed acquisition of Kosmos Line by, 166; neutrality of, enforced, 166, 235, 319, 321, 342, 343, 374–5; British apology to, 379 n 2

China, coasting trade of, 118; trade with, 121; effect of war on trade of, 126, 135, 137–8, 148, 275–6

China Seas, trade in, and its protection, 117–9, 124, 132–8, 143, 219

Chittagong, trade of, 117, 139 n, 215, 216 n, 219, 219 n, 274, 275 n; shipping held up at, 206

Churchill, Rt. Hon. Winston, First Lord of the Admiralty, cited, 48 n

Clearances, normal, 5; during war, 194, 303, 388, 416; to N. America and Caribbean, 113; to India, 219–20, 276, 332; to S. America, 227, 227 n, 265, 345 n; to France, 287; at Indian ports, 274, 332

Clinton-Baker, Capt. Lewis (BERWICK), S.N.O. in W. Indies, 110–2

Clopet, Capt., Master of *Southport*, 152

Clyde, trade diverted to, 358; congested, 403

Coal supply, of commerce destroyers, 21–3, 22 n

Coal, weight of exports, 5; restrictions on export of, 85, 109, 188, 190; exports of, during war, 98, 194, 265, 296, 358, 391; price of, 402; American exports of, 109; Indian exports of, 132, 140; Australian exports of, 145, 149; shortage of, in S. America, 166, 169, 343; in Germany, 201; suspected contraband, 295–6

Coasting traffic, extent of, 5; effect of war on, 192, 196, 306, 368, 402

Cocoa, imports and consumption of, 3 n 2, 104, 156

Cocos Is., EMDEN at, 278, 326–8

Coffee, sources of supply, 104, 159; effect of war on Brazilian exports of, 168, 171, 177, 227, 369

Colombo, focal point at, 116–9, 126–7, 271, 277, 279, 327; uncovered, 140, 143, 204; shipping held up at, 206–11, 214–6, 271–2; EMDEN off, 211–4, 268–72

Committee of Imperial Defence, 35, 53 n

Compagnie Générale Transatlantique, sailings resumed, 109, 197

Constantinople, GOEBEN at, 63; situation at, 65–7, 85, 289–90

Contraband, law as to, 70–2; British and Allied declarations as to, 72–3, 284, 297–8; stoppage of, 60, 70, 72–4, 76, 240, 293–9, 362–4; German treatment of, 204, 256, 256 n, 282–4, 358–9, 376–7

Convoy, mercantile, under steam, 24; appeals for, 272–3, 322

Convoys, military, interfere with trade defence, 62, 74, 140, 204, 208, 218, 240, 272–3; escorts protect trade, 140–1, 211, 242, 271, 326–8, 332

Copenhagen, German trade through, 296

Copper, importance of imports, 4; war demand for, 101, 301; sources of supply of, 121, 156; effect of war on supply of, 126, 195, 302 n 1, 342, 350, 394, 419; price of, 408, 419; as contraband, 293–4, 296, 363

Coquimbo, copper port, 156; shipping held up at, 344

INDEX II

Corbett, Sir Julian S., cited, 27 n, 53 n, 63 n
Coronel, DRESDEN off, 228; action off, 319–20
Coruña, watch on, 75–6
Cotton, stocks and imports of, 4 n 2, 101, 156; effect of war on trade and supplies, 109, 113–4, 120, 139 n 1, 190–1, 195, 211, 211 n, 274, 276, 294–5, 302, 302 n 2, 305, 360, 394, 419; price of, 408, 419; enemy supplies of, 202, 294–5, 364
Cradock, R.-Ad. Sir Christopher, commands 4th Cr.Sq., 104; protects and encourages trade, 107–10; on S. American station, 110, 175–6, 221–6, 234–5, 237, 238, 244, 252, 267, 313, 317; his defeat and death, 319–20
Credit, importance of in maintaining seaborne trade, 28–9
Cunard Line, sailings maintained, 109–10
Curaçao, KARLSRUHE supplied from, 108, 111, 246–7

Dairy produce, dependence on imported fodder, 3 n 2; effect of war on supply of, 96–8, 195, 282. See also "Butter," "Cheese," "Eggs," "Milk"
Dardanelles, GOEBEN at, 63; mines in, 65–6; effects of closing of, 66–7, 85–6, 96, 185, 289–92, 301, 354, 406–7
Dar-es-Salaam, German base, 123, 124, 130
Days of Grace, 55–6, 65, 83
de Chair, R.-Ad. D. R. S., commands 10th Cr.Sq., 57
Declaration of London, provisions of, 20, 70–2, 166, 283; not ratified by Great Britain, 20 n 1, 71; modifications of, 72–3, 297–8
Declaration of Paris, 17, 48
Dedeagatch, services transferred to, 290
Defensively armed merchantmen, 48–9, 262–3, 381
Denmark, shipping of, 17, 18 n 2; trade with, 97–8, 282; German trade through, 200–1, 295–6
de Robeck, R.-Ad. John M., commands 9th Cr.Sq., 58–60; protects trade in Atlantic, 75–6, 83, 108, 176, 241, 287
Deutsche Amerikanische Petroleum Gesellschaft, ships transferred to U.S., 294

Deviation, steamers' power of, 23–4; Admiralty instructions for, 46, 81, 135, 142, 175, 217; difficulties of, 174, 213–4, 269–70, 274, 334; shipping saved by, 264, 266, 274, 334, 377, 382
Diego Garcia, EMDEN at, 268–9
Diversion of Shipping Committee, 45–6, 187
Dobell, Brig.-Gen. C. M., 243
Duala, capture of, 242–3, 280
Dundee, jute shortage at, 334; congested, 403
Dyestuffs, effect of war on supply of, 392

Easter I., German rendezvous, 232, 234, 313, 316, 371, 374
East Indies, Dutch, trade and communications of, 118–21; neutrality enforced in, 141–2; trade with, 276. See also "Borneo," "Java"
Ecuador, trade and communications of, 156–7; effect of war on trade of, 234–5; neutrality of, enforced, 233
Eggs, imports and consumption of, 3 n 2; effect of war on supply of, 96–7, 282, 393, 419; price of, 408, 419
Eight Degree Channel. See "Minikoi"
Entrances, normal, 5; during war, 194, 302, 353, 362, 388, 416; from N. America and Caribbean, 113; from S. America, 227, 227 n, 265, 345 n; from India, 332; at Indian ports, 140 n, 332
Esquimalt, British base, 136, 148, 162–3, 165, 179, 230, 236
Eten, ships held up at, 231
Evans, Sir Samuel, President of the Prize Court, cited, 55 n 2
Exports, normal, 2–3, 5; prohibition of, 187–8; effect of war on, 195, 303–4, 353, 364, 390–1, 417, Table XI

Fanning I., cable cut at, 151
Fernando Noronha, raiders operate near, 172, 228, 244, 248, 253–4, 263–4, 346, 377
Ferrol, watch on, 83
Fiji, alarm for, 225
Financial Crisis, in Great Britain, 34; world-wide, 60, 77, 185–6; in India and Far East, 125–6; in Australia, 137; in S. America, 160, 168, 171, 177

Finisterre, Cape, patrol off, 58, 76, 83
Finland, Gulf of, closed, 95, 284
Fish, effect of war on supply of, 98, 393, 419; price of, 419
Fitzmaurice, Capt. M. S. (TRIUMPH), observes Tsingtau, 133–6
Flag, transfer of, law as to, 19–20, 66, 166; of British ships to U.S., 385; of German ships to U.S., 107, 111, 236, 294, 364; to Chile, 166
Flax, stocks of, 4 n 2; effect of war on supply of, 360, 394, 419; price of, 419
Flushing, services suspended, 98
Fodder, importance of imports to Germany, 16, 201, 311, 388
Food supplies, British, proportion of imports to consumption, 3, 3 n 2; threatened stoppage of, 34–5; maintenance of, 195, 304, 361, 392–3. *See* also under separate commodities
——, German, extent of dependence on imports, 15–16; effect of war on, 201, 310–2, 363–4, 387–8
Forth, Firth of, closed, 357–8
France, trade and shipping of, 11–12, 18 n 2; shipbuilding in, 19; effects of war on, 84–5, 196–8, 287, 308–9, 383–4, 384 n
Freight markets, effect of war on, 30, 34–5, 77, 185, 188, 190, 193–4, 196, 306–7; in N. America, 105–6, 109, 113; in India and Far East, 125–6, 132, 139, 219, 274; at Plate, 168–9, 171, 177, 226, 238–9
Freights, fall in, 194, 194 n 2; general rise in, 308, 361, 395–6; its causes, 396–405; liner surcharges, 191, 191 n, 193; on particular routes, 96, 132, 135, 139, 149, 171, 176, 219, 239, 276; on grain, 417–18, Tables XIII, XIV
Fremantle, protection of focal point off, 127
Fruit, imports and consumption of, 3 n 2, 104; effect of war on supply of, 85, 195
Fuchau, effect of war on trade of, 137
Fuller, Capt. Cyril T. M. (CUMBERLAND), at Duala, 243

Galapagos Is., LEIPZIG at, 230, 233
Gefle, trade through, 96, 284, 365

Genoa, German liners at, 62, 63–4; German trade through, 199, 309, 310; congested, 400
George, Rt. Hon. David Lloyd, Chancellor of Exchequer, 35, 40
Germany, trade and shipping of, 13–16, 18 n 2; shipbuilding, 19; economic position in, 198–202, 309–12, 363–4, 386–8
Giacopolo, Capt., Master of *Loredano*, 206–7
Gibraltar, ships held up at, 63
Gibraltar, Straits of, British command of, 61, 77, 363
Glasgow, congested, 403–4
Glen Line, service suspended, 138
Glossop, Capt. John C. T. (SYDNEY), destroys EMDEN, 328
Gordon, Mr. C. W., President, Chamber of Shipping, 39
Gorleston Raid, 312
Gothenburg, safety of route to, 96; trade through, 359; German trade through, 199
Grangemouth, closed, 358
Grant, Capt. Henry W. (HAMPSHIRE), operates against EMDEN, 208–9, 214, 218, 268–9, 271, 279, 327
Grant, Capt. Noel (CARMANIA), sinks CAP TRAFALGAR, 223–4
Granton, trade transferred to, 358
Great Belt, mined, 95
Great Britain. *See* " United Kingdom "
Great Circle Tracks, Atlantic, 103; Pacific, 145–6
Great Eastern Ry. Co., service transferred, 282 n
Greece, shipping of, 18, 18 n 2; trade with, 289
Grey, Rt. Hon. Sir Edward, Foreign Secretary, 31, 33–4
Grimsby, trade of, 98, 282
Guam, GEIER interned at, 351
Guayaquil, terminal port, 157; LEIPZIG off, 231; ships held up at, 340
Gunny bags and cloth. *See* " Jute "

Hague Conventions, 22 n, 48, 55–6, 59, 87–9, 170 n, 281
Hamburg, British ships detained at, 33–4; entrepôt port, 139, 159; export bank at, 199
Hamburg-Amerika Line, services suspended, 32; coal depôt at St. Thomas, 111

INDEX II

Hams. *See* "Bacon"
Hankau, effect of war on trade of, 137
Hankey, Capt. M. P. A., Secretary, Insurance Committee, 36
Hann, Capt. (LEIPZIG), avoids RAINBOW, 164; his plans, 230; arranges for supplies, 232; joins Ad. von Spee, 232, 314
Haparanda, Russian trade through, 365
Hartlepool, bombarded, 356
Harwich, British base, 90, 280
Havre, trade of, 12; submarines off, 367-8: congested, 400 n l
Hawaii. *See* "Honolulu"
Hemp, imports of, 4, 121; effect of war on supply of, 360, 394, 419; price of, 419
Hides and skins, stocks of, 4 n 2; effect of war on supply of, 238, 274
Higgins, Mr. A. Pearce, cited, 22 n, 48 n 2 and 3, 55 n 1, 72 n 1, 88 n
Hill, Sir A. Norman, member Insurance Committee, 36, 39
Holland, shipping of, 18, 18 n 2; shipbuilding in, 19; trade with, 98-9, 282, 358; and German trade, 200, 296-7, 363; neutrality of, enforced, 142, 286
Holland-Amerika Line, increased trade of, 296-7
Hongkong, British base, 118, 127, 141, 218; protection of tracks to, 135-7, 142
Honolulu, focal point at, 145-6; NÜRNBERG at, 124, 148, 151, 154, 232; GEIER at, 277, 329
Horn, Cape, route round, 119, 145, 158-9; DRESDEN rounds, 222; PRINZ EITEL FRIEDRICH rounds, 374
Hornby, R.-Ad. R. S. Phipps, commands 11th Cr.Sq., 57, 74, 108; on N. American station, 110-1
Hough, Mr. B. Olney, cited, 10 n l
Huelva, iron from, 287
Hull, Mr. I., cited, 88 n
Humber, minefield off, 91-2, 280

Immingham, partially closed, 280
Imports, normal, 2-3, 5; effect of war on, 195-6, 302-4, 360-1, 364, 391-5, 417. Tables XI, XII. *See* also under separate commodities.

India, British, communications and trade of, 116-20; effect of war on trade of, 125, 132, 138-40, 210-20, 274-6, 331-5, 335 n
Indo-China Line, service maintained, 138
Indra Line, service maintained, 138
Industries, British, dependence on imports, 4-5; effect of war on, 303, 390-1
—, Enemy, dependence on imports,15-16; effect of war on, 201, 202, 309, 387
Insurance, Marine, increased cost of, 191
Intelligence Officers, Naval, functions of, 46-7
Investments, foreign, in relation to seaborne trade, 161-2, 390
Iquiqui, shipping released at, 344
Irish Sea, submarines in, 366-8
Iron Ore, imports and stocks of, 4, 4 n 2; effect of war on supply of, 85, 195, 393-4, 419; price of, 419; Swedish export to Germany, 201, 284
Iron, Pig and Wrought, effect of war on supply of, 97, 392
Italy, shipping of, 18, 18 n 2; neutrality of, 61, 63-4; trade with, 85, 288-9; German trade through, 201, 297, 310, 363; protests against Austrian minelaying, 288

Jackson, Rt. Hon. Fredk. Huth, Chairman Insurance Committee, 36
Japan, shipping of, 13, 18 n 2; trade and communications of, 117-9, 120-1, 145-6; enters the war, 134-7; effect of war on trade of, 126, 135-8, 148-9, 164, 218-9, 275-6
Java, sugar from, 121, 204, 211, 218, 275, 307, 361
Java Seas, search of, 142, 203-4
Jellicoe, V.-Ad. Sir John R., commands Grand Fleet, 49
Jerram, V.-Ad. Sir Thomas, commands China Sq., 122; protects trade, 127, 132-6, 141-3, 148, 151; his measures against EMDEN, 208, 218, 326-7; 164, 204
Jute, imports and stocks of, 4, 4 n 2, 119; effect of war on supply of, 140, 210, 215, 274,

334–5, 335 n, 361, 394; price of, 409

Karachi, trade of, 116, 132, 139 n, 211, 216, 216 n, 219, 219 n, 274, 275 n, 332, 335 n
Karimata Strait, 118; search of, 142
Khedivial Mail, service suspended, 289–90
Kiddle, Capt. Edward B. (MINOTAUR), 326–7
King-Hall, R.-Ad. Herbert G., commands on Cape Station, 123, 126, 130
Kinneir, Capt. Douglas (SS. *Ortega*), escapes DRESDEN, 225–6
Köhler, Capt. Erich (KARLSRUHE), his plans, 246–8; his methods, 249–51, 257; his operations in mid-Atlantic, 248–67, 317–8, 329–30; his treatment of prisoners, 258, 261 n, 317–8; his good luck, 249, 254; his difficulties, 266–7; plans raid on West Indies, 264–5, 317, 330; his death, 330
Kola, ice-free port, 365
Korean Strait, 117–8; EMDEN operates in, 133
Kosmos Line, proposed transfer of ships to Chile, 166; controversy with Chilian Government, 343

Laccadive Is., navigation restricted by, 116, 214
Lard, effect of war on supply of, 113, 419; price of, 419; excessive Danish imports of, 296
Las Palmas, news of captures received at, 81, 373; German ships interned at, 82, 380
Lead, imports of, 4; effect of war on supply of, 85, 419; price of, 419
Leather, stocks and imports of, 4 n 2, 101, 120; effect of war on supply of, 210
Lebon, M. André, cited, 384 n
Leith, trade of, 97, 282, 358; congested, 401
Lindley, Mr. Arthur, member Insurance Committee, 36
Liners, functions of, 7–8, 102; foodstuffs carried by, 194, 303. *See* also "Services, fixed"
Lisbon, watch on, 75–6, 241
Liverpool, congested, 401, 403, 404
Lloyds, Corporation of, 26, 46, 47, 91
London, services from, 98, 282; insurance market, 10, 310; wool market, 118; rubber market, 159; money market, 199; metal exchange closed, 126; coal supply, 402; congested, 403–4
Loring, Commr. C. F., cited, 25 n 2
Luce, Capt. John (GLASGOW), on S. American station, 167; encourages shipping, 167–8, 170, 172, 247; 174, 176, 234–5
Lüdecke, Capt. (DRESDEN), releases prizes, 169–70; avoids trade routes, 172–4, 221–2; with Ad. von Spee, 314; inactive after Falklands, 370, 379; 382
Luleå, trade with Germany, 284
Lumber. *See* "Timber"

Madeira, focal point at and watch on, 58, 70, 75–6, 83, 84, 158
Madras, trade of, 117, 139 n, 216 n, 219, 219 n, 275 n, 335 n; bombarded, 209–11, 215–6, 331, 334
Magellan, Straits of, 154–5; DRESDEN avoids, 222; search of, 225–6
Mahlstedt, Paymaster A., cited, 262 n 1
Maize, imports of, 159, 219 n 2; effect of war on supply of, 168, 171, 177, 226, 238, 238 n 2, 265, 291 n 2, 361, 369, 370 n, 393, 419; price of, 407–8, 419
Majunga, KÖNIGSBERG at, 141
Malacca Strait, trade in and defence of, 117, 127, 141–2, 218, 279
Malay Peninsula, trade and communications of, 119–20; effect of war on trade of, 211, 275
Maldive Is., navigation restricted by, 116, 213–4; searched for EMDEN, 268–9, 271
Malmö, German trade through, 296
Manchester, congested, 403–4
Maranham, crew of *Bowes Castle* landed at, 176, 248
Margarine, imports and consumption of, 3 n 2; effect of war on supply of, 419; price of, 408, 419
Marquesas Is., Ad. von Spee at, 232, 234
Marseilles, trade of, 12, 139
Marshall, Capt H. J. T., commands N.Z. Div., 123
Marshall Is., Ad. von Spee at, 148, 150; occupied, 277
Mas-a-fuera, German warships at, 228–9, 233, 316, 321–3, 340, 349
Mauritius, sugar from, 307
Meat, imports and consumption of,

INDEX II

3 n 2, 121, 158-9; effects of war on supply of, 176-7, 226, 238, 238 n 2, 239, 239 n 3, 265, 369, 370 n, 393, 393 n, 419; price of, 408, 419
Mediterranean, trade and operations in, 51, 61-5, 67-8, 84-5, 109, 287-9
Messageries Maritimes, variation of service, 289-90
Methil, trade transferred to, 358
Milk, price of, 408
Miller, Mr. H. R., Secretary, London Group of War Risk Associations, 39
Milne, Ad. Sir A. Berkeley, commands in Mediterranean, 61-2
Mines, Submarine, law as to, 87-9
Minefields, Austrian, in Adriatic, 65, 288
—, British in North Sea, 281; prepared at Vancouver, 236
—, French, in Adriatic, 288
—, German, in Elbe, 54; reported off Port Said, 63; in North Sea, 89-91, 312, 356-7; in Baltic, 95; off Tory I., 285-6, 352
—, losses caused by, 54, 65, 90-1, 93, 93 n, 95, 281, 281 n 3, 285-6, 288, 290, 312, 353, 356-7, 357 n, 365, 412-5, Tables I, III, V, VIII
—, their effect on trade, 93, 97-9, 181, 192, 196, 280-2, 282 n, 286, 400-1
Mine-sweeping, 63, 91-3, 99, 352-3, 357. *See* also " Swept Channel "
Minikoi, focal point at, 116, 127, 279; EMDEN off, 212-13, 268-71
Mohair, stocks of, 4 n 2; effect of war on supply of, 394
Montenegro, blockade of, 64
Monte Video. *See* " Plate, River "
Müller, Capt. von (EMDEN), operates in Bay of Bengal, 203-10; off Colombo, 211-4, 269-71; disappointed at Diego Garcia, 268; raids Penang, 278; defeated, 325-8; his methods, 214; his good luck, 203, 204, 268-9; his difficulties, 333; his treatment of prisoners, 205, 207; 249-50, 266

Nauru, German W/T station, captured, 277
Navigation, restrictions on, 187, 280-1, 298-9, 357-8
Navy, Austrian, ill equipped for attack on commerce, 61; inactivity of, 198, 240

Navy, British, functions of, 1, 5; readiness of, 49, 51-3
—, French, co-operation and activities of, 52, 58-9, 62, 64, 83-4, 287, 288
—, German, inactivity of, 198, 240
—, Japanese, co-operation of, 137, 149-51, 218, 235, 237, 277, 324
—, Russian, co-operation of, 52; in Black Sea, 291.
See also Index I
Netherlands Oversea Trust, 363
Neu Pommern, captured, 141, 152. *See* also " Rabaul "
Newcastle, N.S.W., trade of, 145, 149
New Guinea, German, captured, 149, 152
Newport, congested, 404
Newport News, raiders interned at, 378-80
New York, German liners at, 104-5, 108; shipping held up at, 106-9; watch on, 110
New Zealand, trade and communications of, 118-19, 121, 145, 159; imports from, 239, 239 n 3, 369, 370 n
Nicobar Is., search of, 209, 271, 278
Nine Degree Channel. *See* " Minikoi "
Nippon Yusen Kaisha, Australian service suspended, 149; trade transferred to, 164
Nitrate, a Chilian monopoly, 156, 166; effect of war on Chilian exports of, 265, 342-3, 350, 369, 370 n, 394; importance of, to Germany, 16, 156, 311; German cargoes captured, 74-5, 240 n
Norddeutscher Lloyd, services suspended, 32
North-about Passage, 50, 57, 94, 181, 299
North Sea, British command of, 50, 69, 87, 94-5, 108, 365; minefields in, 89-93, 281, 312, 352-3, 356-7, 365; trade in, 94-9, 282, 358; submarines in, 285, 365; military area in, 298-9
Norway, shipping of, 17, 18 n 2; British trade with, 97-8, 282; German trade with, 201, 295-6; neutrality of enforced, 352

Oats, imports of, 156, 159, 291 n 2; effect of war on supply of, 113,

291 n 2, 302 n 1, 369, 370 n, 393, 419; price of, 407, 419
Oil Fuel, 23 n, 246 n 2, 261, 264
Oil Seeds, effect of war on trade in, 120, 139, 238, 274–5, 369
Oporto, wine trade, 85, 287
Orange Bay, DRESDEN at, 222; search of, 226
Osaka Yusen Kaisha, trade transferred to, 164
Ottley, Capt. C. L., R. N., 87
Owen, Sir Douglas, Chairman, Advisory Board, State Insurance Scheme, 44; cited, 10 n 1

Pacific Steam Navigation Co., services held up, 231, 340, 342, 348
Pagan I., Ad. von Spee at, 134, 146-7; 203
Panama, terminal and tranship-ment port, 145, 155–7; shipping held up at, 163–4, 237, 321
Panama Canal, 154–5, 179, 236–7, 314–15, 324, 342
Paper, from Scandinavia, 97
Papieté, bombarded, 217, 224–5
Para, rubber port, 156, 160; news of captures received at, 322, 329
Patey, R.-Ad. Sir George E., commands Australian Fleet, 122, 137, 141, 148
Peirse, R.-Ad. Richard H., commands E.I.Sq., 122, 204
Penang, focal point at, 117, 127; EMDEN raids, 278–9
Peninsular & Oriental Line, A.M.C. requisitioned from, 127; service maintained, 138
Pernambuco, focal port, 158, 160; port of call for instructions, 167, 172; MONMOUTH at, 173; Ad. Cradock at, 175; Ad. Stoddart at, 244, 267; shipping held up at, 173; news of captures received at, 379
Persian Gulf, defence of trade in, 336
Peru, trade and communications of, 156–7, 161; effect of war on trade of, 165–6, 231, 233–5, 342–4; neutrality of enforced, 233, 344, 375
Petroleum, stocks and imports of, 4 n 2, 101, 121; effect of war on supply of, 113, 195, 301, 302 n 1, 336, 394; as contraband, 293–5
Philippine Is., communications and trade of, 117, 119, 121; German steamers in, and watch on, 142, 147, 152, 217–8, 277, 279

Pit-props, imports of, 4; effect of war on supply of, 85, 95–6, 195, 282–3, 358–60
Plate, River, trade of, 158–61, 168–9, 171, 176–7, 226, 238–9; shipping held up at, 173, 175; alarm at, 221, 322–3, 345; British warships at, 176, 221, 224, 323, 340, 347; DRESDEN off, 174, 179; KRONPRINZ WILHELM off, 262, 338–9
Ponape, Ad. von Spee at, 145–6
Pork, effect of war on supply of, 98
Port Said, mines reported off, 63; demand for Indian coal at, 132
Ports, requisitioning of accommodation at, and closing of, 187, 280, 358; congestion of French, 197, 287, 399–400; of British, 361, 399–405. *See also* under names of ports
Portugal, attitude of, 76, 241; safety of trade with, 85, 287
Powlett, Capt. F. A. (NEWCASTLE), S.N.O. in N. Pacific, 179; his measures for trade defence, 179, 229–31, 235–6
Prices, effect of war on, 34–5, 361, 395, 405–9, 418–9
Prize Courts, British, cases cited, *Möwe*, 55 n 2; *Chile*, 56 n 4; *Perkeo*, 59 n 2; at Alexandria, 128
—, German, cases cited, *Maria*, 256, 256 n: *Alfred Hage*, 256 n, 359 n 4; *Modig*, 256 n, *Belle Ille*, 359 n 3; *Helicon*, 323
Prizes, employment of, 399, 402
Puget Sound, trade of, 156, 232, 236–7; shipping held up at, 163–4
Punta Arenas, Ad. Cradock at, 226; shipping held up at, 321, 340; DRESDEN coals at, 370

Rabaul, German base, 124, 145, 146, 149. *See also* " Neu Pommern "
Railways, congestion of, 401–2
Rangoon, trade of, 117, 139 n, 215, 216 n, 219, 219 n, 274, 275 n, 335 n; shipping held up at, 208, 210
Raumo, route through, 96, 284, 365
Red Sea, protection of trade in, 129, 290, 329
Red Star Line, services transferred to England, 196, 286
Requisitioning of shipping, effects of, 60, 135, 140, 149, 188–9, 307–8, 362, 397–8

INDEX II

Rice, imports of, 120; French imports of, 219
Riga, Gulf of, closed, 284
Rio de Oro, KAISER WILHELM at, 81-2
Rio de Janeiro, trade of, 160-1; news of captures received at, 173, 175, 227-8; GLASGOW at, 167, 340
Rocas Reef, KARLSRUHE at or near, 248-9, 263
Rotterdam, services to, 98; German trade through, 199; replaces Antwerp as *entrepôt*, 297
Rouen, congested, 400 n 1
Roumania, grain supplies from, 67 n 1, 289, 291 n 2
Royal Mail Steam Packet Co., service suspended, 171; resumed, 177, 227
Rubber, stocks and imports of, 4 n 2, 119-20, 121, 156, 159; crisis in Brazil, 168; effect of war on supply of, 177, 274-5, 361, 394, 419; price of, 409, 419; reaches Germany, 296
Rufiji R., KÖNIGSBERG in, 276, 279, 329
Runciman, Mr. Philip, cited, 404 n
Russia, trade and shipping of, 12-13, 18 n 2; effect of war on trade of, 95-6, 99, 196, 284-5, 289, 291 n 2, 360, 364-5, 383-4
Russian Steam Navigation Co., service maintained, 290
Russian Volunteer Fleet, replaces C.P.R. service, 232
Rymann, Capt. (KAISER WILHELM DER GROSSE), operations of, 78-82; humane conduct of, 78-9; his plans, 83

Saigon, Allied base, 118, 218; trade of, 219
Sailing Vessels, employment of, 145, 157, 323, 323 n 2; State Insurance Scheme extended to, 183
St. Lucia, protection of focal point at, 112
St. Nazaire, British base, 181; congested, 197
St. Paul Rocks, 175, 228, 346, 369, 373
St. Quentin Bay, Germans coal in, 228, 341-2, 347
St. Thomas, Ger. base of supplies, 111-2, 247
St. Vincent, Cape, patrol off, 76
St. Vincent, Cape Verde, news of KARLSRUHE received at, 228, 255
Salmon, canned, from North Pacific, 155, 163, 236-7

Samoa, alarm for, 225
San Francisco, trade held up at, 163-4, 179, 266
San Juan, Porto Rico, KARLSRUHE coals at, 108, 246; *Farn* interned at, 330 n; *Odenwald* stopped at, 380
San Roque, Cape, focal point off, 158, 244; KARLSRUHE operates near, 179, 222, 244, 248-65; KRONPRINZ WILHELM operates near, 369
Santander, iron ore from, 287
Santos, coffee port, 158, 160, 161, 345; prisoners landed at, 227
Satow, Sir Ernest, 87, 88
Scarborough, bombarded, 356; minefield off, 356-7, 357 n, 365
Schlieper, R.-Ad. von on s/m warfare, 355
Seattle. See "Puget Sound"
Services, fixed, suspended, varied, or maintained, 98, 109-10, 113, 125, 138-9, 149, 162, 171, 177, 187, 190, 191-2, 197, 232-3, 282, 282 n, 288, 289-90, 306
Shimonoseki, services suspended, 138
Shipbuilding, 19, 385
Shipping, Mercantile, British, functions, character, and extent of, 5-8, 18 n 2; value of, 10 n 2; molested before outbreak of war, 33, 34, 54; detained on outbreak of war, 54; locked up in Baltic and Black Sea, 95, 95 n; seized in Turkish ports, 291, 291 n; confidence displayed by, 77, 84, 165, 178, 345; losses of, 273, 384-5, 412, 415. See also "Clearances," "Entrances," "Flag, transfer of," "Freight Markets," "Liners," "Services, fixed," "Tramps," "Tonnage"
—, Allied, extent and character of, 11-13, 18 n 2; detained on outbreak of war, 54; losses of, 386, 413; effect of war on French, 197-8, 308-9; on Japanese, 135, 149, 164, 219; Belgian transferred to British ports, 196, 286-7
—, Enemy, extent and character of, 13-16, 18 n 2; suspension of services, 31-2, 58; detained on outbreak of war, 56-7, 64-5, 127-8, 128 n, 291; held up in neutral ports, 64-5, 67, 75-6, 83-4, 94, 104-5, 111, 113, 129, 162-3, 167,

170, 178, 178 n, 198, 242, 387, 414; British cargoes in, 198 n 2; blocked at Antwerp, 286; paralysis of, 99, 114, 165, 198, 293, 386–7; losses of, 198, 386, 413–4; financial position of, 386–7. *See* also "Flag, transfer of"

Shipping, Mercantile, Neutral, extent and character of, 16–19, 18 n 2; activity of, in British trade, 85, 97–9, 282, 284, 308, 416; in enemy trade, 293, 310–1, 362–3; in supply of enemy cruisers, 77, 111–2; preference to, at Plate, 239; losses of, from mines, 415, Table VIII

Shire Line, service suspended, 138

Silk, stocks and imports of, 4 n 2, 121; effect of war on supply of, 126, 275, 361, 394, 419; price of, 409, 419

Silver, Capt. H. L. (MELBOURNE), 326–8

Simalur, EMDEN at, 204, 325

Singapore, focal port and Allied base, 117, 141–2, 218, 279, 327

Slade V.-Ad. Sir Edmond J. W., Chairman, Diversion Committee, 45; cited, 27 n

Smith, Sir H. Llewellyn, Secretary, Board of Trade, 35, 39

Society Is., trade of, 225

Sound, mined, 95

South Africa, British, immunity of trade of, 182, 242; de Wet's rebellion in, 302

Southampton, closed, 110, 110 n, 187

Southwold, minefield off, 89–92, 281

Spain, neutrality of, enforced, 76, 82; trade with, 85, 287, 289

Spee, V.-Ad. Graf von, commands Ger. Pacific Sq., 123; situation and plans of, 144–8, 150; his operations in the Pacific, 150–1, 224–5, 232–3; his intentions discovered, 234; on S. American coast, 314–6, 319–23, 340–1, 347–50; his opportunities and plans, 314–6, 320–2; his defeat and death, 349–50

State Insurance Scheme, British, genesis of, 35–40; provisions and importance of, 40–7; developments of, 183, 193; extended to Belgian shipping, 286–7; voyages excluded from, 65, 85, 95–8, 288; hull premiums under, 45, 176, 183, 193, 354, 389; cargo premiums under, 45, 109, 174, 176, 183–4, 193, 354, 361; effects of, 53, 60, 77, 82, 109, 138, 143, 167, 175, 182, 184–5, 189, 195, 211, 239, 245, 272, 301, 336, 345, 368, 392, 410; criticisms of, 304–5

State Insurance Scheme, American, 364; French, 197; German, 199; Japanese, 219; Russian, 284–5; Swedish, 97, 359

Steam, influence of, on attack and defence of trade, 20–4, 27

Steel, effect of war on supply of, 392

Stoddart, R.-Ad. Archibald P., commands 5th Cr.Sq., 58; protects Atlantic routes, 76–7, 108, 173, 176, 241, 249; on S. American coast, 244, 267, 313, 317–8, 323, 324, 340, 346

Straits Settlements. *See* "Malay Peninsula"

Studt, Korvetten-Kapitän, cited, 246

Sturdee, V.-Ad. Sir F. Doveton, operates against Ad. von Spee, 324, 340, 346–50

Submarines in Baltic, 284; in North Sea, 285, 312; as commerce destroyers, 20 n 2, 50 n, 53, 285, 353, 355–6, 365–8, 376, 409–10, 412. *See* also Index I

Suez Canal, trade of, 118–9, 121; German liners shelter in, 127–8; anxiety regarding, 290, 336, 354

Sugar, imports and consumption of, 3 n 2; 104, 121, 156; effect of war on supply of, 98, 195, 211, 234, 275, 307, 310, 350, 361, 419; price of, 408, 419; Indian import of, 140; German export of, 309–10; Royal Sugar Commission, 307, 310, 401, 408

Sunda Strait, 116, 279, 325, 327

Swansea, congested, 404

Sweden, shipping of, 17, 18 n 2; trade with, 96–7, 282–4, 358–60, 360 n; Russian trade through, 96, 282, 284, 365; German trade with and through, 201, 284, 295–6, 363

Swept Channel, 91–3, 282, 312, 357

Switzerland, German trade through, 201, 310

Tagus, patrol off, 76, 241

Talcahuano, shipping held up at, 344, 348

Tea, imports of, 119, 121; effect of war on supply of, 126, 137, 210,

INDEX II 441

274–5, 334–5, 335 n, 361, 419; price of, 419

Tenerife, news of captures received at, 77, 81 n, 244, 261

Terminal Waters, defence of trade in, 50, 52, 57–8, 69–70, 74–85, 108, 165, 240–1, 280

Territorial Waters, use of to escape attack, 24, 46, 96, 174, 225, 229, 319, 321, 340, 343–4, 348, 371

Thames, channels closed in, 280

Thierfelder, Capt. (KRONPRINZ WILHELM), his methods, 252, 338–9, 371–4, 376–8, 381–2; his good fortune in capture of colliers, 372, 377, 379, 382; in escaping British cruisers, 373; accepts internment, 380

Thierichsens, Capt. (PRINZ EITEL FRIEDRICH), his bold course after Falklands, 370–1, 374, 381; his disregard of neutrality, 374, 376; unlucky as regards coal, 377–8; seeks internment, 377–9

Tilbury, services transferred to, 282, 282 n

Timber, imports and stocks of, 4, 4 n 2, 101, 155; effect of war on supply of, 95–8, 163, 195, 237, 282–3, 358–60, 360 n, 393, 419; price of, 419

Tin, imports of, 4, 119–20, 156; effect of war on supply of, 195, 234, 275, 342, 369, 370 n, 394, 419; price of, 409, 419

Tirpitz, Grand Ad. von, on s/m warfare, 355–6, 365–6

Tobacco, Liverpool congested by, 404

Tochinai, V.-Ad. S., 279, 327

Todd. Mr. J. Stanley, Secretary, North of England Protecting and Indemnity Association, 39

Togoland, occupation of, 241–2

Tonnage, shortage of, at Indian ports, 140, 219–20; at Chilian ports, 165–6; at Brazilian ports, 177; at Plate, 226, 238–9; at Australian ports, 275; general, 361, 397–9

Tornea, route through, 365

Tory I., minefield off, 285–6, 357

Trade, Seaborne, importance of in modern war, 1–2; attack and defence of, 20–8; processes of, 28–9; British share in world's, 6

—, British, nature and extent of, 2–6, 10–1; effects of war on, 60, 84–5, 185–96, 300–8, 360–2, 390–409; percentage losses, 388–9,

415. *See* also "Exports," "Food Supplies," "Imports"

Trade, Seaborne, Allied, nature and extent of, 11–13; effect of war on Belgian, 196, 286; on French, 196–8, 308–9, 383–4; on Japanese, 126, 219; on Russian, 96, 196, 284–5, 360, 383–4

—, Enemy, nature and extent of, 13–16; effect of war on, 58, 198–202, 309–11, 363–4, 383, 386–8

Trade Routes:

—, Australian-American, 10, 145–6, 156; trade of during war, 149

—, Cape, or South African, 9, 10 n 1; defence of, 241–4; trade of during war, 242, 280, 302

—, Caribbean, 9, 103–4; defence of, 104, 107, 110–3, 314–5, 324; trade of during war 113

—, North American, 9, 100–4; defence of, 104–8, 110–1; trade of during war, 105–10, 113–4, 301–2

—, North Pacific, 10, 145–6, 156; defence of, 164, 179, 230, 235–7; trade of during war, 148–9, 162–4, 232–3, 344

—, Oriental, 9, 10 n 1, 115–21; defence of, 121–137, 140–3, 147–8, 204, 208–9, 214, 217–8, 268–9, 276–7, 279, 326–9, 336–7; trade of during war, 125–6, 132, 135, 137–40, 142–3, 210–11, 214–20, 273–6, 278–9, 326, 331–6, 394; percentages of losses on, 332

—, South American, 9, 10 n 1, 155–62; defence of, 154–5, 162–4, 167, 170, 175–6, 179–80, 221–30, 234–7, 238, 244, 267, 313–7, 319–20, 323–4, 340, 346–7, 349–50, 369–70, 373, 378–80; trade of during war, 162–80, 226–8, 231, 233–7, 238–9, 244–5, 265, 318–9, 321–3, 340, 342–5, 347–8, 350, 369, 370 n, 394; percentage of losses on, 265

Tramps, functions of, 8

Transports, refrigerated space reserved on, 275

Trinidada, German base at, 174, 174 n, 222–4, 253, 253 n, 381

Trondhjem, trade through, 96, 359; BERLIN interned at, 352

Tryon, Ad. Sir George, 37

Tsingtau, German base, 118, 122, 124, 133–7, 141, 145–6, 277, 329

Turkey, shipping of, 18 n 2; attitude of, 65–7, 85–6; outbreak of war with, 289–91

Tyne, minefield off, 91–2, 281; shipping diverted from, 93; congested, 403

United Kingdom, trade and shipping of, 1–11, 18 n 2; shipbuilding in, 19; declares war against Germany, 44; against Austria, 64; against Turkey, 290–1

United S.S. Co. of Copenhagen, service transferred, 282 n

United States, shipping of, 17, 18 n 2; trade and communications of, 100–4, 145–6, 155–6, 158, 160; effect of war on trade of, 106–14, 148–9, 162–4, 232–3, 236–7, 292, 294–5, 301–2, 302 n; controversies with, 293–5, 363–4; neutrality of, 108, 110, 111, 142, 380; projected purchase of German shipping by, 111, 364; German ships transferred to, 107, 293–4, 364

Uruguay, trade and communications of, 158–62; trade with, 176–7, 226–7, 238 n 2, 345 n 2, 369, 370 n

Ushant, patrols off, 75, 83

Valetta, port of refuge, 62–3

Valparaiso, trade of, 156–7; GLASGOW and MONMOUTH at, 235, 313; Ger.Pac.Sq. off and at, 316, 318–19, 321–2, 338; shipping held up at, 319, 321–2, 340, 344

Vancouver, terminal port, 146, 156, 232; shipping held up at, 163; preparations for defence of, 235–6

Vegetables, imports and consumption of, 3 n 2; effect of war on supply of, 85, 195

Venice, ships held up at, 65, 288

Vigo, Ger. loadings stopped at, 32; watch on, 75–6, 83

Villagarcia, watch on, 75

Vladivostok, terminal port and Russian base, 117, 118, 122, 133, 137

War Risks Associations, value of shipping entered in, 10 n. See also "State Insurance Scheme"

War Risks, guaranteed by Government on wheat, 35; underwriters' quotations for, 30–2, 34, 109, 149, 174, 182–4, 192–3, 211, 274, 286, 304, 306, 322, 336, 354; cost of insurance against, 171, 191, 389–90, 402. See also "State Insurance Scheme"

Webb, Capt. Richard, Director of Trade Division, Admiralty, 45

Wemyss, R.-Ad. Rosslyn E., commands 12th Cr.Sq., 58, 74, 108, 240

West Africa, British, trade of, 9–10, 182, 242–3, 302

West Indies, trade and communications of, 103–4; KARLSRUHE's projected raid on, 265, 317–18, 330, sugar from, 307

Wheat, imports and consumption of, 67 n, 100, 119–20, 121, 155, 156, 159, 291 n 2; effect of war on supply of, 113, 132, 163, 171, 195, 216, 219, 236–7, 274, 291 n 2, 301, 301 n 2, 361, 369, 370 n, 393, 406–7, 407 n, 419; price of, 292, 405–7, 418–9

Whitby, bombarded, 356

White Sea, trade of, 96, 284, 360, 364–5

Wilson Line, sailings resumed, 98; transferred, 282 n

Wine, from Portugal, 85

Wireless Telegraphy, advantages and dangers of, 25–8, 80, 217; shipping saved by, 206; intercepted messages, 78, 134, 142, 147, 207, 209, 214, 218, 226, 234, 253, 371; raiders alarmed by, 223, 252, 253, 258, 267, 377; use of, by KARLSRUHE, 250–1; apparatus on captured ships, 78, 79, 80, 170, 205, 253, 254, 263, 272, 373; refitted after release, 80, 208; German wireless stations captured or destroyed, 134, 148, 149, 242–3, 277

Wood pulp, effect of war on supply of, 97, 98, 358

Wool, stocks and imports of, 4, 4 n 2, 121, 156, 159; effect of war on supply of, 137, 195, 238, 360–1, 369, 370 n, 419; price of, 409, 419

Yap, Ger. wireless base, 134, 146, 148, 277

Yellow Sea Patrol, 134–5

Yokohama, terminal port, 117, 145, 146; shipping held up at, 164

Zeeland Line, service maintained, 98

www.ingramcontent.com/pod-product-compliance
Lightning Source LLC
Chambersburg PA
CBHW032007300426
44117CB00008B/934